Collectible Correctables

by

John Artman

illustrated by Vanessa Filkins

Cover by Vanessa Filkins

ISBN No. 0-86653-214-5

Printing No. 9

GOOD APPLE, INC.
BOX 299
CARTHAGE, IL 62321-0299

Table of Contents

Introduction

In my twenty-five years of teaching language arts, at several different levels, I have constantly been aware of a large number of errors that a great majority of students make daily both in speaking and writing.

This book *Collectible Correctables* concentrates on correcting the major errors students make day after day in language arts. Problems such as commonly misspelled words, confused words, the double negative, the double comparison, redundant words, the run-on sentence, singular to plural errors, *could of*, *would of*, *should of*, and wacky words such as *kinda*, *gonna*, etc., are worked on in interesting and varied activities.

Each section of this book presents the error, discusses it, corrects it, offers information to conquer the error and then presents several activities to work on correcting the error.

Some activities present information for the student to memorize and master. These are very important activities, and I feel that you must ask each student to memorize the presented information and work on it over and over until he/she masters it.

Each section is complete by itself so it does not matter in what order you use the sections. However you use them, I wish you success in helping your students master these major language arts errors.

To the Teacher

The main objective of this book is to help your students overcome problems in language arts. I believe that if they complete the units provided in a careful and diligent manner that they will master these errors.

With every lesson, explain very slowly and patiently what you wish for you and your class to accomplish. You should do a great deal of oral work on each lesson. In other words, after the students have worked on *there*, *their*, and *they're* on the chalkboard or mimeographed sheets, give them oral sentence after sentence where they must give you the correct form of the pronoun in their answers.

Allow the students to make up activities similar to the ones presented in this book. This will give your students practice in correcting errors, provide you with additional exercises and provide the children with the opportunity to help each other.

In every lesson, employ patience, humor, and kindness. A free and open atmosphere of mutual trust and understanding is a must for anyone attempting to learn and master any kind of information.

There is an answer key at the back of the book to provide quick answers and save time finding the answers.

Commonly Misspelled Words

There are certain words that many writers of our language misspell. The following list contains forty-five spelling words that students have problems spelling correctly:

1. lose
2. loose
3. February
4. coming
5. beginning
6. finally
7. privilege
8. grammar
9. disappear
10. necessary
11. disappoint
12. business
13. principal
14. principle
15. until
16. believe
17. receive
18. separate
19. foreign
20. vacuum
21. library
22. weather
23. sincerely
24. deceive
25. niece
26. embarrass
27. friend
28. sophomore
29. ninety
30. written
31. Wednesday
32. calendar
33. rhythm
34. definite
35. existence
36. truly
37. disease
38. commercial
39. opportunity
40. lieutenant
41. misspell
42. excellent
43. writing
44. accomplish
45. achieve

1. Go over this entire list with the class. Ask if there is any word the class does not understand the meaning of. If there is, supply the meaning(s). Ask that the students study the words and memorize their spellings. Each day give speed drills of five to ten words at the beginning of the class. Continue all year until the children master the spelling of each word.

2. Tell the class that everyone is going to write a paragraph with the ten words you are going to give orally from this list of forty-five words. Slowly, give ten words from the list. Ask the students to attempt to write a paragraph that makes sense.

3. It is possible that some of your students will be able to write a paragraph using twenty-five or more of the spelling words.

4. Have the members of your class give each other words as many times as possible until they are able to master them.

5. Your children will be able to improve their spelling by using a dictionary, keeping track of their individual spelling errors and constantly helping each other in their spelling improvement.

Work Sheet #1
Commonly Misspelled Words

Some of the following words are spelled incorrectly. If a word is not correct, write the correct spelling of that word on the line to the right. If it is correct, write "correct."

1. grammer ______________________
2. untill ______________________
3. writen ______________________
4. acheive ______________________
5. excellent ______________________
6. seperate ______________________
7. ninety ______________________
8. recieve ______________________
9. truely ______________________
10. Wednesday ______________________
11. rhythm ______________________
12. definate ______________________
13. vacuum ______________________
14. sophmore ______________________
15. necessary ______________________

student's name ______________________

date ______________________

Confusing Words

6. Circle the correct word in each sentence.

   A. (It's, Its) a beautiful day.

   B. The dog has (it's, its) doghouse.

   C. The boys are over (their, there).

   D. (There, They're) bigger than you are.

   E. (Their, There) house is new.

   F. Is he better (than, then) you?

   G. We had better go (than, then).

   H. You do that (good, well).

   I. Everyone can go (except, accept) you.

   J. Will he (except, accept) the gift?

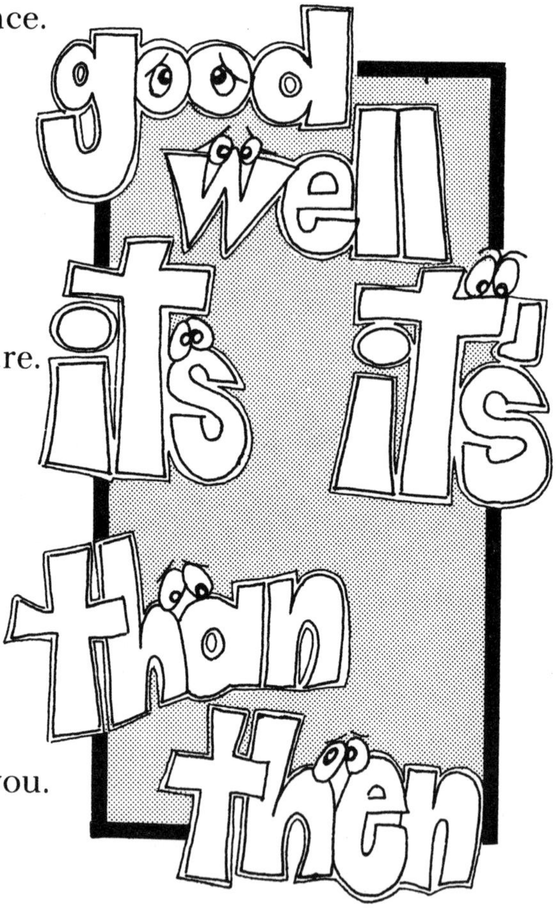

Write these sentences on the chalkboard or mimeograph copies and ask each child to do the activity.

7. The directions for this activity are the same as Activity #6.

   A. Mary is bigger (then, than) Jane.

   B. Will you (except, accept) the book?

   C. Everyone is here (accept, except) Bess.

   D. He is over (there, their).

   E. That tree has lost (it's, its) branches.

   F. (There, Their) uncle has arrived.

   G. My food tastes (good, well).

   H. (They're, Their) all at Ben's house.

   I. My mother is nicer (then, than) any mother.

   J. (Its, It's) a beautiful day.

8. Ask each student to look up the meaning of *its*, *it's*, *there*, *their*, *they're*, *then*, *than*, *good*, *well*, *accept*, and *except* in a dictionary. He/She is to discuss the meaning of each word with you and then use every word in a sentence. These sentences will be turned in to you.

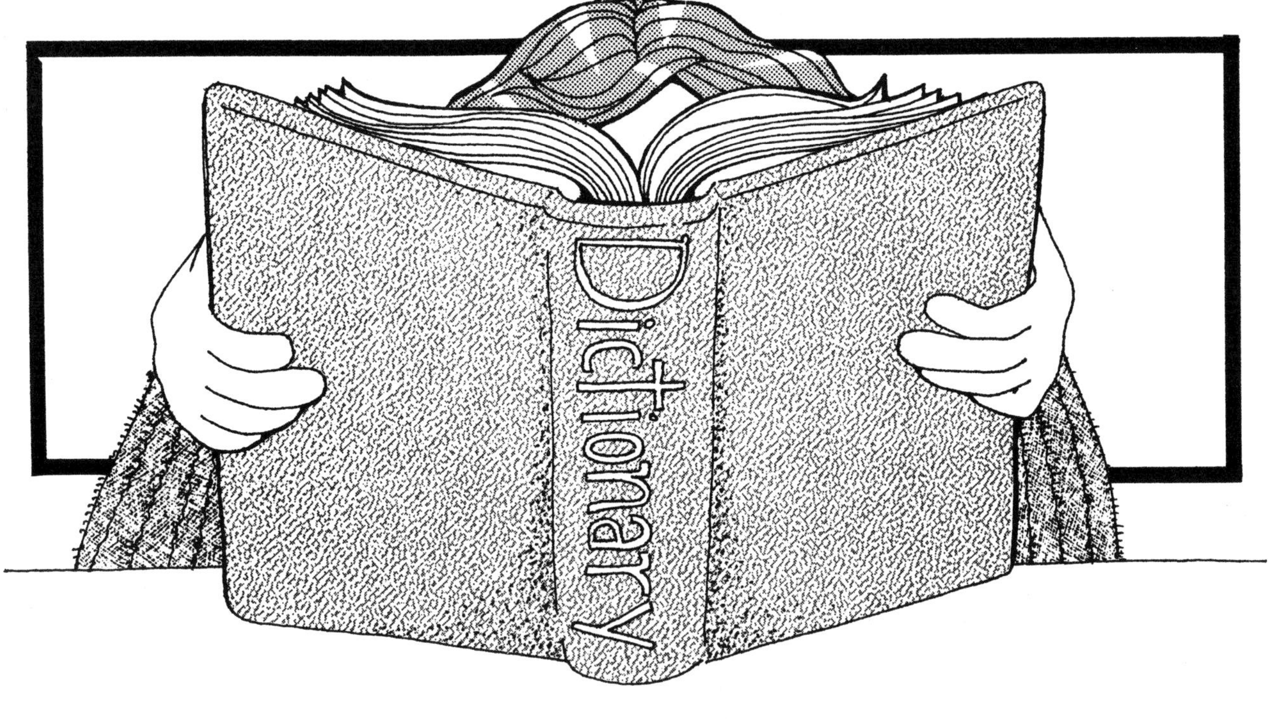

9. The children are to study these words and master their meanings.

A. *It's* is a contraction meaning "it is."

B. *Its* is the possessive of *it.*

C. Food tastes *good.*

D. You do *well*—not *good.*

E. A person is *well* but he can be in *good* health.

F. *Then* tells us when.

G. *Than* is used to compare people or things.

H. *Accept* means to receive something or to be willing to receive something.

I. *Except* means to leave something or someone out, to omit something.

10. The student will write a sentence for each of the following words:

A. its

B. accept

C. than

D. there

E. good

F. it's

G. their

H. they're

I. then

J. except

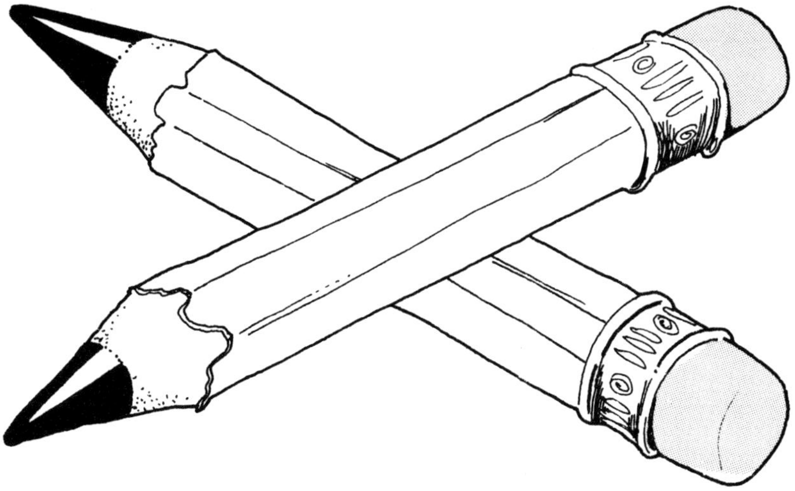

11. Start a list of words that are similar in spelling and pronunciation that confuse your students. Each student is to also keep an individual list of such words. Have the students work in groups of two or four. The groups are to help each student master confusing words.

Work Sheet #2
Confused Words

Circle the correct word in each sentence.

1. Please (except, accept) my gift.
2. (Their, There) he is.
3. (It's, Its) time to go home.
4. I can do better (then, than) that.
5. Everyone went (accept, except) Bill.
6. That tastes (well, good).
7. That is (there, their) house.
8. (There, They're) all going with us.
9. Our family will go (than, then).
10. Should each town have (its, it's) own fire department?
11. Did you (accept, except) the job?
12. That car over (their, there) is mine.
13. He plays (good, well).
14. (It's, Its) a good thing you like apples.
15. We will do better (than, then) the other team.

teacher______________________

student______________________

Misspelled and Misused Words

12. The student is to circle the correct word. Write these sentences on a mimeographed sheet for each child.

    A. We bought (alot, a lot) of candy.

    B. Is that (alright, all right)?

    C. I (am not, ain't) going.

    D. (Them, Those) boys are here.

    E. Wait (till, untill, until) we get there.

    F. We can't go (cause, because) we are not ready.

    G. The food is (tuff, tough).

    H. We (snuck, sneaked) home.

    I. Can (them, those) girls swim?

    J. Mary has (a lot, alot) of friends.

13. Do the same in this activity.

A. The enemy (sneaked, snuck) behind us.

B. That is (alright, all right).

C. She has (a lot, alot) of money.

D. The presents won't arrive (till, until, untill) summer.

E. That is (tuff, tough) luck.

F. She isn't happy (because, cause) of you.

G. Betty (ain't, isn't) going to the store.

H. That's (alot, a lot) of work for us to do.

I. Those boys (snuck, sneaked) up on us.

J. We can't start working (till, until, untill) my father is here.

14. Each member of the class is to look up the meanings of *a lot*, *all right*, *them*, *those*, *until*, *because*, *tough*, and *sneak(ed)* in a dictionary. The student will discuss each meaning with you and then write a sentence for each of the words. He/She will share these sentences with you and several of his/her classmates.

15. Ask the students to study this list and attempt to master the use and meaning of each word.

   A. *A lot* is two words. It is *never* used as one word. Do *not* use the one word *alot*!

   B. *All right* is two words. Do *not* use the one word *alright.*

   C. *Ain't* is not used in educated speech and writing. Use *am not*, *are not*, or *is not.*

   D. Do *not* use *till* or *untill* for the word *until.*

   E. Use the word *because* when you wish to present a reason. The word *cause* means "something that brings about an effect or a result."

   F. Use the word *tough. Tuff* is a misspelled and misused word for *tough.*

   G. *Sneak* or *sneaked* means "to go stealthily or furtively." *Snuck* is a misspelled and misused word for *sneak(ed).*

   H. Do *not* use *them* before a noun. *Them* girls, *them* boys is incorrect. We say *those* girls, *those* boys. We write "We saw them" or "The women brought them a gift."

16. Make a copy of this exercise for each student.

This is a headline on the sports page of a recent issue of a large midwestern newspaper. Notice that *tuff* is used when the word *tough* is called for.

Today, sports writers and advertising people are using the word *tuff* a great deal. Perhaps they think this is "hip," but we don't want you using this word unless you knowingly use it.

Go to a dictionary and look up the definition of "tough." Write the definition down on a sheet of paper. On the same sheet, write down five different sentences using the word *tough*. Turn your words into your teacher.

17. The student will write a sentence using each of the following words:

A. until

B. all right

C. a lot

D. tough

E. because

F. them

G. those

H. sneak(ed)

18. Each time you encounter a word such as "tuff, alot, or snuck," write the word down and also write down the word it is replacing. Ask each of the students to keep a similar list.

Work Sheet #3
Misspelled and Misused Words

Circle the correct word in each sentence.

1. Can (them, those) guys go with us?
2. We will be there (till, until, untill) the game is over.
3. (Alright, All right), you win!
4. He (snuck, sneaked) into the old house.
5. She knows (alot, a lot) about trees.
6. (Isn't, Ain't) he here?
7. The food is very (tough, tuff).
8. There (isn't, ain't) a great deal we can do.
9. Wait (until, till) summer is over.
10. I want (a lot, alot) of candy.
11. (Alright, All right), all of you may go.
12. He's (alot, a lot) like your father.
13. We saw (those, them) people at the game.
14. (Isn't, Ain't) Janey going to the show?
15. Wait (until, till) we get some more money.

your name____________________

Doubles

ative

ntences on the chalkboard.

nothing.

B. They don't have no money.

C. Betty couldn't hardly work.

D. It don't make no sense.

E. Bill never has no food.

F. George can't hardly move.

Ask the students to look at the sentences in order to see if they are clear and correct in meaning. If any student can correct the error in each sentence, allow him or her to go to the chalkboard and correct each sentence.

The sentences should look something like these.

Inform your class that negative words such as *don't*, *doesn't*, *can't*, *couldn't*, *no*, *not*, *nothing*, *never*, *none*, *hardly*, and *scarcely* should never be used as pairs in any sentence. When we use two such words in a sentence, we call these words "the double negative." This doubling of words causes confusion in sentence clarity.

20. Ask each child to rewrite each sentence in this activity correctly.

    A. The book doesn't make no sense.

    B. Mary hasn't done nothing.

    C. Jane never has no schoolwork.

    D. We don't hardly ever practice.

    E. Bill couldn't hardly say anything.

The Double Comparison

21. Write the following sentences on the chalkboard:

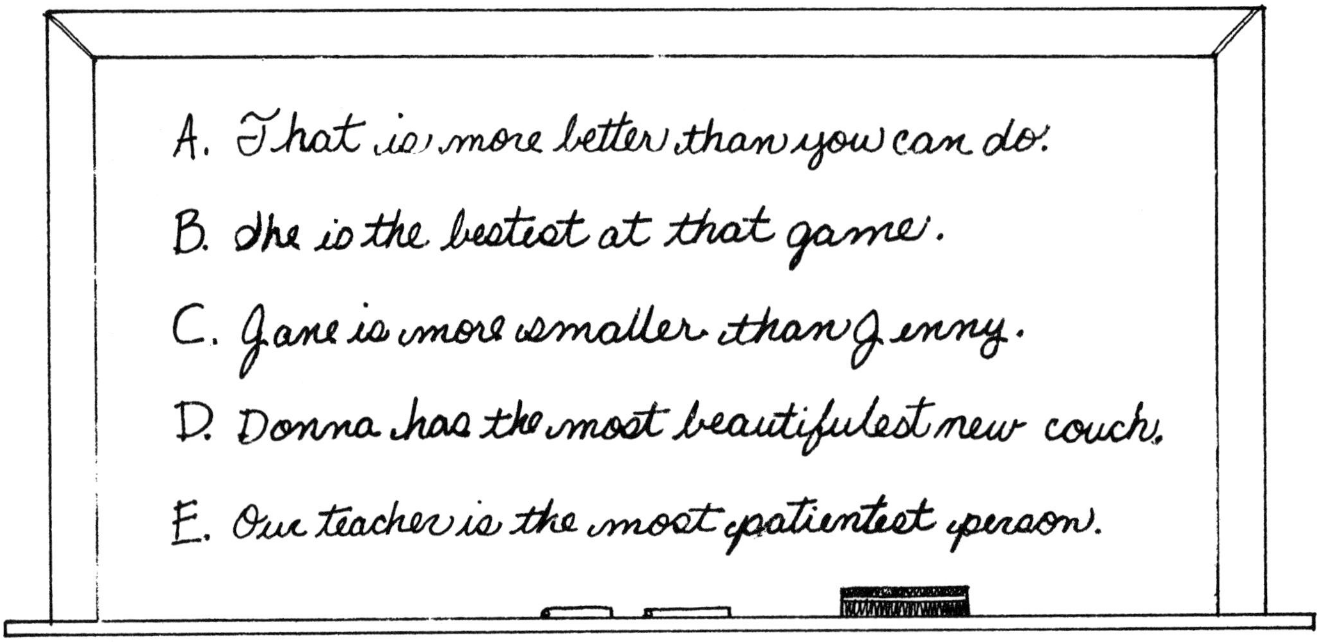

Allow the class to look at the sentences. You read each sentence aloud so the children are able to "hear" the sentences. You and the class discuss each sentence and then attempt to revise it in order to make it clear. Each sentence has a "double comparison."

The sentences should be revised like this:

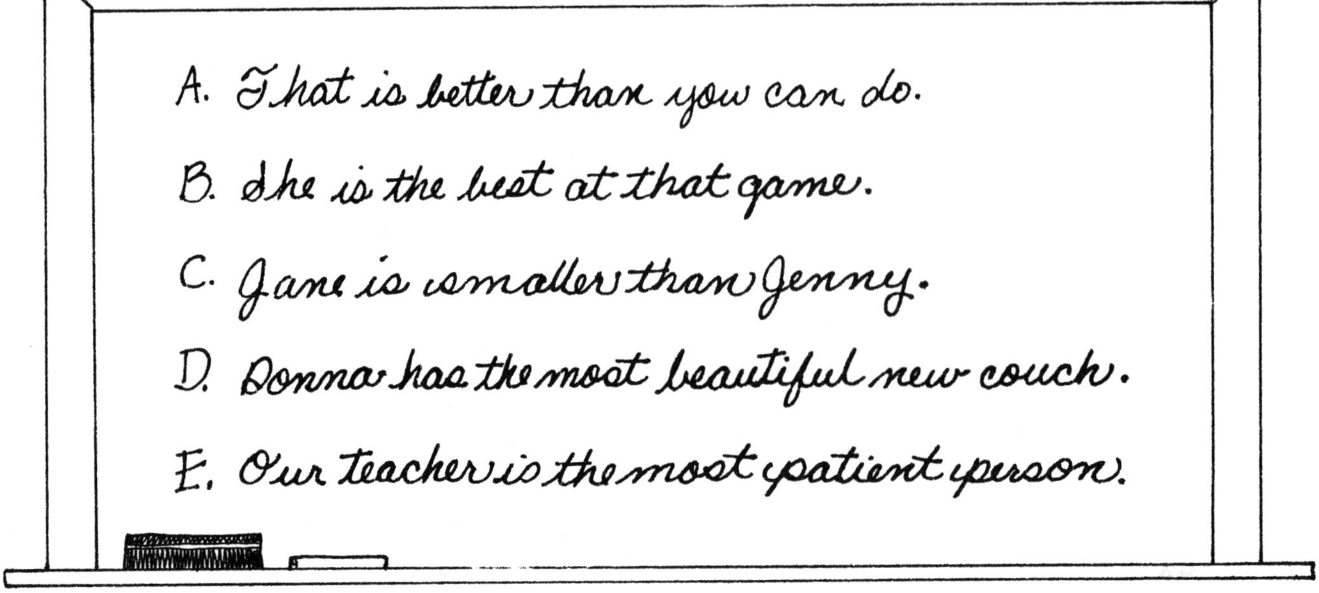

22. Inform your students that we compare adjectives in three degrees of comparison. These degrees are called *positive*, *comparative*, and *superlative*. Show the following to the class either on the chalkboard or on mimeographed sheets.

Positive	**Comparative**	**Superlative**
bad	worse	worst
big	bigger	biggest
good	better	best
weak	weaker	weakest
pretty	prettier	prettiest
foolish	more foolish	most foolish
well	better	best
gracious	more gracious	most gracious

Ask each student to write a sentence for each three degrees of comparison. Here is an example.

A. He is a *bad* boy.

B. She is *worse* than Martha.

C. That man is the *worst* player I have ever seen.

After they have written all of the sentences, you look them over to see if they understand the comparison of modifiers (adjectives).

23. The students should understand that the positive degree is the basic adjective. The comparative degree uses the adjective in a comparison when a writer is comparing two things. The comparative form has an ending on it like the *er* in *weaker* (see Activity 22), or it is a different word like *worse* whose positive degree is *bad* or puts *more* before the adjective like *more gracious.* The superlative degree compares three or more things.

All five sentences in Activity 21 are examples of "the double comparison." We wish to avoid the double comparison because it destroys the clarity of a sentence. A student creates a "double comparison" when he/she adds *er* or *est* to the modifier and/or puts *more* or *most* before the modifier. Therefore, the sentence "Donna has the *most beautifulest* new couch" makes no sense because the three comparisons are *beautiful*, *more beautiful*, and *most beautiful.*

24. The best way to have your students avoid the double comparison is to have them learn the correct use of modifiers.

Positive	**Comparative**	**Superlative**
simple	simpler	simplest
pretty	prettier	prettiest
big	bigger	biggest
dark	darker	darkest
kind	kinder	kindest
bad	worse	worst
good	better	best
well	better	best
weak	weaker	weakest
small	smaller	smallest
loud	louder	loudest
foolish	more foolish	most foolish
fearful	more fearful	most fearful
modern	more modern	most modern
gracious	more gracious	most gracious

Here is a list they can begin to memorize. Have them work on this list until they master all the comparisons. Then ask each child to write a separate sentence for each degree of each word.

25. Find many more comparisons of modifiers for your students to master, and *constantly* be on the alert for the "the double comparison" in their writing and speaking.

Work Sheet #4
Doubles

Correct each sentence on the line provided.

1. I ain't got nothing.

____

2. She never has no money.

____

3. That doesn't make no sense.

____

4. She is more taller than I.

____

5. Bill hasn't done nothing.

____

Now write five sentences that contain double negatives. Ask a friend to correct each sentence.

1. ______________________________
2. ______________________________
3. ______________________________
4. ______________________________
5. ______________________________

your name______________________

Redundant Words

26. Place these sentences on the chalkboard.

A. Now today we are able to produce a great deal of food in this country.

B. The camp was not visible to the eye.

C. In its present state of affairs today the nation must be aware of a possible war.

D. To me the book is good.

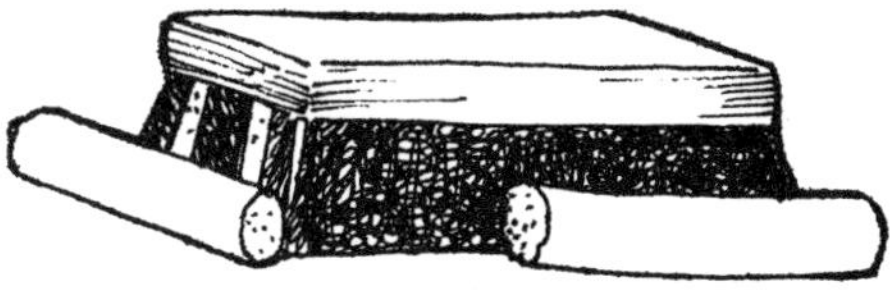

E. I myself think this is foolish.

Allow the class to read the sentences. Then ask five students to read one sentence aloud. Inform the children that this is an exercise on unnecessary words. There are one or more words in each sentence that merely repeat what has been stated. We call this sort of wordiness superfluous words or redundant words. Ask if anyone is able to mark out the words not needed. If any boy or girl is able to do so, allow him/her to come to the chalkboard and cross out the superfluous words.

27. Write these corrected sentences on mimeographed sheets and give each child a copy.

A. Now we are able to produce a great deal of food in this country.

B. The camp was not visible.

C. In its present state of affairs the nation must be aware of a possible war.

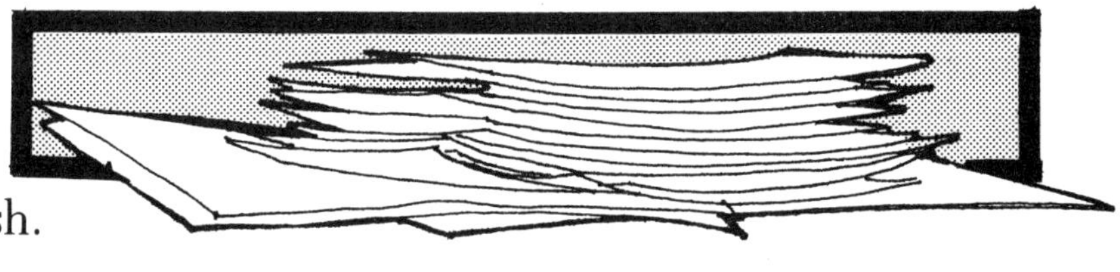

D. The book is good.

E. I think this is foolish.

Explain why the unnecessary elements have been crossed out in each sentence.

28. The student is to study the following information until he/she masters it:

    A. Do not use "To me" at the beginning of a sentence. You are the speaker or the writer so the "To me" is unnecessary.

    B. Never use the construction "I myself." Simply use "I."

    C. Words like "now today" or "modern trains of today" merely repeat. Avoid such repetition.

    D. Words such as "great big" repeat. Say "big" or "large."

    E. Be aware of superfluous words at all times.

29. Every child is to look up the meanings of *superfluous*, *redundant*, and *repetition*. He/She will write a definition for each word and also a sentence for each word. The student will show his/her work to the teacher.
30. The entire class will start a collection of redundant statements and/or sentences. Each time a student finds such unnecessary repetition, have him/her write the example on a piece of paper. Tape these examples up all over one wall of the classroom.

Work Sheet #5
Redundant Words

There are unnecessary words in all of these sentences. Cross out the superfluous words.

1. To me there are too many people here.

2. Now today America is stronger than ever.

3. I myself do not care.

4. The cabin was not visible to the eye.

5. She herself really works hard.

6. The great big bear roared at us.

7. The picture really looks nice to me.

8. He himself drove the tractor.

9. Things are easier now today.

10. Was the mountain visible to the eye?

your name____________________

date____________________

Some Comma Problems

The Run-On Sentence

31. Write these sentences on your chalkboard.

A. I went to town, Mary stayed at home.

B. Our car will not start, maybe we need a new battery.

C. I woke up early Monday morning it was my birthday.

D. Mother ran the vacuum Dad dusted the furniture.

E. Our team won the game, we were very happy.

Give the children time to look at the sentences. Then call for volunteers to go to the chalkboard and correct the error in each sentence. Ask the students to explain what is wrong with each sentence.

The following sentences are corrected:

A. I went to town; Mary stayed at home.

I went to town. Mary stayed at home.

B. Our car will not start; maybe we need a new battery.

Our car will not start. Maybe we need a new battery.

C. I woke up early Monday morning. It was my birthday.

I woke up early Monday morning; it was my birthday.

D. Mother ran the vacuum. Dad dusted the furniture.

Mother ran the vacuum; Dad dusted the furniture.

E. Our team won the game; we were very happy.

Our team won the game. We were very happy.

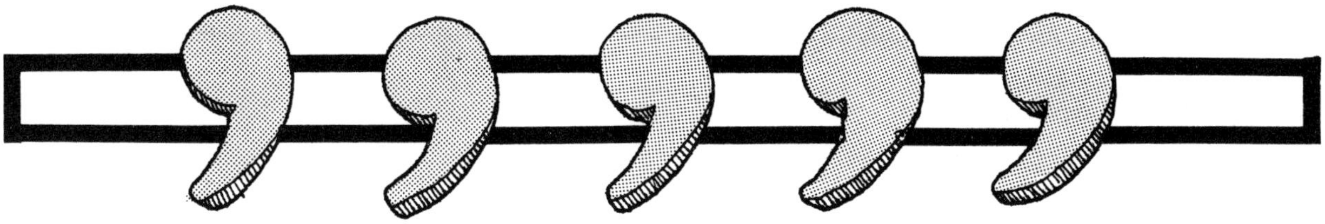

Tell the class they have been correcting run-on sentences. A run-on sentence is two or more sentences that have no punctuation mark separating them or that have only a comma separating them. In this type of sentence, one sentence "runs on" into the next sentence. The end of a sentence should be punctuated with a period, a question mark, or an exclamation point. Be certain your students understand this.

32. Each child is to correctly punctuate the following sentences:

   A. Betty bought a coat, I bought a new hat.

   B. Our class is going to Chicago we won this trip by selling the most magazines.

   C. Where is Uncle George he is supposed to go with us.

   D. Jack helped Bill paint the house, he enjoyed the hard work.

   E. Don't go over there, there is a mean dog in the yard.

Introductory Adverbial Clause

33. The following sentences can be written on the chalkboard or on mimeographed sheets:

    A. When I was a little kid I was scared of the dark.

    B. If I go to town I will buy you a new coat.

    C. When I was twelve years old I went to Chicago.

    D. If you see Jim tell him "hello."

    E. When Lynn was celebrating her tenth birthday her older sister Becky was at college.

Allow each student to attempt to correct these sentences. Each of these sentences begins with an introductory adverbial clause and a comma is required at the *end* of the clause.

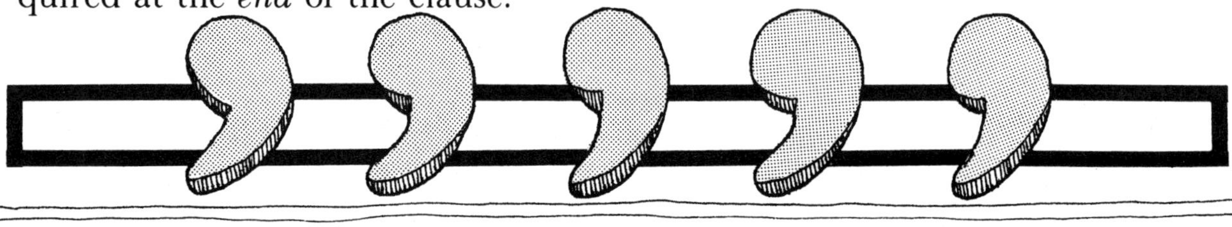

Explain to the children that *any* time they see a sentence that begins with "If," "When," "Since," or "While," that beginning will probably be an introductory adverbial clause that requires a comma at the end of it.

After the class has worked at correcting the sentences for Activity 33, you might put the sentences on the chalkboard. Correct and explain each sentence.

A. When I was a little kid, I was scared to death of the dark.

B. If I go to town, I will buy you a new coat.

C. When I was about twelve years old, I went to Chicago.

D. If you see Jim, (you) tell him "hello."

E. When Lynn was celebrating her tenth birthday, her older sister Becky was in college.

34. A. If ________________________________

B. When ________________________________

C. Since ________________________________

D. While ________________________________

Every child is to finish each of the above sentences. He/She will have a comma after each introductory adverbial clause and a period at the end of each sentence.

Comma at the End of a State or Nation

35. Write these sentences on your chalkboard.

    A. We drove to Carthage, Illinois to buy gas.

    B. They flew over Bombay, India on their way to China.

    C. In Chicago, Illinois we saw the Bears play.

    D. At Keokuk, Iowa they saw the statue of Chief Keokuk.

    E. In London, England we visited the Tower.

Allow the class to read the sentences. Then, put a comma after "Illinois," "India," "Illinois," "Iowa," and "England."

Every student must be aware that in a sentence which has the town before the state or country and that state or country is not the last word in the sentence, then a comma must be placed after the state or the country.

36. Ask each child to write ten sentences similar to the ones in Activity 35. He/She is to punctuate each sentence correctly.

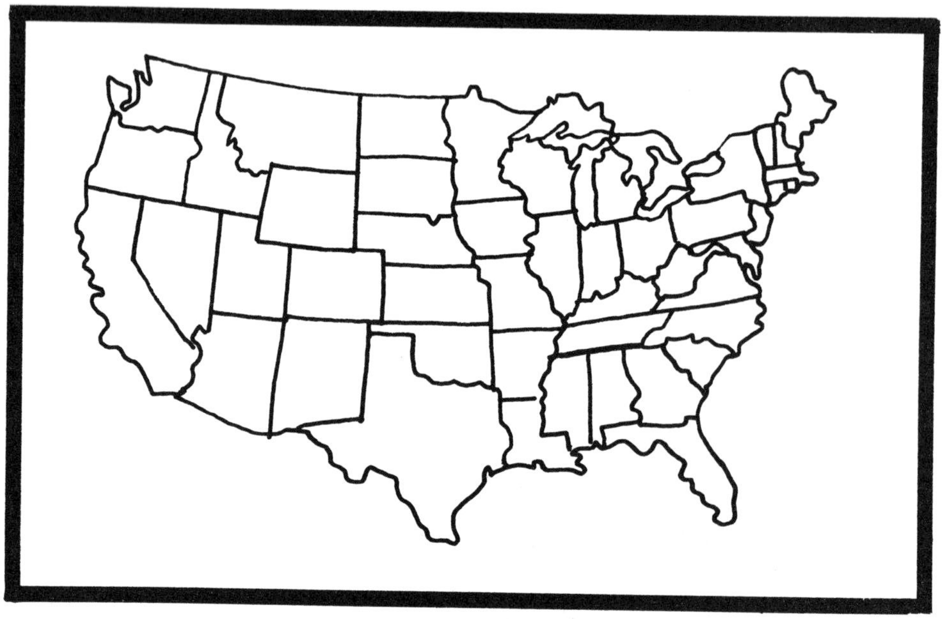

Work Sheet #6
Some Comma Problems

Correct the punctuation errors in these sentences.

1. I went to town Bill stayed home.
2. Mother painted the walls, Dad painted the ceiling.
3. Betty sold tickets, Nancy took in the money.
4. If I see your friend I will tell him you are here.
5. When we get to Chicago we will go to the Art Institue.
6. While we are at Uncle Bill's you will be able to go fishing.
7. He went to Basco Illinois to see his friend.
8. In Munich Germany we bought a beautiful set of dishes.
9. At Seton Ohio we had a picnic.
10. Jim bought gas, Joe bought groceries.

your name______________________________

teacher's name______________________________

Singular-Plural Errors

37. Mimeograph copies of the following sentences or write on the chalkboard:

    A. Everyone did their work.

    B. Each of the players did their part.

    C. Someone in the class did not do their share of the work.

    D. Anyone will be able to do their role in the play well.

    E. Each of the students forgot to do their work.

Call for volunteers to correct the sentences. Discuss each sentence as it is being corrected.

Now write the correction on the chalkboard.

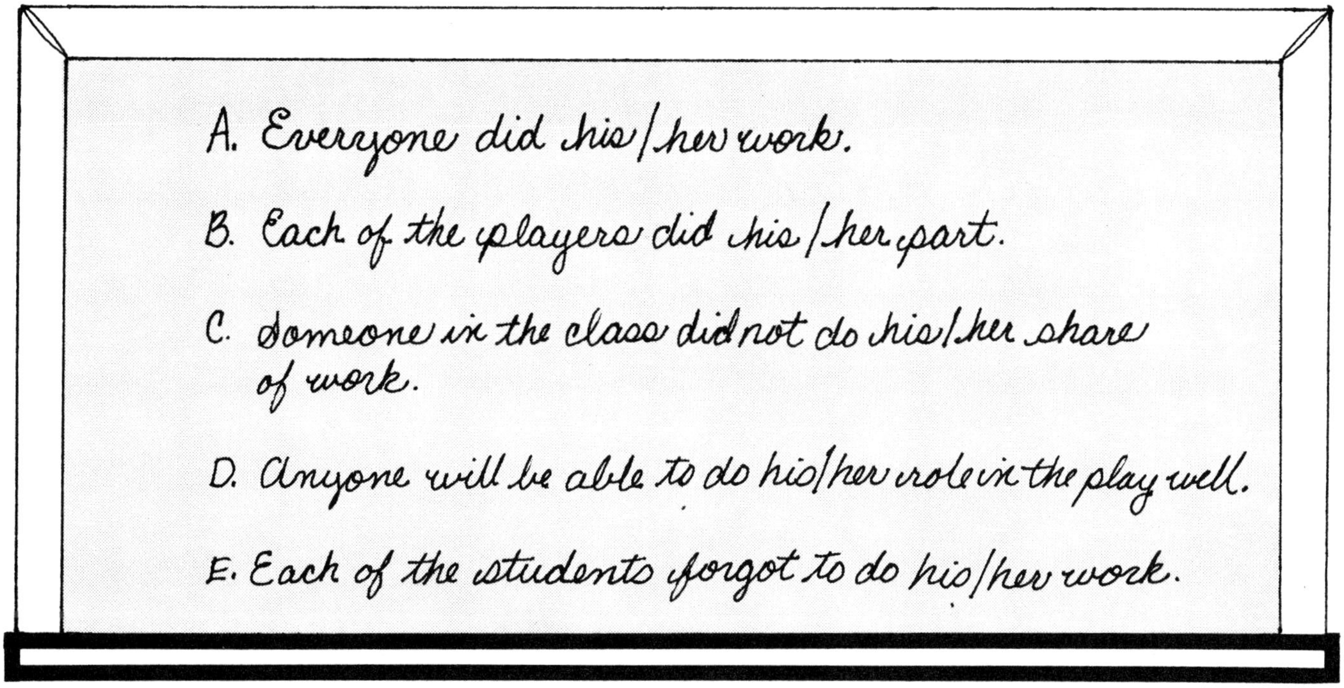

Explain that a writer cannot have a singular subject and have a plural pronoun referring to that singular subject. *Each*, *everyone*, *everybody*, *one*, *nobody*, *anybody*, *someone*, *somebody*, and *anyone* are singular and are referred to by singular pronouns.

38. Each member of the class is to correct each of the following sentences:

    A. Somebody must have left their supplies here.

    B. Each person did their best.

    C. One of the members of the class moved their chair.

    D. Nobody should leave their clothes on the floor.

    E. Everyone ate everything on their plate.

39. Ask the children to memorize the singular pronouns and to use each one in a sentence.

Work Sheet #7
Singular-Plural Errors

Correct the singular-plural errors in these sentences. Rewrite each sentence on the line provided.

1. Everyone ate their dinner at 12:30 p.m.

   ____

2. Someone in the house did not do their chores.

   ____

3. Each of the girls brought their clothes.

   ____

4. Anyone may bring their favorite records.

   ____

5. Each of the children put their toys in the play area.

   ____

student's name______________________

date______________________

Could of, Would Of

40. Ask the class to look at these two sentences.

A. I *could of* done that.

B. She *would of* gone if Mary had asked her.

Tell the children that neither of these sentences makes any sense because of the constructions *could of* and *would of*. *Of* is a preposition. It is not a verb. You need the verb *have* after the verbs *could* and *would*. A person would not say "I *of* a ball" or "They *of* a great deal of money." Instead, he would say "I *have* a ball" and "They *have* a great deal of money." So the first two sentences should be:

A. I *could have* done that.

B. She *would have* gone if Mary had asked her.

41. If any of your students have been using constructions like *could of*, *would of*, or *should of*, ask them to start correcting these constructions to *could have*, *would have*, and *should have*. Ask them to talk to their friends about such constructions. Also, ask them to work together to help each other in correcting such errors.

42. The student is to study and master the following information:

A. Do *not* use the constructions *would of*, *could of*, and *should of*.

B. *Of* is a preposition. It *cannot* be used as a verb.

C. *Have* is a verb. *Have* goes after *would*, *could*, and *should*.

43. Each member of the class is to write ten sentences using *would have*, ten using *could have*, and ten using *should have*.

Work Sheet #8
Could of, Would Of

Write five sentences using *could have.*

1. ____________________
2. ____________________
3. ____________________
4. ____________________
5. ____________________

Write five sentences using *would have.*

1. ____________________
2. ____________________
3. ____________________
4. ____________________
5. ____________________

Correct the errors in these sentences by changing *of* to *have.*

1. She should of gone to town.
2. George would of done that for you.
3. Marge could of baked another pie.
4. The boys would of done the work for you.
5. All of them should of helped out.

your name____________________

Wacky Words

44. Put these sentences on the chalkboard.

    A. "Do you like these boots?" "*Kinda.*"

    B. "I'm *gonna* do it."

    C. "What type of girl is she?" "Oh, you know. *Lika* those girls we know."

None of your students use wacky words such as *kinda*, *gonna*, *lika*, or *dunno*, do they? I hope not because they confuse anyone a person is speaking to or writing to. What does *kinda* mean? You like the boots a little? Is there such a word as *kinda*? *Gonna*, now there's a strange word for going. Perhaps it's easier to say or write for some people, but it makes no sense to the listener or the reader. Is *gonna* a word? Ask the children if they can find it in the dictionary. And what about the word *lika*? Whenever someone uses *lika* around me, I'm totally confused. Does the speaker or writer mean *like* when he/she uses *lika*? If so, why not use the word *like*?

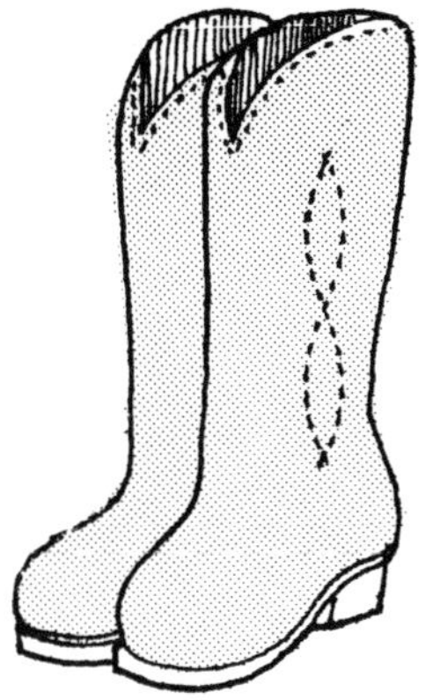

Now, show these sentences to your class.

A. "Do you like these boots?" "Yes, no, a little."

B. "I'm going to do it."

C. "What type of girl is she?" "Oh, you know. Like those girls we know."

45. Print the words *lika*, *kinda*, *gonna*, and *dunno* on separate pieces of poster board. You might even draw a crazy figure above each word. Several times a day, have the class look at these words, as you hold up a poster board, and decide that they will never use these wacky words in speaking and writing.

Work Sheet #9
Wacky Words

This is a "monster drawing" contest. In the square below, draw a "dunno" monster or a "lika" monster or a "kinda" monster. Color the monster and print the correct label beneath it.

Monster Drawing

student's name________________________

The Period and Comma Inside Double Quotation Marks

46. The following sentences should be presented to your class:

A. She said, "I will go".

B. "Close the door", the man stated.

C. "Do not go over there", Mary said.

D. The man said, "Bill is here".

They are to look at the sentences to see if there are any marks of punctuation out of place. Some of the children may be able to spot the errors. If so, allow them to correct the errors.

47. Now show the students the sentences with all the punctuation marks in the correct places.

A. She said, "I will go."

B. "Close the door," the man stated.

C. "Do not go over there," Mary said.

D. The man said, "Bill is here."

48. Explain to the class that periods and commas *always* go *inside* of double quotation marks. Discuss this point over and over, and write sentences on the chalkboard as correct examples of this point.

49. Every student is to write ten sentences with commas inside the double quotation marks.

50. Each child will also write ten sentences with periods inside the double quotation marks.

Work Sheet #10
The Period and Comma Inside Double Quotation Marks

Write a dialogue between Betty and Bill. Be sure you put the periods and commas *inside* the quotes. The first two sentences have been done for you.

Betty: "Bill, please come in."

Bill: "Thank you. How have you been?"

Betty: ______________________________

Bill: ______________________________

Betty: ______________________________

Bill: ______________________________

Betty: ______________________________

Bill: ______________________________

Betty: ______________________________

Bill: ______________________________

student's name______________________

Lay, Seen

51. Either write these sentences on a chalkboard or write them on a mimeographed sheet for the class.

A. I seen the kid yesterday.

B. Mary is laying down.

C. He seen what she did.

D. I think I will lay down.

Allow the children time to look at these sentences and to tell you the error in each sentence, if they are able to.

The errors are *seen* and *lay*. Most students and many adults use *seen* and *lay* when they should use *saw* and *lie*.

Now show the class the four sentences in their corrected form.

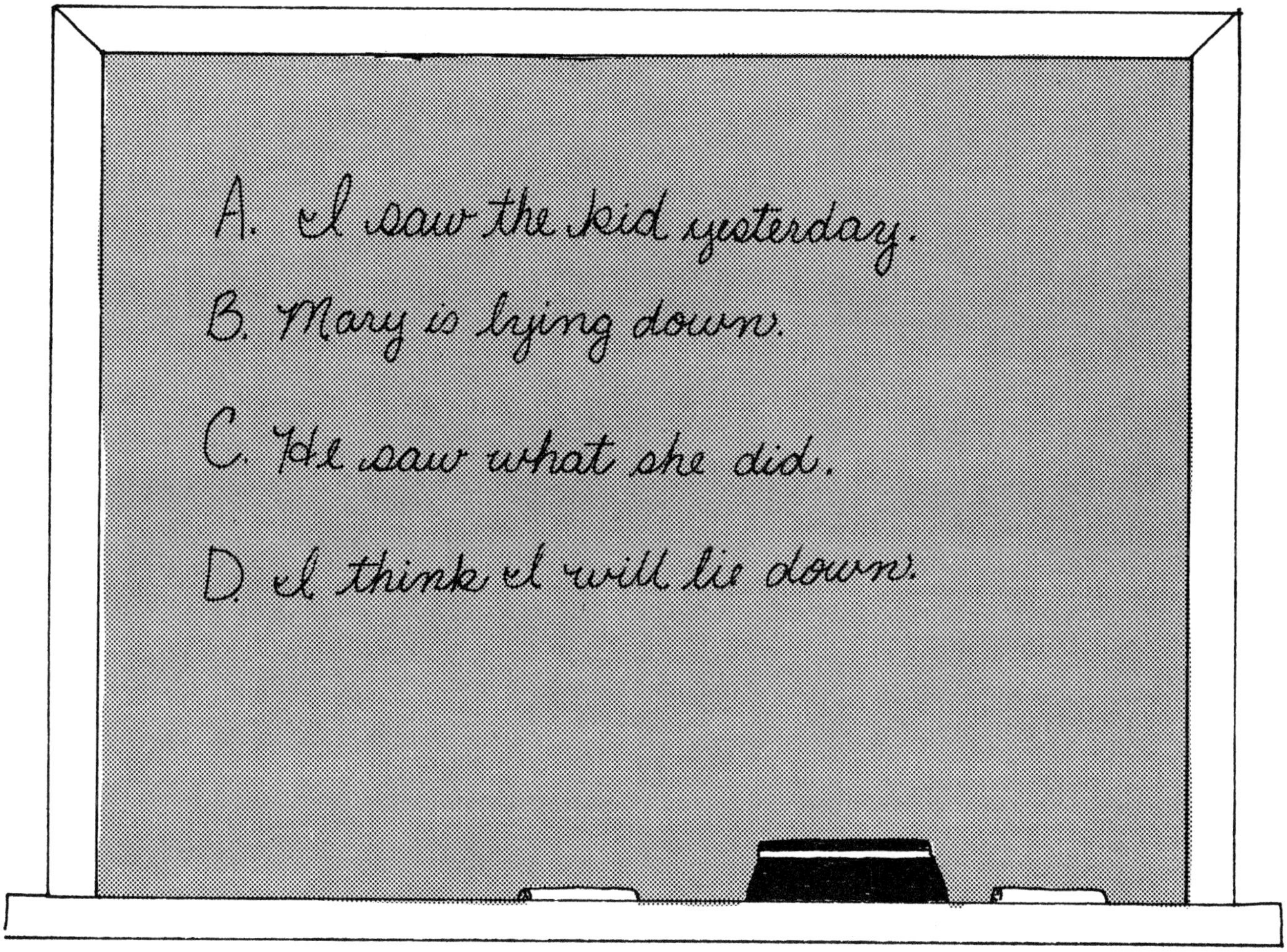

52. Each member of the class is to study the following information and memorize it:

A. People *lie* down. They don't *lay* down. You say or write "I will *lie* down," or "She is *lying* down."

B. Never use *seen* after I, we, or a person's name. You don't say "I *seen*" or "We *seen*" or "Jane *seen*." You state "I *saw*" or "We *saw*" or "Jane *saw*." *Seen* is used with words like *was* or *have*. "She *was seen*," or "They *have seen*."

53. Each child is to draw a person lying down. This can be done on half a sheet of poster board. The student may color the poster board any way he/she wishes. Someplace on the poster board the student is to write or print, "He/She is *lying* down." "I think I will *lie* down." Hang the poster boards up all over the room.

54. Do the same thing for the word *saw*. Each class member will draw a picture of a person looking at something. The child will print "He/She saw ______________________."

55. Practice with the class every day orally using *lie* and *saw* in many different sentences.

Work Sheet #11
Lay, Seen

Complete these sentences using *lie*, *saw*, *seen*, and *lying* correctly. One sentence has been done for you.

1. ____________ lie ____
2. ____________ saw ____
3. ____________ lying ____
4. ____________ saw ____
5. Aunt Mary is lying on the couch.
6. ____________ saw ____
7. ____________ seen ____
8. ____________ lying ____
9. ____________ seen ____
10. ____________ lie ____

student's name____________________

date____________________

Is When, Is Where

56. Write these sentences on your chalkboard.

A. That is when we go to town.

B. The barn is where we keep the hay.

C. This is when we all pull together to win.

D. Our garage is where Dad keeps his tools.

Read these sentences to the class. Allow the children to "hear" the sentences. Next, tell them *not* to use the constructions "is when" and "is where."

Write the corrected sentences on the chalkboard.

A. That is the time we go to town.

B. The barn is the place in which we keep the hay.

C. This is the moment (*or* the time) we all pull together to win.

D. Our garage is the place in which Dad keeps his tools.

57. Ask the children to correct the following sentences:

A. This is when I like to work.

B. The office is where my father works.

C. That is when they all start school.

D. A forest is where there are many animals.

58. Have one or two students make this sign to hang up in the classroom.

NOT CORRECT
is when
is where

CORRECT
is the time
is the place

Work Sheet #12
Is When, Is Where

Correct the *is when* and *is where* errors in these sentences. Write the corrected sentences on the lines provided.

1. The old house is where we play.

   ____

2. This is when Dad comes home.

   ____

3. My grandmother's farm is where we go to have picnics.

   ____

4. That is when all the students go to school.

   ____

5. The river is where we all go fishing.

   ____

Now write five *is when* and *is where* sentences for your friends to correct.

1. ______________________________
2. ______________________________
3. ______________________________
4. ______________________________
5. ______________________________

your name______________________

The Use of One and You

59. Mimeograph the following paragraph and give each child a copy:

When one plays basketball, it is best if he is in good condition. You must get plenty of sleep, and you must exercise daily. One should also have a balanced diet. One could also do some light workouts with weights at least three times a week. If one does all these things, you should be in good condition.

Ask the class if they understand this paragraph. Discuss with the class ways to make the paragraph stronger. Then give each student a copy of this new paragraph.

When a *person* plays basketball, it is best if he is in good condition. A *player* must get plenty of sleep, and *he* must exercise daily. The *player* should also have a balanced diet. *He* could also do some light workouts with weights at least three times a week. If a *player* does all these things, *he* should be in good condition.

60. The students are to study and master this information.

A. Use *one* as a number. Do *not* use it when you are writing or talking about a person. It is too vague. If you use *one*, people will ask "One what?" (However, be aware that *one* can be used to mean people in general.)

B. Do *not* use *you* unless you are directly talking to or writing to one person. Do *not* use *you* when you are writing or talking about a person. Say "the player, or he, or the workman, etc."

61. Each member of the class is to replace the *ones* and *yous* in this paragraph with nouns or pronouns.

You will need all of your skills to write a strong paragraph. One must be able to write a strong topic sentence. You must also organize and develop the paragraph. One must attempt to build a paragraph of at least 150 words. You must also use interesting adjectives in order to make your paragraph interesting. All of these items are important for one to write a good paragraph.

62. Every boy and girl in the class will look up the meanings of *you* and *one* in a dictionary. He/She will also write down each definition. He/She will show his/her work to you and discuss the definitions with you.

Work Sheet #13
The Use of One and You

Rewrite this paragraph in the space provided at the bottom of the page. Replace the *ones* and *yous* with appropriate pronouns or nouns.

One should always help around the house. You should help your mother and your father whenever you can. One can help mow the yard and one can help rake it. You can take out the trash, help dry dishes, and help keep the house neat by picking up things. One can also set the table, and one can help Mother bring food to the table. You should do as much as possible in helping around the house.

your name______________________

The Correct Form of Numbers

63. Write these sentences on the chalkboard.

A. I have 25 cents.

B. The dress costs 40 dollars.

C. Will you please pay him the 200 dollars we owe for the rent?

D. The groceries came to a total of 83 dollars and 49 cents.

E. Our house repairs will be about 1400 dollars.

F. That will be 37 cents, please.

After the students have read the sentences, go to the chalkboard and make the following corrections:

A. I have twenty-five cents.

B. The dress costs forty dollars.

C. Will you please pay him the two hundred dollars we owe for the rent?

D. The groceries total eighty-three dollars and forty-nine cents.

E. Our house repairs will be about fourteen hundred dollars.

F. That will be thirty-seven cents, please.

64. The following information is for your children to study and master:

A. If the number can be written in one or two words, write it out—two, thirty-four, ninety-nine, one thousand, six hundred, etc. Otherwise, use figures—656, 497, etc.

B. You will use a hyphen in all compound numbers between twenty-one and ninety-nine.

10 ··· Ten ··· 6 ··· Six ··· 3

Work Sheet #14
The Correct Form of Numbers

Cross out the errors in the incorrect sentences, and write in the corrections. Some of the sentences are correct.

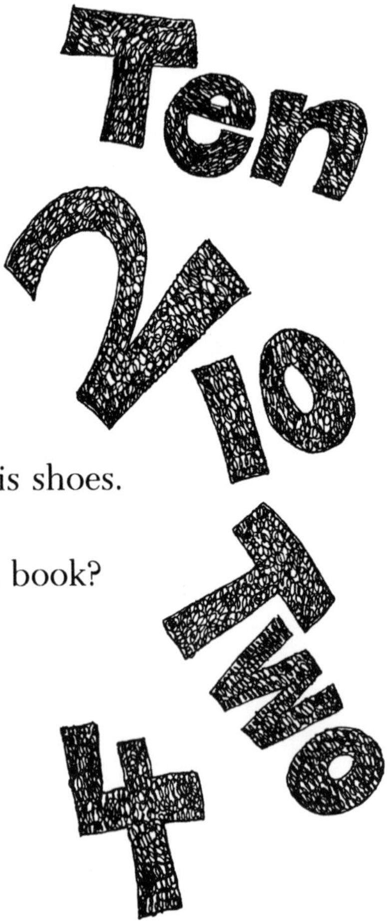

1. Aunt Jane paid 25 dollars for her new dress.
2. I will give you 50 cents for a piece of pie.
3. My father paid 4,000 dollars for his new car.
4. The team scored eighty-six points.
5. My brother had to pay 10 dollars for his tennis shoes.
6. Is fifty-five cents too much to give for this old book?
7. Our weekly grocery bill is 92 dollars.
8. Give the salesman forty-two dollars, please.
9. Billy gave 25 cents for the fishing plug.
10. Don't pay anymore than 10 dollars for that.
11. My dad gives me five dollars and 45 cents a week for my allowance.
12. We earn 8 dollars and 65 cents an hour.
13. They paid 20,000 dollars for the house.
14. Give me 22 cents for the ball.
15. I gave 15 dollars for the new rake. your name____________________

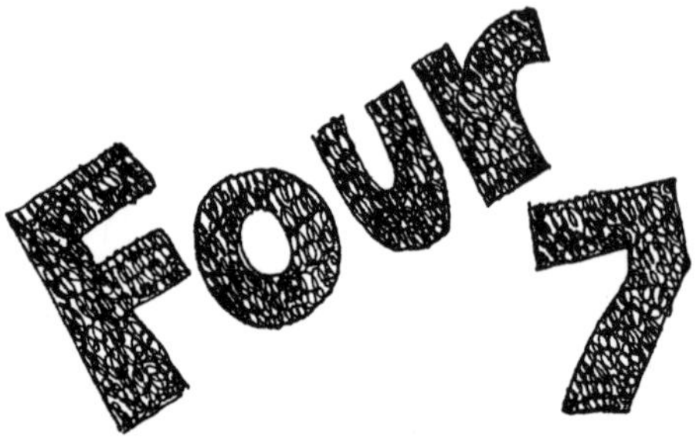

ANSWER KEY

Activity 6 — A. It's B. its C. there D. They're E. Their F. than G. then H. well I. except J. accept

Activity 7 — A. than B. accept C. except D. there E. its F. Their G. good H. They're I. than J. It's

Activity 12 — A. a lot B. all right C. am not D. Those E. until F. because G. tough H. sneaked I. those J. a lot

Activity 13 — A. sneaked B. all right C. a lot D. until E. tough F. because G. isn't H. a lot I. sneaked J. until

Activity 20 — A. The book makes no sense.
The book doesn't make any sense.

B. Mary has not done anything.
Mary has done nothing.

C. Jane never has any schoolwork.

D. We hardly ever practice.

E. Bill could hardly say anything.

Activity 32 — A. Betty bought a coat. I bought a new hat.
Betty bought a coat; I bought a new hat.

B. Our class is going to Chicago; we won this trip by selling the most magazines.
Our class is going to Chicago. We won this trip by selling the most magazines.

C. Where is Uncle George? He is supposed to go with us.

D. Jack helped Bill paint the house. He enjoyed the hard work.
Jack helped Bill paint the house; he enjoyed the hard work.

E. Don't go over there; there is a mean dog in the yard.
Don't go over there. There is a mean dog in the yard.

Activity 38 — A. Somebody must have left his/her supplies here.

B. Each person did his/her best.

C. One of the members of the class moved his/her chair.

D. Nobody should leave his/her clothes on the floor.

E. Everyone ate everything on his/her plate.

Activity 57 — A. This is the time I like to work.

B. The office is the place in which my father works.

C. That is the time they all start school.

D. A forest is the place in which there are many animals.

Work Sheet#1 — 1. grammar 2. until 3. written 4. achieve 5. correct 6. separate 7. correct 8. receive 9. truly 10. correct 11. correct 12. definite 13. correct 14. sophomore 15. correct

Work Sheet#2 — 1. accept 2. There 3. It's 4. than 5. except 6. good 7. their 8. They're 9. then 10. its 11. accept 12. there 13. well 14. It's 15. than

Work Sheet#3 — 1. those 2. until 3. All right 4. sneaked 5. a lot 6. Isn't 7. tough 8. isn't 9. until 10. a lot 11. All right 12. a lot 13. those 14. Isn't 15. until

Work Sheet#4 — 1. I do not have anything.

2. She never has any money.

3. That doesn't make any sense.

4. She is taller than I.

5. Bill has not done anything.

Work Sheet#5 — 1. There are too many people here.

2. Today America is stronger than ever.
Now America is stronger than ever.

3. I do not care.

4. The cabin was not visible.

5. She really works hard.

6. The big bear roared at us.

7. The picture really looks nice.

8. He drove the tractor.

9. Things are easier today.
Things are easier now.

10. Was the mountain visible?

Work Sheet#6 — 1. I went to town. Bill stayed home.
I went to town; Bill stayed home.

2. Mother painted the walls; Dad painted the ceiling.
Mother painted the walls. Dad painted the ceiling.

3. Betty sold tickets; Nancy took in the money.
Betty sold tickets. Nancy took in the money.

4. If I see your friend, I will tell him you are here.

5. When we get to Chicago, we will go to the Art Institute.

6. While we are at Uncle Bill's, you will be able to go fishing.

7. He went to Basco, Illinois, to see his friend.

8. In Munich, Germany, we bought a beautiful set of dishes.

9. At Seton, Ohio, we had a picnic.

10. Jim bought gas; Joe bought groceries.
Jim bought gas. Joe bought groceries.

Work Sheet#7 — 1. Everyone ate his dinner at 12:30 p.m.

2. Someone in the house did not do his/her chores.

3. Each of the girls brought her clothes.

4. Anyone may bring his/her favorite record.

5. Each of the children put his/her toys in the play area.

Work Sheet #12 —

1. The old house is the place in which we play.
2. This is the time Dad comes home.
3. My grandmother's farm is the place in which we go to have picnics.
4. That is the time all the students go to school.
5. The river is the place in which we all go fishing.

Work Sheet #14 —

1. Aunt Jane paid twenty-five dollars for her new dress.
2. I will give you fifty cents for a piece of pie.
3. My father paid four thousand dollars for his new car.
4. Correct
5. My brother had to pay ten dollars for his tennis shoes.
6. Correct
7. Our weekly grocery bill is ninety-two dollars.
8. Correct
9. Billy gave twenty-five cents for his fishing plug.
10. Don't pay any more than ten dollars for that.
11. My dad gives me five dollars and forty-five cents a week for my allowance.
12. We earn eight dollars and sixty-five cents an hour.
13. They paid twenty thousand dollars for the house.
14. Give me twenty-two cents for the ball.
15. I gave fifteen dollars for the new rake.

Multimedia Foundations

Additional Photograph Credits

Figure 1.3: Liviu Ionut Pantelimon/Shutterstock.com
Figure 1.7: kentoh; Laser0114/Shutterstock.com
Figure 1.9: Oxlock/Shutterstock.com
Figure 1.10: Iakiv Pekarskyi; egd; jocic; graphit; Oxlock; file404/Shutterstock.com
Figure 1.16: Pete Saloutos/Shutterstock.com
Figure 1.18: Sergii Korolko; Leigh Prather/Shutterstock.com
Figure 1.19: EugenP; Renata Novackova; B. Melo; Mushakesa/Shutterstock.com
Figure 1.22: Francisco Caravana/Shutterstock.com
Figure 2.1: aceshot1/Shutterstock.com
Figure 2.2: Adrio Communications Ltd/Shutterstock.com
Figure 2.7: Kitch Bain/Shutterstock.com
Figure 2.8: Tudor Voinea/Shutterstock.com
Figure 2.10: Norman Chan/Shutterstock.com
Figure 2.11: terekhov igor; iadams/Shutterstock.com
Figure 2.12: Jesus Cervantes; nasirkhan/Shutterstock.com
Figure 2.14: thaikrit; Yanas/Shutterstock.com
Figure 2.15–2.17: vlastas/Shutterstock.com
Figure 2.20: Vtldtlm; Sofia Santos; sgame; Janfilip; Diego Cervo/Shutterstock.com
Figure 2.22: Gentleface/Shutterstock.com/Shutterstock.com
Figure 2.23: Miguel Angel Salinas; Biehler, Michael; Andrey Kekyalyaynen/Shutterstock.com
Figure 2.25: Oleksiy Mark/Shutterstock.com
Figure 2.26: Andrea Danti/Shutterstock.com
Figure 2.27: Martin Spurny; dofmaster/Shutterstock.com
Figure 2.28: cobalt88; Agan; romvo/Shutterstock.com
Figure 2.29: Tatiana Popova; buonarrotidesig; alexwhite; kenjito; Lukiyanova Natalia/frenta/Shutterstock.com
Figure 2.30: ravl; ronfromyork/Shutterstock.com
Figure 3.1: Michael D Brown/Shutterstock.com
Figure 3.2: Tubol Evgeniya/Shutterstock.com
Figure 3.3: maigi/Shutterstock.com
Figure 3.4: Lukiyanova Natalia/frenta; leedsn; Vitaly Korovin; fotoluminate/Shutterstock.com
Figure 3.5: Sergio Hayashi; astudio; Vladimir Koletic; weissdesign; BLANKartist; claudia veja/Shutterstock.com
Figure 3.6: Ben Roach Studios; Alkestida; Sergii Korolko; photovibes; Slaven/Shutterstock.com
Figure 3.7: Turovsky/Shutterstock.com
Figure 3.8: almagami/Shutterstock.com
Figure 3.9: marekuliasz/Shutterstock.com
Figure 4.1: Adriano Castelli; Terry Chan/Shutterstock.com
Figure 4.3: Suzanne Tucker; Flower_Power/Shutterstock.com
Figure 4.4: shooarts; 55662019/Shutterstock.com
Figure 4.5: Krivosheev Vitaly; Gorilla/Shutterstock.com
Figure 4.7: Henrik Lehnerer; eddtoro/Shutterstock.com
Figure 4.8: vladislav_studio/Shutterstock.com
Figure 4.9: Noedelhap/Shutterstock.com
Figure 4.10: Goran Bogicevic; Leenvdb; Nemeziya; Clive Watts; CoolR; ollirg/Shutterstock.com
Figure 4.11: P Phillips/Shutterstock.com
Figure 4.12: Peter Kirillov/Shutterstock.com
Figure 4.13: Yevgen Kotyukh/Shutterstock.com
Figure 4.14: Vasca; rudall30/Shutterstock.com
Figure 4.15: SomeSun/Shutterstock.com
Figure 4.16: Tamara Kulikova; wong yu liang; Chris Howey; Palto/Shutterstock.com
Figure 4.17: Angela Waye/Shutterstock.com
Figure 4.19: Eskemar; 28769977/Shutterstock.com
Figure 4.20: Hubis/Shutterstock.com
Figure 4.21: Kailash K Soni; Ivelin Radkov; Matt Tilghman; dragon_fang/Shutterstock.com
Figure 4.22: Sylvie Bouchard; Patrickma/Shutterstock.com
Figure 4.23: Stuart Jenner; Jeffrey M. Frank/Shutterstock.com
Figure 4.24: Guilu; bikeriderlondon; Walter G. Arce/Shutterstock.com/Shutterstock.com
Figure 5.7: Sooolnce/Shutterstock.com
Figure 5.8: jstan; Eugene Sim/Shutterstock.com
Figure 5.9: silavsale; Roberts/Shutterstock.com
Figure 5.10: 68853748/Shutterstock.com
Figure 5.11: oriontrail/Shutterstock.com
Figure 5.14: zhuda/Shutterstock.com
Figure 5.15: R. Cherubin/Shutterstock.com
Figure 5.18: Blaze986; pics721; pics72; Frank Fennema; v2; Sir Armstrong/Shutterstock.com
Figure 6.1: Annette Shaff/Shutterstock.com
Figure 6.2: Barone Firenze/Shutterstock.com
Figure 6.4: spline09; pcruciatti/Shutterstock.com
Figure 6.5: Schmid Christophe/Shutterstock.com
Figure 8.1: Jupiter Images Corporation/schools.clipart.com
Figure 8.2: maigi/Shutterstock.com/Shutterstock.com
Figure 8.3: Andrea Danti; krugloff/Shutterstock.com
Figure 8.9: Steven Newton/Shutterstock.com
Figure 8.16a: Jupiter Images Corporation/schools.clipart.com
Figure 8.16b: Neale Cousland/Shutterstock.com
Figure 8.16c: Stephen Denness/Shutterstock.com
Figure 8.19–8.20: Zeljko Radojko/Shutterstock.com
Figure 8.22: Yes Man/Shutterstock.com
Figure 8.27: OZaiachin/Shutterstock.com
Figure 8.28: berkut/Shutterstock.com
Figure 8.29: Dario Sabljak; Vladru/Shutterstock.com
Figure 9.1: Ahmad Faizal Yahya/Shutterstock.com
Figure 9.24: nasirkhan; Sergey Kamshylin/Shutterstock.com
Figure 9.25: Patryk Kosmider/Shutterstock.com
Figure 9.26: Graeme Shannon; Vaclav Volrab/Shutterstock.com
Figure 10.4: Vatikaki/Shutterstock.com
Figure 10.25: Kletr/Shutterstock.com
Figure 11.1: Clipart design/Shutterstock.com
Figure 11.2: Monkey Business Images/Shutterstock.com
Figure 11.3: MilanB/Shutterstock.com
Figure 11.4: Jezper; MilanB/Shutterstock.com
Figure 11.5: Paul Picone/Shutterstock.com
Figure 11.6: Mart; Steve Collender/Shutterstock.com
Figure 11.7: MilanB/Shutterstock.com
Figure 11.12: MaxFX/Shutterstock.com
Figure 11.16: Mike Flippo/Shutterstock.com
Figure 11.17: Robert Kneschke/Shutterstock.com
Figure 11.24: Miguel Angel Salinas; James Weston/Shutterstock.com
Figure 11.26: Galoff; Aleksandar Bunevski/Shutterstock.com
Figure 11.27: shalex84; Cyriel; Adrian Grosu; shupian; Studio 1a Photography; caimacanul/Shutterstock.com
Figure 11.30: Goran J/Shutterstock.com
Figure 12.1: James Steidl/Shutterstock.com
Figure 12.2: Borat; asliuzunoglu; Shmer/Shutterstock.com
Figure 12.3: Viktor Gmyria; Soundsnaps/Shutterstock.com
Figure 12.4: ID1974/Shutterstock.com
Figure 12.6: Panom; jcjgphotography; Sergio Schnitzler/Shutterstock.com
Figure 12.7: Bruce C. Murray/Shutterstock.com
Figure 12.8: Leo/Shutterstock.com/Shutterstock.com
Figure 12.10: Zoltan Pataki; esbobeldijk/Shutterstock.com
Figure 12.11: Andrey Zyk; Ivonne Wierink; keellla/Shutterstock.com
Figure 12.12: lznogood; Bruce Rolff/Shutterstock.com
Figure 12.13: Kitch Bain/Shutterstock.com
Figure 12.17: SeDmi/Shutterstock.com
Figure 12.21: Kovalev Sergey; Panom/Shutterstock.com
Figure 13.1: Suzanne Tucker/Shutterstock.com
Figure 13.2: withGod; tele52/Shutterstock.com
Figure 13.3: Claudia Veja/Shutterstock.com
Figure 13.5: Claudia Veja/Shutterstock.com
Figure 13.6: David Burrows; Stocksnapper/Shutterstock.com
Figure 13.14: Claudia Veja/Shutterstock.com
Figure 13.15: Claudia Veja; Selena/Shutterstock.com

Multimedia Foundations

Core Concepts for Digital Design

Vic Costello

with Susan A. Youngblood and
Norman E. Youngblood

Focal Press
Taylor & Francis Group
NEW YORK AND LONDON

First published 2012
This edition published 2013
by Focal Press
70 Blanchard Road, Suite 402, Burlington, MA 01803

Simultaneously published in the UK
By Focal Press
2 Park Square, Milton Park, Abingdon, Oxon OX14 4RN

Focal Press is an imprint of the Taylor & Francis Group, an informa business

Library of Congress Cataloging-in-Publication Data
Application submitted

British Library Cataloguing-in-Publication Data
A catalogue record for this book is available from the British Library

ISBN 13: 978-0-240-81394-3 (pbk)

Typeset by: diacriTech, Chennai, India

Dedication

To the Giver of light for the gift of multimedia.

Contents

Contents

Contents

SECTION 3 • Static Media

SECTION 4 • Time-Based Media

Acknowledgements

I want to thank everyone who participated in the development of this book and supported me as I've worked on it. At the top of the list are Susan Youngblood and Ed (Norman) Youngblood, who coauthored and illustrated Chapter 7, "Web Design," and edited nine other chapters. Ed has worked in the field of web and interactive media design since 1994, and he has taught web design courses since 1999. Susan's specialty is in technical writing and editing. Together they produced an excellent chapter that will be of great value to the readers of this book. In their editorial role, Ed and Susan conducted background research, verified facts and terminology used throughout the book, polished the clarity and consistency of the writing, and contributed new material that the reviewers wanted to see included or expanded upon. Their contribution of time and expertise is most appreciated.

Along the way, Ed and Susan introduced me to Chris Walker, a professional photojournalist whose storied works have been published by numerous media outlets, including the Associated Press, *New York Times*, *Scientific America*, and *Smithsonian Magazine* (online). Chris was brought in initially to review Chapter 10, "Photography." However, after hearing about the book and reading the chapter, he became excited about the project and wanted to do more. Chris offered to illustrate Chapter 10 with his own photographs and captions. He even wrote a short piece entitled "The Decisive Moment" that you won't want to miss. Chris' work brings the photography chapter to life and is a terrific visual accompaniment to the text.

Qian Xu, my colleague in the School of Communications at Elon University, wrote Chapter 6, "Interface Design and Usability." Like the field of web design in general, the companion field of interface design has evolved over the years into a sophisticated branch of study; and as such, it remains a highly specialized and technical component of multimedia design. Chapter 6 was a perfect fit for Qian, whose research and teaching interests include the social and psychological impact of media technology, user experience of online media, and online strategic communication.

I also wish to thank a number of individuals for kindly providing feedback and commentary throughout the various stages of development of this book: Dana Allison, Barton Community College; Jeff Bird, Swinburne University of Technology; Bob Carey, Gardner-Webb University; Candace Egan, California State University-Fresno; Anthony Galvez, Rhode Island College; Howard Goldbaum, University of Nevada-Reno; Christopher R. Harris, Middle Tennessee State University; Tom Hill, Bournemouth University; Sundeep Muppidi, University of Hartford; Andrew J. Ryan, Montgomery College; Staci Saltz, Elon University;

Jeffrey S. Wilkinson, United International College; Norman E. Youngblood, Auburn University.

This book would not have been possible without the support of Elon University and my colleagues in the School of Communications where I've taught since 2001. I also want to thank my students. They teach and inspire me daily about what works and doesn't work in the classroom regarding multimedia education and the instructional pedagogies I employ and often modify. I hope for them that this book hits the mark and that it will serve them and other readers well for many years to come. I also want to recognize a few of my students who played a more active role by posing for some of the photographs used to illustrate Chapter 11, "Audio Production:" Samantha Chambers, Brent Edwards, Jared Gilbert, Andrew Hirsh, Katherine Hodges, Anne Lukens, and John Tinkelenberg.

As a first-time author, I had absolutely no idea what I was getting myself into and how challenging it would be to write and illustrate a first edition of a textbook of this magnitude. My Focal Press editor, Michele Cronin, has stuck by me and encouraged me through countless delays and missed deadlines (more than either of us wishes to remember). Thank you so much for your saintly patience and unwavering support.

Finally, I want to thank Beth, my wife of nearly thirty years, my children, and a great host of friends and colleagues too numerous to mention, for your many prayers, kind words, and encouragements. You have sustained me in ways that you can't imagine, and I am extremely grateful for each and every one of you.

—Vic Costello

About the Author

Dr. Vic Costello has more than twenty years of experience in media education. He is currently an Associate Professor in the School of Communications at Elon University, where he has taught numerous courses in multimedia production since 2001. Before transitioning into academics, he worked professionally for seven years in broadcasting and corporate communications. Throughout much of his career, he has also worked concurrently as a freelance technical director, video producer, and creative consultant for corporate meetings, live events, and awards shows. Costello is a longstanding member of the Broadcast Education Association (BEA) and has served as both Producer and Chair of the BEA Festival of Media Arts.

He received a Ph.D. in Communication from the University of Tennessee–Knoxville, an M.A. in Communication from Regent University, and a B.S. in Radio-Television Production from Western Carolina University. His doctoral dissertation "Interactivity and the 'Cyber-Fan': An Exploration of Audience Involvement Within the Electronic Fan Culture of the Internet" received the Kenneth Harwood Outstanding Dissertation of the Year Award from BEA in 2000. Since 2004, he has chaired the Technology Committee for his school, for which he received an Excellence in Leadership Award in 2008.

About the Website

Teaching and learning the foundational concepts of multimedia entirely with printed words and illustrations is a great start, but the instruction only begins with *Multimedia Foundations: Core Concepts for Digital Design*. The companion website (http://www.focalpress.com/9780240813943) to this textbook contains additional material designed to illuminate more fully the many concepts and ideas covered here. As I set out to write this book, I knew from the start that I did not want to write another how-to book that would become outdated in six months or less. Thus, the focus of this book has been on what endures over time—the concepts and principles of design that transcend the technologies, software programs, hardware platforms, and creative workflows of multimedia, which are in a constant state of flux. The Web gives me a channel for posting time-sensitive and program-specific content that I think you will enjoy and find useful. The Web also provides a way for keeping ancillary materials like these up-to-date between subsequent editions of the textbook. The website features video tutorials for each chapter as well as other relevant content designed to reinforce the material covered here and perhaps take you even deeper into the subject. You will also find the glossary for the book on the website.

Please follow the registration instructions on the website to gain access to all of the materials.

Please visit the site: http://www.focalpress.com/9780240813943

Introduction

The idea for this book emerged from a course that I helped create in 2003 and have been teaching ever since. Digital Media Convergence, or DMC as the students like to call it, is a rapid-fire survey course that introduces students to foundational concepts and skills used across a wide range of multimedia technologies and design and production workflows. In DMC, students learn the basics of visual theory, graphic design, digital photography, sound and video recording and editing, and Web design—all in a one-semester course. To accomplish such a feat, this course focuses on breadth rather than depth. Students gain an expansive view of multimedia theory and practice, the language of audio and visual design, and the essential concepts and principles they need to understand before moving into advanced courses designed to take them deeper. One of the biggest challenges in teaching this course has been finding a textbook that adequately covers all the bases. We've looked long and hard to no avail. And with that, I set out to write one.

Multimedia Foundations: Core Concepts for Digital Design brings together in one work a myriad of essential principles and concepts common to all forms of digital artistry. In today's world of new media and convergent technologies, the starting point for entry into the digital arts is remarkably the same whether you aspire to be a journalist or art director, a photographer or filmmaker, a web designer or graphic artist, or a recording engineer or video producer. The digital revolution established a common denominator for all human acts of creative expression—namely, bits, those tiny binary morsels of digital information (0s and 1s) that proliferate invisibly across time and space bringing countless millions of multimedia messages to the masses every day.

For better or worse, the computer has become the central tool of multimedia design and production. Living in a digital age means that all of our devices and acquisition tools are nothing shy of mini computers designed to capture the physical elements of the material world (light, sound, motion, etc.) and convert them into immaterial coded streams of data that a computer or digital appliance can decipher, process, and manipulate. Your digital camera, smart phone, iPad, Android tablet, MP3 player, and smart TV serve as extensions of your digital footprint and toolset. The media you produce and consume eventually comes home to rest on a physical drive connected to your laptop or desktop computer, or more frequently today, in the Cloud—on a remote server housed at an undisclosed location by a multimedia service provider with a name like Google, Facebook, YouTube, iCloud, or WordPress.

The ubiquitous products of an ever-growing, always there, multimedia culture spill into our lives from every direction, affecting us personally (how we communicate, stay informed, shop, relax, manage our public identity, etc.) and professionally (how we conduct business, communicate ideas, manage and share information, produce goods, etc.). Today's user migrates effortlessly across the once compartmentalized roles of content producer, publisher, and consumer. With a few clicks of a mouse, you can be all three in a matter of moments, as opposed to days or weeks. The traditional lines have blurred and have perhaps disappeared altogether. Seemingly overnight, the media systems and workflows we have enjoyed for decades have changed forever; and yet, just as true, they have converged, making the world smaller, democratizing media, and bringing together under one roof a splendid assortment of previously noncombinable crafts and tools.

Multimedia Foundations looks broadly across the digital terrain and points out the common ground. It focuses on transferrable concepts and ideas that are relevant to all forms of digital creativity that you are likely to encounter as you pursue varied pathways of study and learning. I hope this book proves to be a good starting point for you as you explore the lay of the land and venture forth into the emerging fields of multimedia.

HOW THIS BOOK IS ORGANIZED

Each chapter covers a single facet of multimedia design. Thus, in one sense, the book is organized fluidly so that the instructor or reader can interact with the material nonlinearly in any manner he or she wishes. For those of you who prefer to progress through a book one chapter at a time in the order presented, I have tried to arrange the chapters in a way that makes sense and that progresses logically from beginning to end. The book is divided into four sections that address the areas of multimedia foundations, multimedia design, static media, and time-based media.

Multimedia Foundations

Section I is intended to give the reader a broad foundational understanding of the field along with an introduction to some essential tools and processes used in multimedia design. Chapter 1 sets out to define multimedia. It explores the characteristics of old and new media from an historical and theoretical perspective, and it provides an overview of how multimedia technologies have evolved during key moments of change and innovation. Chapter 2 looks at the computer. No matter what area of multimedia design you end up pursuing, you will spend lots of time in front of a computer screen, planning, conceptualizing, designing, and producing multimedia. The computer is more than a box filled with high-tech hardware components, it is an invaluable personal assistant, running the tools and programs you need to create, publish, and consume multimedia. Chapter 3 introduces readers to the planning and design process. All too often, the planning process is underestimated, rushed, or eliminated entirely from the producer's workflow. Good outcomes are highly dependent on good planning, vision, and intentionality on the front end of a multimedia project.

Multimedia Design

Section II includes four chapters on professional practices and theories that guide and inform the multimedia design process. Chapter 4 draws upon the field of visual communication, introducing the reader to core elements and principles of design related to aesthetics, a branch of study dealing with human perceptions of visual form and presentation. This chapter provides a conceptual framework to help you objectively assess, discuss, and critique the presentation of content (or form) within a visual design. Chapter 5 looks at page design, which has its roots in print media such as newspapers and magazines. In multimedia, the concept of page design extends into the realm of screen space as well, and digital displays come in a seemingly endless array of sizes and shapes. This chapter explores concepts related to page layout and design within the context of two-dimensional digital space. Chapter 6 looks specifically at interface design and the often-related concept of usability. The multimedia experience is primarily a nonlinear one in which users rely on the content creator to provide a well-designed interface to guide them past mountains of irrelevant information to find what they actually need. You can have the most exciting and compelling content on your website, but if users can't find it or get frustrated trying, they will click off your site as quickly as they landed. Making the multimedia experience commonsensical and user-friendly is what this chapter is all about. Chapter 7 looks at web design. While the field of multimedia encompasses much more than the Web, the ubiquitous Web is what many of us are most familiar with. For now, it remains the dominant distribution channel for disseminating multimedia content to the masses. This chapter explains how the Web works and provides an excellent overview of the terminology and concepts you need to begin designing, authoring, and publishing content online via the Web.

Static Media

Section III introduces you to three branches of static media. Static media, as defined here, refers to media or visual elements that can be presented or viewed instantaneously, in a fixed moment of time. For example, while you can gaze endlessly at a photograph, the entire photograph is available to you all at once. You do not have to wait for it to unfold or reveal itself over time. An exploration of static media begins with Chapter 8, which takes you into the field of graphic design and the rudimentary principles used for rendering raster graphics and bitmap images. Chapter 9 looks at the important field of typography. Readers will learn concepts related to the placement and design of text-based information in a multimedia design. Rounding out this section is Chapter 10 on digital photography. This is a beautifully illustrated chapter that covers a wealth of information about camera imaging and photographic techniques.

Time-Based Media

Section IV is concerned with the unique products of time-based media, namely audio and video, which by definition reveal information to the listener or viewer linearly over time. Chapter 11 explores the nature of sound and the production tools and techniques used for capturing and processing digital audio. Chapter 12 explores the historic roots of the audio and video recording process and the development of analog and digital recording formats over time. Chapter 13 deals with nonlinear editing (NLE) systems and their use in professional audio and video postproduction. While animation is included in most definitions of multimedia as a time-based element, space did not permit its inclusion in this edition. I intend to cover the topic of animation in the next edition of this book, as well as online on the companion website (see page xxi for the website address and instructions).

HOW THE CHAPTERS ARE ORGANIZED

Historical Quotes and Predictions

Each chapter begins with an historical prediction or quote about multimedia or the technologies behind it. Many of these came from the predictions database at Imagining the Internet, a website created by my colleague Janna Quitney Anderson as a part of the Pew Internet and American Life Project. The database includes thousands of predictions such as these:

> In the world of the future, people will use low-cost Radio Shack equipment to spy on themselves to find out who they are.
>
> **—Eric Hughes, 1992**

> I'm looking forward to the day when my daughter finds a rolled-up 1,000-pixel-by-1,000-pixel color screen in her cereal packet, with a magnetic back so it sticks to the fridge.
>
> **—Tim Berners-Lee, 1995**

It's fun to read and think about what people have said throughout the years about the Internet and other technologies that impact us daily. Take a moment and visit the site to see what you can find: http://www.elon.edu/e-web/predictions/early90s/

Chapter Highlights

Each chapter also includes a list of bullet points that highlights material examined in the chapter. The bulleted preview section provides a quick snapshot of the chapter's content and may be helpful for review as well.

Key Terms

One of my goals for this book is that the reader will gain a greater understanding of the language of multimedia design. The key terms section features a vocabulary list of important words mentioned in the chapter. Increasing your knowledge and understanding of industry terminology will help you to communicate with professionals who use these terms every day. Definitions for each *key term* can be found online in the chapter glossaries (see page xxi for the website address and instructions).

Boxes

Throughout the book, boxes are used to showcase material under three broad subject headings: Flashback, Great Ideas, and Tech Talk.

FLASHBACK

In order to understand the present, you need to know something about the past. Flashback segments point to a significant past accomplishment, event, or individual work.

GREAT IDEAS

The field of multimedia has been affected by countless ideas, inventions, and innovations that have significantly impacted the way we design and create multimedia. A great idea is not necessarily a good or lasting one, but one that has left a mark or that has had a transformative effect on the profession and those who work in it. A great idea may be something as grand as a theory or as simple as a workflow tip or technique.

TECH TALK

One the biggest challenges I faced in writing this book was deciding how deep to go into any one particular topic or subject area. Remember, this book was designed to focus more on breadth than depth. The risk here is that for some, I will not have gone deep enough and for others I will have gone far beyond what they were looking for in an introductory textbook. A partial solution to this dilemma is Tech Talk. Tech Talk delves deeper into advanced technical concepts and issues associated with multimedia. At times, it also covers practical techniques or applications that go beyond that of a cursory glance.

SECTION 1
Multimedia Foundations

Marish/Shutterstock.com

CHAPTER 1

Understanding Multimedia

We become what we behold. We shape our tools and then our tools shape us.

—Marshall McLuhan, Communication Theorist

The digital revolution is far more significant than the invention of writing or even of printing.

—Douglas Engelbart, Inventor of the Computer Mouse

Key Terms
Algorithm
Analog
Animation
Audio
Automation
Batch Processing
Bit
Blog
Broadcasting
Communication
Content Sharing
Convergence
Digital
Digitization
Graphics
Hypertext/Hypermedia
Hyperconnectivity
Interactive Media (Rich Media)
Internet
Linear
Mass Audience
Mass Media
Media
Microblog
Mobile Media
Multimedia
Narrowcasting
New Media
Niche Audience
Nonlinear
Numerical Representation
Old Media
Paradigm Shift
Rendering
Rich Internet Application (RIA)
Social Bookmarking

Chapter Highlights

This chapter examines:

- Multimedia as an extension of traditional media industries and practices
- The five elements of a multimedia experience
- Three characteristics of old media
- The new media paradigm shift
- Five principles of new media in a digital age

WHAT IT IS ... IS MULTIMEDIA!

In 1953, legendary comedian Andy Griffith recorded a monologue about a country preacher's trip to a college town during a home football game. In this fictional tale, the preacher has traveled to the "big city" to conduct a tent meeting, but his plans are interrupted when he is unexpectedly caught up by a frenzied crowd as they make their way to a football stadium on game day. What follows is a hilarious first-person account about the culture and sport of football as witnessed through the eyes of someone who has never seen or played the game. With a limited vocabulary and frame of reference, he begins to describe the events around him using the only terms he understands. He refers to referees as convicts because of their striped uniforms. The football is called a pumpkin. And the playing surface is compared to a cow pasture that players enter through a "great big outhouse" on either end of the field. The skit, titled "What it Was, Was Football," launched Griffith's professional career, leading to a guest appearance on the Ed Sullivan show in 1954. The live radio recording remains a cult classic and is one of the biggest selling comedy recordings of all time.

Social Media
Social Networking
Structural Modularity
Text
User-Generated Content
Vlog
Web 1.0/2.0/3.0
World Wide Web

At one time or another, all of us have been caught by surprise by a new experience or trend that sneaks up on us at lightning speed, challenging old ways and habits and leaving us scratching our heads in bewilderment. The country preacher's first game of football reminds me of the challenge my mother must have experienced as she learned to send an email message or open a file attachment for the very first time. She was born in the 1930s, and spent most of her life relying on pen, paper, and the U.S. postal system for sending and receiving correspondence. To her, this newfangled thing called email must have seemed like a strange and foreign idea. Perhaps you can think of a friend, grandparent, or child who has struggled finding the right words to describe social networking, online shopping, or surfing the Web. How does someone raised in the 1950s come to understand the World Wide Web? How does someone raised in the 1970s adapt to Facebook, Twitter, WordPress, and other social media channels?

For some of you, engaging in a formal study of multimedia will resemble the country preacher's first time at a football game. The landscape will appear strange and foreign to you at first, as you struggle for meaning in a sea of unfamiliar objects and ideas—even though you've probably spent plenty of time online. In time, a sense of comfort and familiarity will set in as you catch a glimpse of the big picture and develop a grasp of some fundamental concepts and rules. To begin, let's take a peek at something that you are probably very familiar with that may serve as a common reference point for understanding multimedia.

Social Media

Social media is a broad term used to describe a growing host of tools and services that enable computer-mediated interpersonal, group, and mass communication (see Figure 1.1). Social media can be broken down into many different categories of services as related to their general purpose and focus. A few of the most popular channels are included below.

- **Social networking** sites such as Facebook, MySpace, LinkedIn, etc., connect people with common interests, backgrounds, and associations. Such services provide numerous opportunities for synchronous and asynchronous communication through features such as live chatting, email, message board posting, event announcements, image galleries, embedded video, etc.
- **Blogging** engines such as Blogger and WordPress provide users with an online publishing tool for the regular posting of written stories or narrative commentaries. The term *blog* is a blended form of the phrase "web log." Blogs often focus on a particular subject or offer news and insight from a specific point of view. They also can serve as a public space for personal reflections, such as you might find in a diary or travel journal. Celebrities, media practitioners, and organizations (journalists, critics, actors, singers, authors, public relations firms, etc.) use blogs for interacting with fans, consumers, or the general public. Video blogging or **vlogging** (pronounced *V-logging*) is a hybrid form of blogging that uses video in place of a written narrative.

Vlogs typically feature a headshot of the individual as he or she communicates directly to the audience through a webcam attached to a personal computer. **Microblogging** is a variation of the blogging concept that limits communication to short strings of text or video. Microblogging services such as Tumblr and Twitter integrate the text-messaging capabilities of mobile technologies such as the cell phone with the enhanced distribution channels of the Web and mobile apps.

- A **wiki** is a tool that allows users to collaboratively create and edit documents and web pages online. Wikipedia, an online encyclopedic resource founded in 2001, is one of the most popular wikis. Entries in the Wikipedia database are posted and compiled interactively by a community of volunteers from around the world. Wikipedia is based on the MediaWiki platform. Like many of the wiki platforms, MediaWiki is free.
- **Content sharing** sites enable the exchange of various forms of multimedia content. Commercial photo sharing services such as Flickr and Shutterfly allow users to order photographic prints, albums, cards, and other products from content uploaded by family members and friends. Video sharing tools such as YouTube and Vimeo allow users to upload video content for potential distribution to a mass audience. Other services enable users to share music, audio resources, music playlists, and channels (as with the integration of Pandora Radio's online music service into Facebook and Twitter).
- **Social bookmarking** services (such as Delicious) and **news aggregators** (such as Digg) allow users to rate and share the most popular sites and news articles on the Web.

FIGURE 1.1
The rapid proliferation of social media sites like these has led to a phenomenon called hyperconnectivity; whereby people and machines stay perpetually connected via an ever expanding network of diverse communication channels. *Illustrator: Sarah Beth Costello.*

DEFINING MULTIMEDIA

The word *media* means "ways of transmission" and encompasses all of the various technologies we use to record information and transmit it to others. For example, videotape is a recording medium (singular) used for storing moving images and sound onto the physical surface of a magnetic strip. Television broadcasting and DVD (digital versatile disc) are transmission media (plural) used to deliver a video recording or live event to an audience. Likewise, printing is a medium whereby ideas are encoded as letterforms in ink onto the surface of a page, while books, newspapers, and magazines are the distribution channels or media through which intellectual content is delivered to a reader.

GREAT IDEAS

The Use of Metaphors

It's natural for us to draw upon past experiences when confronted with a new tool, system, or way of doing something. Familiar frames of reference, along with established patterns and workflows, can help us to make sense of new technologies and methods of productivity. This may explain why metaphors are used so often to describe a new communication object or activity (see Figure 1.2). For example, a computer's main interface is called "the desktop" because it represents the virtual version of a real space where tools and documents reside for conducting everyday business. Folder icons metaphorically symbolize the place where paper files are stored in cardboard sleeves. We're told to think of the hard drive as a file cabinet. We refer to online content as a "web page" because the book analogy makes sense to those of us familiar with print media and the structure of content arranged in a linear format. On Facebook and other social networks we write messages on "the wall" and we refer to the included members of our social networks as "friends." Metaphors are handy devices used to frame complex ideas in a way that nearly everyone can understand.

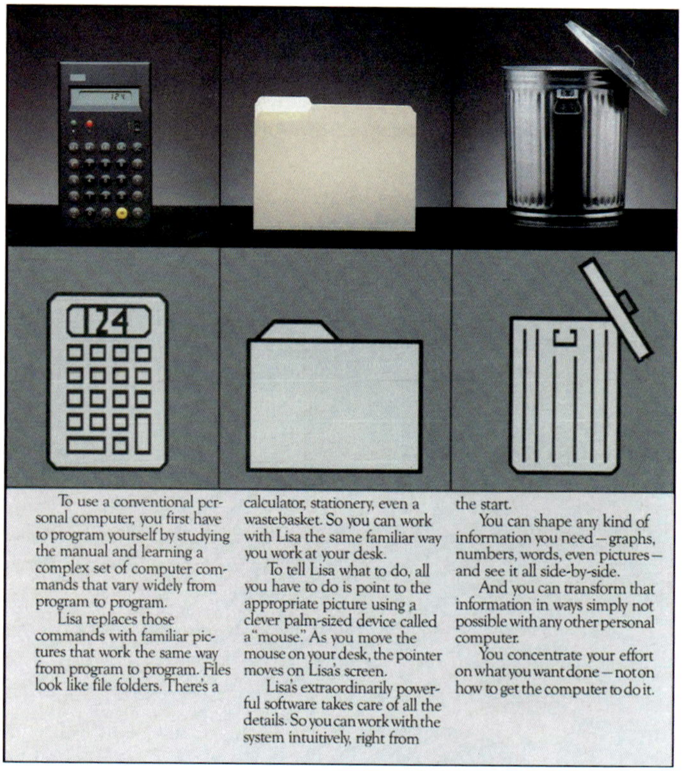

FIGURE 1.2
A 1983 promotional brochure from Apple Computer illustrates the power of a good metaphor. The Apple Lisa computer used these familiar picture icons to represent virtual versions of common everyday objects in a real office.
Image Courtesy of Computer History Museum.

A medium can be thought of as a pathway or channel through which ideas, information, and meaning flow as they travel from one place or person to another. Every medium has a native form and structure through which it delivers content. A sound recording produces pressure waves that can be understood aurally through the organs of hearing. A book transmits ideas with text and still pictures. Video and film convey stories through moving images and sound. Traditional media products such as these have a physical structure that is rigid and fixed and cannot be easily modified or adapted by the user or content producer.

For more than twenty years, the Web has been the centerpiece of multimedia culture. And for many people today, it still is. However, the Web's longstanding monopoly status as the dominant distribution platform for multimedia content is being challenged by newer technologies. While the web browser remains a popular gateway to the multimedia experience, more and more, users are producing and consuming multimedia content through a growing cadre of "smart" devices and mobile media apps. Smart phones, smart TVs, tablet computers, gaming consoles, and similar devices are being touted as "multimedia-enabled" by virtue of their

GREAT IDEAS
Multimedia

Multimedia is any combination of text, graphics, video, audio, and animation in a distributable format that consumers can interact with using a digital device. Multimedia can be thought of as a super-medium of sorts, because it represents the blending together of previously distinct, and noncombinable, forms of human expression.

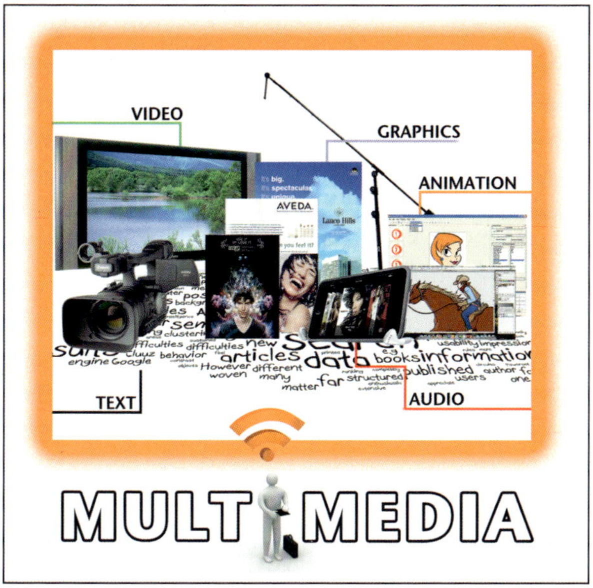

FIGURE 1.3
Illustrator: Sarah Beth Costello.

FIGURE 1.4
USA Today is reaching out to the next generation of news consumers with its "Mobile Marketplace." In addition to delivering content through traditional print and online media channels, it offers its readers access to news through a growing cadre of digital devices and gaming apps.
Source: usatoday.com

ability to rapidly access nearly any form of media content from within the Cloud or on the Web, through wireless or 3G/4G cellular connections (see Figure 1.4).

Understanding Multimedia

Today, much of the media content we consume is available in a variety of formats, intended to serve multiple purposes and audiences. For example, a book usually starts out as a print-only product. However, if the market demand is large enough, it may also be published in a spoken-word format and delivered via compact disc or MP3. With the right equipment, you can avoid paper altogether by downloading the e-book, a digital version of the text designed for reading on a computer screen or a handheld device such as the Kindle or iPad. The website for a bestseller may offer bonus material or

FIGURE 1.5
Visitors to J. K. Rowling's official website (jkrowling.com) are treated to an interactive virtual desktop. Clicking any object on screen reveals information about the author and her bestselling Harry Potter books.
Source: jkrowling.com

value-added content to online users through a gamut of multimedia channels—featuring audio excerpts, video interviews, background stories, pictures, and more (see Figure 1.5). With such a vast sea of information and social networking potential, you can easily imagine many of the other possibilities that exist. The opportunities for shaping content to meet the diverse needs and habits of different user groups are numerous, and they are changing rapidly, as the culture of multimedia continues to grow and permeate nearly every aspect of our personal and professional lives.

Multimedia is the grand culmination of many ideas rooted in the centuries-old traditions of human communication and content production. In one sense, the meaning of all that we have ever known about the communication process, mass media, and social interaction reaches its apex in multimedia, encompassing anything and everything having to do with the multisensory exchange of information and stories within a culture. Yet, in another way, the constant influx of bleeding-edge technologies means that there is always something new to discover or learn. Old habits, processes, and workflows need to be reexamined and modified from time to time as the tools of media production, distribution, and presentation change. That said, many of the established rules and conventions used in the design process rarely lose their relevance. Good design is still good design regardless of changes made to multimedia software and delivery platforms. Understanding multimedia requires bridging the past with the present while maintaining an ever-present eye on the horizon. The second you think you have it all figured out, something is sure to change.

Tech Talk

Hypermedia The term *hypermedia* refers to a host of digital technologies that enable the presentation of multimedia content in a nonlinear form. Traditional media such as books and vinyl records have a native linear structure. The contents are arranged in a logical order of presentation from beginning to end. This structure is fixed and cannot be changed or modified by the reader. The digital revolution introduced the concept of hypermedia into the language of media design and production. Hypermedia is not dependent on linear presentation alone, but allows the user to experience content in a nonlinear fashion. The path can vary depending on user-directed choices or spontaneous detours encountered along the way. Hypermedia is an extension of *hypertext*, a term coined in 1963 by technology pioneer and author Ted Nelson to describe text that is linked to other text, allowing the user to move between sections of text, within the same page or between linked documents. In the case of hypermedia, the principle is applied to nontext elements. Hypertext and hypermedia are core elements of the World Wide Web, though the principles extend beyond the Web to any type of digital product that allows users to randomly access content in a nonlinear way. The compact disc is a hypermedia technology because it allows users to skip tracks or change the location of the play head rapidly rather than having to fast-forward through a tape.

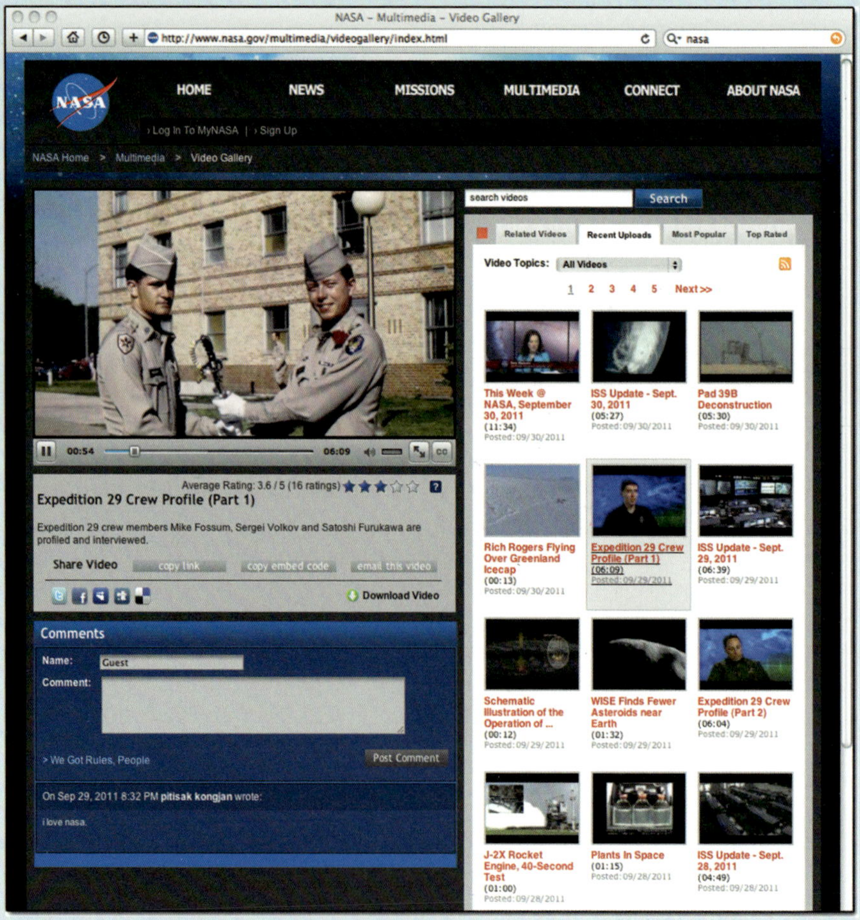

FIGURE 1.6
Hypermedia makes watching a video online a more interactive and nonlinear experience. Visitors to NASA's video gallery can search the video library, post comments, and control viewing and listening options using the media player's visual interface.
Source: nasa.gov

FLASHBACK

Three Generations of the Web

The evolution of the World Wide Web can be traced through three key stages of development known as Web 1.0, 2.0, and 3.0. The first generation of the Web, known as Web 1.0, covers the first decade of its existence from 1991 to 2001. This era was characterized by one-way communication and point-to-point exchanges of information. Web pages of this era usually mirrored the linear presentation and structure of a printed book. Static content, made up mostly of text and images, was consumed linearly in a traditional manner by reading from left to right and from top to bottom. User-generated content was unheard of, and there were few opportunities for interactivity, collaboration, or customization of the user experience. For most people, access to Web 1.0 was made possible through a low-bandwidth connection using a dial-up modem. While this was an adequate pipeline for the exchange of text and low-resolution graphics, it was not sufficient for handling the high-bandwidth transmissions of large files such as high-resolution images and streaming audio and video files.

Web 2.0 came into its own around 2001 following the dot-com bubble of the late 1990s. This generation of the Web ushered in the era of rich media content, dynamic web pages, content management systems, content sharing and collaboration sites, tagging, wikis, blogging, social networks, and more. Web 2.0 was made possible in large part by the release of program authoring tools used for creating Rich Internet Applications (RIAs). An RIA is a web-based application such as Adobe Flash, Oracle, Java, Microsoft Silverlight, or HTML5. RIAs typically require the use of a supported browser, media player, or browser plug-in (such as Flash Player or QuickTime) to run programs and view content. RIAs are used for deploying "rich media" or "interactive multimedia" content to consumers. As the name implies, rich media is designed to enrich the user's online experience by increasing opportunities for interactivity, customization, and personal control of a multimedia experience.

FIGURE 1.7
World Wide Web is the name given to the vast system of interconnected servers used in the transmission of digital documents formatted using Hypertext Markup Language (HTML) via the Internet.

(Continued)

> Timothy Berners-Lee, the inventor of World Wide Web, coined the term *Semantic Web* to describe Web 3.0, which many see as the next significant iteration of the Web. The Semantic Web is defined as "a web of data that can be processed directly and indirectly by machines."[1] Web 3.0 will likely involve the creation of new standards and protocols for unifying the way that content is coded, organized, and analyzed by computers monitoring the Web. This may involve transforming the Web into a massive unified database akin to a virtual library. Such a vast library will require more sophisticated computers and search engines to categorize and make sense of its holdings. As computers become "smarter" and the engineering behind the Web grows more sophisticated, many believe that we will see a significant increase in computer-generated content. Web 3.0 signals, in part, a larger role for computers as creators of intellectual content. Is a day coming when you will no longer be able to distinguish between content written by humans and machines? Has it already arrived?
>
> [1]Berners-Lee, T., Hendler, J., & Lassila, O. (2001, May 17). The semantic Web: A new form of Web content that is meaningful to computers will unleash a revolution of new possibilities. *Scientific American Magazine* 284(5), 34–43.

Evolving Media Industries

Traditional media are often defined as a set of monolithic industries with discrete practices and workflows that are proprietary to specific segments of the creative workforce. Journalists work with paper, ink, and words; photographers are the masters of communicating through the still image; graphic designers create visual illustrations and page layouts; and video producers, sound engineers, and filmmakers are the primary producers of time-based media content. This is no longer "exclusively" the case. Today, a growing number of photographers routinely shoot and edit their own video stories; graphic designers are busy retraining as web designers in order to retain a job or advance in a career; video and film have become nearly synonymous terms, having been unified (at least in part) through significant advancements in digital imaging and editing technologies; and journalists are fighting for survival as traditional products of the information age, such as the newspaper, are growing less viable in a digital marketplace driven by instant access, free content, and mobile delivery. More than ever before, media professionals are crossing historic lines that have previously defined who they are and how they produce and deliver content to consumers. What lies on the other side can be exciting or scary, depending on your point of view and ability to adapt rapidly to change.

In the same way that the mass media functioned as the primary shapers of culture in the 20th century, multimedia serves as one of the most prevalent forces of human communication in the 21st century. Multimedia is the melting pot that has brought all storytellers and content producers into the same creative crucible. The previously autonomous silos of producing and publishing are being replaced by new, dynamic, and converging infrastructures, which favor collaboration and content fluidity over rigid specialization and fixed distribution models. The term *melting pot* is an appropriate metaphor for describing the blending together of heterogeneous people into a homogenous team of professional designers and producers. The multimedia melting pot represents the corporate synthesis of creative people and workflows into a collaborative multimedia culture that is shaped more by what people have in common than by the divergent forms of creative expression they prefer or are most familiar with.

FLASHBACK

My Introduction to the Web

The year was 1993 and I was in a study lounge with fellow graduate students at the University of Tennessee in Knoxville. We were seated around a small desk exploring a new software program that had just been installed on a Windows workstation. The program, called Mosaic (see Figure 1.8), was one of the first web browsers that could combine colored images with text on the same screen. The more I discovered about Mosaic's web-surfing capabilities, the more I began comparing the experience to that of my parents' generation, when people gazed upon moving television images for the very first time. Little did I know then that this nascent technology would change the world forever and impact me directly in my career as a video producer and educator.

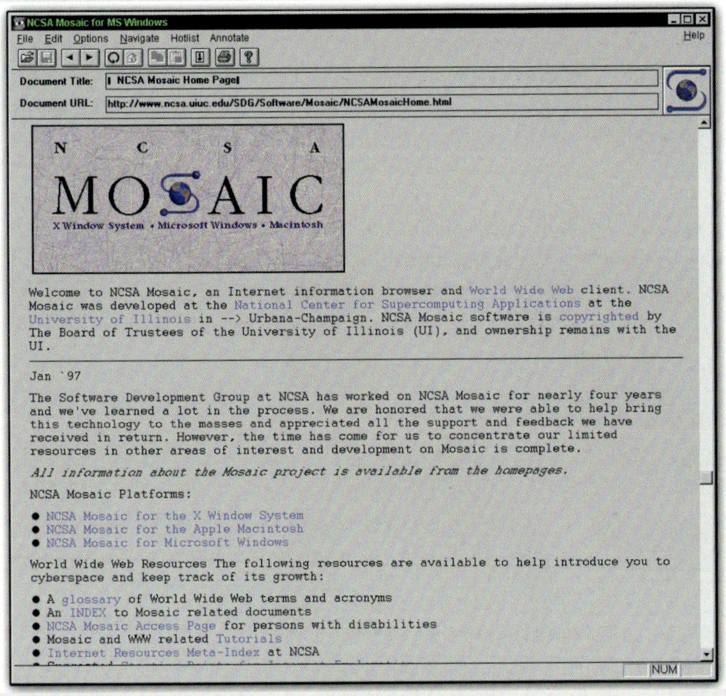

FIGURE 1.8
Mosaic 1.0 for Microsoft Windows was released in 1993 by the National Center for Supercomputing Applications. NCSA discontinued development and support for the browser in 1997.
Source: NCSA Image Archives.

(Continued)

Mosaic faded into obscurity nearly as quickly as it came into existence, eclipsed by Netscape Navigator in 1994. Despite its short lifespan, Mosaic was known as the "killer application" of the 1990s and was the catalyst for making the Internet accessible to the general public. While the Internet had been in existence for two decades, the human interface was text-based, cryptic, and visually uninteresting. Mosaic was one of the first web browsers to feature a graphical user interface (GUI), an object-oriented design that was visually intuitive and easy to use. Mosaic introduced the Web to the masses and took the Internet mainstream.

FROM OLD MEDIA TO NEW MEDIA

The term *old media* has become synonymous with the seven traditional forms of mass communication: books, newspapers, magazines, film, sound recordings, radio, and television (see Figure 1.10). The term *new media* is used to describe the relatively recent emergence of digital technologies that have changed the way that content is produced, distributed, and consumed.

The Characteristics of Old Media

Newspapers, television, motion pictures, and other media are still with us. Being "old" does not mean that they have disappeared or that they no longer provide a viable commodity for consumers. Rather it reminds us that the previous century's models of mass media, which took many years to refine, are based on a different paradigm from those used by the new media platforms of the 21st century.

FIGURE 1.9
These vintage icons of old media juxtaposed with a modern day "play" button remind us that the old media haven't died, but rather, they've merely adapted to new methods of content delivery and consumption.

FLASHBACK

Paradigm Shift

Thomas Kuhn coined the term *paradigm shift* in 1962 as a way of describing monumental changes in the meanings of terms and concepts that would shake up the status quo, challenging the scientific community's preconceived ideas and assumptions about natural phenomena. Kuhn was a proponent of aggressive puzzle-solving science, the sort of out-of-the-box thinking that would break new ground, pushing his colleagues away from routine practices of "normal" science that were rooted in established theories and methodologies. With Kuhn's help, it may be better for us to think of old media as normal and new media as the inventive type, the kind that allows us to advance new ideas and methodologies of information sharing and social interaction. The old media were slow to change because of the tremendous investment in the physical infrastructure (television towers, printing presses, recording studios, etc.) and the high cost of producing and distributing content. The digital revolution and the birth of the World Wide Web represent two of the most important defining moments in the history of communication. The paradigm of old media was suddenly confronted with new ways of creating, delivering and consuming content. A paradigm shift of epic proportions has occurred and things will never be the same.

In the 1950s sociologist Charles Wright examined the mass media and found that they share three defining characteristics:

1. The mass media are the product of large organizations that operate with great expense.
2. The mass media are directed towards a relatively large, heterogeneous, and anonymous audience.
3. The mass media are publicly transmitted and timed to reach the most audience members simultaneously.

LARGE ORGANIZATIONS

The first characteristic of old media is that they are the product of large organizations that operate with great expense. Hollywood movie studios, metro city newspapers, recording houses, television networks, broadcast television and radio stations, and book and magazine publishers, are large entities employing many people with highly specialized skills and job functions. The concentration of media ownership has increased significantly over the years, leading to fewer and fewer companies owning more and more of the world's mass media outlets.

In 2010, *Fortune Magazine* listed The Walt Disney Company as the largest entertainment and media conglomerate in the United States with net revenues of $36.1 billion. The top five also included News Corporation, Time Warner, Viacom, and CBS. These are household names to many of us. Millions of people are touched daily by content delivered or produced by one of these five companies. The start-up costs for a conventional media operation are high, which

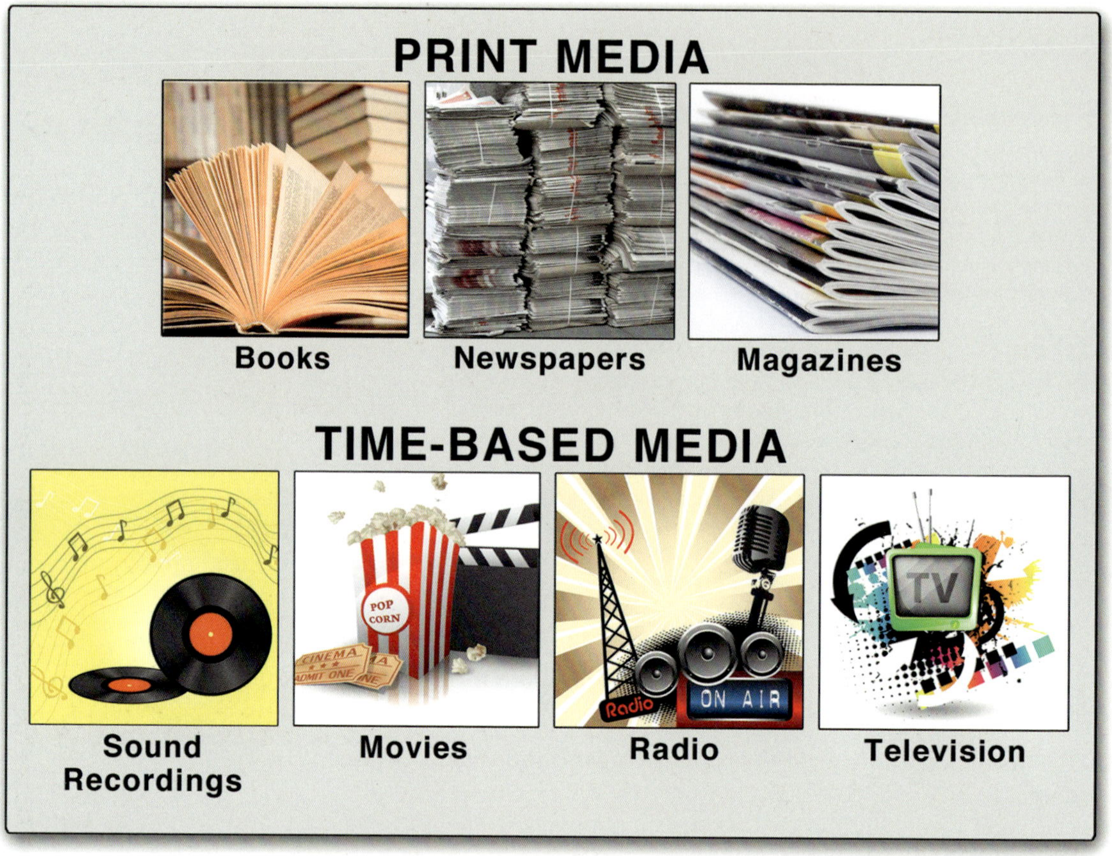

FIGURE 1.10
Old Media. Seven industries are often grouped under the broad heading of mass media. The print media include books, newspapers, and magazines. Time-based media (also known as electronic media) include sound recordings, movies, radio, and television.

means that most people will never be able to own a television station or movie studio. Also, professional programming and content is difficult and expensive to create. A single episode of a primetime dramatic series can easily cost more than $10 million to produce.

The Consumer as Producer: The New Media Paradigm Shift

Consumers no longer have to rely solely on large organizations to provide them with news and entertainment. The shift to new media means that anyone can produce and deliver content to a public audience. User-generated content (UGC), or consumer-generated media (CGM), bypasses the formal gatekeeping functions and monopolistic control that characterize the old media factories of cultural production. This paradigm shift is sometimes referred to as the *democratization of media* because it empowers the individual with a multitude of outlets for personal expression. With a little bit of new media know-how, you can self-publish a book or compact disc, rule a country in SecondLife, post a video on YouTube, send an iReport to CNN as a citizen

FIGURE 1.11
Launched in 2006, CNN iReport gives users of CNN.com a public outlet for posting opinion pieces, news reports, photos, and video. The best submissions carry the CNN iReport red stamp of approval, meaning they have been vetted and cleared for mainstream distribution on CNN.
Source: ireport.cnn.com

journalist, maintain a blog or Twitter feed, create a website, manage a radio station, host a podcast, and so much more. The opportunities for self-expression and commercial enterprise are virtually unlimited (see Figures 1.11 and 1.12). If the content you publish is compelling enough, you could develop a significant following. Almost daily, we hear of people rising to celebrity status, sometimes almost overnight, by publishing an item of sensational interest on the Web. Word of such things travels quickly through the new media channels of social networking as well as through mainstream media outlets as they monitor and report on Internet trends and sensations. As Andy Warhol so aptly predicted in 1968, "in the future, everyone will be world-famous for 15-minutes." With new media and the Web, this has never been more likely.

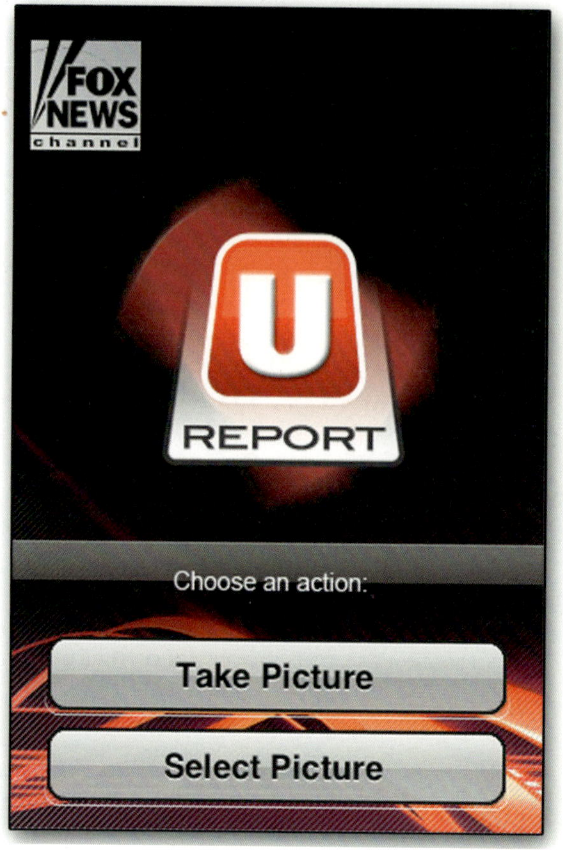

FIGURE 1.12
Fox News provides the uReport iPhone app to citizen journalists for instant filing of user-generated photos.
Source: ureport.foxnews .com

LARGE AUDIENCE

The institutions of old media were optimized to reach a large, anonymous, and heterogeneous audience. This characteristic identifies the receiver of a mass media message as a large group of people collectively known as "the audience." For this reason, they are sometimes called the "mass audience." The model of advertiser-supported media, which has been in use in the United States since the modern era of commercial printing and broadcasting, makes content available to consumers for virtually free, or at a partially subsidized cost. With this model, a media company's expenses and profits are paid for indirectly through the sale of commercial advertisements. A "mass" audience ensures a sufficient return on investment. Television programs will continue or be discontinued based on their ability to maintain a large following. When audience numbers fall below a pre-determined threshold or break-even point, a program is cut to minimize losses.

While market research companies such as Nielsen and Arbitron can provide aggregate data about the size and composition of a mass audience, the individual identities of people consuming mass media messages are largely unknown (see Table 1.1 and 1.2). An exception occurs with subscription services such as newspapers and magazines. Still, for every known person who subscribes, there are many anonymous users who acquire print products through point-of-purchase displays, magazine racks, street vendors, and the like.

The term *broadcasting* is a metaphor taken from earlier days when farmers sowed seeds manually by tossing them into the air with a sweeping movement of the hand. The farmer's "broadcast" method of planting his fields ensured that the seed would be evenly dispersed in the air before hitting the ground. Done correctly, this would produce a healthy crop of evenly spaced plants. Radio and television broadcasters use this principle to transmit programming to a mass audience. Based on the frequency and power allocation awarded to them by the FCC, they have a specific geographic region in which to operate. The broadcast signal is dispersed evenly over this area, falling randomly on home receivers that happen to be tuned in at any given moment. The opportunity to receive a broadcast signal is open to the public at large. While social and economic factors will prevent some people from owning a receiver, the wide distribution of the broadcast signal ensures delivery of the content to a diverse and heterogeneous audience. In order to appeal to a large and diverse audience, programming has to be broadly appealing to the average person. While programming can be targeted to specific groups such as men and woman, narrowing the focus too much can result in an audience size that's too small to offset expenses or the support of advertisers who subsidize the cost of over-the-air broadcasting.

Table 1.1 U.S. Broadcast TV Ratings for Week of September 19, 2011

Rank	Program	Network	Rating	Viewers (000)
1	*Two and a Half Men*	CBS	16.7	28,743
2	*Dancing With the Stars*	ABC	12.3	19,033
3	*NBC Sunday Night Football*	NBC	12.2	20,357
4	*NCIS*	CBS	12.2	19,958
5	*2 Broke Girls*	CBS	11.5	19,368
6	*NCIS: Los Angeles*	CBS	10.3	16,712
7	*Dancing W/Stars Results*	ABC	9.8	14,787
8	*Sunday Night NFL Pre-Kick*	NBC	9.3	15,975
9	*Unforgettable*	CBS	9.0	14,085
10	*Big Bang Theory, the - Sp(S)*	CBS	8.8	14,939
11	*Criminal Minds*	CBS	8.8	14,137

Media companies and advertisers rely on audience research firms like Nielsen for statistical data about the consumption patterns of television viewers.

Source: The Nielsen Company. Viewing estimates on this page include live viewing and DVR playback on the same day, defined as 3:00 a.m. to 3:00 a.m. Ratings are the percentage of TV homes in the United States tuned into television.

Table 1.2 Internet: Top 10 Global Web Parent Companies

Rank	Parent	Unique Audience (000)	Active Reach %	Time Per Person (Hh:mm:ss)
1	Google	373,418	84.8%	2:30:31
2	Microsoft	324,767	73.8%	2:26:48
3	Facebook	280,334	63.7%	6:00:28
4	YAHOO!	235,378	53.5%	1:43:59
5	Wikimedia Foundation	157,527	35.8%	0:13:54
6	EBay	131,274	29.8%	1:28:03
7	Interactive Corp	127,847	29.0%	0:08:46
8	Amazon	122,460	27.8%	0:25:38
9	Apple Computer	115,192	26.2%	1:02:51
10	AOL, Inc.	100,620	22.9%	2:13:44

In response to industry changes, Nielsen has extended its services beyond traditional media analysis into the burgeoning field of new media research and web analytics.
Source: The Nielsen Company, March 2011.

Narrowcasting: The New Media Paradigm Shift

With new media, consumers have greater access to content that interests them the most. Tuned in to a traditional radio broadcast signal, a listener must conform to the linear presentation of a playlist as determined by the on-air announcer or music director of the station. While it's possible to switch to a different station on the radio dial at any time, the presentation of musical selections is fixed and cannot be altered by the listener to fit their personal tastes and preferences. A new media paradigm shift has occurred with services such as Pandora, an Internet radio service (see Figure 1.13). Pandora calls itself "a new kind of radio—stations that play only the music you like." With Pandora, a user can enter the name of a favorite song or artist. The Pandora search engine will analyze the selection and generate a playlist based on similar styles of music. You can skip a song that you do not like and a new song will begin. User feedback in the form of approvals, disapprovals, and skips provides Pandora with information that it uses to improve future selections and playlists. The term *narrowcasting* is used to describe the new media technique of delivering content of value to a niche audience with shared values and interests. Narrowcasting shifts power to consumers, enabling them to access the content they enjoy most, more quickly, and without having to be bound to linear and fixed methods of content distribution.

SIMULTANEOUS DELIVERY

Wright's second characteristic states that the mass media are publicly transmitted and timed to reach the most audience members simultaneously. The mass media industries use expensive distribution systems to ensure that a product is delivered to consumers in a timely manner. A new motion picture must reach all theaters

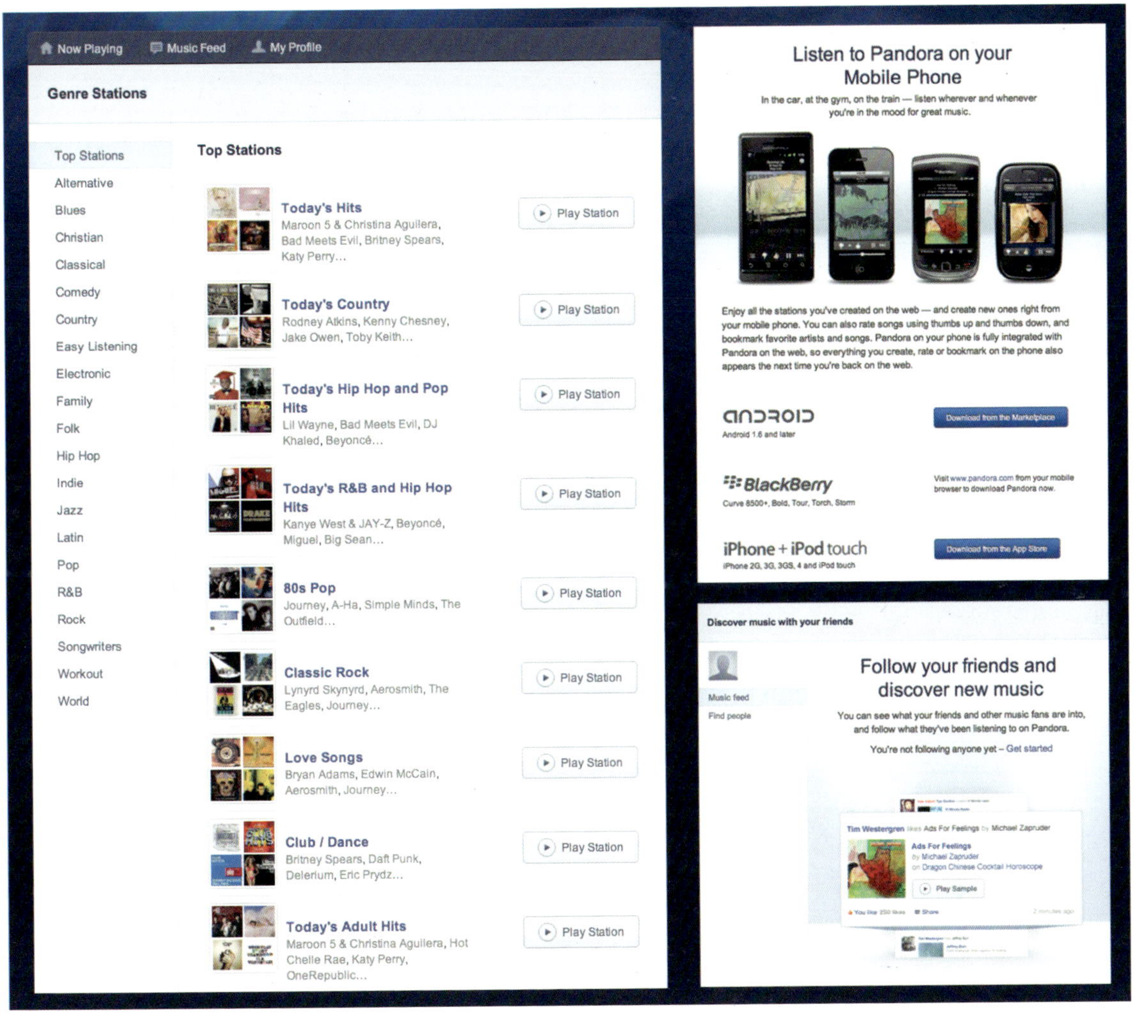

FIGURE 1.13
Pandora Radio provides free access to an unlimited number of virtual radio stations. In addition to choosing from the list of top stations on the left, users can create their own stations or music channels based on a favorite song, artist, or genre. With support for mobile apps and social media, Pandora's reach extends far beyond the Web.

on the targeted release date. The *Wall Street Journal* arrives in a subscriber's mailbox on the publication date whether he resides in Atlanta or Milwaukie. Television networks go through great pains and lots of research to determine the best day and time of a week to air their programming. Once the schedule is set, consumers must align their schedules and expectations to fit the producer's timetable.

Old media are also transient in nature. Mass mediated messages are available for a season, and once they've aired or become outdated, they are removed from circulation. Newspapers have a shelf life of only one day for a daily paper or seven days for a weekly edition. Before the invention of personal electronic recording devices such as the VCR or TiVo, consumers of electronic media were forced to conform to a broadcaster's fixed program schedule. It was not unusual for families to alter their lifestyle to accommodate the viewing of a favorite television program.

CHARACTERISTICS OF NEW MEDIA

The transition to new media began in the early 1980s with the proliferation of the personal computer (see Figure 1.14). The digital revolution, as it is often called, fundamentally changed many of the ways that people work, produce, and interact with one another. It also opened up many new methods for the production and distribution of media content. In *Being Digital*, Nicolas Negroponte uses the phrase "from atoms to bits" to describe the revolutionary shift in the production of intellectual content from a material form consisting of *atoms* (film; printed matter such as books, magazines, and newspapers; phonograph records and cassette tapes; etc.) into an electronic format made up of *bits* (the invisible output of computers).[2]

Moving from atoms to bits is reflected in the transition from a print newspaper to an online version that readers consume on a computer screen. It means shifting from a physical book to a virtual one using a Kindle or iPad. It means moving away from the distribution of content in a purely tangible format such as a record, tape, or compact disc, to an electronic format that comes to us as a digital download. With bit-based content, a computer or digital appliance is needed to decode information from an encrypted format (or digital cipher) into human symbols and forms that we can understand and make sense of. Material content (made of atoms) must be transported by hand (person-to-person, postal service,

FIGURE 1.14
New media extends the reach and capabilities of all forms of media content to consumers through a host of new methods and delivery channels.

[2]Negroponte, N. (1996). *Being digital.* New York: Vintage Books.

FedEx, etc.). Digital information is more easily disseminated. The distribution possibilities are nearly endless. Bits can travel across telephone lines, fiber optic cable, or through the airwaves using wireless transmission systems.

For decades, media producers had little choice but to use physical media (made of atoms) for recording and archiving content. Early photographic images were recorded on metal and glass plates and later on celluloid film. Animations used to be entirely hand-drawn by the artist frame by frame on a transparent sheet of thermoplastic called a *cel* (short for the *celluloid* material it was made from). Sound and video was captured and edited on magnetic tape. Books and printed materials were published using mechanical typesetting equipment and paper. Being digital means moving away from many of these traditional processes that have relied so heavily on proprietary platforms of creative expression.

In his book *The Language of New Media*, author Lev Manovich uses the phrase "the computerization of media" to highlight what he sees as the primary distinctions between old and new media. According to Manovich, "just as the printing press in the fourteenth century and photography in the nineteenth century had a revolutionary impact on the development of modern society and culture, today we are in the middle of a new media revolution—the shift of all culture to computer-mediated forms of production, distribution, and communication."[3] In the new media era, the computer assumes a dominant role as the universal instrument of inspiration, creation, distribution, and consumption, radically transforming old methods and workflows that have defined media production and cultural transmission for centuries (see Figure 1.15).

FIGURE 1.15
Like many newspapers, the *New York Times* has expanded its business model by adding new media channels into the advertising mix. Businesses can continue to reach readers through traditional methods of print advertising and/or through new media channels of content delivery via the Web (online), mobile, and tablet technologies.
Soures: NY Time.com

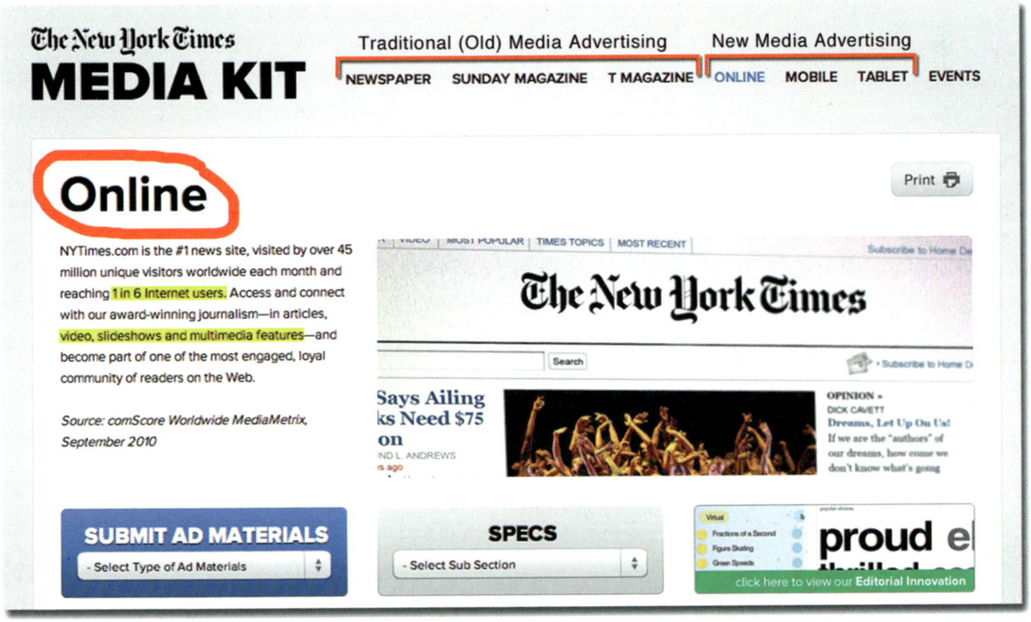

---

[3]Manovich, L. (2001). *The language of new media*. Cambridge, MA: The MIT Press.

Five Principles of New Media

Manovich lists five principles of new media that he says reflect the "general tendencies of a culture undergoing computerization." While not entirely exclusive to new media, this list identifies some of the most significant differences between the media of today and those of previous generations.

NUMERICAL REPRESENTATION

The first principle of new media is called "numerical representation," and states that new media objects can be defined numerically as a formal equation or mathematical function. The computer reduces every act of human communication to a binary expression made up of zeros and ones.

Old media relied on analog methods of reproduction and distribution. An analog audio or video recording is represented by a continuous signal, whose physical qualities vary across time along a linear path. For example, when listening to a phonograph recording, the stylus is placed in the groove of a vinyl record. As the record spins, the stylus (usually a diamond or other hard stone) advances along a spiral path while sensing minute variations in the structure of the groove. The stylus stays in direct contact with the record at all times, producing a continuous signal without interruption. The vibrations picked up by the stylus correspond directly to the fluctuating properties of a live sound performance across time. The term *analog* is used to describe this type of process, because the manmade recording is directly comparable to the physical properties of the original sound source.

The digital sound recording process is different. A digital audio recorder converts the properties of sound to a numerical value at discrete intervals of time. Each point of measurement is called a *sample*. In professional audio recording, sound is sampled at 48 kHz (or 48,000 times per second). This means that every 1/48,000th of a second, the computer measures the sound source's physical properties and records them as a data file. In a digital recording, the value of each sample is retained in numerical form, allowing it to be individually addressed and affected mathematically. While it would be difficult and impractical to try to edit 48,000 individual samples of a one-second audio clip, the fact that a digital signal is numerical opens up opportunities that were impossible to achieve before computerization. New media, because they are digital, are naturally subject to algorithmic control and manipulation.

Tech Talk

Algorithm An *algorithm* is a mathematical sequence or set of instructions for solving a problem. The software tools used in multimedia design and editing employ mathematical algorithms to systematically rewrite the numerical data structure of a computer file. This results in a wonderful partnership between people and machines. The designer can focus on the creative tasks of authoring and content creation while the computer performs the math, crunching numbers at an amazing speed behind the scenes while you work.

FIGURE 1.16
Using Adobe Photoshop CS5, various filters were applied to this image of a hurdler to produce a series of visual effects. The software program performs a mathematical algorithm whenever a filter, tool, or setting is applied.

Like digital audio recorders, still and motion digital cameras use sampling to create a digital image. Before computerization, photography involved the production of a "continuous" tone image on a sheet of film emulsion. Held up to a light and magnified, one could notice that the negative imprint of the image was uninterrupted, a perfect analog of the intensity of light captured by the photographer through the lens of the camera. Using a digital still camera, the image plane is broken down into a grid made up of millions of individual light-sensing picture elements. The computer converts each sample, or pixel, into a numeric value stored in a data file. Math is an integral part of the process, and the computer uses algorithms to both compress and modify the pixel values. For example, painting with the blur tool in Photoshop causes the pixels in the path of the tool's brush to lose focus and soften. As you move the brush across the screen, the image is visibly affected by the application of the tool. In the background, however, what's really happening is that the numerical value of each affected pixel is being changed to reflect the altered state of its new appearance. As you change the properties of a tool (e.g., make the brush tip bigger or lighten the stroke intensity, etc.), the underlying algorithm is adjusted to yield the desired effect (see Figure 1.16).

Convergence

Convergence is a term that's used often to describe the merging together of previously discrete technologies into a unified whole. A digital smart phone is the perfect example of convergence at work in a new media device. The primary

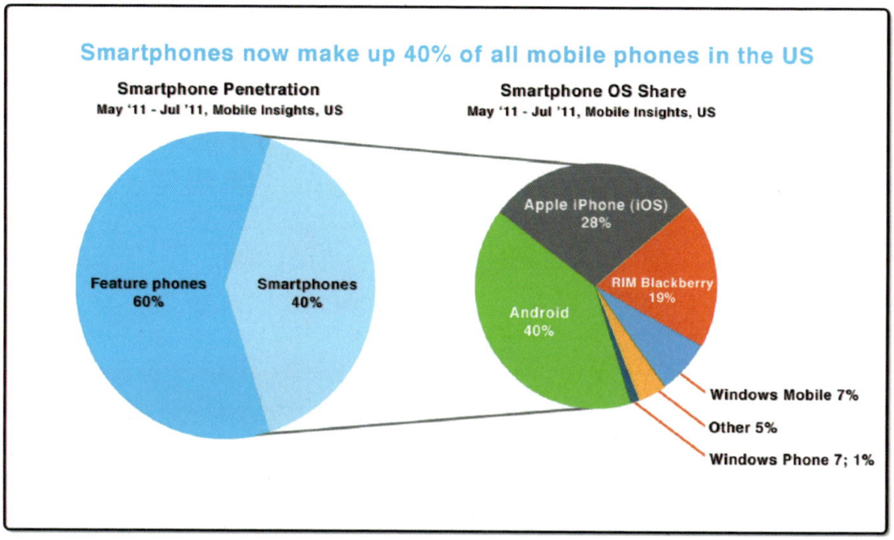

FIGURE 1.17
Consumers are relying more and more on "multimedia enabled" smart phones for 24/7 access to Web- or Cloud-based services and content from virtually any location with a mobile 3G/4G signal.

function of a smart phone is telecommunication, enabling the user to have a conversation with a distant party on the other end of the line. This function preserves the original purpose of the telephone as an instrument of person-to-person voice communication. The smart phone, however, is much more than a telephone appliance—it's a mobile wireless device capable of (1) surfing the Web; (2) capturing still images, video, and sound; (3) texting using the industry-wide SMS protocol (or Short Message Service); (4) sending and receiving images, video, sound, newsfeeds, ringtones, etc., using the industry-wide MMS protocol (Multimedia Messaging Service); (5) downloading, uploading, and storing digital content; (6) running games and other types of phone apps; (7) serving as a navigation instrument (with a built-in GPS); and (8) serving as an MP3 player. A smart phone is essentially a computer. It has a microprocessor, operating system, RAM, and storage media. Because of this, the smart phone can become anything a computer software application will allow it to become (see Figure 1.17).

Convergence is a product of the digital revolution, made possible by the commonalities of a shared binary language system. Before the computerization of communication media, each system and tool functioned according to the principles of a proprietary design and system architecture. The tools of old media—cameras, televisions, cassette tape recorders, telephones, etc.—were discrete inventions designed to perform a single primary function. Combining such a divergent mishmash of technology together was like mixing oil and water. In the absence of a common structural platform, convergence was not possible (see Figure 1.18).

STRUCTURAL MODULARITY

As we continue our discussion of Manovich's principles of new media, you will notice that they are somewhat interdependent and often build upon previous

FIGURE 1.18
In the not-too-distant past, a phone was just a phone. It was used for the sole purpose of establishing voice communication between two people. Today, the smart phone represents the convergence of many previously discrete communication technologies. It is a "multimedia enabled" device that functions more like a computer than the telephone some of us remember from earlier days.

attributes in the list. Thus, we can say that the second principle of new media, called *modularity*, is made possible because of new media's property of numerical representation. Modularity means that a new media object retains its individuality when combined with other objects in a large-scale project. This is only possible because the computer sees each structural element in a design as a distinct mathematical object or expression.

The principle of modularity isn't limited to text alone. To illustrate, let's take a look at a common multimedia task that many of you may be familiar with. A PowerPoint presentation is a good example of structural modularity at work in the new media age. The digital multimedia slideshow is made up of a collection of slides positioned and arranged in a logical order of presentation. The designer can apply a unique transition or timing function to each slide individually, or he or she may choose to assign a single effect globally to all of the slides in the presentation. Each slide is populated with its own unique content and design elements (text, graphics, video, sound, background image, etc.). Each content element has various properties and attributes associated with it (position, size, style, etc.). Modularity allows you to build a project from the ground up, one step at a time, without losing independent control of each element in the project. Changes can be made at any time, to any object, without having to go back to the beginning or to an earlier stage in the design process.

In PowerPoint, as in numerous other programs, a designer can interact with a project's content on multiple levels. On the macro level, you can edit global properties such as the slide template and background colors. It's also possible to interact with multiple objects simultaneously by selecting them together and manipulating them as a group. On a micro level, you can make changes to a single element on a particular slide. An image on the first slide can be cropped or resized without affecting content on the second slide. Likewise, a style can be applied to a single letter, word, sentence, or paragraph, simply by selecting the portion of text you wish to transform (see Figure 1.19).

Modularity typically works only up to the point of project output and distribution. Most multimedia production software tools, such as those used for photo, video, and audio editing, are designed to give you a tremendous amount of control during the editing and production process. These typically rely on a master project file. This file gives you relatively easy access to the structural elements of the media and is designed to make the editing process easier. Once the project is finished, however, you'll usually finalize the project into a more compact, portable, and less editable format for distribution. As an example, one of the most common master project file formats in Photoshop is the PSD (Photoshop Document) format. When you add text to a PSD image, you can easily go back and edit the text. When you get ready to put the image online, however, you'll need to convert it to a JPG or GIF file (we'll learn more about these later)—smaller and more universally readable formats that merge the text and image layers into a single image—in which the text is no longer readily editable.

AUTOMATION

According to Manovich, digitization and structural modularity are the antecedents upon which the third principle of automation is predicated. With automation, the computer can be programmed to serve as an agent of content design and production. In the age of new media, low-level creative tasks can be

FIGURE 1.19
This composite image, created in Adobe Photoshop CS5, is constructed of four separate elements: sky, sun, house, and person. Each element resides on its own editable layer, allowing the designer to easily change any part of the design without affecting the others.

carried out through automated machine processes and preprogrammed batch sequences. This feature can save time and often requires little expertise on the part of the user.

An example of this is SimpleViewer, a free plug-in that can be used for making a web-based photo gallery. A plug-in is a software component that adds capabilities and functionality to an existing program. The SimpleViewer plug-in is designed to be used within Photoshop. Once installed, the user executes the SimpleViewer script. A data entry screen appears, prompting the user to provide basic information about the design of the gallery and the photo assets that will be used in the project. Since the script is designed to create a multi-image gallery, the user is asked to designate the location of the "input" folder containing the images to be used in the gallery. An "output" folder must also be designated as a location for saving the master project files as they are created. As with many automated processes, some preproduction work by the user is required. In this case, it's advisable to copy the original images (in JPEG, or .jpg, format) to a separate folder, naming them sequentially in the order that they should appear in the gallery (image001.jpg, image002.jpg, image003.jpg, etc.). Once this is done and the required fields are filled in, the script can be run and the gallery created.

SimpleViewer allows the user to create a professional-looking image gallery in a matter of minutes without having a programmer's knowledge of Flash, ActionScript, JavaScript, HTML, or XML. With a little bit of time and effort, even an amateur designer can learn to edit the XML document to customize and enhance the appearance of the gallery before posting it online (see Figure 1.20).

FIGURE 1.20
The photo gallery on the right was created in Adobe Photoshop CS5 using the SimpleViewer plug-in. Once a user submits the project properties form on the left, SimpleViewer excutes an automated sequence of events called a script. In a matter of seconds, a professional-looking photo gallery is created that would have taken hours of time and a great deal of sophisticated knowledge to create manually. *Photographer: Kate Rabatsky.*

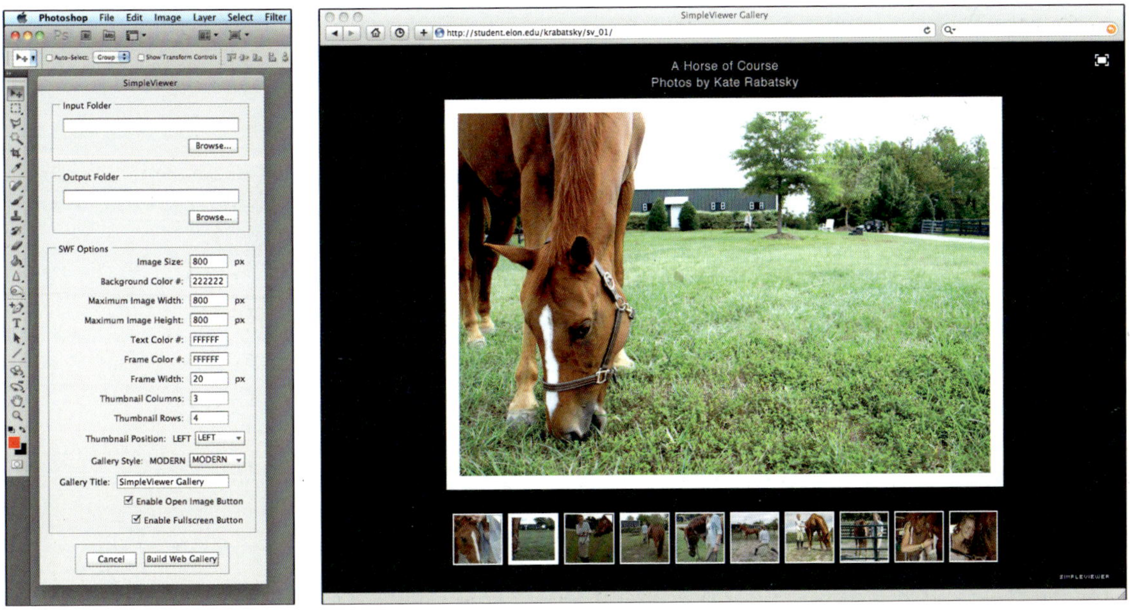

Tech Talk

Batch Processing Batch processing is the execution of a series of sequential actions performed by a digital device or software application. In the SimpleViewer illustration, I mentioned the preproduction process of renaming a series of images using a sequential file-naming protocol. This action requires two steps. First, I need to determine the order that the images will appear in the gallery. Second, I must rename each image so that when the list of files is sorted alphanumerically, the images will appear in ascending order from first to last. Workflow automation comes in handy whenever you have a series of repeated actions such as this to perform. You can take on a task such as this manually or you can turn to a computer application to carry out a series of repetitive actions more quickly and with greater precision. For this task, I will turn to Adobe Bridge. Using the virtual light box in Bridge, I can shuffle the order of my images by dragging and dropping them into position. Next, I can choose the Batch Rename function from the Tools menu to apply a renaming algorithm to the images in the folder. The Batch Rename properties window provides me with several options for specifying a file name prefix and sequencing method. Once the options have been selected, I can carry out the renaming function automatically for the entire series of images in the folder. Let's assume that there are 30 images in the source folder. Without automation, it will take a great deal of time and effort to manually change the names of each individual file. Automating the procedure will save lots of time and guarantee that mistakes do not occur because of typographical errors introduced by a human typist. A savvy multimedia producer is constantly on the lookout for tools and automated processes that can enhance workflow performance and productivity, leaving more time for creativity in the design process.

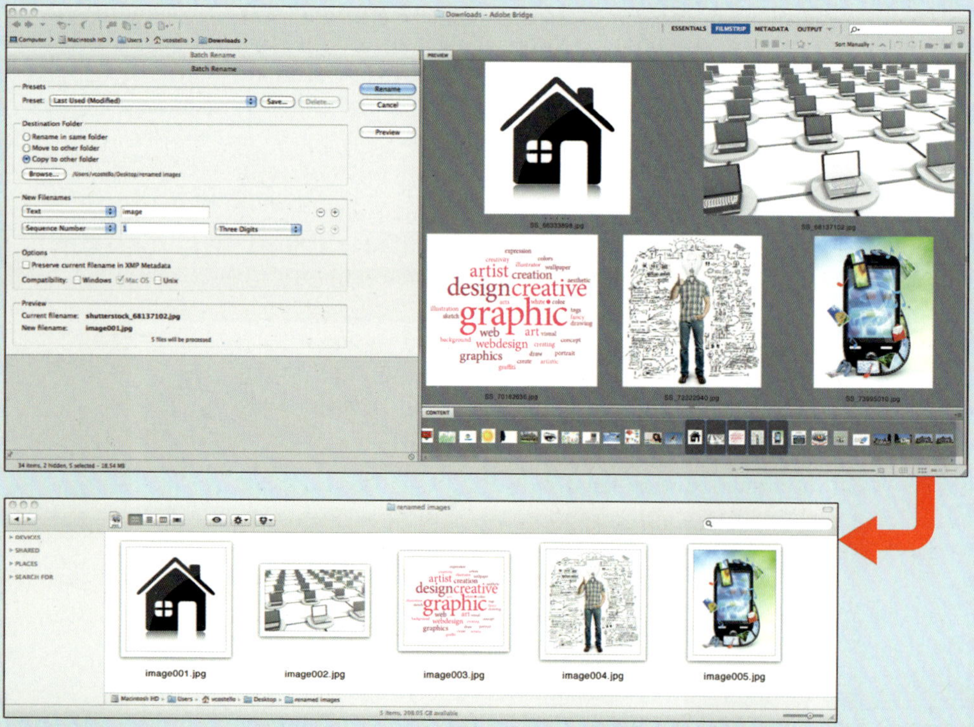

FIGURE 1.21
The Batch Rename tool in Adobe Bridge CS5 is used to automatically rename the five selected images (top) and copy them to a new folder (bottom).

Tech Talk

Rendering Rendering describes the automated background processes that are activated whenever numerical calculations or transformations are performed by a computer application. Graphic design, illustration, audio and video editing, and animation programs are just a few of the software applications that incorporate rendering engines designed to perform repetitive algorithmic operations. In photo editing, the simple act of resizing a digital image involves reconstituting the data structure for every pixel in the image. Given the number of pixels in a high-resolution image, such an activity would be mindboggling to attempt by hand; but with a computer and a good algorithm, the data can be automatically coded by machine. With video rendering, the process is even more intensive given that each second of video is made up of 30 individual frames. Depending on the complexity of an effect or manipulation, rendering even a short segment of video can involve millions of mathematical calculations for each of the affected frames and pixels in a sequence.

The software and web-based tools of media creation are growing more sophisticated every year. Prebuilt templates, user-interface components, widgets, scripts, and style sheets offer users a way to fully or partially automate complex operations that would normally require extensive programming expertise to perform. While software tools and web applications are increasingly more intuitive and intelligent with each new release, computerized automation has yet to replace the human element. Producers should strive to embrace the potential efficiencies of workflow automation without sacrificing the autonomy and aesthetic sensibilities of the content creator. Some tasks ought never to be delegated to the computer.

VARIABILITY

New media objects are not bound to a single fixed form but can exist, and often do, in a "potentially infinite" number of versions. When working within digital workflows, it's quite common to create and edit projects in one format, while distributing them in another. For this reason, new documents and media assets are saved first in the native file format of the application or device that create them. For example, a Microsoft Word document begins as a .doc or .docx file. A Photoshop project is saved using the .psd file format. Professional sound recordings start out as uncompressed WAV or AIFF audio files. And a digital video project may include source material recorded in a DV, QuickTime, or MPEG4 compression codec.

Before publishing a Word document online I will usually convert it to a more widely accessible format such as PDF. PDF is a universal file format that nearly everyone with a computer and Internet access will be able to download and view. Having done so, the same document will now exist in two different formats. I will retain a copy of the MS Word version (.docx) in case I ever need to make changes to the original document or export it in a different format. The PDF version will be used only as a distribution format for making the document available to others.

Likewise, I often use Adobe Photoshop to create graphics for the Web. However, before publishing a graphic online, it must be saved to a Web-friendly format such as JPEG, GIF, or PNG. To minimize file size and conserve bandwidth during transmission, online music files and audio podcasts are distributed in the popular MP3 file format. As a final example, in order for a video project to be burned to a standard definition DVD, the native video file must be encoded to conform to the DVD standard (MPEG2 for video and AC3 for audio).

The principle of variability enables the new media producer to quickly repurpose digital content for a variety of distribution and publishing scenarios. Because the content is digital and modular, the data structure remains fluid, allowing files to be re-encoded any time the need arises (see Figure 1.22).

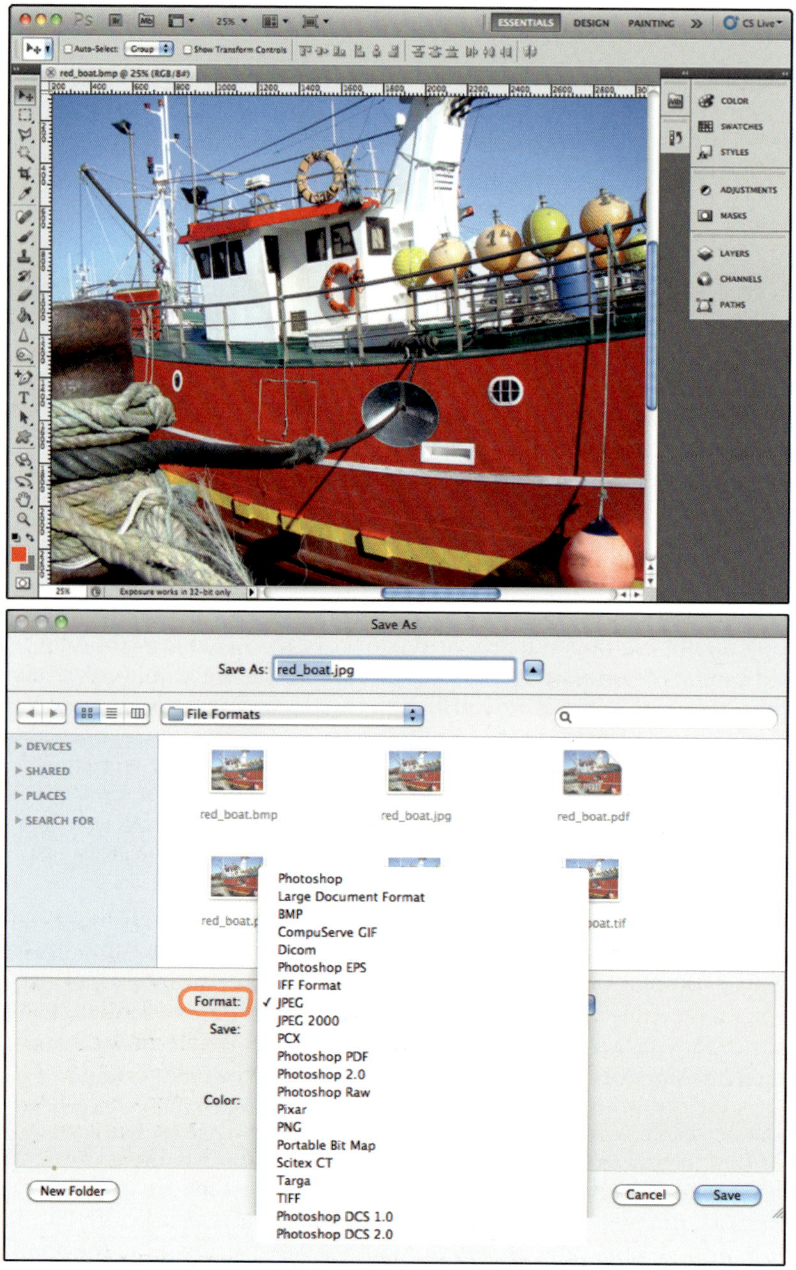

FIGURE 1.22
This image of a red boat was saved first in Adobe Photoshop's native PSD file format. However, the program offers lots of options for saving a document file in a different image format.

CULTURAL TRANSCODING

Manovich's fifth principle of new media delves deeply into the theoretical implications of using computers to represent the various products of human culture. He uses the term *cultural transcoding* to describe the bi-directional influence of computers and human culture acting reciprocally upon one another. With old media, the methods of production and distribution were based largely on organic processes that conformed to the natural properties of a specific medium and method of reproduction. Sound and light were captured and stored in a way that preserved the continuous structure and form of the content in a natural way. Manovich believes that new media is partitioned into two competing parts, what he calls the "cultural layer" and the "computer layer," and that each layer is constantly at work influencing the other. The merging of the two layers is producing a new "computer culture"—"a blend of human and computer meanings, of traditional ways in which human culture modeled the world and the computer's own means of representing it." In the words of Marshall McLuhan, "We become what we behold. We shape our tools and then our tools shape us."[4]

CHAPTER SUMMARY

In the mid-1990s, Nicholas Negroponte, then director of MIT's Media Lab, argued that the world's economy was moving rapidly from the production of material objects comprised of atoms to immaterial ones made of bits. He knew that any object of human creativity that could be digitized could also, then, be delivered to consumers via the world's growing networks of computer and telecommunication systems. Digital platforms would become the dominant means for designing, producing, and distributing ideas in the next information age. Less than twenty years later, we know that this is true. As of 2011, Amazon now sells more e-books per year than physical books; YouTube is the largest distributer of online video content in the world; and if Facebook was a country, we're told that based on users it would be the third-largest nation in the world. This move from physical to digital production and consumption has rapidly reshaped how people communicate and how users consume the media products that professionals create. We are no longer satisfied consuming media on an à la carte basis, especially at the whim of producers using proprietary methods and fixed delivery systems. With new media, the consumer is potentially just as influential as the producer. In fact, we can no longer speak in such archaic ways about consumers and producers. In the multimedia age, everyone can be both and often is.

In this first chapter, we have defined multimedia as any communication event that involves the combination of text, graphics, video, audio, and animation though a digital channel or device. Understanding multimedia requires an appreciation for the legacy media and systems that have influenced human communication for more than a hundred years. Traditional television, books, newspapers, etc. haven't left us, per se; but rather, they are changing and evolving under a radically new paradigm and production rubric. Likewise, we need to understand what has been added to our knowledge as a result of new media. The digital revolution brings with it a whole new set of concepts and workflows that must be learned and understood. As with many things, understanding multimedia involves looking forward to the future through the lens of past experience and practice.

---

[4]McLuhan, M. (1964). *Understanding media: The extensions of man.* New York: McGraw-Hill.

CHAPTER 2

The Computer

When we are … connected through our computers, we can achieve collective creative heights. Computers have already changed the way we lead our lives. Doubtlessly they will continue to do so. What is up to us is utilizing the positive potential—figuring out how we'd like them to serve us, and demanding that of our technicians, as we make the Net in our own image.

—Justin Allyn Hall, Computopia: Sharing Stories Humanizes Computer Connections (1995)

Key Terms
Application
ASCII
Bandwidth
Bit
Byte
Clock Speed
Command Line Interface (CLI)
Compact Disc (CD-ROM)
CPU
DVD
ENIAC
File
Fixed Storage
Flash Memory
Floppy Disk
Folder
Fragmentation
Gigabyte
Graphical User Interface (GUI)
Hard Disk Drive
Hardware
Human Interface Device (HID)
IBM Compatible (or clone)
IEEE 1394 (Firewire)
iLink
Intel
Keyboard
Kilobyte
Local Area Network
Megabyte
Microcomputer
Microprocessor
Moore's Law
Mouse

Chapter Highlights

This chapter examines:

- Personal computing and the digital revolution
- The role of computer hardware and software as a tool for the multimedia producer
- The factors affecting the speed and efficiency of computer processing
- The Human Interface Device—using the mouse and keyboard to interact with a computer
- The Graphical User Interface—using visual prompts and symbols to interact with a computer
- Storage solutions for saving, retrieving, and managing digital files and project assets

THE DIGITAL REVOLUTION

I recently ran across a t-shirt emblazoned with "There are only 10 kinds of people in the world, those who understand binary and those who don't." While a few of you may be chuckling to yourselves (or perhaps even groaning), my bet is that many of you are wondering why there are ten types of people, but only two options. The answer is that the number 10 is in binary (base-2) rather than in base-10, the decimal system we work with on a daily basis. In the decimal system, we use the digits 0–9 to make up numbers. In the binary system, the only digits are 0 and 1. Table 2.1

MS-DOS
Network-Attached Storage
Operating System
OS X
PC
QWERTY
RAM
Removable Storage
Serial Bus
Software
Terabyte
USB
Windows

Table 2.1 Decimal to Binary

0	0
1	1
2	10
3	11
4	100
5	101
6	110
7	111
8	1000
9	1001
10	1010

converts the decimal numbers 0–10 into binary, and you'll notice that the number 2 in binary is 10.

What's that you say? Why is this important in a book on multimedia production? Good question! It's important because the binary system is a critical component of the computer. When researchers were looking at ways to use electricity to do mathematical calculations, they realized that they could harness the fact that an electrical circuit was either on or off, if they used binary rather than decimal numbers—an idea very similar to that used by Samuel Morse with the telegraph. In a computer, each instance of a zero or one is called a bit. Binary numbers (*bits*) are still at the heart of how the computer stores and processes information, even if contemporary computers shield us from them. Bits are a critical component of what Nicholas Negroponte talked about in the early 1990s when he argued the economy was making a transition from atoms to bits, the move from physical items such as paperback books to digital items, such as Amazon's Kindle e-book reader. Part of the process of becoming a multimedia professional is learning the basics of what is happening inside the box of electronics that sits on or near your desk, and what each of the parts do. Understanding this will help you in selecting the appropriate tools for a job, and being able to talk coherently about the technology increases your credibility and your chances for employment.

From Bits to Bytes

A string of eight consecutive bits is called a *byte* and is used as one of the basic building blocks for encoding information into digital form. A byte can be arranged 256 (2^8) different ways by altering the order of the zeros or ones in the string. Like the series of dots and dashes used in Morse code, bytes can be assigned to represent letters, numbers, punctuation marks, and other characters.

Early computers often used different schema for converting letters into digital form, making it difficult to share information between systems.

In the early 1960s, the American Standards Association began work on ASCII (pronounced *as-KE*), the American Standard Code for Information Interchange, to provide an industry standard and make it easier to move data between computer systems. ASCII translates its 128-character set, including most of the symbols found on a typewriter keyboard, into a binary format (see Table 2.2). While ASCII and regional variants have dominated the computing industry, it is gradually being replaced by UCS Transformation—8 bit (UTF-8), particularly on the Web, though the UTF-8's first 128 characters are the same as those in ASCII.

Using the ASCII character set, the phrase "smiley face" can be translated into binary code as 11 bytes (or 88 bits) of digital data (see Table 2.3).

As you can see, it takes a lot of zeros and ones to represent a very simple two-word phrase. The more complex the information, the more bits and bytes will be needed to encode it into a form that a digital device can recognize.

Table 2.2 ASCII Character Chart for the English Alphabet

A	01000001	a	01100001	N	01001110	n	01101110
B	01000010	b	01100010	O	01001111	o	01101111
C	01000011	c	01100011	P	01010000	p	01110000
D	01000100	d	01100100	Q	01010001	q	01110001
E	01000101	e	01100101	R	01010010	r	01110010
F	01000110	f	01100110	S	01010011	s	01110011
G	01000111	g	01100111	T	01010100	t	01110100
H	01001000	h	01101000	U	01010101	u	01110101
I	01001001	i	01101001	V	01010110	v	01110110
J	01001010	j	01101010	W	01010111	w	01110111
K	01001011	k	01101011	X	01011000	x	01111000
L	01001100	l	01101100	Y	01011001	y	01111001
M	01001101	m	01101101	Z	01011010	z	01111010
space	00100000						

Table 2.3 The Phrase "Smiley Face" Represented with Binary Code Consumes 88 Bits

s	**m**	**i**	**l**	**e**	**y**
01110011	01101101	01101001	01101100	01100101	01111001
space	**f**	**a**	**c**	**e**	
00100000	01100110	01100001	01100011	01100101	

GREAT IDEAS

Communicating with Binary Numbers

He said to his friend,—"If the British march
By land or sea from the town to-night,
Hang a lantern aloft in the belfry-arch
Of the North Church tower as a signal light,—
One if by land, and two if by sea;
And I on the opposite shore will be,
Ready to ride and spread the alarm
Through every Middlesex village and farm,
For the country folk to be up and to arm."

Henry Wadsworth Longfellow, "Paul Revere's Ride" (1861)

Longfellow's classic line, "one if by land, and two if by sea," illustrates the usefulness of a binary code for communicating a message. On the eve of the American Revolutionary War, Paul Revere and his associates developed a surefire plan for

FIGURE 2.1
This statue of Paul Revere stands within walking distance of the Old North Church in Boston.

warning the patriots of the British army's route of attack. If the British approached by land, a single lantern was to be hung in the steeple at the Old North Church; if they crossed the Charles River, two lanterns would sound the alarm. To eliminate confusion, there were only two possibilities, and only Revere held the key to deciphering the meaning of the two lamps. This binary cipher is part of a long line of attempts to communicate across time and space using binary communication. The introduction of the telegraph the next century turned binary signaling into an international communication tool.

The way that a computer processes digital information today is similar to how a human telegraph operator would have encoded or decoded transmissions over a copper wire in the 19th century, only much faster. Invented by Samuel Morse and Alfred Vail in the 1830s, Morse code is a binary encoding scheme that uses dots and dashes to represent letters, numbers, and punctuation marks. By tapping with a device called a telegraph key, the operator can momentarily complete an electric circuit, allowing electricity to flow across the telegraph wire. A short tap of the key produces a dot, while a long tap results in a dash (see Figure 2.2).

Each character in a Morse code transmission is a carefully crafted series of short and long electrical bursts. For example, one dot followed by one dash represents the letter "A." One dash followed by three dots corresponds to the letter "B." At best, an experienced telegraph operator could send or receive 250–300 characters (or 40–50 words) per minute. By comparison, computers are capable of processing billions of bits of data per second.

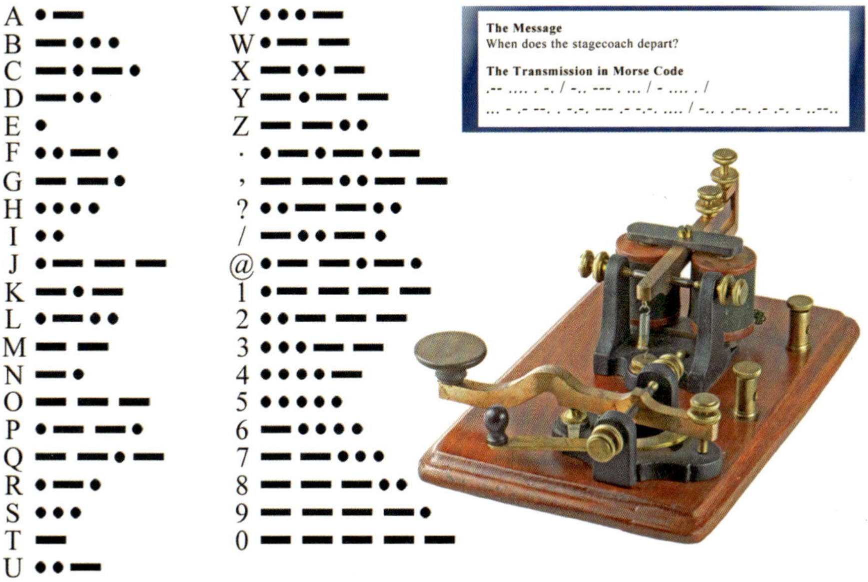

FIGURE 2.2
A telegraph key such as this one was used to encode messages in Morse code, an early system of binary transmission using dots and dashes.

History of the Personal Computer

While we are used to a computer fitting comfortably on a table, desk, or even in a pocket, many early computers were quite large. The 1946 Electronic Numerical Integrator and Calculator (ENIAC) weighed 30 tons, used over 19,000 radio tubes, and filled 1800 square feet (see Figure 2.3). As technology improved, computers became smaller and more reliable, particularly with the transition from tubes to transistors. By the late 1950s, computers were down to the size of three or four large refrigerators, but they had a limitation—they were designed to run one program at a time, a process known as "batch computing." In 1961, researchers at MIT developed CTSS (Compatible Time Sharing System), an experimental multi-user computer system. CTSS helped shift the way people interacted with computers, opening the door to off-site computer access using the telephone system to connect users via remote terminals. Computer availability grew rapidly in the 1960s, but personal computers were well out of reach until the development of the microprocessor in 1971. The microprocessor combined core-computing functions on a single chip, and although the first microprocessor, designed for a calculator, only did basic math, it wasn't long before microprocessors were available for more complicated use.

In 1975, Micro Instrumentation and Telemetry Systems (MITS) released the Altair 8800 microcomputer based on the Intel 8080 microprocessor

FIGURE 2.3
A large space was required to house the massive components of the ENIAC at the U.S. Army Research Lab in Adelphi, Maryland.
Source: K. Kempf, U.S. Army Research Lab.

(see Figure 2.4). While MITS hoped to sell a few hundred systems the first year, it was deluged with thousands of orders following an advertisement in *Popular Electronics*. Microsoft (originally MicroSoft), founded by Paul Allen and Bill Gates, got its start by developing software for the new Altair. The next year, two friends in California, Steve Wozniak and Steve Jobs, formed a small computer company called Apple to market a kit-based computer, the Apple I. The next year, they introduced the Apple II, a fully functional computer. The age of personal computing had arrived.

In 1981, pushed in part by the success of Apple and others, IBM introduced the IBM 5150—the IBM PC. It sold well, buoyed in part by IBM's reputation for mainframe computing and by IBM's decision to use "open architecture" hardware, which meant that technical specifications were made public, encouraging other companies to build add-ons. This also allowed other companies to find ways to build "clones," systems that mimicked the IBM PC. IBM decided to have another company, Microsoft, develop the operating system (OS) and let Microsoft retain ownership. This decision meant that Microsoft could license its OS, MS-DOS (**M**icro**S**oft-**D**isk **O**perating **S**ystem) to other companies.

Microsoft's retention of the right to market MS-DOS helped propel the company to international fame, and the abbreviation PC evolved into a generic nickname for many computers based on IBM's original design. The social and economic impact of the microcomputer was felt around the world, securing it as one of the most influential technological breakthroughs of the 20th century. Less than 10 years after the introduction of the microcomputer, the newsmagazine *Time* selected the computer as its "Man of the Year" for 1982.

FIGURE 2.4
The Altair 8800 Microcomputer was released in 1975.
Source: Ed Uthman, Creative Commons License BY-SA-2.0, via Wikimedia Commons.

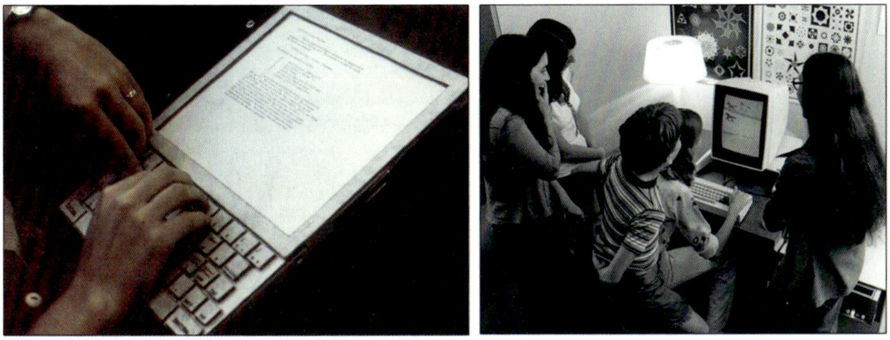

FIGURE 2.5
Computer scientist Alan Kay created this mockup prototype of the Dynabook tablet computer (left) in 1968. While tablet computers like the iPad are a relatively recent phenomenon, the idea for them was hatched over 40 years ago. On the right, students explore the visual interface of the Alto PC, developed at Xerox PARC in 1973. The Alto was the first desktop computer to utilize a graphical user interface and mouse.
Source: PARC Media Library.

FIGURE 2.6
This collection of magazine covers from 1978 to 2010 chronicles consumers' infatuation with computer technology over three decades of product innovation.

Two years later, Apple introduced the Macintosh, simplifying the way users interact with the computer and helping Apple to solidify a profitable niche in the burgeoning desktop publishing industry, a professional sector that Apple's advancements in computers and laser printers helped fuel. Apple's commitment to desktop publishing, and its subsequent foray into desktop video editing, fostered a loyal base of support among multimedia professionals. Except for a brief stint in the 1990s, Apple has refused to license its operating system to other manufacturers of desktop and laptop computers.

COMPUTER HARDWARE AND SOFTWARE

The multimedia producer's tools are classified into two broad categories: hardware and software. In this case, the term *hardware* refers not to the scores of nuts, bolts, screws, and fittings you might find at your local home improvement store, but to the physical computers and electronic devices used to carry out specific design and production activities. The term *software* refers to a computer program (a set of instructions for the computer) or set of programs designed to perform a specific set of tasks or functions, and that needs to be loaded into the computer's memory (RAM, or Random Access Memory) to be able to be used. A computer program that is permanently installed by the manufacturer on a hardware chip within a portable digital device (like a cell phone or digital camera) is usually referred to as *firmware*.

The operating system is the most important software application on a computer and must be loaded first in order for the computer to launch and run other applications. The act of turning on a computer initiates a "boot sequence" or set of command functions that launches the computer's operating system. We call this process "booting up." The act of restarting a computer (or "rebooting" it), repeats the boot sequence—refreshing the operating system and restoring the system to its default configuration. Other software, or applications, are designed to perform specific tasks. Be aware that some of the software you use as a multimedia professional may not be on your computer, it may be on the Web. This trend includes distribution tools such as YouTube but also, increasingly, productivity tools ranging from word processors and spread sheets such as Google Docs to online photo-editing tools such as Photoshop Express.

It may be helpful to think about hardware and software as you would think about a book. The physical substance of a book—the binding, cover, pages, and ink—are like hardware, while the intellectual substance of a book, encoded in

Tech Talk

Inside the Box

- *Motherboard*: A large printed circuit board that is a central computer component. It is home to the microprocessor and RAM and allows other components to be connected to the system.
- *Power Supply*: Sometimes abbreviated PSU, the power supply regulates the power coming into the computer, often converting it from AC to DC power, and supplies power to the motherboard and other computer components.
- *CPU*: Short for central processing unit, the CPU serves as the brains of the computer.
- *Video Card*: Outputs data from the computer to a video display (monitor).
- *RAM*: Random Access Memory (RAM) temporarily stores programs actively running on the computer, including the operating system. RAM is volatile memory, which means that data is not retained if there is no power.
- *Hard Drive*: A storage device for data files, a hard drive is nonvolatile memory, meaning that it retains information even when not powered. Traditionally based on magnetic storage, some hard drives are now solid-state drives (SSD).
- *Optical Drive*: CDs, DVDs, and Blu-Ray discs relying on lasers to store and read data.
- *Network Card*: A device that allows the computer to interface with other computers on either a wired or wireless network.

FIGURE 2.7
A computer is a carefully engineered collection of individual components.

the form of words, is like the software, providing meaning and significance to the reader. In short, a computer without software is about as meaningful as a book filled with empty pages.

Computer Hardware Basics

The phrase *inside the box* is used to describe the hidden components that make up a computer system (see Figure 2.7). Whether it's a desktop or laptop computer, *inside the box* items include the motherboard, CPU, memory chips, hard drive, and power supply. The quality of these components determines the speed and performance capabilities of a computer system. Computer software makers provide recommendations for the minimum system requirements for running their applications. The system requirements are printed on the software packaging and can usually be found online at the product manufacturer's web site. Table 2.4 shows the recommended system requirements for running Adobe Photoshop CS5 on either a Windows PC or Macintosh computer. Be careful about system requirements. These are the *minimum* requirements, not the ideal

Table 2.4 System Requirements for Adobe Photoshop CS5

Windows	Macintosh
Intel® Pentium® 4 or AMD Athlon® 64 processor	Multicore Intel Processor
1GB of RAM	1GB of RAM
1GB of available hard-disk space for installation; additional free space required during installation (cannot install on removable flash-based storage devices)	2GB of available hard-disk space for installation; additional free space required during installation (cannot install on a volume that uses a case-sensitive file system or on removable flash-based storage devices)
Microsoft® Windows® XP with Service Pack 3; Windows Vista® Home Premium, Business, Ultimate, or Enterprise with Service Pack 1 (Service Pack 2 recommended); or Windows 7	Mac OS X v10.5.7 or v10.6
1024x768 display (1280x800 recommended) with qualified hardware-accelerated OpenGL graphics card, 16-bit color, and 256MB of VRAM	1024x768 display (1280x800 recommended) with qualified hardware-accelerated OpenGL graphics card, 16-bit color, and 256MB of VRAM
DVD-ROM drive	DVD-ROM drive
QuickTime 7.6.2 software required for multimedia features	QuickTime 7.6.2 software required for multimedia features

Source: www.adobe.com

requirements. If possible, you'd want substantially more RAM than what Adobe lists as the minimum, particularly if you are working with large images and if you plan to have any other software applications running at the same time as Photoshop.

PROCESSOR SPEED

Located prominently on the computer motherboard is a large silicon chip called the *central processing unit* (CPU), or more simply, the processor (see Figure 2.8). It serves as the brain of the computer and plays an important role in determining the overall speed and efficiency of the system. Intel is the leading manufacturer of microprocessors.

Chip manufacturers can improve the performance capabilities of microprocessors in several ways. First, they can increase the microprocessor's transistor density, the physical number of transistors on the chip's surface. Second, they can increase the rate at which a processor performs basic operations—the processor's "clock speed," the rate at which a processor can execute instructions. Clock speed is measured in millions of cycles per second, expressed as megahertz (MHz); or in billions of cycles per second, expressed as gigahertz (GHz). It's important to understand that the processor with the highest clock speed is not always the fastest processor. Some processors have more efficient instruction sets than others, and manufacturers are building multicore CPUs, CPUs that have multiple independent processors (or cores) on a single chip. Dual-core (2), quad-core (4), and 8-core processors are now quite common. It appears that the old adage "two heads are better than one" applies to the brainpower of a computer as well. In order to take advantage of multicore processing, operating system and application software must be written to support it.

FIGURE 2.8
Don't be fooled by its small size. The CPU is a silicon chip or wafer containing millions of tiny switches called *transistors*. It functions as the brain of a computer, performing all of the mathematical operations required of the operating system and program software.

FLASHBACK

Moore's Law

In 1965, Intel cofounder, Gordon Moore, predicted that the number of transistors per square inch on integrated circuits (the predecessor of the microprocessor) would double about every two years for the foreseeable future. The prediction, now referred to as "Moore's law," has proved markedly accurate. Intel introduced its first microprocessor, the 4004, in 1971. It used 2300 transistors. The Intel 8088 (1979) used in the original IBM PC, had 29,000. The Pentium III processor was introduced in 1999 and contained 9.5 million transistors. In 2010, Intel announced release of the Itanium 2 processor, a family of multicore chips with more than 2 billion transistors.

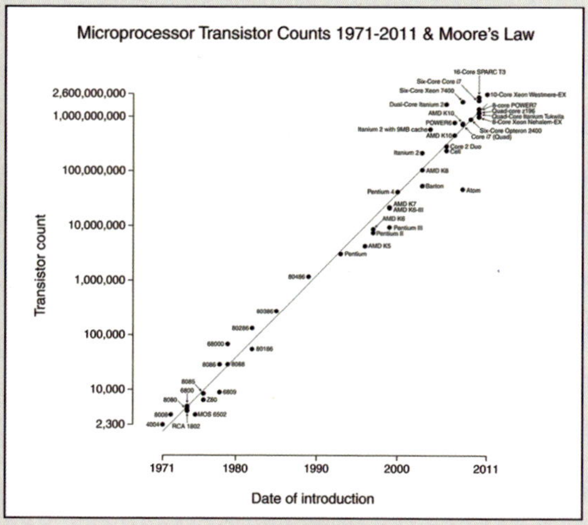

FIGURE 2.9
Gordon Moore (pictured left) accurately predicted the exponential growth in the number of transistors on a CPU.
Source: Intel
The chart (pictured right) illustrates Moore's law across the span of four decades.
Source: Wgsimon. Creative Commons License BY-SA-3.0, via Wikimedia Commons

SYSTEM MEMORY

Memory is a critical part of the computer. It typically falls into one of two categories. The first type is memory used for data storage, such as hard drives, which are nonvolatile, meaning that they retain information even when the computer is off. We'll be talking about that type of memory later in the chapter. The second type, and the topic at hand, is system memory, often called RAM (Random Access Memory). RAM is used to temporarily store operating system software and program files while a computer is running. This type of memory is volatile memory, which means that data is retained in RAM only as long as an electrical current is provided to the memory chips. System memory is erased (or refreshed) each time the computer is turned off or restarted.

When a program like Photoshop CS5 is launched, the files necessary to run the program are loaded into RAM and will remain there until the program shuts

FIGURE 2.10
A RAM chip is carefully inserted into a designated slot on the computer's motherboard.

down (the user quits or exits the application). Computers do this because reading data from RAM is much faster than reading it directly off of the hard drive. The speed of RAM is rated in nanoseconds (billionths of a second), while hard drive speed is rated in milliseconds (thousandths of a second). As we'll see in a minute, this is one of the reasons that it is critical to make sure your computer has plenty of RAM.

Manufacturers preconfigure computer systems with a minimum amount of system memory. This is like selling a car with only standard features. Upgrades are available, but they come at an additional cost. Editing and design programs tend to require more system memory than programs like Internet browsers and word processors (see Table 2.5).

Software memory recommendations do not factor in the likelihood that users will work with more than one application at a time. The more applications you have open on your computer at one time, the more RAM you will need to run the software. At some point, you will simply run out of RAM and not be allowed to open any additional programs until you begin shutting things down. As a general rule, it's better to err on the side of having more RAM than you think you'll ever need than having to live with sluggish performance and perpetual system crashes brought about by not having enough system memory. Adding more RAM to a computer system is one of the best things you can do to increase the speed and performance of software applications. One of the reasons adding RAM helps is that the less RAM you have, the more often the computer has to write information to the hard drive and writing information to and from the hard drive is much, much slower than writing it to RAM.

As you read system requirements for software packages, you'll also notice that some of them talk about specifications for the video card—the piece of hardware that gets information from the computer to the computer screen (see Figure 2.11); we'll talk more about the screen itself in Chapter 8, "Graphics." As graphics became a more and more important part of the computing experience, particularly with graphics-intensive video games, computer designers began including graphics processing

Table 2.5 A Comparison of Memory Recommendations

Software Application	Recommended Memory (RAM)
Windows 7 OS	1–2 GB
Mac OS X (Lion)	2 GB
Mozilla Firefox	128 MB
Microsoft Office for Mac 2011	1 GB
Adobe Flash Professional CS5	2 GB
Pro Tools 9	4 GB
Final Cut Pro X	4 GB
Avid Media Composer 4	4 GB

FIGURE 2.11
A video card (also known as a *video adapter* or *graphics card*) like this one is attached directly to the computer's motherboard. The video signal is fed to a computer monitor via a cable connected to an output connector on the outside of the box.

units (GPUs) on video cards to take the graphic processing load off of the CPU. Better video cards will have their own RAM, separate from what's on the motherboard. Programs that put a strain on video cards, such as video editing and 3D modeling, often have minimum requirements for the GPU and for the amount of RAM available on the video card. Some will even require a specific brand of video card.

THE HUMAN INTERFACE

Computers, like many machines, require a human interface, a system of hardware and software controls used by people to operate the appliance. In an automobile, the ignition, steering wheel, gas pedal, brake, and speedometer make up part of the human interface needed by the driver to operate the vehicle.

While the original Altair 8800 was programmed using flip switches on the front panel, most of the subsequent first-generation PCs used a command line interface (CLI), a text-only system that allowed the user to input commands using a keyboard and view the results on a monitor, typically either a monochrome monitor, or in some cases, a repurposed television. In the absence of onscreen prompts, the operator needed a lot of technical know-how to interact with the software features of the computer. Two related innovations led the way for moving beyond the limitations of the CLI to an interface design that was natively more user-friendly: (1) the invention of the mouse to supplement the keyboard for navigation and data input, and (2) the development of the graphical user interface.

The Mouse and the GUI

In 1963, Douglas Englebart, an engineer at the Stanford Research Institute, invented the X-Y Position Indicator for a Display System (see Figure 2.12). Nicknamed *mouse* by its creators because of the tail-like cable protruding out of the back of the unit, Englebart's device was one of the first human interface devices (HIDs) to rely on an onscreen pointer to execute commands. In 1968, Englebart's research team released a text user interface (TUI) that displayed visual hyperlinks on the screen that a user could activate by pointing with the mouse. The hyperlinks contained embedded instructions that were executed when selected by the mouse. The TUI was more user-friendly (easier to use) than the CLI because it allowed the user to choose from a list of available options without having to recall the command line syntax for executing an action.

Xerox's Palo Alto Research Center (PARC) further refined the mouse and the human computer interface during the 1970s, including the introduction of the mouse ball and the development of the first desktop-based graphical user interface (GUI). The GUI (pronounced *GOO-ey*), used visual metaphors such as buttons, folders, and windows to make the computer interface more intuitive. While the GUI was introduced by Xerox on the experimental ALTO (1973) and the commercially available Star (1981), Apple was responsible for bringing the GUI to a broader audience, with the Lisa (1983) (see Figure 2.13) and more importantly, the Macintosh (1984). Microsoft moved toward a GUI-based interface in 1985, with Windows 1.0, though it would take some time before

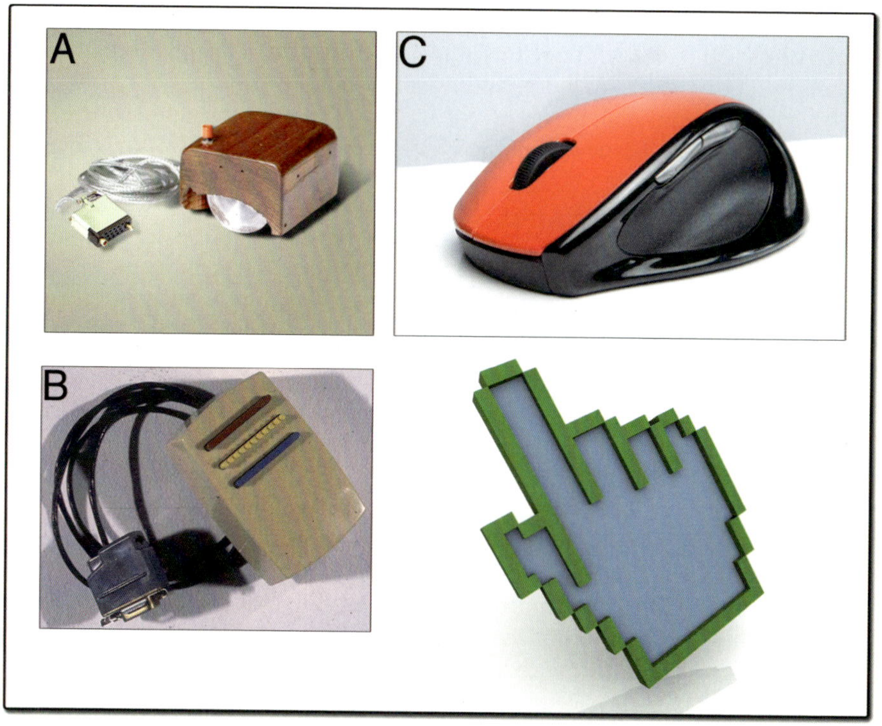

FIGURE 2.12
The evolution of the computer mouse.
(A) The original mouse prototype invented by Douglas Englebart in 1963.
Source: SRI International.
(B) The first commercial three-button mouse developed by Xerox PARC.
Source: PARC Library.
(C) A modern wireless mouse.

FIGURE 2.13
Apple produced this marketing piece in 1983 to highlight Lisa's user-friendly graphical user interface (GUI). *Image courtesy of Computer History Museum.*

Windows caught up with the Macintosh. Today, the GUI is the norm for most operating systems, even if CLI-level access is still available.

The Keyboard

Despite the importance of the mouse and other input devices such as touch-based screens and tablets, the keyboard is still one of the main input devices used for entering data into the computer. While there is no universal standard for the layout of a computer keyboard, most English language keyboards use the QWERTY (pronounced *KWER-tee*) arrangement for the layout of the alphanumeric keys (see Figure 2.14). So named because the top row of alphabetic characters begins with the letters *q, w, e, r, t, y,* the keyboard was designed in 1878 to space out the most commonly used keys to prevent the typing mechanism from jamming. While jamming is not an issue with electronic keyboards, widespread familiarity with QWERTY keyboards has limited the adoption of other systems. Although similar in appearance to typewriter keyboards, computer keyboards have more keys with specialized functions, and the user can often redefine how specialty keys work. For example, in text-oriented applications, the space bar is used to insert a space between characters. However, in most video editing programs, the space bar also functions as a play/pause control for starting and stopping video segments.

KEYBOARD BASICS

There are three main categories of keys on a computer keyboard: character keys, modifier keys, and function keys.

FIGURE 2.14
The QWERTY layout dates back to the 1800s and is still used today on English language keyboards.

FIGURE 2.15
The Character keys consume most of the space on a standard computer keyboard.

Character Keys

Character keys are used to insert letters, numbers, and punctuation symbols into a document or text-box window (see Figure 2.15). They also include several related keys used for document formatting and data entry.

- *Space Bar*. The space bar is most commonly used to insert a space between characters and words. In audio and video applications, it is often used to stop and start playback.
- *Tab Key*. In word-processing applications, the Tab key is used to move the insertion point for text to the next predefined tab stop located along the horizontal ruler at the top of the document. Tab stops generally occur at regular intervals such as every half-inch. In non-text-oriented applications, the Tab key can be used to advance the location of the cursor to the next item in a sequence. For example, when completing an online form in a web browser, selecting the Tab key will advance you to next entry field. The Tab key is also used for advancing from cell to cell in a table or spreadsheet.
- *Return/Enter Key*. When working with text, the Return key is used to advance the insertion point to the beginning of the next line. When performing data entry, the Return key completes the input of data in one cell and moves the insertion point to the next entry field. The Enter key is located on the numeric keypad and in most cases functions the same as the Return key.
- *Backspace and Delete Keys*. Depressing either the Backspace or Delete keys will remove selected text or objects from a project. In this case, both buttons function pretty much the same. However, when typing text, the Backspace key deletes characters located before the insertion point, while the Delete key removes characters located after the insertion point. The Backspace key may be labeled *backspace, delete, del,* or simply have an icon of a backward-facing arrow. The Delete key may also be labeled *delete* or *del*, or have an icon of a forward-facing arrow.

Modifier Keys

Modifier keys are used to alter the actions of other keys or mouse clicks (see Figure 2.16).

Modifier Keys

FIGURE 2.16 Modifier keys are used in combination with other keys to alter their function.

- *Shift Key*. The Shift key is used to change the display of a character to its uppercase form or to select the upper character of a dual-purpose key such as using SHIFT+5 to create the percent symbol (%). The Caps-Lock key forces all letters to appear as capitals, though it doesn't lock the other keys the same way.
- *Control/Command Keys*. The Control key on a PC and the Command key on a Mac usually function the same way. Older Mac keyboards may have an Apple on the Command key. Command is used most often in combination with other keys to provide shortcuts for menu item commands. For example, on a PC, CTRL+S (CMD+S on a Mac) is usually the keyboard shortcut for saving the current file.
- *Alt/Option Keys*. In Windows, the Alt key is used in combination with letters to open the drop-down menus on the menu bar. For example, selecting ALT+F opens the File menu; ALT+E opens the Edit menu; etc. On an Apple keyboard, the Alt key is called the *Option key*, but it behaves rather differently than the Alt key on a PC. When combined with other keys, the Option key can be used to generate special text symbols. For example, selecting OPTION+G on a Mac produces the international copyright symbol (©). The Option key can also be used to modify the effect of a mouse click or drag.
- *Escape Key*. Originally designed to cancel or abort a running command or procedure, the Escape key is used most often in combination with other keys and less often as a standalone key function.

Function Keys

Function keys are dedicated to performing specific tasks (see Figure 2.17).

- *F-keys*. Programmable function keys labeled F1, F2, etc. are located across the top row of the keyboard. These keys perform different functions depending on what type of computer you are working on and what application you are currently working in. Many applications allow the user to assign frequently-used-tasks to specific function numbers to speed up the process of executing repetitive actions.
- *Home/End*. In some programs, such as Adobe Acrobat, the Home and End keys let you move to the top or bottom of a document. In text editing

FIGURE 2.17
Function keys may perform specific tasks as assigned by the user or the system operating software or computer program being used.

programs such as Microsoft Word, home and end will move the insertion point to the beginning or end of a sentence. In video editing programs such as Final Cut Pro, the Home key will move the play head in the editing timeline to the beginning of the program. The End key will move it to the end of the timeline. Did we mention some keys will work differently depending on what program you are using?

- *Page Up/Page Down*. Depressing Page Up or Page Down scrolls the viewable area of a document or a window up or down one page or screen at a time.
- *Arrow Keys*. In text editing, arrow keys can be used to reposition the insertion point to the left or right one space at a time, or up and down one line at a time. When used with the Shift key, arrow keys can be used to expand or collapse the selection of words, sentences, and paragraphs. In graphic design programs such as Photoshop, the arrow keys can be used to nudge the position of an object one pixel at a time in either direction. In tables and menus, the arrow keys are used to move horizontally and vertically from cell to cell or item to item.

Keyboard Shortcuts

Keyboard shortcuts can help save time and improve workflow productivity. System-specific shortcuts (see Table 2.6) are built into the operating system software and will normally work with any platform-compatible software application, though this is not always the case. Application-specific shortcuts (see Table 2.7) are designed to work only within a specific software application and will vary from program to program. A convenient way to learn about shortcuts is to explore the program's drop-down menus. If a shortcut for a specific action is available, it will usually be displayed to the right of the command line description.

Keystroke Combinations

Keystroke combinations are typically written in an annotated style where the key name or abbreviation is connected to another key name by either a hyphen (-) or plus sign (+). For example, the infamous Windows shortcut CTRL+ALT+DEL instructs the operator to depress and hold the Control key, followed by the Alt key, followed by the Delete key, until all three keys are simultaneously depressed. In Windows XP, the CTRL+ALT+DEL keystroke is used to end a task or exit from an

Table 2.6 Examples of System-Specific Shortcuts

Windows XP Shortcut	MAC OS X Shortcut	Action
CTRL+O	CMD+O	Open File
CTRL+N	CMD+N	New File or New Finder Window
CTRL+P	CMD+P	Print
CTRL+S	CMD+S	Save
CTRL+W	CMD+W	Close File
CTRL+X	CMD-Q	Exit/Quit Current Application
ALT+Tab	CMD+Tab	Switch between open applications
CTRL+A	CMD+A	Select All
CTRL+F	CMD+F	Find
CTRL+C	CMD+C	Copy
CTRL+X	CMD+X	Cut
CTRL+V	CMD+V	Paste
CTRL+Z	CMD+Z	Undo
Right-Click	Right-Click or CTRL+Click (with a 1-button mouse)	Opens Contextual Menu

Table 2.7 Examples of Application-Specific Shortcuts in Adobe Photoshop CS5

Keyboard Shortcut	Action
CTRL+ +	Zoom In
CTRL+ -	Zoom Out
V	Activates the Move tool
CTRL+T	Free Transform

unresponsive program. In Mac OS X, a user would perform the OPT+CMD+ESC (Option, Command, Escape) keystroke to *force quit* a frozen application.

SAVING AND MANAGING DIGITAL FILES AND PROJECT ASSETS

As a multimedia producer, the content you create or manage on behalf of a client can represent a significant investment of time and money. You need to protect it with care. The act of saving a project in any software application results in the creation of a digital file that consumes a fixed amount of space on a digital storage device. The more work you generate with a computer, the more files you will generate, and the more options you will need for managing, storing, retrieving, and moving files. Computer storage devices are rated in terms of how much binary data they can hold. In 1998, the International Electrotechnical Commission (IEC) approved the following units of measurement for system memory chips and computer storage devices:

kilobyte (KB) = 2^{10} or 1,024 bytes of data
megabyte (MB) = 2^{20} 1,048,576 bytes of data
gigabyte (GB) = 2^{30} or 1,073,741,824 bytes of data
terabyte (TB) = 2^{40} or 1,099,511,627,776 bytes of data
petabyte (PB) = 2^{50} or 1,125,899,906,842,624 bytes of data
exabyte (EB) = 2^{60} or 1,152,921,504,606,846,976 bytes of data

While these base-2 equivalents are technically correct, the practice of rounding off has become commonplace for consumers and manufacturers alike. With numbers this large, many people find it easier to think of a kilobyte

Tech Talk

Mastering the File System Browser An active producer can quickly amass thousands of folders and files spread across a vast array of personal storage devices and remote hosting sites. With so much data to keep track of, it is imperative to develop good habits for storing and managing data and efficient techniques for locating files when they go missing, or when they have been mislabeled and/or saved in the wrong location. Fortunately, your operating system comes with a powerful little application known as a *file manager* or *file system browser* (see Figure 2.18). For PCs running a Windows-based OS, this application is called *Windows Explorer* (this not to be confused with Internet Explorer, the Microsoft web browser). On Mac operating systems its called *The Finder*. The file system browser is used for interacting with all of your digital assets, whether they are stored locally on a physical drive, or remotely on a network server or hosting site.

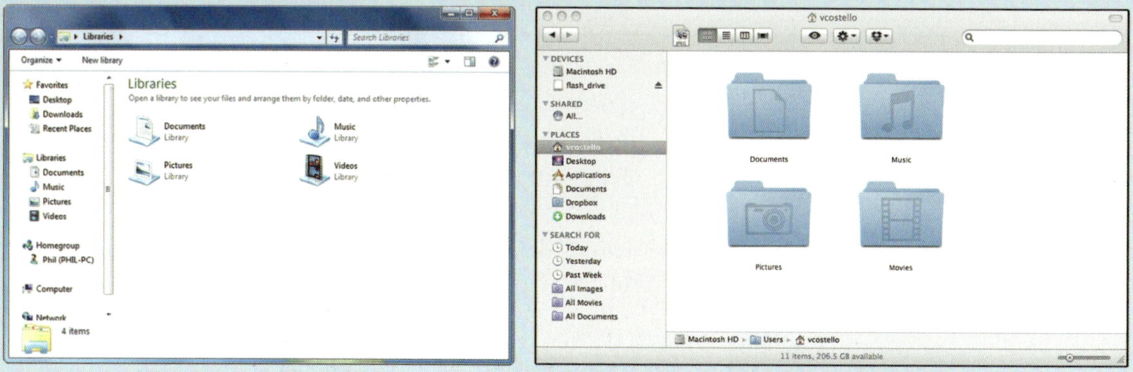

Windows 7 Explorer **Mac OS X Finder**

FIGURE 2.18
The file system browser of a computer functions virtually the same, regardless of whether you are using a PC or a Mac. On a PC, Windows Explorer (left) is used to access and manage applications, folders, and files. On a Mac, the Finder application performs many of the same functions.

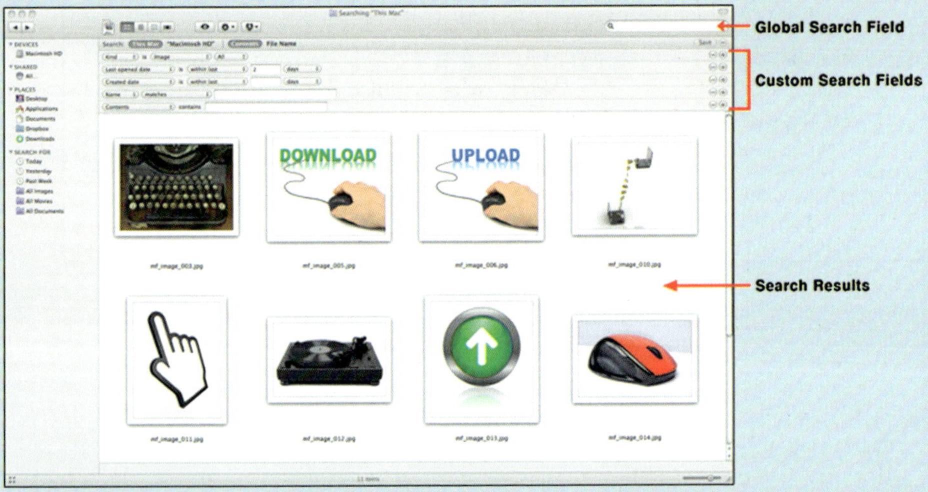

FIGURE 2.19
The file system browser gives users many options for conducting advanced searches. For example, the Finder in Mac OS X allows you to search specific fields associated with your digital contents such as: Date Created, Date Modified, File Name, Kind (folder document, movie, presentation, etc.), and Contents.

as one thousand, a megabyte as one million, and a gigabyte as one billion, but as the numbers increase into the petabyte and exabyte range, the error introduced by rounding down becomes more significant.

To put such numbers in context, in 1983 IBM released the PC/XT, the first personal computer with an internal hard drive. The XT's hard drive could store 10 MBs of data. Given the software applications in use at the time, this was considered a generous allocation of space. As computers evolved, the storage needs of program applications and end-users have increased significantly. Today, hard drives in the megabyte range are no longer available, having been supplanted by storage units capable of holding gigabytes and terabytes of data.

Text consumes only a small amount of digital real estate compared to other types of data. Computer graphics, digital images, sound, and video, are much more greedy when it comes to gobbling up precious drive and storage space. In a previous example, we saw that the phrase "smiley face" could be digitally encoded as 11 bytes of binary data. Contrast this with the high-resolution JPEG image of a smiley face in Figure 2.20. This graphic has a file size of 757 KB. Carrying this example a bit further (no pun intended), a digitally recorded speech about the origins of the smiley face, saved as an uncompressed CD-quality audio file, will take up 10 MBs of disk space for every running minute of content. Finally, a DV-quality video recording of the same speech requires approximately 1 GB of data storage for every five minutes of actual footage. This translates to 200 million bytes (or 1.6 billion bits) of data per running minute of video. HD video consumes even more.

FIGURE 2.20
A comparison of data storage requirements for different types of multimedia content. Audio and video files consume much more space on a digital storage drive than simple text and graphics.

Tech Talk

File Management 101 One of the worst ways to pack a storage building is to randomly toss items into the unit one at a time until nothing else can fit. Doing so will create a mess and make it extremely difficult for the owner or anyone else to locate and retrieve specific items at a later time. You'll also waste a lot of precious space in the process. A savvy packer will approach this task more thoughtfully. For example, one could begin by packing items into boxes along with other items of a related nature. Each box could then be labeled according to its contents (kitchen items, toys, crafts, tools, books, Christmas decorations, etc.).

This kind of organizational system has been used for years to manage physical documents. For example, a doctor keeps tabs on your medical history by updating your file each time you come in for a checkup. Your medical file is placed in a folder labeled with your name or patient ID number. The folder is stored alphabetically or alphanumerically in a specific drawer or section of the file cabinet. Like the boxes in our storage facility, the folder serves as a physical container keeping all of your information together in one place and separate from that of other patients. Proper labeling and sorting helps the office staff to easily locate your file among the thousands of identical folders in the cabinet.

Because this system was so widely understood, it was adopted metaphorically for managing data on computer storage drives. Thus, any digital storage device, such as a hard drive, flash drive, memory card, etc., can be thought of as a virtual file cabinet designed for holding electronic documents. To avoid clutter, files are placed strategically into named folders or subfolders containing related

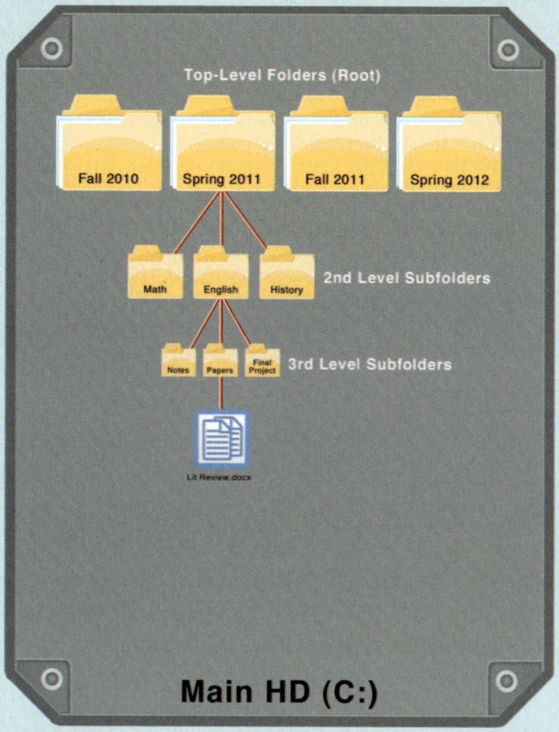

FIGURE 2.21
Folders and subfolders are used to organize electronic files systematically on a hard drive. A structural hierarchy is formed by nesting—the act of placing one folder inside another and so on. The folder at the top of a nested collection of subfolders is called the *root* or *parent folder*.

content. Figure 2.21 illustrates how a college student might organize course-related content on a computer hard drive. In this example, the top-level folders are given date-related names to identify a specific semester of study. A second-level subfolder is created for each course taken during a specific semester. A third-level subfolder is used to further divide the coursework files into logical categories based on type (notes, papers, final projects, etc.).

A computer identifies the address of a saved file with a path statement that specifies its location within the hierarchy of folders and subfolders on the drive (sometimes called the directory tree). For example, the path for the document file "Lit Review.docx" would be written as follows:

- **Mac OS X:** Main HD/Spring 2011/English/Papers/Lit Review.docx
- **Windows:** C:\Spring 2011\English\Papers\Lit Review.docx

The exact form of a path statement can differ slightly between PCs and Macs and various operating systems. Windows systems recognize either the forward slash ("/") or the backslash character ("\") as the delimiter between each directory level or folder name. Unix and Mac systems recognize only the forward slash delimiter in a file path statement.

File management is of critical importance in the professional workplace. The system you adopt not only has to make sense to you, but it should make sense to others as well. What will happen on that day when you're out of the office and your boss or coworker needs to retrieve a critical file from your computer for a client meeting at 2:00 p.m.? As they peruse your hard drive, will they be frustrated, confused, or lost in a sea of informational chaos, or overjoyed to see an organized file system hierarchy that is user-friendly and easy to navigate?

Digital Storage Solutions

The term *storage* is used to describe any number of devices that can be used to permanently record and store digital information. Unlike RAM, digital storage media are nonvolatile, meaning they retain data after the computer is turned off. There are three main types of digital storage solutions: (1) fixed storage, also known as *direct-attached storage* (DAS); (2) removable storage; and (3) network-attached storage (NAS).

FIXED STORAGE

Fixed storage refers to a nonremovable chip or drive permanently installed within the chassis of a computer or digital device. Fixed storage can usually be replaced or upgraded, but it's not designed to be quickly moved from one computer to another. The most common type of fixed storage medium is a hard-disk drive (abbreviated as HDD or hard drive (see Figure 2.22). A hard drive is a mechanical device that reads and writes data onto magnetically charged spinning platters located within a sealed compartment. Hard drives come in a variety of sizes and styles but can be broadly classified into two main types: internal and external (see Figure 2.23).

FIGURE 2.22
A vector illustration of a mechanical hard drive.

Internal and External Drives

Internal hard drives fall under the category of fixed storage, as they are located out of sight, inside the chassis of a laptop or desktop computer. The internal hard drive of a computer

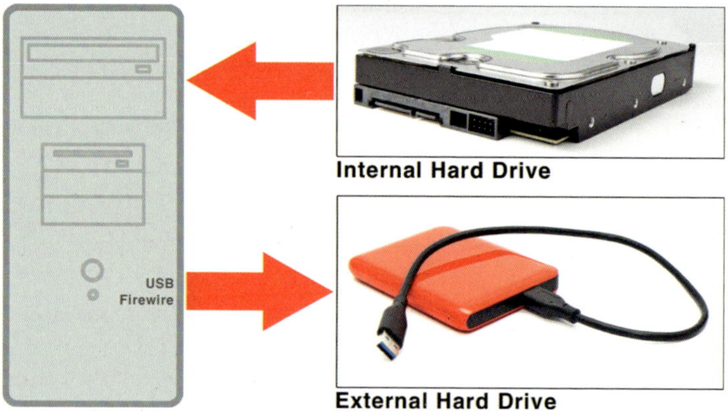

FIGURE 2.23
An internal hard drive is mounted inside the chassis of a desktop or laptop computer. An external hard drive is connected to a computer via an interface cable (typically USB or Firewire). External drives sometimes require a second cable to provide electrical power to the device.

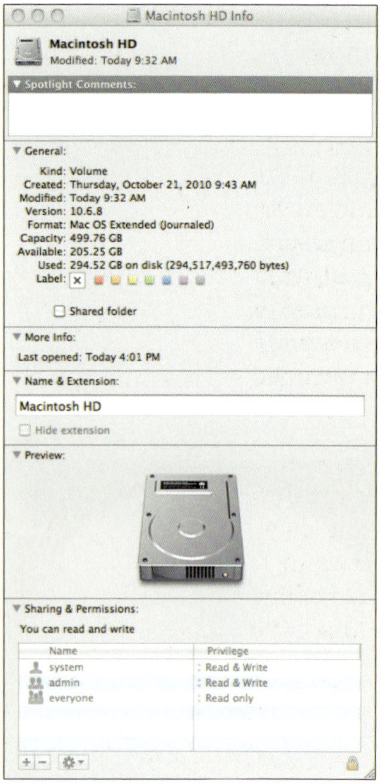

FIGURE 2.24
A window displays basic information about the internal hard drive of my MacBook Pro laptop computer. Among other things, it tells me that I have roughly 205 GB of space left on the drive. The total capacity of the drive is 500 GB.

is used to store the operating system, and software application files installed on the computer, as well as storing user data files. External hard drives are designed to sit outside of the box and must be physically connected to the computer with a serial interface cable. External drives are handy for storing user data and project files. Because external drives can be easily disconnected and moved from machine to machine, they fall under the category of removable storage that we'll cover in a moment.

Hard Drive Capacity

The capacity of a hard drive is rated according to how much data it can hold (in gigabytes, terabytes, etc.). While a 2TB hard drive and a 500GB model may have identical external dimensions, one would say that the first drive is bigger because it can hold more data. In terms of capacity, it's four times as large as the smaller unit. The cost for digital storage has dropped significantly since 1980 when drives were only available in the megabyte range, and the adjusted cost per gigabyte was an astounding $193,000. Today, multiterabyte drives can be purchased at an average rate of 10 cents per gigabyte or less.

To determine the value of two competing models based on capacity, it's helpful to calculate the "cost per gigabyte" of digital space. This figure can be achieved by dividing the total cost of the drive by its size. For example, if you were faced with a choice between a 2TB drive for $120 and a 500GB drive for $42, the cost per gigabyte would break down as follows:

Hard Drive Model	Size	Cost	Cost per Gigabyte
A	2TB	$120	6¢/GB
B	500GB	$42	8.4¢/GB

All things being equal, drive A is the better value, even though the total cost of the unit is higher than drive B.

Hard Drive Speed

While capacity is important, the mechanical performance of a hard drive plays an important role in how well computer programs will run. Hard drive performance is determined by several factors, including the rotational speed of the spindle, average seek time, and data transfer rate.

The platters in a hard drive are mounted to a spindle that rotates at an exceptionally high rate of speed. The *rotational speed* of the spindle is measured in revolutions per minute (rpm). Typical speeds range from 3600 to 10,000 rpm (sometimes referred to as "10K"). The faster the rotational speed of the discs, the faster the drive is able to access data and process information. While 4800–5400 rpm drives are acceptable for most applications, 7200 rpm drives or faster are better for more intensive processing and rendering applications like video editing.

The *average seek time* of a drive is shown in milliseconds and measures how fast, on average, the read/write head of the drive is able to locate individual pieces of data. The read/write head is located on the tip of an actuator arm that moves back and forth across the surface of the platter. Hard drives can contain several platters, and since data can be stored on both sides of a disc, multiple read/write heads are required. The read/write heads move in tandem, meaning that they are always located at the same position on each platter. However, only one head is active at a time. In the case of average seek times, the smaller the number, the faster the drive.

Data transfer rate refers to how fast digital information can flow in and out of the hard drive to the computer's microprocessor. Data transfer rates are stated as *bits-per-second* (bps). The greater the data transfer rate, the faster the hard drive. Network data rates are also measured in bits-per-second. Remember that bits-per-second is different than bytes-per-second. You'll need to divide the number of bits by eight to get bytes-per-second and get a reasonable estimate of how long a file might take to transfer. As I said at the beginning, the whole bit and byte business is actually fairly important.

In the last few years, some manufacturers have started using platter-free solid state drives (SSD), similar to a USB flash drive or the data card you use in a camera (see Figure 2.25). With no moving parts, SSDs tend to be a bit hardier than regular hard drives, have faster access times, and allow the computer to boot faster. On the downside, SSDs will slow down as they fill up and are much more expensive on a cost-per-gigabyte basis.

FIGURE 2.25
A solid-state hard drive (SSD) contains no moving parts.

Hard Drive Maintenance and Optimization

Hard drives must be formatted before data can be stored on them. During the formatting process, the surface area of each platter is divided into a series of concentric circles called *tracks*. Each track is divided into smaller areas called *sectors*. Each of the tracks and sectors are numbered, providing the computer with a unique physical address for each piece of data stored on the hard drive.

It's important to note that hard drives do not store information the same way that people do. A person might store a printed copy of a ten-page report in a folder located in a file cabinet, or in a pile on a desk. When a computer stores the electronic version of the same report, it begins by copying the file bit by bit into available space in an open sector. Given the size of the file, the computer may or may not be able to fit all of the data into one sector. When a sector fills up, the computer will continue writing the file to another sector. Very large files such as video clips and photographs are often written across multiple sectors.

While you would never think about cutting up a ten-page report into five sections and storing each piece in a separate folder, to a computer, this is an ordinary way of managing data. Under normal conditions, the computer is able to keep track of the individual pieces of digital information perfectly, deconstructing and reconstructing the data files as necessary. However, as a hard drive fills up, especially under conditions of intense usage over time, it can become fragmented. Fragmentation is a condition whereby the files on the drive become increasingly scattered among nonadjacent sectors, slowing down the ability of the hard drive to access data. A fragmented hard drive can reduce a computer's performance and operating efficiency. In Windows, you can use Microsoft's built-in Disk Defragmenter to maintain your drive, and Windows will even let you schedule the maintenance so that it happens automatically. Apple's OSX handles much of this automatically without you needing to take any action. It's worth noting that file fragmentation is much less of an issue with SSDs.

In addition to disk fragmentation, individual sectors on a hard drive can become damaged, preventing the computer from reading, or writing to, specific areas of the disk. Depending on the project and the amount of time and effort that went into it, the loss or damage of critical information can be a significant and costly setback that most of us would prefer to avoid. While there's no way to guarantee that a mechanical or system failure will never occur, preventative measures can be taken to significantly reduce the risk of hard drive failure and the resulting loss or corruption of data.

REMOVABLE STORAGE

The second category of computer storage is broadly referred to as *removable storage*, and as the name suggests, it refers to a portable storage medium that's designed to easily move data from one computer to another. Removable storage

Tech Talk

Backing Up Your Data Think about how much stuff you have on your computer. What would happen if your computer disappeared or quit working? What about those assignments due tomorrow that you've almost finished? One of the best things you can do to safeguard your data is to regularly backup important files. Backing up involves storing duplicate copies of files either on a separate physical drive connected directly to your computer, or to a network storage device either in your home or elsewhere. If your computer crashes, or if a file becomes corrupted, having a backup copy will let you recover files that might otherwise be lost forever. Most operating systems provide a way of systematically backing up data on a regular schedule. Apple's Time Machine actually backs up the entire computer and can restore to a new system if needed. Third-party software is also available to ease the task of keeping track of your data backup files and restoring them when needed. A number of companies, such as DropBox and Mozy, offer online backup services, giving you an extra layer of data protection in the event your computer is damaged or stolen. Understand that it's not a question of *if* your hardware will fail, it's a question of *when*—and invariably, it's at the worst possible moment.

is classified into three categories based on the underlying technology: optical disks, flash memory, and magnetic storage (typically an external version of the hard drives we talked about earlier).

Optical Storage

Optical storage devices use a laser beam to read and encode data onto the reflective inner surface of a hard plastic disk. The laser beam encodes binary data as a series of pits and lands. *Pits* are microscopic depressions burned onto the surface of the disc. *Lands* are the unaffected regions between the pits. The transition from a pit to a land or from a land to a pit is interpreted as a one, while no change (pit to pit or land to land) indicates a zero. Pits are recorded along a single, continuous spiral track from the inside of the disc to the outer edge.

The Compact Disc While video laserdiscs hit the market in the late 1970s, the Sony/Phillips audio compact disc (1982), or CD, was the first widely adopted optical storage technology. An audio CD can hold 74 minutes of uncompressed audio. As the first consumer digital audio format, the CD was lauded for its size, superior sound quality, durability, and random accessing of music tracks. Other uses for CD technology evolved, and in 1985 a variant of the compact disc was released called the *CD-ROM* (compact disc read-only memory). With a storage capacity of 700 MB, a CD-ROM can hold as much data as 486 floppy disks. As a result, CD-ROMs quickly eclipsed floppies as the primary distribution medium for software. When the Windows 95 operating system was first introduced, it was made available to consumers on either 30 floppy disks or a single CD-ROM. For customers with a CD-ROM drive on their computer, the installation was much easier and faster to complete. To illustrate just how densely information is stored on a compact disc, if the concentric data track was stretched into a straight line, it would be .5 microns wide by 3.5 miles long (5.6 kilometers). A micron is one millionth of a meter. The average width of human hair is approximately 100 microns.

FIGURE 2.26
A red or blue laser beam is used to write and read data on an optical disc.

While certainly a step forward, the CD-ROM was limited because data was permanently stored on the disc and could not be erased or rerecorded. The acronym WORM (write once, read many) is used to describe this type of recordable medium. A significant breakthrough occurred with the development of CD-R and CD-RW consumer disks and drives. CD-R technology allows for the recording of digital information onto a blank disc providing a convenient way of backing up or archiving large amounts of data. Like CD-ROMs, CD-Rs can only be written to once. CD-RW (ReWritable) disks work the same way, but they can be erased and reused more than once.

DVD The second type of optical storage technology is the DVD, short for *digital versatile disc* or *digital videodisc.* DVD technology was developed by Toshiba and released as an international standard in 1995. Toshiba designed the DVD as an alternative to distributing video on videotape—do you remember VCRs? A standard DVD holds 4.38 GB of data, more than six times the capacity of a compact disc, and it can hold up to 133 minutes of standard definition video. The DVD-ROM version of the technology, along with the subsequent development of DVD±R/RW recordable drives, has made this an ideal medium for high-density removable storage. DVDs are backwards compatible, meaning that an audio CD will play in a DVD device. While employing the same basic technology as the compact disc, DVDs can hold more data because the tracks are narrower and closer together. If you could stretch out the data track of a DVD into a straight

FIGURE 2.27
While physically identical in size, the capacity of an optical disc differs widely depending on what type of media is being used.

line, it would be 7.5 miles long (12 kilometers). Newer Dual Layer DVDs hold around 8.5 GB of data, but the media is relatively expensive and is already being made obsolete by Blu-Ray discs.

Red or Blue Laser Technologies Optical discs have traditionally used a red laser beam to read and write data on a CD or DVD. Blu-Ray was developed by a large consortium of manufacturers in the consumer electronics, personal computer, and entertainment industries. The recording system uses a blue laser beam, giving it a shorter wavelength than traditional red-laser DVDs, and producing a narrower beam with a much higher degree of precision. Blu-Ray discs can hold up to 25 GBs of data on a single-sided disc and 50 GBs of data on a two-sided disc. The additional storage capacity permits manufacturers to distribute high definition (HD) video content and movies to consumers, significantly enhancing the home theater viewing experience. Blu-Ray is backwards compatible with all existing red-laser optical media.

Flash Memory

Also developed by Toshiba, flash memory is a solid-state chip technology used in a variety of digital appliances. Originally designed as a removable storage solution for portable devices like digital cameras and cell phones, flash memory is compact, lightweight, and extremely fast. Unlike magnetic and optical storage solutions, flash memory chips contain no moving parts, therefore providing exceptionally fast seek times and high data transfer rates. As discussed earlier, this is the same technology SSDs use.

There are two main types of flash memory products available: flash memory cards and flash drives. Flash memory cards come in many shapes and sizes and are used as a local source of removable storage for portable electronic devices like cameras and digital voice recorders. Some of the more popular card formats are branded as Compact Flash, SmartMedia, Secure Digital (SD), and Memory Stick. A card reader is required in order for a computer or printer to read the contents of a flash memory card.

FIGURE 2.28
Each of the 3.5-inch floppy disks pictured above had a capacity of 1.44 MB. It would take 2845 of these disks to equal the capacity of a 4 GB SD memory card (roughly the size of a thumbnail).

A flash drive is a small portable device designed to connect directly to a computer through a standard serial interface port on the outside of the chassis. Flash drives (also known as *USB drives*, *jump drives*, and *thumb drives*) are small enough to fit on a keychain and can store up to 256 GB of digital information. Since flash drives utilize a standard serial bus protocol (USB), they can be attached to virtually any computer regardless of the platform or operating system.

NETWORK-ATTACHED STORAGE (NAS)

The third category of computer storage is network-attached storage. Using the same technology that allows computers to interact with each other across the Internet, computers can be set up to access the storage drive of a remote computer located in another room or building. Network-attached storage is often available for people who work in organizational settings where computers are connected to a Local Area Network (LAN). Authorized members of the organization can log onto a network drive from any computer that's attached to the LAN. Once connected, the network drive functions the same as a local hard drive. Depending on the amount of space that's allocated to each user, a network drive can be used for backing up important files, making files available to other people on the network, or simply as a convenient location for quickly accessing files from remote locations. Using network-attached storage, a university student could write a paper in the library, save it to her network drive, and access it later from a computer located in her campus apartment. As discussed above, a number of companies now offer Internet-based file storage, allowing access from anywhere you have an Internet connection.

GREAT IDEAS

Cloud Storage

Cloud storage is a method of saving data to servers located off-site and managed by a third-party vendor. It has many of the same features as network-attached storage, with the added benefit of giving you, and others whom you designate, access to your data at any time via the Internet or through mobile devices and apps. A network-attached storage system is intended for a single user, or at best, a team of users attached to a local area network (LAN). People outside the network firewall are generally forbidden access to files stored on your personal NAS account.

Cloud storage addresses this limitation by allowing users to transmit and share documents across open networks. Have you ever tried to send a large file such as a hi-resolution photo or video to someone as an email attachment, only to find out later that it did not go through because the file size exceeded the limits of the system? With cloud storage, you can upload folders and files that others can instantly view, download, and edit at any time. Most cloud storage providers offer free accounts with 1–2 GB of storage. Heavy users can acquire more space by paying a monthly hosting fee. A major benefit of cloud storage is collaboration. The author of an uploaded file can invite others to edit the document online, granting them the status of a collaborator. Changes and revisions to cloud-hosted documents can be tracked, allowing users to revert back to an earlier version at any time. With cloud storage, project collaborators no longer have to be physically present in the same office. In fact, they don't even have to reside in the same country.

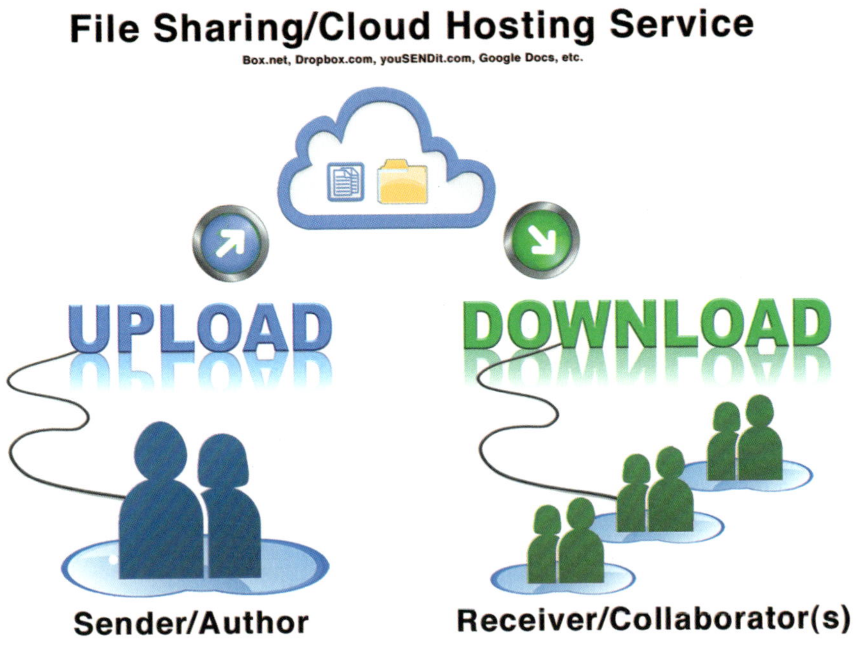

FIGURE 2.29 Cloud storage enables multiple users to collaborate on the development of a single document or body of work. The author of a shared file or folder defines the *permissions*, a set of rules that determines the level of access granted to collaborators. For example, one person can be limited to read-only privileges, allowing them to view a document online; while others are permitted to download a file or make changes to it online.

CONNECTING DRIVES AND DEVICES

Devices such as external hard drives and printers are collectively known as hardware peripherals, since they are not essential to the basic operation of a computer. With the exception of wireless devices, external peripherals are attached with a cable that plugs into a serial bus connector located on the outside of the computer. The serial bus connector is a port, or interface, used for interconnecting digital electronic devices. The term *serial bus* is used to describe any type of data transfer protocol where digital information is transmitted sequentially, one bit at a time. Internal buses handle the transfer of data to and from the processor to other internal components of the system. External buses are dedicated to the transfer of data from the computer to devices located outside of the box.

USB and IEEE 1394 have emerged as two of the most popular external bus protocols in use today. The Universal Serial Bus, or USB, was introduced in 1995 by a consortium of seven computer and telecommunications companies: Compaq, Digital Equipment Corporation, IBM, Intel, Microsoft, NEC, and Northern Telecom. USB ports first appeared on PCs in 1997 and quickly became the international standard for connecting digital devices like printers and scanners. USB was easy to use, and it was fast.

The term *bandwidth*, another word for data transfer rate, is used to describe the speed at which digital information is transmitted from one device to another. Bandwidth is usually stated as the number of bits per second (bps) that can flow across the wire. USB has a bandwidth of 12 Mbps (stated as 12 million bits per second). This is lightning fast compared to a serial port (115 Kbps) or a standard parallel port (920 Kbps), two of the most common interfaces used throughout the 1990s. While serial and parallel buses work fine for keyboards, mice, and other types of low-bandwidth peripherals, they are woefully inadequate for handling the high-bandwidth needs of digital photography, audio, and video. To put this in perspective, downloading a 1.2 MB image from a digital camera to a computer with a USB cable takes approximately 8/10th of a second. The same image traveling across a traditional serial bus interface, would take approximately 84 seconds to download. USB ports are found on both PCs and Macs and can be used to connect up to 127 peripheral devices simultaneously.

The development of USB was a historic leap forward in many ways, yet the standard was still not fast enough to handle the high-bandwidth needs of audio and video processing. As an alternative to USB, Apple Computer developed a serial bus interface capable of transmitting data at 400 Mbps. Apple called its advanced serial bus protocol *Firewire* because of its remarkably fast throughput. In 1995, the Institute of Electrical and Electronics Engineers (IEEE) adopted Firewire as an international standard. While technically known as IEEE 1394, Apple has branded it as Firewire, while Sony refers to it as iLink.

In an ongoing battle of one-upmanship, High-Speed USB (also known as USB 2.0) was developed in 2000, surpassing the data throughput of IEEE 1394 with a speed of 480 Mbps. Not to be outdone, Apple introduced an advanced Firewire

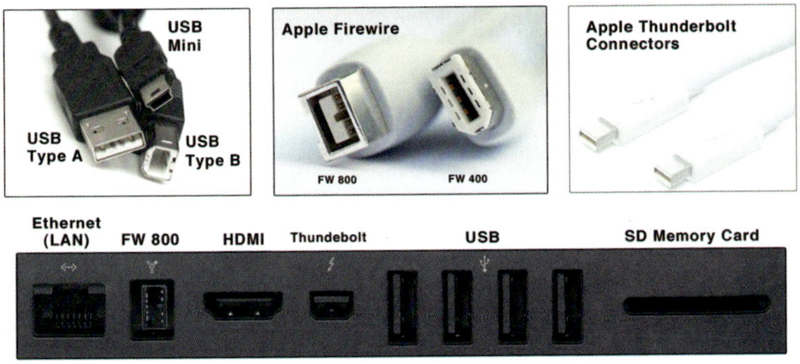

Apple Mac mini I/O Interface Panel

FIGURE 2.30
USB (1.0, 2.0, and 3.0) and IEEE 1394 (Firewire) are two of the most common protocols used today for connecting an external device to a computer. For Mac users, Thunderbolt may eventually replace Firewire 800 as manufactures provide connectivity support for the new interface.

protocol (IEEE 1394b) in 2002 with a new connector design and a bandwidth of 800 Mbps. The terms *Firewire 400* and *400-iLink* are used to describe products with the original IEEE 1394 interface. *Firewire 800* and *800-iLink* are used to describe devices equipped with the advanced IEEE 1394b connector. For a while, Apple provided both Firewire 400 and 800 ports on its computers. Today, only the 800 version of the connector is supported. Fortunately, an adapter cable or hub can be used to connect a Firewire 400 device to a Firewire 800 connector.

The most recent contenders in the connector wars are USB 3.0 and Thunderbolt. USB 3.0 builds on the older USB standards but increases data throughput to 3 Gbit/s. Thunderbolt, the most recent option, provides up to a 10 Gbit/s of data throughput and allows users to connect an even broader assortment of devices, including high-resolution video displays.

CHAPTER SUMMARY

The personal computer is the core hardware technology used by multimedia producers to plan, create, and distribute creative projects. Like Morse code, computers use a binary language system comprised of only two characters (zero and one). Each instance of a zero or a one is called a *bit*. Combining eight zeros and ones into a single data string forms a byte. The more complex the information, the more bits and bytes will be needed to represent the information in digital form. The digital revolution has made it possible for any form of human communication, including text, graphics, photographic images, moving video, sound, and animation, to be translated into the language of computers. Computer speed and performance comes down to how fast the various components of a computer system and its peripheral hardware can process streams of binary data. The term *storage* is used to describe the numerous devices capable of recording digital information. The three main categories of computer storage are fixed storage, removable storage, and network-attached storage.

CHAPTER 3

Planning and Design

Among all the types of paper documents, narrative fiction is one of the few that will not benefit from electronic organization. Almost every reference book has an index, but novels don't because there is no need to be able to look something up in a novel. Novels are linear. Likewise, we'll continue to watch most movies from start to finish. This isn't a technological judgment—it is an artistic one. Their linearity is intrinsic to the storytelling process. New forms of interactive fiction are being invented that take advantage of the electronic world, but linear novels and movies will still be popular.

—Bill Gates, *The Road Ahead* (1995)

Key Terms

Audience
AV Script
Client
Concept Development
Copyright
Demographics
Idea Generation
Intellectual Property
Mockup
Planning
Postproduction
Preproduction
Previsualization Tools
Producer
Production
Protype
Screenplay
Script
Storyboard
Target Audience
Treatment
Usability Testing
Visualization
Wireframe

Chapter Highlights

This chapter examines:

- The importance of planning and process in multimedia design
- The use of conceptual frameworks for guiding design and production processes
- The relationship between client and producer
- The Previsualization tools used in the design process
- The steps and substeps involved in multimedia design and usability testing

A ROAD MAP

A famous adage in advertising and marketing circles proclaims, "If you aim at nothing, you will hit it every time!" This simple, yet profound cliché is a call to the masses to be purposeful and intentional in planning for success. A carefully hatched plan provides direction, a road map for helping you get to your intended destination. Without it, you will have no idea where you are going or how to get there.

Imagine for a moment someone embarking on a 3,000-mile road trip across the country without any planning or preparation. They didn't pack any clothes or provisions. They have no money or credit card. They didn't even bother to consult a map or install a GPS for guidance. Chances are they won't get very far or have much fun along the way. While it's difficult to fathom anyone like this setting out on a journey so ill prepared, many people approach multimedia design with a similar disdain for planning and process. Give a person a video camera and he wants to start shooting right away. Tell another person to create a website and she immediately sets off to build it. After all, planning is so boring, and we want to get to the fun stuff as soon as possible.

In reality however, the time and effort you put into planning a multimedia project will determine the degree to which the project, once completed, hits its mark. It matters little what the plan looks like. What matters most is that you have one; and that it sufficiently addresses the needs of the client, the design team, and the users of the product. A good plan is one that is thoughtfully crafted, thorough, and realistic. A plan is your road map and serves as the foundational visionary framework undergirding the creative enterprise.

GREAT IDEAS

Target Market and Target Audiences

A *target market* is a group of consumers that a company has strategically identified as having potential to purchase and use its goods and services. Manufacturers seldom produce a product that everyone wants or can afford. Because of this, they will go through incredible lengths to find out as much as possible about consumers who are the most likely candidates for using their products. The more they know about their target market, the more successful they will be in designing and delivering effective messages and product campaigns. When it comes to consumers of media products such as television programs, newspapers, and websites, you're more likely to hear the target market referred to as the *target audience*. In effect, these are synonymous terms. By understanding more about their target audience, media organizations can do a better job of selling advertisements to companies looking to reach a specific target market.

FIGURE 3.1
"If you aim at nothing, you will hit it every time." Identifying the target audience or user for your multimedia product is a critical first step in the planning and design process.

CREATIVITY

Experts in the field of creativity research generally agree that creativity is a process that "involves the production of novel, useful products."[1] This definition suits us well, as the focus of this book is about making multimedia products designed to communicate a message with deliberate thought and intentionality. It's not about art for art's sake, not that anything is wrong with that per se; but it is about the process of creating a meaningful communication experience for the benefit of an audience. Such value will rarely emerge without giving proper attention to planning and process.

Observe a young child at play and you will see that creativity can flow spontaneously out of an active imagination without any forethought or predetermined goals (see Figure 3.2). Hand a child a drawing tablet and some crayons, and in no time at all the paper will be filled with lines, shapes, outlines, and colors. The recognizability of such primitive doodlings will depend entirely on the child's age and skill. Sometimes children will begin with an idea, but oftentimes they are content to create on the fly without any preconceived notions of where their creativity and talent will lead them.

FIGURE 3.2
For the multimedia producer, creativity is a process that "involves the production of novel, useful products."

While there is a place for such unstructured moments of creative expression, aspirations and needs mature as we grow older. A carpenter will not embark on building a house until the blueprints for the design and layout of the construction have been completed and approved. Likewise, a professional web designer must have a plan before the actual coding and design work can begin. A formal process of some sort is necessary for translating any sophisticated idea or concept into a multimedia product that people will find useful. A project of any great size will require a process with numerous steps from start to finish and involve the work of many people with specialized knowledge and skills.

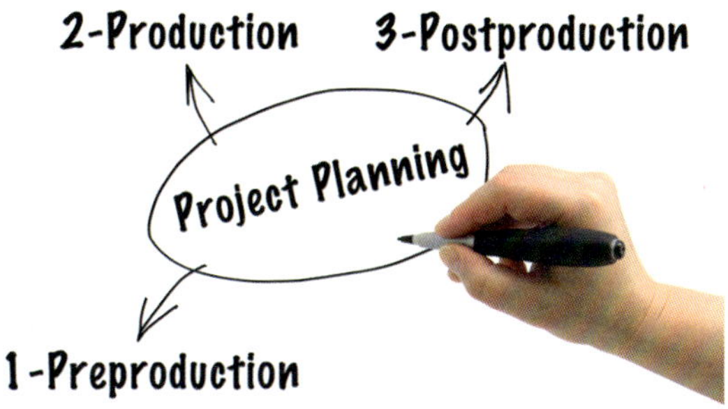

FIGURE 3.3
The Three Ps Production Model.

The Three Ps

For many years, film and video producers have utilized a popular process model known as the three Ps: preproduction, production, and postproduction (see Figure 3.3). The elegance and simplicity of this

[1]Mumford, Michael D. (2003). Where have we been, where are we going? Taking stock in creativity research. *Creativity Research Journal*, 15(2 & 3), pp. 107–120.

FIGURE 3.4
Preproduction is the planning phase of the design process and includes a broad set of activities required for a successful outcome.

three-phase model have contributed to its widespread adoption as a conceptual framework for the production process. A model like this is helpful because it consolidates the individual steps of a complex process into a smaller subset of related categories that are easier to remember and track. Like the older media it represents, the three Ps is a linear model. Preproduction comes first, followed by production and postproduction.

PREPRODUCTION

Preproduction is the preparation phase of a project and involves many steps, including: problem identification and needs assessment, idea generation, concept development, research, audience analysis, scriptwriting, budgeting, scheduling, staffing the production team or crew, auditioning, scouting locations, etc. (see Figure 3.4). Preproduction activities are meant to establish the scope, direction, timeframe, and cost of a project before spending one dollar on the actual production. When done well, preproduction saves time and money during subsequent phases of a project, which are almost always more expensive.

PRODUCTION

Production is the acquisition or design phase of a project (see Figure 3.5). In a film or video project, this is the recording phase and includes: (1) all of the work that goes into preparing for a shoot or recording session, such as building sets, hanging lights, miking instruments, applying makeup, setting up the equipment, etc.; (2) the actual recording of shots, scenes, and tracks that will be edited together to tell a story; and (3) striking the set, packing up the equipment, and vacating the premises at the end of the day. When tape begins to roll and the director hollers "ACTION!" you know that production is in full swing. More generally, production involves the creation of any media asset, including static graphics, photographs, time-based media, or animations that are needed for inclusion in the final product.

FIGURE 3.5
Production is the acquisition or design phase of a project where the individual pieces of a multimedia project are acquired or produced.

GREAT IDEAS
Intellectual Property

While production often focuses on the creation of original content by the designers and producers of a work, it can also include the legal acquisition of media resources owned by others. *Intellectual property* is a term used to describe many types of created works that are protected by copyright, trademark, or patent law. Just because an image or piece of music can be easily downloaded from the Internet doesn't mean you can legally use it in your own work. Whether you intend to materially profit from the use or not, or whether the work is intended for commercial or noncommercial use, doesn't always matter. Copyright law is complicated, and without the expert advice of a lawyer who specializes in such matters, it is often difficult to know for sure what permissible uses the law will, or will not, allow. When in doubt, it is always better to err on the side of caution. The good news is that there are many avenues available to the multimedia professional for acquiring photographs, music, clip art, stock video, film footage, animations, and more from companies specializing in the sale of royalty-free or licensed content.

It is also easy to find sites publicizing content that is free or in the public domain. While some of these sites do indeed offer legitimate ways for securing legal rights to use another person's intellectual property, you need to be careful and discerning. You also need to read the fine print. For example, a media resource may be allowed for publication on the Internet but not in a program aired on television or in a derivative work for sale, such as a DVD. As with anything, you need to choose your sources carefully and dig deep to discover all the facts. In a court of law, you're usually no less culpable because you didn't know any better, or because you were mistakenly led to believe that it was okay to use content downloaded from an Internet site or scanned from a book. For this reason, it is best to rely on companies with an established reputation, who own the rights to the material you want to use, and who have the legal authority to grant permissions for its use.

POSTPRODUCTION

So you've been out on location, or in a design suite, recording studio, or sound stage, and all of the raw footage and material you need for your project has been acquired or gathered. Now is the time for putting it all together. *Postproduction*

FIGURE 3.6 Postproduction brings together the individual components of a multimedia project into a unified finished product. The postproduction workflows you adopt will vary depending on the project, for example, whether you are editing a film, building a content management system, or constructing an online photo gallery.

POSTPRODUCTION

is the assembly phase of a project (see Figure 3.6). In traditional time-based workflows, postproduction is spent almost entirely on video and audio editing. However, it also includes the creation of titles, motion graphics, and video effects. A *rough cut* is the first complete edited copy of a program. Depending on a project's complexity and the demands of the producers, a rough cut may go through several rounds of revisions before being approved. The approved edited master program, called a *final cut*, moves on for one final round of polishing, a process that may involve audio sweetening, color correction, and other forms of fine tuning.

THE CLIENT AND PRODUCER

Multimedia production can be a solo endeavor with a design team of just one person, but more often than not it is a collaborative process involving many people representing one of two parties: the client and the producer. In the corporate sector, the client may be an individual but more likely is a business or organization. The client is the content expert. Clients are the ones most familiar with the mission, goals, and needs of the organization they represent.

Likewise, the producer may be an individual as well. The market is full of freelance producers and directors who operate independently on a work-for-hire basis. More likely, however, the producer is a creative agency or production company. The producer is the message design expert. Producers are the ones most familiar with the process and tools for crafting an effective message and deploying it strategically to a target audience.

While some companies can turn to an in-house department or creative unit to handle a communication problem, others don't have this option; and even if they did, they will sometimes choose to hire an out-of-house producer to get the job done. Their corporate colleagues may be booked solid and unable to meet the project deadline, or perhaps they just want the objectivity and fresh eyes of an independent producer who is free of company bias and old ideas.

Initial Client Meeting

The starting point for nearly every project is the initial client meeting, a general fact-finding session involving the client and producer and their respective team members. No matter how the teams are constituted, each party will have a designated leader or point-person. For example, a company's marketing director or communications officer might be assigned to head up the client team. Other members may include the department head of the unit requesting the project and a couple of content experts with hands-on knowledge of the problem or need. A team leader or project director also heads up the production team (or design team). The composition of the production team depends on the nature of the assignment and the project requirements, but will typically include key creative and technical experts such as writers, visual designers, and programmers.

NEEDS ASSESSMENT, FACT GATHERING, AND RESEARCH

Let's assume from the outset that the producer knows very little about the client, its corporate mission, and needs. Believe it or not, this is a common starting point. The members of the design team need information, and lots of it, before they can fully assess the problem and begin offering solutions. The client is a vast reservoir of institutional knowledge and content expertise. During the initial client meeting, the project director will often take the lead by asking lots of questions and taking copious notes. Some typical questions to explore at this point include:

- What is the mission and purpose of the organization and/or department funding the project?
- Who are you trying to reach, and why?
- What is the primary purpose of the project? To educate? To train? Persuade? Inform? Something else?
- Will the project be for internal use by a specific department or set of employees (such as members of a regional sales force or assembly-line workers), or will it be for external constituents such as board members, stockholders, vendors, suppliers, or customers?
- How will the project be deployed?
- What's the project deadline?
- Do you have a specific idea or concept in mind?
- Have budget parameters been set for the project?

Questions will become more specific as the discussion unfolds and the project moves forward. The initial client meeting will rarely lead to a concrete idea or conceptual road map. Its purpose is purely informational, to gather the facts and to give the design team enough information to begin working on an idea, theme, or concept for the project.

Idea Generation and Concept Development

The next step in the process is to begin developing a general idea or concept for the project. The process model for idea generation can vary widely depending on whether you're designing a website, an interactive photo gallery, an educational training video, or something else. After all, each multimedia project or program genre has unique attributes and conceptual workflows associated with it. But oftentimes the starting point is the same.

GREAT IDEAS

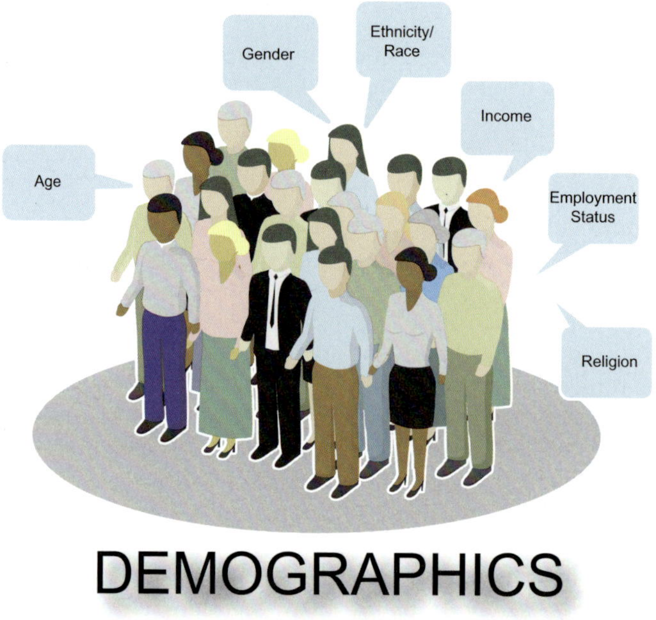

FIGURE 3.7
Demographic variables such as age, gender, and ethnicity are used to describe the shared traits of a user group or target audience. Once this information is known, producers can use it to shape the message to fit the intended audience. For example, one would expect the content and design of a fitness website targeting 30-to-34-year-old business executives to look decidedly different from one intended for teenage girls in middle school.

FIGURE 3.8
Ideas drive the creative process and are a wonderful product of human brainstorming and interaction.

An idea is sort of like a snowball accelerating down an alpine slope. It takes a while to get it started, but once it begins to roll on its own, it rapidly builds up mass and momentum. During the early stages of idea generation, lots of ideas will be thrown out. It's a good idea to write all of them down, even the ones you don't like or don't think are particularly good.

Previsualization Tools

Legendary photographer Ansel Adams defines visualization as "the ability to anticipate a finished image before making the exposure."[2] In other words, a good photographer can compose an image in her head before framing it in the viewfinder

[2]Adams, A. (1995). *The Camera*. Boston: Bulfinch Press.

and releasing the shutter. Under normal circumstances, she doesn't need to spend hours of preproduction time making sketches or thumbnails of shots that will be taken tomorrow or next month. However, when producing something more complex, such as a film, website, or user interface, it pays to refine and expand the concept on paper before proceeding to the production phase of the project.

Since ideas are hatched in the mind, they must be put into a transferable form before they can be communicated to others. Verbal brainstorming is a great way to get the creative juices flowing during the formative stages of idea generation and concept development. However, as an idea begins to take root and grow, the methods used to develop it and communicate it to others need to grow as well. Previsualization is a term that has been used for years to describe the act of putting an idea or concept into a visual form that can be better understood by the author of the idea and shared with others. Let's look briefly at six previsualization tools that have been widely used in multimedia design: treatment, storyboard, script, wireframe, mockup, and prototype.

GREAT IDEAS
Think Outside the Box

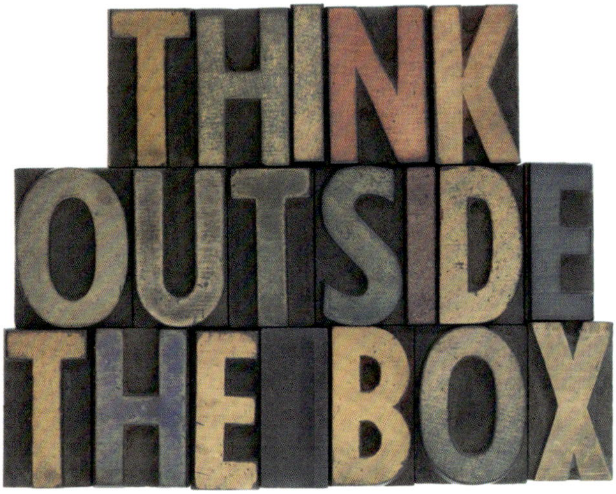

FIGURE 3.9

"Think outside the box" is a popular expression used by creative people to encourage the imagination to think beyond the obvious, familiar, and conventional. Our personal likes and dislikes, predispositions, experiences, established work and design preferences, unconscious habits and workflows, etc. can keep us from solving a problem or developing an idea in a truly innovative way. Thinking outside the box means traveling beyond the routine pathways of our mind that we are naturally inclined to follow.

TREATMENT

A *treatment* is a short narrative description of a project. It provides the reader with a concisely written summary about a concept or story idea. A treatment should include sufficient details to address the basic *who, what, when, where,* and *why* types of questions. As appropriate, it should also include information such as the project title, purpose, goals, audience, and genre. Treatments are often used for pitching narrative film and video projects. A treatment is similar in purpose to an executive summary or resume. It is a short-form device used to cast a vision or sell an idea. The length of a treatment depends on the type of project being proposed. A treatment for a feature-length screenplay for a motion picture film might be four to five pages long, while one for a news story or television commercial could be done in half a page or less. Treatments can be used for describing any type of multimedia project, including web pages and interface components.

STORYBOARD

A *storyboard* combines words and pictures together to communicate an idea (see Figure 3.10). It is an organized panel of images and text used for previsualizing a linear or nonlinear sequence of actions or steps. In the 1930s, Walt Disney popularized the storyboard format to assist artists in the production of animated films. Today, storyboards are used routinely in multimedia production from planning short-form motion picture projects such as television commercials and "webisodes," to interactive narratives used in web and interface design.

Resembling pages from a comic book, a storyboard is made up of a series of boxlike frames depicting the visual portion of a story. Written copy is placed adjacent to each frame (usually below it) to describe its contents. The text can be purely descriptive or include spoken voiceover copy or dialogue. Before computers, storyboards were drawn by hand. Today, they can be generated any number of ways using sophisticated previsualization software, page layout and design programs, or online tools. In fact, a storyboard template is probably available for your favorite word processing program.

SCRIPT

A *script* is a written narrative framework for organizing the visual and audio portions of a multimedia presentation. Scripts are most often used for time-based media projects and increasingly for interactive narratives.

AV Script Format

The two-column AV format is ideal for the producers of radio and television commercials, music videos, promotional videos, education and training programs, documentaries, interactive narratives, and more (see Figure 3.11). It is one of the most common and versatile script formats used in commercial production today. This format features a divided page with two vertical columns. The column on the left takes up about one-third of the width of the page and includes information about the video portion of the program. The wider column on the right is used for audio information such as music cues, voiceover

FIGURE 3.10
This storyboard was created to help visualize scenes from the screenplay *Cupcake*, written by Paul Castro. Filmmakers and advertising agencies will often hire a storyboard artist to illustrate a script prior to shooting a film or television commercial. (*Courtesy of Paul Castro*)

1.

Agency	NA	**Writer**	Willie Wordsmith
Client	NC Open Government Coalition	**Producer**	Tammy Taskmaster
Title	Sunshine Laws in North Carolina	**Director**	Cindy Callshot

VIDEO	AUDIO
CU OF U.S. AND STATE FLAGS EXT CAPITOL BUILDING	(MUSIC UP)
EXTERIOR STATE CAPITOL TWO-SHOT: ON-CAMERA HOSTS CU: ALISON CU: JACKIE WS: OF VOTING MACHINES WS: CHATHAM COUNTY SEA MS: CONCERNED RESIDENT	JACKIE: HI, I'M JACKIE ________. ALISON: AND I"M ALISON ________. WE'RE HERE OUTSIDE THE STATE CAPITOL IN RALEIGH TO INVESTIGATE SUNSHINE LAWS IN NORTH CAROLINA. SUNSHINE LAWS KEEP GOVERNMENT MEETINGS AND RECORDS OPEN TO THE PUBLIC. JACKIE: IN 2006, THE CHATHAM COUNTY BOARD OF ELECTIONS HELD THREE OFFICIAL MEETINGS WITHOUT GIVING THE PUBLIC ANY NOTICE AHEAD OF TIME. DURING THESE MEETINGS, THE BOARD AUTHORIZED THE PURCHASE AND IMPLEMENTATION OF CONTROVERSIAL NEW ELECTRONIC VOTING MACHINES. CONCERNED RESIDENT ______ REALIZED THE POTENTIAL IMPACT ON HER COMMUNITY AND SOUGHT TO UNDERSTAND THE ACTIONS TAKEN BY HER LOCAL GOVERNMENT.
CU: CONCERNED RESIDENT	CONCERNED RESIDENT: THE OLD MACHINES WERE PAPER BALLOTS WHERE YOU WROTE ON THEM WITH A MAGIC MARKER... AN INDELIBLE MAGIC MARKER... SO YOU WROTE YOUR OWN LITTLE LINES. THERE WAS REALLY NO WAY THAT I COULD SEE THAT ANYBODY COULD FIDDLE WITH THE VOTES YOU KNOW. YOU JUST MARKED YOUR BALLOT ON PAPER AND PUT IT INTO A BOX AND IT WAS COUNTED.

FIGURE 3.11
This two-column AV style script was used in the production of an educational video program.

copy, or actor dialogue. The AV script format is used in both single-camera and multicamera production settings.

Screenplay Format

The screenplay is the Hollywood studio format used in the production of motion picture films and prescripted television comedy and drama programs (see Figure 3.13). This format features a single-column layout where each page translates to roughly one-minute of on-screen action. Full-length

1.

Agency	NA	**Writer**	Willie Wordsmith
Client	NC Open Government Coalition	**Producer**	Tammy Taskmaster
Title	Sunshine Laws in North Carolina	**Director**	Cindy Callshot

(MUSIC UP)

JACKIE:	HI, I'M JACKIE __________.
ALISON:	AND I"M ALISON __________.
	WE'RE HERE OUTSIDE THE STATE CAPITOL IN RALEIGH TO INVESTIGATE SUNSHINE LAWS IN NORTH CAROLINA.
	SUNSHINE LAWS KEEP GOVERNMENT MEETINGS AND RECORDS OPEN TO THE PUBLIC.
JACKIE:	IN 2006, THE CHATHAM COUNTY BOARD OF ELECTIONS HELD THREE OFFICIAL MEETINGS WITHOUT GIVING THE PUBLIC ANY NOTICE AHEAD OF TIME. DURING THESE MEETINGS, THE BOARD AUTHORIZED THE PURCHASE
	AND IMPLEMENTATION OF CONTROVERSIAL NEW ELECTRONIC VOTING MACHINES.
	CONCERNED RESIDENT _______ REALIZED THE POTENTIAL IMPACT ON HER COMMUNITY AND SOUGHT TO UNDERSTAND THE ACTIONS TAKEN BY HER LOCAL GOVERNMENT.
CONCERNED RESIDENT:	THE OLD MACHINES WERE PAPER BALLOTS WHERE YOU WROTE ON THEM WITH A MAGIC MARKER... AN INDELIBLE MAGIC MARKER... SO YOU WROTE YOUR OWN LITTLE LINES. THERE WAS REALLY NO WAY THAT I COULD SEE THAT ANYBODY COULD FIDDLE WITH THE VOTES YOU KNOW. YOU JUST MARKED YOUR BALLOT ON PAPER AND PUT IT INTO A BOX AND IT WAS COUNTED.

FIGURE 3.12
The script in Figure 3.11 was quickly transformed into this single-column layout using Final Draft AV, a popular scriptwriting program. Script formats vary widely depending on the company or industry you work for.

screenplays are usually 90 to 120 pages long. This is a highly prescriptive format that must be followed carefully at the risk of being rejected on technical grounds. A common practice is to use a professional scriptwriting program such as Final Draft or Movie Magic Screenwriter to ensure that the formatting of the script conforms to acceptable industry standards.

WIREFRAME

The design process for a new website often begins with a series of drawings or sketches called *wireframes* (see Figures 3.14 and 3.16). A wireframe is a visual representation of the layout or skeletal structure of a page. A designer will often use a wireframe to experiment and pitch various ideas for the placement of content and interface components that address the client's needs and goals. First-generation wireframes are often very simple and crude. In the beginning stages of a project, the designer will often produce multiple wireframes for the client to evaluate and choose from. Sometimes there's a clear winner, and sometimes the client doesn't like any of them, forcing the design team back to the drawing board for a second try. Another possibility is that the client

83.

139 INT. SCHOOL CONFERENCE ROOM - DAY 139

DISTINGUISHED ADMINISTRATORS huddle in padded leather chairs at the end of a long table. A Secretary escorts August in. He looks around this scary place. Busts and pictures of famous composers dot the dark wood-paneled conference room.

After a few moments the Dean beckons to August.

DEAN
Mr. Rush.

He motions for August to join them. August eyes pages of sheet music on the table. The title simply says, "August's Symphony." All eyes are on the boy.

AUGUST
I'm sorry.

DEAN
Why are you apologizing, August?

AUGUST
Sometimes I don't listen well and I don't do the homework like I'm supposed to.

The Dean smiles. So do the others.

DEAN
Well, I'm sure you'll do better in the future.

August nods hoping that was it. But then...

DEAN
The New York Philharmonic Orchestra has a concert this spring... In the history of this school we've never performed the work of a first year student. Certainly no one of your age. But now, we have asked if they could perform your composition. Would you like that?

His Professor gives him a reassuring smile. August nods.

DEAN
Good. Good --

Out of the blue...

AUGUST
How many people will hear it?

(CONTINUED)

FIGURE 3.13
This is a sample page from the screenplay *August Rush*. The screenplay format is an industry-standard scripting convention and is used widely throughout the motion picture and television industries.
(*Courtesy of Paul Castro*).

might like a design element in one wireframe and ask to have it incorporated with features in another. Wireframes are a great tool for honing in on the aesthetic tastes and sensibilities of the client without exhausting a lot of time and money on the front end of a new project.

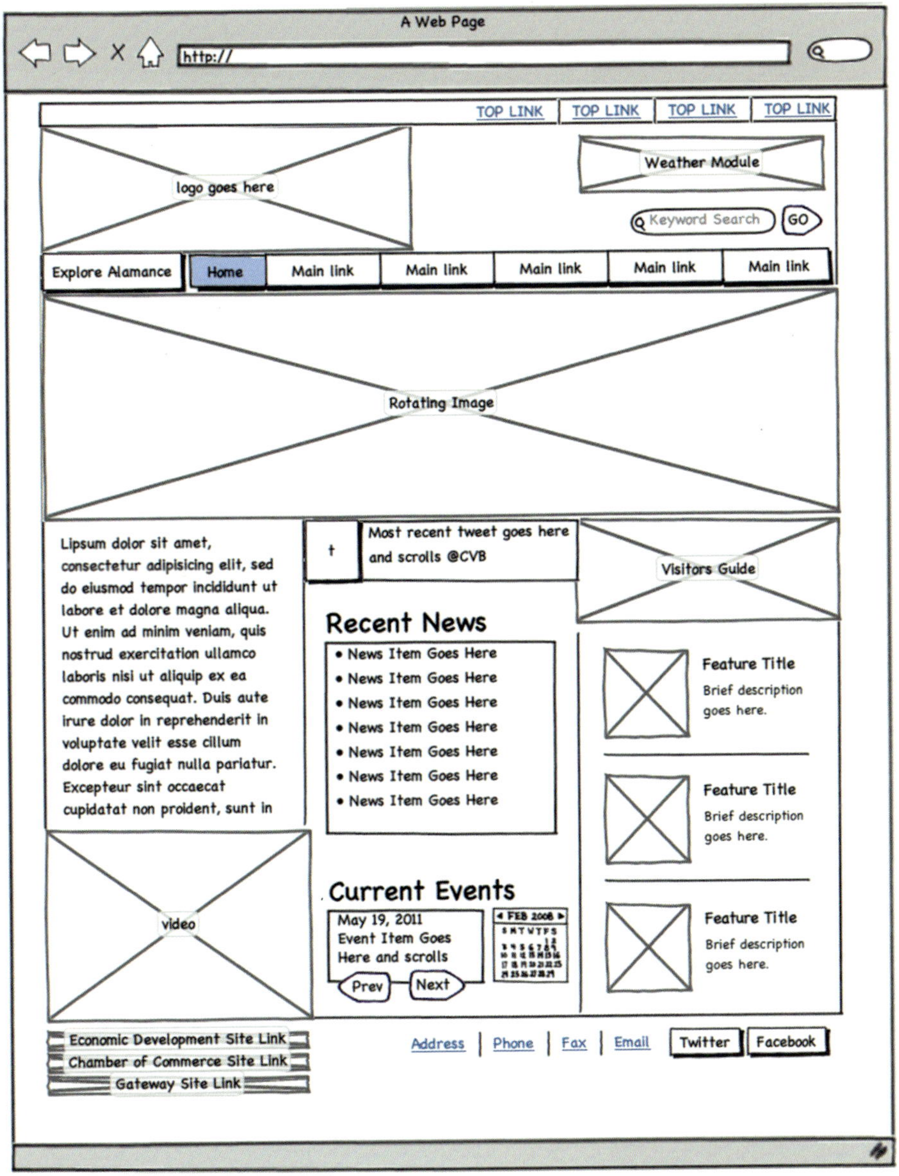

FIGURE 3.14
A graphic designer created this wireframe for previsualizing the structural layout of a new web page and its contents. The drawing was created with a computer software program called Balsamiq, a visual mockup tool used by professional web designers.
(Courtesy of North Star Marketing and the Burlington/Alamance County NC Convention and Visitors Bureau).

MOCKUP

Once a wireframe has been approved, designers will often create a more refined visual rendering known as a *mockup* (see Figure 3.15). A mockup is a detailed actual-size version of the page, usually created by a graphic designer with a program like Adobe Photoshop or Fireworks. It can include either actual copy and artwork or temporary content such as image placeholders and dummy text. A mockup also shows the color scheme and style elements of the page. The purpose of the mockup is to provide the client and design team with a detailed visual model of what the web page or interface component will look like when finished. As with wireframes, multiple versions of a mockup will usually be shown to the client.

PROTOTYPE

Wireframes and mockups are great for experimenting with the visual look and layout of a page or interface, however, they won't help much when it comes to

FIGURE 3.15
Once approved by the client, the rough wireframe sketch shown in Figure 3.14 was transformed into this detailed and colorful mockup using Adobe Photoshop. The nonsensical Latin text (commonly known as filler or dummy text) was used as a temporary placeholder to help the client and design team more fully envision what the page will look like in its final form.
(Courtesy of North Star Marketing and the Burlington/Alamance County NC Convention and Visitors Bureau).

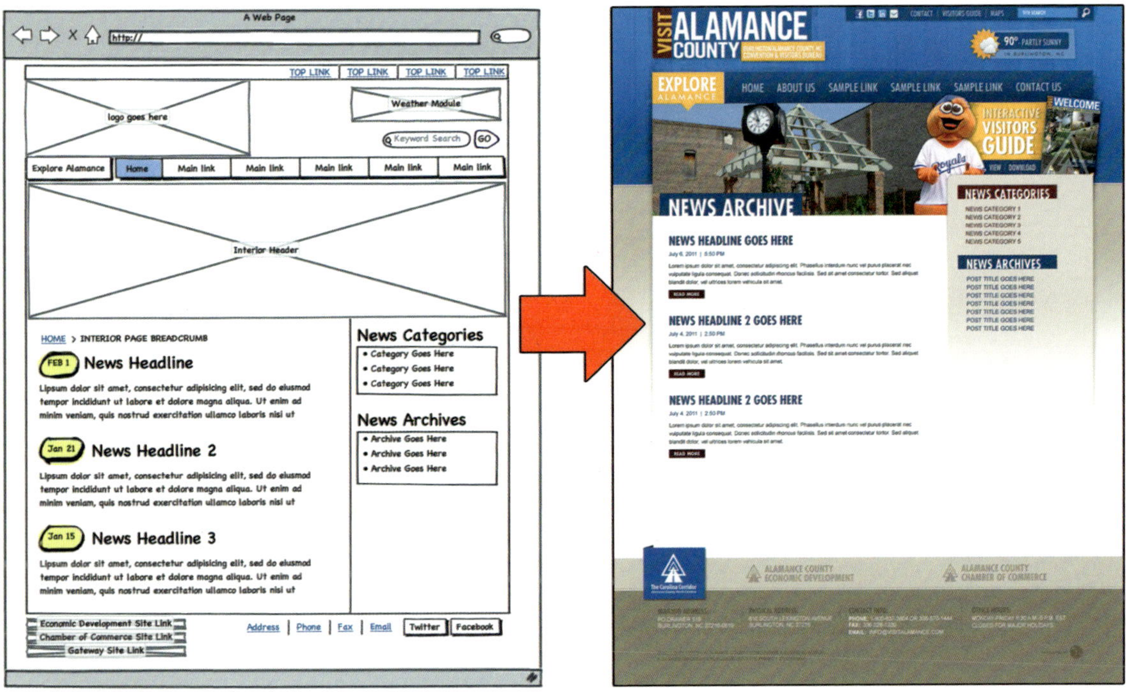

FIGURE 3.16
For this project, the design team created wireframes and mockups for every section (or main page) of the website. Such careful planning on the front end of a project helps ensure that time and money will not be wasted when the project moves forward into production. (*Courtesy of North Star Marketing and the Burlington/Alamance County NC Convention and Visitors Bureau*).

testing the usability of a design. At some point before production begins, you need to verify that a design is functional and will work as intended. Otherwise, a great deal of time and money may be put into creating a project that is technically flawed or doomed from the start. For this you need a prototype.

A *prototype* is a paper or working model of the project designed for simulation and testing. As the name suggests, a paper prototype is built on paper or cards and can be constructed using simple sketches or drawings. If time and money allow, the quality of a paper prototype can be refined using computer-generated artwork. Unfortunately, some functions, like scrolling or drop-down menus, are difficult to mimic in a paper prototype, creating limits on how much "real-life" testing can be done with a paper model. To overcome such limits, professional designers will often use a prototyping software application like Adobe Fireworks. Using application software, a designer can build a computer-based prototype that more realistically simulates the multimedia experience for the end-user. A prototype is like the blueprint of a house. Once approved, the web development team and programmers can begin the more time-intensive and costly step of actual construction.

THE DESIGN PROCESS

Multimedia design is a complex process involving many steps and substeps. While every project is different, there are at least four steps that must be followed to move a project from the concept phase to completion:

- Specify requirements (identify the scope of the project)
- Analyze users (define the target audience)
- Build a working prototype or finished product (construct the product)
- Evaluate and revise based on feedback (improve the product)

Although these steps can be applied to nearly any type of multimedia project, let's look at how they work in creating a website.

Specify Requirements

Specifying requirements helps establish the scope of your project, or the range of content and pages or screens. During this phase, your design team will meet with the client to identify business needs and requirements, existing problems, and potential users. You'll also develop functional solutions and decide what to include in the project and what to leave out.

Begin with a process known as *benchmarking*. Look at similar projects to see what they contain and how they are organized. Do you want similar types of screens? Different screens? Figure out the number and types of screens (or web pages) you need. Give each a temporary name, then sort them into logical groups and headings based on content. You can refine these categories later when you work with real users by having them do card sorting, creating your main navigation by letting them sort content into groups with predetermined names or by naming groups themselves.

Analyze Users

Next, you will conduct research to define your target users by demographic characteristics and/or their technology skills. You will explore when, where, and how target users will use the interface. You'll also learn about their previous experience with similar interfaces. The client is the best resource for this information and can tell you who the primary and secondary users of the site will be. However, don't assume the client will tell you all you need to know about the users. The client may have a fixed vision of what the site should include but may have missed some obvious—or not so obvious—user concerns. Your job is to ask the right questions.

If your client asks you to create a recycling website, first ask whom they intend the site to serve. Will the site target people looking for a place to drop off their used appliances? Or will it be aimed at local manufacturers trying to understand recycling laws as they apply to small businesses? Or maybe it will be aimed at grade-school teachers.

Many interfaces, whether websites or other multimedia projects, will have two types of audiences: a target audience (the audience you intend to reach) and ancillary audiences (users who will use the interface for other reasons). Your first concern is the target audience. This is the group of people your client most wants to reach. If the site is designed to reach teachers, they are your primary audience. If your client also wants to have information for local residents and businesses, these are your secondary target audiences. Focus on designing for your primary audience, but keep the site usable for secondary audiences too.

If you can meet with a few people who will use your interface, do it. If you can't, try to find people who are similar to real users. If that still doesn't work, do your best to think like real users. Start by answering the following questions about your target audience:

- *Who are the users?* Start with this, the most obvious question. How old are they? How much do they use this technology, or a computer in general? What do they use the technology for? Are they part of a particular organization? And so on. If you're designing a site for people in their 50s, tiny fonts are a bad idea.
- *What tasks will they try to accomplish?* What might they use this system or site for? What are the most important of these tasks?
- *What conventions are my users used to?* Look at other interfaces to develop your design criteria (benchmarking). What do similar interfaces look like? Does this one need to tie into a theme from a parent corporation? Don't copy another organization's interface or site, but look for patterns.
- *What do they like about similar interfaces?* What works on those interfaces in terms of navigation, color, organization, and so on?
- *What do they find frustrating about similar interfaces?*
- *What type of equipment and connections do my users have?* If you're building a website or application, what types of computers and software do they have? What size monitors and resolutions do they use? What types of handheld devices will they use? How fast are their Internet connections? If you're designing a phone app, plan for a small interface. If you're designing a website that will be used by children in school or people who work on small laptops, plan to design for a smaller screen.
- *What colors and images do they prefer?*

Build a Working Prototype

The design and initial production stage involves planning your layout with a wireframe, creating a mockup or paper prototype, getting initial user feedback, and creating a working prototype. Your team will first develop a conceptual model of the interface, addressing target users' needs and incorporating functional solutions. You will first implement your conceptual model roughly, then on specific physical platforms (for instance, online or on an iPad 2), and you'll get user feedback along the way.

Once you've divided content into sections, you need to choose how much space to devote to various components, for instance, how many items to include in a horizontal menu. The number of menu items will affect the size, and therefore look, of your buttons or bar. Next, figure out what components you are going to include on a given part of the interface. Consult with the client to see what they want on it. List the various options they have. If you don't, you'll find that they will often add components after you've worked hard on a design that doesn't have space for extra items. Put these items in a wireframe, a line drawing showing the main components (main navigation, logo, footer, etc.), and get their feedback. You can create a wireframe on the computer or using pencil and paper.

It is often much easier to create a more detailed picture of what one page will look like than to create a working screen or page. Then, when you find major mistakes, you haven't wasted valuable time. More importantly, you won't be so committed to the design (because of all of your hard work) that you refuse to make necessary changes. The mockup is a more photorealistic version of a page than a wireframe. Choose a medium you can work with easily. If you're good at Photoshop or a similar application, create a sample page using that application. Or use a drag-and-drop mockup or wireframing application (such as Mockflow and MockingBird) to easily make a visual of an interface, including using your own pictures.

Create three or more options for your client to evaluate, and let them choose an initial design. Then, have a few users look at your mockup. You can either get general feedback on the design, or you can test your paper prototype, conducting a mini-version of the testing you'll do later on a working prototype. You don't need more than a few mocked-up pages or screens to test, and a prototype test can save you lots of work later. After all, it would be disappointing to go through the hard work of creating pop-up menus only to learn that your users don't like them. Usability testing, which we'll cover later, is best done early and often.

Next, turn your design into a working prototype with at least some functionality.

Evaluate and Revise

Before turning the prototype into the actual interface that you'll give users, your team needs to evaluate and refine it. Begin by testing the interface yourself and fixing obvious problems. Then usability test it and fix the remaining problems.

Devote time to fixing any problems you can find yourself: text and color problems, functionality problems ("this button doesn't work like it should"), loading times, the appearance of a screen or page when a user magnifies it, and so forth. If you're building a website interface, test it for cross-platform compatibility, which we'll cover in Chapter 7, "Web Design." Then conduct usability tests, tests of your site with real users. After your tests, you may have to rename links, change your layout and design, "re-chunk" your information, or alter your images. Some of these changes may hurt, especially if you are overcommitted to

DME 110

Chap 1 by 1/27
Read & Quiz

Web 115

Unit 1 INTRO
Chap 1 + Assig
Chap 2 + Ass
+ Study Guide
END of Chap

your design. No matter how painful, fix the problems now so your users will be happy. And test again to be sure your changes work.

CHAPTER SUMMARY

The preproduction process for a multimedia project includes all of the activities leading up to the client's approval of the concept and initial design. Whether you're producing a video, website, or content management system, this process will likely begin with an in-depth conversation between you and the client and all of the key stakeholders in the project. Since creativity is largely a subjective process, a multimedia message can be designed an infinite number of ways and still be successful. Don't waste your time trying to nail down what you think is the only right way to go. Instead, spend your time wisely, listening and asking lots of questions. The best ideas often emerge from a process that is thorough, thoughtful, inclusive, and collaborative.

SECTION 2
Multimedia Design

Marco Rullkoetter/Shutterstock.com

CHAPTER 4
Visual Communication

Design is the method of putting form and content together. Design, just as art, has multiple definitions; there is no single definition. Design can be art. Design can be aesthetics. Design is so simple, that's why it is so complicated. Without aesthetic, design is either the humdrum repetition of familiar clichés or a wild scramble for novelty. Without the aesthetic, the computer is but a mindless speed machine, producing effects without substance, form without relevant content, or content without meaningful form.

— Paul Rand, American Author and Graphic Designer

Chapter Highlights

This chapter examines:

- The process of visual communication
- The role of content and form in visual space
- Eight elements of design: space, dot, line, shape, form, texture, pattern, and color
- Twelve principles of design affecting human perceptions of visual form in two dimensional space.
  - Unity: proximity, alignment, similarity, and repetition
  - Emphasis: contrast, color, depth and proportion
  - Perceptual Forces: balance, continuation, figure-ground, and psychological closure

Key Terms

Elements of Design
Space
Dot
Line
Shape
Form
Color
Texture
Pattern
Principles of Design
Unity
Alignment
Proximity
Similarity
Repetition
Emphasis
Contrast (Value)
Color
Depth
Proportion
Perceptual Forces
Balance
Continuation
Figure-Ground
Psychological Closure
Aesthetics
Aspect Ratio
Asymmetrical Balance
Axis
Canvas
Composition
Content and Form
Depth
Design
Dutch Tilt
Eye Candy

VISUAL COMMUNICATION

Visual communication (sometimes referred to as *vis-com*) is an area of study that investigates the transmission of ideas and information through visual forms and symbols. On a deeper level, it also looks at the cognitive and affective processes that affect the way we perceive (or sense) visual stimuli. Seeing is one thing and perceiving is another. The former has to do with the objective realities of sight, while the latter has to do with the transmission of culture and meaning. Two people with equal vision can stand in front of a painting and physically "see"

Field of View
Focal Point
Frame
Gestalt Psychology
Graphic Vector
Grayscale
Halftone Image
High-Key Image
Hue
Index Vector
Less is More
Low-Key Image
Motion Vector
Negative Space
Perception
Perspective
Positive Space
Rule of Thirds
Saturation
Symmetrical Balance
Tonal Range
Three-Dimensional Space
Two-Dimensional Space
Vector
Visual Communication
White Space
Workspace

FIGURE 4.1
Seeing and perceiving are two different things. The patrons in this art gallery "see" the artwork on the wall in much the same way (assuming equal vision). However, their perceptions of aesthetic value and beauty are individually constructed. What one person likes, another may disdain.
Photographer: Adriano Castelli/Shutterstock.com

the same thing. The "seeing" part of the event will be pretty much the same for both participants. However, each person's experience, point of view, knowledge, and aesthetic sensibilities, will shape his or her personal judgments about the painting's beauty or the artist's ability. One of them may like what he or she sees while the other may not (see Figure 4.1).

Content and Form

Visual communication involves the interaction of content and form. *Content* is the tangible essence of a work: the stories, ideas, and information that we exchange with others. *Form* is the manner in which content is designed, packaged, and delivered for consumption (see Figure 4.2). Put another way, content can be thought of as a person's body, while form is the makeup, clothing, jewelry, and accessories used to accentuate physical appearance. Content relates to what we want to say, while form has to do with how we choose to express it or communicate it. We would not expect a history teacher to explain an event that took place during World War II in the same way to a second-grader as he or she would to a college student. While the material substance of the content may be the same, differences in the age, skill level, and maturity of the audience inform decisions about how best to tell the story and shape its presentation.

FIGURE 4.2
The Congressional lawmakers who penned the Bill of Rights provided the content for this illustration of the First Amendment. A graphic designer created its form. *Courtesy of the Freedom Forum.*

Content and form are complementary components of a visual design. Both are required for success. Without good content, even the best designs and visual treatments will fall flat. The phrase "eye candy" has become a popular cliché for describing something that is visually appealing but lacking in substantive value. In multimedia, there are many tools at our fingertips that we can use to create an eye-catching first impression. We sometimes call it the WOW-factor or hook. While the WOW-factor can play a useful role in gaining the attention of the audience, without meaningful content, people will quickly lose interest and move on. There's simply no substitute for a good message, and in the absence of a compelling story or idea, good designs are nothing more than eye candy.

Likewise, without an appealing visual design, even the best messages can pass by unnoticed. Good form enhances the pleasure of consuming good content. A well-designed presentation reduces eyestrain and provides cues to the audience to help them navigate through visual information quickly, to find what is most important to them at any given moment. Form should never be a distraction, but instead should complement the message in such a way as to optimize the effectiveness of communication with an individual or group.

Communication theorist Marshall McLuhan is renowned for his classic statement, "the medium is the message." While interpretations of this phrase vary, one reading suggests that if the form of the medium dominates the content, the message can be adversely affected. While McLuhan was speaking in a larger sense about mass media technologies such as television and radio, the principle holds true for individual designs and presentations of visual media. The delivery medium or form, when elevated above content, can overshadow the message to the point where communication with an audience is diminished or made entirely ineffective.

FLASHBACK

The Medium Is the Message

> The electric light is pure information. It is a medium without a message, as it were, unless it is used to spell out some verbal ad or name. This fact, characteristic of all media, means that the "content" of any medium is always another medium. The content of writing is speech, just as the written word is the content of print, and print is the content of the telegraph. If it is asked, "What is the content of speech?," it is necessary to say, "It is an actual process of thought, which is in itself nonverbal." An abstract painting represents direct manifestation of creative thought processes as they might appear in computer designs. What we are considering here, however, are the psychic and social consequences of the designs or patterns as they amplify or accelerate existing processes. For the "message" of any medium or technology is the change of scale or pace or pattern that it introduces into human affairs.

Marshall McLuhan,
Understanding Media: The Extensions of Man (1964)

Adobe's Flash authoring tool is an excellent example of McLuhan's idea in practice. Although Flash-based content is ubiquitous on the Web, we continue to debate about an overemphasis on the WOW-factor in many Flash projects or websites. Flash is a tool that can be easily overused, to the point where it trumps "the message," leaving the audience with an empty candy wrapper and a craving for a more significant and satisfying meal.

We need to remember that the phrase "content is king," coined by Bill Gates, still holds true. Although form plays an essential role in the visual design process, it is a secondary role that must be carefully handled by the visual designer. The expression "less is more" is a popular saying that encourages a minimalist approach. "Less is more" promotes a healthy sense of self-restraint in the application of form with a focus on simplicity and the fundamental elements of design. This is good advice for the beginner or amateur designer. Adding bells and whistles to a project just because you can or because you think it's cool, will not necessarily impress the client or contribute to the overall effectiveness of a communication product. It usually does just the opposite. These bells and whistles can make a product less usable, in part by impairing its efficiency, its ability to be learned, and its ability to satisfy users. We'll talk more about usability in Chapter 6, "Interface Design and Usability."

Aesthetics

We make perceptual judgments about visual beauty every day. We might observe that a certain website looks amazing while another one appears drab and unattractive. We turn up our nose at unsightly outfits in a store that grate against our personal taste, then rave when we find the one that's just right for us. Likewise, people have diverse, and often pronounced, sensibilities regarding color. Some of us favor blue, while others prefer red. Think about the color and style preferences that have

FIGURE 4.3
Our aesthetic sensibilities vary widely depending on many factors including context and place. Which armchair is more appropriate for a fishing lodge in the Appalachian Mountains? Which one would you rather see in the office of a lawyer?

influenced your selection of a new car, a pair of shoes, eyeglasses, or laptop computer (see Figure 4.3). While content, function, and usability are important, our affinity for things is greatly affected by our perceptions of outward beauty or appearance. This is true for the physical objects we eat, wear, drive, live in, or otherwise enjoy; as well as for artistic works or media products that we interact with visually.

People can be passionate when expressing their personal judgments about appearance. One person may exclaim, "I hate green!" Another shouts out, "I wouldn't be caught dead wearing that in broad daylight!" Likewise, someone might comment on a piece of pottery, "This is the most beautiful bowl I have ever seen!" While another gasps in disgust as he thinks about how ugly it looks. How can two people respond so differently to the same visual stimuli? This question and others like it are explored in the field of aesthetics, a theoretical branch of visual communication that deals with the nature of beauty and human perceptions of visual form and presentation.

For professional designers, the field of applied aesthetics addresses the need for industry-specific rules and guidelines used in trade crafts such as cinematography, graphic design, television production, website design, and photography. Each field is guided by its own design rules and guidelines, a set of formal and informal practices that influence the choices made during each phase of the creative process. Learning and practicing the principles of applied aesthetics is essential for developing a professional framework through which you can critically examine your own work as well as the design choices of others. Applied aesthetics moves us away from unfounded judgments that are rooted in personal bias and opinion, and to the place where we begin to make reasoned and informed observations based on formal theory and research. Thus, a photojournalist has to learn how to articulate the difference between a well-composed shot and one that is poorly framed. In the same way, a film critic has to assess the difference between a movie that gets five stars (Hollywood Oscar material) and one that falls flat at the box office (a candidate for the Razzies, perhaps).

The work of professional designers is persistently subject to the aesthetic judgments of others, and on occasion, you may receive more feedback than you want on your work. Sometimes the comments may be overwhelmingly positive; at other times they may be severe, mercilessly harsh, sending you back to the proverbial drawing board to start over. More often than not, they will fall somewhere in the middle, prompting you to reconsider certain aspects of your design and make changes accordingly. An old proverb says, "There is wisdom in a multitude of counselors." This doesn't mean that every tidbit of advice you receive from others will be constructive or helpful. But it does suggest that the more eyeballs you have evaluating the aesthetic value of your work, the more direction you will have for improving its presentation. Because aesthetic sensibilities are so diverse and wide-ranging, you need the input of others to help you see past your personal tastes. Just remember, the point of criticism is not to attack the messenger (or designer), but to objectively assess creative output in an effort to optimize a message's effectiveness. Learning elements of design can help you provide effective feedback, too, and ground your criticism in theory.

ELEMENTS OF DESIGN

Design is the strategic arrangement of visual elements within a two-dimensional space to form a unified and holistic impression. Sometimes, the word *composition* is used as an alternative way of describing the same process. For example, in one situation it may be appropriate to say, "I like the *design* of your web page or corporate logo," while in another it makes more sense to say, "I like the way you *composed* this shot" or "the *composition* is well-balanced." In both cases, I am referring to same thing: the intentional organization of a visual space.

The elements of design are the fundamental building blocks of visual content. In the same way that a house is constructed of essential components like the foundation, floors, walls, windows, doors, and roof, graphic images are formed using the elements of design. This section focuses on eight elements of design that are common to all forms of visual communication: space, dot, line, shape, form, texture, pattern, and color.

A popular cooking program pits two skilled chefs in a timed competition. Each chef is given one hour to prepare a multicourse meal for a panel of judges. At the beginning of each program, the host reveals the "secret ingredient," a specific food component such as corn, honey, fish, or peppers that must be featured in each dish. Among other things, contestants are judged on their ability to incorporate the secret ingredient into every course. They will use other ingredients, but their goal is to make the secret ingredient stand out as the star attraction. It may be helpful for you to think of the elements of design as a master list of ingredients that you can use when designing a graphic or composing an image. Typically, one or two of the elements in a design will contend for the starring role of "secret" ingredient. Rarely do you see a design that will incorporate every element within a single visual representation. Sometimes, the designer will choose to accentuate the element of line. At other times the designer may want to highlight form or color. By combining the elements of design, we can create an endless array of variations.

Understanding the elements of design and their influence on human perception will help you become a better visual communicator and media consumer. It will also strengthen your ability to make informed judgments about the overall quality and beauty of a visual design. Learning the language of visual design will help you better defend and critique your own work as well as that of others. Doing so will help you complete the sentence, "I like this because . . . " or "Photograph 'A' is better than Photograph 'B' because. . . . "

Space

Like a traditional artist, a digital designer begins with a blank surface or design space that comes to life as the creative process unfolds (see Figure 4.4). In Adobe Photoshop and Illustrator, the document window or workspace is referred to metaphorically as the canvas. Like an artist's canvas, the digital canvas is flat

FIGURE 4.4
A visual communicator's job is to fill empty space with meaningful content that communicates a message.

FIGURE 4.5
A camera sees only what the photographer wants it to see. The design space is composed within the frame of a camera's viewfinder and is referred to as the *field of view*.

and boxy. It has an outer frame that defines the area of the design surface where visual elements reside. The designer's job is to fill this empty space with meaningful visual content that communicates a message.

In photography, the design space is called the *field of view*. The field of view is the area of a scene that is visible to the camera at any given moment in time (see Figure 4.5). Looking through the viewfinder, a camera operator can change the field of view by zooming the lens in or out, or by moving closer to or farther away from the subject. "Framing a shot" involves making conscious decisions about what to include and exclude (crop) from within the frame. The spatial area of the scene the camera "sees" is controlled by the person composing the shot.

TWO-DIMENSIONAL SPACE

Digital workspaces only have two dimensions: width and height. These dimensions are measured in pixels—rectangular or square picture elements, or tiny blocks of color—rather than by using an absolute unit of measurement, such as inches or centimeters (see Figure 4.6). As a result, the size is relative, because the actual appearance of the spatial area will vary depending on the settings of the display device rendering the design on-screen. We'll talk more about pixels in Chapter 8, "Graphics." The workspace's width is measured along its *x-axis* (horizontally), and its height is measured on its *y-axis* (vertically). When we refer to coordinates within the workspace, an x:y position, we set the upper left-hand corner as zero, counting pixels from left to right and from top to bottom.

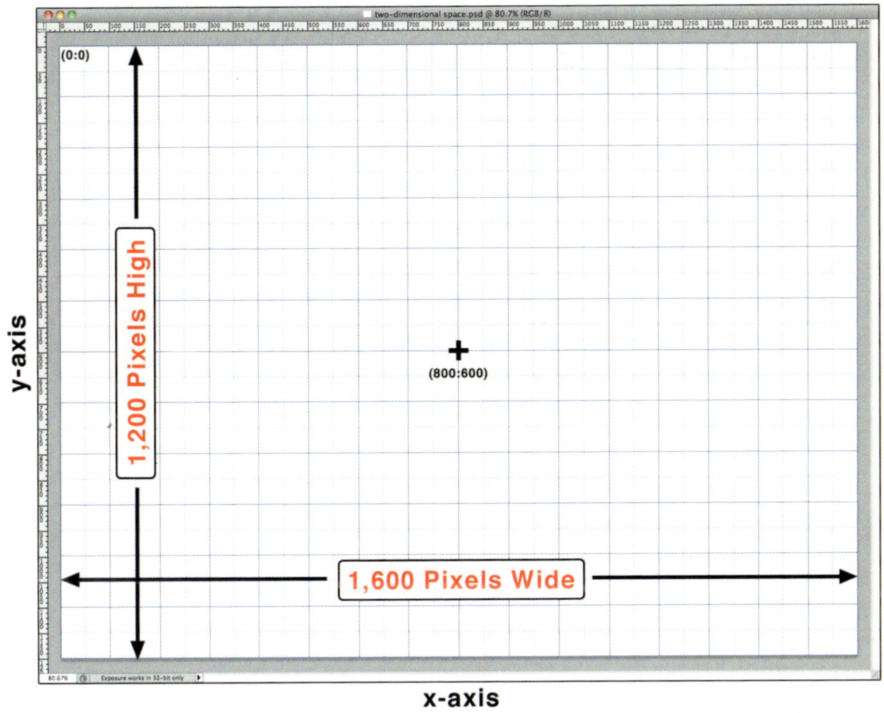

FIGURE 4.6
This is a screen shot of the design space (or "canvas") in Adobe Photoshop CS5. The blue gridlines are a designer's tool used for placing and aligning visual elements within the frame.

Digital spaces are rectangular, so they conform to the boxlike frames of electronic displays and projectors. The term *aspect ratio* refers to the relationship between the width and height of a design space. A 4:3 space is 4 units wide by 3 units high. A 16:9 space is 16 units wide by 9 units high. Although the physical dimensions of a display monitor or viewfinder can vary from small to large, as long as the aspect ratios are compatible, images will stay true to their original proportions. Using compatible aspect ratios for output or presentation prevents unwanted distortion.

Digital spaces are physically limited to width and height, but people have the ability to perceive the third dimension of depth when viewing two-dimensional representations. Depth in two-dimensional space is only a perceptual illusion. Through skilled control of lighting, perspective, shading, texture, color, contrast, relative speed (for media with movement), etc., visual designs can be made to look remarkably three-dimensional. Depth is represented by the *z-axis*, an imaginary sight vector that extends away from the viewer and into the center of the design. Our ability to perceive depth depends on our ability to make sense of the relative position of background, mid-ground, and foreground elements along the z-axis. As creatures of three-dimensional space, we tend to favor designs that promote a sense of depth. A design or image that is lacking in depth is said to be flat.

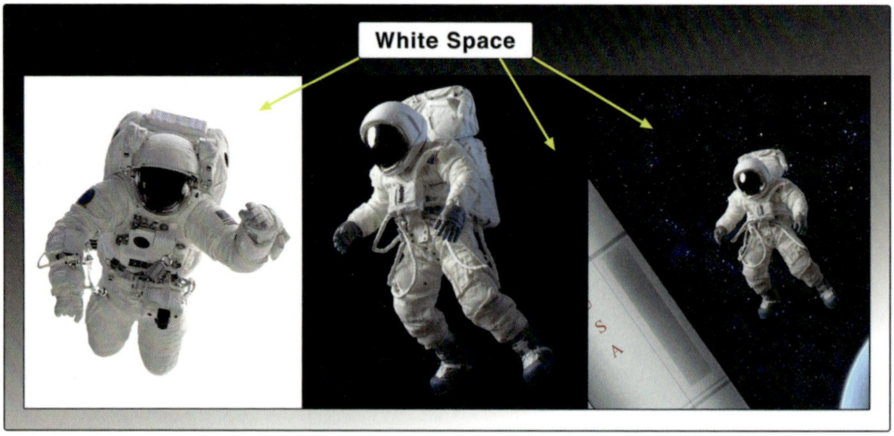

FIGURE 4.7
White space (also called negative space) doesn't have to be white.

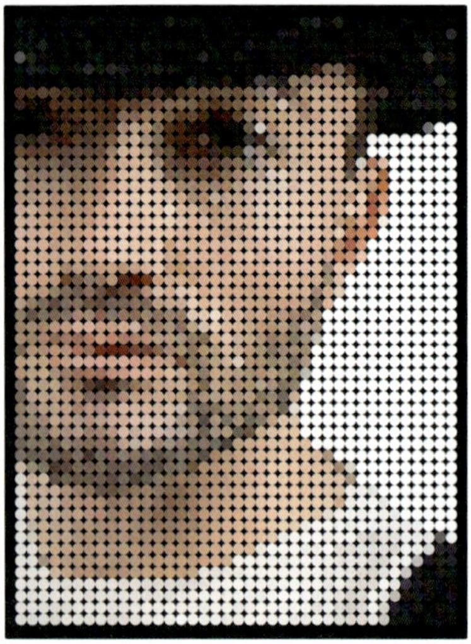

FIGURE 4.8
This image is formed entirely of colored dots. Close up, the dots are more noticeable. The further back you are, the more they coalesce to form a composite image.

POSITIVE AND NEGATIVE SPACE

The design window is divided into areas of positive and negative space. *Positive space* is the portion of an image where visual elements (lines, shapes, forms, etc.) reside. *Negative space* is the rest of an image, where no visual content exists. In a book, the letters, words, sentences, paragraphs, and illustrations make up the positive space on a page. In this example, you can think of positive space as every part of the page that has been pressed with ink to form a visual impression. Negative space is everything else. Since paper stock for books, newspapers, and magazines is often white, the terms *white space* and *negative space* are used interchangeably. So, even if the background of a web page is blue, most designers will refer to the empty portions of the design as white space (see Figure 4.7).

White space is essential because it adds breathing room to visual information, making it easier for users to consume content and navigate the page. The terms *margins, padding, tabs, spaces,* and *line breaks* describe specific instances of negative space. Research indicates that we read faster when white space separates lines of text and forms margins at the edges of a page. The same is true for content that's presented on an electronic display. Without sufficient white space, designs can become visually cluttered and difficult to read.

Dot

The most basic representation of form is the *dot*. It's the starting point for all other elements of design. A line begins and ends with a dot, but more importantly, dots can be combined in large numbers to portray complex visual objects and images (see Figure 4.8). Under a magnifying glass, you can see that a printed newspaper image (or half tone print) is made up of dots (positive space) surrounded by white space. From a proper reading distance, the dots merge, they coalesce, completing the optical illusion of a continuous tone image in our visual receptors.

Tech Talk

Halftone Image In the 1850s, William Henry Fox Talbot came up with a method for printing photographic images in newsprint. Using a special large-format camera, a printer would reshoot a photograph through a perforated screen containing hundreds of small holes. The holes in the screen served to break up the continuous tonal structure of the image into discrete points of light represented by a single color or shade of gray. Talbot's procedure—similar to the technique of sampling that's used in digital imaging today—produced a halftone version of the original image made up entirely of dots of varying sizes along a uniform linear grid (see Figure 4.9).

The size of each dot in the grid is directly proportional to the intensity of color at that given point. In black and white halftone printing, the darkest areas of the image are represented by the largest dots, and the lighter areas are made up of smaller dots. The size of the dots in the halftone screen regulate how much black ink is applied to the paper, producing varying shades of gray (from black to white) with a single shade of pigment.

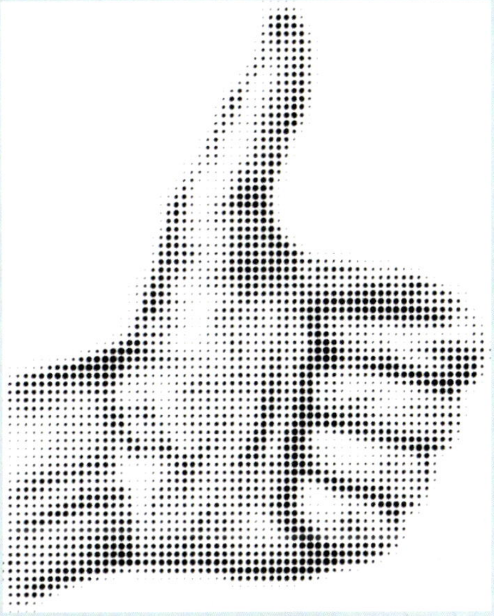

FIGURE 4.9
This halftone image is formed with black dots of various sizes and shades.

The process has become more sophisticated over the years, but we still use halftone printing today. In process printing, printers make screens for each primary color channel: cyan, magenta, yellow, and black, or CMYK. During printing, each primary color is applied separately to control the density of its ink droplets. Under the microscope, color dots appear as clusters of four dots of varying sizes, each representing the intensity of the color pigment needed to make the final color. And we use similar principles to form electronic images. Television and computer images are made of millions of pixels—each one using various intensities of red, green, and blue to create a tiny square of color. In printing, we refer to the tiny droplets of ink on a page as *dots*. In digital imaging, we refer to the square points of light on a display screen or projection as *pixels*.

Line

A line is the visual connector between two points in space. Lines can be real or implied. For example, a white line painted on the edge of a road is real. We know that the line did not just appear. It was intentionally painted to warn drivers not to run off the road. Lines can also be implied by natural alignment or the

FIGURE 4.10
Lines can be horizontal, vertical, curved, or diagonal, and can be combined in an infinite number of ways. The visual world is full of them in a myriad array of shapes, sizes, and colors. Take a look around you. What kind of lines do you see? Can you describe them?

purposeful placement of objects within a graphic composition. The top of a rail fence, a distant horizon, a row of trees, the edge of a skyscraper, and a winding road all imply the element of line. In visual design, lines can be used to stir the emotions or to create a specific mood or atmosphere (see Figure 4.10). Some lines have the effect of relaxing a design and putting the viewer at ease. Other lines connote a sense of direction, movement, or visual energy.

STRAIGHT LINES

Straight lines can be *static* (horizontal or vertical) or *dynamic* (diagonal). *Horizontal lines* often communicate a sense of peace and calm. Perhaps this is tied to the fact that we lie down to rest and stand up to move and walk around. Placing a flat object on a level surface such as a desk or countertop, we would expect it not to move. The laws of physics should ensure a period of stasis. We perceive horizontal lines in much the same way. They are a natural and reliable reference point that can reinforce a sense of balance and stability within

FIGURE 4.11
The parallel tracks appear to converge along the z-axis, contributing to an illusion of depth in this two-dimensional photograph.

a design. *Vertical lines* reach upward, promoting a sense of power, strength, grandeur, and awe. They too are stable, because gravity holds them in place. We naturally associate vertical lines with height. Intersecting horizontal and vertical lines form strong visual frameworks, much like a building's intersection of studs and joists increases its structural strength.

Diagonal lines hold the greatest potential for energizing a visual design. They exude a sense of speed, movement, and depth. Photographing the façade of a building head-on will evoke a relatively stable response from the viewer, because the natural lines produced by structural elements such as bricks, windows, doorframes, etc. are largely parallel or perpendicular to the ground. If you shift the angle of view along the x- or y-axis, you capture diagonal lines, and the previously stable lines now appear to converge into a distant vanishing point. A similar effect occurs when photographing a set of railroad tracks along the z-axis. We know that railroad tracks are always parallel, but perceptually, their lines appear to converge and seemingly will meet at some distant point (see Figure 4.11). This is just a perceptual illusion, of course. In art, this technique is called *perspective* and is used to create the illusion of a third dimension in a two-dimensional frame. Perspective breaks up the visual monotony of a stable image by emphasizing depth and distance through the use of diagonal lines.

CURVED LINES

Curved lines can create a sense of peace and tranquility in a design. The smooth edges of a curved element provide a sense of flow and directionality and are easy for the eye to follow without abrupt stops or interruptions. Car bodies are typically curved to improve the aerodynamic performance of the vehicle, but curves also improve the appearance of a car, making it look sleek and stylish. Curves accentuate the shape and form of other elements and are among the most common lines found in nature.

Tech Talk

Vertigo and 3D The vestibular system, comprised of organs of the inner ear, sends messages to the brain that enable us to retain our balance and spatial orientation. When this system fails, we can experience vertigo, sensing the feeling of movement when we are stationary. Vertigo can make you feel dizzy or nauseated. Using visual trickery, we can lead people into a momentary state of vertigo, affecting their sense of equilibrium. IMAX, 3D and 4D film, and Circle-Vision 360° are cinematic technologies used to add a physical sense of movement to a 2D viewing experience.

In most cases, accentuating angles and diagonal lines in a still image will not induce a case of vertigo. But this technique can help the viewer perceive motion in a scene, enhancing the visual dynamic. The *Dutch tilt* is a cinematic technique that involves tilting the camera so the horizon is not parallel to the bottom of the frame (see Figure 4.12). This technique, also known as the *canted angle*, is popular in sports and action photography. Tilting the camera destabilizes an image and can give the viewer a heightened sense of movement and tension in the shot. If used heavily, the effect can add a comic-book feel, as it does in the late-1960s Batman television series.

FIGURE 4.12
Use of the Dutch tilt adds visual energy to this shot of a lone competitor in the Tour de France.
Photographer: Peter Kirillov/Shutterstock.com

FIGURE 4.13
In this photo, an S-curve is used to gently guide the viewer's eye along a linear path to the main subject.

Diagonals and curves are particularly effective when used as leading line elements in a design (see Figure 4.13). A leading line steers the eyes of the viewer through a design, guiding them from one element to another or directly to the main subject or focal point.

Shape

A *shape* is a two-dimensional element formed by the enclosure of dots and lines (see Figure 4.14). We perceive shapes as flat objects without depth (either real or implied). A shape can be as simple as a circle or as complex and intricately conceived as a snowflake. The basic geometric shapes are *circles*, *triangles*, and *squares*. When we combine them in various ways, they can form virtually any other shape imaginable. They are called *geometric shapes* because they can be rendered mathematically using formal rules of construction.

Organic shapes are so called because they resemble objects in the natural world. Organic shapes have an imperfect, soft,

FIGURE 4.14
Shapes often connote a sense of the familiar. Like lines, they can be combined in an infinite number of ways to form new, more complex shapes.

and flowing appearance. They are often constructed of continuous curves or circular elements. For this reason, curvilinear and freeform shapes frequently fall into the same category. Organic shapes are often based on familiar objects such as animals, clouds, insects, leaves, plants, fruits, and vegetables. The famous logo for Apple computers is a great example of how a company has used an organic shape for branding its public identity.

Shapes can be powerful visual forces in design. Shapes can evoke the memory of objects or symbols with which we have established points of reference or emotional connections. The shape of a flower can stir up the memory of a fragrance. The shape of a male or female silhouette reminds us instantly which restroom to use in a public space. The recognizable shapes of the Manhattan skyline and Statute of Liberty transport us immediately to New York City, potentially unlocking memories or impressions from past experiences. Shapes often have symbolic meanings that can be used as visual shorthand to elicit a feeling or thought. What shape comes to mind first when you think of things like love, peace, warmth, or money? Perhaps, like me, you envisioned a heart, a dove, the sun, and a dollar sign.

Form

Form adds the dimension of depth to shape. *Form* is three-dimensional and connects us more fully to the way we see objects in the natural world (see Figure 4.15). In terms of geometric elements, it may be helpful to compare the two-dimensional shapes of a circle and square to their three-dimensional counterparts, the sphere and the cube. In order to show depth within a two-dimensional design space, a designer or photographer must learn to manipulate lighting, shading, color, and contrast within the frame. In film, a single

FIGURE 4.15
A 3D modeling program was used to create these visual forms. Form adds a sense of depth, a perceptual illusion that can be produced by manipulating light, shadow, color, and other elements within 2D space.

backlight can create the shape or silhouette of a person on screen. To create form, more sophisticated lighting from multiple angles is required. In graphic design, 3D modeling tools and software can be used to create the illusion of form. With such programs, you can add and manipulate virtual lighting to the same end. One medium relies on natural light and physical instruments to do the job. The other uses virtual instruments and algorithms to do the trick. As discussed earlier, using perspective also enhances the viewer's ability to perceive depth along the z-axis.

LIGHTING

As we've already established, lighting affects forms. Good designers carefully plan their lighting when they take photographs, capture video, and create graphics. We describe light as having both color temperature and hardness. Color temperatures, described in degrees Kelvin, can be low on the scale and warm (orange or reddish) or high on the scale and cool (bluish), giving images different qualities. Hard lighting from distant or narrow light sources casts shadows and will give your image an illusion of volume and emphasize textures. If you angle a light to the side of a texture (called *short lighting* in portrait photography), small shadows will emphasize the lines in a face or the grains of sand of a dune. Soft lighting from broad (frontally placed), multiple, close, or diffused (scattered) light sources—even lighting diffused by clouds or from backlighting—can soften an image, making an older subject appear a bit younger or creating an ethereal quality.

Low light, universal light, and light falloff also affect an image. In low light, a still-image camera has to keep its shutter open longer, and objects in motion can become blurry; in video, the image becomes grainy. And when you work with images and graphics in editing applications such as Photoshop, using universal lighting will make light-dependent effects (drop shadows and beveling, for instance) more cohesive. Universal lighting makes the illusion of light consistent, so light appears to come from only one angle. Finally, you can light a scene to emphasize selective parts of a composition, taking advantage of light falloff, or the lower illumination of objects farther from your light source.

Texture

Texture is the surface attribute of a visual object that evokes a sense of tactile interaction, and it can be implied in images. We perceive texture with the sense of touch. Some surfaces feel smooth whereas others are coarse. Some are wet, and others are dry. Some are soft, others are hard. Texture can affect us on a multisensory level, evoking in us a sense of touch, smell, and even taste. A digital image can only imply a sensory response, but the power of suggestion is real. As with shape, the visual element of texture can stir up memories and associations in the user. The sight of grill marks on a hamburger can remind us of the sound of sizzling fat and stir up thoughts of familiar smells and flavors. The grill marks attest not only to how the meat was cooked, but also may bring to mind positive recollections of summer cookouts and backyard parties. Of course, those who don't eat meat may respond entirely differently to such a visual prompt. Knowing your audience and its associations is important, especially when your audience is intercultural.

Looking at a familiar texture on screen, you can easily imagine what it might feel like. Adding sound to the experience makes the connection even stronger. What if you could hear the burger sizzle? Just imagine the grinding sound of sandpaper rubbing up and down the edge of a board, and the relative graininess of the surface becomes all the more apparent. What about the sound of feet walking on a gravel road? Does it change depending on the size of the gravel?

Texture ignites the imagination, allowing us to interact with a design at a deeper cognitive level. For example, the texture of a person's skin can tell us a lot about an individual. We associate soft, smooth skin with the touch of a baby's face. Likewise, we expect older people to have dry, cracked, or wrinkled skin that is weathered by age and the elements of life. Rust and peeling paint also speak to us about age and the passing of time. And the designs of many websites and applications play to our expectations of current technology as smooth and sleek.

Texture also serves to break up visual monotony. It adds visual depth, since most textures rise above the surface of an object. When properly incorporated into a design, texture can enhance the interest and perceived realism of a visual work.

Pattern

Pattern is the reoccurrence of a visual element within a design space. Clothing, furniture, and wallpaper are often identified by the characteristic pattern they employ (checkerboard, herringbone, polka dot, paisley, plaid, etc.). As with texture, pattern can add visual interest to an otherwise plain and monochromatic object. Like shape, pattern can be geometric or organic. The Spirograph toy, invented in the 1960s, is a popular plaything that enables kids to draw intricate geometric patterns of lines, shapes, and colors. The device, made up of a drawing frame and design templates with gears and tracks to control movement, allows the child to combine curves, circles, loops, and lines to form highly complex patterns and designs. The long-term popularity of this toy testifies to our innate fascination with repetition and pattern.

FIGURE 4.16
1) Lighting, 2) texture, 3) pattern, and 4) color can be intentionally highlighted to achieve a desired effect or mood. As with all visual elements, they can be mixed. The umbrella shot equally combines the use of pattern and repetition.

Organic patterns are found in nature, such as a flock of geese flying in formation, the woven matrix of a spider web, or an aerial view of a pumpkin patch at harvest time. Patterns can be uniform and predictable as in the repetition of colors and shapes in the American flag. The random or natural scattering of similar elements within a shared space can also lead to interesting patterns, such as hieroglyphics on a cave wall or shots of sunbathers strewn along a crowded beach.

Color

Color has three dimensions: hue, saturation, and brightness. *Hue* is the color shade of an object as a single point on the color spectrum. We refer to colors most often by their hue (red, green, blue, etc.). *Saturation* is the strength or purity of a color. The red in a stop sign is a highly saturated hue, whereas pink is a desaturated version of the same color. A completely desaturated color contains only variations of white and black as measured along the grayscale. *Brightness* (also called *value*) is the relative lightness or darkness of a color. Brightness can be thought of as the dimmer control on a light switch that raises or lowers the level of light in a room.

FIGURE 4.17
Boy or girl? What role does color play in your decision?

We can use color to set tone and mood, to elicit instant associations, to attract attention, and even to help users remember things. In the beginning of the movie *Catch Me If You Can*, Leonardo DiCaprio's character is in control of his life, and the palette is subdued. The colors become vivid as he loses control and takes bigger chances. You might buy a beach towel with an orange and red design because the colors bring to mind oceanside sunsets and stir up related emotions. And the orange can generate positive emotions on its own, without bringing a past trip to mind. Or you might paint a baby's room a pale, desaturated green to create a soothing environment.

Colors also have cultural associations. What sex is a baby dressed in blue? (see Figure 4.17) Does a website with a pink background target men or women? These are purely learned associations: in Western nations and prior to the end of World War II, pink and blue were often used interchangeably across genders. What does red mean to you? That depends on where you're from. In the United States, red is associated with danger and passion, among other things, whereas in China, it has a number of other associations, such as luck. If you want to attract attention to an element on a page, what color would you use? Brown would not be your first choice! And psychologists have tied color to memory, too. If you have used a coloring book to study anatomy, color may have helped you pass your exams.

THE PRINCIPLES OF DESIGN

In the previous section, I referred to the elements of design as the "ingredients" used in making visual art. If the elements are the ingredients, then the principles of design can be thought of as the recipe for combining elements within a visual space. The principles of design are formal rules and concepts for optimizing the arrangement and presentation of two-dimensional visual elements. The 12 general principles covered in this section fall into the broad categories of (1) unity, (2) emphasis, and (3) perceptual forces. The principles of *unity* can be thought of as the perceptual glue that holds a design together and maintains a sense of visual harmony. The principles of *emphasis* address the need for maintaining a visual focal point. They also relate to the way designers designate the importance or weight of the subject matter. Emphasis is often used to communicate to the viewer the relative importance of visual objects or information in a design. Finally, the principles of *perceptual force* help us to understand some of the psychological processes that affect the way we interact with visual content within a frame.

Unity

You have heard the saying, "the whole is greater than the sum of its parts." In visual theory, this means that the viewer should be able to grasp the essence of the "big picture" without being distracted by the individual elements of a design. This is the principle of *unity*, which is achieved when the visual subcomponents of a design coalesce to form a holistic impression. Unity means that the constituent parts of a work reside together in harmony. In a good design, each visual element or group of elements should contribute to the whole without competing against other elements or distracting the viewer from the primary point of interest.

In 1923, German psychologist Max Wertheimer (1880–1943) developed the theory of perceptual grouping as a part of a larger set of axioms dealing with perceptual organization. Rooted in Gestalt psychology, a branch of study dealing with the self-organizing tendencies of the mind and brain, the laws of perceptual organization suggest that the human brain favors whole forms over random smatterings of disconnected elements. To this end, the brain strives for unity by organizing visual information into meaningful clusters or groups. This tendency enables people to retain holistic impressions of shapes and patterns while ignoring the constituent parts used in their construction.

When visual content is haphazardly arranged and disorganized, the brain must work harder to make sense it. When information conforms to known principles of organization, the brain can work faster and communication is more effective. These unifying principles include proximity, alignment, similarity, and repetition (see Figures 4.19 and 4.20).

PROXIMITY

The law of *proximity* states that objects are more likely to be perceived as related when they are positioned close together. Think for a moment about how Google returns search results (see Figure 4.18). Google gives you a series of search snippets, each with a linked web page title, URL (web address), and excerpt or page description. Evenly distributed spaces separate the listings, allowing you to identify each separate snippet: all of its material is grouped together.

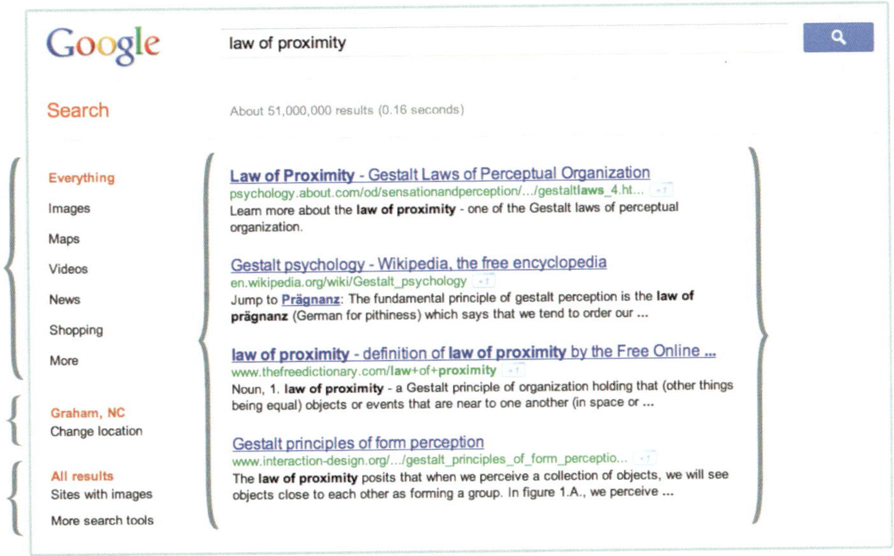

FIGURE 4.18
Observe how proximity is used to group related elements in the layout of a Google search results page. Perceptual grouping makes it easier for the viewer to process and consume visual information while enhancing the overall unity of a design.
Source: google.com

Proximity reminds me to keep captions close to the images and illustrations they refer to. It informs us that titles should appear near the first line of text in an article. It also reminds us never to scatter the location of buttons on a toolbar that belong together by virtue of a similar function. White space is often associated with proximity. If you add too much white space between related objects in a design, the audience may fail to see that they are connected. If there's not enough white space, then clutter may result, making it difficult for people to perceive the presence of individual elements.

ALIGNMENT

The principle of *alignment* encourages designers to position objects that belong together along a common edge or implied line. Visual objects—text, graphics, etc.—are normally aligned along their outer edges (left, right, top, or bottom) or centers. However, any line will do, as long as the placement is thoughtful and consistent. When composing text, we use the terms left, right, and center justified to indicate which edge to line up against. To enhance readability, we almost always left justify paragraph text or body copy, providing readers with a consistent starting point at the beginning of each line.

Depending on the designer's preferences and the nature of the content, the right edge can remain ragged (uneven) or each edge can be justified (both flush left and flush right). Leaving the right side ragged preserves the uniformity of the word spacing and gives readers visual reference points in longer blocks of text, which enhance readability. Justifying both sides of a paragraph adds spaces between words to expand each line to its outer limits; it affects readability but gives a design a clean look.

Within a single design frame or multipage layout, alignments should be consistent. Mixing them is normally not recommended. If you choose to left justify the body copy on one page, be sure to apply the same formatting to every page in the site. Alignment can also be used to unify different, yet related, visual elements. For example, left justifying a photo caption along the left side of the image it refers to ties both elements together along a common vertical edge. This lets the viewer know that they belong together. Be careful not to have too many implied lines: a handful of well-chosen lines enhances a design, but too many make it look cluttered.

SIMILARITY

The law of *similarity* states that the brain will perceive visual objects as belonging together when their style attributes are similar and uniform.

For example, the unity of this paragraph is diminished by the ARBITRARY ANd random mixing of dissimilar **STYLES**.

Here, a lack of similarity results in poor organization of the content and diminished readability of the text. The more objects are alike, the more likely they will stick together naturally as a group. The more dissimilar they are, the more likely they will resist grouping and pull apart. The law of similarity does not presuppose that all of the elements in a group should be identically styled. If this were the case, many designs would be rather boring and flat in terms of visual contrast. Designers often take advantage of the fact that dissimilar objects pull apart in order in order to create emphasis.

REPETITION

Repetition is related to similarity and suggests that repeating visual elements such as lines, colors, shapes, and patterns help strengthen the overall unity of a design. In web design, repetition can be used to bring harmony and consistency to the look of a multipage website. Repeating important symbols or components such as a banner graphic or menu bar at the top of each page enhances usability and brings visual synergy to the site. Similarly, it's common to see visual elements or scenes from a movie repeated in the jacket design of a DVD and on the movie poster and website promoting the film. Repeating elements can help a company to preserve its visual brand identification across multiple communication channels as it promotes its products and services to consumers.

Repetition occurs frequently in nature, and photographers enjoy capturing it on film. Repetition produces pattern, and patterns are intriguing to the eye. Think about how stable and fascinating the pattern of a honeycomb is. There's something innately interesting about its uniform structure and appearance that captures our interest and provides a natural sense of awe and wonder.

FIGURE 4.19
The color pencils in the first vector illustration are haphazardly arranged. The second illustration features a more purposeful arrangement, applying the laws of proximity and alignment. How is your perception of each version influenced by the use of proximity, alignment, similarity, and repetition?

FIGURE 4.20
How are proximity, alignment, similarity, and repetition used in the layout of this web page design template?

Emphasis

The principle of *emphasis* suggests that a good design must have a primary focal point or center of interest. In a newspaper, the headline type is set to a very large font size in order to draw the attention of the reader to what the editor believes is the most important story of the day.

Emphasis can be used to quickly guide the viewer's attention to the main subject or message in a communication exchange. Large bold headings on a web page help you navigate quickly to the item or information you are most interested in. Google's homepage clearly emphasizes the text entry window to make it easy for users to enter keywords in a search. Just imagine if all of the text in a newspaper or on a website were exactly the same size, style, and color. The usability of the content would suffer tremendously, and users would quickly get frustrated and lose interest. Since our eyes are naturally drawn to larger objects in a design, varying the size of spatial elements is a common way to connote emphasis. Although there are many ways to create emphasis in a design, we will look briefly at contrast, color, depth, and proportion (see Figure 4.21).

CONTRAST (VALUE)

The term *value* describes the range of light and dark portions in an image or design. In photography, film, and television, value is usually expressed as *contrast*. The strongest visible contrast is represented by the difference between black and white. One of the reasons that books are traditionally produced with black text on a white page is because this method creates the best contrast for reading. The text "pops" out against the lighter background and makes reading more pleasant and efficient. The text is the main event, and the background should not present a distraction by competing for the reader's attention.

The number of colors or gradient steps in a composition that fall between the bipolar extremes of black and white is called *tonal range*. The greater the tonal range, the greater the contrast, and the more interesting a composition will generally appear. The eye is attracted first to the areas of a composition with highest contrast (or *high-key*), regardless of whether they contain color.

Increasing contrast is one of the easiest ways to emphasize the main subject or visual object. In photography, contrast impacts image detail, clarity, and mood. A *low-key* image contains mostly dark tones or color levels and communicates a serious, somber, or reflective mood. Such images can also ignite a sense of foreboding, mystery, horror, and fright. Photographic film was touted for years because of its ability to reproduce quality low-key images. Most narrative filmmakers prefer shooting on film for this very reason. Achieving low-key tonality is necessary in order to create realistic and compelling moments of heightened visual drama. Digital cameras have come a long way, though some professionals still prefer film's ability to handle low-contrast lighting situations. A high-key image is characterized by bright tones with very few dark areas, and a *mid-key* image falls in between. The higher the overall contrast in an image, the brighter and more cheerful the overall impression will be. In photography, film, and videography, pushing contrast too far in either direction will lead to an unusable image. This occurs when an image is under- or overexposed due to poor lighting in the scene or on the main subject.

FIGURE 4.21
Contrast, color, depth, and proportion work to emphasize elements in a design.

Contrast is at work in other components of multimedia design as well. Multimedia works are often combinations of elements, and the contrast in each may vary. A web page or animation's background is often more than a solid color. It may be a graphic or have images. Designers often make such backgrounds low-key to keep these elements from competing with the design's secret ingredient, its star attraction.

COLOR

Color is a powerful tool for enhancing contrast in visual design space, and *color contrast* has been used particularly well in the advertising industry. Perhaps you've seen a print or television ad in which a single colored object (like a hat or a can of soda) stood out against the backdrop of a black and white or monochromatic setting. A selective splash of color can immediately grab our attention, providing a sense of focus and direction for the viewer.

Colors are classified as warm, cool, or neutral, depending on which portion of the color spectrum they fall into. Warm colors reside near the orange area of the spectrum and include shades of red and orange, as well as warm greens. The human eye is attracted to the warm color regions of a design first. We tend to perceive warm colors as breaking free from the background and advancing toward us from a printed page or screen. A designer can use this effect to bring attention to an object by increasing the figure-ground contrast. But be careful! Too much warm color in a design can be visually overwhelming. Cool colors such as violets, blues, and cool greens seem to recede away from us into the background, appearing distant and detached. Cool colors are calm, soothing, and placid, like the blue waters of a still mountain lake. A design can accommodate large areas of cool colors without visually overwhelming the user. Neutral colors are achromatic (effectively lack hues). We'll get more into color in Chapter 8, "Graphics," but white, black, and achromatic grays work well with warm and cool colors. Another caution: many grays are not achromatic, and their hint of hue limits how effectively they can be used.

DEPTH

Depth is related to the principle of *figure-ground*, or what we perceive in the foreground or background, which we'll discuss later. It is a powerful tool for achieving emphasis in a design. In photography, film, and videography, the term *depth of field* describes the portion of the z-axis that viewers perceive as being in focus at any one time. When this distance is small, the image is said to have a shallow depth of field. When the distance is large, we refer to depth of field as being great or expanded. You can emphasize the main subject by keeping it in focus (sharp and clear) and the background clutter or dead space out of focus. In graphic design, drop shadows, lighting, perspective, and other visual effects can be applied to a foreground image to simulate the appearance of depth.

PROPORTION

Proportion is the scale of an object relative to other elements within a composition. Our perception of an object's size is related to the size and position of other objects within the field of view. Decreasing the size of an object makes it recede into the distance, creating the perception that it is getting farther and farther away. Increasing the size of an object elevates its visual status, making it appear closer to the viewer. The location of an object also affects our perception of size. Objects placed near the top of the screen appear smaller and farther away than objects placed near the bottom. Including familiar objects of a known size within a design can help a viewer to make accurate perceptual judgments about the actual, or relative, size of other elements nearby.

Perceptual Forces

When we look at a graphic representation within a frame (still picture or moving image), our brains are constantly processing the relative push and pull of perceptual field forces within the visual space. For example, regardless of whether we view a photograph when it is lying flat on a table, hanging on a wall, or even rotated a quarter turn, we tend to perceive the top of the image as up and the bottom of the image as down. The bottom of the frame simulates the natural gravitational field of our human experience. But unlike gravity, which acts upon us from only one direction, perceptual field forces can tug at visual matter from any direction.

When a visual element is positioned too close to the edge of the frame, the attraction between the object and the side of the frame increases. The effect is similar to bringing the opposite poles of two magnets within close range. As the magnets get closer, the attraction increases, until they eventually snap together. White space can provide necessary breathing room around visual objects and will help counteract the natural pull of the frame. When we discuss the perceptual forces humans experience, we talk about the principles of balance, continuation, figure-ground, and psychological closure.

BALANCE

A *balanced composition* is achieved when the visual weight of objects is equally dispersed within the frame, producing a perceived state of equilibrium. On occasion, the designer may want to purposely destabilize an image for effect, but generally our goal is to achieve balance in design. The size, color, and position of graphical elements affect our sense of balance or instability within a composition. Like a set of scales, the frame rests on an imaginary fulcrum at the center of its baseline. To the viewer, some objects will naturally appear heavier or lighter than others. Typically, we perceive large or dark-colored objects as heavier than small or light-colored ones. If the designer places a large dark-colored sphere in the upper left-hand corner of the frame, then an object, or multiple objects, of equal combined mass will need to be positioned in the lower right hand corner to achieve balance. Compositional balance can be achieved using either a symmetrical or asymmetrical approach (see Figure 4.22).

Symmetrical Balance

In a *symmetrical composition*, objects of similar shape, color, and size are weighted equally on opposite sides of the frame. This can be accomplished by centering the subject, or multiple visual elements, along the vertical or horizontal dividing line of the frame, with the weight of the elements evenly distributed in each half. Symmetrical balance is analogous to a seesaw whose pivot point or fulcrum is centered, and children of equal weight are positioned on opposite ends. This approach is also called *formal balance* because it leads to designs that are perceived as tranquil, elegant, traditional, and conservative. Symmetrical balance can lead to a somewhat predictable and less-creative visual design.

Asymmetrical Balance

With *asymmetrical* or *informal balance*, equilibrium is established with objects of differing size, color, and tone. This approach is analogous to a seesaw whose fulcrum is located in an off-center position. In this configuration, placing two children of equal size on opposite ends of the seesaw will not lead to balance. More weight must be added to one side in order to compensate for the new pivot point. Asymmetrical, or informal, compositions are much more interesting to design and compose, and can appear more visually interesting and dynamic.

FIGURE 4.22
Symmetrical balance (top) and asymmetrical balance (bottom) work in different ways to create visual equilibrium.

Tech Talk

Rule of Thirds The *rule of thirds* is a compositional tool used to produce visually appealing images using asymmetrical balance. With the rule of thirds, the area of an image is figuratively divided into thirds, both horizontally and vertically, to produce a 3 × 3 grid. Four points are created by the intersection of the lines. The points and lines serve as a guide to the designer or photographer for optimally placing subjects. The four intersection points are the most visually compelling areas within the frame. Likewise, the weakest area of the design space is in the middle of the frame, in the center box (see Figure 4.23).

According to the rule of thirds, the focal point of the image should be located at one of the four intersection points. These are the natural landing points for the eye. However, people do not perceive the left and right side of the frame equally. In Western cultures, our eyes tend to land first on the left side of the frame then flow to the right in search of a resting place. We often place the main subject on the left side of the frame and dead space on the right. Professionals vary the intersections at which they place subjects and background matter, depending on whether they have a single or group subject, have background matter, want to create tension, and so forth. The rule of thirds is not a hard and fast rule, but adopting this simple technique will allow you to quickly boost the effectiveness of a two-dimensional design or photographic image.

The purpose of the vertical and horizontal lines is to guide the placement of subjects to an off-center position, approximately one-third in from each side of the frame. It also reminds us to avoid the practice of dividing screen space in half along either its vertical or horizontal center. For example, a dominant vertical element like a street lamp, tree trunk, or flagpole should be positioned approximately one-third to the left or right of center. Likewise, the horizon is best positioned along the upper or lower third of the frame.

The term *lower-third* comes from the rule of thirds convention. The lower-third is the horizontal line nearest to the bottom of the frame. Television producers routinely superimpose the name and title of the person speaking on camera along this line. When you hear someone say that they need to insert a lower-third, they are referring to this type of a title graphic.

To aid photographers in composing shots, many cameras now come with a rule-of-thirds overlay feature. When activated, the rule-of-thirds grid is superimposed in the viewfinder of the camera. This is a great tool for amateur photographers. However, if your device lacks this feature, you just need a little bit of practice to learn how to mentally break up the frame into thirds. Incidentally, the rule of thirds works regardless of the size or aspect ratio of the frame, or the visual medium you are designing in. It works just as well if you're designing a business card, taking a digital photo, or composing a 16:9 high-definition image for a documentary.

FIGURE 4.23
Using the rule of thirds as a guide, how would you critique the composition of these two photographs?

CONTINUATION

The law of *continuation* suggests that our brains tend to process what we see as continuing along lines that are predictable and free of obstacles, and that don't abruptly change direction. So in a design with overlapping curves, our brains interpret each vector (line) as a smooth curve; we don't see each as changing direction at their intersection. More precisely, vectors are directional forces within the frame that guide the eye from one point to another. Three types of vectors occur most often in visual space: graphic vectors, index vectors, and motion vectors (see Figure 4.24).

Graphic vectors are created by strategically placing stationary line elements within the frame. The lines can be real or implied through the placement of other visual elements. They focus the viewer's gaze in a specific direction or guide them along a visual path. In photography, these pathways are called leading lines because they "lead" the eyes from point to point or directly to the primary focal point of the image. A barbed wire fence stretching across a landscape, the line created by the water's edge at the beach, and a row of people waiting for a movie are all examples of graphic vectors.

Index vectors are created by placing objects that conspicuously point in a specific direction. A crowd gazing upward, a road sign with a large arrow pointing to the right, and a hitchhiker with his hand extended are visual examples of index vectors.

Motion vectors are created by the real or apparent movement of subjects within the frame. Motion connotes a sense of directionality. We can usually tell which direction a person or object is moving by observing which way it is facing. Although best demonstrated with time-based media, motion vectors can be implied in a still image or graphic. The addition of a motion blur or trailing edge can intensify the perception of speed and directionality.

FIGURE-GROUND

In Gestalt psychology an element that appears in the foreground of our perceptual field is called a *figure*, whereas everything behind it is the ground. In nature,

FIGURE 4.24
Visual examples of graphic, index, and motion vectors (L-R). Continuation works to guide our eyes from one point to another within the frame.

FIGURE 4.25
Some optical illusions work by playing with the figure-ground relationship. What do you see in this image? Relax your focus and look again. How about now?

the phenomenon of depth perception enables us to distinguish between figure and ground (see Figure 4.25). In two-dimensional space, we must rely on visual cues within the frame to provide a sense of order along the z-axis. You need to remember that the viewer wants to make sense of what he or she is seeing. Our brain is wired to organize the visual field into meaningful figure-ground relationships. The degree to which the viewer can do so effectively attests to the skill of the designer or photographer. Providing good contrast between the foreground and background elements in the frame is the best way to keep viewers from being perceptually confused or overwhelmed.

PSYCHOLOGICAL CLOSURE

The final perceptual force we will look at is psychological closure. One of the most powerful abilities we have is to mentally complete a visual pattern or impression when only partial information is provided. *Psychological closure* is the human equivalent of connecting the dots or filling in the gaps. For this reason, objects within the frame can extend past the boundary of the frame. As long as enough visual information is provided, an individual can complete a picture in her head, thus maintaining a stable perceptual experience (see Figure 4.26).

The principle of psychological closure is used in visual design all the time. Literal interpretations of words and symbols can be replaced with partial impressions or abstract variations of larger elements. With psychological closure, the brain seeks to create meaningful order out of visual chaos. As long as enough visual cues are provided, the brain will kick in to form a complete mental impression. The extra measure of sensory activity can give us a deeper and more satisfying experience because we are participating and cognitively engaging with the visual stimuli more.

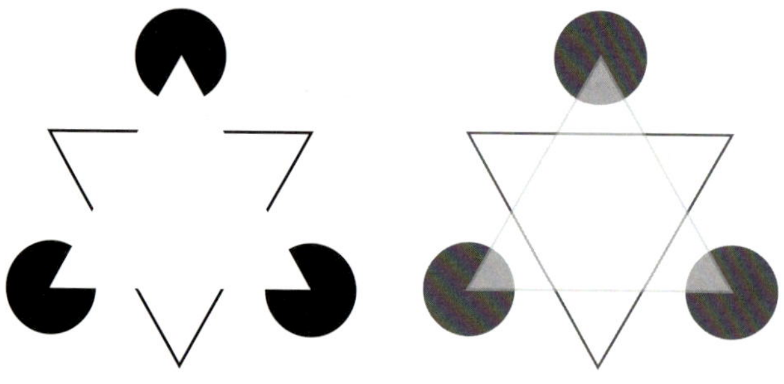

FIGURE 4.26
Kanizsa's Triangle illustrates the principle of closure to suggest a second triangle overlaying the first.

CHAPTER SUMMARY

Content is still king, but if we deliver content without good design, users will not know where to focus, will not make the connections we intend, will not be engaged, and may even misunderstand the message. The elements and principles of design are a designer's foundation. They give you the tools to understand aesthetics and preferences, and to both make and defend sound choices. Rarely do we work solely for our own pleasure. We often work in teams, and we work for clients who hire us for our expertise. Occasionally, others make suggestions that go against our better judgment. Being able to explain why an idea won't work well may make the difference between creating an outstanding graphic or video and getting stuck creating something that will fall flat with its audience.

Ultimately, we create for our users, the people who will visit our websites, see our photos, watch our podcasts, and use our kiosks. Designers strive to make products usable and engaging. Good design makes users' experiences positive and rewarding. Bad design serves no one.

A foundation in design elements and principles inspires not only good practice but also creativity. Return to the foundation when you feel that you are in a creative rut. Do you need to add energy to a graphic? Perhaps you can add dynamic lines. Are your action photographs missing the action? A canted angle might help. Does your video need to evoke other senses? Consider lighting your subject so it has more texture, and add appropriate sounds. Are you at a loss for how to create a new logo? The principle of closure may suggest a creative solution. The combinations are limitless, but be judicious: don't emphasize too much. If you do, you might emphasize nothing at all, leaving your users to wonder what your secret ingredient was supposed to be.

CHAPTER 5

Multimedia Page Design

The more personal computer displays become like lightweight books, the more people are going to feel comfortable reading from them. A PC that you can open up and physically handle easily, that has the right kind of battery and display, will give the same visual impression as a page.

—John Warnock, Inventor of PostScript and the Founder of Adobe Systems (1994)

Chapter Highlights

This chapter examines:

- Strategies for the effective placement of visual content within the page
- The influence of visual hierarchy on viewing behavior
- Use of the grid system for managing page and screen space
- Commonly used layouts in multimedia page design
- Design tips when using page templates and style sheets

Key Terms

Body Copy
Border
Box Model
Cell
Chunking
Column
Dynamic Page
F-Layout
Fixed Layout
Float
Fluid Layout
Golden Ratio
Grid System
Gutenberg Diagram
Headings
Headline
Layout
Margin
Modular Grid
Multicolumn Grid
Padding
Page
Page Template
Row
Sidebar
Single-column Grid
Splash Page
Static Page
Style Sheet
Table
Typographic Grid
Visual Hierarchy
Z-layout

ORGANIZING CONTENT ON A PAGE

Page layout is the area of graphic design that refers to the visual arrangement of text and images on a page. It is essentially the role of visual information management, using the general principles of design and typography to bring order and structure to a page. The term originated in the printing industry as the specialized craft of designing the physical pages in books, magazines, and newspapers. In publishing houses, agencies, and newsrooms, it's the job of authors, reporters, copywriters, editors, and the like to generate the text (or *copy*) for visual pages, while photographers, illustrators, and graphic designers produce the images. It's the job of a layout artist or page compositor to combine the various elements of visual information (text and graphics) within the page, creating a presentation that is both pleasing to the eye and easy to consume.

Programs like Quark Xpress and Adobe InDesign are professional software tools used in the desktop publishing industry for the prepress layout and design of printed pages. In multimedia, the concept of page layout has migrated metaphorically from the kinds of physical pages that you can touch and turn, to digital pages that appear on a computer screen or monitor. The page metaphor was extended into the field of web design, but can also be more broadly applied to any type of screen space where visual information must be arranged and ordered for presentation. In multimedia work, the principles of page design can be applied to the creation of a DVD menu screen, a full-screen title graphic in a television commercial, or to the welcome screen of a micro app running on a tablet computer or smart phone. Anytime you combine visual content within the fixed or fluid space of a digital page or screen, you are engaging the activity of page design (see Figure 5.1).

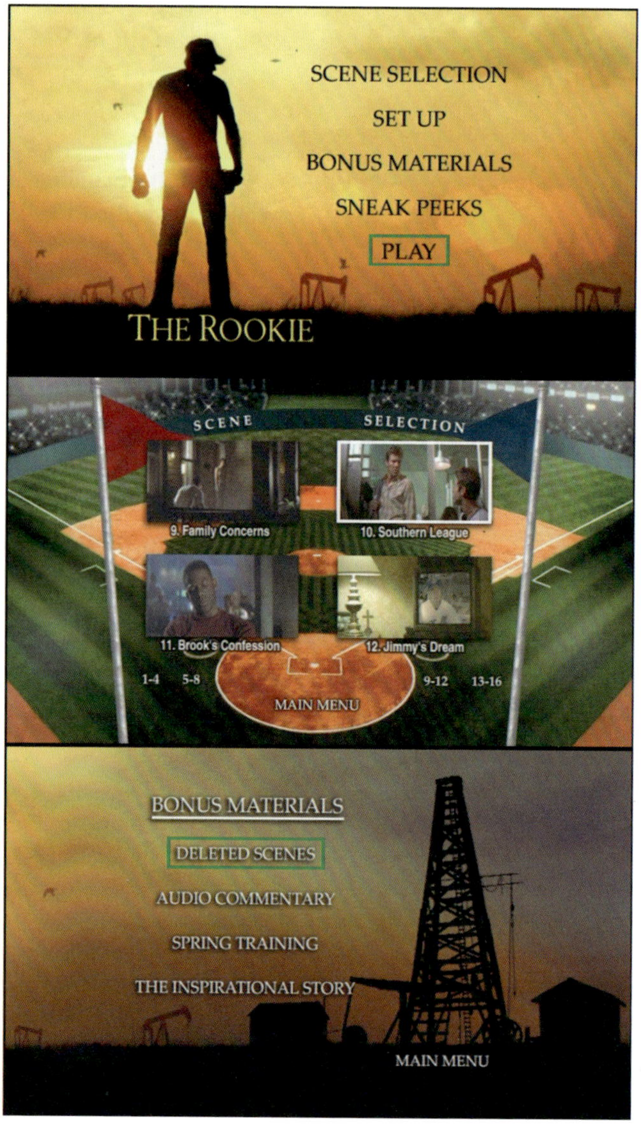

FIGURE 5.1
The DVD menu system for the Walt Disney film *The Rookie* includes a main menu, a scene selection submenu, and a bonus materials submenu (pictured here). The visual layout of each menu is the product of multimedia page design, where diverse visual elements such as video, graphics, text, and animation are arranged within the screen space of a 16 × 9 television frame. While not a visual element, audio is also present, adding to the richness of the multimedia experience.

THE GUTENBERG DIAGRAM

In the early days of printing, page layouts were densely populated with text. While early printing systems, like the Gutenberg press, could easily mass-produce the transfer of letterforms on paper, they were not equipped to reproduce artwork, illustrations, or other visual elements that are commonly used today to break up the heavy flow of printed text. If artwork was included, it was drawn by hand after the pages were printed.

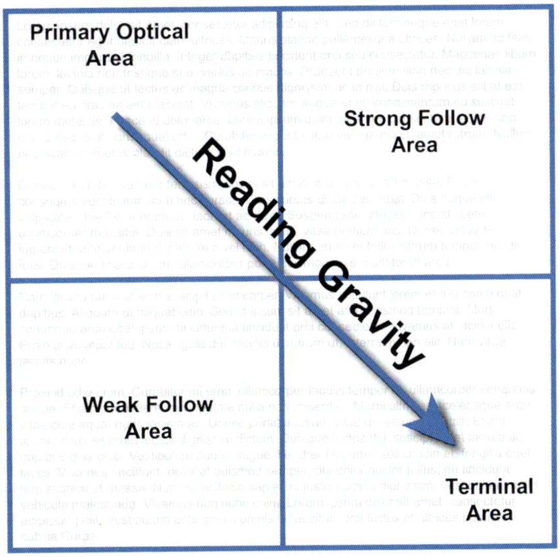

FIGURE 5.2
The Gutenberg Diagram illustrates the general pattern the eyes follow as they scan visual information within a page. It applies primarily to text-dominant layouts where there is little to no visual hierarchy, such as a page from a novel containing only printed words and sentences.

The *Gutenberg Diagram* is a primitive eye-tracking model that is used to show how readers scan through a page comprised entirely of evenly distributed text (see Figure 5.2). The Gutenberg Diagram divides a page across its horizontal and vertical centers to produce four equal quadrants. A reader's interaction with the text begins in the top left quadrant on the page. This is the dominant section of the page known as the *primary optical area*. Next, they move across each line of text, from left to right, in a series of horizontal sweeps or scans referred to as the *axis of orientation*. Metaphorically, reading exerts a gravitational force on the user that continually pushes their gaze downward and to the right. As a result, the eye is persistently led along a diagonal path from the primary optical area in the top left part of the page to the terminal area located in the bottom right. The strong fallow area (in the upper right) and the weak fallow area (in the lower left) lie beyond this path, and as such, are demoted in terms of their visual influence. A reader typically pays less attention to content that's placed in these regions of the page.

BREAKING OUT OF THE BOX

The layout of a page directly impacts the way a user scans its contents. As page designs have shifted from print to digital forms, and from heavy text-based layouts to visually dynamic designs with rich media content, users have adopted more sophisticated methods for scanning pages. Two familiar scanning methods are often talked about with regard to how users interact with web pages online.

F-Layout

The *F-layout* is one of the most common page layouts on the Web. As the name suggests, the reader's gaze is directed though the page in a pattern that resembles the letter *F* (see Figure 5.3). As with most layouts, this one encourages the user to begin reading in the top left part of the page. He then proceeds to make a full scan from left to right across the first row of visual information. Next, the user makes a partial scan of the second row. This pass rarely extends to the end of the line or column. Each subsequent row of information is scanned in short bursts from left to right as the user settles into a normal rhythm and pattern for processing the main content on the page.

FIGURE 5.3 The Library of Congress homepage features the classic F-layout design. A prominent vertical side bar along the left edge of the page serves as a visual anchor for the eyes as the user scans from left to right in progressively shorter bursts from top to bottom.

Humans are creatures of habit. For this reason, the F-pattern is an all-too-familiar format for people who spend any amount of time in front of a computer surfing the Web. We have grown accustomed to the most important information being placed along the top edge of the page, usually in the form of an eye-catching masthead or banner graphic. The masthead provides important visual cues about the contents of the page. It can be scanned quickly and will often influence a user's next step. Will he continue scanning or bail from the page? The second row of a web page often contains navigational prompts like menu buttons or hyperlinks. If the first scan did its job by hooking the user's attention, then the second scan will take on more meaning as he seeks to understand how the page and site contents are organized. A sidebar along the left edge of a page often comes into play on the third scan. It pulls the user's gaze towards the left edge of the document window, directing him downward into a series of shorter bursts of scanning activity. Research shows that conforming layouts to the F-pattern will enhance the usability of the page, making it easier for users to glean information in an expedient manner.

Z-Layout

A less popular format, the *Z-layout* is a variation of the Gutenberg Diagram (see Figure 5.4). Scanning begins with a full visual sweep across the top row of the page. The second scan flows diagonally through the center of the page in

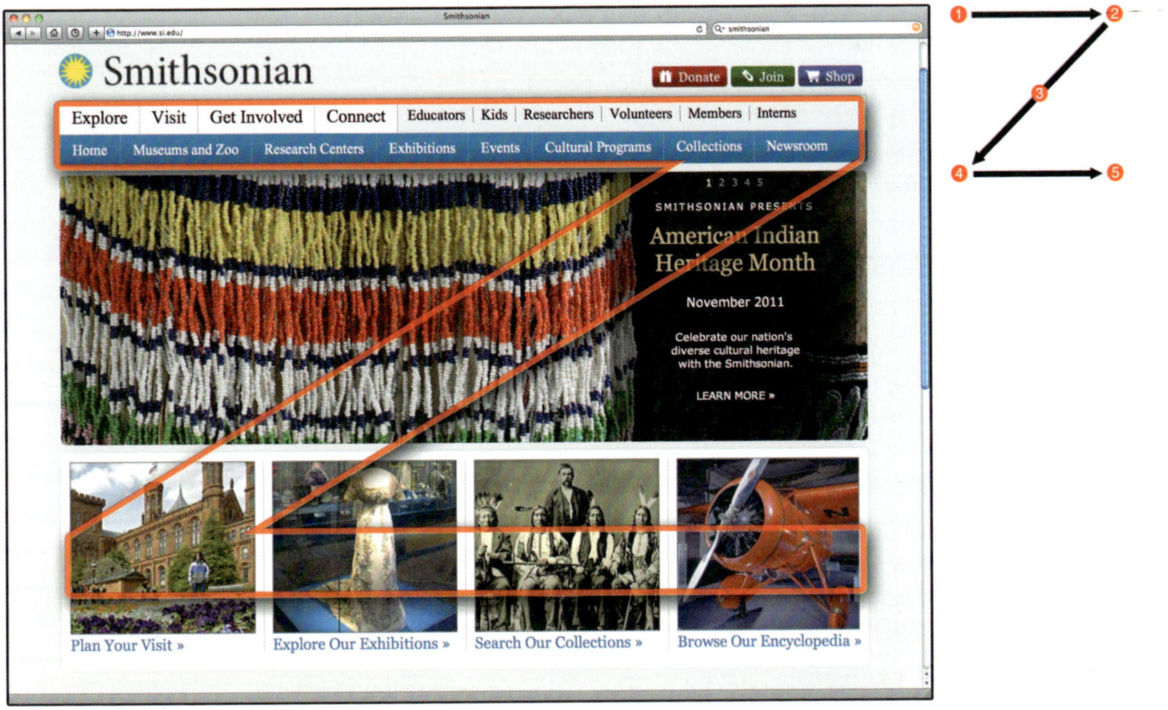

FIGURE 5.4
The Smithsonian homepage pictured here guides the user's eyes through the page along a Z-shaped path. Can you locate other examples of the F-layout and Z-layout in action?

a downward movement towards the bottom left-hand corner. The final scan is a horizontal sweep across the bottom of the page. Important visual elements should be placed along the path of the Z. While the Z-layout suggests a rigid zigzag path, the chiseled angles of the Z-pattern can be softened to produce a more organic S-curve feel. The Z-layout works best when a large visual element or content region (like a single photo or visual montage) is placed in the center of the page, between two rows of linear information. It is a simple layout to create and can be used effectively for pages containing only a handful of key elements that need to be communicated quickly without a lot of visual clutter.

GREAT IDEAS

Visual Hierarchy

The term *visual hierarchy* refers to the perceived ordering of content within a page by the reader. A page that consists only of text that is equally spaced and uniform in size is perceptually flat. In such a design, every word carries the same weight, and therefore nothing rises to the forefront of the reader's perception. However, when certain words or phrases are set apart stylistically using the principles of design covered in Chapter 4, "Visual Communication," such as alignment, color, emphasis, proportion, etc., they will rise above the background noise of the page, vying for attention.

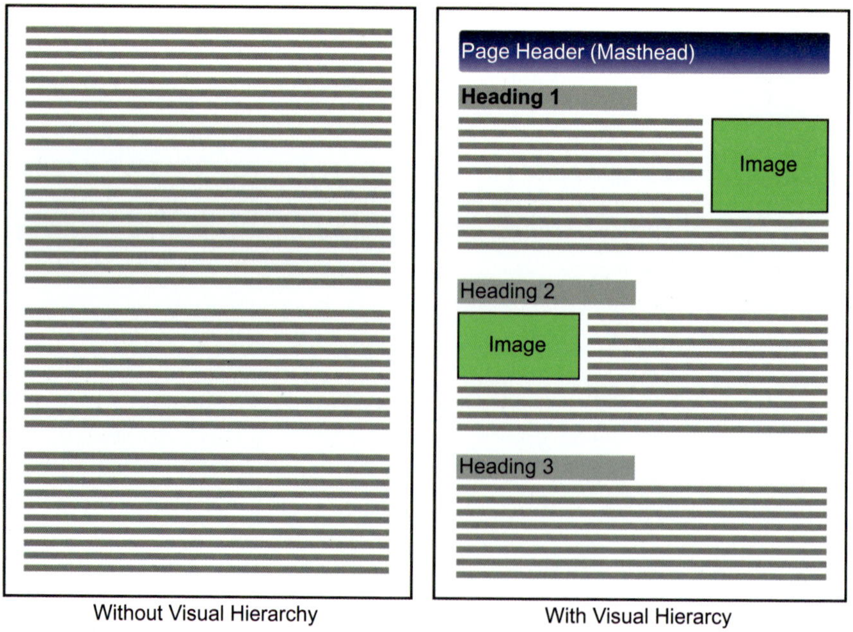

FIGURE 5.5
A thoughtfully constructed visual hierarchy can improve the order and flow of content on a multimedia page.

Chunking Body Copy

One of the easiest ways to begin establishing visual hierarchy in a page is to subdivide large blocks of body copy into smaller segments or chunks. *Body copy* is the main text of a published document or advertisement, and it is often the most plentiful source of content on a page. *Chunking* is a practice that involves the visual consolidation of related sentences or ideas into small blocks of information that can be quickly and easily digested. Paragraphs are a common chunking tool, as are lists, callouts, and text boxes. From a consumer's point of view, chunking is like eating a steak. The meat is easier to ingest after it is cut into smaller bite-sized pieces. Placing too much text on the screen at a time, or within a specific region of the page, can overwhelm the senses and lead to eye fatigue. A reader can quickly tire out or lose interest. Chunking is highly recommended when writing copy for multimedia consumption, since reading on a low-resolution digital display is more difficult than reading the same text in a high-resolution print publication. Chunking reduces the visual density of the text on a page. It transforms unwieldy blocks of strung-together words and sentences into manageable parcels of visual information.

Headings

The next thing you can do to bring order and structure to the presentation of text is to add section headings and subheadings. A *heading* is a short descriptive title or subtitle used to mark the beginning of a paragraph or content area. Magazines and newspapers use headings routinely to set stories apart and to provide readers with a brief informative prompt as they scan the page for what interests them most. In a newspaper, the most important story of the day is given visual prominence by placing it on the front page, above the fold, and under a special type of heading called the *headline*. The headline carries the biggest and boldest font style on the page. Less significant stories are attached to progressively smaller headings or subheadings.

In web page design, HTML specifies six levels of headings, identified with the tags <h1>, <h2>, <h3>, <h4>, <h5>, and <h6> (see Figure 5.6). Heading 1 is the largest and is often used for the masthead (master heading) to identify the title of a page. Sectional content areas often begin with heading 2 or heading 3. Subsections within each area can be further delineated with headings 4 to 6. To distinguish them from body copy, headings are set in a larger font and weight, typically from 24pt down to 10pt in steadily declining increments. However, headings can be customized to any size. They can also be assigned a custom typeface, color, or border (see Figure 5.7). It's important to keep heading styles consistent within the page and across a series of connected pages. For example, heading 1 should look the same on page 1 as it does when reused on pages 2 and 3; doing so reinforces the design principle of repetition.

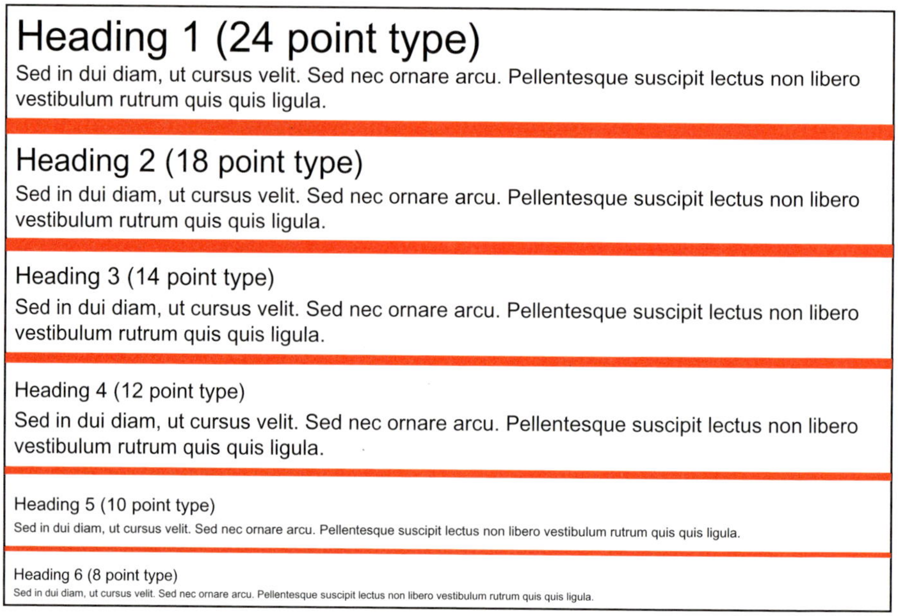

FIGURE 5.6
HTML specifies six levels of headings with default sizes that get progressively smaller from first to last.

FIGURE 5.7
Headings are often custom designed as a part of the overall theme of a page layout. The principles of alignment, proximity, and repetition are critical ingredients for creating a meaningful and aesthetically pleasing visual hierarchy.

GREAT IDEAS

The Golden Ratio

The *Golden Ratio* is a mathematical construct that has been widely used for determining the proportions of a visual space. It can be seen in architecture, painting, printing, and photography, and more recently in new media and the Web. Also known as the *Divine Proportion*, the ratio is defined by the numerical constant *Phi* or 1.61803. As a ratio, it suggests that the optimum visual space is a rectangle whose height is slightly longer than one and a half times its width (see Figure 5.8). The vast majority of books printed prior to 1800 conformed to the Golden Ratio, which served for centuries as a near universal standard for page proportions. Whether horizontal or vertical in orientation, humans tend to favor visual pages and screens that closely mirror the Golden Ratio. For this reason, it is still embraced by many today, albeit more loosely. The Golden Ratio has greatly influenced the design of page and screen spaces used today in multimedia design.

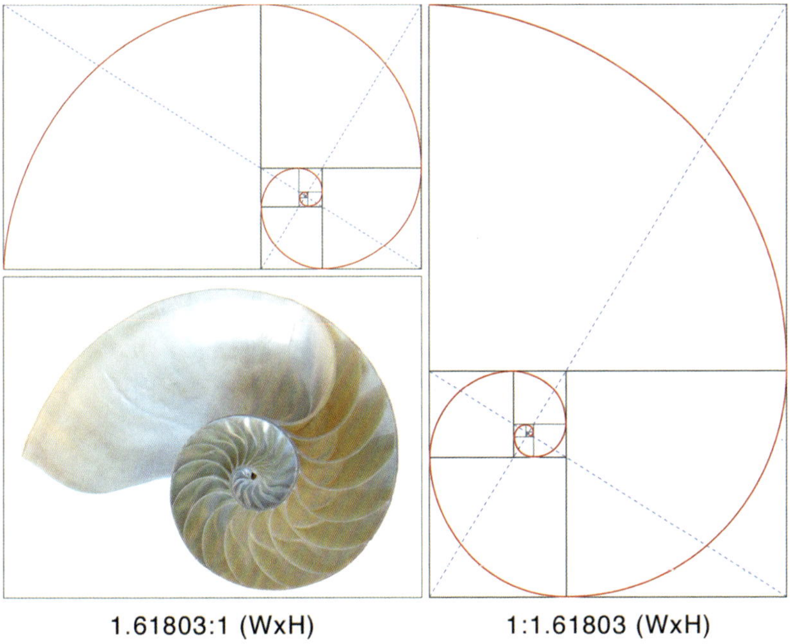

FIGURE 5.8
The spiral form of a nautilus shell closely conforms to *Phi*, the golden number.

BRINGING ORDER TO CHAOS

Imagine for a moment that you live in a house with only four walls. You step through the front door, and because there are no visual obstructions, you are able to see the entire footprint of the house. There's no living room, no bedrooms,

FIGURE 5.9
Staring at a blank page is a bit like walking into a house without walls. Where to start? For a designer, the first step is to subdivide the vast unitary space of a blank page into smaller editable regions that can be individually arranged and populated with content.

no bathroom, kitchen, closets or garage—just one large area of uninterrupted space. A house like this has no internally defined spaces that can be arranged or decorated independently. Making a change to one area of the house affects the entire house, because spatially, everything is connected. Very few architects would design a house like this, and if given a choice, most people would not want to live in one. The walls and rooms of a house are functional features that create order and meaning for its occupants. Without them, a home would look empty and bare or constantly cluttered and disorganized.

A blank page is very much like a house without walls. It is an empty two-dimensional shell with fixed boundaries on four sides (see Figure 5.9). One of the first things a page designer must do is to break up the unitary real estate of an empty page into modular regions that can be independently managed and populated with content. As you become acquainted with some of the different page design programs and workflows, you will see that each one uses slightly different terminology and techniques for breaking up the page into modular regions. We can't possibly go into all of the specific methods and applications here but will instead deal with some general concepts and provide a few examples.

The Grid System

The typographic grid system is a popular conceptual tool for breaking up pages into smaller editable parts. While many variations of the grid system have been formulated, all of them are based on the fundamental idea of using horizontal and vertical lines for subdividing a page into modular units of space (see Figure 5.10).

FIGURE 5.10
The design of a new web page often begins with simple sketches like this one showing how the screen space will be broken apart into various content regions.

GRAPH PAPER GRID SYSTEM

While designed primarily for use in engineering and mathematics, graph paper is a handy visual aid that you can use for creating mockups of multimedia pages. Graph paper is overlaid with thin ruled lines that are evenly spaced at set distances across the width and length of the page. In the United States, an off-the-shelf brand of graph paper typically comes printed with four grid lines per inch. This grid structure produces a page that is covered edge-to-edge with an array of ¼-inch square blocks.

The first step in creating a mockup on graph paper is specifying the grid scale and unit of measurement. A scale is required for conforming the paper grid to the actual dimensions of a digital page as defined in pixels (see Figure 5.11). For example, you may decide that each square on the graph paper represents an area of 400 pixels (20px × 20px). Using this scale, the length of a 100-pixel line can be represented on graph paper as a line five block units wide (5px × 20px). Likewise, a 200-pixel wide column can be drawn on the page using a grid width of 10 block units. White space separating visual elements on the page can be visualized on the grid as a margin of 20 pixels, or one block unit. In this example, the graph paper serves as a conceptual framework, on top of which a designer can specify the size and shape of columns and boxes used for holding visual information. Used correctly, a grid can provide a uniform page structure where elements are consistently aligned and sized in proportion to the page as a whole, and to other elements within the shared space of the page.

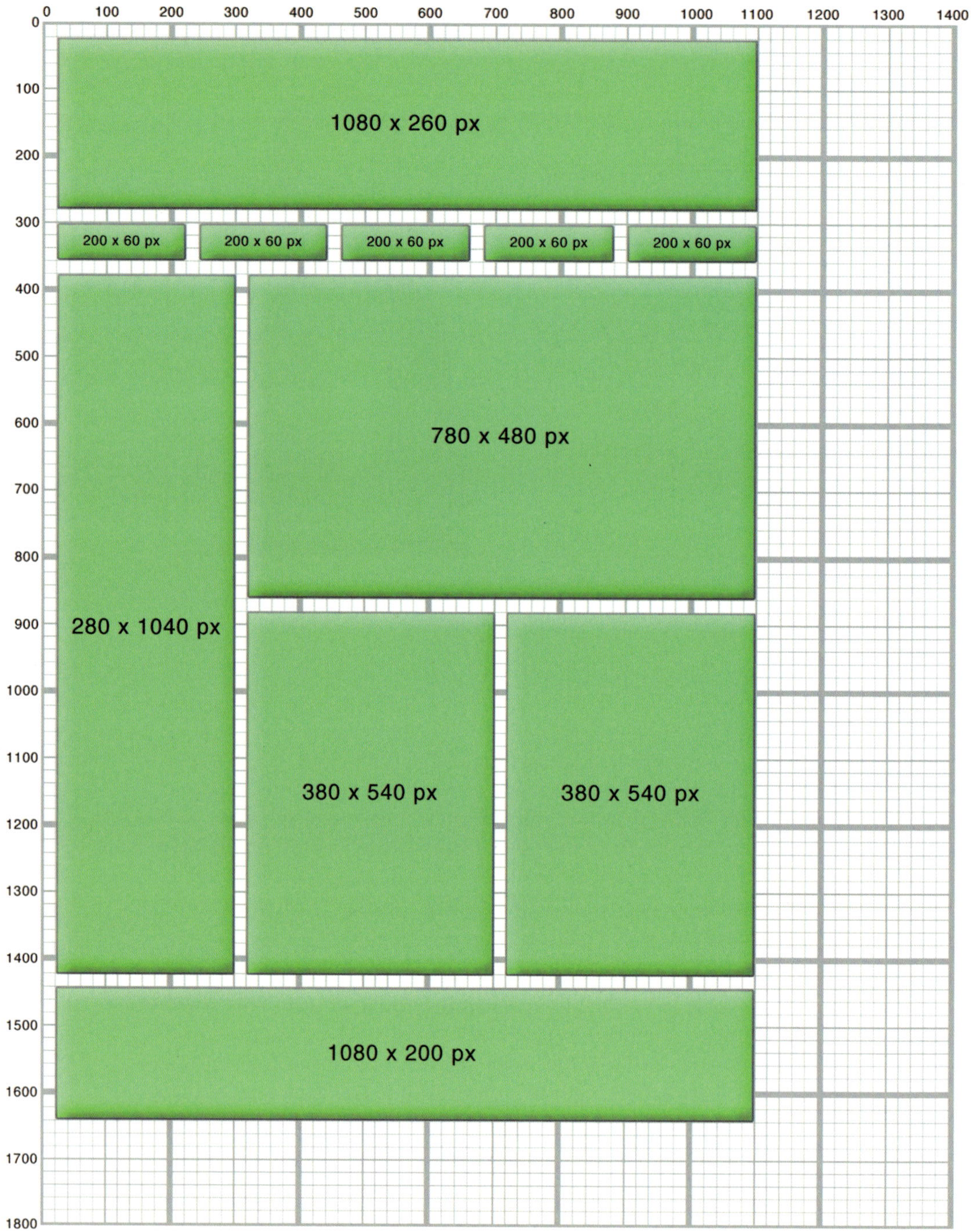

FIGURE 5.11
Graph paper can be used to break up a page into a variety of subspaces.

Tech Talk

The Anatomy of a Grid In his seminal work on the subject, *Making and Breaking the Grid*, author Timothy Samara notes that "a grid consists of a distinct set of alignment-based relationships that act as guides for distributing elements across a format. Every grid contains the same basic parts, no matter how complex the grid becomes. Each part fulfills a specific function; the parts can be combined as needed, or omitted from the overall structure at the designer's discretion, depending on how they interpret the informational requirements of the material."[1]

The Parts of a Grid

Columns. A column is a vertically oriented space that is typically taller than it is wide. Columns are often used as holding areas for continuous running text and visual information.

Rows. A row breaks up space into horizontal strips that flow from left to right. Rows establish linear flowlines that can help guide the reader's eye across a design.

Modules. A module is a uniform square unit of space created by the intersection of perpendicular lines in a grid. Independently, modules are the smallest spatial unit in a grid.

Spatial Zones. A spatial zone is formed when two or more modules are grouped together. Spatial zones can be large or small, square or rectangular in shape. There are a seemingly endless numbers of ways that modules can be combined to form spatial zones of various shapes and sizes.

Margins. A margin is the negative space between modules and the outside edges of a page or spatial zone.

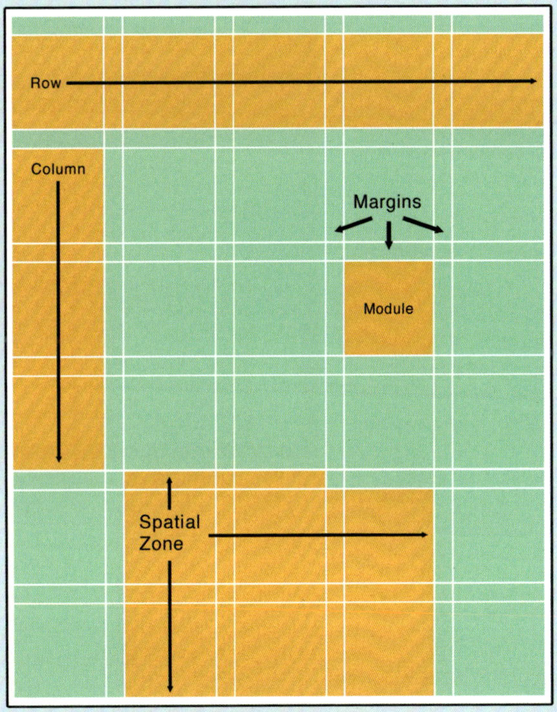

FIGURE 5.12
The Typographic Grid.

[1]Samara, T. (2002). *Making and Breaking the Grid.* Beverly, MA: Rockport Publishers.

COMMON GRID STRUCTURES

The starting point for designing a new layout often begins with defining the grid structure of the page. However, for this process to be successful, the designer needs to have some idea of the scope, size, and proportionality of the content that will fill the page. Once a grid is created and populated with content, it cannot be altered without affecting the arrangement of the visual information within

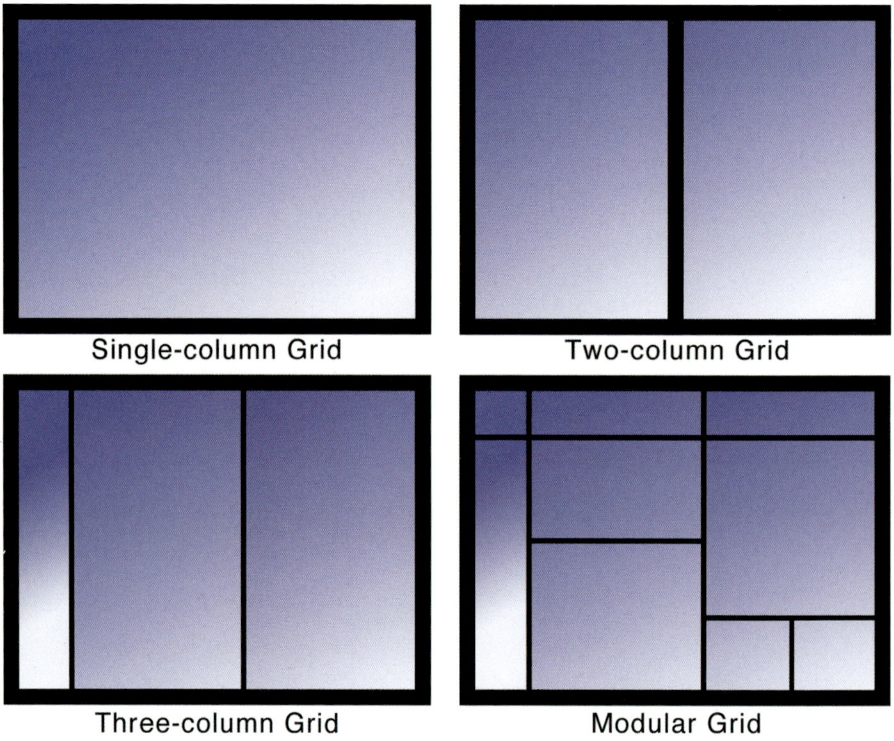

FIGURE 5.13
By altering the grid structure, a design space can be subdivided in an infinite number of ways.

the page. Thus it is very important to have a vision and plan on the front end for how a page will look when completed. The size of text and graphics needs to be established early on to ensure that the columns and spatial zones formed by the grid are made sufficiently large or small enough to hold the intended contents. Proper planning is essential! A prudent designer will rarely embark on creating a grid without giving long and careful forethought to the intended structure and contents of the page. With this word of caution established, let's take a look at three of the most common grid structures used in page design: (1) the single-column grid, (2) the multicolumn grid, and (3) the modular grid (see Figure 5.13).

SINGLE-COLUMN GRID

The simplest grid system features a single-column of visual information bordered by margins on either side of the page. Also called the *manuscript grid*, this layout is commonly used for document processing and book publishing, where the content consists mostly of continuous text and few images. It is the simplest grid to design. In fact, many programs, such as word processors, use the single-column grid as a default starting point when a new document is created. Because single-column formats are most often associated with high-density text-based layouts, they are also most susceptible to the effects of the Gutenberg Diagram.

MULTICOLUMN GRID

A *multicolumn grid* breaks up the page with vertical divisions from left to right, providing greater flexibility for integrating text and graphics within the page. Multicolumn grids come in many varieties, with two- and three-column formats being the most popular. Establishing a visual hierarchy is made easier in a multicolumn grid because columns can be assigned different roles for handling different kinds of content. For example, on a web page, a narrow sidebar column might be used for small snippets of visual information such as links, menu buttons, and short chunks of text that can be quickly scanned by the user. A wider column might contain running text for displaying the main content of a page. Columns can be equal in width or different. They can be independent of other columns on the page, or connected, allowing text and images to spill over from the end of one column into the next.

With a multicolumn grid, text no longer needs to flow in an uninterrupted stream of continuous lines from the top of the page to the bottom. Columns can contain negative space, headings, and illustrations, allowing text to stop and resume less predictably at various points in the page. All things being equal, reading text on a computer monitor is improved when it is formatted into columns, as opposed to running across the full width of the screen. Doing so changes the start and stop points in a line, reducing the distance that the eye has to travel back and forth with each scan. For smaller screens, like those on smart phones and book readers, single-column layouts tend to be more common.

Tech Talk

Inline and Floating Graphics An *inline graphic* is an image or illustration that is inserted into a text-based column or spatial area. By default, an inline graphic behaves just like a text character. It dissects the line at the point of insertion, pushing adjacent text to the right and thereby producing a gap in the line for it to reside in. The size of the gap depends on the width of the image. The bottom of an inline graphic aligns with the baseline of the text that it is joined to. If the height of an inline graphic is the same height as the line, then the layout of the paragraph or column will be largely unaffected. However, graphics often exceed the height of the lines they are combined with. When this happens, the line height (or *leading*) will automatically expand to match the height of the inline image. This increases the white space around the image and can cause unintended consequences affecting the layout of the page.

To fix this problem, many layout programs, including the CSS standard in web page design, offer a feature called *image floating*. When an inline graphic is floated, the surrounding text will wrap around it to the left and/or the right, creating a more pleasing interaction between the two. Floating a graphic to the left locks it to the left edge of the column, causing text to wrap around it to the right. Floating it to the right yields the opposite effect. Floating a graphic in the center causes text to wrap around it evenly on either side. After an image is floated, it is generally a good idea to add padding between the image, the text, and column edges. Padding adds negative space and breathing room to the newly formed union of image and text (see Figure 5.14).

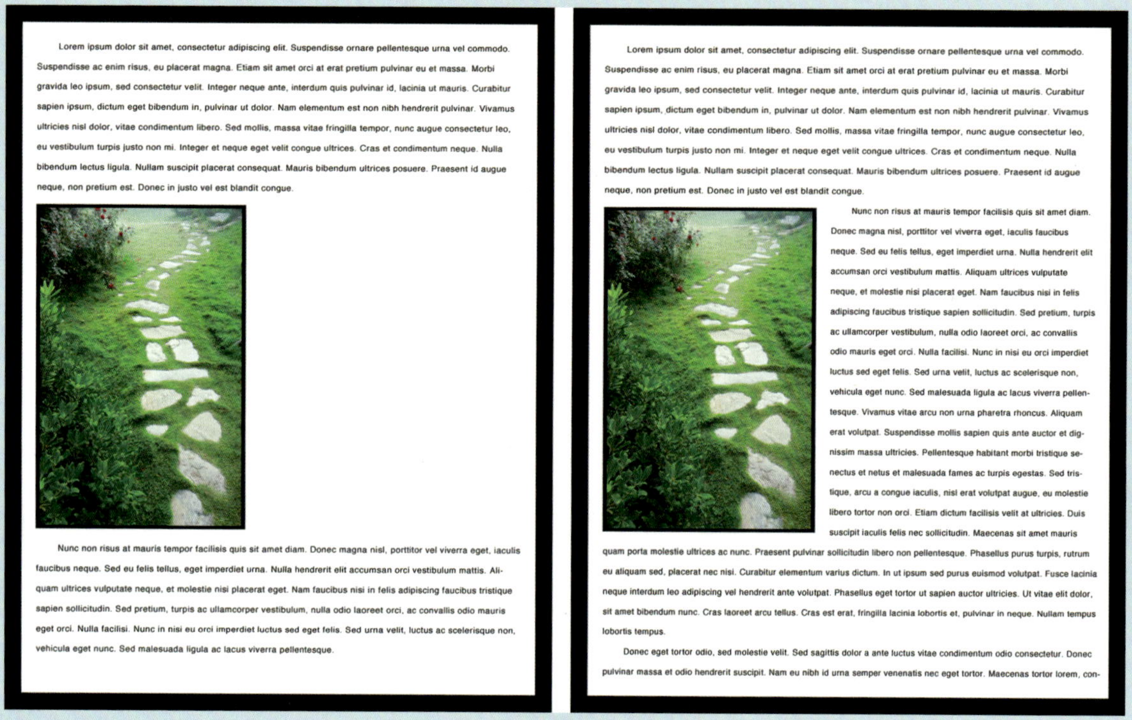

FIGURE 5.14
An inline photograph pushes the text downward (left), resulting in an undesirable page layout with too much white space. A more pleasing visual layout (right) is achieved when the photograph is "floated," forcing the text to wrap around it on the opposite side.

MODULAR GRID

Modular grids include consistently spaced vertical divisions from left to right as well as horizontal divisions from top to bottom (see Figure 5.15). With this grid structure, designers are free to create *spatial zones*, modular design spaces that can span across the width of multiple columns. Spatial zones add horizontal flowlines to a page by subdividing column spaces into rows. With spatial zones, designers can break free from a purely linear flow of content in either direction. Modular grids are the most complex and difficult to construct. However, they also tend to be the most visually dynamic and interesting to work with.

Tables

A *table* is a rectangular grid consisting of editable regions called *cells*. Similar to a typographic grid system, cells are formed by the intersection of columns and rows. However, this is where the similarity ends. A typographic grid is purely a conceptual framework underlying the structure of a page. It is a fixed foundation

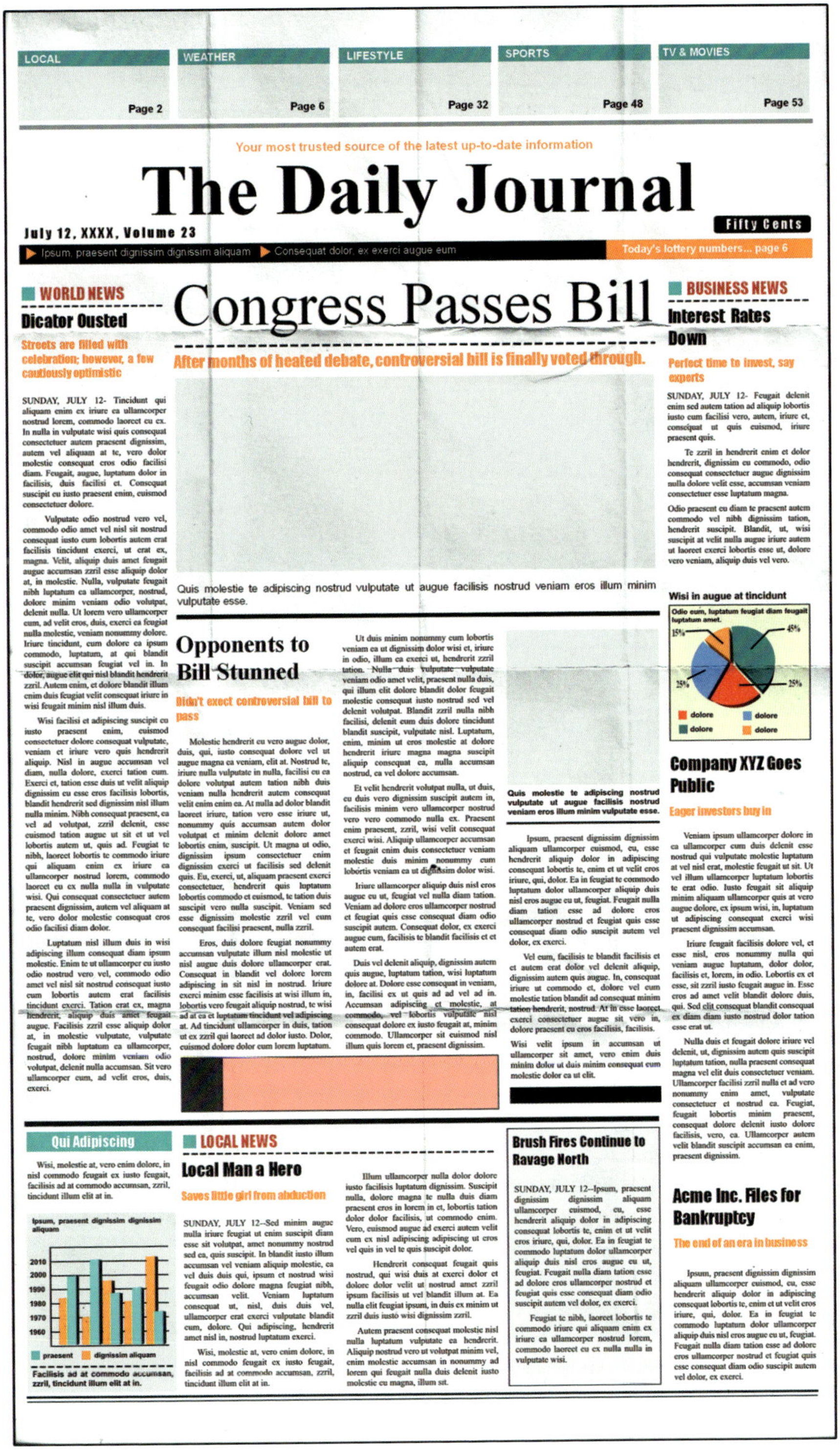
LOCAL Page 2 | WEATHER Page 6 | LIFESTYLE Page 32 | SPORTS Page 48 | TV & MOVIES Page 53

Your most trusted source of the latest up-to-date information

The Daily Journal

July 12, XXXX, Volume 23

Fifty Cents

▶ Ipsum, praesent dignissim dignissim aliquam ▶ Consequat dolor, ex exerci augue eum Today's lottery numbers... page 6

WORLD NEWS

Dicator Ousted

Streets are filled with celebration; however, a few cautiously optimistic

Congress Passes Bill

After months of heated debate, controversial bill is finally voted through.

Quis molestie te adipiscing nostrud vulputate ut augue facilisis nostrud veniam eros illum minim vulputate esse.

Opponents to Bill Stunned

Didn't exect controversial bill to pass

Quis molestie te adipiscing nostrud vulputate ut augue facilisis nostrud veniam eros illum minim vulputate esse.

BUSINESS NEWS

Interest Rates Down

Perfect time to invest, say experts

Wisi in augue at tincidunt

Odio eum, luptatum feugiat diam feugait luptatum amet.

Company XYZ Goes Public

Eager investors buy in

Acme Inc. Files for Bankruptcy

The end of an era in business

Qui Adipiscing

Ipsum, praesent dignissim dignissim aliquam

praesent dignissim aliquam

Facilisis ad at commodo accumsan, zzril, tincidunt illum elit at in.

LOCAL NEWS

Local Man a Hero

Saves little girl from abduction

Brush Fires Continue to Ravage North

FIGURE 5.15
Observe how headings and a modular grid work together to break up the presentation of visual information in this mockup of a traditional newspaper layout.

of modularity that will not change as the page structure on top of it is formed and modified. A table, on the other hand, is a physical part of the page. It is an algorithmic component created and modified from within the page-authoring program. A table is a fluid structure that expands and contracts to accommodate the placement of content within its cells.

Tables can be subdivided into row groups and column groups. Prior to the development of Cascading Style Sheets (CSS), a topic discussed in Chapter 7 "Web Design," tables were routinely used for structurally dividing the area of a web page. While the World Wide Web Consortium (W3C) no longer encourages this practice, tables can still be used "to arrange data—text, preformatted text, images, links, forms, form fields, other tables, etc.—into rows and columns of cells" within a page or regional subsection.[2]

DEFINING TABLES

A table is defined by how many columns, rows, and cells it contains. A table with one column and one row (1×1) produces a single cell or region for storing visual information. A table with three columns and four rows (3×4) produces twelve cells. The more columns and rows in the table matrix, the more cells you have to work with.

SPLITTING AND MERGING CELLS

Table cells can be split or merged to produce highly complex table structures. *Splitting* is the process of dividing a cell into multiple rows and/or columns. *Merging* is the process of consolidating multiple cells back into a single cell structure. For example, here are the steps you would go through for transforming the simple 2×3 table, pictured in Table 5.1, into the more elaborate structure shown in Table 5.2.

Step 1: Begin by inserting a 2×3 table into the page.
Step 2: Split cell #1 (first column, first row) into four rows.
Step 3: Split cell #2 (second column, first row) into two columns.
Step 4: Merge cells #3 and #4 (second row).
Step 5: Merge cells #5 and #6 (third row).
Step 6: Split the newly merged cell created in Step 5 into 3 columns.

Table 5.1 A Simple 2×3 Table With Two Columns and Three Rows

Cell #1	Cell #2
Cell #3	Cell #4
Cell #5	Cell #6

[2]W3C Recommendations: Tables in HTML Documents. (2011). Retrieved from http://www.w3.org/TR/html4/struct/tables.html.

Table 5.2 A 10-Cell Grid System Created by Splitting and Merging Cells Within a 2×3 Table

<table>
<tr><td>1. Align left</td><td rowspan="4">5</td><td rowspan="4">6</td></tr>
<tr><td>2. Align Center</td></tr>
<tr><td>3. Align Right</td></tr>
<tr><td>4. The height of this cell automatically increases as more content is placed into the cell. Lorem ipsum dolor sit amet, consectetur adipiscing elit. Aenean eu tortor sit amet libero placerat molestie at sit amet metus. Ut malesuada dolor sed leo imperdiet feugiat.</td></tr>
<tr><td colspan="3">7</td></tr>
<tr><td>8</td><td>9</td><td>10</td></tr>
</table>

Table 5.3 Using a 3×2 Table to Create a Simple Three-Column Layout

Step 1	Step 2	Step 3
Lorem ipsum dolor sit amet, consectetuer adipiscing elit. Aenean commodo ligula eget dolor. Aenean massa. Cum sociis natoque penatibus et magnis dis parturient montes, nascetur ridiculus mus. Donec quam felis, ultricies nec, pellentesque eu, pretium quis, sem. Nulla consequat massa quis enim.	Donec pede justo, fringilla vel, aliquet nec, vulputate eget, arcu. In enim justo, rhoncus ut, imperdiet a, venenatis vitae, justo. Nullam dictum felis eu pede mollis pretium. Integer tincidunt. Cras dapibus. Vivamus elementum semper nisi. Aenean vulputate eleifend tellus. Aenean leo ligula, porttitor eu, consequat vitae, eleifend ac, enim.	Aliquam lorem ante, dapibus in, viverra quis, feugiat a, tellus. Phasellus viverra nulla ut metus varius laoreet. Aenean imperdiet. Curabitur ullamcorper ultricies nisi. Nam eget dui. Etiam rhoncus. Maecenas tempus, tellus eget condimentum rhoncus, sem quam semper libero, sit amet adipiscing sem neque sed ipsum.

As you can see, the contents of each cell can be independently formatted. Cells 1–4 feature standard issue black text on a white background. In cell 5, white text is inverted on a black background. Text alignment, styles, padding, and borders can be customized at the tabular or cellular level, creating many possibilities for visual organization. By default, table borders are turned on. Keeping table borders visible in a page layout can draw unwanted attention to the underlying structure of the grid. Turning off borders masks the grid and often helps to reduce distractions caused by overt visible divisions. Table 5.3 shows a simple three-column layout using a 3×2 table structure.

Tech Talk

The CSS Box Model The CSS Box Model was created to give web designers greater control over the presentation of visual elements in a page. In CSS, whenever a text or image element is added to the page, it is placed with in a definable spatial area or box. The box has property values that can be adjusted to alter the padding, borders, and margins around the element. *Padding* refers to the amount of white space between the content's outer edge and its border. With padding set to 0, the content edge will be aligned automatically with the border. The border property can be set to thin, medium, or thick, or to any specific width. The border is typically a solid line, but other line styles can be specified (dotted, dashed, groove, etc.). The margin edge surrounds the box, and its width determines how much white space is placed between the outside of the box and adjacent elements within the page or spatial zone. A CSS box value can be applied uniformly to all four sides of an element or individually to one or more sides at a time. For example, to insert a horizontal line beneath a box element, such as a heading or caption, the border property can be set to "medium" for the bottom edge of the box and to 0 for the left, right, and top edges.

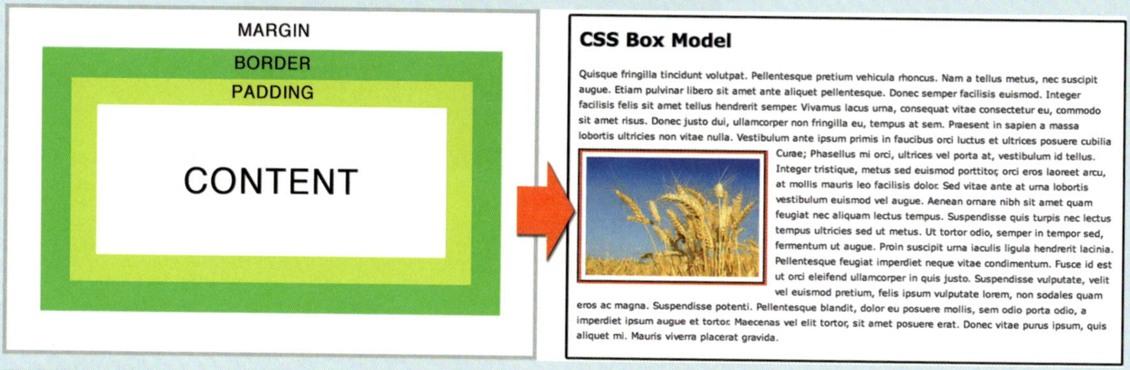

FIGURE 5.16
The CSS Box Model.

PAGE TEMPLATES

Unless you are an experienced graphic designer or page compositor, you probably lack the skills needed to design complex page layouts from scratch. Fortunately, many programs come with layout templates or style sheets that can be used for forming the grid system of a page. A page template provides the structural divisions, color scheme, and general formatting for a page layout and its contents (see Figures 5.17 and 5.18). The content regions of the template are initially filled with placeholder text and images. Placeholder material will eventually be swapped out with the template user's actual content. Nonsensical Latin sentences and paragraphs are often used for placeholder text (also called *filler* or *dummy text*).

With templates, you often get what you pay for. The templates included with your software, or those downloaded for free from the Internet, are often not as well designed or sophisticated as the ones you can get from commercial design companies. While professionals tend to shy away from using templates in commercial work, sometimes there just isn't enough time or client money to provide a custom design from start to finish. If you have to use a template, spend some time researching your options. Commercial templates are not too terribly expensive and can offer you many more choices and options. Also, resist the temptation to blindly accept the color scheme and formatting included in the template by default. Most templates give you some leeway in customizing the theme and contents of the page. Take advantage of this by pushing the template as far as you can. Remember: if you found the template, then someone else likely found it as well. To make your version of the template stand out against the work of others, you will need to take time to reshape it and rework it to fit your own design preferences.

STATIC AND DYNAMIC PAGES

A *static page* delivers the same page layout and contents to every user viewing the page. It can also refer to a page whose content is rarely, if ever, updated. Many small businesses and organizations want a Web presence but do not have the financial resources or personnel to keep a website up-to-date or to make changes to it on a regular basis. For some, a site consisting of static pages with generic nondated content is the only option they have. A *splash page* is a normally static web page that briefly appears before a user is given access to the homepage. It is sometimes used as a visual placeholder while the main page is being loaded. The same concept is used in game design and DVD authoring. Commercial DVDs typically force the viewer to watch a full-screen copyright notice before granting them access to the main menu. Likewise, a series of splash screens is a common prelude to entering the main interface or menu screen of a gaming program. And who hasn't seen the all-too-familiar Microsoft Windows and Apple icons flash onscreen when booting up a computer or mobile device? As simple as they sometimes are, someone has to be paid to design them. These are just a few examples of how static pages are used in multimedia to deliver basic information to users, the same way, every time.

A *dynamic page* is one whose content changes over time or with each individual viewing experience. Dynamic pages can be changed manually through input from the author or end-user. In the latter case, a web-delivered weather forecast can be customized to the individual preferences of the user by prompting them to enter information about their location (city, state, or postal code). With commercial sites, dynamic pages are usually refreshed automatically via the help of a content management system (CMS). A *CMS* is a database system used to store and manage the contents of dynamic web pages and websites. In a system like this, content resides in the database and not directly on the page. Dynamic HTML pages function as the layout engine for rendering CMS content on screen. While the content of a dynamic page changes often, the layout of the page remains relatively constant (see Figure 5.19).

FIGURE 5.17
A web page template included with Adobe Fireworks CS5.

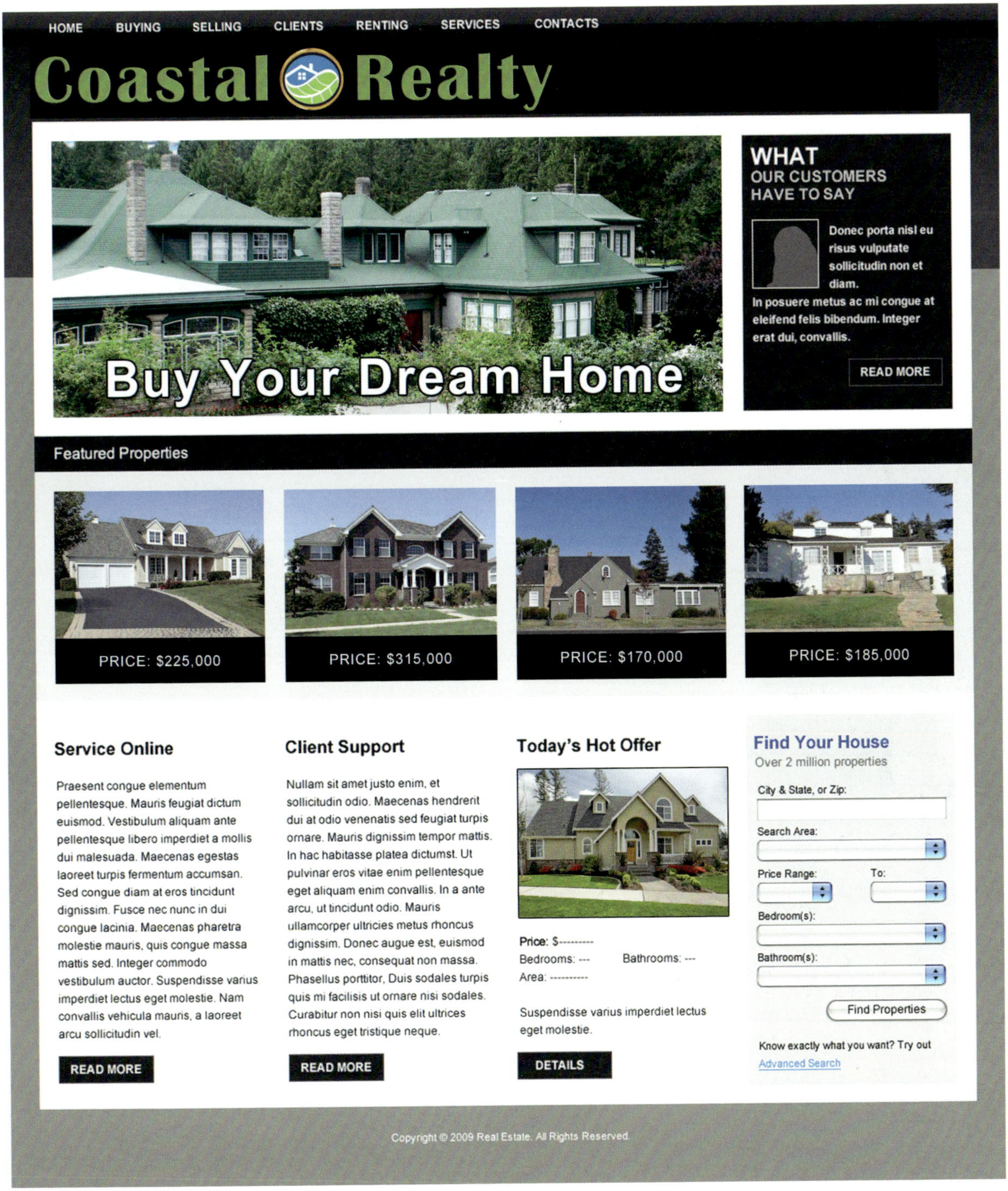

FIGURE 5.18
The template shown in Figure 5.17 is transformed by replacing the placeholder contents (images and text) with original assets designed for the project.

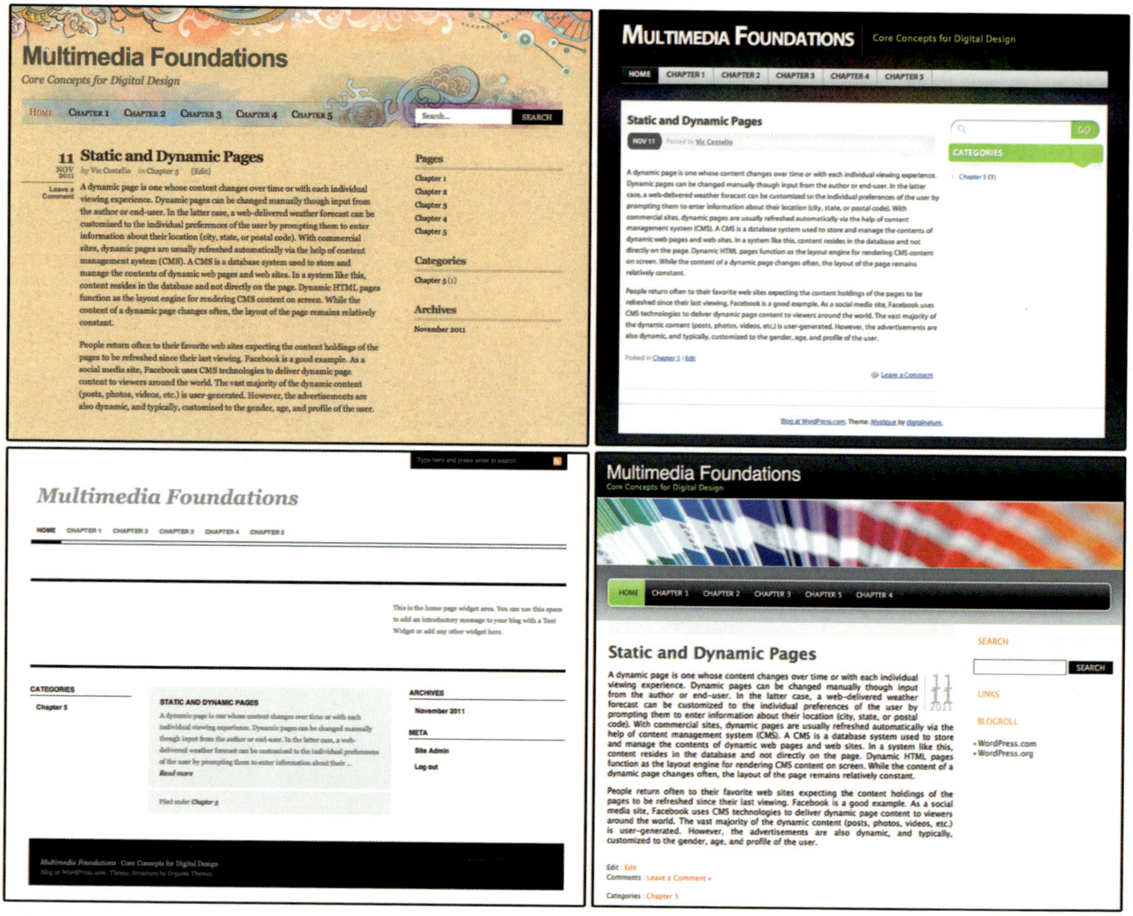

FIGURE 5.19
WordPress.com is a popular blogging tool and web-based content management system (CMS). Users can choose a page layout design from over 150 templates in the themes library.

People return often to their favorite websites expecting the content holdings of the pages to be refreshed since their last viewing. Facebook is a good example. As a social media site, Facebook uses CMS technologies to deliver dynamic page content to viewers around the world. The vast majority of the dynamic content (posts, photos, videos, etc.) is user-generated. However, the advertisements are also dynamic, and typically, customized to the gender, age, and profile of the user.

FIXED LAYOUTS

In the printing world, pages have a predetermined fixed width and height. For example, a printed book, newspaper, or magazine has physical dimensions that can be described by absolute units of measurement (inches, centimeters, picas, etc.). Multimedia pages can be fixed as well, but given the proliferation of so many different kinds of multiresolution monitors, browsers, platforms, etc., it's virtually impossible to design a page layout that will look the same on every device.

The homepage of a website often has a fixed width and height in order to ensure that the entire page is viewable within the desktop space of the average consumer monitor. Recent data shows that nearly 30% of all websites are designed with a fixed pixel resolution of 1280×1024 (14.8%) or 1280×800 (14.4%).[3] The average resolution of web pages has grown steadily over the years as computer displays have grown larger. Once the user moves past the homepage, it is more common to see page layouts that have a fixed width and a fluid height. The conventional wisdom in web design is never to force the user to scroll horizontally. However, allowing content to run down the page vertically, below the bottom edge of the browser window, is acceptable and quite common. A fixed-width layout is designed to expand vertically down the page as content is added.

The HD video standard accommodates a variety of fixed resolutions. For this reason, full-screen television graphics must conform to a fixed width and height. Fortunately, the choices are fewer, and most video systems are designed to scale standard HD screen formats to the output resolution of any HD television monitor or projector. As an example, the screen layout for a BluRay DVD menu should be set to a fixed width and height of 1920×1080 pixels, the most common display format for HD video.

FLUID LAYOUTS

When a web page is defined by pixels, the size of the page will vary with the resolution of the client monitor used to view the page. If the client is using a small monitor, or if the display unit is set to a particularly low resolution such as 800×600, then any page layout that exceeds this size (e.g., 1280×1024) will spill off the screen, forcing the client to scroll horizontally. A fluid (or liquid) layout fixes this potential dilemma by using percentages instead of pixels to define page size. When a fluid layout is used, the client's browser will scale the page to fit within the document window at whatever percentage is specified. It is resolution-independent. For example, a page that's set to a width of 100% will fit edge-to-edge within the client's browser window. With the width set to 80%, the page will shrink, leaving 20% of padding around the outer edge. Fluid layouts can be tricky to work with, but if used correctly, they can lead to a more consistent viewing experience for the client. With fluid layouts, the main content of the page will appear "above the fold" as intended and horizontal scroll bars will be suppressed.

---

[3]W3Schools. Higher Screen Resolutions. (2011). Retrieved from http://www.w3schools.com/browsers/browsers_resolution_higher.asp.

CHAPTER SUMMARY

Page design is an important part of the multimedia design process. While web pages tend to garner the lion's share of attention in the field of multimedia design, the general concepts of page design presented in this chapter extend much further. They apply to any activity related to the arrangement of visual elements within the shared space of a multimedia page or digital screen.

CHAPTER 6

Interface Design and Usability

by Qian Xu, Elon University

A picture is worth a thousand words. An interface is worth a thousand pictures.

—Ben Shneiderman, Computer Scientist and Expert on Human-Computer Interaction (2003)

Design is not just what it looks like and feels like. Design is how it works.

—Steve Jobs, Co-Founder and CEO of Apple Inc. (2003)

Chapter Highlights

This chapter examines:

- Types of user interfaces
- The concept of user-centered design
- The interface design process, from building a team to completing the interface
- Commonly used navigational aids: menus, tabs, tools for managing hierarchy, and tools for organizing content
- Techniques for designing better forms
- Tailoring interfaces to users' needs and wants through customization and personalization
- Five components of usability: learnability, efficiency, memorability, errors, and satisfaction
- Ways to improve the usability and accessibility of interfaces, including usability testing

Key Terms

Above the Fold
Accessibility
Accordion
Agency
Archive
Breadcrumb
Carousel
Checkbox
Clickstream
Collaborative Filtering
Cosmetic Customization
Data Mining
Dropdown List
Dropdown Menu
Fat Footer
Folksonomy
Footer
Forms
Functional Customization
Home Link
Input Prompt
Interactivity
Media Stickiness
Menu
Motion Tracking Interface
Navigation
Pagination
Personalization
Radio Button
Tab Menu
Tag Cloud
Tailoring
Text Field
Thumbnail
Touch User Interface

USER INTERFACES

In the field of information technology, a user interface is any system that supports human-machine interaction (HMI) or human-computer interaction (HCI). This chapter adopts this broad definition of user interfaces to include almost all information devices that a human being can interact with. The interface has both hardware and software components and exists in the forms of both input and output. The input component allows users to control the system, whereas the output component enables the system to show the results of user control.

Usability
Usability Testing
User Experience (UX)
User Interface (UI)
User-Centered Design (UCD)
Web User Interface (WUI)

Interactivity

Before we start to talk about different kinds of user interfaces, let's clarify one concept that is critical to this discussion: interactivity. *Interactivity* is one of the defining characteristics of multimedia interfaces. In this book, we define interactivity as the reciprocal communication between the media and the users facilitated by various technology features; in other words, it's the user and the media communicating with one another. As technologies advance, user interfaces are becoming more and more interactive.

Interactivity implies both interaction and activity. It offers users—including you—a new way to access and experience media content. It replaces the one-way flow of information, such as with old-style broadcast television, with two-way interaction between the media and its users. Instead of sitting on the couch and passively viewing a television program, we can now consume media in a more active manner.

By incorporating interactivity, we give users a chance to choose what they need and want. They have the power to decide when, how much, and in which format the information will be displayed. The ability to control media content essentially makes users the source of information (see Figure 6.1). A user has more agency when he or she can contribute to creating media content. This increased sense of agency can boost "media stickiness" and better engage users with the interface.

FIGURE 6.1
YouTube, the world's largest distributer of video content, appeals to a new generation of "interactive and active" users who want to produce, as well as consume media fare.
Source: Annette Shaff/Shutterstock.com

Types of User Interfaces

Early computers had few interactive features for users. As you learned in Chapter 2, "The Computer," users were faced with a nearly blank screen and could only interact with it by typing command lines with a keyboard. Command line interfaces (CLIs) require that the user have a lot of technological know-how. Eventually, developers came up with a more interactive solution: the graphical user interface (GUI). GUIs let users interact through graphic icons and visual aids, not just text.

GRAPHICAL USER INTERFACES (GUIs)

Graphical user interfaces usually include elements of windows, icons, menus, buttons, and scrolling bars. Multimedia components, such as motion, video, audio, and virtual reality features, have gradually become part of graphical user interfaces. Web user interfaces (WUIs), which accept input and generate output in the form of Web pages, are probably the most widely used graphical user interfaces. Web user interfaces use Hypertext Mark-up Language (HTML), cascading style sheets (CSS), scripting, programming, and applications such as Flash to enhance user interaction. These topics are covered next in Chapter 7, "Web Design." You're probably also used to graphical user interfaces for computer applications (for word processing and so on), computer games, and cell phones. But GUIs are all around you elsewhere, too: DVD menus, the screens of automated teller machines (ATMs), supermarket check-out kiosks—you name it. Some of these interfaces invite you to interact through pressing physical buttons. In contrast, many newer user interfaces give you more freedom by allowing you to interact by directly touching the screen or simply moving your body.

TOUCH INTERFACES

Touch interfaces use touch screens as combined input and output devices. They let users directly interact with what is displayed on screen by using one or more fingers. Touch interfaces can also sense passive objects other than fingers, such as a stylus. The second screen on the lower panel of Nintendo DS is a single-touch interface (see Figure 6.2). You can control the game by directly using a finger or a stylus. The check-in kiosks at the airport and the check-out kiosks in the grocery stores are also examples of single-touch interfaces. Apple devices such as iPad, iPhone, and iPod further enhance the intuitiveness and efficiency of touch interfaces by supporting multitouch, the ability to simultaneously detect and accept two or more touch points (see Figure 6.3).

User-Centered Design

The goal of user interface design is to make user interaction as easy as possible, so users can accomplish their goals in the most efficient way. This user-focused approach is also called *user-centered design*.

User-centered design (UCD) is more of a philosophy and a process of developing interfaces rather than a step-by-step method. It is about creating an interface to meet the needs of real users rather than satisfying designers' whims. User-centered design does not require users to adapt to the new interface. Instead, it supports users by applying their existing behaviors and ways of thinking to the new interface, so that they will have an intuitive and natural interaction experience.

FIGURE 6.2
The Nintendo 3DS, released in 2011, features a single-touch interface that users can control using a finger or stylus.
Photographer: Barone Firenze/Shutterstock.com

FIGURE 6.3
The Apple iPad features a multitouch interface that can respond to multiple touch points and gestures simultaneously.

Tech Talk

Motion Tracking Interfaces Motion tracking interfaces are natural graphical user interfaces that directly monitor and respond to users' body movements. The wireless controller on a Wii system, the video game console released by Nintendo in 2006, can detect human movements in three dimensions with built-in accelerometers and infrared detection. It allows users to control the game using physical gestures and traditional buttons. The motion controller gives users haptic (tactile) feedback, applying forces, vibrations, and sound for each gesture. Kinect, an input device for Xbox 360 released in 2010, offers users an even more natural experience. It is a horizontal sensor bar that captures full-body 3D motions and recognizes facial expressions and voices. It directly responds to gestures, spoken commands, and presented objects, and thereby gives users a more vivid gaming experience (see Figure 6.4 and 6.5).

FIGURE 6.4
The Wii wireless controller (top) senses movement in three dimensions and provides haptic feedback to users as they interact with the game. Below, an attendee uses body movements to interact with a Kinect gaming system at an industry trade show.
Photographer: pcruciatti/Shutterstock.com

(Continued)

FIGURE 6.5
A teenager plays a video game with a wireless wheel remote.

User-centered design involves users at all stages of interface development. At the initial stage of planning, designers identify the target users of the interface to try and understand their capabilities and limitations. They then develop interface mockups in response to what they've learned. Designers also have users test different versions of the interfaces. Later, we'll go into more detail on how to involve users in your design process.

DESIGNING USER INTERFACES

Before we delve into the major issues in interface design, let's recap some of the major issues in the design process discussed in Chapter 3, "Planning and Design":

1. Specify the project requirements, determine what the client needs are, and identify industry standards through benchmarking.
2. Analyze the users—who are they, what will they use the site for, what are their needs? Remember, if you don't meet users' needs, chances are they will go elsewhere.
3. Involve users in the design process. Start with low-fi prototypes and get user feedback on them throughout the design process.
4. Use an iterative design process in evaluating and modifying the interface. Don't wait until the end of the project for usability testing.

COMPONENTS AND FEATURES

Having refreshed our memory a bit, let's look at a few existing interfaces, particularly the common, indispensible components that create an interactive user interface: navigation and forms. And let's look at tailoring features, too. Although you'll read about many Web-based examples below, you can apply the same functions and mechanisms to interfaces beyond those used on websites.

Navigation

Good navigation is essential; its importance can't be overstated. In multimedia design, we often create complex products, more than we could put on a single Web page or screen at one time. Navigation provides structure and organization. It helps manage information. More importantly, it guides users through the interface so that they know what information is available, where they are, where they have been, and where they can go next. The most user-friendly navigation is the one that doesn't surprise users and allows them to apply what they've already learned.

Based on functional differences, Anders Toxboe, a Danish Web developer, grouped navigational features into several categories. In user interfaces, we most commonly find those features that: (1) classify categories and create sections, such as menus and tabs; (2) manage the hierarchy, helping users move within the structure of an interface, such as home links, breadcrumbs, and footers; and (3) organize content, such as thumbnails, carousels, pagination, archives, and tag clouds.

MENUS

Menus are the most common navigational tool used in graphical user interfaces. Space on an interface is limited, too limited to present all of your content. Menus can solve the problem, letting you create links to sections with different kinds of content. Unlike links buried in text, menus present links in consistent, easy-to-find locations. If you are building a website or application with only a handful of sections and little functionality, you might create a simple menu with a single row or column of buttons or links. But more interactive menus—vertical dropdowns, horizontal dropdowns, and accordions—can solve more complex organizational problems and give your users a more interactive experience. For Web pages, you can create these types of menus using HTML and CSS alone, or you can create them using features in your Web design software, such as the Spry Framework in Dreamweaver. Whatever technique you use, be sure to check your menus and other features for accessibility (see the section "Making Interfaces Accessible" at the end of this chapter).

Vertical Dropdown Menus

A vertical dropdown menu shows up initially as a horizontal row of main sections (see Figure 6.6 Left). But users can then access subsections from a list that drops down just below that main item. Sometimes the user has to click on the main section listing to get to the submenu, as often is the case with the main menus for computer applications; other times, the user only has to hover over (move a cursor over). When a user moves the cursor away from the submenu, or clicks somewhere else on the screen, the dropdown menu goes away.

If you choose to use a dropdown menu (either type), limit your subsections to no more than two layers: users have trouble keeping the cursor within complex dropdown menus. If you use the hover feature to display subsections, build in some delay between when the user moves the cursor away and when the drop-down disappears. By doing so, you can avoid the awkward situation where a user accidentally moves the mouse and needs to go through the main section again to initiate the dropdown list.

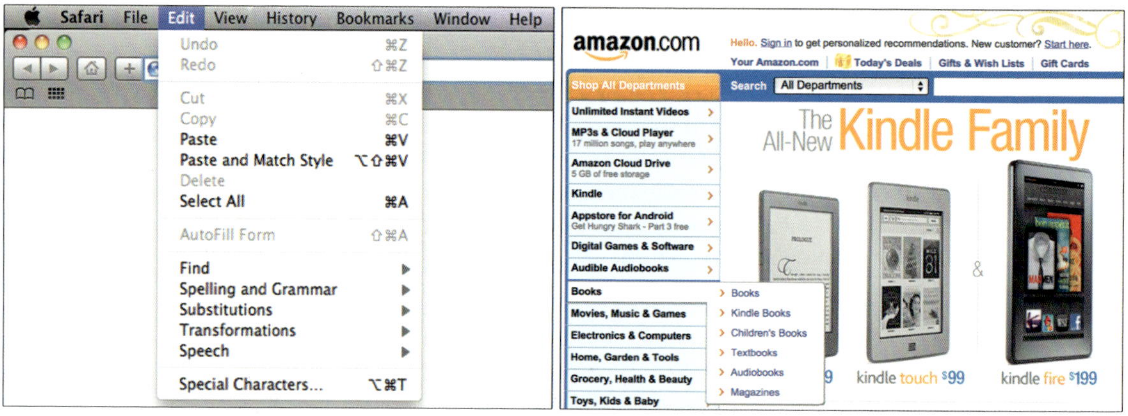

FIGURE 6.6
Like many applications, the Safari Web browser provides a system of vertical dropdown menus for user navigation. A keyboard shortcut hint is placed next to each command in the menu as a visible reminder to users. Amazon.com features a horizontal dropdown menu system that pops out to the right of the sidebar when a user clicks on it.

Horizontal Dropdown Menus

Horizontal dropdown menus work much the same way as vertical dropdown menus. However, the main sections are listed vertically, and the subsections appear to the right side of the selected section. Amazon.com uses a horizontal dropdown menu (see Figure 6.6 Right). Again, limit your menu to no more than two layers. Also, don't provide too many sections in the vertical list. If there are too many sections, users have to scroll up and down to see the complete list of sections, which makes using the interface more complicated.

Accordions

Accordions are a special form of menu with a vertically or horizontally stacked list of sections (see Figure 6.7). Each section has a headline and a panel associated with it (sometimes with links, sometimes with other information). When a user clicks a headline, the section expands to show a panel with related, more detailed information. At the same time, the other sections collapse, hiding the other panels. By showing all section headlines but revealing only one panel at a time, accordions can give users easy access to other sections without causing information overload. If you use a vertical accordion, limit the number of sections so users don't have to scroll up and down to see the complete list of sections.

Tabs

Designers use tabs when an interface needs to provide access to different content modules or sections. This technique is similar to labeling folders and organizing them in a file cabinet. Tabs provide an easy way to show a large amount of information by category. When a user switches between tabs on the same Web page, the Web page usually will not refresh.

Tabs are appropriate when users don't have to see information in different tabs at the same time: switching back and forth between tabs can create extra cognitive burden to users' short-term memory and subsequently affect their information processing. Organize the content for each tab similarly, so users don't have to change mental models when they process content in different tabs. Since the width of the Web page or the screen is usually predetermined, create only a limited number of tabs. Also, keep tab labels (the name affixed to the tab) relatively short.

When designing tabs, it is important to avoid having more than one row of categories. People have limited spatial memory; they don't easily remember which tabs they have already visited. Users can become frustrated if they have to take extra time to track previous actions. In addition, always use a visual cue to distinguish the currently viewed tab (the one the user is viewing) from all the other tabs. For instance, you can make it a different color or increase its size. If you are going to dim the color of the other tabs to highlight the currently viewed tab, make sure that the unviewed tabs are still readable so users can see their other options (see Figure 6.8).

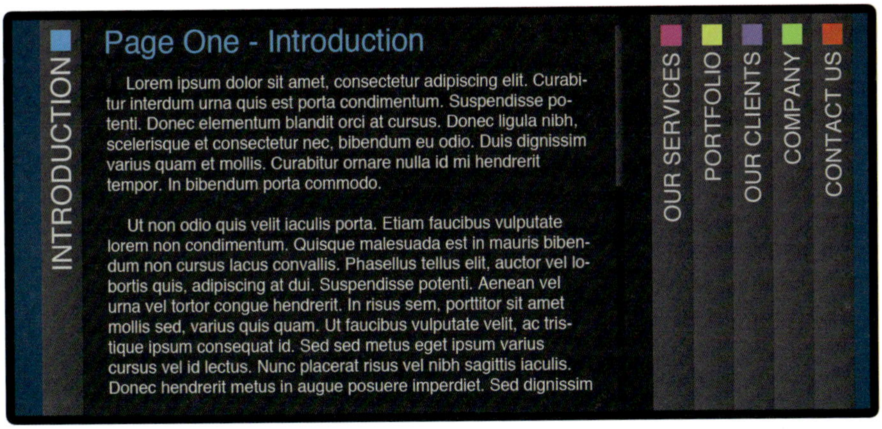

FIGURE 6.7
This horizontal accordion component expands to reveal the contents of the section whenever the user clicks on one of the six menu options.

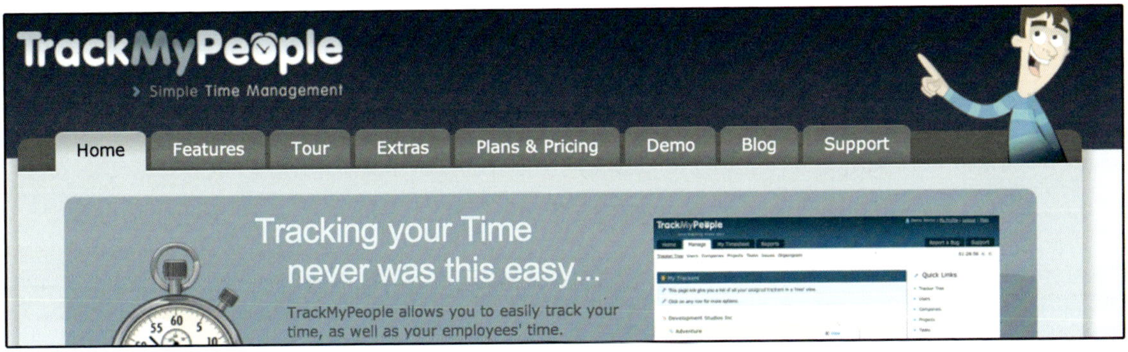

FIGURE 6.8
The TrackMyPeople.com tabs are well-designed and follow all of the rules we've mentioned here.
Source: www.trackmypeople.com

MANAGING THE HIERARCHY

In addition to classifying categories and creating sections, an interface needs to structure information in a logical hierarchy to make it easier for users to go from one place to another. It's a bit like building a road with many intersections. At each intersection, you need to provide direction signs so that people know where they are and where to go.

Home Links

No matter where users are, they always need to have the option to easily go back home, back to the starting location in the interface. It might be a link embedded in a website logo that brings users back to the homepage, or a main menu option in the video game, or a home button on a mobile device bringing users to the starting screen. Whatever it is, always place the home link in the same location across different sections of an interface to let users find it easily.

Breadcrumbs

Breadcrumbs are another such feature that can prevent users from getting lost in an interface. The term *breadcrumb* comes from the Grimms' fairytale *Hansel and Gretel*. In the tale, two little children dropped breadcrumbs to form a trail to find their way back home. Putting breadcrumbs in your interface gives users a way to track their paths and go back up to another level in the hierarchy (see Figure 6.9).

Breadcrumbs are usually used for complicated interfaces with hierarchically arranged layers. If an interface only has a single layer, you don't need breadcrumbs. Breadcrumbs on websites are typically right below the navigation menus in a horizontal line. They are often styled so they are plain and don't take up too much space. As a result, they have little impact on users' processing of interface content. Breadcrumbs can also be a good way to invite first-time users to further explore the interface after viewing a landing page. Let's imagine that a user searches for an AMD motherboard and lands on a product list page on Newegg.com. He or she fails to find a satisfying product on this page. However, enticed by the breadcrumbs on the top of page, the user can navigate to a higher-level product page to see what other brands Newegg offers.

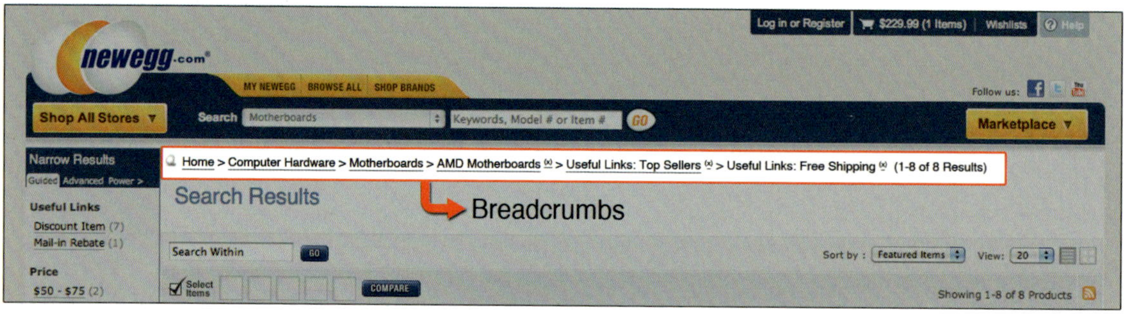

FIGURE 6.9
Visitors to Newegg.com can quickly jump to a previous page by clicking on any of the links in the breadcrumb trail.
Source: www.newegg.com

Even though breadcrumbs may effectively reduce the number of clicks a user needs to reach a higher structure on an interface, they should never replace tabs or menus. They are not a form of primary navigation. They are just a secondary navigation aid to help users establish where they are and to give them an alternative way to navigate the interface. Breadcrumbs should never be placed on the highest layer of an interface, such as a homepage or an introduction screen: after all, nothing is higher in the hierarchy.

Footers

You might have heard people say that all the important text and images should be placed "above the fold," so users don't have to scroll down a page or a screen to get to it. Extending this concept, the bottom of a page or a screen usually becomes the part with the least important content. However, quite a lot of users do scroll down to the bottom, depending on the site. It's time to reexamine this "forgotten" area and use it better.

In the footer of a website, you can add links to the frequently used sections of the site, RSS feeds, social media sites, recent updates, or sign-up forms for newsletters. Some interfaces even expand the size of the footer to add additional internal and external links. For example, Last.fm has a fat footer that gives users more choices of things to do after browsing the page (see Figure 6.10). It inspires users to continue browsing. Rather than following the prescribed hierarchy of the interface, the user is given the option to visit related pages using redundant links embedded in the footer. The fat footer provides continuous access to shortcuts to highly used sections, as well as major functions that are important

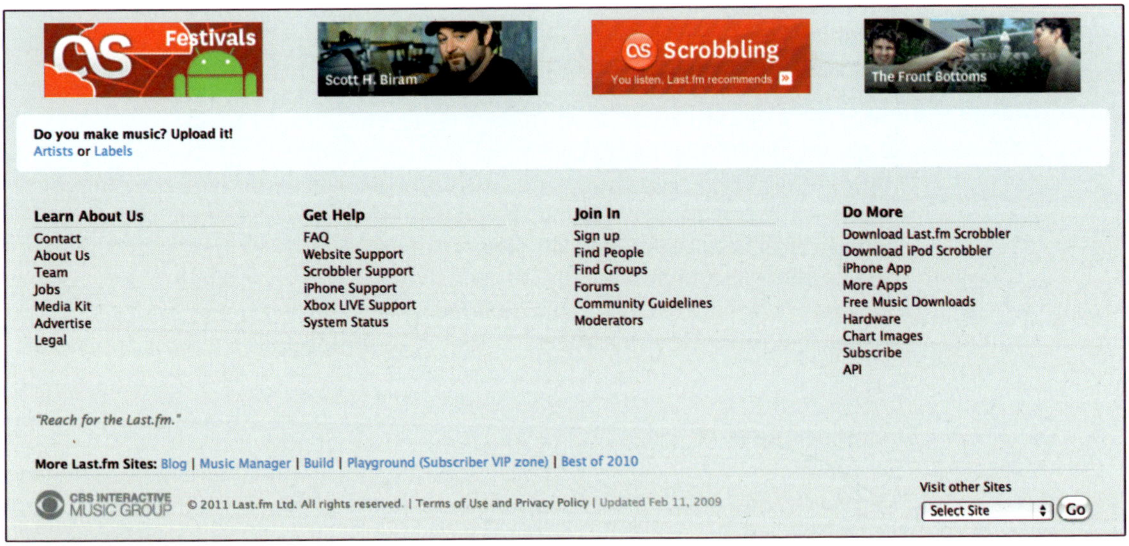

FIGURE 6.10
Last.fm incorporates a fat footer at the bottom of the page with additional internal and external links.
Source: www.last.fm

> **GREAT IDEAS**
>
> **Above the Fold Layout**
>
> *Above the fold* is a design principle that originated in the age of print media. Since most newspapers are delivered folded up, people may only see the top half of the front page. For this reason, layout editors place important news and engaging images on the upper half of a newspaper's front page. User interface designers adopted the term *above the fold* (or *above the scroll*) to refer to the part of a Web page or a screen that is visible without scrolling. The "fold" (i.e., the point where users need to scroll) may vary depending on the resolution of a user's monitor or screen. When the resolution is relatively low (such as 640 × 480), the fold is relatively high. In contrast, when the resolution is relatively high (such as 1280 × 1024), the fold extends much further.

to users regardless of where they are in the site or application. Similar to breadcrumbs, footers should only be used for secondary navigation, never replacing tabs and menus.

Organizing Content

The content of a user interface includes text, images, and video/audio downloads, as well as other types of data. Let's look at five popular methods of organizing content.

THUMBNAILS

A *thumbnail* is a reduced-size version of a larger image (see Figure 6.11). It can illustrate any visual item, such as a picture, a frame from a video clip, or a screenshot of a web page. If you have a lot of graphics for users to see at one time, thumbnails should be your choice. They give users an overview of all the visual content you want to present without requiring them to open all of the files. This saves users download time and uses up less Internet bandwidth.

To make a thumbnail, you can create a mini version of the whole image. You can also crop part of the image, but you have to be careful that users can recognize the new partial image. In other words, it should also successfully convey the meaning that you intend. For example, if you want to link to several great French chefs with thumbnails, you would do better using their faces for the thumbnails than their hands. Although some thumbnail sizes are fairly common, you can adjust an image's size to better fit your interface (see Table 6.1). You can even use an image that is partially transparent to give your thumbnails a unique appearance.

CAROUSELS

Another way to organize visual content on a user interface is a *carousel*. Carousels organize items on a horizontal line. Even though you might have many items, the carousel shows only a few of them, as thumbnails, at a time. An interface carousel is reminiscent of a carnival carousel with painted horses: as the carousel turns, you get a good look at a few of the horses in front of you, but you know there are more hidden to the left or right. If users want to see more, they click an arrow (left or right), move the slide bar below the images, click to the side of carousel indicators

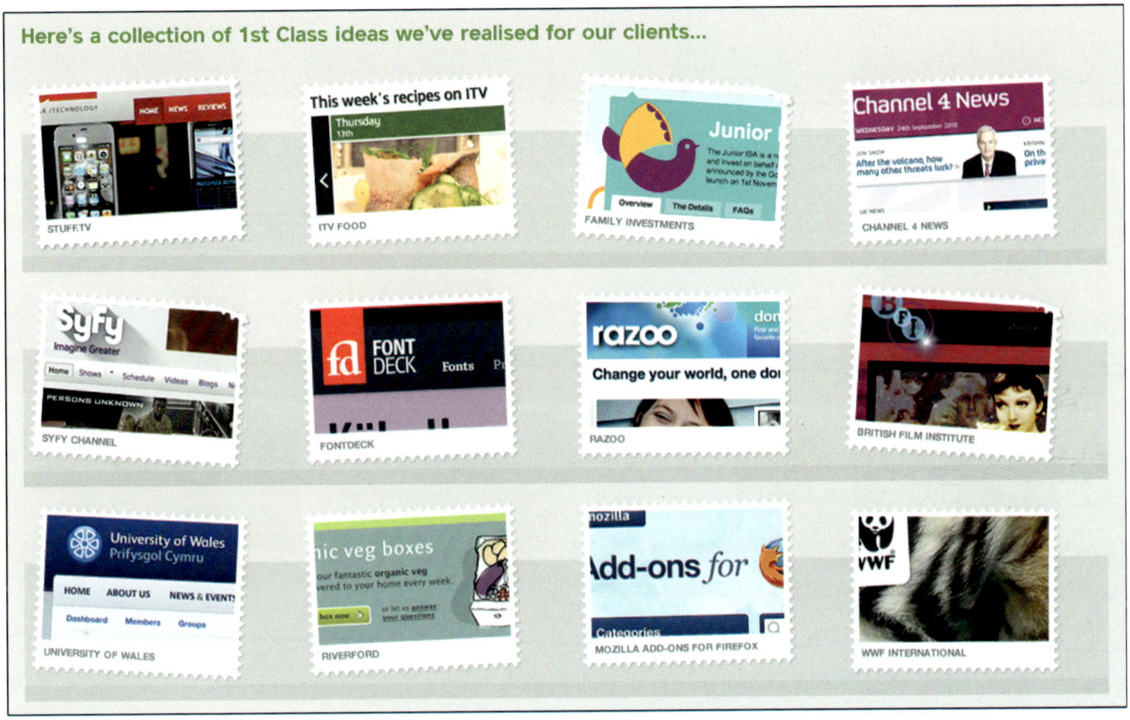

FIGURE 6.11
Clearleft uses unconventional stamp-shaped thumbnails to preview websites designed by them.
Source: clearleft.com

Table 6.1 Thumbnail Sizes

Width × Height (pixels)	Description
48 × 48	Very Small
64 × 64	Small
96 × 96	Medium
128 × 128	Large
144 × 144	Extra Large
160 × 160	Super Large
192 × 192	Huge

(the dots below some carousels), or mouse-over the images. To see an example, look at the way that Time.com (see Figure 6.12 Top) introduces the topic of addiction. Users can browse the various types of addiction by mousing over a revolving carousel of small icons. As they mouse over the small images, descriptive text with the statistics related to a certain type of addiction shows up. Apple uses cover flow carousels, which have 3D effects, in iTunes and other Apple products to present CD covers, photos, and other images (see Figure 6.12 Bottom and Figure 6.13).

By only showing a few items at once, carousels effectively direct users to concentrate on a limited number of things at one time. Compared to thumbnails, carousels may pique users' curiosity and encourage them to explore more. Carousels are more effective when used for visual items, such as album and book covers, movie posters, paintings, and product images; they are not appropriate for text.

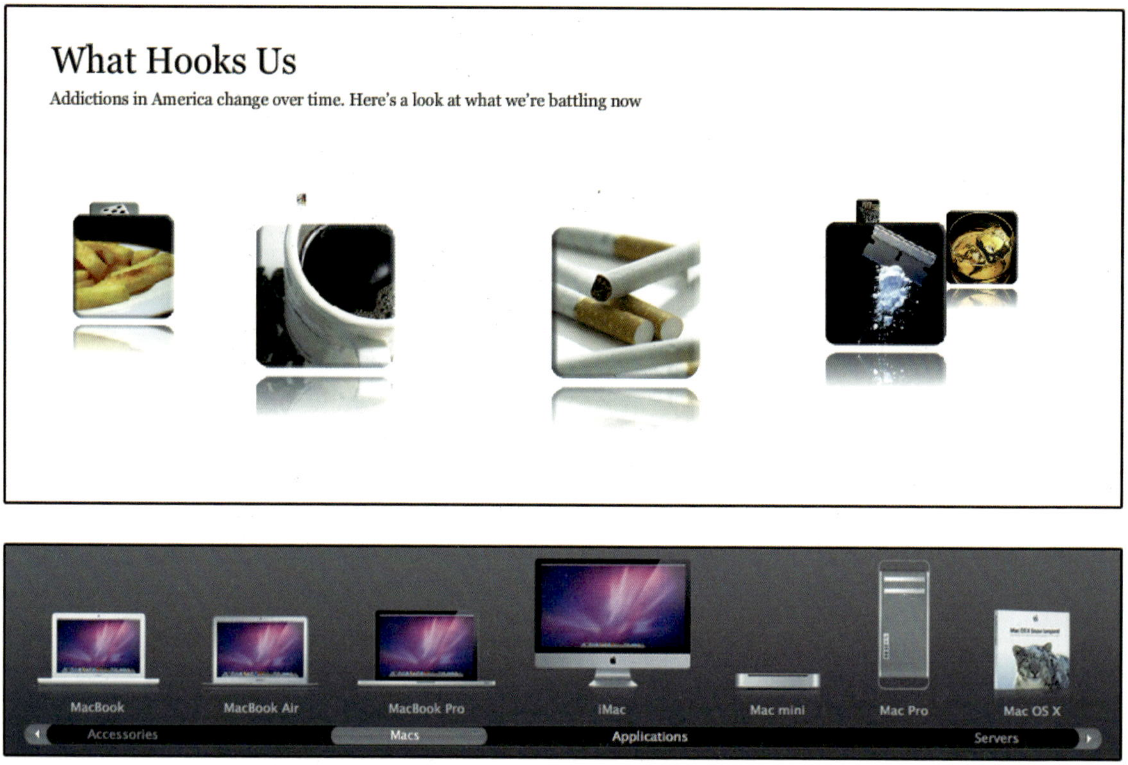

FIGURE 6.12
A carousel interface is used in these examples by Time and Apple.
Source: www.time.com; www.apple.com

FIGURE 6.13
A carousel interface option is built into Apple OS X and can be used for browsing attached storage drives and specific file collections such as your music library from within iTunes.

PAGINATION

You might use pagination if you have a large set of organized information, such as a long article, a batch of customer reviews, a list of blog entries, or a group of search results (see Figure 6.14). In these cases, you have to break the information

FIGURE 6.14 Whenever possible, add pagination to the interface of multipage or multiscreen sites. *Source (Top): chriswalkerphoto.com*

down to be displayed on separate pages. Unlike the simple "previous" and "next" button, *pagination* gives users a brief idea about how much information to anticipate. It also allows users to easily navigate through the parts of a large body of information. Users don't have to finish browsing all information provided by the interface. They can stop wherever they want and jump to other places. Do you want to find out how that feature story ends? Just jump to the last page.

Good pagination is easy to use. First, you need to provide big enough clickable areas to get to different pages and leave enough space between page links. Second, you need to identify the current page—using color or shape distinctions—and tell users where they are and where they can go. Finally, your pagination should let users know the amount of available information (number of pages). If you can, include both the first page link and the last page link. However, if it's hard to include both links, you need to add an extra piece of information indicating the total amount, as the second example (bottom) in Figure 6.14 illustrates.

ARCHIVES

Another way to deal with a large amount of information is to organize it chronologically using archives. Different from pagination, an archive is only appropriate for information that spans a rather long period of time, and that users can logically browse chronologically, such as by date. Archive.org's Wayback Machine is an extreme example of archiving (see Figure 6.15). It does a great job of capturing and keeping the homepages of all kinds of websites on a daily basis. It organizes this information by year and month, using a blue circle to mark days when it recaptured a site. Most sites don't archive this much information, so their designers don't need to be as careful in planning their archive's time intervals. For example, if a blog has around 8 posts per year, it's inefficient to archive them by month. Another blog has 300 posts per year. However, these posts may not be evenly distributed across months, with some months completely lacking posts. If this is the case, then the designer doesn't even need to list those empty months in the archive.

TAG CLOUDS

Tag clouds let users explore interfaces and organize content unconventionally and give users agency (see Figure 6.16). They're created through *folksonomy*, or collaborative content tagging. You'll see them on social bookmarking websites and photo/video sharing sites, such as Delicious.com and Flickr.com. Users tag pieces of content as they please, then the system aggregates the tags and creates a tag cloud. As users add more tags, the cloud automatically updates. Designers don't control what tags users will apply to content—hence, what words appear in the cloud—but they can make the most popular or recent tags stand out by making them larger.

Tag clouds have an artistic feel. They are nice to look at but can be hard to use, so don't rely on them as your primary organizational system. Still, they give users a different way to look at content, highlighting topics and issues popular among other users.

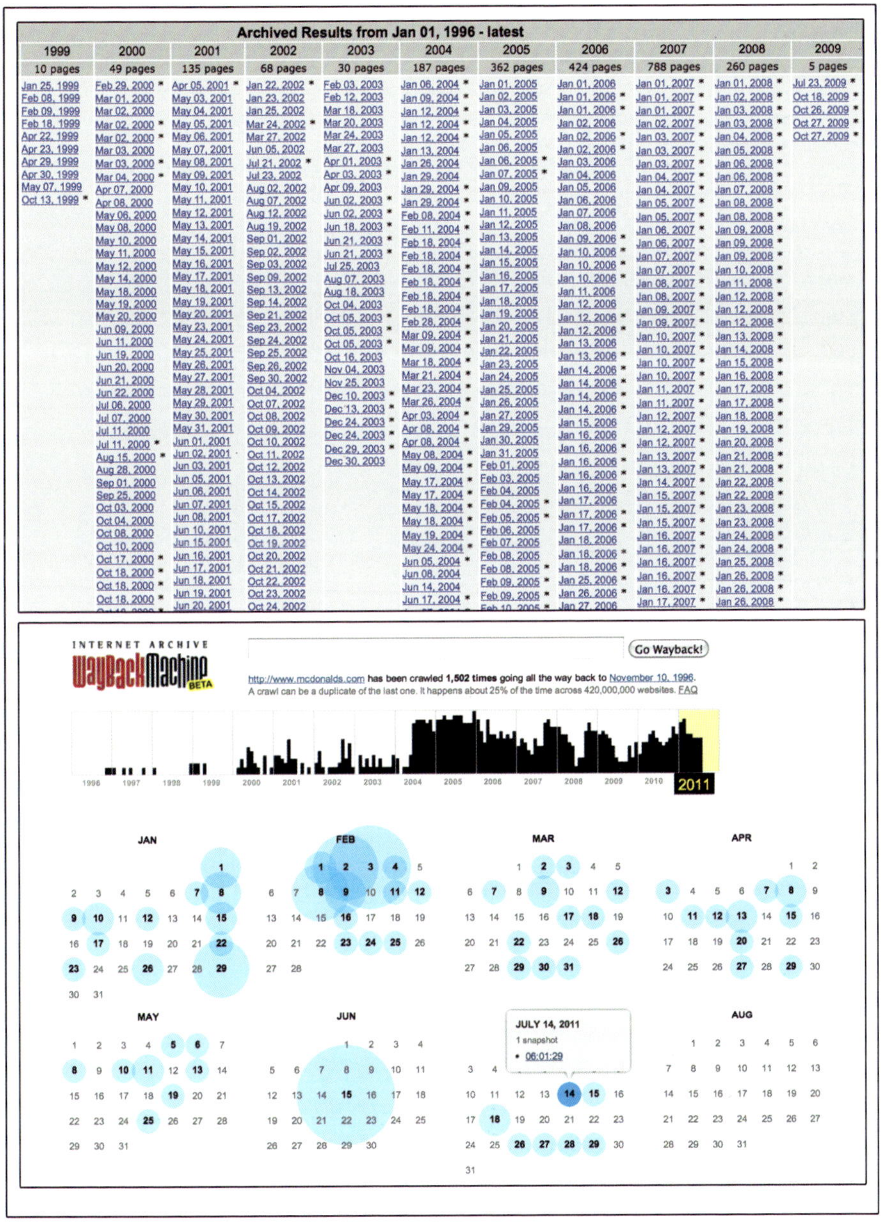

FIGURE 6.15 Which interface would you rather work with, the one on top or the one on bottom? Navigating online databases and archives can be an arduous task. Making the interface fun and visual can make the process more enjoyable for users and keep them coming back to your site.
Source: wayback .archive.org

FORMS

You probably use electronic forms frequently: shopping online, logging into a game system, registering software, downloading phone apps, and such. In essence, you enter information and get feedback. Maybe your information goes to another party—Amazon.com needs your order, payment information, and

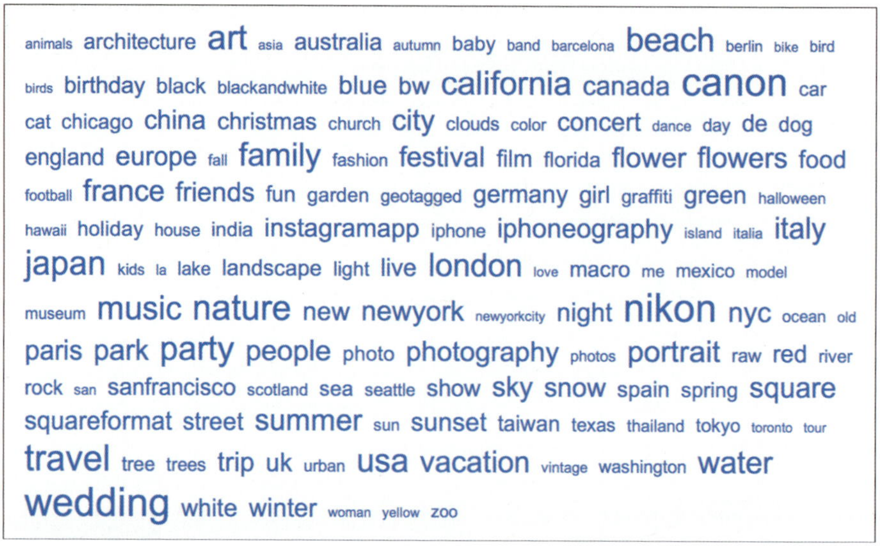

FIGURE 6.16
This tag cloud displays a collection of the "all-time" most popular tags generated by the users of Flickr's photo sharing website.
Source: www.flickr.com

address. But some forms just give you feedback, such as an inch-to-centimeter conversion calculator. The bottom line to making your forms successful is keeping them short and intuitive. The less you ask people to fill in, and the easier you make the process, the more likely they will actually complete and submit the form. Also, the more you avoid asking for sensitive information or information they might not readily have on hand, the more complete forms you'll get back.

When you create a form, you can give users preset options to choose from with checkboxes, radio buttons, and dropdown lists, or you can have them type content into text fields (see Figure 6.17). Here are a few options:

- *Checkboxes* (small squares) let users select multiple options, even all of them, if they'd like (e.g., interests: reading, playing music, playing sports, cooking).
- *Radio buttons* (small circles) let users choose among mutually exclusive options (e.g., yes or no; red, green, or orange).
- *Dropdown lists* (text followed by a triangular down arrow) also let users choose among mutually exclusive options, but you can reasonably include more options in a dropdown list than with radio buttons (e.g., a list of states to let you identify the state you live in).

Text fields let users type in what they want. Human beings are cognitive misers. We try to fill out those online forms as quickly as possible. Sometimes, we might not even bother to read instructions or labels when filling out a form. You can help your users fill in the blanks with less effort in several ways: by using autofill, prompt prefills, and tabbing. You should already be familiar with autofill and autosuggestions: many email editors and search engines use them. For instance,

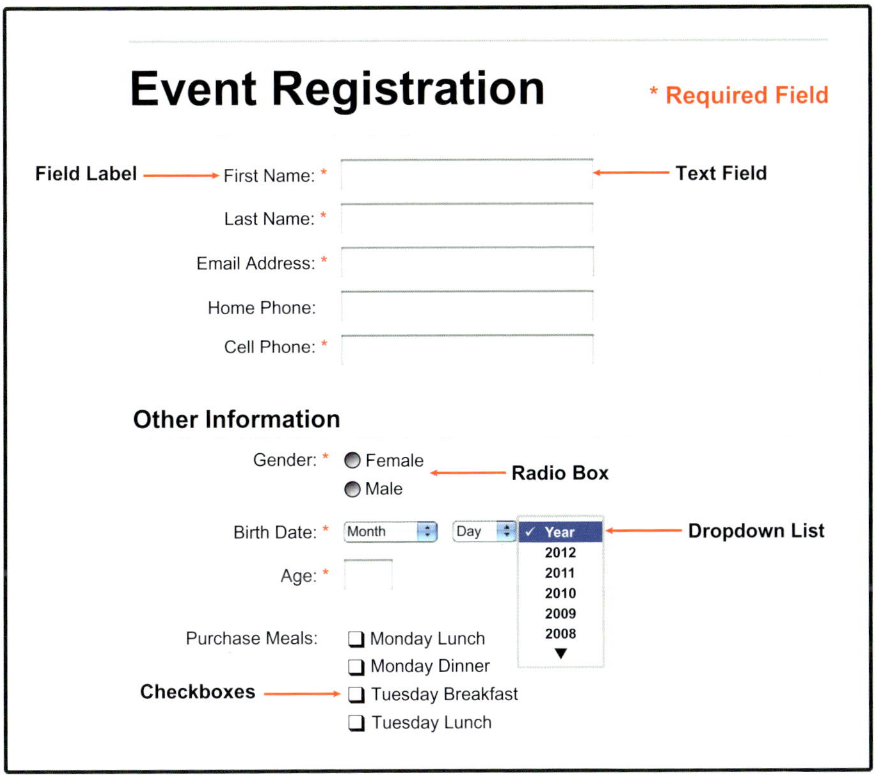

FIGURE 6.17
A typical form layout with text fields, dropdown lists, radio buttons, and checkboxes for user input.

as you enter the first few letters of a contact's name or an email address, some email editors use autofill and automatically fill in a complete address. As you type "multimedia" in Google.com's search field, you get an autosuggested list below the search box: "multimedia audio controller," "multimedia fusion 2," "multimedia audio controller driver," and more. And if you type two words, "multimedia website," you get more detailed suggestions of "multimedia website template," "multimedia website design," and others. Autofill and autosuggestion work best for the most commonly searched terms. If you try to look for something less common or rarely used, the system probably will not be able to provide good suggestions.

How often do you read all of the text on a form you complete? Input prompts prefill a text field with a prompt, telling you what to type. The website of EveryBlock New York City gives users a way to search for local news. The search fields are prefilled with an example—"e.g., 175 5th Ave., Manhattan, Williamsburg"—making the form field self-explanatory (see Figure 6.18). Without such input hints, users might quickly scan a site and miss or ignore the other hints below or next to text fields. But an input prompt that sits right where you start typing will

FIGURE 6.18
Input prompts provide a visual hint to users entering data into a form field.
Source: nyc.everyblock.com

grab your attention right away. Ideally, you should also use a script that clears the prompt text once your user starts to type. Also, if you design your forms so users can tab through them, they won't have to reposition the cursor to get to each new field.

TAILORING

In the early days of computing, every visitor to a website received the same interface. Web pages looked the same regardless who you were. Likewise, applications displayed the same screen no matter who the users were. Some sites and applications are still designed that way, but many interfaces now adapt to individual users, giving people tailored experiences. There are two types of tailoring: *personalization*, in which the system makes the changes, and *customization*, in which the user makes the changes.

Personalization

When a computer system personalizes your interface, it's using your previous actions (sometimes information you put in a profile) to predict your interests. In other words, it relies on your implicit interests rather than your explicitly expressed ones. For instance, Netflix.com might recommend *Avatar* based on the fact that you've rented other science fiction and fantasy movies. Facebook.com examines your profile and gives you relevant advertisements. Sometimes the process isn't perfect.

A system needs data to make effective predictions and recommendations. It might ask you to submit a questionnaire—collecting demographic, lifestyle, and content preference information—when you register with a website or an application. The system then applies rules and gives you a preset category of content that fits your profile. Another way it can collect that data is by data mining—such as with a website *clickstream*, or a record of your clicks—to anticipate what action you might take next. Both these approaches require you to log in to your own account. But it can collect data even if you don't have an account. Using cookies saved on your hard drive, the system can identify you and your browser, then give you an individualized welcome message and recommendations. But if you use a friend's computer or a public computer without first logging in to the site, you won't get a truly personalized interface.

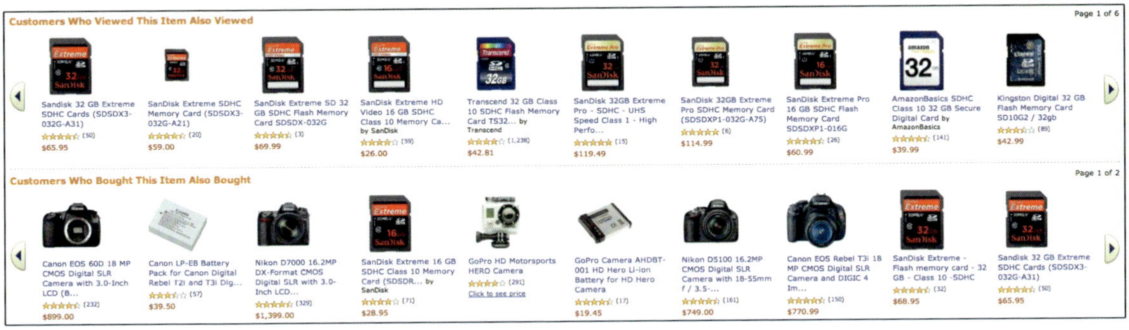

FIGURE 6.19
With every search, Amazon.com acquires valuable information about the shopping and buying habits of its customers. Through collaborative filtering, this information is personalized and shared with other shoppers who are conducting a similar search.
Source: www.amazon.com

One of the best ways to personalize an interface is with *collaborative filtering*. Collaborative filtering technology examines both your profile and the action you're taking, such as viewing a book on Amazon.com. It then bases feedback on what similar people who took that same action did. The group of like-minded people you are being compared to constantly changes based on what you're doing (see Figure 6.19).

Customization

Unlike personalization, customization allows users to deliberately tailor content, giving them agency. As a user, you can directly choose options or even create new content. As researcher Sampada Marathe explains, customization can be either cosmetic or functional.[1] *Cosmetic customization* lets you control presentation, such as the background, color, font, layout, graphics, and your profile photo. For instance, with a Wii, you can create an avatar of yourself, selecting a gender, hair and skin color, facial features, name, and body type. At the "feature" level of its interface, Facebook lets you hide your friend Bob's posts. And on iGoogle.com, you can change the background color and theme of the site (see Figure 6.20). As the name implies, *functional customization* lets you change the functionality of your interface. MyYahoo.com lets you add and remove applications on your page and even drag-and-drop to rearrange the order of applications. In Skype, you can create a specialized ringtone for contacts in your address book. A ringtone might be a statement, such as "Mike is calling," a song, or some other sound.

Sometimes personalization and customization work together in one interface. On YouTube.com, you can customize your own channel, changing its title, creating tags, changing the background theme and color, adding and removing functional modules. At the same time, YouTube.com will also suggest videos that you might be interested in based on what you recently viewed.

[1]Marathe, S. S. (2009). Investigating the psychology of task-based and presentation-based UI customization. CHI Extended Abstracts, 3129–3132.

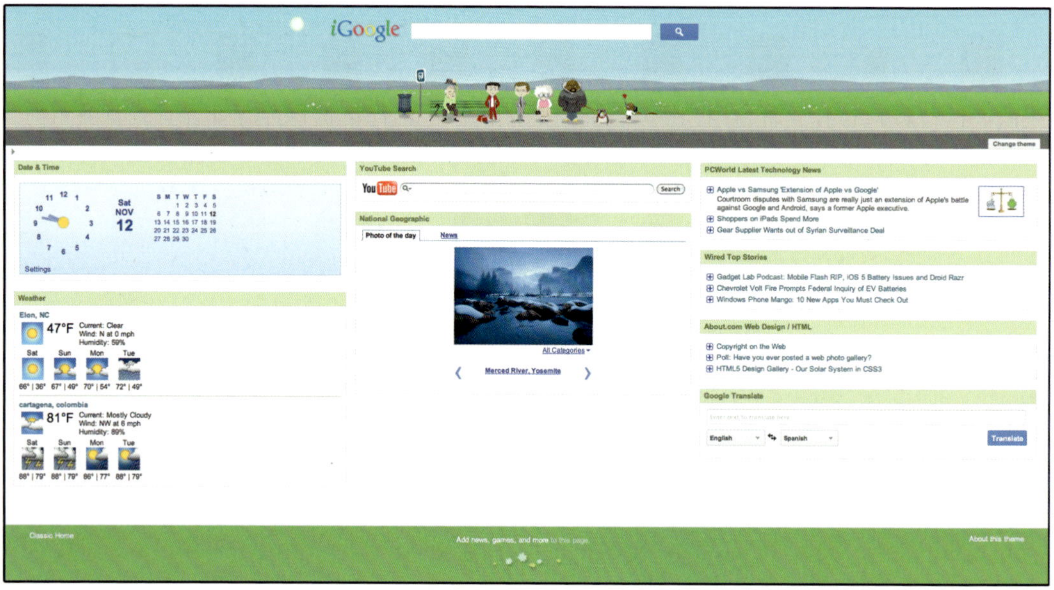

FIGURE 6.20
You can customize your iGoogle interface cosmetically by changing the theme and functionally by adding or removing gadgets.
Source: www.google.com

USABILITY

Have you ever used a website that isn't well organized or is complex but doesn't have a help menu? Perhaps you've used an online course management system that requires extra steps to upload an assignment, a word processor that loses a document because of one accidental click, a remote control with more buttons than you actually need, or a touch screen that does not respond quickly enough to the fine movement of your fingers. These are usability problems. Designers can identify many of these problems—and fix them—by focusing on usability during the design process: they apply usability methods, including usability testing, to make sure their products meet usability criteria.

Usability is a measure of people's experience with a user interface. We can apply the concept to anything a user uses, from software to hardware. Often, we apply it to user interfaces because they are what users interact with. Usability refers to the extent to which users can achieve their context-specific goals effectively, efficiently, and with satisfaction. Can users successfully achieve their goals? How much effort do they need to spend to complete a given task? And how much do they enjoy the experience? In other words, usability is about the user. It focuses on how to make the interface easier for people to use, rather than how to train people to better adapt to a poorly designed interface. It's hard to change the habits of a large group of users, and if an interface is hard to use, many users will find an alternative product or website that's easier to use. In the end, it's easier—and more profitable—to make the interface more usable. Check for usability early and often!

Jakob Nielsen identifies five essential criteria that make something usable: learnability, efficiency, memorability, error management, and satisfaction.[2]

Learnability

Learnability is how fast a user can accomplish the basic tasks on an interface that they have never used before. An interface will be easier to learn if its design taps into the core psychology of how we learn, and we learn well when something is familiar, generalizable, predictable, consistent, and simple. If the design of an interface is similar to the ones that users are familiar with, they will be able to navigate through it by generalizing what they've learned in the past. They will be able to predict what will happen when they click a certain button or figure out how to go back to the homepage. If you keep the design pattern of the interface consistent across different sections, users will be less confused and will need to adapt their behavior less. Learning is fast when there is not much to learn. Less complexity also can improve learnability.

Efficiency

Efficiency is how fast a user can perform tasks after learning how to use the interface. While learnability is about users' initial interactions with the interface, efficiency is about the effort users expend during repeated visits. For example, two shopping websites can be equally learnable if their check-out buttons are well placed, making it easy for users to complete a purchase. But one may be more efficient than the other. One may require a single step for completing the purchase, while the other may take four steps and require users to fill in several forms. An efficient website can ultimately save users a lot of time, make them happy about their experience, and boost both ratings and repeat business.

Memorability

If a user has used the interface before, can he or she still remember enough to use it effectively after being away from it for a while? This is the issue of *memorability*. It's not surprising that users tend to forget how to use interfaces they only use occasionally. If they use several different systems at the same time, such as three different banking websites, they'll have an even harder time. Relearning a system every time they come back takes extra time and effort, and some people may take their business elsewhere. Memorable feedback helps users, and familiar visual cues make an interface both more learnable and memorable.

Error Management

Although usability is primarily focused on eliminating design mistakes rather than blaming users, we realize that people will click buttons we didn't expect them to click and make other decisions we might think of as errors. A good interface: (1) reduces the number of errors users might make; (2) decreases the severity of each error, and (3) makes it easy for users to recover from errors. If

---

[2]Nielson, J. (2010). Usability 101: Introduction to usability. Retrieved December 2nd 2010 from http://www.useit.com/alertbox/20030825.html.

possible, avoid creating situations in which users are likely to make mistakes. For example, if you expect users to look for content or a feature that's on another page, add a link to it on the current page. And if a user submits a form with an empty required field, send the user back to the partially completed form—not an empty one—and point out what's missing.

Satisfaction

Satisfaction is about enjoyment. How pleasant is the user's experience? How much do users like the interface, and how satisfied are they with it? We can learn about the other three elements of usability by watching users interact with the interface. Not so much with satisfaction: to understand satisfaction, we need to ask for users' subjective feedback.

If you are designing something only you will use, you can do almost anything. But most interface design is a creative activity bounded by constraints: time, money, environment, and more. Usability is just another constraint, an essential one. Checking usability lets you explicitly identify users' needs. You learn how people usually perform on interfaces similar to what you plan to design. It sheds light on real issues that you need to consider and inspires ideas for improvement. Usability is never the enemy of creativity. You, as the designer, ultimately choose the details of your design. But usability principles and testing give you a way to ensure that people will actually want to use your website, play your game, or visit your kiosk.

Usability Testing

If you want to ensure the usability of an interface, you need to conduct usability tests early on and again when you develop a working prototype. They are the best way to understand how users really experience your interface and where your design isn't intuitive. If you're faithfully following the design process we've discussed, you've already identified the target users of your interface and developed the prototypes mimicking the entire interface or the part of it you are interested in. Now recruit your test participants: several users or good user proxies. You can catch about 80% of the problems with your interface if you choose five to eight good users and design your test carefully. You can conduct usability tests in a lab or in a more natural setting, where the interface is supposed to be used.

There are several ways to conduct a usability test. Let's look at two: (1) *unobtrusive observation*, and (2) think-aloud protocols, also called *obtrusive observation*.

Whichever method you choose, avoid bias by using a script (such as the Test Facilitator's Guide available on Usability.gov) so each participant receives the same instructions when you explain tasks. Also, make participants comfortable with the process. People often have anxiety about testing, even when there's no grade involved. Remember to explain that the interface is being tested, not them. Tell them that any problems they have are problems with the interface and that they are helping you when they find problems.

With each method, you usually give participants one or more tasks to complete. With the unobtrusive observation method, after you give participants the basic instructions, you observe what they do without talking to them. You can record how much time they need to finish a task, how many errors they encounter, whether they are confused by a certain function, as well as their physical and emotional reactions. Even if you only have a paper prototype, you can give them tasks to complete (e.g., find out how to email the Vice President of Operations), have them point to where they would click, and watch what they do. In contrast, when you use the think-aloud method, you will not only keep a record of what they do, but also encourage them to talk about their experience as they interact with the interface. Is it hard or easy? What do they expect to happen when clicking a thumbnail or image? If they were to encounter a similar problem in a different interface, how would they solve it?

If you are testing a fuller prototype, give participants tasks that will require them to use or interact with at least the following types of components:

- main menu and submenus
- interactive components (forms, search boxes, popups, and so on)
- text and informative statements
- images (especially icons)

Ask your users to go to specific pages or screens, use forms, complete tasks that involve icons, and find answers to questions that require them to go to pages or screens buried in your architecture. Ask them to do anything an average user might do. If you have pages or screens that they can't get to in one or two clicks, choose some tasks that require them to go to these deeper spots. If you have submenus, choose tasks that require the users to use them. For instance, if you are designing a website for a club, and you have membership information that they can get to only from a submenu, ask a question about membership (e.g., How much are dues?). Make sure your design isn't missing features they want, like search boxes, contact links, and such. Get their reaction to the colors, fonts, layout, images, and other traits of your design.

With the think-aloud method, you can collect users' responses and understand their decision-making in real-time. You can also collect much of the same data you would in unobtrusive observation; however, you might interrupt the normal flow of users' interaction with the interface, making the interaction unnatural and some data meaningless. What will a users' "time on task" (the time it took them to complete a task) mean if you interrupted them to talk about what they were doing at length?

In addition to observing users' actions, you can carry out focus group research, letting users sit together and discuss their experiences with the interface. You can also collect their opinions in one-to-one interviews to get more in-depth feedback. Questionnaires, both pencil-and-paper and online, are yet another way to collect users' feedback after they finish interacting with the interface. If you would like to compare two types of interfaces or two functions of an interface, conduct an experiment.

Soliciting and Applying Feedback

Show users your prototype, but don't say, "It's great, isn't it? You like it, don't you?" Instead, ask them what they like and what they find problematic. As you watch each user, avoid giving help. Yes, of course you know how to find that piece of information: you put it there. You're not being tested: the interface is. The test is useless if you help your participant complete the task and then assume your design is good. If you're using the think-aloud method, neutral prompting is okay. Don't be afraid to prompt quiet users to share their thoughts, particularly if they look grumpy or confused. Pay attention to your users' reactions. If some of your users look irritated as they search again and again for a piece of content, your design probably has a problem.

If your users tell you that they don't like parts of your design, don't get upset. The point of getting feedback is to get honest critiques that will help you make necessary changes. You will probably find it helpful to have someone else ask the questions to make the process as neutral as possible. Designing is like writing: a sentence may sound great to you, and you might have written it as a sincere response to a problem, but it may confuse your reader or come across with the wrong tone. If you're upset, put the project aside for a while, and come back to working on it when you can consider the feedback without taking offense.

Use your test findings to help you refine design ideas, make the changes, and improve the interface. Again, you should carry out several iterations of usability testing throughout the interface design process.

MAKING INTERFACES ACCESSIBLE

Accessibility is a fundamental principle of user interface design. We typically define accessibility in terms of making sure users with disabilities can access your content, but an accessible interface can also help people with technological constraints, making it usable by as many people as possible. Let's examine how you can do both.

Accessibility features should addresses all kinds of disabilities that may affect people's use of interfaces, including visual, auditory, physical, and cognitive problems (both short- and long-term). People who can't see rely on assistive technologies such as screen readers, which read websites and other electronic documents aloud. But screen readers can't describe images if designers don't add alternative text (textual synopses that accompany the images and can be read aloud), so if you design an interface that relies on images, those users won't understand all of the content or even be able to access all of it. (We'll address this issue more in Chapter 7, "Web Design.") Interfaces with small fonts and tiny images are difficult for users with weak vision to read. Older people who lack fine motor control might not be able to precisely control the movement of a mouse or a joystick to interact with an interface. These are a few cases in which designers need to focus more on accessibility to guarantee equal access and equal opportunity for people with special needs.

GREAT IDEAS

Accessibility and the Law

A number of government acts call for accessibility. We'll talk about two. Section 508 of the Rehabilitation Act requires Federal agencies to make their information technology, such as websites, accessible to people with disabilities; this is frequently a requirement of organizations receiving Federal funding or doing business with the Federal government. Section 255 of the 1996 Telecommunications Act also calls for electronic media to be made accessible. Over the last few years, there have been a number of lawsuits regarding websites based on these and other laws. While many of them are still undecided, the last thing you want to do is open you or your client up to legal action.

Accessibility features tend to make interfaces more usable overall. In particular they benefit people without disabilities who use an interface under situational limitations. Environmental circumstances might constrain users' activities. In a quiet environment, such as a library, users might be uncomfortable if the interface makes unexpected sounds. If you build your interface with an easy-to-use mute option that still gives them the cues they need, you will help users avoid embarrassment. In contrast, it's hard for users to hear clearly in a noisy environment. Interfaces that show the content of conversation or the script of a video or audio clip benefit these users, not only those with hearing loss. Many people browse the Web on mobile devices; these users welcome websites with simpler navigation and input methods. When you design an interface, consider other usage situations, too, such as strong sunlight, slow Internet connections, and differences in operating systems and browsers.

Making sure your interface gracefully degrades, or changes with older technology, is important. Not every user will have the latest version of a browser or the most recent model of a mobile device. An accessible interface makes sure these differences in technology don't become an obstacle, preventing people from accessing content. That doesn't mean that we need to design interfaces based on the least advanced technology. But designers do need to consider average users' needs rather than developing an interface only for the latest technology. When designing a website, try turning off all the images and audio/video clips you've embedded to see how the layout would change without these elements. When developing content with Flash, consider how it would look on devices that don't support Flash, such as some mobile phones and iPads.

If you separate your content from its presentation (fonts, layouts, and so on), you'll have an easier time making it accessible. In Web design, you can accomplish this separation with cascading style sheets (CSS is discussed more fully in Chapter 7, "Web Design"). A set of well-designed style sheets allows users with disabilities to override your styles and apply idiosyncratic

GREAT IDEAS
Accessibility and Usability

Accessibility is related to usability. However, accessibility should not be confused with usability. Whereas usability refers to designing an effective, efficient, and satisfying interface, accessibility focuses on allowing more people, especially those with disabilities, to use that interface under more circumstances.

preferences: reverse-contrast text and larger headings for low-vision users, color schemes for color blind users, and more. And you can create separate style sheets for mobile devices and printing.

CHAPTER SUMMARY

The way that we interact with technology has evolved significantly through the years, and it continues to change. Motion tracking interfaces and multitouch interfaces probably will become more popular in the near future. Interface designers are also working on developing more natural input devices, some controlled by a user's natural eye gaze or even by brainwaves. The display devices we use are becoming lighter and more flexible, and upcoming devices will likely break some of our current conventions. Samsung recently demonstrated a transparent display that could be used for MP3 players, and LG has developed flexible e-paper that can be bent. In general, interfaces are becoming more intuitive and giving us more interactive experiences.

No matter what type of interface you create, it's essential to focus on real users throughout the design process. When you plan navigation features, consider how they will be used. When you design forms, make them easy to use. Consider tailoring your interface to give users a better experience. Whatever your ultimate design, work to ensure it is usable and accessible, not just trendy.

ABOUT THE AUTHOR

Qian Xu is an assistant professor in the School of Communications at Elon University, where she teaches graduate courses in Interactive Media. She received her Ph.D. from Penn State University. Her research and teaching interests focus on the social and psychological impact of media technology, user experience of online media, and online strategic communication.

CHAPTER 7

Web Design

—Susan A. Youngblood and Norman E. Youngblood

The future of cyberspace is not really about technology. Although it will obviously continue to develop, the essential technology is already here in one form or another. The thing we have to start recognizing is that cyberspace must be content-driven rather than technology-driven.

—Rick Schremp, *Cyberspace 2020* (Govtech.com), (1995)

Chapter Highlights

This chapter examines:

- The World Wide Web and Hypertext Markup Language (HTML)
- The basics of HTML code and the technology behind client/server networks
- How to create and manage project files and website assets
- The process for researching, planning, designing, producing, uploading, and testing a basic website
- The importance of separating meaning from presentation and designing accessible sites for all audiences

Key Terms

Accessibility
Absolute URL
Alternative Text
ARPANET
Attribute
Audience
Background Image
Bandwidth
Benchmarking
Block-Level Element
Body
Breadcrumb Trail
Broadband
Browser
Button
Button State
Cascading Style Sheets (CSS)
Compliant Browser
DHCP
Dial-up
Domain Name
Drop-down Menu
Element
File Transfer Protocol (FTP)
Forms
Frames
Head
Headings
HTTP
Hyperlink
Hypertext Markup Language (HTML)
Index Page
Inline Element
Internet
IP Address
Local Area Network (LAN)

HOW THE WEB WORKS

So what is this thing we call "the Web"? Perhaps the first thing to understand is that the World Wide Web (WWW) and the Internet are not the same thing, even if many people use the terms synonymously. The Web is a part of the Internet, usually the part we use through a web browser by entering an address beginning "http://." So what's the Internet? In his book, *Weaving the Web*, Tim Berners-Lee,[1] the inventor of the WWW, defines the Internet as a "global network of networks through which computers communicate by sending information in packets. Each network consists of computers connected by cables or wireless links." These computers communicate using a variety of network protocols (rules for communicating). The Internet encompass a wide variety of technologies, including email, the Web, File Transfer Protocol (FTP), and many others.

[1]Berners-Lee, T. (2000). Weaving the Web: The original and ultimate destiny of the World Wide Web by its inventor. New York: HarperCollins. p. 223.

Margins
Menu
Mockup
Navigation Bar
Nesting
Network
Nonbreaking Space
Padding
Plug-in
Property
Protocol
Quirks Mode
Relative URL
Rollover
Root Folder
Server
Site Design
Splash Page
Submenu
Tables
Tag
Tag Name
Title
Uniform Resource Locator (URL)
Usability
Virtual Private Network (VPN)
World Wide Web (WWW)
World Wide Web Consortium (W3C)

FLASHBACK

A Brief History of the Internet and the World Wide Web

In 1957, the Soviet Union launched Sputnik, the first manmade satellite. Concerned that the United States had fallen behind in scientific and military research, the Department of Defense established the Advanced Research Projects Agency (ARPA). In 1962, shortly before becoming the head of computer research at ARPA, computer scientist J.C.R. Licklider began talking about a “Galactic Network” of computers that would stretch across the globe. In 1966, ARPA researchers began work on the first iteration of his idea, ARPANET. Unveiled to the public in 1972, ARPANET connected a number of academic research centers across the United States. Email was added to the system the same year. Over the next 20 years, ARPANET was supplemented by other networks, most notably the National Science Foundation’s NSFNET in 1986.

In 1989, Tim Berners-Lee, a researcher at the European Organization for Nuclear Research (CERN), submitted a proposal to CERN to help researchers communicate by linking together documents located on different networked computers using hypertext: words in a document that, when selected, allow the user to move to another document. His project was accepted, and over the next year he developed the underpinnings of what is now the World Wide Web, including Hypertext Markup Language (HTML), the Uniform Resource Locator (URL), the web server, and, of course, the web browser. CERN connected to ARPANET in 1990, and CERN’s first web server went online on December 25, 1990.

The World Wide Web developed rapidly. In 1992, four Finnish college students released Erwise, the first graphical web browser. In 1993, the National Center for Supercomputing Applications (NCSA) released its own graphical web browser, Mosaic. A year later, Marc Andreessen, who had worked on Mosaic, released Netscape, a commercial graphical web browser. Also in 1994, Tim Berners-Lee and others involved in the creation of the Web established the World Wide Web Consortium (W3C) to create web standards, including how HTML should be written and how web browsers should interpret it. In 1995, Microsoft introduced its first browser, Internet Explorer. As the Web caught on, the number of sites grew exponentially. In January 1995, Jakob Nielsen estimated that the number of web servers was doubling every 53 days. To put that in perspective, there were around 1000 websites in March 1994 and over 10,000 by July 1995. While the doubling of web servers slowed to every 173 days by early 1997, the number of websites was well over 1,000,000 by mid-year—not bad growth given that the first web server went online in December 1990. The volume of material on the Web continues to increase rapidly. The search engine Google, which once listed how many pages it indexed, now just refers to billions.

HTML

Web pages are built using Hypertext Markup Language. Rather than being a programming language, HTML lets you put tags (markup) around your text so that the browser knows how to display it on the screen, which words or other objects are links, and where to go if you select the link, among other things. This chapter talks about the latest version, HTML 5, which has new features such as built-in support for playing media files, but mostly addresses those parts of HTML 5 that are compatible with HTML 4.01. That way, you can easily make your websites available to people using browsers that don't yet support HTML 5. The newer HTML 5 will be a much more versatile standard. If you are planning to work in the online industry, you will need to keep your knowledge current, though the finalized version isn't slated for release until 2014. In addition to adding new elements, HTML 5 should free developers from having to rely so heavily on JavaScript and plug-ins such as Flash. Keep tabs on the latest HTML 5 decisions on the W3C website; if the information on that site is too technical for you, read the latest tech blogs and other well-updated sites about HTML 5.

HTML files are just text. Although many people use web design software such as Dreamweaver and Expression Web to create web pages, you can create them with nothing more than a basic text editor such as Notepad in Windows. The graphics used in a web page are not actually inside the text document, but are referenced in the code and then uploaded along with the HTML file to the server. Formatting the text works much like a word processor, assuming you had to type in the commands to make things bold, italicized, etc., which once upon a time you actually had to do. Most, but not all, elements have a *start tag* and an *end tag* (also called *opening* and *closing tags*), which tell the browser to start doing something and to stop doing something. Figure 7.1, shows one way to render text in bold.

In addition to marking up how things look graphically, you can also mark up the text semantically, giving different parts meaning, as in labeling some text as a paragraph (<p></p>). Instead of marking something as being in bold (<b></b>), you can mark it as being strong (<strong></strong>). The same is true for italicizing. You could mark up the text to be presented in italics (<i></i>), but it's better to mark it up semantically as emphasized text (<em></em>). If you decide later to make text tagged with <em> bolded rather than italicized, you can do that without changing the HTML tags.

Good designers try to use semantic—or meaningful—markup rather than markup that controls presentation alone. So they opt for <em> tags rather than tags like <i> and control how the emphasized text looks in a style sheet, usually in a separate file. We'll get more into that later. For now, picture labeling your text in meaningful ways—with chunks marked up as headings, paragraphs, lists, block quotes, images, links, and emphasized text—and having a separate file control how it all looks. You might have a 500-page site, but at a whim, you could change that one style sheet file and make all of the paragraphs display in Arial rather than in Times New Roman without changing anything in those 500 pages. Handy, no?

The <b> tells the browser to start making the text bold, and the </b> tells it to stop making it bold.

You can also tell the browser to change the font, size, and color of the text. We'll look at this in more detail a bit later.

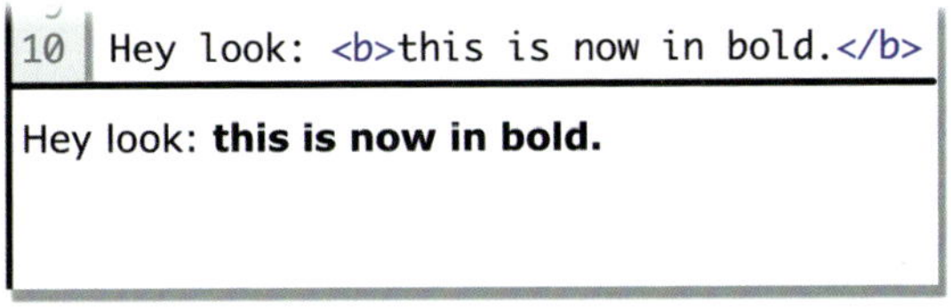

FIGURE 7.1
How tagging works.

Tech Talk

Sections of an HTML Document Your HTML document is divided into three sections:

Declarations. At the very top of the document, you should include at least a "doctype" declaration. This bit of code has to be exactly right for the browser to interpret the page correctly. The browser needs to know whether the code it's interpreting is HTML 5 or an older version of HTML with a few now-out-of-date conventions. Also, you might include a character encoding declaration that tells the browser what character set the server uses to store and transmit your site's information. This second declaration is optional and only one of several ways to accomplish this task.

Head. Like the head on a body, to some extent it controls what the body does. Most information you put into your head is invisible to the user. This section of code is at the top of your page between the head tags (<head> </head>).

Body. Most of the information you place in the body is information you want the user to see or code that directly controls how and where this information shows up. This section of code is below the head and between the body tags (<body></body>).

The declaration(s) come first, and the head and body are between the HTML tags. Your basic tags for an HTML 5 page will look something like Figure 7.2.

```
<!DOCTYPE html>
<html>
<head>
  <title>Appears in the browser's top and the browser's tab.</title>
</head>

<body>
  <p>Here's the text that the user will see.</p>
</body>
</html>
```

Here's the text that the user will see.

FIGURE 7.2
HTML 5 sample.

This technique is a much better way to manage a big site. It also lets you include a separate style sheet for mobile devices so users can easily get to your information on their phones and tablets. Also important, it gives visually impaired users who rely on assistive technology (including screen readers that read pages aloud) an idea of what your text means. Instead of marking up a piece of text so it's presented as Arial 14 pt bold, you could mark it up as a heading, and the screen reader would read it aloud as a heading!

Look back at that sample of code above. Notice how the head and body tags above are inside the HTML tags? This is called *nesting*. Have you ever had a set of nesting dolls, the two-part hollow dolls that stack inside each other? Tags work the same way. You have to make sure the start and end tags in one pair of tags fit completely inside the start and end tags of another pair. Just like it wouldn't work if you tried to put the head of a small doll on once the bottom is already sealed in a larger doll, as you can see in Figure 7.3, your HTML won't work if you don't nest the tags properly. HTML 5 lets you leave the end tags

```
<body>
  <p>This is a paragraph, and here is some <strong>bolded</strong>
  text. It will display correctly because the beginning and ending
  bold tags are both between the paragraph tags.</p>
```

This is a paragraph, and here is some **bolded** text. It will display correctly because the beginning and ending bold tags are both between the paragraph tags.

```
<body>
  <p>This is a paragraph, but it <strong>may not display correctly,
  </p> and when you make similar mistakes with other tags, you could
  cause serious problems on the page.</strong>
```

This is a paragraph, but it **may not display correctly,**

and when you make similar mistakes with other tags, you could cause serious problems on the page.

FIGURE 7.3
Nesting HTML tags.

off of certain elements, but you can also include those end tags. Because older versions of HTML require them for most elements—as do many elements in HTML 5—consistently using end tags is a good practice, with exceptions.

Some types of elements often deal with bigger chunks of information than others and usually begin on a new line. These are called *block-level elements*. Examples include paragraphs, lists, and list items (the separate bulleted or numbered items in a list). In contrast, *inline elements* such as strong tags, often control small chunks of information and are used within a block-level element. In the example shown in Figure 7.3, the paragraph element is block-level, and the strong element is inline. You can nest some block-level elements in others, and you can nest inline elements in block-level elements, but you can't nest block-level elements in inline elements (so you can't put paragraph tags between bold tags).

Let's take another look at the parts of an HTML page. While the browser knows it's looking at HTML, without the doctype declaration, it doesn't know which type of HTML. The W3C periodically issues new HTML standards, and the browser needs to know which version (doctype) is being used so that it can correctly interpret and render the page. If you don't include a doctype, the browser may not render the page correctly. Once all browsers support (correctly interpret and render) HTML 5, you'll be able to reliably use that simple piece of code: <!DOCTYPE html>. Although people are beginning to use the draft version of HTML 5, it is still being developed and refined, so this doctype isn't standard yet. HTML 5 offers new features, but the code in this chapter is common to both HTML 5 and HTML 4.01, so you shouldn't have any problems. If browsers aren't displaying your page correctly, try using the "strict" doctype for HTML 4.01, a complicated piece of code that is best copied and pasted right from a reliable source, such as W3C. Here's what it looks like:

```
<!DOCTYPE HTML PUBLIC "-//W3C//DTD HTML 4.01//EN"
"http://www.w3.org/TR/html4/strict.dtd" >
```

Tech Talk

HTML Head Content Your web page head controls what the user sees at the top of the browser and in the tab. You have to include title tags (<title></title>); what's between them will appear as text on the tab and at the top of the browser. You might also include a link to a tiny image called a *favicon*, the little icon that appears in the browser tab next to the title. Now for the invisible head content:

- links to external style sheets (separate files that control how the pages look, maybe even for printing)
- style information (if you choose to control styles within the file rather than from a separate file)
- meta data—information about the HTML document such as the author, language of the content, character encoding, key words that help a search engine find your page, and so on—in meta tags (<meta> </meta>)
- links to other external script files, such as separate files with JavaScript
- tags that indicate which scripts are used in the body.

FIGURE 7.4
Anatomy of a basic tag.

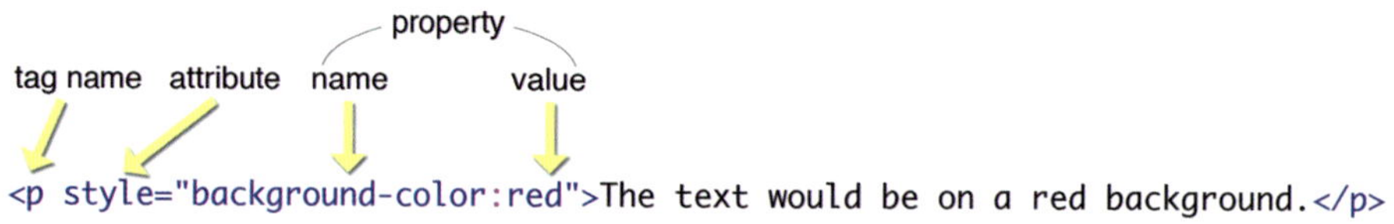

FIGURE 7.5
Anatomy of a complex tag.

Now let's look at some body tags, which control what the user sees. Although the tags in Figures 7.1 to 7.3 are simple, they get more complex. There can be several parts to a tag, as with the hyperlink in Figure 7.4.

Some resources call the tag the *element*, but technically the element here is everything from the start tag to the end tag and in between. HTML 5 will streamline code, making it cleaner (less cluttered and more efficient) and pushing developers to control presentation in external style sheets. You will find examples of older approaches to coding as you analyze pages to see how other people made cool things work, but you are better off controlling styles externally. In older code, especially, you might see examples of more complex attributes as shown in Figure 7.5. Again, though, you are better off controlling colors and other presentation characteristics from a separate style sheet file rather than within the element.

Let's look at a couple of things in the examples you just read. Did you notice that every time you saw an equal sign, it was always followed by quotation marks? This is a handy thing to remember as you start writing your own code. You'll probably read elsewhere that these quotation marks are optional in HTML 5, but since you sometimes need them to make your code work right, get in the habit of using them consistently. Also, did you notice that some of the code above was indented? Indenting your code can make it much easier to read and brings up another point: browsers ignore multiple spaces in HTML. If you put twenty spaces between two words, it's the same as putting one space between the words. Browsers also ignore blank lines you put between your words, as shown in Figure 7.6.

If the browser doesn't see a command telling it to put extra space between the words, it won't put the space in. HTML is generally not case-sensitive; even though the doctype is in uppercase, that's only by convention. Among the exceptions are special character commands, which have to be lowercase. Using lowercase is the best practice because these exceptions exist, and because lowercase is easier to read, most developers use lowercase, and the practice of using lowercase will prepare you to branch out into similar coding that is case-sensitive.

```
<body>
  <p>Here's a paragraph of text. It has two sentences.</p>
  <p>Here's a paragraph of text.
  It has two                      sentences.</p>
  <p>The two sentences look the same, even with the spaces.</p>
```

Here's a paragraph of text. It has two sentences.

Here's a paragraph of text. It has two sentences.

The two sentences look the same, even with the spaces.

FIGURE 7.6
Blank spaces in HTML.

Tech Talk

Special Characters Special character commands are great. They allow you to use symbols that are not part of the standard HTML character set, such as a copyright symbol © and quotation marks. Displaying symbols like these requires you to use special characters, © and " in this case. Special characters always begin with an ampersand (&) and end with a semicolon. Special character commands can also solve other problems. Above, you learned that HTML treats five spaces the same way it does a single space. But what if you want five spaces between the words? The special character command   (nonbreaking space) will come to the rescue, as Figure 7.7 shows.

```
<body>
<p>Here's a paragraph of text.     It has
two sentences.</p>
<p>By the way, you need a special character to make an
ampersand-&amp;.</p>
```

Here's a paragraph of text.   It has two sentences.

By the way, you need a special character to make an ampersand-&.

FIGURE 7.7
Special characters in HTML.

In addition to formatting and defining elements in a web page, you can, of course, create hyperlinks—this is why we use HTML, right? You can create links to spots within your web page, to other pages in your site, and to web pages on other websites. You do this by using the anchor tag with a hypertext reference attribute (<a href></a>). For example, the code in Figure 7.4 would take you to the Focal Press website when you click on the text "Link to Focal Press."

Browsers

One of the challenges to designing web pages is that what looks good in one browser may not always look good in another—the browsers don't always interpret HTML and other elements the same way. And there a number of web browsers: Firefox, Chrome, Internet Explorer, and Safari, to name a few. Not only is code sometimes interpreted differently between browsers, but different versions of the same browser may behave differently, and the same version of a browser may interpret code a bit differently when run on different platforms (Windows, versus Linux, versus Apple's OS X). Part of the problem is that HTML is an evolving language. The meanings of HTML tags sometimes change, new tags are added, and old tags are deprecated (made obsolete and invalid). Watch out for browsers that don't follow W3C standards. One of the most notorious is IE 6, which often requires special coding. Although it came out in 2001, there are still people using it, particularly outside of the U.S.

One thing most graphical browsers have in common is that they rely on plug-ins to show non-HTML-based material, such as video, Flash, Adobe Acrobat, and Microsoft Word files. Plug-ins allow you to run a program inside your web browser and have become an integral part of the Web. When you are designing a web page, you need to be careful about relying too heavily on content that requires plug-ins. If your end user doesn't have the plug-in, the page won't work correctly. Also, consider how many people browse the Web on mobile phones and other devices, such as the Kindle. Many types of devices have browsers that may not support all plug-ins. For instance, Flash isn't currently supported by Apple on the iPhone or iPad. As we move from HTML 4.01 to HTML 5, plug-ins are becoming less necessary. That said, HTML 5 won't be fully supported for several years.

When you develop a page, you need to make sure that users of graphical browsers will see what you want them to see, that mobile users can easily access materials—and the page isn't just a hard-to-read mini-version of the one you designed for the person using a desktop computer—and that other users can too. While most of us are familiar with graphical web browsers like the ones listed above, some text-based browsers are still in use, including Lynx and Bobcat. And you should also think about how users with assistive technology "see" your page. We'll talk more about that later.

The Network

THE URL: YOUR ADDRESS ON THE WEB

Communicating on the Web is a bit like communicating with postal mail—assuming you had to mail off a request for information every time you wanted

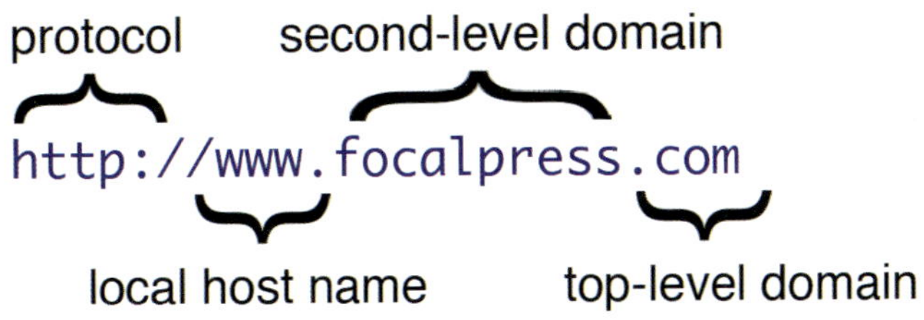

FIGURE 7.8
Anatomy of a uniform resource locator (URL).

something. Clicking on a link is like sending a request to a company for a brochure: you have to have the right address for the company (the web address), and you have to have a return address of sorts (at least a temporary address for the company to mail the brochure to). Focal Press's web address—http://www.focalpress.com—is an example of a Uniform Resource Locator (URL). The URL includes the protocol, or the set of rules that controls how data are exchanged over a network: in this case Hypertext Transfer Protocol (HTTP). Figure 7.8 breaks down the component parts of the URL. It also includes the domain name of the server, focalpress.com, and the local host name, www (the part that says "look on the server Focal Press has named *www*"). It could include the name of a specific file as well, set off with a slash (as with http://www.focalpress.com/web.aspx), and even a list of folders the computer has to look in to find that file (the path, between slashes after the domain name—/books/film_and_video/—show the folder structure). Browsers are not limited to just using HTTP. They can also read HTTPS, which is secure HTTP; FTP (File Transfer Protocol), which is used for uploading and downloading files; RTSP (Real-Time Streaming Protocol), which is used for streaming media; and a variety of other protocols.

The server name can be broken down as well, and we do this by reading the dot-separated domains from right to left. The last section, the .com, is a top-level domain (TLD). In this case, it indicates that the site is a commercial domain. A site ending in .gov would be a government (probably American) site. There are currently about 280 top-level domains. In addition to indicating what type of site a page is on, a top-level domain can also indicate what country the site is located in, for example, .us (United States), .uk (United Kingdom), and .de (Germany—from Deutschland). The middle section, the .focalpress, is a subdomain, or a second-level domain, and usually refers to the name of the organization to which the site belongs. In some cases, organizations may even use third- and fourth-level domains. The front section, in this case www, is a local host name.

If you want to choose a cool domain name—something meaningful and easy to remember—go to a domain name registry service and search to see if the name you want is available. Once you find an available name, you can pay the fee to have that name licensed to you for the year (or prepay to have it licensed for multiple years). You'll also need a web hosting service, or space you can rent on a server that's always on. The web host will let you associate your domain name with their IP address. Some web hosting companies provide both domain name licenses and hosting.

SERVERS AND IP ADDRESSES

For others to access a website, the files have to be on a server, or a computer that receives requests for data over the Web and then sends back the right data. If you are creating a website, you won't have any visitors until the site is published on a server (just like a budding author won't have readers until the publisher prints and distributes that best-seller-to-be).

To get the Focal Press home page when you type in http://www.focalpress.com, the network has to send the request to the right computer, and that computer has a number. The entire domain name is linked to an IP address, a unique numerical address that computers use to identify each other over a network. Focal Press's IP address is 216.139.220.211. If you type in http://216.139.220.211, you'll reach the same page you would if you typed in the easier-to-remember http://www.focalpress.com. Computers that function as servers usually have static IP addresses; that is, their IP addresses don't change. Your personal computer has to have an IP address to work on a network (some place for the server to send the page you request when you click or type in a URL), but it may instead be a dynamic IP address—it may change from time to time. Your computer acquires a dynamic IP address from a Dynamic Host Configuration Protocol (DHCP) server. IT administrators typically use DHCP to reduce the number of IP addresses they need and to make it easier for them to keep up with which IP addresses are in use. This is important. If you have two computers with the same IP address on a network, one of them won't connect to the network correctly. This can be a disaster if the machine with the problem is a server.

You can load your files onto the server in a number of ways. The most common way is using File Transfer Protocol, or FTP, a protocol or set of rules for transferring files. You don't need to know much about FTP to use it: although you can get standalone FTP client software—software that allows you to transfer files this way—most commercial web design software will have a built in FTP client. Any time your computer is connected to a server, it becomes a client of that server. It doesn't matter what information the server is providing. As you spend more time working with computers, you'll probably encounter other types of servers, including print servers (computers that provide you with access to an attached printer) and file servers (computers that let you store and retrieve documents).

INTRANETS

We tend to think about web content as being something we use on the Internet; however, designers also build content for use on *Intranets*. Intranets frequently work much like the Internet itself and rely on many of the same protocols, including HTTP. Whereas the Internet is generally considered a public arena, Intranets are private and are usually restricted to employees of a company. In many cases, a company will restrict the use of its Intranet to computers with IP addresses owned by the company. Users outside the company's local area network (LAN) have to log in to a Virtual Private Network (VPN) server so that they can get an authorized IP address and gain access to the company's Intranet. If you are in college, you may already be logging in to a VPN to get access to resources not otherwise available from off campus (such as library databases), or possibly to use the campus wireless network.

PLANNING SITE STRUCTURE AND NAVIGATION

You have a great idea for the content of a website, but a good site depends on good organization and good file naming schemes. One of the keys to managing your website is understanding what files go where and how to name your files. In most cases you won't be building your site directly on the web server. Instead, you'll create the site on your computer and then transfer the site to the server. This method has several advantages. First, it gives you a chance to preview the site before it's available to the world on the web server. Second, it allows you to keep a backup of the website on your local system. Commercially maintained web servers keep backups, but you'll always do well to have your own copy. Computers fail; it's a fact of life. Even if the people who maintain the server keep meticulous backups, a fire or other disaster might destroy the backups, particularly if they are stored in the same building and the same area as the server.

Defining a Site and the "Root Folder"

When you are setting up your site, you'll need to set up a *root folder* on your local computer (e.g., mysite). This is the folder in which you will store the files for your website. All the files you are using for the site must be in this folder, or in folders inside the root folder. Eventually, you'll need to find the information for publishing your website to the server. Again, unless you are using an older version of Expression Web (Microsoft's replacement for FrontPage), you will probably be publishing your files using FTP. You'll need to know the name of the FTP server too; this is probably, but not always, going to be the name of the web server and your root folder on the server. You'll also need your username and password.

GREAT IDEAS

File Naming Conventions

How you name your files is critical. Here are some general guidelines:

The main page of your website should be called index.htm or index.html. Most web servers are set up to display a default file if the user doesn't specify one; the names index.htm and index.html are standard options. When users type in http://epa.gov, the server sends them to http://epa.gov/index.html, the EPA's default home page. If you don't have a file with this name in your directory, the server will either give users a complete list of the files in the directory or give them an error message such as "Directory Listing Denied."

(Continued)

Be consistent with which file extensions you use for your web pages. A file extension is a suffix used to indicate a kind of file. Develop a religious-like devotion to .htm or .html, the two file extensions that tell the computer you have an HTML file. You can use either .htm or .html, but if you are not consistent, you risk ending up with both a project.htm and a project.html file and changing or uploading the wrong one. You can run into similar problems with naming JPEG graphic files. You're better off using the more standard .jpg instead of .jpeg.

Keep your file names lowercase. Lowercase file names tend to be easier to read. In addition, most web servers can tell the difference between uppercase and lowercase file names. Some servers are case-sensitive: even if you only have a Projects.htm file, the server may not find it if the user types the URL in lowercase. Also, you don't want to get caught in the trap of having a projects.htm file and a Projects.htm file and linking the wrong one.

Don't put spaces in your file names. Most web servers will not display spaces in a file name. Instead, they will fill the space with a %20, so the file name "my projects.htm" ends up being "my%20projects.htm." Not only does this look ugly, but it also makes it difficult for users to type in a file name. If you feel compelled to put spaces in, use an underscore: "my_projects.htm."

Don't use characters that aren't a letter, number, underscore, or hyphen. Such characters may cause problems with some servers and can make it difficult for people to remember or type a file name. You should also avoid using non-English letters such as ë.

Avoid extra periods. For example, my.project.htm. Periods in file names are generally used only to separate the name from the file extension.

Many of the above guidelines apply to non-HTML files as well, including graphics and video files. Some organizations have their own naming conventions. When you are working for others, make sure you learn their naming conventions and use them.

Establishing a Hierarchy

Most websites have a hierarchy, often with three main page levels, as shown in Figure 7.9:

- home (your default page, index.htm or index.html)
- main pages (linked from a main menu)
- content pages (linked from local navigation and from other content pages)

A first step in site design is deciding how many pages you need to link to in the main navigation on your home page and whether you'll need a submenu (also called *local navigation*). Your navigation area needs to be big enough to accommodate your major links. As you plan what users will click on to reach their destinations, create a chart to figure out how pages can be reached. Try to plan your site so users can reach any page with three or fewer clicks from the homepage. Main menus usually run along the top of the page or the left-hand side of the page. Users are used to navigation being in these areas. Avoid the right and bottom for main navigation.

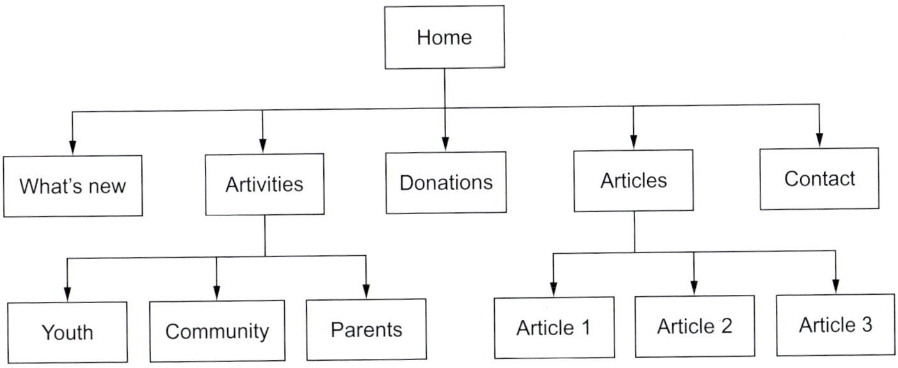

FIGURE 7.9 A hierarchical site map.

Maintaining Site Uniformity and Consistency

Repeating components, particularly the navigation, should be in the same location on each page. Users get frustrated when components move. Here are two approaches to make sure each page looks about the same:

- Design your basic page as a template, and create other pages in your site only from your template. Some web development software allows you to design one page as a template—a page that controls how all of the others look—and to make site-wide changes on that one page, making them ideal for larger sites.
- Design one page as index.html; copy the page, rename and save your copy, and edit it, adding a new title and new content.

PAGE DESIGN AND LAYOUT

Focus on creating a user-centered design from the start. What tasks do users need to complete? What information are they looking for? Use this information to define your site's scope and structure. Next, create a wireframe and mockup to work out ideas and to get client and user feedback. Choose a layout, select colors, and plan the items you want on your pages. Plan what a typical page of a site will look like well before coding it in HTML. Decide whether the pages will be fixed-width, elastic (growing and shrinking based on the browser's width), or liquid (stretching to fill the browser). As we discussed in Chapter 5, "Multimedia Page Design," and Chapter 6, "Interface Design and Usability," pay attention to what resolution your users typically use.

If you're working on your personal website and don't need a client's approval, your wireframe (rough sketch) may evolve from a series of rough pencil sketches, and you'll probably quickly move into creating a mockup. After your pencil sketch, make a more detailed mockup in something other than your web editing software so you can focus solely on design without becoming distracted by coding problems. If you're skilled at using a program like Adobe Photoshop, you can drop in blocks of color, add images, and add samples of text. Alternatively, you could work with a drag-and-drop wireframe/mockup application or create more precise paper and pencil drawings. But how do you begin that mockup?

Careful planning can prevent having to rebuild an entire site. Decide what components your web page needs, and create a space for each component. If you plan to have other pages with different components, set aside space for those, too, so you are not changing the existing design as you make new pages. As in a newspaper, make sure the most important information is "above the fold" and doesn't require the user to scroll down. Don't make users scroll horizontally. An inverted L (flipped top to bottom, not rotated) is a classic site design, and it's a good place to begin for your first website. As shown in Figure 7.10, use the L itself for navigation—your menus—and items like your site title or logo. Use the area framed by the L for text and additional images. Place informative statements at the bottom. In Chapter 5, "Multimedia Page Design," you learned about the basics of the CSS Box Model. Use these boxes, or *divs* (divisions), to put the main components of your web page in. You'll use a style sheet to control the size, position, and appearance of each box.

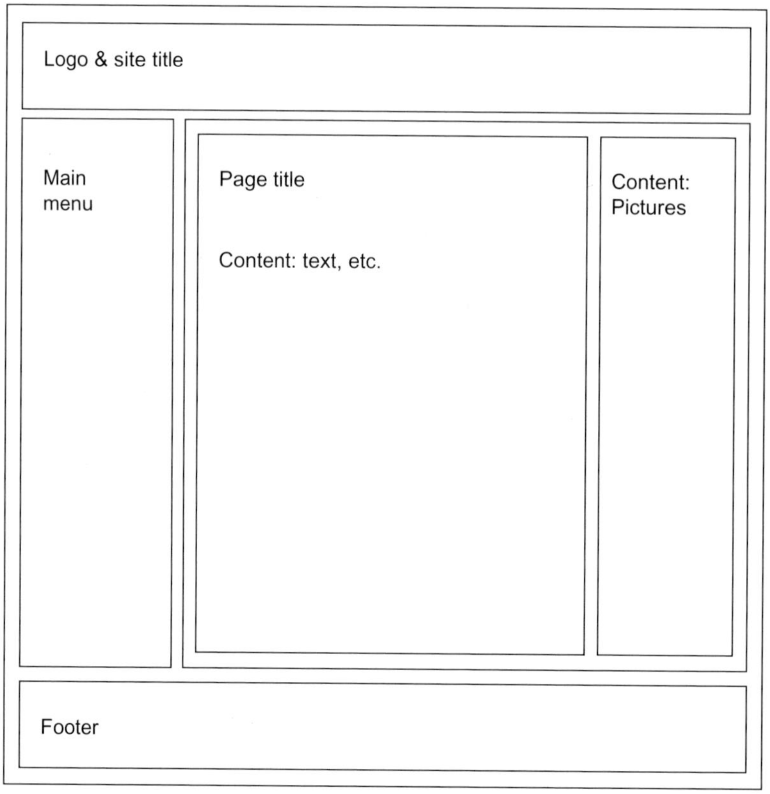

FIGURE 7.10
The box layout.

ENSURING SITE USABILITY

Design is a process. As we discussed in Chapter 3, "Planning and Design," before you even write any code, you need to

- plan the scope of your site
- learn about your users
- sketch layouts (draw wireframes) to plan where your page components will go
- solicit preliminary user feedback
- and create a mockup

Learn about your users' needs and conduct usability testing along the way. Follow the process in Chapter 3 as you design, and make sure you check your code and test for crossplatform compatibility, as we will discuss later in this chapter. Test to see how long your page takes to download—many web-design tools, such as Adobe Dreamweaver, can help with this. Research suggests that 40% of users will leave a site if it takes more than 3 seconds to load.

You have a plan for a representative page. Now for the dirty work: creating a working prototype. Start with one master page or template, and test it, as you are working, on multiple browsers and operating systems (platforms). This may be the most labor-intensive page you create. Make sure you can implement your design without lots of problems. If you can't get something to work, modify your design before you create multiple pages.

Figure 7.11 shows the basic boxes for a page and the accompanying code. Each of the boxes is created by a div element. Look at each div and its id attribute (essentially, a label for a unique item on the page): the section where a header graphic might go is <div id="header">, the box for the navigation is <div id="nav">, and

Here's a basic page. The dotted lines won't be visible to users.

Once you define widths and heights or add content, you will have something like this:

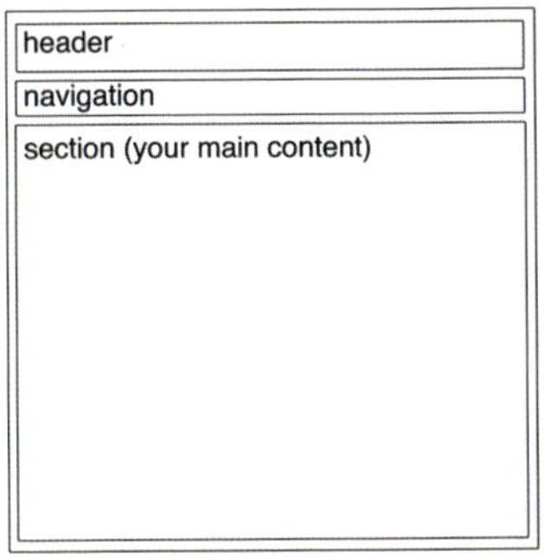


```
<body>
  <div id="wrapper">
    <div id="header">header</div>
     <div id="nav">nav</div>
    <div id="section">section</div>
  </div>
  <!--End of the "wrapper." This comment
  will not be displayed to users.-->
```

FIGURE 7.11
Coding the box layout.

the box for your main text or other information is <div id="section">. You'll notice that all three of these are contained in a larger box: <div id="container">. The properties for each div, such as its position, margin, background, or font characteristics, will be controlled by setting the properties for that id in a style sheet. The id attribute assumes that the label will only be use once on any given page. If you need to reuse a label more than once on a page, you need to use the class attribute. For example, if you were to add another div that you wanted styled the same way as the one labeled "section," you would need to use a class for each, not an id: <div class="section">. We'll talk more about class and id and style sheets a bit later in the chapter.

The boxes in Figure 7.11 are all made with generic div tags, and all current browsers will recognize them. Notice how, without the indenting, it might be hard to see which div an end tag closes? It gets harder when you make more complex pages and fill them with content. As HTML 5 becomes standard, move toward using semantic tags for most of these boxes (e.g., <nav> and <header>, <article> for syndicated-style articles, <section> for general content, etc.). For now, use divs and label them semantically (e.g., <div id="nav">) so you can transform them easily in the future, and so you can figure out which is which. Learn how to add HTML comments, like the one in Figure 7.11, to label the div end tags and add other important comments.

Notice, too, how the header, nav, and section divs are all nested inside the wrapper div? This structure gives you control, in CSS, to position the main part of the site as a whole (all the items in "wrapper"), perhaps against a larger color background that fills the whole browser, and also to position items within "wrapper" in relationship to the larger div and to each other. Without any fancy positioning, the items would show up in the normal flow from top to bottom, just as they are placed in the code. With a little CSS coding, you could move them around in relationship to one another—for instance, with the menu on the left—without changing your HTML. That's beyond the scope of this chapter, though.

When you pull up a web page in your browser, you'll see page title (<title> </title>) information above your browser's buttons. The page title, controlled in the head, is especially useful if you have multiple pages open, because each window or tab shows the page title, helping you find the right page when you move back and forth. The title makes the page more usable. Choose a meaningful title. Also, either choose a short title, or choose a title that has the basic site information in the first word or two: when titles appear in tabs, you'll usually see only the words at the beginning of the title. For example, if you were shopping for shirts online and had five pages open, a title that starts with the store name would be more useful than a title that starts with the word "shirts." Perhaps the title will include a pipe (|) separating the company name from the page name.

MARKING UP YOUR CONTENT

Add your content, marked up with HTML. Every chunk of text in your page needs to be labeled semantically, or in a meaningful way. If you don't put your text between semantic tags, the browser won't put spaces between your paragraphs and headings. You may cause other problems, too. Again, some elements are block-level and others are inline.

Headings

You will probably use headings throughout your website, much like a textbook uses headings. Headings give users a sense of the structure of a site at first glance, and assistive technology allows users to review the headings on a page without wading through all of the content. HTML gives you six options for heading sizes: h1 (the largest because it is the first level heading) through h6 (the smallest). You can define how these headings look by using a style sheet, but the headings will be easy to read and tell apart even if you don't use a style sheet. Headings automatically appear with space above and below them.

Paragraphs and Block Quotes

Much of your remaining text will be paragraphs, and you may also use block quotes for indented text. Browsers will put space above and below text with these tags, too.

Lists

Another useful way to mark text is with list tags. You may choose a bulleted list (an unordered list, or <ul>) for items that don't have to go in a particular order, or a numbered list (an ordered list, or <ol>) for items that are sequential; each uses list items (<li>). Alternatively, you might use a definition list (<dl>), in which each item is broken into two pieces, the definition term <dt> and the definition data <dd>. Figure 7.12, outlines the structure of each type list.

HTML Lists

Unorderd List:

```
<ul>
  <li>item 1</li>
  <li>item 2</li>
  <li>item 3</li>
</ul>
```

Ordered List:

```
<ol>
  <li>item 1</li>
  <li>item 2</li>
  <li>item 3</li>
</ol>
```

Definition List:

```
<dl>
  <dt>term 1</dt>
  <dd>definition 1</dd>
  <dt>term 2</dt>
  <dd>definition 2</dd>
  <dt>term 3</dt>
  <dd>definition 3</dd>
</dl>
```

Rendered Lists

Unorderd List:

- item 1
- item 2
- item 3

Ordered List:

1. item 1
2. item 2
3. item 3

Definition List:

term 1
    definition 1
term 2
    definition 2
term 3
    definition 3

FIGURE 7.12 The three types of lists.

Creating and Managing Hyperlinks

LINKING WITHIN THE WEBSITE

Links can be a bit tricky at first, because you use the same element (<a></a>) to put in an anchor and to create a link to that anchor or to another file. An *anchor* is a piece of code that tells the browser where to jump to on a page. Of course, the browser needs to receive instructions to make the jump, and those instructions come when you click on a link that directs it to the anchor. Figure 7.13 shows you how to create a link to content on the same page and to separate pages, both within and outside of your site.

Linking to other pages, whether on your site or not, uses the same principle: an anchor element with a hypertext reference. That hypertext reference will either be a path through your files to one of your documents (a *relative URL*) or a URL from someone else's site (an *absolute URL*), which includes the protocol (e.g., HTTP).

Use a relative URL to link to files in your website. A relative URL is the name of the file and cues to show where it is in your file structure relative to the current page. With this type of URL, you can post your site in another folder on the server but still have all of your internal links work. Also, if you change the folder structure as you work, some web design applications will give you the option to automatically rename your URLs so they continue to work. If you use absolute links by mistake, your links likely won't work correctly when you upload your files, and you'll have a maintenance headache.

If you want to link to a file in a different folder, you need to indicate the *path*, or the steps the browser has take to find the file. Figure 7.14 illustrates a sample file structure.

To link to:		
a different spot on the same page	Choose a name for that spot. Then put in an anchor. In this example, your anchor would be at the top of the page.	<a name="top"></a>
	Next, use the <a> element and the href attribute to set up your link. Use a hashmark (number sign) and the anchor name as the value. Think "a for anchor" and "href for hypertext reference" to remember how to write this tag.	<a href="#top">click here to return to the top</a>
a file in the same folder	Use a ***relative URL*** (listing the file location relative to the file with the link). Use the file name as your value.	<a href="index.htm">Visit my homepage.</a> <a href="resume.pdf">Download my resume.</a>
external pages	Use an ***absolute URL*** (listing the file location *independent* of the file with the link). Use an anchor element with a hypertext reference.	<a href= "http://www.focalpress.com"> Focal Press</a>
To control:		
how the file opens	Use the target attribute. Target values begin with an underscore. "_blank" makes the page open in a new window.	<a href= "http://www.focalpress.com" target="_blank"> Focal Press</a>

FIGURE 7.13
Linking content on the page and linking files.

Your site's file structure should be logical.

The example to the right has
- a **homepage** (index.html)
- three **main pages** (e.g., about.htm)
- three **main folders** (e.g., samples), each with one or two more files
- one **sub-folder** (grants) with files

Alternatively, you might design a site so all related files are in the same folder.

For instance, the **samples** folder could include the main page for portfolios, **portfolio.htm**, where you link to you shows and posters:

samples
portfolio.htm
shows.htm
posters.htm

index.htm

about.htm
about
resume.pdf

portfolio.htm
samples
shows.htm
posters.htm
writing.htm
grants
communityfoundationgrant.htm
ruralenergygrant.htm

design.htm
design
principles.htm
examples.htm

contact.htm

FIGURE 7.14
A sample file structure.

To link to a file:

down 1 folder	Set your href value as the folder name, a slash, and the file name. E.g., from the homepage (index.htm) to the resume.	`<a href="about/resume.pdf">My Resume</a>`
down 2 folders	Set your href value as the first folder name, a slash, the second folder name, a slash, and the file name. Make sure you list the folders in the correct order. E.g., from the homepage (index.htm) to the rural energy sample grant.	`<a href="samples/grants/ruralenergygrant.htm">Rural Energy Grant</a>`
up 1 folder (from a deeper page)	Set your href value as two periods (or dots), a slash, and the file name. E.g., from the principles page (in the design folder) to the homepage.	`<a href="../index.htm">Home</a>`
up 2 folders (from a deeper page)	Set your href value as *two* sets of dots and slashes. E.g., from the Rural Energy Grant page to the homepage.	`<a href="../../about.htm">About</a>`
up 1 folder, then down 1 folder	Use these techniques in combination to create more complicated paths. In this case, two dots and a slash bring you up a folder, and the folder name, slash, and file name bring you down to the file. E.g., a link from the principles page to the resume in the about folder.	`<a href="../about/resume.pdf">My Resume</a>`

FIGURE 7.15
Navigating directory paths in HTML.

Let's say you have everything in a folder named My Work. When you upload your site, you'll upload the contents of My Work, but not the folder itself. For now, you're working on the site offline (not the version on the server). A few files would be in that main folder: your homepage (index.htm) and your main pages (about.htm, portfolio.htm, design.htm, and contact.htm). Notice that the site has only one index.htm file, and it's in the main folder. That folder contains other folders with simple names to organize deeper site content. If this site had images, it would probably have an images folder. Figure 7.15 shows how to structure links between some the files shown on the right of Figure 7.14, including navigating up and down the directory structure. These navigation rules apply to your image files as well, not just HTML files.

Usually, when you click on a link that pulls up another part of the same website, the new page fills the same window or tab that the old page filled. This is one cue that you're still in the same site. This is the default way the browser opens links.

LINKING TO EXTERNAL SITES

Do you want to link to files (web pages, documents, audiovisuals) outside of your site? If you do, you need to use an absolute URL. Instead of showing the path to the right page or file, this link provides the complete URL, like the one you see in the address window of your browser:

```
<a href="http://www.focalpress.com">Visit our publisher, Focal Press.</a>
```

Sometimes, links to external sites open files in a new window using a target attribute, as you see in the last example in Figure 7.13.

THE NAVIGATION BAR

Links in the text are great, but you also need a navigation bar to get to the main pages and subpages. Navigation bars are often just images or styled text with links:

- ***Text.*** You can control the appearance of text-based buttons with a style sheet. Text links can display with background colors, change colors when you mouse over them, and so on.
- ***Separate images.*** Separate images can act as buttons, coded to swap out with other images when you mouse over them.
- ***Image maps.*** Single images can have designated hot spots, or places that trigger the browser to read URLs. These have drawbacks, though: they can be slow loading, problematic if they don't load, and cause accessibility problems.

Tech Talk

Creating an Email Link Have you ever clicked on an email address and had your computer pull up the email client (like Outlook or Mac Mail)? It's easy to get set up an email link. Start with the same structure as a text link (<a href=), but change the property: instead of using a URL, use mailto and add the email address:

```
<a href="mailto:usbkinfo@elsevier.com">Email
to order this book.</a>
```

Consider your audience before you add an email link like this. Many people don't have their email client set up because they either find it difficult to set up or are working on shared computers, as in a computer lab. Instead, they use web interfaces for email: they might go to yahoo.com and Yahoo's mail service without ever opening Outlook. For these people, it's a hassle when Outlook or another email client loads unexpectedly. If you choose to add an email link, use the email address as the linked text so (1) people can copy and paste it, and (2) people don't click on a name expecting to get more information about the person. Be aware that automated software collects email addresses for spam. This software collects links typed into web pages and included in email links. As you become more advanced, look into other options for including email addresses.

Navigation bars can be simple or complicated. You can use other types of code, like JavaScript, to create navigation bars, but some of these scripts slow down the browser or pose accessibility problems.

Linking Images and Adding Image Information

The image element (<img>) allows you to tell the browser to insert an image into the web page. It's important to understand that the image is a separate file from the HTML document. As shown in Figure 7.16, there are four critical attributes that need to accompany an img element:

- src: the source, or the location and name of the image file
- width: the image's width, measured in pixels
- height: the image's height, measured in pixels
- alt: an alternative text description of the image

Although most elements have both a start and end tag, the image element is a void element, meaning it doesn't have an end tag: all of its information is within one tag. Sometimes you'll see a slash within a void element, right before the last bracket; this is most commonly found in XHTML, a variant of HTLM. It's not used in HTML 4.01, and it's optional in HTML 5. Linking images is much like linking text. Instead of putting text between the start and end <a> tags, you need to refer to the image file you want to link, as you see in Figure 7.16.

Most of your users will be able to see the image just fine. Some, however, won't. Blind users have screen readers to tell them what's on the page. When these readers encounter a link like the one in Figure 7.16, they can't tell the user what the picture represents. This problem is particularly frustrating if the image is a

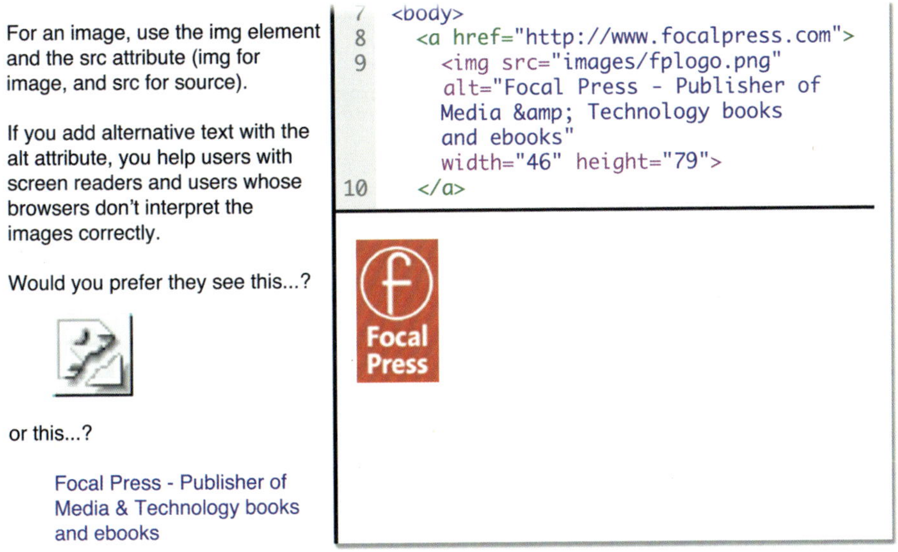

FIGURE 7.16
Linking images and using alternative text.

graphic button. Even if you create a site for visual artists and expect only sighted users, some images may not be rendered. Do you recall pulling up a page and seeing a box with an *X* or an odd error icon in it where the image should have been? That's a rendering problem. To make sure that content is still usable, add an alt attribute to your img element to describe it.

Creating Tables

Originally, HTML tables were designed to hold tabular data—and that is a great use for them. Some designers, unfortunately, use them to lay out web pages by turning off the borders and using the cells to place images, colors, and text right where they want. Don't fall into this trap. Tables are not as flexible as divs: they make your content harder to scale (harder to magnify and shrink) and your job of preparing the page for a different presentation—such as on a mobile phone—tricky, and they frustrate users who rely on assistive technologies like screen readers. (Among other things, imagine having to hear about the table as you listened to a web page being read: "Table with two columns and four rows. Welcome to ... "). Tables are still used to hold tabular data, though, so you might use one to show a menu of upcoming yoga courses and their prices at a gym.

Tables are built row by row. Essentially, you tell the browser you want a table; within that table you want a row; and inside that row you want a cell, another cell, and yet another cell. Then you add another row and continue. Imagine listening to a screen reader read these cells aloud as they are written in the code. You could create quite a mess for your users. So as you develop a table, make sure you build it correctly and use semantic, or meaningful, markup so assistive technology can help readers make sense of the information. Good tables include a summary attribute in the <table> tag, start with a caption, and are then built by row groups in up to three sections in this order:

- ***Table summary*** <table summary="Your summary.">. Summarize the content this way.
- ***Table caption*** <caption>. This caption serves as a title for the whole table.
- ***Table head*** <thead>. This row group contains labels (table headers) for each column. This row group must come first.
- ***Table foot*** <tfoot>. This row group contains a footer. Leave it out if you don't need it. If you include it, though, place the tags right after the end tag for the head.
- ***Table body*** <tbody>. This row group contains the cells in the body of the table, or the table data.

Within row groups, create rows and cells:

- ***Table rows*** <tr>. In your table head, your row will contain the next elements, the table headers. In your table foot and table body, your rows will contain table data (normal cells).

- ***Table headers*** <th>. You can (and should) add a header to each column to label what comes below.
- ***Table data*** <td>. Your cells (other than headers) are in table data elements.

Let's look at a simple table in Figure 7.17. You'll notice that the width is set to 400 pixels, and the border is set to 1 pixel. You can get rid of the border by setting it equal to zero.

```
<table border="1" width="400" summary="This table is an example of
how you should structure table code.">
<caption>Table 1. An example of an HTML table.</caption>
  <thead>
    <tr>
      <th>Col. 1</th>
      <th>Col. 2</th>
     </tr>
   </thead>
   <tfoot>
    <tr>
      <td>col. 1 info</td>
      <td>col. 2 info</td>
    </tr>
  </tfoot>
  <tbody>
    <tr>
      <td>col. 1, row 1</td>
      <td>col. 2, row 1</td>
     </tr>
     <tr>
      <td>col. 1, row 2</td>
      <td>col. 2, row 2</td>
     </tr>
  </tbody>
</table>
```

Table 1. An example of an HTML table.

Col. 1	Col. 2
col. 1, row 1	col. 2, row 1
col. 1, row 2	col. 2, row 2
col. 1 info	col. 2 info

FIGURE 7.17
The structure of a table.

Tech Talk

Controlling a Table's Appearance Now we've covered the basics, but how do you control the presentation, or how the table looks? If you put lots of text in your cells, your table will grow. How do you get control of your table size for layout? How can you merge and split cells, add space, and otherwise manage your table? Most web design applications let you skip typing the HTML to control your table's appearance and the table's structure. Even so, when your application asks you to set the characteristics of your table, you need to know what each characteristic controls. Here are a few basic characteristics you can control:

- **Table size.** You can control the width of your table as a whole (or by cell). Also, you can control height, setting a height for a cell, a row, or the whole table.
- **Merging cells.** You can merge cells by controlling the number of columns you want a cell to span or stretch across. For instance, if you wanted to add a title that stretched across the table in Figure 7.17, you could add a row at the top. Unless you use the colspan attribute, your title will only stretch across the first column. If you use colspan and add the value 2 (which tells the cell to "span 2 columns"), your cell will stretch across both columns.

(Continued)

- **Splitting cells.** You can split cells into two, with one stacking on top of the other, by using the rowspan attribute. If you'd like to split a cell into two side-by-side cells, add an extra cell (using the <td> element).
- **Grouping columns.** You can group a set of columns (e.g., the first five) using the <colgroup> element to control their width and alignment.

Let's look at a sample of other things you can control in your table. The presentation of your table (borders, spacing, alignment) is best controlled through CSS. If you are using an HTML editor to create the code, it may ask you for table characteristics and add the code to the table itself as attributes in various tags:

- **Alignment.** You can control the horizontal alignment of your cell contents (using the align attribute), and you can also control the vertical alignment (using valign).
- **Border.** You can control the line at the boundaries of each cell. You can control the thickness and color, or you can leave the border out.
- **Cell spacing.** You can control the space between cells. As you add cell spacing, the space between cell boundaries expands. Many web tables have borders with a 3D look because the designers added a bit of cell spacing: as the user, you see a border around each cell, and the borders have space between them.
- **Cell padding.** You can control the buffer space inside the cell, or the space between the edge of the cell and the contents of the cell.

CONTROLLING APPEARANCE: CASCADING STYLE SHEETS

There are four ways to control how something appears on the screen:

- ***Use standard HTML tags in the body.*** Choose semantic tags such as <em> and <strong>, rather than tags that only focus on presentation, such as <i> and <b>. Semantic tags will let you adjust the appearance of the tagged content elsewhere, such as in an external style sheet.
- ***Use style tags in the body (inline styles).*** If you want to adjust how one section of a page looks, you can use the style tag with just that section. A better practice, though, is to label that section and control it in an external style sheet.
- ***Use a style tag in the head (an internal style sheet) of your page.*** This tag will allow you to set font types, font sizes, margins, the appearance of headings and other text, the appearance of links, background colors, and so forth. If you are making a single-page site, this approach is okay. Otherwise, use an external style sheet.
- ***Use an external style sheet (a cascading style sheet).*** An external style sheet is a separate file (a .css file) that you refer to in the head. The browser reads both the HTML file and the .css file, which tells the browser how the page should look.

The best option is usually an external style sheet. These are called *cascading style sheets* (CSS) because of the way the rules for styles fall into a cascade, or how one rule overrides another: if you need one page to look different from the rest, you can override the CSS by using an internal style sheet or tags in the body. Or you might even refer to a separate external style sheet on that page. Even though there is a cascade in internal and inline styles—a background color you set inline in the body will override one you set in the head—when people refer to cascading style sheets, they generally mean external style sheets. If you have a large site and want to make a change to all your pages, you only need to change one piece of code in one CSS file. You might have a 100-page site, but you can change the color of all of your paragraphs with one small change to your style sheet. Much like regular HTML, most good web design tools like Dreamweaver will help you create your styles without getting too heavily into the code. Also like HTLM, CSS has different versions. Although the W3C is working on CSS 3, CSS 1 is the most widely supported version.

External style sheets use *selectors* to tell the browser what characteristics to apply the rule to. For instance, you might choose to make all first-level headings (<h1>s) blue. In your style sheet, you would write a bit of code (essentially a short sentence) to change all of those headings at once. In that case, h1 is your selector. You can select most elements and control their appearance and sometimes behavior in CSS. In addition, if you have a special element on your page that you want to treat differently, you could create an id selector that applies only to one element on a page and format it differently. In the HTML, you'd label the code using the id attribute. Perhaps you want to control your navigation div's position, fonts, and so on from your external style sheet (<div id="nav"></div>). Perhaps you want the button with the id "thispage" (the page you're on) to be a different color than all of your other navigation so the site's menu can indicate what page the user is on. Or you could create a class selector that can apply to several different tags, perhaps bits of text you want to put boxes around (<p class="boxed"></p>).

When you are debating whether to use a class or id when writing your code, think about how the section will be used. If it is a section of the page that is only going to be used once per page, such as a page footer, it should be an id. Otherwise, set it up as a class. Having trouble keeping track of this? Here's a helpful mnemonic—a student may have many classes, but should have only one student id card.

CHARACTERISTICS OF APPEARANCE

You have a basic structure and content. The properties that follow (using CSS) let you control the look. These characteristics can be controlled by inline styles or internal style sheets, but they are best controlled by external style sheets. Remember, separate the meaning of your content from the presentation to make the code easier to understand (somebody needs to maintain the pages), to make sitewide changes easier, and to make the content more accessible to users with disabilities.

Margins

Web page real estate is valuable. Although large margins are good on paper, most designers like to have small margins. When you set top and bottom margins, you are setting the space above and below your text and images. This space is added to the very top and bottom of your page. It is not a buffer of space, so it disappears when you scroll down. Left/right margins work in a similar way.

Define the value of your margins using the number of pixels (px) or one of several other measurement units (for instance, % for percent of the page width or height; pt for points; mm for millimeters; or em for em widths, the width of an "m" in whatever font size you use or whatever font the user's browser displays). You can define top and bottom margins, and you can also define left and right margins.

Background and Text Colors

Pay attention to your users' preferences and whether or not you need to tie in a client's color scheme. Let common sense and color theory guide your choices. Purchase a color wheel or look one up online (you don't need a precise example to make basic choices). Colors on opposite sides of the wheel, especially intense colors like bright blue and orange or red and green, will appear to vibrate if they're next to each other. Inverse text (light on dark) can strain your readers' eyes. Some combinations cause problems for colorblind users. Choose your color scheme carefully, view it on different monitors to make sure the colors look good, and use a visuals checker, such as Vischeck's free online checker, to make sure the contrast is adequate.

You can use color names for basic colors like blue and yellow. To achieve subtle variations, use hexadecimal codes for other colors (six-digit color codes, each digit using a number 0-9 or letter A-F, such as 0000FF for a common blue). These codes tell your browser how to combine red, green, and blue, giving you well over 16 million colors to choose from. Select colors from the web-safe colors—your web design application will have a palate that will let you choose from 256 colors—or select colors from the color wheel or spectrum in your design application. Most people now have browsers that do a good job of interpreting colors that are not on the web-safe list. Like other presentation characteristics, colors can be set in CSS.

Tech Talk

Background Images If you want to use an image as your background, choose one with a small file size to shorten the page-loading time. Images online don't need to be high resolution to make your page look good. A typical resolution for web images is 72 ppi (pixels per inch). Your image will be in a separate file (usually in an images folder), and you will refer to it in the HTML. The browser will read your code and pull the image into your web page. You control the background image with the body tag or CSS. You can use one large image as your background (which slows loading time), or you can use a small image and make it repeat, like tiles on a floor. Usually, if you use a tiled image, the image is designed to blend with the next tile, so it looks like a seamless pattern.

Font Type and Style

First, keep your lines of text short (about 40 to 60 characters per line), and avoid using all capital letters: they make text hard to read. Refer to Chapter 9, "Text," for more tips on designing type for on-screen display.

You've got a lot of content to fit on one page. A small font seems like a good idea, but is it really? Probably not. People generally prefer to see a larger font onscreen than on paper. Also, you may have users who are aging or wear glasses. Don't make your site hard for them to read. Another thing to keep in mind is that font size is relative to the font type you choose. In a word processor, 12 point Times New Roman will have smaller letters than 12 point Arial. The same is true for web pages: some font types are larger than others.

ABSOLUTE SIZES

One way to set your font size in HTML is by using absolute values. Instead of using points (as you would in a word processor), you'll use numbers, with 1 being the smallest font and 7 being the largest. If you don't set a font size, your paragraph text will be displayed in size 3 font (16 point font).

RELATIVE SIZES

Another way to set your font size in HTML is by using relative values. To use relative values, you first need to set your base font size (reset the default font size in the page properties window). Then, you select the relative sizes +1 to +6 for larger fonts and −1 to −6 for smaller fonts. The difference in font size will always be relative to the base font size you established for the site.

Link Characteristics

How do users know what text on a web page is a link or which links they have already followed? A site is more usable if users can identify links and tell which links they clicked on. Designers set different characteristics for links to make navigating easier using pseudo-classes, such as a:hover, which changes the properties of a link when the cursor is over the link or a: visited, which changes the color of links to already visited pages. Although links are often to web pages or other files, you can also use them to take users to a specific part of a web page.

If you don't want your linked text to be blue and underlined, you can change how it appears, but make sure you give the user good cues that the text is linked. Create your links in a distinct color, and style them so the browser adds underlining when you move the cursor over them (*mouse over* or *hover*). You can be creative, but apply color theory (such as by choosing colors for effect and selecting color analogs for your link pseudo-classes), and be consistent with link colors throughout your site.

To control text link appearance and states (how the link appears before, during, and after the user interacts with it), use an external style sheet. In your style sheet, you can control these and other states with pseudo-classes (a selector followed by information about the element's state):

- *Unvisited.* This is how your link shows up before you click on it. It should stand out from the page. Use the selector a:link.
- *Hover.* This is how your link appears when you mouse over, or move the cursor over, the link. Use the selector a:hover.
- *Active.* This is how your link shows up when you are clicking on the link and haven't yet released the mouse button. Use the selector a:active.
- *Visited.* This is how your link shows up after you have visited that page or document. Use the selector a:visited.

Like any text, you can control all sorts of properties of your links: margins, background colors, background images, borders, text decoration (like underlining), and so on, creating text-based buttons styled in CSS. The key is setting properties for separate states. Figure 7.18 shows how you can change link colors and make the underlining appear only when you move the cursor over the links

```
@charset "UTF-8";
/* CSS Document */

a:link {color: #9900FF; text-decoration: none;}
a:visited {color: #9966FF; text-decoration: none;}
a:hover {color: #660066;}
a:active {color: #336666;}
/* active color shows
when the link is
clicked */
```

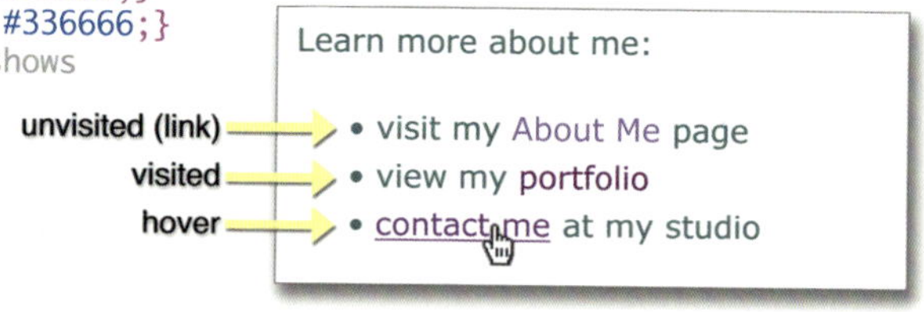

FIGURE 7.18
Controlling link pseudo-classes in CSS.

Tech Talk

Buttons and JavaScript How about image-based buttons? How can you get the same cool effects with buttons? Like text links, you set properties for different states. For each state, your web page can use an event handler to tell the browser to swap out images when you take a particular action (for instance, swap the silver button with the blue button when the cursor touches the image). Here are two common states used in JavaScript:

- ***onmouseover.*** This triggers the swap when you move the cursor over the linked image that serves as the button.
- ***onmouseout.*** This triggers a second swap (usually to the original image) when you move the cursor off the button.

These events are usually handled with JavaScript. Not to worry, though: your web design application should be able to create the JavaScript for you.

Interactive and Multimedia Web Content

We've just skimmed the surface of HTML 5 and CSS. You've probably visited sites with numerous visual effects, forms, music, videos, games, and so on. Many of these pages don't yet use HTML 5 to work, but instead use an older version of HTML, often relying on JavaScript or another scripting language—essentially bits of programming code that are inserted into the HTML. If you insert interactive features such as accordions (parts of the content that expand and contract when clicked) using Dreamweaver, the editor creates them using JavaScript. JavaScript is usually used as a client-side script, meaning it runs on the user's computer. It's free, simple—at least when you compare it to full programming languages—and well supported. Some features use server-side scripting, such as PHP (Hypertext Preprocessor) or ASP (Active Server Pages). These scripting languages are processed (run) by the server and send data back and forth between the user's computer and the server. If you think you'll need a server-side scripting language, learn more about your needs and options, and choose one before you choose a host for your site: you'll have to select a hosting package that supports that language.

In HTML 5, your job as a designer will be easier: some of the work of these scripting languages will be done by HTML elements, though scripting languages will still play a role. Where you once had to use scripts to make a page editable, for instance to let users make a list right on the web page, you'll be able to use the contenteditable tag (<contenteditable></contenteditable>). Where you once had to use a script to pop up a calendar to let someone choose a date for a form, you'll be able to use a simple input tag (e.g., <input type="date">). In other cases, HTML 5 elements will pair with scripting to more easily allow users to interact with the page. The canvas element (<canvas></canvas>) is one such case and will let users draw graphs and other things on the web page. HTML 5 will also allow you to more easily create drag-and-drop features. If you want to create a form for users to register with your site, you'll still need a server-side script, because you'll still need to get that data back to your server; however, many design tasks will be easier to accomplish.

To include media—music and video—designers have had to rely on the embed element (<embed></embed>) with lots of extra information in additional tags and hope the user had the right plug-in. Once HTML 5 is standard, you'll reliably be able to use more specific elements, such as audio and video (<audio src="mysong.ogg">my song</audio>, <video src="myvideo.ogg">my video</video>), without depending on plug-ins. You'll have to offer the right type of files, though, and HTML 5 compatible browsers are not consistent in which media files they will read. You will be able to control how the video plays, the size of the display, and so forth using attributes in the video tag itself. You can set the music or video to auto-play, but you're better off letting your users decide whether and when to play media. Overall, multimedia features in HTML 5 will let your coding be cleaner, let your media work well with the rest of the page, and give users with disabilities keyboard access to controls.

CHECKING YOUR CODE AND COMPATIBILITY

Along the way, check your code using a validator, or a code checker. W3C has an online HTML validator (http://validator.w3.org) and CSS validator (http://jigsaw.w3.org/css-validator). These tools check to see if your code is well-formed so that browsers display your page correctly. Remember that example early in the chapter when the tags weren't nested properly? Validators detect these problems and more. Some web design software has built-in tools for validating code and checking for compatibility problems, but you should also perform a separate check using the W3C tools.

After you've adjusted your design and created your master page or template, create other pages and *populate* them with content. In other words, fill in the pages with the information and images you or your clients want. Then, publish your site (post the files). If you don't want your users to see the unfinished product, post the site on another domain (at a different address). Once you have a working prototype, continue to check for—and fix—problems with appearance, links, functionality (for all users, including users with disabilities), crossplatform capabilities, and load times.

Test again for crossplatform compatibility. Bring up your site on multiple platforms (at least PC and Mac) and browsers (at a minimum, Firefox, Chrome, Internet Explorer, and Safari). Try viewing your site on older versions of the main browsers as well. If your site doesn't work, don't put up a "best viewed on" message: that message translates as "I didn't know what I was doing, so you'll have to use another computer or other software." Fix the site! Test for color displays and font appearances. Colors and fonts that look fine on a Mac may not look fine on a PC (fonts can vary subtly from platform to platform). Colors also may change between monitors. Average users will not color-correct their monitors: you can't assume that just because you're working on a color-corrected flat screen, your colors will display the same way on other flat screens. Check page-load times using your web design application; if you can't estimate the time, find a friend with a slow connection and try loading your page on your friend's computer. And make sure your site design holds together when you change the text size in your browser. If it doesn't, find the problems and fix them.

Even if you ran usability tests at earlier stages, run another test to catch the remaining problems. You want your site to be as usable as possible.

Accessibility Issues

We've talked about accessibility throughout this chapter and in Chapter 6, "Interface Design and Usability." When you think about your audience, always remember that some of your users may have different needs because of disabilities. The most common issue that you'll hear about is users who have a vision problem. These problems can range from color blindness to problems reading small print, to users who are completely blind and rely on a text reader to use the Web. Other disabilities you should consider are hearing loss; motor control issues (users who can't use a mouse, for instance); and cognitive problems, including, among others, problems with attention, memory, and reading. As you build your site, make sure it's usable for users with disabilities. Here are a few questions you should ask to start off:

- If I took away all of the nice presentation and was left with only text, links, and media …
  - could I access the information?
  - would the site be usable? (Would I be able to skip past a 30-item menu, or would I have to listen to it to reach the main content?)
  - would the information be in a logical order?
- If someone were to read me a list of headings (only what's in the heading tags), would I understand the structure of the page?
- Does every link have text associated with it?
- When I use color to indicate something, like a link, do I provide an alternative indicator too?
- Is the information logically organized so all users could get back to other areas easily?
- When I use sound and video to provide valuable content, do I also provide text to get that content?
- Would my menus be easy to use if my hand had a bit of a tremor?
- Do I have distracting items, such as flashing images?

This set of questions isn't complete. For more information, go to WebAIM.org, a leading accessibility site. Also, visit Section508.gov (see "Evaluate your site").

You can make some accommodations or adjustments for disabled users' needs with small bits of code. One of the easiest accommodations you can make for users with vision problems is putting in alternative text for images, called *alt attributes* (commonly, but mistakenly, called *alt tags*). Most web design applications will give you a spot to put this information when you insert an image in your web page. Without alt attributes, all the text reader will tell the user is that there is an image on the page. Alt attributes are critical when you are using images to create hyperlinks or to replace text. One of the nice things about using alternative text is that it will also make life easier for users on slower connections who might have turned images off in their web browser or people who are using a mobile device. Users with motor skill problems may have to navigate using the tab key—an issue you can address by setting the "tab order" on a page.

Use tools to help you fix accessibility problems, but don't rely on tools alone. Some web design applications have built-in accessibility checkers, and the W3C validator will warn you if you have images that are missing alt attributes. You can and should use online accessibility checkers, too. WAVE (http://wave.webaim.org) will give you a visual of your page and flag the problems it detects with red and yellow icons. Dreamweaver and other design software include similar tools. These are a great start, but they won't detect all problems (such as missing headings). Vischeck will show you how users with common forms of colorblindness will see your page. Mozilla's FANGS add-on will take an open page in Firefox and simulate how a text reader would render it. FANGS will let you see what these users will likely get if they pull up a headings list or a links list, too. Use these tools, but rely on common sense as well. Electronically detectable problems are a start, but you need to develop pages that make sense, pages that are *usable* by users with disabilities. Accessibility specialist Neal Ewers uses a badly designed form as an example: if a blind user has to read through an entire form before reading the context and instructions below it, the form isn't very usable.

Making your page accessible for any of these users will frequently increase the overall usability of the site on both computers and mobile devices. And as you learned in Chapter 6, "Interface Design and Usability," you may have a legal obligation to make your site accessible, too.

UPLOADING THE SITE TO THE SERVER

So you've finished your website and you need to upload it to the web server. Did you proofread your text? Dreamweaver and other editors have built-in spell checkers, but don't rely on them to do all your work, since spell checkers will miss correctly spelled words that are still the wrong word, e.g. there and their. Take a deep breath and push the button to upload your files. If you are using Dreamweaver, you may see a dialog box asking if you want to "include dependent files." What it is asking is whether or not you want to publish the images that the web page needs to display correctly. You'll want to say yes the first time you publish a page. After that, you'll only need to say yes if you need to update the images on the server, that is, you've added additional images or you've modified one of your images. Depending on the software you are using, you may need to upload audio and video files separately. Once you've published the site, pull it up in a web browser to make sure it is where it's supposed to be. If possible, check the website on a machine other than the one you created it on to make sure your pages don't reference any files on your local computer. If you need to change something, fire up your web editor, change the file, and republish it. If you don't have the file on your computer, you can always download it from the server. Remember that you have to enter the site definition on each computer you edit on to ensure that the links you create work properly later and that changes to your template are applied site-wide. If you are using a public machine, be sure to clear your username and password when you finish.

CHAPTER SUMMARY

As the tools and technology for creating and uploading web pages continue to become more user friendly, remember that production software and hardware issues play a relatively small role in determining the effectiveness of a website. The best sites will always be those with good navigational structures that are functional, easy to use, and accessible to all audiences; that provide substantive, timely, and meaningful content for the user; that feature attractive designs and page layouts; and that are maintained and updated by the webmaster on a regular basis. Such a site is only possible with thoughtful research, planning, design, and authoring on the part of the webmaster or production team.

About the Authors

Susan A. Youngblood teaches both graduate and undergraduate web development at Auburn University's Department of English in the Master of Technical and Professional Communication (MTPC) program. Her classes emphasize research-based best practices for design, accessibility, and usability testing. She helped plan the layout of Auburn's Instruction in Design, Evaluation, and Assessment (IDEA) lab—used mostly for teaching usability testing—and consulted on the installation of Auburn's new research-oriented usability and focus-group lab. She teaches students to be advocates not only for end users but also for their colleagues and clients who have to maintain the sites that they create. Susan's research interests include competing communication needs in online environments, usability, and web accessibility. Her work has appeared in the *Journal of Business and Technical Communication*, the *Journal of Technical Writing and Communication,* and in the edited collection *Handbook of Research on Virtual Workplaces and the New Nature of Business Practices,* edited by Pavel Zemliansky and Kirk St. Amant.

Norman E. Youngblood has been teaching courses on web design and interactive media since 2001 and has a background in information technology. He is an assistant professor in the Department of Communication and Journalism at Auburn University and the codirector and cofounder of a new university usability and communication research laboratory.

SECTION 3
Static Media

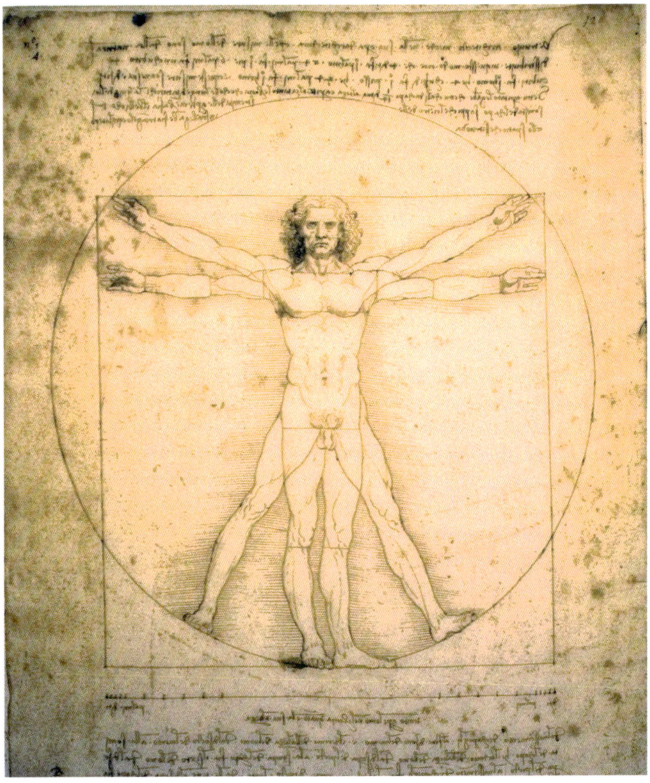

Reeed/Shutterstock.com

CHAPTER 8
Graphics

The whole is greater than the sum of its parts.

—Origins Unknown (but often attributed to Gestalt Psychology, 1920s)

Key Terms
Additive Color Mixing
Aliasing
Anti-aliasing
Aspect Ratio
ATSC
Bit Depth
CMYK
Color Space
Compression
Cropping
Dithering
DTV
DVB
EDTV
Field
Frame
Frame Rate
Graphic
HDTV
Hertz
Image
Interlaced Scanning
JPEG
Moving Image
Native Resolution
NTSC
Optimization
PAL
Path
Persistence of Vision
Pixel
Pixel Count
Pixel Dimensions
Progressive Scanning
Raster Image (or Bitmap)
Refresh Rate

Chapter Highlights

This chapter examines:

- The nature of computer graphics
- The raster image encoding process
- The vector graphics encoding process
- Moving image scanning technologies
- Computer and television display technologies
- World standards for Digital Television (DTV) broadcasting

GRAPHICS AND IMAGES

William Fetter coined the term *computer graphics* in 1960 while working as a graphic designer and art director for the Boeing Company. Today, this phrase describes processes in which pictorial data is encoded and displayed by computers and digital devices. Computer graphics are generally divided into two main categories: graphics and images.

Graphics

A *graphic* is any type of visual presentation that can be displayed on a physical surface like a sheet of paper, wall, poster, blackboard, or computer monitor. Graphics are a product of human imagination and are typically created by hand or with computer-assisted drawing and design tools. Graphics include things like stick figures, symbols, numbers, drawings, typography, logos, web buttons, illustrations, and line art (see Figure 8.1). A graphic designer is a media arts professional who creates graphics for use in print or electronic media.

Resampling
Resolution
RGB
Scaling
Scan Line
Scanning
SDTV
SECAM
Still Image
Subtractive Color Mixing
True Color
Unit of Measurement
Vector Graphic

FIGURE 8.1
This assortment of graphics includes clipart, logos, line art, and symbols.

Images

An *image* is a two- or three-dimensional representation of a person, animal, object, or scene in the natural world (see Figure 8.2). Images can be still or moving. A still or static image is one that is fixed in time. A moving image—or time-based image—is one that changes over time. Photographs, maps, charts, and graphs typically fall into the still image category. Broadcast television, digital video, and motion pictures are examples of moving images. As we'll see later in this chapter, moving images are made by presenting a sequence of still images in rapid succession to simulate the illusion of motion. In reality, there are no moving images, only the optical illusion of movement created by the repetitive presentation of static images.

DIGITAL IMAGING

A film camera uses a plastic strip, coated with a light-sensitive emulsion, to record a scene composed by the photographer. The film negative that's produced is real and can be handled, held up to the light, or passed along "physically" to someone else. In the digital world, everything is reduced to a number, including graphics. For example, a digital camera uses an optical image sensor to convert light into electrons (electrical energy). The electrical signal is converted into a digital recording and saved as a binary file made up of 0s and 1s. While a binary file cannot be touched or held up to the light, it is every bit as real to the computer as the film negative is to the photographer (see Figure 8.3).

FIGURE 8.2
A large collection of photographic images.

FIGURE 8.3
Brothers examine a strip of photographic negatives. (Left) In analog photography, the negative is used to make photographic prints. Because digital images are recorded numerically, they cannot be directly touched or viewed. (Right) A digital device or computer is required to render a binary image for output to a display screen or a printer.

Two methods are commonly used to digitally encode and display computer graphics. The first approach, called *bitmap* or *raster* imaging, uses pixels to define the structure of a digital image. Tiny squares of color, like tiles in a mosaic, make up the graphic. Depending on the number of pixels, or squares, per inch, you may not even notice them in the final digital or printed graphic. The second approach, called *vector imaging*, uses mathematically constructed paths to define a graphic's visual structure. In other words, it records a graphic as a group of interrelated points, lines, curves, and shapes. Table 8.1 compares some of the differences between the two methods.

Table 8.1 A Comparison of the Raster Image and the Vector Graphic

	Raster Image	**Vector Graphic**
Image Structure	Defined using pixels—square picture elements each representing a single color value.	Defined using paths—geometric areas defined by points, lines, curves, and shapes.
Editing Software	Adobe Photoshop, GIMP, Corel Painter, and Corel Paint Shop Pro	Adobe Illustrator, Adobe Flash, CorelDRAW, and Adobe FreeHand
Primary Output Channels	Best format for low-resolution electronic display. Used in digital photography, video, and web pages.	Best format for high-resolution printing and prepress applications. Also used for rendering 2D or 3D computer animation.
Ideal for …	Images with lots of color information and complexity.	Simple drawings, line art, clipart, and logos.
Scalability	Resolution-dependent (fixed number of pixels), so image quality deteriorates when enlarged.	Resolution-independent, so graphic can be resized without losing detail or clarity.
Common File Formats	.bmp, .gif, .jpg, .png, and .tif	.eps, .svg, .swf, and .wmf
File Size	Typically large. Raster images can be compressed to reduce file size. Some compression formats may cause the loss of image details.	Relatively small. Vector encoding is highly efficient.

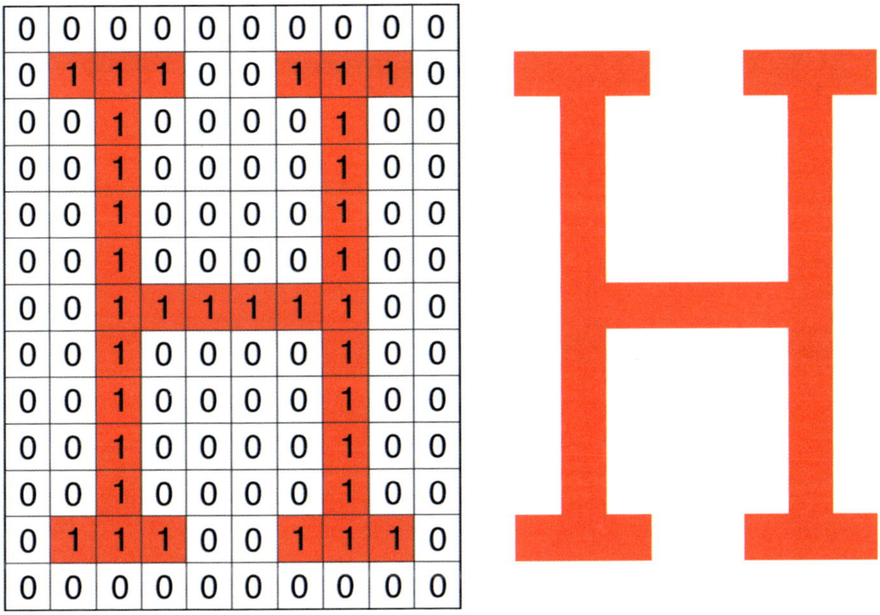

FIGURE 8.4
Thirty-five red pixels coalesce to form this bitmap graphic of a capital letter *H*.

Raster Images

A raster image is formed by dividing the area of an image into a rectangular matrix of rows and columns comprised of pixels (see Figure 8.4). A *pixel*, short for *picture element*, is a square (or occasionally rectangular) area of light representing a single point in a raster image. Every pixel in a raster image is exactly the same size and contains a single color value that's typically stored as a 24-bit string of binary data. The total number of pixels in a raster image is fixed. In order to make a raster image physically larger, more pixels have to be added to the raster matrix. Likewise, pixels need to be discarded when making a raster image smaller. The width and height of a raster image is determined by how many pixels each row and column contains.

On their own, pixels are relatively meaningless, but when combined with hundreds, thousands, and even millions of other pixels, complex patterns and photorealistic images can be formed. German psychologist Max Wertheimer (1880–1943) developed the concept of perceptual grouping to explain the human tendency to perceive whole shapes and patterns from an arrangement of smaller particles of visual information. This concept is commonly expressed as "the whole is greater than the sum of its parts." Take a look at the image in Figure 8.5 to see perceptual grouping at work.

The mosaic façade in this photograph is made up of thousands of individually colored tiles carefully arranged to form an exquisitely detailed composite image. It takes very little effort on the part of the viewer to overlook the individual pieces

FIGURE 8.5
From a distance, the individual pixels forming this image are barely perceptible to the naked eye. In fact, our brain works hard to achieve and maintain a holistic impression. Up close, however, we can see that many small pieces of visual information went into forming this 19th-century mosaic of Christ, the good shepherd.
Source: Historien d'art (Own work) [Public domain], via Wikimedia Commons

FIGURE 8.6
Digital image pixels are much smaller than the bits of tile used in mosaic art. You have to zoom in really close on this image before you'll see the pixels used to form it.

of glass and stone used by the artist. Instead, we're much more inclined to perceive the scene holistically, forming the impression intended by the artists' careful and purposeful arrangement. This technique of using tiny bits of colored material to form a composite visual impression dates back to about 3,000 BC and is still used today in the print and electronic media industries to convey visual information. In Figure 8.6 we see a digital photograph of a fruit basket. This image too is constructed of individual colored tiles. Millions of them in fact! These tiny pixels can be seen by zooming in on the image using a photo editing program such as Adobe Photoshop.

RESOLUTION

Resolution describes the image quality of a raster image and directly relates to the size and quantity of the pixels the image contains. In the illustration in Figure 8.7, the first drawing of the triangle has only three dots, making it a low-resolution image.

As more picture elements are added, the quality of the image improves considerably, moving it along a continuum from low- to high-resolution.

Simply put, the more pixels you have in a given area (for example, in a square inch), the more information you have, and the higher the resolution of the image. In the example in Figure 8.8, artist Peter Roche used nearly 10,000 Jelly Belly jellybeans to form this portrait of President Ronald Reagan (left). By comparison, the official White House portrait of President Reagan (right) consists of more than 4 million pixels.

Jellybeans are a creative medium for artistic expression, but they are quite large compared to the pixels used to from a digital image. Because of this, the image detail in the jellybean artwork pales in comparison to the resolution of the actual photograph. The pixels in the digital photo are so small that they are undetectable with the naked eye.

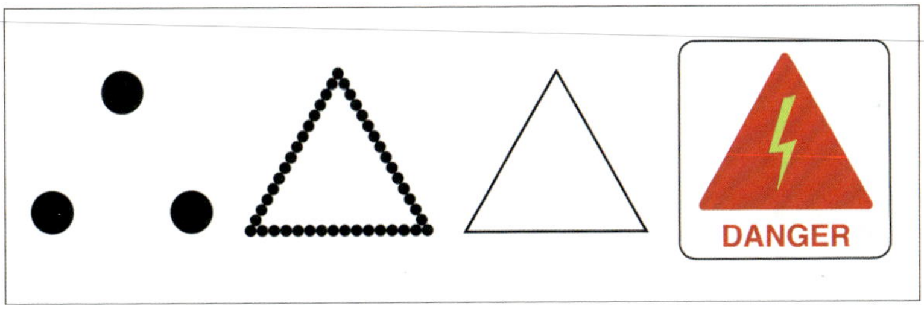

FIGURE 8.7
This sequence of four triangle graphics progresses from low-resolution to high-resolution (left to right) as visual information and detail are added. Interestingly, it only takes three dots to trick the eye into perceiving the shape of a triangle. Remember the principle of psychological closure which we discussed in Chapter 4?

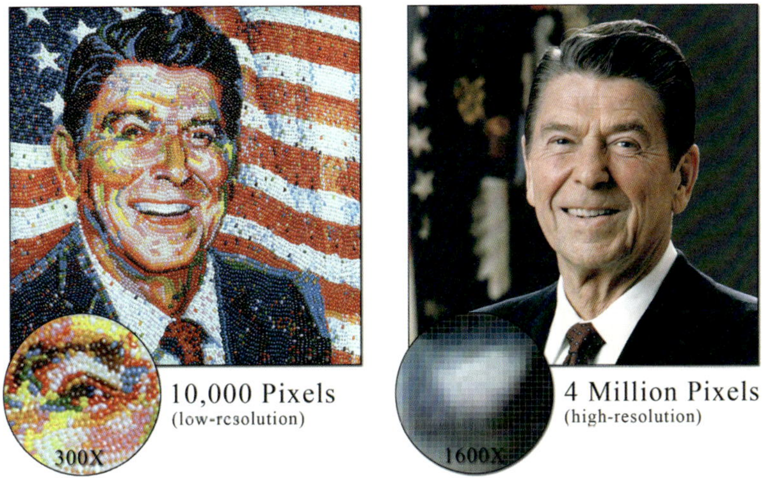

FIGURE 8.8
The first portrait of President Ronald Reagan (left) was commissioned by the Jelly Belly Candy Company. It was later donated to the Ronald Reagan Presidential Library in Simi Valley, California.
(Courtesy of the Ronald Reagan Presidential Foundation and the Jelly Belly Candy Company. Artist: Peter Roche.)

Tech Talk

Color Space We refer to natural sunlight as white light because it appears to the human eye to be colorless. But if you've ever held a prism in front of a window on a sunny day, or if you've seen a rainbow, you know that it's possible to separate white light into a dazzling display of various colors. As light travels through a prism, it's refracted (bent), causing the beam of white light to break apart into its component color wavelengths (see Figure 8.9).

As you learned in grade school, you can mix primary colors to get any color you want. Just add red, yellow, and blue together for any purpose, right? Not exactly. First, those colors are traditional in art, but the pigments used in printing need to be exact, and printers use somewhat different colors. Second, printing is a *subtractive* process: the pigments absorb colors, so when you put all of the colors together, you theoretically get black: each pigment absorbs a different range of light, so no light is reflected back to your eyes. Computer and television displays, on the other hand, emit light. If they put the colors of the rainbow back together, they emit white light. And where they don't emit light, the picture or text is black. They use *additive* color mixing.

RGB Color Model (or Mode)

The primary colors of light are red, green, and blue (RGB). If you vary the intensity of each, you can produce all of the colors in the visible light spectrum (see Figure 8.10). You get white if you add all of the colors equally and black if light is absent. If you were to look at a monitor such as an LCD (Liquid Crystal Display) under a microscope, you'd see that each pixel really displays only the three primary colors of light. How these colors are arranged in a pixel depends on the type of monitor, but in an LCD, they are arranged as stripes. In additive color mixing, red and green make yellow. If you fill a graphic with intense yellow in Photoshop, the pixels really display stripes of intense red and green, with no blue. The individual points of color are tiny, so our brains add the colors together into yellow. If you are designing for electronic display, you will probably create RGB images (see Figure 8.11 Left).

CMYK Color Model (or Mode)

In printing, the primary colors are cyan, magenta, and yellow (CMY) (8.11 Right). You produce colors by combining pigments in paints, inks, or dyes. If you combine equal amounts of each primary color, you should get black, right? At least in theory! To help produce "pure black" (as opposed to just darkening the imprint), printers add premixed black. To print a full-color image using the CMYK

FIGURE 8.9
The primary and secondary colors of white light become visible when light is refracted through a glass prism.

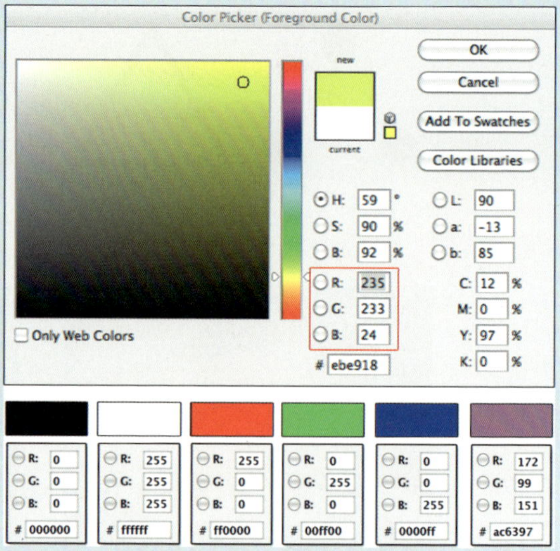

FIGURE 8.10
The Adobe Photoshop CS5 color picker is used for mixing colors. Each color shown here was achieved by changing the values in the red, green, and blue property fields.The hexadecimal code is shown beneath the RGB property fields and is used to quickly identify or pull up a particular color.

process, each page goes through four presses, each inked with a primary color or black pigment. The letter *K* refers to the black and comes from the term *key plate*, a black printing plate. If you are designing for print, you will likely create CMYK images. The challenge, of course, is that you'll be creating them on an RGB color monitor!

Bit Depth or Color Depth

When you capture an image with a digital camera, camcorder, or scanner, the device encodes light into electrical energy, and then into bits for storage in a format that the computer can process and understand. Display devices reverse the process by decoding bits back into electrical energy and light impulses that can be rendered on screen. The more data you collect, the greater the *bit depth*, or number of bits the device uses to record intensity and color components. And the greater the bit depth, the larger the color palette the image will have. Bit depth gets confusing, however: when we talk about 8-bit graphics, we sometimes mean 8 bits total (256 colors), but at other times we mean per channel (per primary color), or 24 bits (16.8 million colors) (see Figure 8.12).

Some display systems can render an even higher bit depth (up to 48 bits), but the 24-bit color standard is currently the most common and will give you a sufficiently large palette for multimedia applications. You may also hear about another channel, the alpha channel. This is an added 8-bit channel that records transparency information in some image formats.

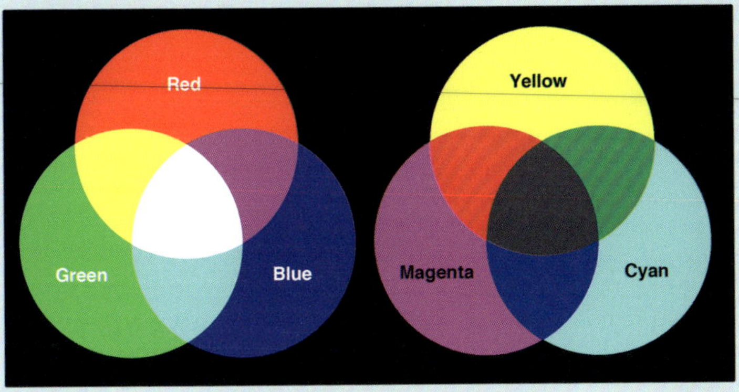

FIGURE 8.11
RGB color space (left) is used for multimedia (Web, animation, and television, etc.). CMYK color space (right) is most often associated with the four-color printing process.

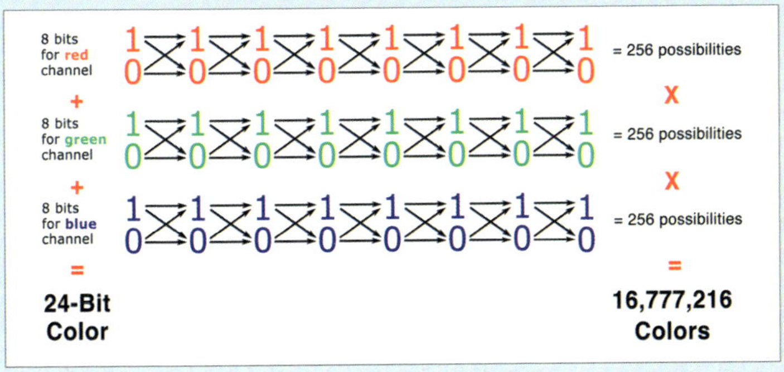

FIGURE 8.12
The possible color combinations for any pixel in an 8-bit graphic (or a 24-bit display). If you follow the arrows through every possible data combination, you'll get 256 (or 2^8) possibilities for each color channel. Combining channels—256 possibilities for red × 256 for green × 256 for blue, or 2^{24} combinations—you'd have about 16.8 million possible combinations.
Illustrator: Susan A. Youngblood.

DEFINING THE RASTER IMAGE

Like the tiny bits of tile in a mosaic, a pixel is the smallest definable element of a raster image. Because of this, image editors rarely have to deal with discrete units of measurement like inches, centimeters, and picas. Instead, editors usually measure graphics in pixels, and pixel count and density determine the physical size and quality of an image.

Pixel Dimensions

When we talk about pixel dimensions, we're not talking about the size of an individual pixel. Instead, we use the term *pixel dimensions* to describe the size of a raster image, expressed as *the number of pixels along the x-axis (width)* by *the number of pixels along the y-axis (height)*. For example, an 800 × 600 pixel image contains 800 pixels across the image from left to right and 600 pixels across the image from top to bottom.

Pixel Count

Pixel count is the total number of pixels in a raster matrix. To determine the pixel count, multiply the horizontal and vertical pixel dimensions. The 30 × 18 pixel image in Figure 8.13 has a pixel count of 540 pixels.

Pixel Density or Resolution

We express the pixel density or resolution of a raster image in pixels per inch (ppi)—this is pixels per linear inch (across or down), not square inch. Although each pixel in an electronic display is a fixed size, the dimensions of a pixel can vary from image to image. The more pixels you have per inch, the smaller each pixel will be.

The resolution determines the maximum size of an image you print. In order to produce a high-quality print of any size, digital photographs need a pixel density of at least 300 ppi—that's 90,000 pixels in a square inch! Generally speaking, the more pixels you have relative to the image's dimensions, the bigger the print you will be able to make without sacrificing image quality. To illustrate

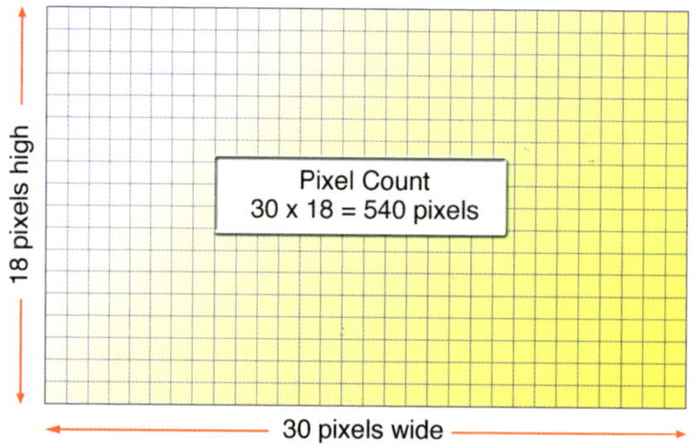

FIGURE 8.13 Pixel count is determined by multiplying the number of pixels across a digital image by the number of pixels high.

10 Megapixel Digital Camera

Recording Pixels	JPEG Compression Ratio	Single Image Data Size (Approx. KB)	Number of Shots per Memory Card	
			4 GB	16 GB
L (Large) 10 M/3648x2736	◢	2565	1471	6026
	▟	1226	3017	12354
M1 (Medium 1) 6 M/2816x2112	◢	1620	2320	9503
	▟	780	4641	19007
M2 (Medium 2) 2 M/1600x1200	◢	558	6352	26010
	▟	278	12069	49420
S (Small) 0.3 M/640x480	◢	150	20116	82367
	▟	84	30174	123550

◢ = Fine Setting (Highest Quality - least amount of compression)
▟ = Normal Setting (Lowest Quality - greatest amount of compression)

FIGURE 8.14
This chart displays the resolution sizes and compression settings for the Canon G12 digital camera.

this point, let's consider the Canon G12 digital camera, which has an effective resolution of about ten million pixels (total pixel count) (see Figure 8.14). With such a large-capacity image sensor, the G12 can produce a photograph with a recorded pixel count of 3,648 × 2,736 pixels. That's a lot of pixels! Dividing both pixel dimensions by 300 allows you to determine the maximum size of a photographic print that can be made from this image with good results.

$$3{,}648\ \text{pixels} \div 300\ \text{pixels/inch} = 12.16\ \text{inches}.$$
$$2{,}736\ \text{pixels} \div 300\ \text{pixels/inch} = 9.12\ \text{inches}.$$

A photographer won't always need to produce a print this large, but having lots of pixels to work with is always better than not having enough.

In multimedia work, we're much more concerned with display resolution and bandwidth than we are with print resolution. Most television and computer monitors have a display resolution of either 72 or 96 ppi (that's a pixel count of 5,184 or 9,216 in a square inch). So images produced for the screen need somewhere between a seventeenth and a tenth as many pixels, respectively, as those produced for print in order to look good. For video and the Web, 72 ppi is the industry standard; on a 72 ppi monitor, each pixel in a 72 ppi image will be displayed by one pixel on the screen. You can go as high as 96 ppi, but anything more than this is simply a waste of file bandwidth and will not increase the overall quality of an image that's displayed electronically.

SCALING

Many software applications allow you to scale an image within an open document by selecting it and adjusting one of eight resizing handles along the outer edge. But raster images are *resolution-dependent*, which means they contain a fixed number of pixels. Resizing (or scaling) a raster image without redefining the structure and pixel count of the array (resampling) can ruin your image.

When you resize this way, you don't change the image matrix (the image's pixel dimensions) or the amount of data stored. You only decrease or increase the size of your pixels. When you scale an image upward (make it larger), each pixel is enlarged, and you lose image detail and sharpness. The more you enlarge a raster image, the softer and fuzzier it becomes. For this reason, professionals try to avoid the enlarging of raster images (see Figure 8.15).

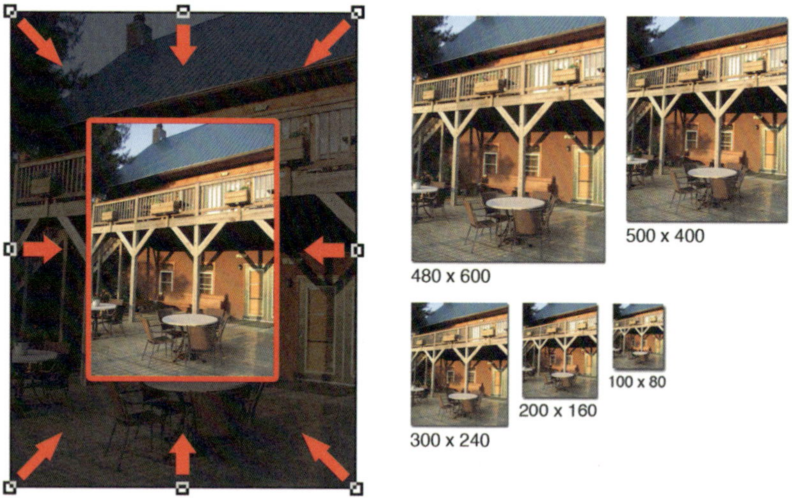

FIGURE 8.15
Scaling is the act of resizing a digital image to make it appear smaller or larger on screen.
Photographer: Sarah Beth Costello

Downscaling a raster image (making it smaller) is done far more often—and with better results. As you shrink an image, pixels become smaller and more tightly compacted together. In some cases, downscaling an image may actually improve image clarity because the pixel density (resolution) is artificially increased. In short, upscaling almost always leads to a bad result and downscaling usually works out okay. There is, however, a better alternative for resizing a raster image (see Figure 8.16).

RESAMPLING

Resampling changes the size of a raster image by increasing or decreasing the image's pixel count. While on the surface this sounds like a simple process, you must remember that each pixel represents a single color value. If you add pixels to an already defined image, what color do you to assign to them, and where do you place them? Which pixels get shifted to make room for the new ones? Likewise, if you delete pixels from an image to make it smaller, which ones get tossed and which ones get to stay? Resampling deals with these challenges by using algorithms to analyze each pixel's color information and using this data to reconstruct an entirely new raster structure. Depending on which resampling method and algorithm you use, some of the original image data may be retained, but much of it may be discarded and replaced. For this reason, you should make a backup copy of your original image before applying changes.

When you resample to enlarge an image, you still lose detail and sharpness. Given the nature of raster images, this just can't be avoided. However, resampling provides more options and typically yields better results than scaling alone.

ANTI-ALIASING

Raster images are also known for producing aliasing artifacts, the visibly jagged distortions along the edge of a line. Aliasing is a stair-step effect caused by using square pixels to define objects with curves or diagonal lines (see Figure 8.17). You can easily see the effect when looking at text on the screen of a small digital device such as a cell phone.

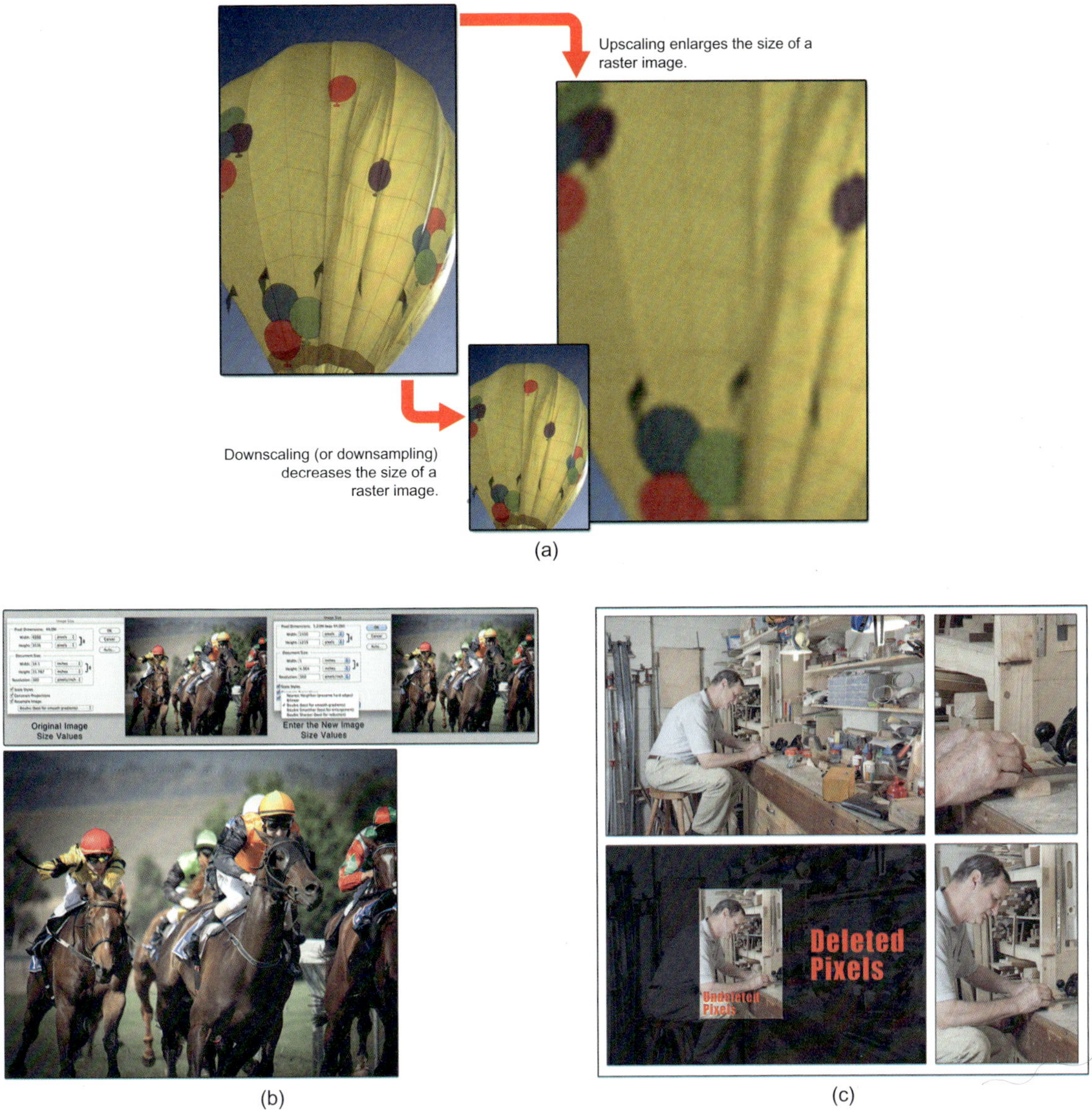

FIGURE 8.16
(a) **Scaling.** Upscaling often results in a noticeable loss of image quality (increased blurriness). When downscaling a high-resolution image, image degradation is rarely a concern; (b) **Resampling.** The original image was too big to fit on this page. I used Adobe Photoshop CS5 to resize (and resample) it to the version you see printed here. Photoshop offers you a choice of five resampling algorithms. Because this image was intended for print, I kept the resolution set to 300 ppi. If I wanted to publish it to the Web, I would have chosen 72 ppi. To reduce the loss of image quality during scaling, be sure to select a resampling method (*Source: Neale Cousland/shutterstock.com*); (c) **Cropping.** The two images on the right were achieved by cropping the original photo (*top left*). Cropping is a photo editing technique used to delete portions of an image in order to enhance the focus of a main subject or improve composition. With scaling, the original composition is preserved by physically resampling the image using fewer pixels (downscaling). With cropping, pixels in the unwanted portion of the image are permanently deleted. The remaining pixels are preserved with their original color values intact. Resampling is not performed. A cropped image will always, by definition, be smaller than the original; however, this reduction in size is due to the deletion of image content (pixels) and not to scaling.

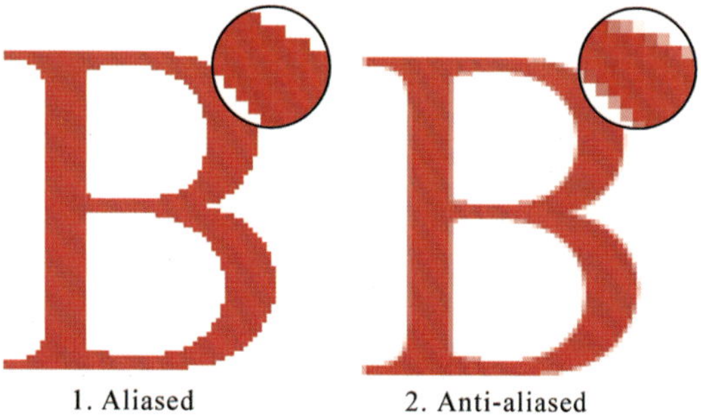

FIGURE 8.17
The stair-step effect known as *aliasing* is seen in a close-up view of the letter *B* in image #1. Aliasing is most pronounced along the curved segments of a stroke. In image #2, an anti-aliasing algorithm was applied. Anti-aliasing softens the perceived jaggedness of a raster image by blending pixels along the edge of the stroke.

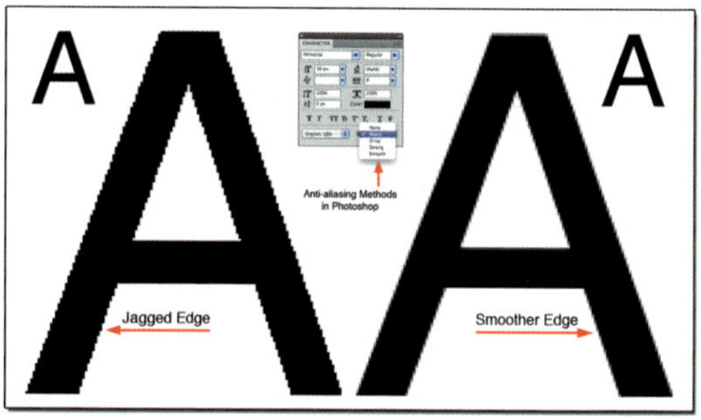

FIGURE 8.18
Bitmap editing programs such as Adobe Photoshop offer different anti-aliasing methods. Which one works the best is often a matter of trial and error.

Anti-aliasing smooths out the edges of jagged type by blending the color transition points, such as the pixels along the edges of a letter (see Figure 8.18). The only major drawback to this is that it increases file size somewhat. In most cases, it's better to have a clean graphic and accept the slightly larger file size. Anti-aliasing typically works best on larger type as the jagged edges of the type are more visible.

Tech Talk

Compression In an uncompressed file format, the graphic file records the individual value of each pixel. Examples of this include the BMP and uncompressed TIFF formats. While these formats give you access to a lot of information, and TIFF in particular is a popular format for photographers, graphics saved in this format tend to be quite large, which is not always a good choice for online projects or storage. Compression can help with this. There are two basic types of compression: *lossless*, which looks for more efficient ways to store the data without losing any information—kind of like putting your sleeping bag in a stuff sack—and *lossy*, which while reducing the file size gets rid of data that you might not need at the moment.

JPEG is the most common lossy format used in multimedia production. Released in 1992 by the Joint Photographic Experts Group, the JPEG standard was designed to reduce the file size of photographic images. File size was a critical issue at the time because computer hard drives were much smaller, and processor speeds weren't nearly as fast as they are today. In addition, data transfer rates were particularly slow online—a fast modem at the time was around 56kpbs. Bits and bytes were precious, and the new JPEG standard greatly improved the photo-imaging workflow. When applied to a raster image, the JPEG compression algorithm evaluates each pixel, looking for ways to "compress" redundant color information into a more efficiently written and structured data file. For example, the high-resolution photo in Figure 8.19 was taken on a clear and sunny day and contains a lot of blue pixels.

The original image size is 4,288 × 2,848 pixels, but notice how the first 100 rows of this image contain largely the same shade of blue. We can compute a rough estimate of the uncompressed file size of this sample as follows:

Pixels Count: 4,288 pixels per row × 100 row
= 248,800 pixels
File Size: 428,800 pixels × 24 bits
= 10,291,200 bits

Saved in an uncompressed TIFF format, this tiny section of blue sky takes up nearly 1.3 MBs of storage space. Using JPEG compression, the same picture information can be rewritten in a new data file that's 68 KB or less.

In photography, you can control the amount of JPEG compression both when you take the photo, and later when you work within an image-editing program. For example, most digital cameras provide at least three JPEG options: Normal (highest compression, smallest file size, lowest image quality); Fine; and Superfine (lowest compression, biggest file size, highest image quality). Photoshop, one of the most popular professional image-editing programs, offers 12 preset levels of JPEG compression and options to customize settings (see Figures 8.20 and 8.21).

It's possible to overcompress an image to the point where its visual integrity is noticeably compromised. The resulting imperfections are called compression artifacts. Image optimization tools such as the *Save for Web & Devices* feature in Photoshop provide a handy way to test and compare compression settings before applying them. Image optimization is critically important for images on the Web because file size is directly related to bandwidth. The smaller the image file, the less time it takes to download from the Internet and render on screen. The goal of image optimization is to create the best-looking image possible, with the smallest file size and no compression artifacts.

FIGURE 8.19
This high-resolution photograph contains lots of redundant color information (blue sky and golden wheat) making it a great candidate for JPEG compression.

FIGURE 8.20
Using Adobe Photoshop's Save for the Web interface allows you to perform a side-by-side comparison of the look and size of the original image on the left, with a preview image on the right. Every time you make a change to the compression settings, the preview image is automatically updated to reflect that change. The goal of image optimization is to produce the highest-quality image with the smallest file size and no compression artifacts.

FIGURE 8.21
Another example of compression at work. At 50%, can you notice any degradation? Which parts of the image are most highly affected by compression?

RASTER IMAGE FORMATS

When you create and work with raster images, you have many options for saving your files. As you work with a file, you should save it in a format that supports layers, probably as a PSD or TIFF with layers, so you can change it in the future or resave the image in a new format for another purpose. But when you prepare a raster image to incorporate into a multimedia project, you'll need a flattened, compressed image. Selecting the right format for your project is important: you need a good-looking image that takes up as little space as possible. Don't fall in to the habit of editing JPEGs. Remember, it's a lossy format. Each time you save it, you lose information. Whenever possible, you should work in an uncompressed or lossless format. Always keep a backup copy. You never know when you might need to reedit the graphic.

When you select the file format and quality settings—how much to compress the image—consider whether the format is lossy (loses information during compression) or lossless. Also consider the nature of your image. Does it have many color variations that need to be captured, such as a photograph? Is it mostly lines and blocks of uniform color? Do you need transparent pixels because you plan to float the image over other elements of a website? You have more than 50 formats to choose from, but here are three of the most common formats used for still images in multimedia:

- **GIF** offers 256 colors and transparency (transparent pixels) and is a lossless compression format. It is common for logos and other images with lines and solid blocks of color. It supports interlacing, so every odd line of pixels loads, then every even line loads, making graphics seem to appear faster (users see the full-sized, half-loaded graphic before the rest of the pixels appear).

- **JPEG** offers 16.8 million colors but does not support transparency (has no transparent pixels). It is a lossy compression format and is used most often for photographs. This format does not support interlacing.
- **PNG** offers 16.8 million colors and transparency, but you can choose to use fewer colors to save file space (PNG 8, or PNG with 8-bit color). It is a lossless compression format and is common for a wide range of images, including ***favicons*** (the small web page icons in browser tabs). Some older web browsers don't support it (Internet Explorer prior to version 4); such browsers have mostly, but not completely, fallen out of use. PNG files can be very small, but for photographs with many colors, they may be larger than comparable JPEGs. This format supports interlacing.

Another option you have with both the GIF and PNG formats is *dithering*, or scattering the pixels to achieve blending without using as many colors. Dithering is useful if you have an image with a drop shadow and want to superimpose it cleanly on a background.

Vector Graphics

Vector imaging defines the area of a picture using *paths* made up of points, lines, curves and shapes. Each vector path forms the outline of a geometric region containing color information. Because paths can be mathematically resized, vector graphics can be scaled up or down without losing any picture clarity. Clipart and typefaces (fonts) are often created and stored as vector graphics because designers want the ability to scale them to any size (see Figure 8.22).

FIGURE 8.22
Vector graphics have crisp edges with no aliasing. They can be resized up or down to any size without negative consequences.

FIGURE 8.23
To complete a paint-by-numbers piece like this one, each numbered region must be filled in with a single color. A vector graphic is rendered geometrically in much the same way using paths defined by points, lines, curves, and shapes. (*Courtesy of Pam Snow, Mesa, AZ*)

The concept behind vector graphics is like painting with numbers. A paint-by-numbers set normally includes a black and white line drawing and a set of numbered paints. The artist fills in each numbered region with the appropriate color, carefully staying within the bordered outline of each defined area. When all of the regions are filled with color, the picture is complete. As with raster images, the phenomenon of perceptual grouping leads us to ignore the individual paths used to form the holistic impression (see Figure 8.23).

Vector graphics can render curves and diagonal lines that are crisp, smooth, and sharp. Aliasing is not a problem because pixels are not used in their construction. So vector graphics are an ideal choice for prepress applications requiring higher-resolution pictures with finer line detail.

When you enlarge a raster image, the file size grows in proportion to the size of the image: as you add pixels to the array, you need more data to represent the image. Because vector encoding uses mathematical equations to record visual information, the size of a vector data file stays consistent, regardless of how large or small you make the graphic. If you are creating a still graphic, you can enlarge the graphic to any size you want, then rasterize it, saving it to whichever file format suits your purpose best.

You could also use vector graphics to create an animation, such as with Flash. Instead of drawing every separate frame of your project—with 24 frames appearing each second—you could create two different graphics for a segment and let your animation software mathematically interpolate the positions of the components in the in-between frames (a technique known as tweening).

DISPLAY SCREEN STANDARDS

Television and computer monitors have a fixed number of image pixels (see Figure 8.24). We call its fixed pixel dimensions its *native resolution*. As monitors increase in size, their native resolution also increases, as more and more pixels are added to the display. I'm currently typing on a laptop computer that has a 17-inch screen and a native resolution of 1920 × 1200 pixels. My computer is refreshing the color properties of 2,304,000 points of light (pixels) 85 times per second. That's impressive!

When a raster image is displayed in full size on a screen that's set to the native resolution of the monitor, there's a one-to-one correlation between the pixel data in the source file and the pixels rendered on screen. In this scenario, the source image will look it's very best and is said to be "pixel perfect." Unfortunately, user preferences can quickly get in the way of viewing a pixel perfect image every time. For instance,

1. A user may not have his or her screen set to the native resolution of the monitor. On my laptop, I can choose from a number of display resolutions, including: 640 × 480, 720 × 480, 800 × 600, 1024 × 768, 1280 × 1024, 1680 × 1050, and finally, 1920 × 1200 (native). Choosing a display setting that's lower than the native resolution of the monitor produces the effect of zooming in. This is a helpful option for someone like me, whose vision is less than perfect. However, the benefit of enlarging the text and icons on screen has two potentially negative tradeoffs: (a) it reduces the desktop real estate or screen space, and (b) it compromises the quality of the screen image

10-inch Apple iPad 2
768 x 1024
132 ppi

7-inch BlackBerry Playbook
1024 x 600
169 ppi

Apple iPhone 4
640 x 960
325 ppi

Nokia C1-01
128 x 160
114 ppi

FIGURE 8.24
A comparison of digital screen sizes and resolutions for a handful of mobile devices.

(the image becomes fuzzier as you stray further from the native resolution of the monitor).

2. A user may not have the screen set to its native resolution but may be zoomed in on an active document window. For example, you could be viewing an online newspaper article using a web browser like Firefox, Chrome, Internet Explorer, or Safari. Most browsers allow you to zoom in on a page to get a better view of the content. Doing so enlarges the view of both text and images, however, with each increase you'll lose clarity, particularly with images (see Figure 8.25).

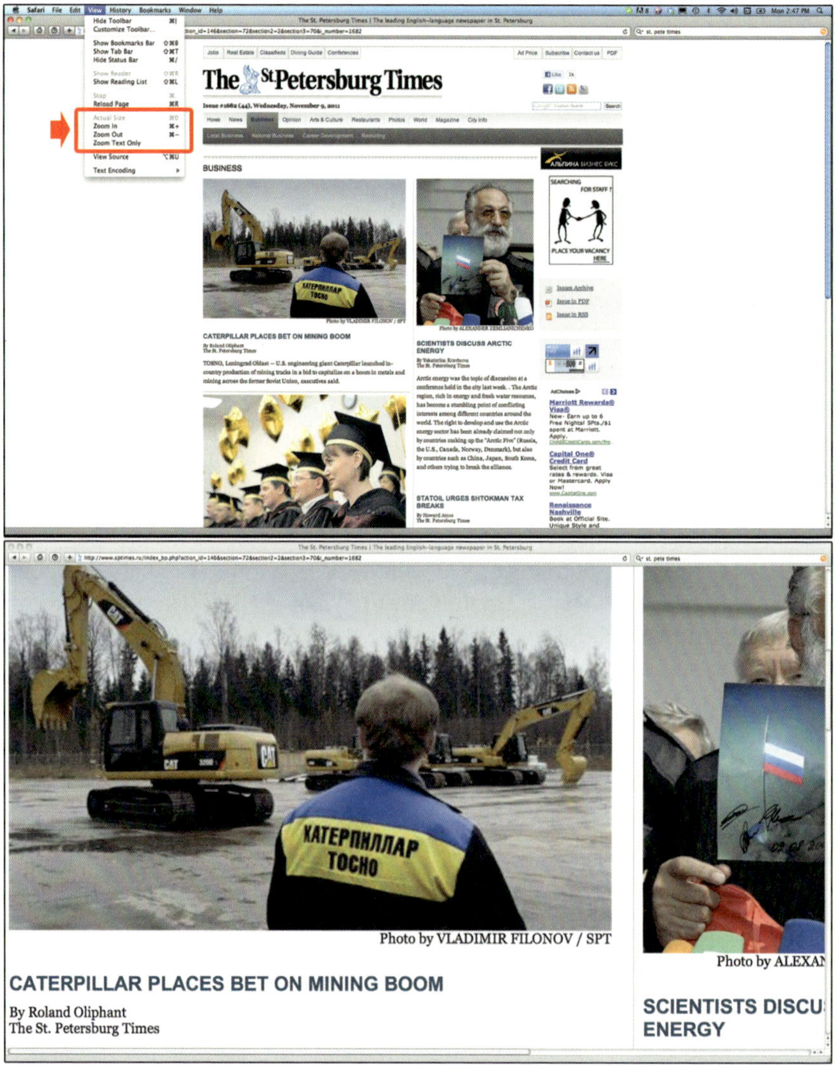

FIGURE 8.25
A web page is viewed natively in its actual size (top). The close-up view (bottom) was achieved using the browser's zoom control.
Source: www.sptimes.ru

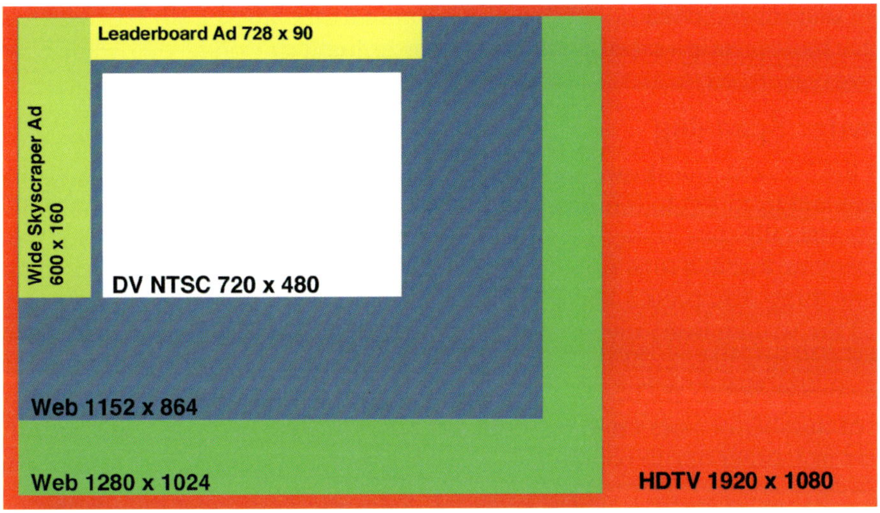

FIGURE 8.26
A comparison of some common display resolutions used in multimedia design. Do you notice how the aspect ratio varies?

In both of these examples, there's no longer a one-to-one correlation between the native raster structure of the source image and the display screen. The image is no longer pixel perfect and will have to be scaled up or down to conform to the raster structure of the screen. And as we've already learned, scaling alters the quality of a raster image, especially when it is enlarged.

Aspect Ratio

In addition to describing the screen attributes in absolute terms (screen size and native resolution), monitors are classified by their *aspect ratio*. Aspect ratio is an indicator of the proportional relationship of the width to the height of the screen and is depicted with the expression *x:y*, where *x* equals the number of units wide and *y* equals the number of units high. While the physical size of a display screen can vary, the aspect ratio remains constant. The two most common aspect ratios in use today are 4:3 and 16:9. The standard 4:3 (pronounced *4 by 3*) aspect ratio predates television and produces a familiar and somewhat boxy-looking shape. The other popular aspect ratio is 16:9 and is usually referred to as *widescreen* because it more closely matches the shape of a theatrical movie screen. While television and computer monitors are available in many shapes and sizes, they almost always conform to either a 4:3 or 16:9 aspect ratio.

MOVING IMAGES

Many people's daily experience is filled with moving images. Some come from televisions and movie theaters. Others come from personal computers, game systems, mobile phones, handheld devices, even GPS interfaces and self-checkout kiosks at supermarkets. Regardless of the content, they are typically based on the same basic principles. Let's look at how this technology works.

Raster Scanning

In the Western world, people tend to process visual information from left to right and from top to bottom. Think about it! When you write a letter or note, you generally start in the upper left-hand corner of the page and work your way down one line at a time from left to right. On a typewriter, you do basically the same thing. You press a key to produce an imprint of a character on the page, and the writing head advances to the next space on the line. You advance one character at a time until the end of a line, then the writing head shifts leftward and downward to the beginning of the next line of text. A sheet of paper has a fixed number of lines on it, so when you reach the end of a page, you need to load in another one to continue.

The process of *raster scanning* works in much the same way, only faster. In television and computer display systems, individual video frames and computer images are reproduced on the screen, one pixel at a time, in a process called *scanning*. An electron beam or impulse mechanism illuminates each screen pixel as it progresses through the raster matrix. Each row of pixels is called a *scan line*. A *scanning cycle* is one complete pass of all of the scan lines in the display. When the scanning beam reaches the last pixel on the last scan line, it moves to the top and begins the next cycle. A *frame* is one complete scanning pass of all of the lines in a picture, or one complete scanning cycle.

The *refresh rate* is the number of complete scanning cycles per second and is measured in Hertz (Hz), a unit of frequency equal to one cycle per second. If the refresh rate is below 50 Hz, the image will appear to flicker. Most displays have refresh rates of 60 Hz or more. The faster the refresh rate, the sharper the image quality will be and the less eyestrain the user will experience. The larger the screen, the higher the refresh rate should be. Large computer monitors typically have a refresh rate of 85 Hz or higher.

PROGRESSIVE SCANNING

Contemporary computer monitors and some televisions reproduce images using *progressive scanning*, consecutively scanning the lines of the picture from top to bottom, just as you type on a typewriter. Progressive scanning helps combat eyestrain, which is why it's a given on computer monitors. That's not, however, necessarily the case for television.

INTERLACED SCANNING

Early television standards adopted a method of raster scanning called *interlaced scanning* to minimize both bandwidth use and flickering. With an interlace system, each frame of an image is captured in two parts and transmitted separately, one field at a time. The odd lines are scanned first, followed by a second pass of the even lines. So you're really only seeing half of each new image at once, but the screen draws so quickly you don't notice.

FIGURE 8.27
Broadcast television images are typically interlaced (left) while video on the Web is often de-interlaced (right), delivered progressively.

Interlaced scanning reduces the bandwidth requirements of standard broadcast television by half compared to a progressively scanned image. Using this standard helped cut the cost of broadcast equipment and, perhaps more importantly, freed up valuable broadcasting bandwidth. While broadcasting standards have changed with the move to digital television, interlaced signals are still an integral part of the broadcast mix (see Figure 8.27).

Fields

One complete scanning pass of either the odd or even scan lines is called a *field*. So two fields, the odd and even, produce one frame. As you can imagine, the electronic raster scanning process has to be fast to give you a good picture. Let's say you're watching a movie on a television with interlacing and a frame rate of 30 frames per second (usually stated as 30 *fps*) that has 480 lines in its raster (a comparatively small number). This means that one scanning pass of the 240 odd-numbered scan lines, or one field, occurs in just 1/60th of a second. Double that to get a full frame. Put another way, 14,400 scan lines of picture information are rendered on your television monitor every second.

Television Standards

Since multimedia projects are often viewed on televisions, you need to consider television standards. A great deal of money goes into supporting the infrastructure of terrestrial broadcasting systems, so countries have developed technical standards—some more widely adopted than others—for the production of television-related equipment. While it doesn't always work out this way, such standards help to ensur e that consumers have access to equipment that's compatible with the delivery systems used by content providers for program

GREAT IDEAS

The Illusion of Apparent Movement

The foundation of all moving image technology rests on the ability of the human eye and the brain to process a series of rapidly projected frames or scan lines as a continuous and uninterrupted picture. The motion we observe on the screen, whether in a movie house or on a television or computer monitor, is a perceptual illusion. Film, video, and moving digital images appear to have motion because of the phenomenon of *short-range apparent motion*. Our brains process successive images that have small changes between them as movement, in much the same way that they process real motion.

In order to pull off the illusion of motion we get from film, video, and animation, individual pictures in a sequence must advance quickly. If the frame rate is set too low, the transition from one image to the next will appear jerky or stilted. The target speed is known as the *flicker fusion threshold*, the frequency at which the momentary flicker of intermittent light between each frame disappears from human perception.

Early on, the motion picture film industry adopted a frame rate of 24 fps as an international standard. However, an image pulsating at 24 fps is well below the flicker fusion threshold for human perception. To compensate, a projector displays each frame of motion picture film twice. A rotating shutter momentarily blocks out the projector's light each time the frame is advanced and between each repeated exposure of a single frame, fixing the image in one spot and keeping us from seeing a blur. We don't notice the brief black spots because of persistence of vision, the phenomenon in which our retinas hold a visual impression of light for a fraction of a second. The result is a flicker-free viewing experience for the audience.

FIGURE 8.28
Moving images are a perceptual illusion, achieved by the rapid projection of individual still frames of film or video.

distribution. In an ideal world, every nation would use the same standards for every type of electronic technology, but this just isn't the case. As it's sometimes hard to get two people to agree on something, it's even more difficult to get the governing bodies of entire nations to agree on a universal set of technical specifications.

As you develop media products to be used on multiple devices—computers, phones, game systems, and so on—keep in mind how those products will work and look on each device, including television.

FLASHBACK

The Legacy of Analog Television

Television signals used to be broadcast in analog formats. In analog broadcasts, continuous waves carried the sound and picture information.

Much of the world has made the switch to digital formats, and many (but not all) remaining countries have plans to switch to digital formats before 2020. There are three major analog television standards: the NTSC (National Television Standards Committee) standard developed in the United States, the PAL (Phase Alternating Line) standard developed in Germany, and the SECAM (Sequential Color and Memory) standard developed in France.

Each analog format had a 4:3 aspect ratio, set to mimic the dimensions of the film that was in use when television was born. Later, movie industries moved to wider-format film to offer viewers something different from television in their theater experience. With the release of high-definition digital television, the aspect ratio was changed to the now popular 16:9 widescreen format, bringing television back into conformity with the theatrical viewing experience.

FIGURE 8.29 Television entertainment technologies have evolved rapidly in recent years. The standalone single-piece television receiver your parents may remember can't compete with today's high-tech home theater system, complete with wall-mounted flat-screen monitor and 5.1 surround sound.

DIGITAL TELEVISION

Digital television (DTV) offers many advantages over legacy analog formats. Content created for digital media is more fluid: it can be easily repurposed and distributed through secondary channels of communication, making DTV more compatible with computer and Internet-based systems and services.

DTV also offers less signal interference and uses less bandwidth than an equivalent analog television broadcast, which is an advantage because the amount of broadcast bandwidth is finite. The switch to DTV has meant that more stations can be broadcast in the same viewing area, while using the same or less bandwidth as analog television. DTV also offers the option of using a 16:9 format, similar to that used in the movie theater, as well as high-definition (HD) video—video with over twice the resolution of the old NTSC standard. When professionals shoot and edit television programs digitally, the DTV infrastructure preserves the quality of the original material during transmission. In order to transmit digital content through an analog system, programs must first be downconverted to an analog format, resulting in a loss of image quality.

ATSC

The United States adopted the ATSC (Advanced Television Research Consortium) terrestrial broadcasting standard in 1996. In the same year, WRAL in Raleigh, North Carolina, became the first television station in the country to begin broadcasting a high-definition television signal. The U.S. transition to HDTV was fraught with many delays and took more than a decade to complete. On June 12, 2009, U.S. analog transmissions ceased and NTSC broadcasting officially ended in the United States.

The NTSC format has a fixed resolution, aspect ratio, scan mode, and frame rate. The newer ATSC standard is more fluid, providing up to 18 different display formats, which are categorized into three groups: standard definition television (SDTV), enhanced definition television (EDTV), and high-definition television (HDTV) (see Table 8.2). ATSC emphasizes progressive scanning and square pixels, bringing television technology closer to current standards for computer imaging. It also improves audio distribution, enabling a theater-style experience with 5.1-channel Dolby Digital Surround Sound. The ATSC standard has been adopted in much of the Americas and in U.S. territories. Canada made the switch in 2011, and Mexico is preparing for the switch and is simulcasting in both digital and analog formats. Other countries also have introduced the ATSC format but have not fully switched. And, of course, the ATSC is working on new standards: as ATSC 2.0 comes out, look for features such as video on demand and possibly even 3D programming.

DVB

The DVB (Digital Video Broadcasting) terrestrial broadcasting standard was established in 1997. The following year, the first commercial DVB broadcast was transmitted in the United Kingdom. Because European consumers depend more on cable and satellite distribution for television and less on over-the-air

Table 8.2 The ATSC Television Formats

	DTV Format	Vertical Resolution	Horizontal Resolution	Aspect Ratio	Scan Mode	Frame Rate
High-Definition Television **(HDTV)** Best Quality	1080p	1080	1920	16:9	Progressive Progressive	24 fps 30 fps
	1080i	1080	1920	16:9	Interlaced	30 fps
	720p	720	1280	16:9	Progressive	24 fps 30 fps 60 fps
Enhanced Definition Television **(EDTV)** Medium Quality	480p	480	740	16:9	Progressive	24 fps 30 fps 60 fps
				4:3	Progressive	24 fps 30 fps 60 fps
		480	640	4:3	Progressive	24 fps 30 fps 60 fps
Standard Definition Television **(SDTV)** Good Quality	480i	480	704	16:9	Interlaced	30 fps
				4:3	Interlaced	30 fps
		480	640	4:3	Interlaced	30 fps

The ATSC DTV Standard established 18 display formats and three levels of image resolution.

terrestrial broadcasting, their transition to a DTV infrastructure has been easier. The DVB standard has been adopted throughout Europe and in Australia. Not all areas have followed the U.S. model of a decade-long digital conversion. Berlin, the capital of Germany, made the change on August 4, 2003, making it the first city to convert to a DTV-only terrestrial broadcasting system.

CHAPTER SUMMARY

Digital images are constructed of thousands to millions of tiny visual elements called *pixels* that are arranged in rows and columns on a screen to form a composite visual representation. The more pixels in an image, the higher its resolution and perceived quality will be. Digital imaging would not be possible without light. Digital images are captured using light-sensitive sensors and displayed using electronic monitors that scan the image onto the screen with light. Since the primary colors of light are red, green, and blue, RGB color space is the standard in digital imaging, whereas CMYK color space is the printing industry standard. The way an image or graphic is defined—either as separate pixels or as mathematical relationships—constrains what you can do with it. And as you create, transform, and incorporate images and graphics into multimedia projects, the final format you choose affects how good the user's experience will be. The final format should also guide your workflow as you don't want to risk starting off working at a lower resolution than your final format needs to be.

CHAPTER 9

Text

Yes, it is a press, certainly, but a press from which shall flow in inexhaustible streams the most abundant and most marvelous liquor that has ever flowed to relieve the thirst of men. Through it, God will spread His word; a spring of pure truth shall flow from it; like a new star it shall scatter the darkness of ignorance, and cause a light hithertofore unknown to shine among men.

—Attributed to Johannes Gutenberg, inventor and pioneer of the modern printing era (1398–1468)

Key Terms
Alignment
All Caps
Ascender
Baseline
Baseline Shift
Bevel
Blackletter Font
Boldface
Capline
Condensed Type
Counter
Decorative Font
Descender
Distribution
Drop Shadow
Emboss
Expanded Type
Faux Font Style
Font Family
Font Management
Gridlines
Inner Glow
Italic
Justification
Kerning
Leading
Legibility
Letterform
Meanline
Modern Font
Oblique
Old Style Font
Outer Glow
Points
Posture
Ragged
Readability
Roman

Chapter Highlights

This chapter examines:

- The origins of typography and the modern use of electronic type in multimedia designs
- Styles and classifications for electronic typefaces in graphic design
- Tools and techniques for managing the appearance of text
- Tools and techniques for controlling character and line spacing, text placement, and alignment
- Ideas for maximizing the readability of screen text in multimedia projects

AN INTRODUCTION TO TYPOGRAPHY

The element of text is one of the most important components of a multimedia experience. Text is the visual representation of intellectual thought as expressed through a human language system. Whether it's in the form of texting, hypertext, tweeting, email, snail mail, or notes on a napkin at lunch, text plays a big role in our lives. The Age of Enlightenment was predicated on humankind's ability to share ideas and information through formally agreed upon conventions of writing. Even in a multimedia age, we continue to rely on text as the primary means of recording, receiving, and transferring human knowledge and ideas. So what is typography? How do you make informed choices about fonts, spacing, and other typesetting and layout options? What makes Times New Roman recognizable and look different from Arial? Let's start at the beginning and get a few terms and ideas straight.

- Sans-Serif Font
- Screen Font
- Script Font
- Serif Font
- Slab Serif Font
- Small Caps
- Snapping
- Strikethrough
- Stroke
- Subscript
- Superscript
- Symbol Font
- Text
- Tracking
- Transitional Font
- Typeface
- Typography
- Underline
- Web-Safe Font
- X-Height

FIGURE 9.1
The shape of a tree is formed by the thoughtful arrangement of stylized text. Here, text is creatively used as an element of both form and content.
Ahmad Faizal Yahya/Shutterstock.com

Type is a character or letterform created for the purpose of communicating written information through printing or electronic means. The term *letterform* implies letters, but it also applies to other characters, such as punctuation, symbols, and numbers. *Typography* is the art of designing and arranging type (see Figure 9.1). You've heard of fonts and typeface; although some people use the terms interchangeably, they have different meanings. Typeface is about design, while font is about executing a version of that design in a particular size. The term *typeface* refers to a particular style of type, such as Times New Roman, where the entire set of alphanumeric characters and symbols—perhaps almost 200—conform to the same design specifications, such as the height of lowercase letters in relationship to capital letters (roughly speaking, the *x-height*) and whether the characters have serifs (decorative accents added to the end of a stroke). A typeface has a unified appearance. The term *font*, on the other hand, refers to the digital or physical means of creating or displaying that typeface in a particular style and size (though the size may be scalable). Times New Roman, for instance, is a typeface, a set of specifications that make the characters look a certain way, no matter the size or medium, but PostScript 12 pt Times New Roman is a font. A collection of related fonts—all of the bolds, italics, and so forth, in their varied sizes—is a *font family* (see Figure 9.2).

Movable type was first invented in Asia, but historians often credit Johannes Gutenberg and his invention of efficient movable type in about 1450 as the starting point of the modern printing era. Gutenberg, a goldsmith and inventor by trade,

Times New Roman Font Family
Times New Roman Regular
Times New Roman Bold
Times New Roman Bold Italic

Helvetica Font Family
Helvetica Regular
Helvetica Light
Helvetica Light Oblique
Helvetica Bold
Helvetica Oblique
Helvetica Bold Oblique

Myriad Pro Font Family
Myriad Pro Condensed
Myriad Pro Condensed Italic
Myriad Pro Bold Condensed
Myriad Pro Bold Condensed Italics
Myriad Pro Regular
Myriad Pro Italic
Myriad Pro Semibold
Myriad Pro Semibold Italic
Myriad Pro Bold
Myriad Pro Bold Italic

FIGURE 9.2
A font family includes all of the variant styles associated with a particular typeface (bold, condensed, light, italic, oblique, etc.). The "regular" style associated with a typeface is its default look or appearance without any stylistic enhancements. Many typefaces have only a regular style.

FIGURE 9.3
This replica of the Gutenberg press is on permanent display at the Gutenberg Museum in Mainz, Germany. Mainz is the birthplace of Johannes Gutenberg.

converted a winepress into a device capable of mass-producing pages of printed text (see Figure 9.3). The Gutenberg press required the printer to manually arrange small pieces of metal type into horizontal rows to form an inverted image of a prepress layout. Each metal block was designed with a single raised letterform on the surface. The side of the metal block containing the raised character was called the *face*, or *typeface*. The width of the blocks varied, with skinny letters such as *l* being narrower than wide letters such as *m*, but the other dimensions were uniform. Other blocks without a raised surface were used as separators between words and sentences. When the layout was complete, the printer would apply a coating of ink to the surface of the blocks. Next, a sheet of paper was placed on top of the blocks. In the final step, the printer would apply pressure to the backside of the paper with the winepress, resulting in a transfer of the ink from the typeface to the surface of the page. As with block printing—carving the text of each page in a block—Gutenberg's process also guaranteed that each printing would result in an identical reproduction of the original page.

While the process of setting the type for a single page was quite time-consuming, the actual printing of the page was very fast, especially when compared to the old-school methods of manual reproduction by human scribes or of block printing.

Printing technology has evolved considerably since Gutenberg's day. Metal type has not wholly been replaced by electronic type, but much typesetting is now done digitally, and digital type is far easier to use and manipulate. With digital type, you have the option of outputting text to a printer, computer screen, or virtually any other type of electronic display. With tens of thousands of typefaces available (at least) and so many easy options for customizing text, you might think good typesetting would be a snap. But good typographic design requires knowledge and careful planning. Good design creates an aesthetically pleasing layout that communicates effectively to the user (the reader, the viewer, or the person interacting with the multimedia). Writing involves the crafting of words, while typography applies the complex rules of design to the presentation of words on a printed page or digital screen to not only present written ideas but also set a tone, connect to users, establish credibility, and set expectations.

LEGIBILITY AND READABILITY

Legibility and readability are related terms. *Legibility* refers to a typeface's characteristics and can change depending on font size. The more legible a typeface, the easier it is at a glance to distinguish and identify letters, numbers, and symbols. A number of factors affect legibility, such as x-height and counter size (the size of the open space either fully or partially enclosed in a letter). In Figure 9.4 (left), compare the letterforms in Playbill, Arial, Rosewood and the other typefaces shown for legibility.

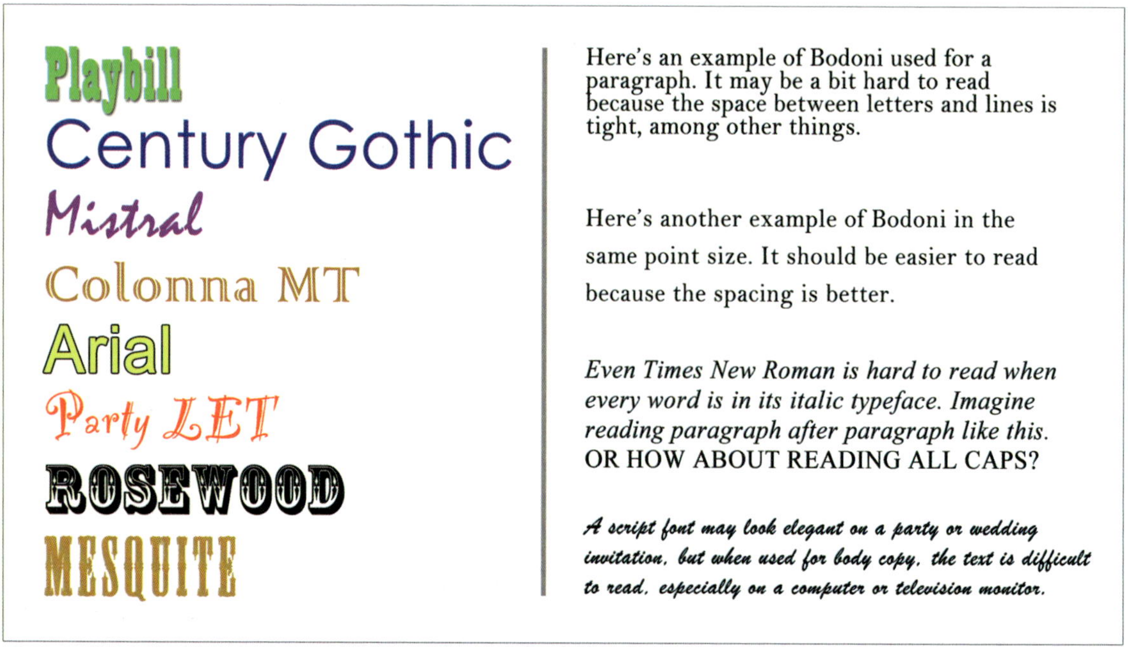

FIGURE 9.4
Legibility and readability are related. What letters and words are easiest to distinguish? Which ones are easiest to read?
Illustrator: Susan A. Youngblood

Readability refers to how easy text is to read in context, not as isolated letters, and depends on a variety of factors, including typeface characteristics such as italics, font size, style, letter spacing, line spacing, alignment, background, capitalization choices, and contrast. Legibility is a factor, of course: if characters are hard to identify, words are hard to read. Good type designs are usually invisible, meaning that the reader's attention is fixed on the words and the meaning of the text, rather than on the stylistic features of individual characters. When typesetting is sloppy and ill-conceived, the readability of text diminishes. When users begin to consciously notice details of a typeface over content, readability is diminished. When users have to strain to read—and when their eyes fatigue because of typesetting choices—readability is diminished. In Figure 9.4 (right), compare the line spacing, styles, and letterforms in Bodoni, Times New Roman, and Script typefaces shown for readability.

CHARACTERISTICS THAT DEFINE TYPEFACES

Many of the traditions surrounding the design and construction of modern-day typefaces are rooted in earlier times when letters were hand-drawn. Typography terms reflect type's origins as do some typeface characteristics, especially early ones. Typographers have well over 40 terms to describe the features of individual letterforms. You may wish to study typography in the future, but the terms that follow will give you a good start.

Stroke, Contrast, and Stress

Before the days of movable type, scribes often used a broad-tipped nib pen dipped in ink to individually construct each stroke in a letterform. A *stroke* could move vertically, horizontally, diagonally, or in a curved direction. In hand lettering, the width of a stroke can vary as the angle and direction of the nib changes with the movement of the pen. This is particularly noticeable in characters with curved strokes, such as in an O, C, and Q.

The transition between the thick and thin areas of a stroke is called *contrast* (see Figure 9.5). Low-contrast typefaces have little to no variation between the thick

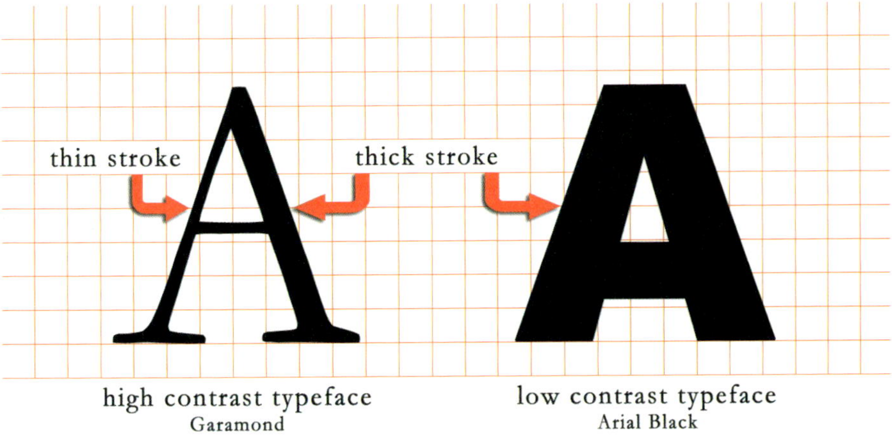

FIGURE 9.5
Garamond is considered a high-contrast font because of the stark difference in the width of the strokes used to form a single character. Arial Black, on the other hand, has a consistent width for each stroke segment.

and thin portions of a stroke. In high-contrast typefaces, the stroke transitions are more pronounced, often allowing users to read the letters more easily. *Stress* is the location or angle of a transition from thick to thin or vice versa. In vertical stress fonts, the transition occurs at the top and bottom of the vertical axis. In angled stress fonts, the transition takes place off-axis, either slightly to the left of center (left-angled) or to the right of center (right-angled).

Weight: Regular, Boldface, and Light

Bold typefaces (also known as *boldface*) increase the width of the stroke and the visual weight of the regular roman letterform. The letterforms, serifs, and character spacing of boldface type are redesigned to accommodate the increase in stroke thickness, so letters have adequate *counterform*, or white space between and within them. *Light typefaces* are the opposite of boldface, with small stroke widths.

Posture: Roman, Oblique, and Italic

Letterforms have *postures*. In typography, the term *Roman* with an uppercase *R* refers to the inspiration of certain typefaces and to categories of typeface. The word *roman* with a lowercase *r*, however, refers to upright typefaces. Letters with other postures—oblique and italic—usually slant to the right, often by about 12°. *Oblique* typefaces have letterforms based on roman counterparts. *Italic* typefaces have features that emulate handwritten forms. A true italic typeface contains visual features consistent with, but not necessarily included in, the roman version of the typeface.

Proportions and Letterform Parts

Figure 9.6 illustrates the basic characteristics of a typeface. In a row of type, the bottom edge of each character's main body rests on an imaginary plane called the *baseline*. Uppercase letters have their tops at the *capline*. Flat-topped lowercase letters have their tops at the *meanline*, and the relative size of a typeface is denoted by its *x-height*, or the distance between the meanline and the baseline, most easily measured using a lowercase *x*. The *counter* is the enclosed or partially enclosed open area in letters such as O and G. Typefaces with larger x-heights and counter sizes are often easier to read. An *ascender* is any part of a lowercase character that extends above the x-height, such as in the vertical stem of the letter *b* or *h*. A *descender* is any part of a character that extends below the baseline; such as in the bottom stroke of a *y* or *p*. Most typefaces are proportional, meaning the type width for each letterform varies, so an *l* sits close to neighboring letters, taking up less space than an *m*. Some typefaces are *monospaced*: spacing is uniform, so an *l* and *m* take up the same horizontal space. Monospaced typefaces are less readable for ordinary purposes, but they are used to illustrate code and in coding applications, such as Dreamweaver for web design, when you need to be able to distinguish each letter.

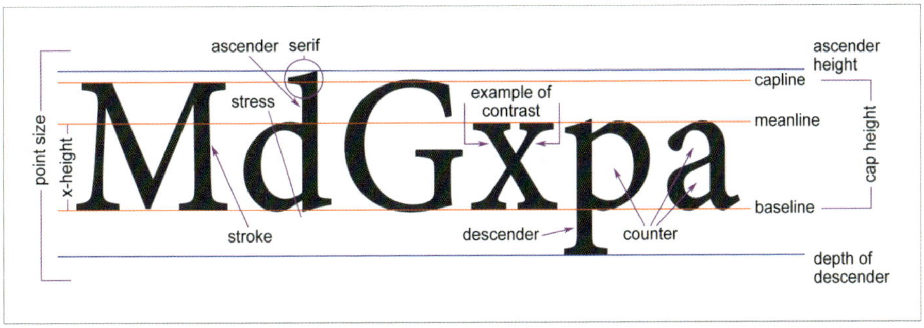

FIGURE 9.6
The characteristics, illustrated here, not only define each typeface but also help determine a typeface's suitability for various uses.
Illustrator: Susan A. Youngblood

FIGURE 9.7
Serifs are decorative accents added to the end of a stroke.

Serifs are small marks located on the ends of a main character stroke (see Figure 9.7). Serif typefaces contain serifs, while sans-serif typefaces do not. Which is better for print, and which is better for electronic display? Even a few years ago, experts would have said that serif typefaces were better for printed materials such as books because the serifs help with horizontal flow, or help guide readers' eyes across long lines of text. Some of this research on print readability has been called into question; at the most, the difference made by serifs is small. Other research suggests that sans-serif typefaces are better for electronic displays. Why? Serifs are small, so lower-resolution displays don't have enough pixels to cleanly render the serifs. Sans-serif typefaces are usually better for computer monitors and video. As you make typeface choices, consider specific font characteristics that improve legibility, not just categories. Also consider what your users expect in a given context, which is often serif typefaces for print and sans-serif for electronic media.

CATEGORIZING TYPEFACES

Typefaces are generally classified into two main groups depending on whether or not they contain serifs, and those groups can be divided many ways. The classification system discussed here is only one way to name and group typefaces.

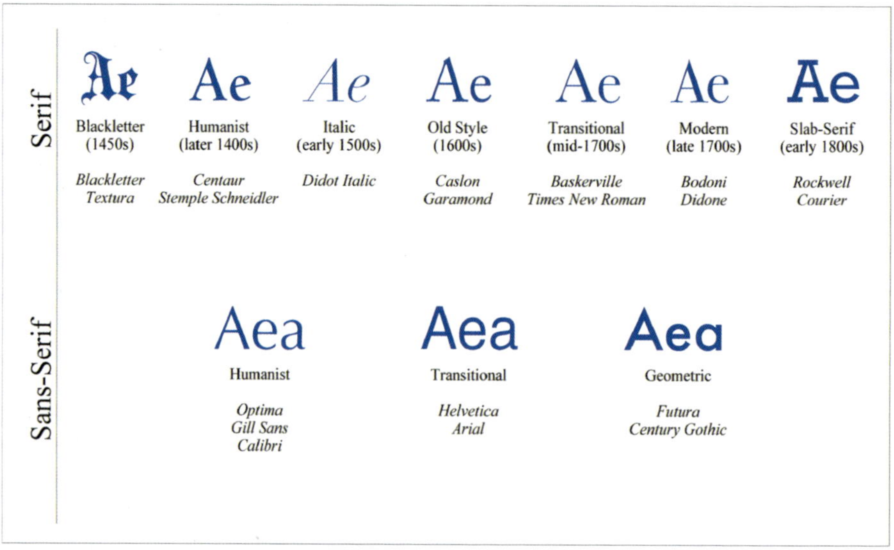

FIGURE 9.8
Typeface development through history. The examples are typical of their categories, but some were created later than the earliest dates listed for a given category.
Illustrator: Susan A. Youngblood

With so many variables, some typefaces are hard to classify. And different systems use some of the same words, such as *Gothic*, to mean different things (see Figure 9.8).

Serif Typefaces

There are six main groups of serif typefaces: Blackletter, Humanist, Old Style, Transitional, Modern, and Slab Serif. Serif typefaces are the industry standard for body copy that's printed in books, magazines, and newspapers. Even if new research calls into question readability differences on paper, readers are used to serif typefaces in these contexts. Digital technology can have trouble displaying serifs, so unless you're using a serif typeface designed for the digital display, such as Georgia, you're usually better off relying on serif typefaces for large headings or for print media.

FROM BLACKLETTER TO OLDSTYLE TYPEFACES

When movable type was invented, typeface designers simply copied the style of written forms onto the surface of metal type. Since traditional pen-based forms were familiar to the pioneers of printing, it seemed natural to them to design movable type in the same style that had been used for centuries. After all, this is what people were visually accustomed to. Because of Gutenberg's origins, it's no surprise that the Gothic script known as *Blackletter* was the first letterform to be widely adapted to metal type throughout the Germanic regions of Europe. While highly decorative, Blackletter type is composed of heavy angular strokes with few curves, making it a rather bold typeface that's difficult to read in small print. The Gutenberg Bible, the first book ever mass-produced with a printing press, used Blackletter type. Gutenberg used a two-column design with forty-two lines of text per page. The typeface could be read because the font was big, but the Gutenberg Bible was quite large and heavy when finished.

As printing moved into southern Europe, the more efficient and elegant forms of Roman lettering greatly influenced the design of metal type. *Humanist* (also known as *Venetian*) typefaces were the result. Like Blackletter, they are dark on the page and have sloped crossbars in the lowercase *e*, but despite their low contrast, they were considered an improvement over their Gothic predecessor. Humanist letterforms have more rounded and gentler strokes and are much easier to read in small print than Blackletter, despite having relatively small x-heights. Many of the serifs on lowercase letters are slanted, and serifs tend to be bracketed: the serifs connect to the main stroke with a curve, providing a smooth and gentle transition from the thick to thin areas of a font. Soon after, italic typefaces were developed; they allowed printers to put more words on a line and are still used for emphasis. *Old Style* (also known as *Garalde*) typefaces are similar to Humanist typefaces but are distinguished by a somewhat more vertical stress and horizontal crossbars in the lowercase *e*. Old Style typefaces include Garamond, Bembo, and Caslon and remain popular.

TRANSITIONAL TYPEFACES

As the name implies, the design attributes of *Transitional* letterforms fall somewhere between those of Old Style and what's to come: Modern-era type. Compared to Old Style type, transitional typefaces, such as Times New Roman and Baskerville, have higher contrast, a larger x-height, vertical stress, wider bracketed serifs, and generally wider letterforms.

Times New Roman is one of the most ubiquitous and well-known typefaces in this category. After being criticized for sloppy printing and the lack of readability in their newsprint, the London-based newspaper *The Times* commissioned the Monotype Corporation in 1931 to develop a new typeface. Released a year later, Times New Roman quickly evolved into the industry standard typeface for the newspaper, magazine, and book publishing industries. Today, Times New Roman is still widely popular and is one of a handful of universal fonts that's included with nearly every computer and operating system in the world.

MODERN TYPEFACES

Modern (also known as *Didone*) typefaces represented the first noticeable departure from typography's historical dependency on pen-based letterforms. Their designs have an extremely high contrast, a small x-height, thin horizontal serifs with little to no bracketing, and vertical stress in the rounded strokes. Modern fonts are not very readable when reduced to small, lengthy sections of text. Their contemporary features make them a better choice for title text and headers.

SLAB-SERIF TYPEFACES

Up until the time of the Industrial Revolution, typefaces were largely designed for setting small body type in newsprint and books. With industrialization came the increased need to promote and advertise goods and services for public consumption using large letter type. *Slab-serif* (also known as *Egyptian*) typefaces were designed specifically for this type of application. Bold and eye-catching, slab-serif typefaces are a good choice for posters, flyers, billboards, and other large format media that demand immediate attention and text recognition. Slab-serif typefaces have low-contrast strokes, thick horizontal serifs that can be either squared-off or slightly bracketed, and vertical stress in the rounded strokes.

Sans-Serif Typefaces

Sans is a French word meaning "without," thus *sans-serif* (also known as *lineal*) typefaces are those that are literally without serifs; they are sometimes also referred to as *gothic* or *grotesque*, because some earlier typeface designers found them unattractive. Sans-serif type was used to emboss pages for blind readers beginning in 1789 and was developed for printing for sighted readers in 1816. The popularity of sans-serif typefaces boomed in the 20th century. Type designers strove to create basic letterforms, devoid of the excessive design elements of modern and slab-serif type. Sans-serif typefaces obviously have no serifs, and usually have uniform strokes with little to no contrast and a vertical stress in rounded strokes. These typefaces are also broken into categories: *Humanist* for varieties that have an angled stress, nongeometric counters, and contrast; *Geometric* for varieties that have vertical stresses, geometric counters, and no contrast; and *Transitional* for those in between.

FIGURE 9.9
These decorative fonts were downloaded under a freeware license from urbanfonts.com. UrbanFonts is a popular font-sharing website that provides access to thousands of fonts. Through this site, and many others like it, users can download fonts for free (as freeware) or on a trial basis (as shareware). In the case of shareware, the cost is often much lower than commercial rates. While known mostly for its large collection of free fonts, urbanfonts.com also sells fonts.

Sans-serif typefaces are ideal for text headings and titles in print and for use in electronic media where lower resolution can make serifs hard to render cleanly. Because of this, sans-serif fonts are often the best choice when designing body copy for the Web or other channels of electronic distribution.

Decorative Typefaces

Decorative typefaces connote a sense of mood, emotion, or attitude (see Figure 9.9). They have personality, which is great for attracting attention but does little for enhancing the readability of the text in small form. Decorative typefaces are characterized by unusual features intended to add splash and pizzazz to a design. Because they're purposely designed to draw lots of attention to themselves, they should be used in moderation.

Script Typefaces

Script typefaces are among the easiest letterforms to categorize because they so clearly attempt to emulate the cursive style of handwriting, or the artistic appearance of calligraphy. Script typefaces are slanted, and a stroke connects adjoining letters and preserves linear flow. Script typefaces are popular with commercial printers when they need to create a formal text design such as in a wedding invitation or certificate of achievement, when readability is less of a concern than the overall feel of the document. Because of their thin strokes and angled form, these typefaces generally have a weak appearance when rendered out to electronic displays.

Symbol Typefaces and Special Characters

There will undoubtedly come a time when you need to insert a special character or symbol that's not found on your keyboard, such as those shown below.

€ å ≠ ± é © ® ¢ Ω ß

Many common symbols—such as currency symbols, mathematical operators, accented letters, and copyright marks—are included in the Universal Character Set established by the ISO/IEC standard 10646. Depending on which program you're using, many special characters can be added to a document by combining a modifier key on the keyboard with a second key or character code (or Unicode). For example, pressing OPTION+G on a Mac keyboard produces ©, the international copyright symbol. On a standard English Windows keyboard, the same character can be inserted by typing ALT+169. The advantage of this method is that the design of the inserted character matches the style of the currently active typeface. It is a part of the same font family, and therefore blends seamlessly with the surrounding type. Unfortunately, the Universal Character Set does not include everything. As an alternative, you can use a dingbat (or symbol) typeface, such as Symbol, Wingding, Webdings, or Zapf Dingbats (see Figure 9.10). Symbol typefaces are popular because they include many ornamental characters not found elsewhere. However, they will not blend as naturally when mixed with another typeface.

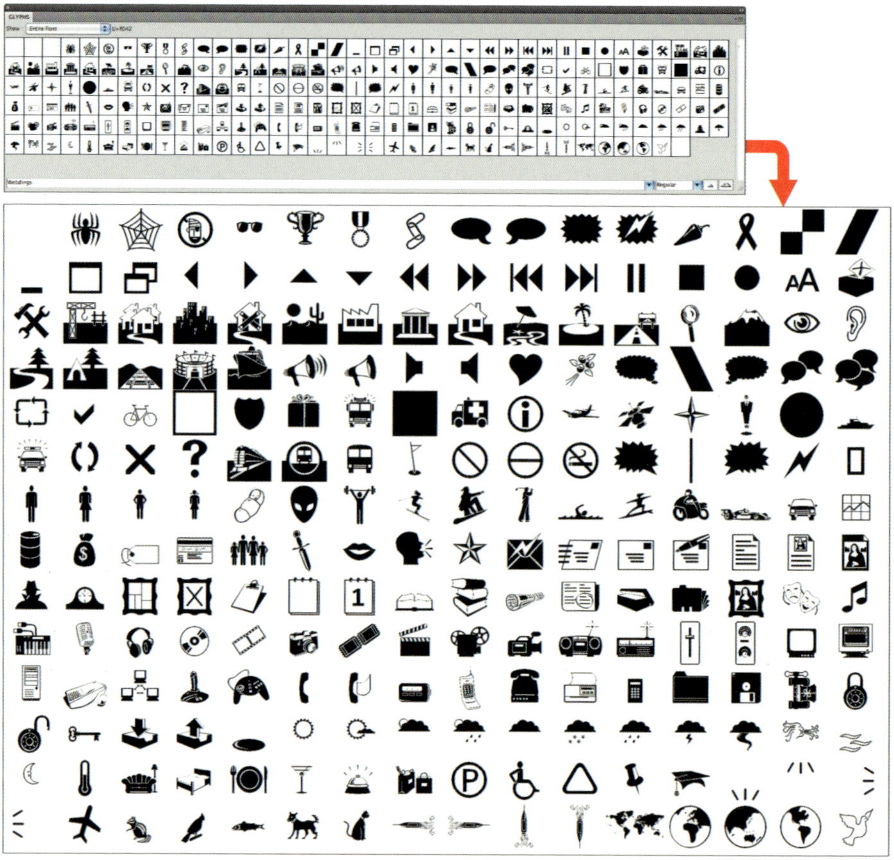

FIGURE 9.10
The Webdings font includes this fun assortment of symbol glyphs. Many programs, including Microsoft and Mac operating systems, include a character map that allows you to view, select, and insert special characters and symbols into an open document. The Glyphs window shown here (top) is available from within Adobe Illustrator.

COMPUTERS AND TYPEFACES

The vast majority of the typefaces (and their fonts) on your computer were designed for the high-resolution medium of printing. When rendered digitally, printer fonts are often difficult to read, especially when they are small, bold, script, italic, have thin strokes, or have tricky-to-display serifs. Georgia and Verdana were among the first typefaces created specifically for display on computer monitors. They have good x-heights, large counters, easily distinguished characters (for instance, uppercase *i* and lowercase *l*), and distinctive bold. In readability testing for the Web, Verdana consistently scores high marks and is one of the most popular screen fonts used for body copy on the Web.

In order for a web browser to accurately display text in a web page, all of the fonts used in its design must reside on the client computer. When the browser is unable to locate a font that's specified in the HTML code, it will perform a font substitution, swapping out the intended typeface with a local one. Font substitution can significantly change the look of a page from what was originally intended. To ensure font compatibility with other systems, select a font from one of the following families: Verdana, Georgia, Arial, Courier New, Times New Roman, Trebuchet MS, Comic Sans, and Symbol. These are standard fonts that come with all Windows and Mac computer systems. They're also considered to be Web-safe, meaning they are supported by all of the most popular web browsers (see Figure 9.11).

Relying solely on safe fonts can limit your creativity. As an alternative, text can be saved as a graphic image and uploaded to the Web in JPEG or GIF format. With the typeface embedded inside the text graphic, users don't need to have the matching font installed on their local computers to view it. However, use images of text only for titles, headers, and display text: search engines do not have the ability locate text when it's embedded in a graphic, and users with disabilities need you to provide alternative text for every image, which can be cumbersome if you have a text-heavy image. If you choose to create limited text in images, consider using an OpenType font: these fonts are scalable and crossplatform, so they'll look right if you move between a Mac and PC during your project.

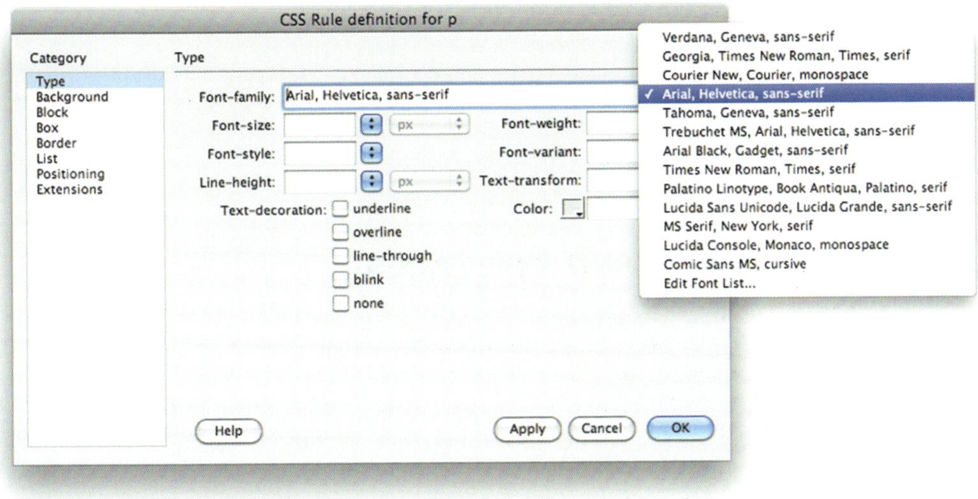

FIGURE 9.11
Like most web authoring programs, Adobe Dreamweaver CS5 displays a relatively small list of fonts to choose from. The fonts shown are ones considered by Adobe to be "Web-safe."

Tech Talk

Category Characteristics
A typeface's characteristics help determine which category it fits in and what it is best used for.

	Serifs	Common Uses	Examples
Blackletter	serifs present; heavy and angular strokes; dark on the page; high contrast; angled stress; few curves	decorative or limited text inspiring an old feel, such as a newspaper textual logo	Blackletter Textura
Humanist	serifs are slanted and bracketed; gentler and rounder strokes; moderate contrast; angled stress; small x-height; sloped crossbar in the lowercase ***e***	printed text; to lend a traditional feel, but other choices may be more readable	Centaur Stemple-Schneidler
Old Style	serifs are wider, bracketed, and rounded; moderate contrast; more vertical stress; small x-height; sloped crossbar in the lowercase *e* open counter	still popular for printed text	Caslon Garamond Bembo
Transitional	serifs are wider, bracketed, slanted, and rounded; moderately high contrast; more vertical stress; larger x-height than Old Style; wider letterforms	very popular for printed text; Georgia was designed for digital text	Baskerville Times New Roman Georgia
Modern	serifs are unbracketed and straight; very high contrast; vertical stress; fairly consistent width of uppercase letters	advertising, headlines	Bodini Didone
Slab-Serif	serifs are wide and squared; often dark on the page; often low contrast; x-height can be large	advertising, such as billboards	Rockwell Courier

	Serifs	Common Uses	Examples
Humanist Sans Serif	no serifs; angled stress	print headings and digital text; Verdana was designed for digital use	Optima Gill SansCalibri Verdana
Transitional Sans Serif	no serifs; low contrast; almost vertical stress	print headings and digital text	Helvetica Arial
Geometric	no serifs; based on geometric forms; vertical stress	advertising	Futura Century Gothic
Italic	angled, but the roman form has been adapted, not just slanted	emphasis, calligraphy	Didot Italic Arial Italic
Decorative	letterforms have decorative touches	limited eye-catching text	Mesquite Std Curlz MT Princetown LET
Script	a subset of Decorative modeled after handwriting strokes	formal invitations	Edwardian Script ITC Lucida Handwriting
Symbol	symbols often not available on the keyboard	for special characters (e.g. - language, currency, mathematical, geometric, and phonetic symbols)	Symbol Wingdings Zapf Dingbats

GREAT IDEAS

Adding to Your Typeface Collection

Typefaces can be added to a computer system (as fonts) in a number of different ways. An assortment of basic fonts is included with the operating system on your computer. Additional fonts are added to the system when new software is installed (word processing applications, graphics programs, etc.). Fonts can also be obtained individually from commercial font foundries and third-party software vendors, and through freeware and shareware services on the Internet (see Figure 9.12). If you have ample patience and a meticulous personality, you can even create your own fonts using software such as FontLab.

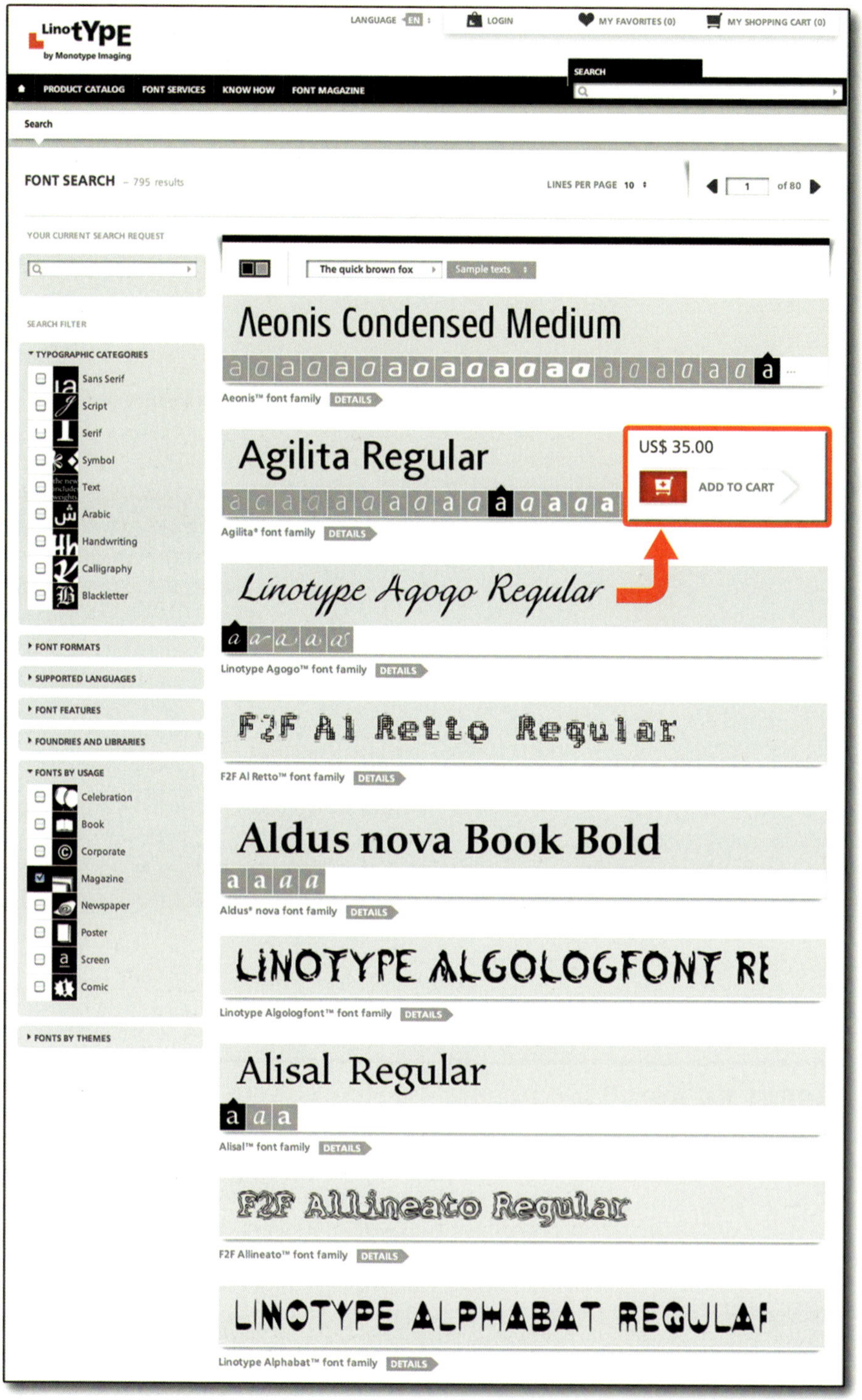

FIGURE 9.12 Linotype is a commercial type foundry that specializes in the design of commercial typefaces for professional designers. Founded in 1886, Linotype designers have created a large collection of fonts including familiar ones such as Gil Sans, Helvetica, Optima, Palatino, and Papyrus.

Adding emphasis to key words, headings, or phrases lets the user know that there is a sense of order and importance in the way that information is presented. When all of the text in a page looks exactly the same, the design becomes visually flat and viewers are left to wander aimlessly through a sea of monotonous pixels. On the other hand, if you emphasize too many text elements at once, the design may appear visually cluttered and confusing. In other words, if you emphasize just about everything, you emphasize nothing. As with all things in design, moderation and balance are important. Text emphasis is most often accomplished by varying the style, size, and color of a typeface (see Figure 9.13).

FONT STYLES: TRUE AND FAUX

Font styles, or font-family variations, are used by designers to add visual variety and emphasis to text by varying the weight, angle, and width of the typeface. Most font families include the four basic styles of roman (upright), bold, italic, and bold italic. Font styles usually look better when they are *true font styles*—ones in which the designer carefully changed each glyph during design—rather than faux font styles—computer-generated effects that simulate font adaptations to create faux-bold and faux-italics. *Faux styles* often produce a look that's different

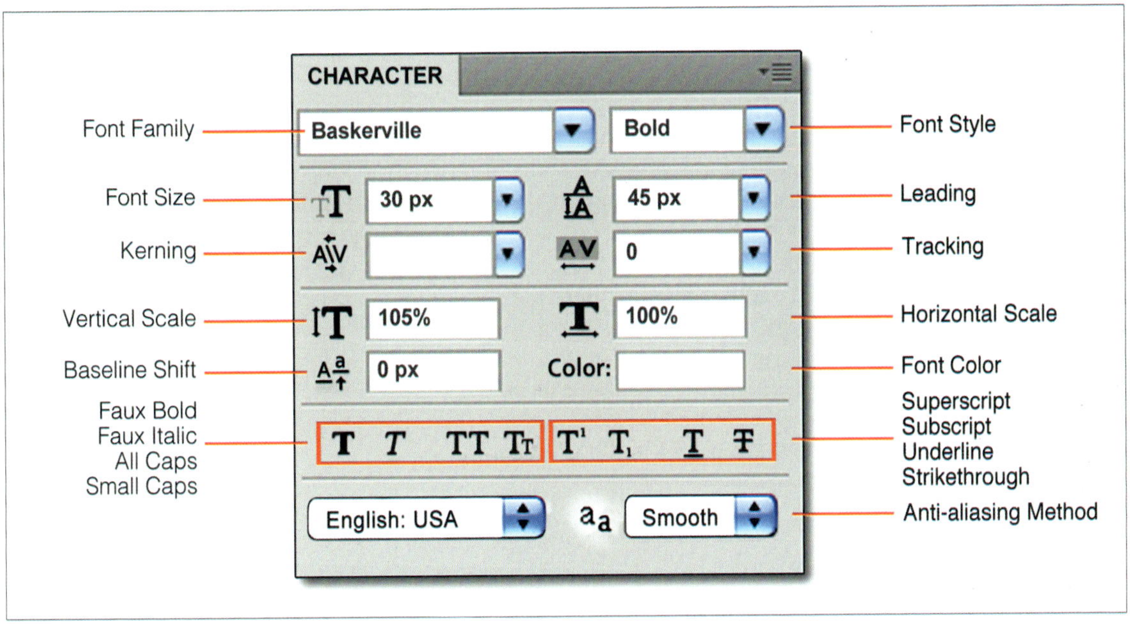

FIGURE 9.13
The Character panel in Adobe Photoshop CS5 can be used for modifying the appearance of selected text in the design window Source: Adobe Photoshop CS 5.
Source: Adobe Photoshop CS 5

Faux Bold	The quick brown fox jumps over a lazy dog.
True Bold	**The quick brown fox jumps over a lazy dog.**
Faux Italic	*The quick brown fox jumps over a lazy dog.*
True Italic	*The quick brown fox jumps over a lazy dog.*
Faux Bold Italic	*The quick brown fox jumps over a lazy dog.*
True Bold Italic	***The quick brown fox jumps over a lazy dog.***

FIGURE 9.14
The difference between true bold and italic styles and faux effects is quite apparent when you compare them side-by-side.

from what the designers of the font intended (see Figure 9.14). Professional designers prefer the authentic look of true font styles, because the size, shape, and spacing of each letterform are custom designed to be consistent with the overall look of the typeface; they tend to avoid faux styles because they are aesthetically less pleasing than the real thing. Some typefaces have more true font styles than others.

Italics and Boldface for Emphasis

When used in moderation, changing a word or short phrase to *italics* can be a subtle, effective, and elegant way to emphasize text. Just be sure not to overdo it, and be careful about italics for digital media: they can be difficult to read. If you want to emphasize text using italics, select a font family that includes a true italic. Like italics, boldface type is used to add emphasis to selected words in body text and headings and should be used sparingly within a design. As the name implies, this typeface style is **Bold!** and will call more attention to the text than its italic counterpart. And some font families—such as Verdana and Georgia—have been designed so the counters (the open spaces in some letters) of their bold versions still appear open on digital displays. These font families also have ample weight differences between their roman and italic fonts, allowing users to pick out bold words easily. Applying a ***faux bold*** effect simply thickens the stroke of an existing roman form without changing a character's style or spacing, producing a proportionally smaller amount of white space in counters and between each character, making text more difficult to read. As with italics, choose a font family with a true boldface.

Condensed or Expanded Type

Some font families include typefaces in which the width and height of the type are purposely disproportional. Condensed typefaces appear tall and thin, while expanded typefaces look somewhat short and fat (see Figure 9.15). Each can be simulated by modifying the selected text with the vertical or horizontal scaling controls in the Photoshop character palette. For normal scaling, both controls should be set to 100%. To increase or decrease the vertical or horizontal scale

Myriad Pro Condensed
Myriad Pro Regular
Myriad Pro - Expanded Tracking

FIGURE 9.15
Type can be condensed, expanded, scaled, and stretched a number of different ways to achieve a desired effect.

of type, adjust the percentages up or down in the appropriate entry field. Vertical and horizontal scaling are virtual effects that merely stretch out type. As a result, they are not nearly as pleasing to the eye as a true condensed or expanded typeface.

All Caps and Small Caps

Normal uppercase letters or *caps* (short for *capitals*) are created by holding down the shift key while typing. In the character palette, you also have the option of formatting text in ALL CAPS or Small Caps. The *all caps* option sets the selected type in uppercase so the top of capital letters touch the normal capline. The *small caps* option also sets type in uppercase, but at a reduced height that's closer to the size of lowercase letters. As a result, small caps are not as visually overwhelming as true uppercase letters. Small caps are often used by designers when it's necessary to type a string of all uppercase letters, as with certain abbreviations and acronyms (P.M., NASA). Using small caps instead of all caps helps keep regular portions of narrative text from being unintentionally overemphasized.

The shape of a word—the letter width, counters, ascenders, and descenders—helps us read, so use uppercase letters sparingly. The brain recognizes words by their physical shape as a unit and not by the individual letters they are composed of. In other words, people do not read letters so much as they read composite shapes in the form of words and phrases. Setting type in all uppercase letters (even small caps) takes away distinctive features, hurting readability. Think about street signs: one labeled "Washington St." is easier to read, especially from a distance, than one labeled "WASHINGTON ST." When words are composed entirely of caps, their distinctive shape is lost and people have to work harder to discern them. As a general principle, avoid using caps to emphasize text, and also avoid mixing upper and lowercase letters together, except when called for by normal writing conventions, such as at the beginning of a sentence or a proper noun.

While designers tend to agree about the pitfalls of using all caps or mixed caps in body text, there's less conformity when it comes to the practice of using caps in titles, headings, and display text, especially when designing for multimedia. The Web in particular demands bolder, larger type, to help compensate for the lowresolution of electronic media, the physical distance between people and the text, and the fatiguing nature of reading off a screen instead of paper. You may be tempted to believe that bigger is better and that caps are justified. All things being equal, though, readability is best served by minimizing the use of caps. All caps also has the stigma of connoting shouting and is considered by many people to be rude and unacceptable in online communication. You be the judge. Which of the following sentences do you think is easier to read?

All caps	THE GOVERNOR IS ARRIVING TODAY AT VICTORIA STATION.
Small caps	THE GOVERNOR IS ARRIVING TODAY AT VICTORIA STATION.
Mixed caps	The Governor Is Arriving Today At Victoria Station.
Normal caps	The Governor is arriving today at Victoria Station.

Underline and ~~Strikethrough~~

Underlining applies a line with the same color as the font to the baseline of selected text, while *strikethrough* adds a line through the horizontal center of type. Neither of these features provides control over stroke thickness or the placement of the line in relation to the text. Underlining text as a method of emphasis is considered taboo by design professionals: it disrupts the shape of the text by cutting through descenders. Like all caps, it makes text more difficult to read. Sometimes conventions have led designers to abandon key principles: for example, on the Web underlining text is a common and standard way of identifying hyperlinks. Readability is impaired, but usability is increased by giving people a visual cue to the clickable text on the page. However, there are many other ways to draw attention to hyperlinks without sacrificing readability. Many sites use code to hide the hyperlink underlines until a cursor moves over them. Using text graphics or visual icons is another way to avoid the unsightly underscores, but be sure to provide alternative text for users who have vision problems and may only hear text descriptions of your images.

Font Size

Digital fonts, whether used to create materials for print or for the screen, are measured in real physical units that correspond to their actual size when the text is printed on paper. But when fonts are displayed in an electronic medium, the actual size of text will vary according to the resolution (in pixels) of the monitor used to view it. You can set font size in several ways, but the point system is the most common method for measuring type. For print, it's customary to set the font size to 10–12 points for body copy. Research and experience have shown these to be good point sizes for text documents when read by most people with normal vision. But just how big is 12-point font?

To begin with, points are a unit of measurement used to define the vertical height of a typeface. Originally, point size referred to the vertical height of the metal block with the raised letterform. Regardless of a character's shape and size, the block for each character in a typeface had the same height. An uppercase *Z*, though, naturally consumes more surface area on its metal block than does a lowercase *i*. And for both metal and digital type, point size reflects the distance from the top of the tallest ascender to the bottom of the lowest descender, plus a bit of additional space on either end. There are 12 points in a pica, and 6 picas in an inch. So there are 72 points in an inch. It's worth mentioning that many monitors, especially Macs, display 72 ppi (points per inch). Does this mean that using a 72-point font will always lead to the production of letters that are exactly one-inch tall? Well no, not really. As long as fonts are limited to display purposes only on electronic screens (as opposed to printed out), the fact that points can be converted to inches really doesn't matter. For the multimedia producer, it's much easier to think of font size in relative rather than absolute terms. The readability of an impression made by different fonts set in the same point size can vary significantly in terms of their visual weight and impact. Even though different fonts of the same point size may use virtual blocks with the same height, one's capital letters may be shorter within the block. Or another's x-height may be greater, making it seem larger. Of course, some fonts, such as Georgia, may have wider letterforms too (see Figure 9.16).

12-point font (Impact)

12-point font (Georgia)

12-point font (Helvetica)

12-point font (Futura Medium)

12-point font (Times New Roman)

FIGURE 9.16
All five lines of type pictured here were set to a 12-point font size in Adobe Illustrator CS5. However, the printed length of each line varies because of variables associated with the design of the each typeface being used. The display size of the fonts shown here was enlarged for comparison.

When creating text in graphics software, always be sure to save it to a layer that is editable so you can resize or revise it later. In graphics software, type is initially created as a vector object, allowing it to be scaled to virtually any size without losing detail. Text can be resized with precision by entering or selecting a discrete point size. When a graphic is saved in a bitmap file format such as JPEG, the text elements within it are permanently *rastorized*, or changed to pixels rather than lines, and can no longer be edited with the type tools or resized without resulting in a loss of image quality and detail.

Font Color

When selecting a font color, be sure to pick a contrasting shade that stands out from the background. Combining a dark-colored font with a dark background, or a light-colored font with a light background, leads to poor contrast, and the text will be difficult to read (see Figure 9.17). Dark type on a light background is generally easier for people to read than light-colored type on a dark background. Even electronic books are normally created with black type on a white background.

When you do choose splashes of color, be careful about the combinations. Some color combinations, such as green and red, seem to vibrate, so they are hard to look at and strain users' eyes. Also, some of your users may be colorblind or have color deficiencies. There are several kinds of problems that affect seeing color, and some color combinations are poor choices. For instance, a person may perceive all red as black, so that the black-on-red website marquis you planned won't work (unless you want the user to see a big black

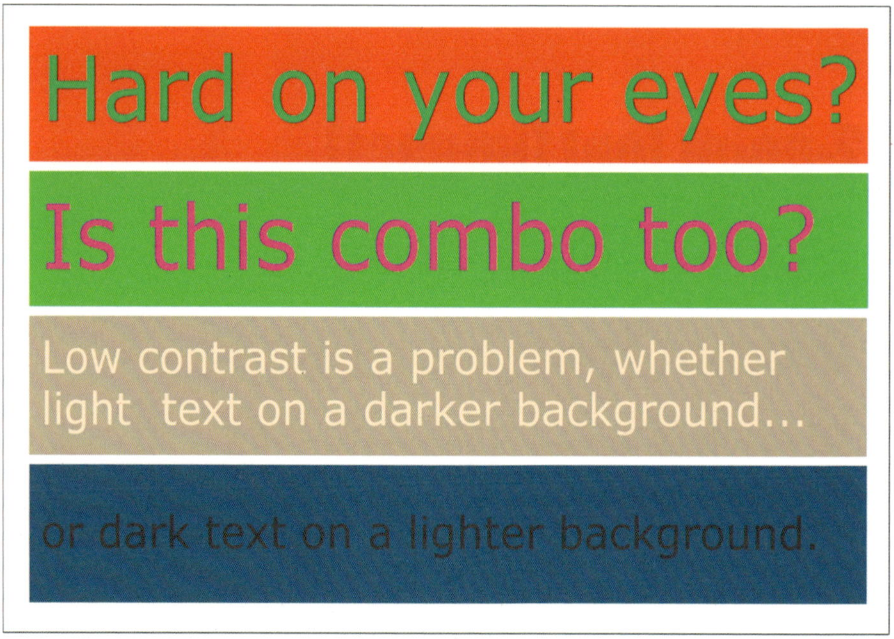

FIGURE 9.17 Color contrast affects readability.
Illustrator: Susan A. Youngblood

box). Whether you're working on graphical text or web text, check your color choices with a tool such as Vischeck.com's online colorblindness simulator.

Baseline Shift

When composing type in a word processing or graphic design program, the software automatically conforms all of the text in a row to a common baseline. Much of the time this works just fine. However, there are other times when the visual aesthetic can be best served by shifting the base of certain characters to a new position. This is particularly true when you attempt to combine different font families, styles, or sizes. You can shift the baseline to move text one point at a time above or below the existing baseline (see Figure 9.18).

Superscript/Subscript

In order to accurately reflect the shorthand notation for special formulas and character symbols, it's sometimes necessary to apply subscript or superscript formatting to text. *Superscript* characters have a smaller point size than the surrounding text and are shifted upward above the baseline. Ordinal numbers are often displayed with a superscript modifier (1st, 2nd, 3rd, etc.). Other uses for superscript formatting include footnote references[1], compass bearings (20° W), and mathematical exponents such as $10^{(2)}$ and $(a^{n})^{-1}$. Subscript characters also have a smaller point size, but are shifted downward below the baseline as in H_2O, the chemical formula for water.

Anti-Aliasing

Because screen fonts are rendered out on screen using square pixels, the edges of the diagonal and curved strokes in a typeface often appear jagged. This stair-step effect is called *aliasing* and is an undesirable consequence of digital typography. *Anti-aliasing* is a technique used in raster (bitmap) editing to smooth out the edges of type. When anti-aliasing is turned on, transition pixels of an intermediate color are added between the jagged edges of a stroke and the surrounding area. The result is a distinctly smoother edge. Anti-aliasing works best on large type and is not generally recommended for font sizes smaller than 10 points because it reduces the readability of text.

FIGURE 9.18
Typically, all type in a row of text sits uniformly on a common baseline (top). Shifting or varying the baseline (bottom) is a creative choice by the designer for achieving a particular visual effect.

---

[1] A superscript footnote reference like the one inserted in the text above, corresponds to a citation or note (like this one) placed at the bottom of the page or at the end of a chapter.

Tech Talk

Font Management Font management software is used for previewing and managing the fonts on a computer system (see Figures 9.19 and 9.20). It can be used to install, remove, view, group, enable, and disable fonts. Fonts are loaded into RAM when your computer is first turned on. The more fonts that are installed, the more RAM your system will need to make those fonts available to running applications. Depending on how many fonts you have, your computer's performance may be improved by temporarily disabling fonts you rarely use. A disabled font remains in the system but will not appear in the fonts list of your design software. As your collection of fonts grows, managing them will become increasingly important.

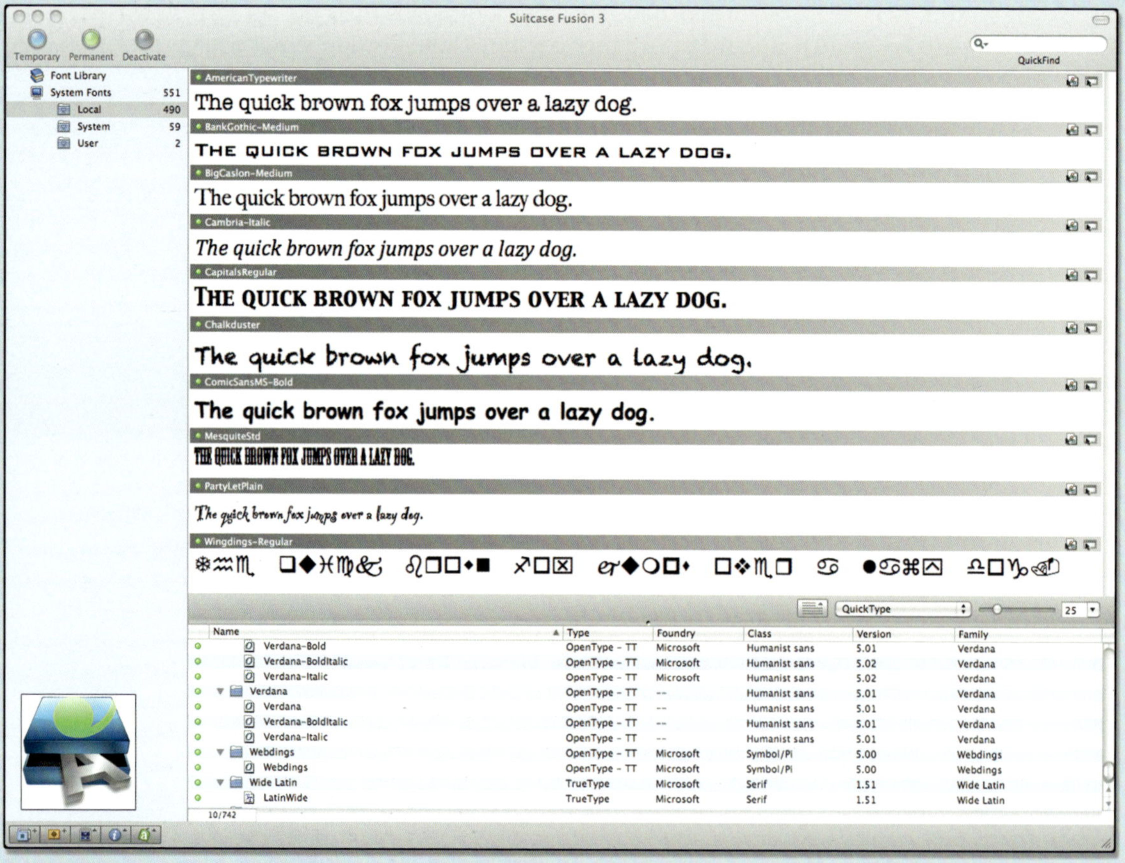

FIGURE 9.19
Suitcase Fusion 3 is a crossplatform font management program compatible with both Mac and Windows.

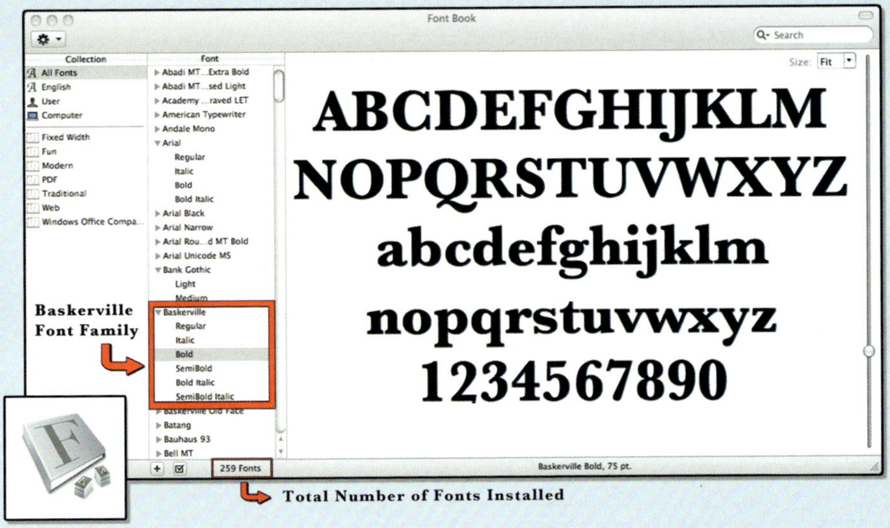

FIGURE 9.20
Font Book is Apple's proprietary font manager utility for computers running OS X. The Baskerville font family is highlighted here as one of 259 resident fonts in the fonts collection.

CHARACTER AND LINE SPACING

Kerning and Tracking

By default, computer graphics programs handle letter spacing automatically according to the built-in design characteristics of each font family. But you often can improve the appearance and readability of text by manually controlling the amount of space between characters with kerning or tracking. *Kerning* selectively varies the amount of space between a single pair of letters and accounts for letter shape, letting letters like *A* and *V* extend into one another's virtual blocks; *tracking* uniformly adjusts letter spacing across a range of selected text. Each can improve the appearance and readability of text by eliminating distracting white space in a text design. They can also loosen up the appearance of type, making it appear less stuffy and congested. However, you need to be careful. Increasing the distance between letters makes the text more difficult to read.

Leading

Leading (pronounced *ledding*) is used to define the amount of space between vertically adjacent lines of text (see Figure 9.21). The term originated during the days of manual typesetting when thin strips of lead of various widths were used to separate the rows of metal typeface. In digital typesetting, leading is measured in points as the distance between the baseline of one row and the baseline of the next. When lines are spaced too closely together or too far apart, readers have trouble advancing their eyes to the next line, and readability diminishes. The computer-generated spacing that's assigned to type by the graphics program is not always appropriate and should never be blindly accepted. For example, large x-height fonts—such as most sans-serifs—usually require additional leading. Extra leading is also needed for longer lines of text and for paragraphs set in boldface type.

Lorem ipsum dolor sit amet, consectetur adipiscing elit. Proin quis erat orci. Maecenas quam nisi, ultrices in lacinia blandit, condimentum lacinia enim. In tortor augue, eleifend non tristique at, molestie id lacus. Morbi a ligula sit amet purus accumsan aliquet. Integer dui nisl, condimentum in interdum vel, bibendum at dolor. Class aptent taciti sociosqu ad litora torquent per conubia nostra, per inceptos himenaeos. Proin ac libero ac dolor posuere tempor vitae non tortor. Etiam et elit massa. In ultrices urna pharetra dui cursus iaculis gravida nisi fermentum.

Lorem ipsum dolor sit amet, consectetur adipiscing elit. Proin quis erat orci. Maecenas quam nisi, ultrices in lacinia blandit, condimentum lacinia enim. In tortor augue, eleifend non tristique at, molestie id lacus. Morbi a ligula sit amet purus accumsan aliquet. Integer dui nisl, condimentum in interdum vel, bibendum at dolor. Class aptent taciti sociosqu ad litora torquent per conubia nostra, per inceptos himenaeos. Proin ac libero ac dolor posuere tempor vitae non tortor. Etiam et elit massa. In ultrices urna pharetra dui cursus iaculis gravida nisi fermentum.

Lorem ipsum dolor sit amet, consectetur adipiscing elit. Proin quis erat orci. Maecenas quam nisi, ultrices in lacinia blandit, condimentum lacinia enim. In tortor augue, eleifend non tristique at, molestie id lacus. Morbi a ligula sit amet purus accumsan aliquet. Integer dui nisl, condimentum in interdum vel, bibendum at dolor. Class aptent taciti sociosqu ad litora torquent per conubia nostra, per inceptos himenaeos. Proin ac libero ac dolor posuere tempor vitae non tortor. Etiam et elit massa. In ultrices urna pharetra dui cursus iaculis gravida nisi fermentum.

FIGURE 9.21
Which of these blocks of text is easier to read? Which is the most difficult to read? Why?

ALIGNMENT, JUSTIFICATION, AND DISTRIBUTION

The terms *alignment* and *justification* refer to the process of lining up objects or text uniformly along their tops, bottoms, sides, or middles. Distribution involves inserting an equal amount of space between the designated edges (left, right, top, or bottom) or centers of visual elements, including text, placed along a vertical or horizontal edge. For example, you're probably accustomed to seeing menu buttons or text labels on a Web page spaced evenly apart. In Western countries, where people read from left to right and from top to bottom, readability is at its best when paragraphs are left justified and the type is evenly distributed. Aligning paragraph text along the left edge produces a consistent starting point for the eye as it shifts to the beginning of each new line. The trend in both print and electronic publishing is to left-align body copy, leaving the right edge of body copy unjustified or *ragged*. The ragged-right edge allows readers to keep track of their place in the paragraph. A ragged edge should be made to look as smooth and natural as possible by controlling the location of line breaks. The technique of curving the right edge inward towards the bottom of a paragraph, adds elegance to the visual flow and shape of the text.

The remaining paragraph alignment options should be used sparingly. A paragraph is considered *justified* when both the left and right edges are aligned. In order to achieve a consistent right edge in a fully-justified paragraph, the graphics program has to increase or decrease space between the words in each line. The irregular and uneven word spacing creates distracting "rivers of white" in paragraphs; it disrupts reading and reduces white space within the page layout. *Right-aligning*text with a left-ragged edge can add variety and interest to a design. However, since readability is diminished with this technique, its best to limit its use to short paragraphs or sentences. *Centered text* produces a symmetrical look that's visually balanced but difficult to read, since both the left and right edges are ragged. Center alignment is not recommended for body copy and only sparingly with headlines and other short sections of text (see Figure 9.22).

It's never a good idea to rely upon your eye or your skill with a mouse when aligning and distributing objects—evenly spacing them out vertically or horizontally—within a layout. Alignment needs to be precise, otherwise you may end up introducing irregularities into the design that are visually distracting to the viewer. You can also align precisely by using gridlines and snapping tools (see Figure 9.23). A *grid* is a matrix of evenly spaced vertical and horizontal lines that are superimposed overtop of the design window. Most multimedia design and editing software includes gridlines or snapping to make it easier to keep objects and text perfectly aligned. If you use *snapping,* as you move a layer close to a gridline, the layer snaps into place.

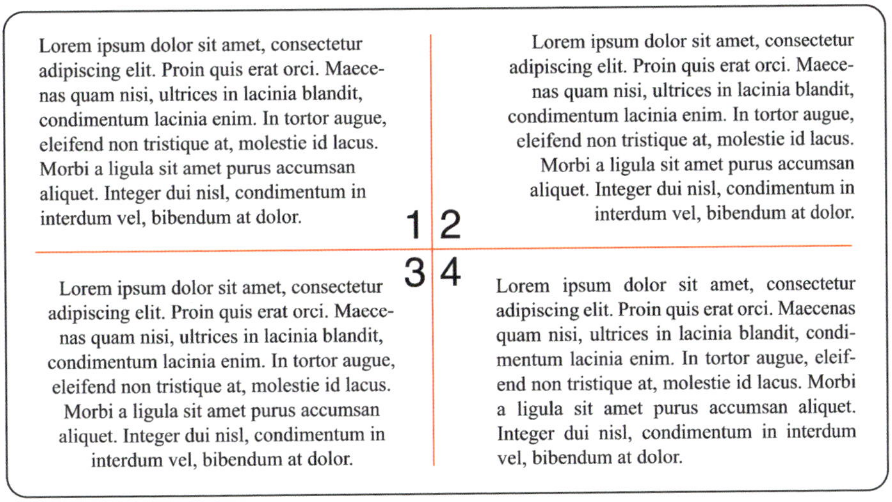

FIGURE 9.22
(1) Ragged-right or left justified (most common for body copy); (2) ragged-left or right justified; (3) centered text; and (4) justified left and right.

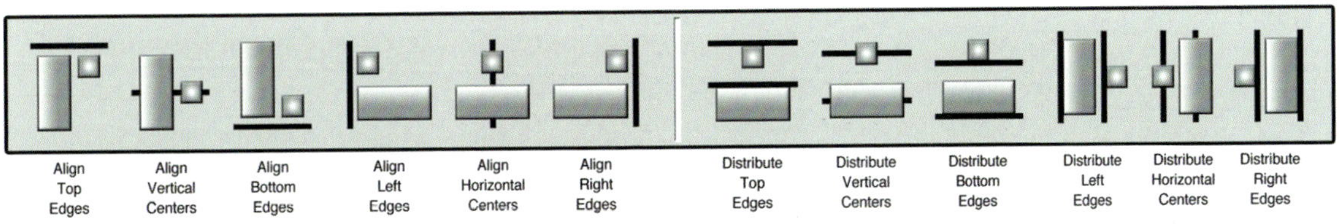

FIGURE 9.23
Most design programs have a set of alignment buttons or menu commands for aligning selected text and objects within the design space. The icons shown here will be familiar to users of Adobe Photoshop CS5.

FONT TRANSFORMATIONS

You can transform type into an element of design to grab the attention of the viewer or to add interest and variety to a page layout (see Figure 9.24). Visual effects can change the appearance of the shape, fill area, and stroke of a typeface in an endless variety of fun and interesting ways (see Figures 9.25 and 9.26). Be careful, though: if the effects aren't subtle, they can be distracting. And many effects, such as drop shadows and beveling, can reduce text's readability.

The following visual effects are fairly common and can be easily applied to text by a designer using a program such as Adobe Photoshop or Illustrator.

- **Color gradients and pattern fills.** While the conventional type in body copy is usually filled with a single color, type can also be filled with a gradient of colors, a pattern texture, or an image.
- **Warping.** Warping bends and distorts a typeface. Text can be arched, inflated, squeezed, twisted, and manipulated a number of other ways to create a variety of text-based shapes.
- **Drop shadows.** Adding a drop shadow is one of the easiest things you can do to add interest and depth to text objects and backgrounds. When applied to text, a drop shadow gives the illusion that words are floating above the background. The more pronounced the drop shadow is, the greater the distance will appear between the text and the background. The perceived foreground-background position of objects in a composite can be manipulated in part by applying different drop shadow settings for each object.

FIGURE 9.24
An assortment of some of the most common effects you can apply to text for enhancing visual contrast and impact. **First Column:** warped text, bevel and emboss; **Second Column:** reversed type, stroke/outline, drop shadow, and inner glow; **Third Column:** pattern fill (grass), gradient fill (three tone color), image fill (flag), and outer glow.

FIGURE 9.25
Top-left: Plain white text (no font transformations applied). Top-right: A drop shadow is applied. Bottom left: A stroke/outline is applied. Bottom-right: A two-color gradient fill and drop shadow are applied. Which version do you think has the best contrast and visual appeal?

FIGURE 9.26
A clipping mask was used in Adobe Photoshop CS5 to create this colorful font-fill effect.

- **Stroke**. A stroke is a colored outline that's placed around the exposed edges of type. Adding a stoke effect can greatly improve the contrast between text elements and the background. An *inside stroke* cuts into the fill area of type, while an *outside stroke* expands outward toward the background. A *center stroke* expands it in both directions at once. A stoke can be a solid color, a gradient color, or a pattern texture.
- **Bevel and emboss**. *Beveling* rounds off the edges of type, giving it the sculpted, graceful look of a raised letterhead, making it appear three-dimensional. *Embossing* produces the opposite effect, making type appear stamped or pressed into the background. The illusion created with these effects varies greatly depending on the settings and the color of background.
- **Inner and outer glow**. An *inner glow* applies colored shading to the inside edge of type to add internal depth or highlights to the fill area. *Outer glow* creates a halo effect around the outside of type to improve contrast and background separation.

Layer styles can be mixed and matched in what seems like an endless number of combinations. The potential for creativity is virtually infinite.

SOME FINAL TIPS

Limit the Number of Typefaces

Most designers suggest limiting the number of typefaces in a design to two. While there are times when more typefaces might be justified, mixing too many typeface families in a design can make it look cluttered and unprofessional. When the need arises to combine typefaces in a design, be sure to choose ones that are totally different from one another. Rather than picking two similar serif typefaces, try combining a serif typeface with a sans serif typeface.

Tech Talk

Designing Text for Screen Display While the typographical principles of print are generally transferable to multimedia, you should take certain precautions when designing text for display on computer screens.

- For body copy, its best to use a 10–14 point sans-serif typeface that's been specifically designed for use on digital displays such as Verdana.
- Do not use a script typeface or other typefaces with thin-line strokes.
- Constrain lengthy sections of text to shorter widths. When text flows across the entire width of the screen, it is difficult to read.
- Apply anti-aliasing to large type to reduce the jagged edges of type.
- While italics work well as a subtle method of emphasizing text in print, the slanted lines and curves lose detail when rendered out as square pixels. Use them sparingly, and experiment with adding color or bold to reduce the unwanted aliasing.
- Remember the low-resolution limitations of computer monitors, and design type for maximum legibility and readability.

Text First, Type Second

While typeface can convey attitude, emotion, and personality, it's the text that communicates ideas and information. Any time the message is overshadowed by the design, communication with your audience is disrupted. Remember, the best typography is often invisible and does not seek to be the star attraction. Designing type for maximum readability should always be your first priority.

Less Is More

There's a popular adage in design circles that says, "less is more." With such an abundance of fonts, styles, and visual effects at your disposal, you may be tempted to throw everything in the pot, wave a magic wand, and see what comes out. *Less is more* suggests that the best styles and effects are often those that are subtle or moderated. You shouldn't have to **SHOUT** to get people's attention. At the right moment, a whisper can be even more effective. So as a final cautionary note, avoid going overboard with all the tools you now have at your disposal. The *less is more* principle implies that a simple and elegant design that communicates effectively is much more valuable than a visual-effects showpiece with no apparent focus or message.

CHAPTER SUMMARY

Typography is one of the most important yet frequently overlooked elements in multimedia design. Whether an interactive menu or web page is *usable* depends on whether the design effectively communicates with text. Text should be designed for maximum legibility and readability. Adding emphasis to text elements in a layout can provide order and focus to the design, and can also direct the user's attention to important visual information and cues. You can add emphasis by varying the style, size, color, and contrast of a typeface. You can also manipulate letter spacing, line spacing, alignment, and distribution to enhance the readability and visual appearance of text, while bringing conformity and unity to the layout. Finally, you can also use layer styles and other types of visual effects to create unique text designs that add visual interest and energy to a page.

CHAPTER 10

Photography

There are always two people in every picture: the photographer and the viewer.

—Ansel Adams, Photographer (1902–1984)

Chapter Highlights

This chapter examines:

- How digital cameras are classified according to their operational features and intended use
- The purpose and function of the imaging chain and each of its basic components
- The variables affecting the proper exposure of a digital image
- The use of fully automatic, semi-automatic, and manual shooting modes
- Strategies for organizing and managing digital image files

Key Terms

35mm
Angle of View
Aperture
Aperture and Shutter Priority Modes
Auto and Manual Focus
Camera RAW
Consumer, Prosumer, and Professional Grade
Decisive Moment
Depth of Field
DSLR
EXIF
Exposure
Exposure Modes
F-Stop
Film
Film Speed
Fisheye Lens
Flash
Focal Length
Focal Length Multiplier
Image Chain
Image Resolution
Image Sensor
Image Stabilization
IPTC
Iris
ISO
Landscape Mode
Lens
Macro Lens
Memory Card
Metadata
Metering
Night Mode

PHOTOGRAPHY

Photography is the process of fixing an image in time through the action of light. In traditional chemical processing, photographic images are created by exposing a light-sensitive emulsion on the surface of film to light in a controlled environment. While some people still shoot with film, the vast majority of the world has crossed over to digital photography, an electronic medium that renders pictures using a digital image sensor. The demise of film was highlighted in 2005 when the Kodak Corporation reported that digital sales accounted for 54% of annual revenue, exceeding film sales for the first time in company history. Sadly, this legendary company founded in 1880, and that pioneered the development of photographic film, filed for Bankruptcy protection in January 2012.

Digital photography offers instantaneous results, producing image files that are easily transferable, and adaptable, for a wide range of multimedia products (see Figure 10.1). The rapid adoption of digital cameras over the last decade can be attributed to many factors, including improvements in reliability and ease of use; better image resolution and print quality; higher-density storage solutions;

Normal Lens
Optical/Digital Zoom
Photography
Portrait Mode
Primary Lens
Reciprocity Law
Red-Eye
Selective Focus
Shutter
Sports/Action Mode
Stich Mode
Telephoto Lens
Tripod
TTL
White Balance
Wide-Angle Lens
Zoom Lens

and greater compatibility with computer hardware and software systems. Digital cameras come in three main varieties: consumer, prosumer, and professional. While the dividing line between each level is somewhat arbitrary, manufacturers use the terms to distinguish between low-, medium-, and high-quality equipment within a product line.

Consumer Cameras

At the lowest end of the consumer spectrum are point-and-shoot cameras designed for users with little to no background in photography. The point-and-shoot camera automatically determines the appropriate focus and exposure settings. Most of these cameras have a built-in flash and are largely menu-driven, with very few controls located on the camera body itself (see Figure 10.2).

Some consumers prefer the body style, features, and quality benefits of a digital single lens reflex camera (DSLR) over the scaled back point-and-shoot. In a DSLR, a mirror located behind the lens directs the image to an optical viewfinder, allowing the photographer to compose and focus a scene while viewing it through the lens (TTL). When the shutter is released, the mirror flips out of the way, allowing the image to strike the image sensor. Experienced photographers prefer to compose through-the-lens because it's more precise. Consumer-grade DSLR cameras normally have a permanently mounted lens, which, while usually much better than the lens on a point-and-shoot camera, may not be as good as that of a prosumer or professional lens. Regardless of the style, consumer cameras are designed for mass-market appeal and are engineered for size, portability, ease of use, and cost. They are not typically designed to give the user easy access to camera settings. The quality of these

FIGURE 10.1
Photography is continuously evolving, both as an art and a science. While the traditional ways often seem archaic, they continue to provide high-quality images. Likewise, while contemporary ways may lack marginally in quality, they make up for it in alacrity and ease of postproduction. Pictured here (L-R), Molly Bartles, a photojournalist for the *Courier & Press* in Evansville, Indiana, shoots with a professional-grade DSLR, as Chris Walker, a documentary photographer who teaches at the University of Southern Indiana, is shown with his 80-year-old wooden 8 × 10. Each is a specific tool that, even in contemporary America, has its place. *Photographers: Chris Walker (left) and Josh Reuck (right).*

FIGURE 10.2
The Apple Store website claims that the iPhone 4S "just might be the only camera you'll ever need." Is the market for the low-end point-and-shoot camera disappearing forever? While resolution is just one benchmark of picture quality, the fact that the iPhone comes with an 8-megapixel image sensor is impressive. Why carry around a camera and a phone when one device may do the trick?
Source: apple.com/iphone

cameras has improved tremendously over the last decade. While one of the differences between consumer and prosumer digital cameras used to be the number of megapixels (the number of light-sensitive elements on the sensor, measured in millions), there is no longer as much difference, and it is not uncommon to find 10- and even 14-megapixel consumer-grade cameras. A high-resolution image from a 10-megapixel-camera will easily print up to an 11 × 14-inch image.

Prosumer and Professional Cameras

The term *prosumer* is a blend of ***pro****fessional con****sumer*** and refers to someone whose level of expertise and needs falls between that of the average consumer and the full-time professional. Prosumer cameras are typically DSLRs with interchangeable lenses, and they have larger and better quality image sensors than consumer cameras. They also allow the user greater and easier control of the camera, providing the user with more versatility and greater control over image acquisition, particularly exposure control. Professional grade cameras improve on these features, particularly lens quality and sensor size. In many cases the lenses and other accessories for professional and prosumer cameras by the same manufacturer are interchangeable, though as we'll see in a bit, the lenses will behave differently when you switch from a prosumer's smaller sensor to the larger full-frame sensor on a professional camera, which is roughly equivalent to 35mm film.

Tech Talk

Focal Length and Angle of View Lenses are classified according to their focal length and angle of view. *Focal length* is a measure of the distance (in millimeters) between the optical center of the lens, when focused at infinity, and the surface of the image sensor. *Angle of view* (also called *field of view*) is a term used to describe the viewable area of a scene that's visible to the lens of the camera. As focal length increases, angle of view decreases, resulting in a narrower field of view and greater image magnification. Decreasing focal length has the opposite effect of increasing angle of view, resulting in a wider angle shot with less image magnification (see Table 10.1).

Table 10.1 The Relationship of Focal Length to Angle of View

Lens Type	Focal Length, Full Frame/ APS-C	Angle of View*
Fisheye	8–15mm/less than 11mm	Up to 180°
Wide-Angle	18–35mm/12–24mm	90° to 54°
Normal	40–60mm/28–40mm	48° to 33°
Telephoto	70–300mm/60–200mm	28° to 7°
Super-Telephoto	Greater than 400mm/200mm	6° to 4°

Video Cameras

While video technology will be discussed in more detail later on, it's worth mentioning here that digital video cameras and digital still cameras share similarities in basic operation, including controls, shooting modes, and exposure settings. Because of this, many of the concepts in this chapter can be applied to the use and operation of video cameras. Given their innate similarities, it should come as no surprise that video cameras today often allow users to capture still images, while many still cameras allow photographers to shoot moving images and sound. As a general rule, however, it's best to use a camera for what it was designed for. Since a video camera is optimized for moving images and sound, its still image processing capabilities and resolution options are generally not as good as a high-end digital camera, though high-end video cameras such as the RED are an exception. Similarly, most still cameras are not ideal for capturing video, particularly from an audio perspective. As with many things, the best results come by choosing the right piece of equipment for the right job (see Figure 10.3).

THE IMAGING CHAIN

The imaging chain of a digital camera is made up of four components: the lens, the iris, the shutter, and the image sensor. Capturing an image is the art of manipulating these four components to achieve desired and intentional effects.

Tech Talk

A Comparison of Still Camera Formats

FIGURE 10.3
Standard camera formats include DSLRs (approximately 16 × 24mm up to medium format), SLRs (24 × 36mm), medium format (2¼" square), and large format (4 × 5 inches and above). In this image, the lens used to make the original 4 × 5 version was a 90mm, which is wide angle for that format. But as the highlighted boxes illustrate, that same lens would render a "normal" angle of view for 2¼", and a slight and medium telephoto for 35mm and a DSLR with an FLM, respectively. The equivalent lens needed to duplicate this image's angle of view with a prosumer DSLR would be approximately 20mm.
Photographer: Chris Walker.

The Lens

In still cameras and video camcorders, the lens is an integrated optical system made up of one or more individual elements of ground glass or molded plastic. The lens is mounted on the front of the camera and is designed to capture and

FIGURE 10.4
A DSLR camera with an assortment of interchangeable lenses.

manipulate light reflected from objects in the camera's line of sight. The lens controls the magnification of the subject being photographed and affects the sharpness and clarity of the image (see Figure 10.4).

PRIME LENSES

Lenses with a single focal length are called *primary* or *fixed focal length* lenses. With a fixed focal-length lens, the only way to affect angle of view is to physically change the distance between the camera and the subject. Serious photographers often own an assortment of prime lenses with a variety of focal lengths, enabling them to manipulate angle of view by simply swapping out the lens. Prime lenses are often classified into one of six main categories: wide-angle, telephoto, normal, novelty (macro and fisheye), and super-telephoto.

Tech Talk

Focal Length Multiplier When you look at lenses for your DSLR, make sure you know whether or not you have a full-frame sensor, because the size of the sensor makes a difference in how a lens performs on a camera. If you are using a prosumer or low-end professional DSLR, your camera probably has a smaller format sensor, most likely based on the APS-C (Advanced Photo System type-C) film format. If you use a full-frame lens on one of these, it will have a narrower field of view than it would on a full-frame camera. As an example, a normal lens for a full-frame camera is usually a 50mm, while a normal lens for an APS-C format DSLR is around a 35mm. This difference in performance is referred to as the *focal length multiplier* (FLM). Most prosumer cameras have an FLM between 1.4 and 1.6. To use the FLM, multiply the lens's actual focal length by the FLM to see what its full-frame equivalent would be. In the example above, a 35mm lens on a camera with a 1.4 FLM is the same as a 49mm (essentially a 50mm) lens on a full frame camera.

- ***Wide-angle lenses*** have a relatively short focal length (18–35mm for full frame, 12–24mm for APS-C) resulting in the wide angle of view. Wide-angle lenses, or *short lenses* as they're sometimes called, are often used for shooting landscape panoramas and vistas where the primary emphasis is on establishing a wide overview of the scene (see Figure 10.5).
- ***Telephoto*** lenses have a long focal length (90–300mm for full frame, 60–200mm for APS-C) resulting in a very narrow angle of view. Telephoto, or *long lenses*, can magnify distant objects, making them appear much closer

FIGURE 10.5
Wide-angle lenses are often used to capture broad vistas, yielding images such as this one.
Photographer: Chris Walker.

FIGURE 10.6
To understand the importance of lens selection, find a subject, like the first red door on this church, and photograph it up close with a wide angle lens. Then measure the distance from your position to the primary subject and double that distance. From that farther spot, zoom in to twice the focal length of your initial image and retake the picture. Your primary subject will retain its original size, but your secondary subjects will become more prominent. Good photographers find their ideal position, and then select the lens that will best depict the scene from that location.
Photographer: Chris Walker.

than they really are. These are the favorite lens of bird watchers, sports photographers, and naturalists for obtaining close-up shots of a subject from a distance (see Figure 10.7-Left).

- *Normal lenses* have a medium focal length (40–60mm for full frame, 28–40mm for APS-C) resulting in an angle of view that falls somewhere in between the extremes of wide-angle and telephoto. Normal lenses are a safe bet for general-purpose shooting activities that do not require extreme close-ups or wide-shots of the subject matter.
- *Novelty lenses* have descriptive names like *macro* and *fisheye*, and feature unique optical characteristics designed for nontypical shooting situations.
- *Macro Lenses* can acquire focus when positioned only a few inches away from the subject. Macro lenses produce high-quality images with low image distortion and are useful for shooting extreme close-ups of small objects like insects or flower blossoms (see Figure 10.7-Right).
- *Fisheye lenses* have an extremely short focal length (8–15mm for full frame, 11mm or less for APS-C), offering an angle of view as high as 180°. However,

FIGURE 10.7
Because of their magnification, telephotos and macros are more likely than other lenses to add camera shake to your image. To help avoid this, a good starting point is to convert the lens's focal length into a fraction and use that as a shutter speed—a 200mm lens would become 1/200th, so it should be hand-held at 1/250th or faster. *Photographer: Chris Walker.*

Tech Talk

Optical Versus Digital Zoom Digital cameras with built-in lenses are often equipped with both an optical zoom and a digital zoom. An *optical zoom* alters the angle of view by changing the actual focal length of the lens elements. Since the lens on most point-and-shoot cameras is relatively small, it's often difficult to achieve a high level of image magnification optically. To compensate, manufacturers have an added feature called the *digital zoom*. With digital zoom, the image sensor creates the zoom artificially, much like enlarging a digital image in a photo editing program. The outer portion of the image is cropped (the pixels are thrown away) and the remaining pixels are enlarged and/or duplicated to simulate the effect of a narrower angle of view. Using a digital zoom can lead to a noticeable loss of image quality and detail.

because of the extreme curvature of glass, images acquired with a fisheye lens are significantly distorted, which results in an interesting hall-of-mirrors type effect.

- ***Super-telephoto lenses*** (400–600mm for full frame) yield the narrowest angle of view while offering extremely high levels of image magnification.

ZOOM LENSES

A *zoom*, or *variable focal-length lens*, can be adjusted to any focal length within a set optical range. For example, using a zoom lens with a range of 28–300mm, the focal length can be set to wide angle (28mm), telephoto (300mm), or anywhere in between. Zoom lenses allow the photographer to quickly change the angle of view without having to swap out the lens. With this type of lens, the photographer zooms in to acquire a narrow angle of view and zooms out to compose a wide-shot. The zoom ratio indicates the magnification capability of a variable focal-length lens. For example, a 3× or 3:1 zoom ratio means that the size of the image at the longest focal length setting (telephoto) is three times greater than the size of the image at the shortest setting (wide angle). High-quality zoom lenses are very expensive. While their optical quality is generally inferior to that of primary lenses, the speed and convenience of zooming can be a worthwhile tradeoff. Zoom lenses are included on most point-and-shoot still cameras as well as on all consumer, prosumer, and professional video cameras.

The Iris

The *iris* is an adjustable plastic or metal diaphragm that regulates the amount of light striking the image sensor (see Figure 10.8). The iris is typically located between the optical elements of the lens. When shooting images that are dimly lit, the iris can be opened up to allow more light to pass through to the image sensor. For brightly lit subjects, the iris can be constricted or "stopped down" to reduce the intensity of the light and keep the image from being overexposed. The term *aperture* is sometimes confused with the iris, but it refers to the actual hole or opening created by the iris and not to the device itself; so when people talk about adjusting the aperture, they are usually talking about adjusting the iris to change the size of the aperture.

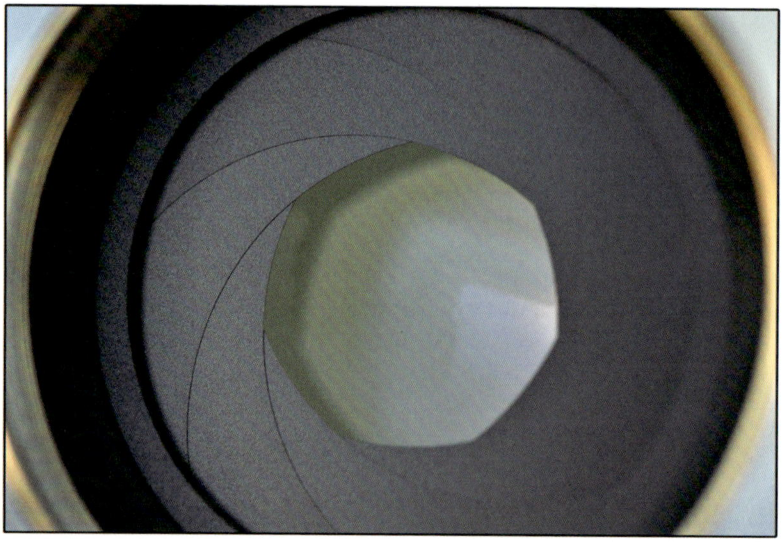

FIGURE 10.8
An iris is typically comprised of a series of metal blades that fold together to form a circle, inside your lens, through which the image passes. *Photographer: Chris Walker.*

Table 10.2 The Diameter of the Aperture is Obtained by Dividing the Focal Length of the Lens by the f-number

	Focal Length of the Lens		
f-number	**18mm**	**50mm**	**300mm**
2.8	6.429mm	17.857mm	107.143mm
4	4.500mm	12.500mm	75.000mm
5.6	3.214mm	8.929mm	53.571mm
8	2.250mm	6.250mm	37.500mm
11	1.636mm	4.545mm	27.273mm
16	1.125mm	3.125mm	18.750mm
22	0.818mm	2.273mm	13.636mm

F-STOP

On professional lenses, the aperture is adjusted by turning the innermost ring on the outside of the lens housing. A series of *f-stop* numbers are printed on the outside surface of the ring indicating the size of the aperture. While shown as a whole number, an f-stop unit is actually a fraction used for calculating the physical diameter of the aperture. For example, an f-stop setting of f/16 means that the diameter of the aperture is equal to 1/16th the focal length of the lens (see Table 10.2). To calculate the aperture of a 50mm lens set to f/16, you would use the following formula:

focal length/f-stop number = aperture diameter
50mm/16 = 3.125mm

Typical f-stop positions include: f/32, f/22, f/16, f/11, f/8, f/5.6, f/4, f/2.8, f/2, and f/1.4, though you typically won't find a single lens that covers the entire range. Because the f-stop number is a fraction, the size of the aperture actually decreases as the f-stop number increases.

Opening the aperture by one full f-stop (e.g., changing from f/11 to f/8), doubles the size of the aperture and the amount of light striking the image sensor. Likewise, closing the aperture by one full stop (e.g., changing from f/1.4 to f/2), reduces the size of the aperture and the amount of incoming light by half. Some lenses allow the aperture to be adjusted in half-stop or third-stop increments for even greater control of light exposure.

The Shutter

The *shutter* is a movable curtain, plate, or other device that controls the amount of time that the image sensor is exposed to light. When the shutter button is depressed, the shutter opens for an instant of time allowing light to strike the surface of the image sensor. The amount of time that the shutter remains open is referred to as *shutter speed* and can commonly range from 1/8000th of a second to several full seconds. Fast shutter speeds in the neighborhood of 1/250th or 1/500th of a second are good for freezing action in a well-lit scene (see Figure 10.9). Much slower shutter speeds are required when shooting under low-light situations.

FIGURE 10.9
The exposure time for this image was approximately 1/1000th of a second. Faster shutter speeds are available on all DSLRs, but it's fairly rare that we use them. *Photographer: Chris Walker.*

> **GREAT IDEAS**
> **The Image Sensor**
>
> A digital camera's image sensor is a small electronic chip used to register the intensity and color of light. It is the digital equivalent of "film," the light-sensitive recording medium used in a traditional analog camera. Light passes through the lens and aperture before striking the surface of the image sensor. The visual data obtained by the sensor is converted into binary form and stored on a flash memory card in the camera body. The image sensor eliminates the need for film and allows the digital photographer to electronically manipulate the size and appearance of a captured image by varying the control settings of the camera. As discussed above, prosumer and professional DSLRs usually use either full-frame or APS-C size sensors.

FILM SPEED

One of the challenges of digital photography is that much of the terminology is rooted in film. One of the best examples of this is the continued use of the ISO Film Speed system. Originally based on a film's ability to respond to light, the ISO rating is now used to describe a sensor's ability to respond to light. The ISO designation follows a logarithmic scale, which means that each jump to a higher ISO number results in a doubling of the film's light-sensitivity (see Table 10.3). This corresponds nicely to the f-stop scale, which works in precisely the same manner. All things being equal, increasing film speed by one ISO level has the same effect on exposure as opening the aperture by one full stop. As film speed increases, however, the sharpness and clarity of an image decreases, and your image will have a grainier, or "noisier," appearance (see Figure 10.10). For the cleanest images, it's best to shoot with the lowest possible film speed setting. Unless you choose to manually override the ISO setting of the camera, your camera will usually set your film speed automatically based on lighting conditions, flash settings, and other selected exposure settings.

FILM SIZE

With photographic film, the surface area of a captured image has a fixed size, based on the type of camera being used (35mm, etc.). In digital cameras, the size of the image sensor is defined by the number of light-sensitive pixels it contains and the

Table 10.3 A Comparison of ISO to Light Sensitivity, Image Contrast, and Graininess

ISO Film Speed Rating	Light Sensitivity	Contrast	Image Grain
50 ISO	low	very high	low
100 ISO	medium	high	medium
200 ISO	medium	medium	medium
400 ISO	high	medium	high
800 ISO	very high	low	very high

FIGURE 10.10
Electronic and analog media share many characteristics, including the degradation of image quality at higher ISOs. As the enlarged view illustrates, the discrepancies between ISOs 200 and 3200 are quite apparent. As technological improvements continue to be made, the distance in quality between low and high ISOs continues to shorten.
Photographer: Chris Walker.

physical dimensions of the chip. Generally speaking, the larger the chip, the larger the acquired image based on its pixel dimensions. For example, a 6-megapixel camera has roughly 6 million pixels and is capable of rendering images up to a maximum resolution of 2,816p × 2,112p. A 3.2 megapixel camera has roughly half as many pixels and a maximum resolution of 2048p × 1536p. While each camera's image sensor is constrained to a fixed maximum size, the resolution settings of the camera can be changed to produce a lower resolution image.

FILE SIZE

Image file size is affected by the resolution setting of the camera and the file format used when saving a picture to memory. Consumer cameras typically process and format images using the popular JPEG compression codec. JPEG compression reduces the size of image files as well as the time it takes for the camera to process sensory data once the picture is snapped. Prosumer and professional cameras also support JPEG encoding, but both usually also provide the option of saving images in uncompressed formats like TIFF or Camera RAW. While these formats produce files that are significantly larger, they offer the advantage of preserving most or all of the original sensor data.

The Camera RAW format records a completely unprocessed version of the image as obtained by the sensor at the point of exposure. Professional photographers prefer the RAW file format because it allows them to retain maximum control of image processing during editing. JPEG and TIFF formatted files are processed prior to encoding, limiting the type of adjustments that can be made in image editing. Camera RAW is a proprietary standard that requires special software or plug-ins from the camera manufacturer in order to edit the image. While Camera RAW is a technically superior format, TIFF and JPEG images are much easier to work with, and their quality is acceptable for the vast majority of multimedia applications.

While the number of options varies by model and manufacturer, most digital cameras allow you to specify the amount of compression you want to apply to a JPEG image. For example, Canon offers three choices called *normal*, *fine*, and *superfine*. As the name implies, superfine produces the highest quality image by applying the smallest amount of compression. There's a dramatic difference between the file size of an image acquired at the smallest resolution and lowest quality JPEG setting and those at the highest quality setting. For example, if you take a picture with Canon EOS Rebel XS set to its lowest resolution (1936 × 1288 pixels), the resulting JPEG image will be around 700K. The same image taken with the camera set to mid-range resolution (2816 × 1880 pixels) would yield a JPEG around 1.2MB. If you were to use the highest JPEG setting (3888 × 2592 pixels), the image would be around 3.8MB. Switching the high-resolution setting to RAW bumps the file size up to almost 10MB. As you can see, it's important to pay attention to the settings you use. Memory cards are relatively inexpensive these days. You need more than one. Keeping a camera set to the highest resolution and best JPEG setting is normally a good choice, though using RAW offers advanced users more flexibility. See Figure 8.14 in the "Graphics" chapter for another example how changing the resolution and JPEG setting affects image file size and the total number of images a memory card can store.

FLASHBACK

The Decisive Moment

For photographers who work on location, the two most important factors in image making are being there and knowing how to capitalize on the situation once you are. In terms of timing, Magnum photographer/founder Henri Cartier-Bresson (1908–2004) believed in the latter with such conviction that he revived the term "the decisive moment" from the writings of a 17th-century French cardinal.

Photographically, *the decisive moment* is that instant when an action is at its peak, when it's stronger than it was the moment before or will be the moment after; it's that singular, perfect, narrow window of time in which the shutter should be released to best depict the emotion of an event. The strength of this moment can be seen through anticipation, the alignment of compositional elements, or in peak action (see Figure 10.11).

FIGURE 10.11
In this set of images, the photographer came upon a couple at a county fair who were arguing. In the first of the 10 photographs (not shown) the young man is yelling at his girlfriend, who'd disappeared for an hour. In the final frame, the couple kissed. The first images held more aggression than desired, and the final seemed overtly sappy, so the 9th image, which held the anticipation of making up, became the chosen photograph in the sequence. *Photographer: Chris Walker.*

It took more than 100 years of photography for the term to be needed, but less than half that for it to become obsolete. In the early years of photography, images were exposed over a period of minutes—so timing was far less important than the photographer's location and composition were. Today we find that technology—the force that, through faster shutter speeds, once created the need for Bresson's statement—has brought us to a point in history where photographers no longer need to exercise such decisiveness in their timing.

Through the ability to extract still images from video, we will soon be freed from the necessity of precision timing, from the need to depress the shutter at the precise moment an action is at its zenith. Almost as retribution, though, we must now further challenge ourselves to be even more decisive in our selection of focal length, depth of field, and composition.

by Chris Walker

EXPOSURE

A digital camera creates a picture by exposing the image sensor to light. Underexposed images have a dark appearance and lack detail while overexposed images often contain bright spots and appear washed out. One of the most important tasks of the photographer is managing the exposure settings of the camera during image acquisition. *Exposure* is the product of two variables: the intensity of light (as controlled by the iris), and the duration of contact with the image sensor (as controlled by the speed of the shutter). This relationship, the *Reciprocity Law,* states that there is an inverse relationship between intensity and time and can be expressed mathematically as:

$$Exposure = Intensity \times Time$$

For example, setting the shutter speed to 1/250th and the aperture to f/8 results in the same exposure level as a setting of 1/125th at f/11 or 1/500th at f/5.6. In this example, doubling time while reducing the aperture by one full stop has the same negligible effect on exposure as halving the time of exposure while increasing the aperture by one full stop. As long as a change to one of the two variables is matched by a reciprocal change in the other, exposure remains constant.

FIGURE 10.12 Light bending as it passes through a lens or small opening is nothing new—the Chinese philosopher Mo Ti first noted this phenomenon 7,000 years ago when viewing images of a solar eclipse being projected on the ground through leaf gaps in overhead trees. So whether it's film, an image sensor, your hand, or a white card for viewing an eclipse, the only magic here lies in what we do with this fantastic medium. *Photographer: Chris Walker.*

FIGURE 10.13
This image was shot at 1/60th at f/22 (left), and at 1/1000th at 5.6 (right). The overall amount of light striking the camera's sensor was virtually the same in each image, but the slower exposure time resulted in the image with the blurred ball. *Photographer: Chris Walker.*

FIGURE 10.14
Correct exposure can only be accomplished in the camera, but Photoshop and other programs allow for some adjustments to be made in postproduction. In the center frame, the Photoshop tool Curves was accessed and highlights and mid-tones were elevated. For the bottom image, the History Brush was used to return the area surrounding the lamp to its original tone, then Curves was again employed to add some magenta to the final color palate. *Photographer/Illustrator: Chris Walker.*

Measuring Light Intensity

Digital cameras have a built-in exposure meter that measures incoming light as it's reflected off objects in the camera's field of view. An *exposure meter* is an electronic instrument with a light-sensitive cell that's activated by partially depressing the camera's shutter button. When the camera is in an automatic shooting mode, the shutter and aperture settings will be set by the camera based on the meter's assessment of light intensity. The way a camera assesses the light intensity of a scene can vary. Most cameras offer a choice of three different metering methods in order to compensate for different lighting scenarios.

EVALUATIVE METERING MODE

With *evaluative metering*, the camera samples the intensity of light at multiple points in the image matrix, and then combines the results with other camera data to determine the best exposure setting. Evaluative metering is the default method used on most cameras because it produces the best overall results, especially for scenes that are unevenly lit.

CENTER-WEIGHTED METERING MODE

Center-weighted metering is identical to the evaluative mode except that more weight is given to data from the center of the image when calculating the exposure settings. This method is recommended for scenes in which the main subject is backlit or surrounded by bright background objects.

SPOT METERING MODE

With *spot metering*, the camera calculates exposure based on the light intensity of the main subject located in the center of the screen. Spot metering is best for high-contrast scenes with varying levels of brightness.

GREAT IDEAS

Flash Control

Using the flash allows you to provide additional fill light for scenes where existing lighting is less than ideal. The range of a flash varies by manufacturer, but most are designed to work within 15 feet of the camera. Be careful when using a flash as it may wash out your image. Don't use a flash unless you really need it. Many cameras allow you to change the output of a flash incrementally from 100% (full), to 75%, 50%, 25%, and off. This feature is helpful when you want to remain close to the subject without overexposing the image or momentarily blinding your subjects. With most cameras, you normally have the option of selecting from a number of different flash modes.

Fill flash (always on)—in this mode, the camera fires the flash every time, even when the exposure meter indicates a sufficient level of natural light. Using a fill flash outdoors on a sunny day can help compensate for excessively bright sunlight, harsh shadows, and uneven backlighting (see Figure 10.15).

FIGURE 10.15
Images made in direct sunlight can often benefit from a little judicious *fill flash*. The objective of using fill flash is to "fill" in the shadowed areas that may be too dark without it. Using too much fill, though, can unnaturally set your subject apart from the background. A good starting point is to set your flash to –1. If you're using a nondedicated unit, try setting the ISO to a higher setting—either way, the flash will get the message that you desire less light on your scene than what it might want to give you. *Photographer: Chris Walker.*

Auto Flash—in this mode, the camera meters the available light and only fires the flash when needed. Limiting the use of the flash helps conserve battery power.

Red-eye reduction—in this mode, the red eyes caused by the reflection of the flash off of the retina of the eye is reduced. When the flash is set to red-eye reduction mode, the camera fires a short burst of light followed by the actual flash. The short burst is intended to shut down the pupil of the eye, thus minimizing the kickback of reflected light. The closer the flash is to the lens, the more prone a camera is to producing red-eye. On professional cameras, the flash is farther away from the lens than on built-in systems, and can often be detached and repositioned. In addition to controlling red-eye with the flash, you may also be able to reduce it by using a wide-angle lens, increasing the amount of existing lighting, or by moving the camera closer to the subject. In a worst case scenario, you may be able to remove it using photo-editing software.

WHITE BALANCE

Our perception of colored objects in the natural world is affected by the type of light source used to illuminate them. Most light sources are not "true white" but rather an uneven mix of the primary color frequencies (red, blue, and green). For example, we know that under certain atmospheric conditions, the physical color of reflected sunlight can appear red, orange, white, yellow, or blue (see

Figure 10.16). In the same way, there are many different types of artificial light sources (fluorescent, halogen, tungsten, etc.), each with its own unique color properties. Light sources are rated according to their color temperature on the Kelvin scale, so named for the British physicist William Thomson, 1st Baron Kelvin of Largs (1824–1907) (see Table 10.4).

While the human eye adjusts rather easily to variations in light, electronic image sensors must be calibrated to the color temperature of the light source they are exposed to in order to accurately capture the color of objects within the field of view. This process of calibration is called *white balance*. The white balance of a camera can be set manually by shooting a white object such as a blank sheet of paper while depressing the manual white balance button. Once a camera "sees" what white looks like under existing light, it can extrapolate the values of all of the other colors in the spectrum. Manual white balance is the most accurate way of calibrating the color space of a digital camera, especially when the source of light is mixed, such as an indoor scene with natural light pouring in from an open window.

Digital cameras often provide white balance presets for several of the most common lighting conditions, including *daylight* and *cloudy* for outdoor situations, and *tungsten* and *fluorescent* for indoors. However, if you forget to change a white balance preset when moving from one light source to another, the color

Table 10.4 The Color Temperature of Common Indoor and Outdoor Lighting Sources (Kelvin Units)

Color Temperature	Light Source
1600 K	sunrise and sunset
1800 K	a candle
2800 K	tungsten lamp (ordinary household incandescent bulb)
3200 K	studio lamps, photofloods
4000 K	indoor fluorescent
5200 K	bright midday sun
5500 K	average daylight, electronic flash
6000 K	lightly overcast sky
6500 K	heavily overcast sky
7000 K	outdoor shade
8000 K	hazy sky
20000 K	deep blue clear sky

Source: en.Wikipedia.org

FIGURE 10.16 This scene was shot late in the day under clear skies. The blue could have been natural had the exposure been longer, but the longer exposure would have caused the drifting fog to blur, so a bluish filter was used to emphasize the blue light while allowing an exposure time that still showed individual wisps of fog. *Photographer: Chris Walker.*

of your newly acquired images will not be true (see Figure 10.17). For this reason, many people take the easy way out and just leave the camera set to *auto white balance* (AWB).

By now, we've become used to the fact that digital cameras include automatic settings for just about every control. While AWB works reasonably well in most cases, you can usually get better results by using a white balance preset based on what type of light you are working with or by manually white balancing your camera.

FOCUS

The *focus control* is used to define the sharpness of an object within the frame by changing the distance between the optical elements of a lens. A camera's focus must be reset each time the distance between the camera and the subject physically changes. Holding the camera steady while depressing the shutter button will prevent unintentional blurring of the image upon capture.

Autofocus (AF)

When a camera is set to *autofocus* mode, it analyzes the area of a scene and then calculates the distance between the camera and the main subject. Point-and-shoot cameras normally use an active autofocus method in which an invisible infrared beam scans objects located within 25 feet of the lens. The camera

FIGURE 10.17
Quality lighting is vital to good photography. In this comparison, the sequence of three images on the left were made at different times of the day; note that the brickwork on the building is reddest during the noon exposure, and shifts as the day goes on due to the amount of blue, ambient light coming from the sky. In the images on the right (top to bottom), the windsurfer was shot moments after dawn, during "the golden hour"; the woman at the wood rack was shot at dusk, where you can see the sky light (blue) mixing with a mercury vapor light coming from the left (green) and tungsten light from her patio and home (orange); the street festival image was balanced for the fluorescent lights in the background, but it also contains "bug lights" within the corn booth (yellow), and high pressure sodium lights from overhead (amber). *Photographer: Chris Walker.*

computes subject distance by analyzing the time it takes for the light to be reflected back to the camera. DSLRs typically use a *passive autofocus* technique that's much more sophisticated and usually more accurate. With this approach, the camera uses a small CCD sensor to detect and analyze changes in the contrast of image pixels. *Active autofocusing* systems can be used in virtual darkness as they provide their own focusing light. Passive systems must have a sufficient amount of light and image contrast in order to work effectively.

AF TARGET POINT

By default, autofocus is usually set to a single target point located in the center of the image. When the main subject is positioned in the center of the frame, this works well. Simply set the focus and snap the image. However, a different focusing strategy must be employed when the subject is placed in an off-center position. With most cameras, this involves the following steps: (1) place the main subject in the center of the screen; (2) acquire and lock the focus by depressing the shutter button halfway; (3) reframe the main subject in an off-center position; and (4) fully depress the shutter button to capture the image. Many cameras provide options for acquiring focus with user-select, single-spot, or multi-spot target points.

While active and passive autofocusing systems have improved dramatically over the years, neither method is foolproof. At some point, autofocus will let you down as the camera miscalculates the proper focus setting. Problems are likely to occur in the following situations:

- When near and distant objects are mixed close together within the frame, the camera may be unable to determine which object in the composition to focus on.
- Moving objects like cars and bikes can confuse the autofocus sensor, causing a focus shift at the point of acquisition.
- Extremely bright lights or subject areas can make it difficult for the camera to lock onto a subject and acquire focus.
- Monochromatic scenes can lack the contrast necessary for acquiring an accurate focus.

Manual Focus (MF)

On professional cameras with interchangeable lenses, focus can be acquired manually by rotating the innermost ring on the circumference of the lens. Turning the ring in either direction changes the sharpness of the image. On less expensive cameras, manual focus will be either unavailable, or controlled through the use of a menu or button. The viewfinder usually displays an MF or AF as a reminder of which mode is currently active. Manual focus should be used whenever you are located more than 25 feet away from the subject, or whenever the camera is unable to isolate the subject or acquire focus automatically.

GREAT IDEAS

Selective Focus

Photographs are two-dimensional. They only have width and height. We infer depth based on visual clues, which can be created using a range of lighting, exposure, and focus techniques. *Selective focus* is a popular technique used by photographers to heighten the interest of an otherwise ordinary composition. Using selective focus, only one primary element in a scene is sharply in focus. The rest of the background and/or foreground elements of the scene are blurred creating a sense of compositional depth.

DEPTH OF FIELD

Depth of field (DOF) refers to the area of a scene in front of and behind the main subject that is in focus. The term *great depth of field* is used to describe a photograph where the majority of the scene is sharply defined. *Shallow depth of field* describes an image where noticeable portions of the foreground and background areas of a scene are out of focus (see Figure 10.18). Photographers will sometimes manipulate DOF to emphasize the focal point of a composition through visual contrast. Background elements can often steal attention away from the main subject in a photograph. For example, when an image is taken of a person positioned directly in front of a tree or wall, the subject and the background appear to merge. The lack of three-dimensional depth creates a flat image lacking in visual contrast. Decreasing DOF in a scene such as this deemphasizes the visual importance of the background by drawing the attention of the viewer to the portion of the scene that is in focus. In some cases, the photographer will use an exceptional shallow depth of field, blurring the background to the point that it may be all but unrecognizable. In photography, this effect is often referred to as bokeh (BOH-ka), from a Japanese term meaning blur or haze.

The factors affecting DOF in an image are rather complex and would require more time than we have to go into here. In the simplest terms, it can be said that DOF is largely affected by three main variables: (1) the size of the lens aperture or f-stop setting; (2) the focal length of the lens; and (3) the distance from the camera to the subject.

Aperture Size

The size of the aperture is inversely related to the DOF of an image. As the size of the aperture decreases, DOF increases, causing more of the scene to appear in focus. As the aperture is enlarged, DOF decreases, creating greater contrast between foreground and background objects. In a brightly lit scene, the aperture is normally small, making it more difficult to acquire shallow depth of field. In situations like this, a larger aperture setting can be obtained by zooming in, or by increasing the camera's shutter speed or decreasing the film speed (see Figure 10.19).

FIGURE 10.18
These images were made almost identically, with the only changes being the shutter speed and aperture. The aperture changes each in a way that alters its success through directing the viewer's gaze. While neither is necessarily "right," the image with less depth of field seems more successful, since in the one with greater depth the decoy's bill seems to be competing for attention with the tools in the background. *Photographer: Chris Walker.*

FIGURE 10.19
Depth of field is the front-to-back distance within a scene that appears to be in focus because of the aperture at which the image was made. In this comparison, the top image, shot at f/2.8, exhibits very shallow depth of field, while the bottom image, shot at f/22, exhibits maximum depth of field. *Illustrator: Adam Bulgatz.*

Focal Length

The focal length of the lens is also inversely related to DOF. As you zoom in on an image, the focal length of the lens increases while DOF decreases. For this reason, wide-angle shots such as landscapes and vistas often have a great depth of field, while narrow-angle shots acquired with a telephoto lens often have a shallow depth of field.

Subject/Camera Distance

The physical distance between the camera and the subject is the third variable affecting DOF in a composition. DOF increases with distance, and decreases as you move the camera physically closer to the subject.

EXPOSURE MODES

Digital cameras feature a variety of exposure modes designed for many of the most common shooting conditions. The exposure mode options vary by camera, but they normally span a range from fully automatic, where control of image exposure is retained entirely by the camera, to fully manual, where the photographer assumes command of all exposure settings. A number of semi-automatic modes exist in between the two extremes, allowing the photographer and camera to share control of exposure settings.

Automatic Modes

FULLY AUTOMATIC MODE

When set to *fully automatic mode*, a camera will analyze the area of a scene and calculate the settings for shutter speed, aperture, ISO, white balance, focus, and flash. Depending on the quality of the camera, shooting in auto mode can produce good results under normal lighting conditions most of the time. While shooting in auto mode makes the camera easier to operate, it significantly reduces the photographer's role in the creative process.

PORTRAIT MODE

In *portrait mode*, the exposure controls of the camera are optimized for shooting close-ups with a shallow depth of field. The objective in this mode is to keep the subject in focus while blurring the background. The camera accomplishes this by raising the shutter speed in conjunction with widening the aperture. Portrait mode works best when the subject is tightly framed and there is considerable distance between the subject and the background. Shallow DOF is always more difficult to achieve when the subject is placed directly against the background.

LANDSCAPE MODE

Landscape mode is the opposite of portrait mode. In this mode, the exposure settings of the camera are optimized for shooting wide shots with a great depth of field. The objective in landscape mode is to keep as much of the scene as possible in focus. To accomplish this, the camera combines a small aperture with a slower shutter speed. As a result, in some cases, you may need to use a tripod to maintain a steady shot.

SPORTS MODE

Sports mode, or *action mode* as it's sometimes called, favors a fast shutter speed and is recommended for shooting a moving subject within a scene. When capturing moving subjects during a bike race or soccer game for example, a fast shutter speed is required in order to freeze the image without blurring. If the shutter speed is too slow, a motion blur will occur. When composing an action scene, a dramatic effect can be achieved by panning the camera along with the moving subject while depressing the shutter button. This technique produces a sharply defined subject while creating an intentional motion blur in the background (see Figure 10.20).

NIGHT MODE

Night mode uses a slow shutter speed combined with the flash when shooting a subject set against a dimly lit backdrop like a sunset or evening sky. The long exposure time allows the details of the background to remain correctly exposed during the firing of the flash to illuminate the subject. A tripod should be used in order to prevent unintentional blurring.

FIGURE 10.20 Sports mode is useful for stopping action and having enough depth of field left to make your images sharp. But sometimes it's good to experiment and "pan" a few frames. *Panning* is the process of selecting a slow shutter speed, such as 1/8th or 1/15th, and triggering the shutter while following the action. This method is not for the impatient; photographers who succeed at panning learn early on to shoot hard and edit harder. *Photographer: Chris Walker.*

Tech Talk

Stitching Mode *Stitching mode* is used for acquiring a sequence of shots that can be joined together in editing to create a large panoramic view of a scene (see Figure 10.21). After taking the first picture in stitch mode, the camera provides a split screen view of the previous shot and the currently framed scene to help you align the end of one frame with the beginning of the next.

FIGURE 10.21
Stitching mode can be used to take a series of photos that will be loaded into Photoshop, or an internal camera program, to "stitch" them together. The key to success lies in overlapping your images—between a third and a half of the area of the previous—so the computer can read the design of one image as it prepares to lace it together with the next one in the series. This stitched image, a tiny courtroom where Lincoln practiced law, is a composite of six vertical photos.
Photographer: Chris Walker.

Semi-Automatic Modes

APERTURE PRIORITY MODE

In *aperture priority mode,* the photographer determines the f-stop setting manually, while the camera sets the remaining exposure variables. The main purpose of using this mode is to control for depth of field in a scene. However, unlike portrait or landscape modes, the photographer retains total control of the aperture.

SHUTTER PRIORITY MODE

In *shutter priority mode*, the photographer sets the shutter speed, while the camera sets all of the remaining exposure variables. This mode is used when the photographer wants to retain precise control of exposure time. For example, when shooting a waterfall, a slow shutter speed can be set in order to accentuate motion by blurring the water while the surrounding area of the scene remains sharp (see Figures 10.22–10.24). Using a fast shutter speed on the same scene can result in the effect of suspended droplets of water hovering in midair for heightened effect.

FIGURE 10.22 Shutter priority mode allows the photographer to choose a shutter speed and leaves it up to the camera's programming to choose the appropriate aperture. For this rainy afternoon, the shutter speed was approximately 12 seconds and the aperture was f/32. *Photographer: Chris Walker.*

FIGURE 10.23 The length of exposure needed for this image ultimately gives the illusion of clouds or fog mingling among the rocks below. In reality, though, it's the frothy heads of crashing waves that have been rendered softly over the course of the 20-minute exposure, cumulatively being gathered as they blur and overlap on a single piece of film. *Photographer: Chris Walker.*

FIGURE 10.24
By opting for a lengthy exposure, the water was allowed plenty of time to blur—about a minute—while the photographer's luck held out and very little wind stirred the leaves in the foreground. *Photographer: Chris Walker.*

PROGRAM MODE

Some cameras offer a *program mode* setting in which the camera determines the correct settings for aperture and shutter speed, while allowing the photographer access to other controls like ISO, white balance, flash, and so on.

Manual Mode

In *full manual mode,* the photographer has control of all of the camera's exposure settings and related controls. While this mode requires the most skill and knowledge, it also allows for the greatest degree of creative control.

IMAGE STABILIZATION

Tripods, monopods, and other camera mounting devices are used in still photography and video production to keep the camera stable when shooting. Even the slightest movement of the camera during acquisition can result in a fuzzy image, or a distracting visual shift when using a video camera. The potential for shakiness increases when the camera is set to a slow shutter speed and/or to a long focal length. Therefore, it's critical to stabilize the camera in low-light conditions or in situations where you are not close to the subject. In video production, shooting from a tripod should be considered the norm rather than the exception. Random or unmotivated camera movements are one of the telltale signs of an amateur production. While using a tripod adds another degree of difficulty to a production setup, having stable shots makes it worth the effort. In situations where using a tripod is not possible, you can help the situation by moving closer to the subject, adjusting the lens to a wide-angle setting, and supplementing existing light, particularly if it is a bit dark.

Video cameras sometimes offer a digital image stabilization mode that works by shifting the pixel matrix in the direction of camera movement in order to counteract the effects of camera motion. While it may work well under certain conditions, it is a digital effect and its use can lead to the creation of unintended visual artifacts, making it a poor substitute for using a tripod.

GREAT IDEAS
Memory Cards

The images captured by a digital camera are usually stored on a removable flash memory card. These cards can best be thought of as a temporary storage solution for digital images until they can be downloaded to a computer or transferred to a more secure location. Since the beginning of digital photography, a variety of different card formats have been introduced, leading to a confusing myriad of storage options. Since the cards are not interchangeable, it's important to know what type of flash memory card your camera uses and what capacity it supports. Here are some of the more common formats used in contemporary cameras.

The CompactFlash (CF) card format was introduced by SanDisk Corporation in 1994 and features a footprint that's a bit smaller than a matchbook and weighs only half an ounce. You can find CF memory cards in a range of storage capacities, including some that will hold over 100GB of data.

FIGURE 10.25
For today's young generation of digital photographers who've never shot with film, the idea of manually loading a spool of 35mm film into an analog camera must seem rather odd and old-fashioned. By comparison, inserting a memory card is a virtual "no-brainer."

(continued)

The Secure Digital (SD) card format was developed jointly by Matsushita, SanDisk, and Toshiba, and was released in 2000. SD cards are roughly half the size of CF cards and are available in capacities up to 4GB. SDHC, a high-capacity version of SD, is available in capacities up to 32GB. Be careful, though, as older SD cameras cannot use the newer SDHC format. Some devices, particularly mobile phones, use smaller versions of the SD format, including miniSD and microSD.

The MultiMediaCard (MMC) format was launched by Siemens AG and SanDisk in 1997. MMCs come in three different sizes, with the smallest version roughly the size of a postage stamp. SD has largely supplanted MMC in most new devices.

Sony developed the Memory Stick (MS) in 1998, as a proprietary format for their line of multimedia products. The Memory Stick Duo (MS Duo) is a variation of the MS, which is smaller in size.

DOWNLOADING IMAGES

Most cameras made today have either a USB or Firewire port built into the camera for connecting directly to a computer to download images. Assuming that all of the necessary hardware drivers are installed, your computer should automatically recognize a camera connection as soon as the cable is attached, the power is turned on, and the camera is placed in playback mode. In Windows 7, plugging in the camera should trigger the AutoPlay box, which will present you with options for viewing, selecting, and downloading images from the camera's memory card to the computer hard drive. Unless you specify a different location, Windows 7 will store downloaded images in the My Pictures folder of the currently logged-in user. In Mac OS X, the default imaging software is iPhoto. On a Mac, images are stored by default in the iPhoto Library subfolder located in the Pictures folder of the current user. Both operating systems also give you the option of manually moving your images from the camera (or memory card) to the computer.

The AutoPlay wizard in Windows 7 is primarily a download interface and contains very few controls for manipulating image content or file details. But iPhoto is a bit more robust in that it can be used to perform a few basic manipulations such as image rotation, red-eye correction, and simple color correction. It also provides some simple cataloging options for managing the image library, resizing, and exporting images. Windows 7 provides some of these same functions through the File and Folder Task Pane of Windows Explorer.

Digital Image Management

Most people download images to a computer giving very little thought as to their location, organization, or potential retrievability. Without proper care, the My Photo or Pictures folder can quickly resemble the overstuffed family shoebox that's filled willy-nilly with 20 years of old photographs. And with digital images, the virtual shoebox is likely to become a cluttered mess all the more quickly. In order to effectively organize and manage an image library, the photographer should take the time to: (1) properly assign a descriptive name to each image file; (2) store related sets of images in topical subfolders; and (3) modify the metadata fields of an image file to include details about the picture's origins and subject matter. While this may seem like busywork it is not. Asset management is an incredibly important part of any multimedia endeavor, and invariably leads to a better workflow.

RENAMING IMAGES

Digital cameras usually assign rather meaningless names to image files. Renaming your image files is one of the first and most important things you can do to bring a sense of order and uniformity to a collection of related images. Programs such as Adobe Bridge and Apple's Aperture can help automate this process. When you rename the files, consider using a standard prefix for related images. For example, for a group of photos taken of Beth on her birthday in 2006, you could use beth_bd06_ as the prefix. As we talk about in Chapter 7, "Web Design," use lowercase names if you plan to use the images online. Similarly, use an underscore instead of a space when you want to separate the character elements in a filename. After establishing the prefix, you need to make the remaining part of the file names sequential. This is where using a program to automate the process really helps. In some cases, you may be able to use part of the file name generated by the camera. This is very helpful for preserving the chronological order of the collection.

IMAGE FOLDERS

Try to avoid the habit of storing all of your digital images in a single master folder. As your image library grows, the folder will swell, and it will become increasingly difficult for you to navigate such a large collection of files in one location. A better method is to use subfolders to store related sets of images. Some of the same naming strategies we've discussed so far can be applied to the naming of image subfolders. Sorting images into subfolders according to project or client name, subject name, or event title, will help alleviate a great deal of confusion and expedite locating image assets.

Tech Talk

Metadata Every time an image is captured and saved by a digital camera, nonpicture information about the image is recorded and saved to the file header. This information is called *metadata* and includes things like the date and time of image acquisition, the camera make and model number, image size, and values for exposure settings like aperture, shutter speed, focal length, ISO, and in some cases GPS data. Most cameras today encode metadata using an international standard called the Exchangeable Image File Format (EXIF). Nearly all image-editing programs are capable of displaying EXIF metadata. In Photoshop, selecting File>File Info opens up a dialog window containing access to EXIF metadata along with a number of blank entry fields that the photographer can use to attach more descriptive details to an image file (see Figure 10.26). Be careful about metadata. It

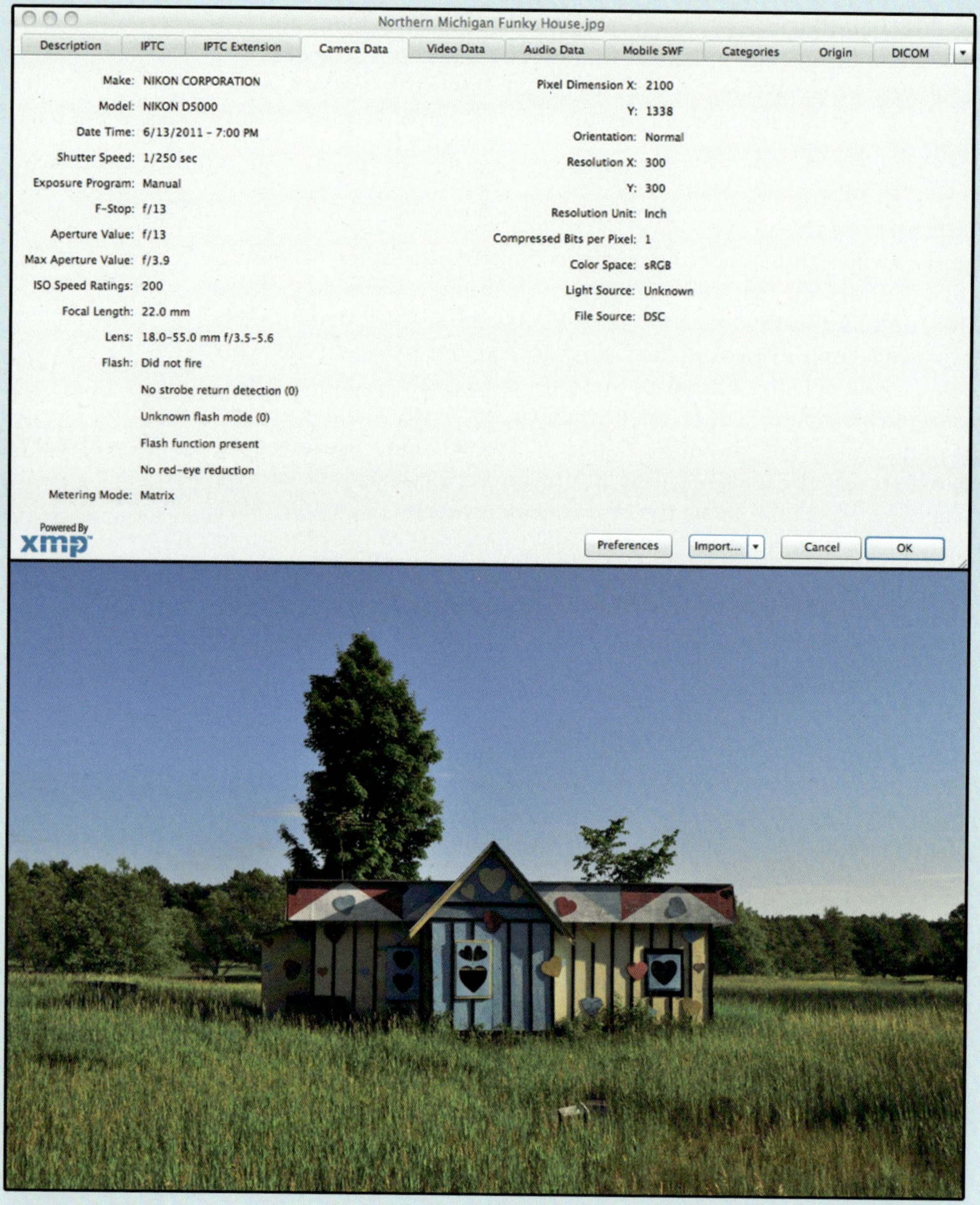

FIGURE 10.26
With each image, the camera gathers a significant amount of data that is available for retrieval long after the photographs from a shoot have been made, edited, retouched, and cataloged. In addition to a complete list of camera settings, some models even gather GPS data, allowing photographers to later identify locations or revisit them for subsequent shoots. *Photographer: Chris Walker.*

often embeds a thumbnail of the original image, which is not necessarily modified when you modify the actual image. This means that if you erase something from the image, it may still be visible in the thumbnail. If your camera has a GPS, you need to know that the GPS data is included in the image—something that is common on GPS-enabled smartphones. While software can use this information to help sort your images, it also means that someone can easily find out where you took the image. Think before you release your images.

In 1979, the International Press Telecommunications Council developed a more extensive set of labeling attributes to give photographers the ability to add descriptive details about the origins and subject matter of an image to the file header. IPTC headers include a variety of informational fields such as object name and title; the city, state, and country of origin; credits; subject category, image caption, and keywords; and special instructions. Professional photographers, digital media producers, and large media organizations typically rely on some type of asset management system for logging, storing, and retrieving digital image files according to embedded IPTC metadata. Programs like Canto Cumulus and Extensis Portfolio provide a visual interface for logging images with IPTC tags; making it possible for content producers to locate and retrieve matching files using keywords and user-specified search criteria.

CHAPTER SUMMARY

A digital camera is one of many tools a multimedia producer can use to create visual assets for a project. The more knowledgeable you are about the imaging process, the more creative freedom you will be able to exercise during the acquisition of digital pictures. This chapter has focused primarily on the mechanical aspects of digital photography by discussing the operational function of imaging components and the management of exposure controls. As the photographer, the degree to which you retain control during the exposure process is determined by which shooting method or mode you adopt. In fully-automatic mode, the camera retains total control of all the exposure variables. In manual mode, the photographer has more latitude and creative freedom but must also possess greater skill and knowledge about the camera, its operation, and intentional outcomes.

SECTION 4
Time-Based Media

Yuliyan Velchev/Shutterstock.com

CHAPTER 11
Audio Production

The notion of media will be completely blended in one digital stream. Moving pictures and static pictures and text and audio—the mix of any of those will be commonplace. Imagine turning the pages of a magazine: every one of the images is a sound clip, and when you put your cursor over one of them, the audio comes. That's absolutely going to be happening in 15 years. Full convergence of media and television and computers.

—Jim Clark, Computer Scientist and Founder of Silicon Graphics Inc. and Netscape, (1994)

Chapter Highlights

This chapter examines:

- The nature of sound and audio
- The audio chain and signal flow
- Microphone element designs, pickup patterns, and form factors
- Microphone placement and recording techniques
- Audio cables, connectors, and cable management

Key Terms

3-Band Equalizer
A/D Converter
Adapter
AGC
AIFF
Ambient Sound
Amplitude
Audio
Balanced Audio
Bass
Bass Roll-Off
Bidirectional
Bit Depth
Bitstream
Boom Pole
Cardioid
Clipping
Codec
Compression
Condenser Microphone
Container Format
Decibel (dB)
Dynamic Microphone
Dynamic Range
EQ
Frequency
Gain
Handheld Microphone
Headphones
High-definition Audio
Hypercardioid
Lavalier Microphone
Microphone
Midrange
Mini Plug
Monitoring
MP3

SOUND AND AUDIO

This chapter looks at sound, one of the key ingredients in the multimedia producer's recipe book. Sound is what we hear and can be featured in a standalone product, such as a song, a podcast, or a radio commercial, or it can be part of a larger product, such as the music or dialog in a feature length film. Think about how boring video games would be without sound effects to go along with the movement of spacecraft and the explosion of weapons. In television production, the phrase *Sound on Tape* (SOT) is used to describe audio captured on location at the time of a video or film recording. For example, during the World Series, the sounds of the ball hitting the bat, the crowd cheering in the background, and the voices of the announcers calling the game, are synchronized in real time with camera shots of the runner rounding third base after hitting a home run. While

Omnidirectional
Over-Under Wrap
Phantom Power
Pitch
Plosives
Polar Pattern
Preamp
Proximity Effect
Pulse-Code Modulation (PCM)
Quantization
Rarefaction
RCA Connector
Ribbon Microphone
Sample Rate
Sampling
Shotgun Microphone
SOT
Sound
Sound Check
Sound Pressure Level (SPL)
Sound Pressure Wave
Supercardioid
Transduction
Treble
TS/TRS Connector
Ultracardioid
Unbalanced Audio
XLR Connector
VU Meter
WAV

the images and sound of a live-event are often acquired at the same moment, the workflows for recording sound for use in a preproduced video or film are not necessarily the same, and it is important to understand the differences. This chapter focuses on the basic concepts, tools, and techniques you need to be aware of as you delve into sound acquisition, recording, and editing.

WHAT IS SOUND?

It's important to distinguish between the physical characteristics of sound as a phenomenon of nature, and the field of audio production—the capture and reproduction of sound. *Sound* is a natural phenomenon that involves pressure and vibration (see Figure 11.1). Understanding how sound and hearing work will help you capture and produce better quality audio. What we perceive as sound traveling across time and distance is actually the invisible moving presence of a sound pressure wave. *Sound waves* are a special type of energy and require a molecular medium for propagation. They can travel though solids, gases, or liquids, but air molecules are the best transmission medium. Despite Hollywood's portrayal of loud space battles, sound cannot travel within the vacuum of space, and in reality, a ship exploding in space would not make a sound as there are no air molecules. We hear by discerning changes in the pressure and movement of the air particles around us. When a tree falls in the forest, the air molecules in its path are momentarily displaced. They are violently pushed out of the way to make room for the falling tree. This sets off a chain reaction as the energy of the

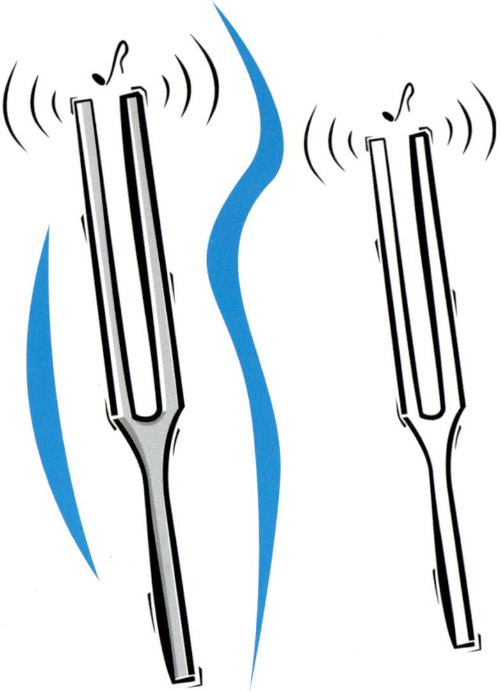

FIGURE 11.1
Striking a tuning fork causes its two prongs to vibrate, which in turn, produces a musical tone.

initial force is passed along to neighboring molecules in all directions. Back and forth they go, oscillating until the energy that caused the disturbance dissipates.

The best way to illustrate the movement of a sound pressure wave is to look at something more visible in nature. When you drop a small rock into a still pond, you see concentric ripples or waves traverse outward from the point of the disruption (see Figure 11.2). Here, water serves as the conduit for energy to flow away from the source. However, the actual water molecules travel only a tiny distance as they bounce back and forth transmitting the energy signature of the wave. As the wave travels further away from the source, the oscillations of the molecules begin to slow down until the pond is once again at rest.

FIGURE 11.2
Concentric ripples are the visible evidence of molecular vibration. Uniform waves progress outward in every direction, as energy is released at the point of disturbance.

Tech Talk

Characteristics of a Sound Wave While sound is invisible to the eyes, the attributes of a sound wave can be measured and visualized. Amplitude and frequency are the two observable dimensions of a sound pressure wave that we are most interested in. *Amplitude* is a sound pressure wave's intensity, or dynamic pressure, and *frequency* is the wave's rate of vibration or oscillation. In hearing, we perceive amplitude as the relative loudness of a sound and frequency as its pitch.

Amplitude

The first thing we tend to notice about sound is how loud it is. Loud sounds capture our attention almost immediately, while soft sounds strain our senses or elude us entirely. Because sound waves are invisible to the human eye, we must use pictures to illustrate their physical qualities and characteristics (see Figure 11.3). A sound wave's height (amplitude) indicates the intensity or magnitude of the pressure wave. *Amplitude* is defined as the distance from the crest of the wave to the trough. The louder the sound, the greater the amplitude, and the taller its waveform will be. The amplitude of a sound is greatest near the source and diminishes over distance and time.

Amplitude is measured in decibel units. The decibel (dB) is a logarithmic unit of measurement used to quantify the sound pressure level (SPL) or magnitude of a sound wave. Humans are capable of hearing a wide range of sounds, from 0 dB to 120 dB. A value of 0 dB represents the least audible sounds that we can hear(just above silence). With each increase of 20 dB on the decibel scale, the amplitude and perceived loudness of sound increases 10 times. Thus, a 20 dB sound pressure wave is 10 times louder than the faintest sound. A 40 dB sound source is 100 times louder than the faintest sound and 10 times louder than sound at 20 dB. When you reach 120 dB, the SPL is 1,000,000 times greater than the level of sound at 0 dB. While adapting to a logarithmic scale can be confusing at first, using a scale with a relatively small number of decibel units is easier to deal with than one with a million or more increments of variation.

The human threshold for pain begins around 140 dB, while permanent hearing loss occurs at 150 dB. Hearing loss most commonly results from repeated exposure to loud sounds over time. With the growing popularity of digital music and MP3 players, concern has emerged over the potentially damaging effects of listening repeatedly to loud music through headphones or earbuds. The close proximity of earbuds to the sensitive organs of the ear makes this an even greater concern and has prompted the makers of personal listening devices to

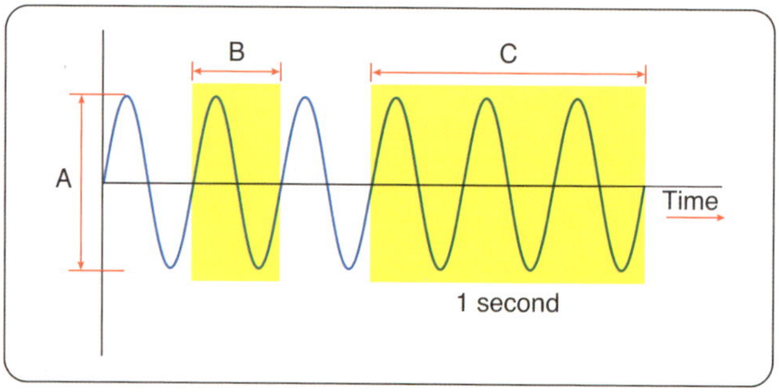

FIGURE 11.3
Sine waves are often used to visualize the repetitive oscillations of sound vibrations. (A) *Amplitude* is represented by the height of the wave. (B) *Wavelength* is the distance traveled during one complete vibration cycle. (C) Frequency is the number of complete wave cycles that occur over a set period of time (usually measured in 1-second intervals).

Tech Talk

Dynamic Range Loudness is rarely constant and tends to vary and fluctuate across time. For example, the human voice can quickly move from a whisper to a shout. Likewise, a classical composition can vary from quiet movements of reflection and solitude to intense moments of drama and passion. This difference in loudness, from the quietest point to the loudest, is called *dynamic range*.

offer volume-limit controls on their units. A volume limiter option allows users to set a maximum listening level based on decibels or the relative volume units of the device. While many factors can contribute to hearing loss or damage, setting a volume limit in place is advisable. By the way, that ringing you get in your ears after a concert—it's called *tinnitus* and can become permanent. Trust us, it's not fun.

Frequency

As sound waves pass through matter, the vibrating molecules experience three phases of movement (see Figure 11.4). As molecules move in an inward direction, they are pushed closer together, leading to an increase in molecular density and sound pressure. This is the *compression phase* and is represented by the portion of the waveform above the horizontal axis (time). The highest point of the waveform is called the *crest* and signifies the moment of greatest sound pressure. Once maximum compression has been reached, elasticity kicks in, causing the molecules to return to their original position. For a fraction of a second, the molecules are at rest as they change direction and begin moving outward. During the *rarefaction phase*, molecules are pulled apart, resulting in a decrease in molecular density and sound pressure. Rarefaction is denoted as the portion of the waveform below the horizontal axis. The lowest point on the waveform is called the *trough* and indicates the moment of lowest sound pressure.

The progression of a sound wave through one phase of rest, compression, and rarefaction is called a *cycle*, and a sound's frequency is based on its number of cycles-per-second. *Frequency* describes a sound's relative low or high pitch. Frequency is measured in hertz (Hz), cycles per second. Every vibration has a unique frequency signature. A common frequency used in audio production for the purposes of calibration is the 1 kHz tone. By the way, 1 kHz is simply 1,000 Hz. Kilohertz (kHz) units can be used as an abbreviated way of referring to particularly high frequencies.

When individually plucked, the strings of an acoustic guitar in standard tuning create the frequencies, or pitch, shown in Table 11.1. Each string can be played separately, producing a single note or pitch. However, most of the time a musician will strike multiple strings at a time, thus creating diverse sounds and harmonics with complex frequency signatures. Most sounds in nature, including human

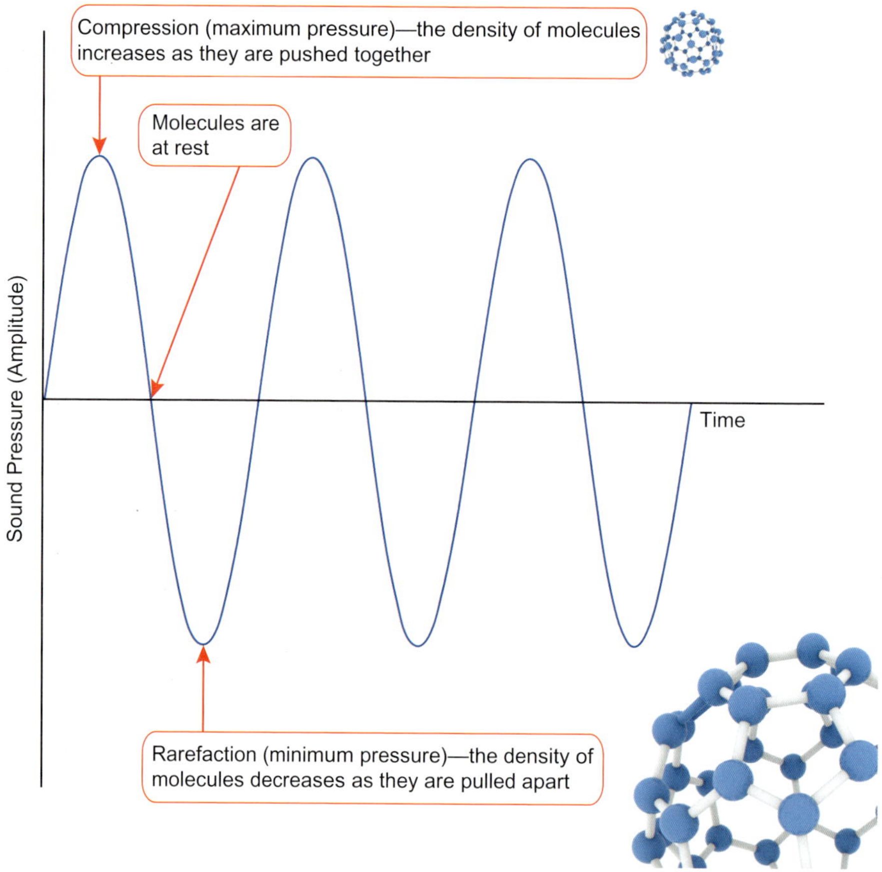

FIGURE 11.4 When the air molecules around us are energized by a sound pressure wave, they begin to oscillate, bouncing rapidly back and forth in unison. As molecules travel inward they are squeezed tightly together (*compression*); as they spring back in the opposite direction, they pull apart and spread out (*rarefaction*). At one brief moment in each wave cycle, when molecules change direction, they are briefly at rest.

Table 11.1 The Frequency Chart for a Six-String Acoustic Guitar

String	Note	Frequency
6th	E	82 Hz
5th	A	110 Hz
4th	D	147 Hz
3rd	G	196 Hz
2nd	B	247 Hz
1st	E	330 Hz

speech, are likewise composed of multiple frequencies interacting together to produce an holistic aural impression.

People with normal hearing are capable of perceiving sound frequencies from 20 to 20,000 Hz. Known as the *human frequency spectrum*, this range is often divided into three subgroups, or bands, called *bass*, *midrange*, and *treble*. The bass frequencies include lower pitch sounds in the range of 20–320 Hz. Midrange frequencies include medium pitch sounds falling between 320 and 5,120 Hz. Treble frequencies, high pitch sounds from 5,120 to 20,000 Hz, represent the largest segment of the frequency spectrum.

GREAT IDEAS

Equalization

Sound systems often allow you to adjust the bass, midrange, and treble output of a program source or channel. This feature is known as a *3-band equalizer* (or EQ) and provides the user with separate controls for raising or lowering the gain of each frequency region or band (see Figure 11.5). For example, "rolling off" or "dialing down" the bass frequencies can add brightness and clarity to the sound output. This may be helpful when listening to news or talk-radio channels, but for music, people often want to feel the deep and penetrating lower frequencies. In such cases, adding bass and rolling off the treble may be more to one's liking.

A 3-band equalizer is simple and inexpensive, but it provides only global controls for adjusting the pitch of the recording or transmission. Professional recording studios and production facilities typically rely on more robust and sophisticated tools for adjusting EQ. The better systems break the frequency spectrum into many more bands, allowing for precise isolation and manipulation of individual frequencies. You'll find a virtual version of this tool in most audio and video editing software.

FIGURE 11.5 A 3-band equalizer, like the one pictured here (top), is a standard feature on most audio mixing consoles and on many electronic sound devices (car stereos, amplifiers, etc.). On the bottom is a screen shot of the new graphic equalizer in Final Cut Pro X. With this interface, users can select between 10 and 31 bands of equalization.

DIGITAL AUDIO SAMPLING

Analog recording devices like the phonograph and cassette tape recorder were designed to capture the continuous linear fluctuations of an analog sound signal. When listening to a vinyl record, the stylus or needle stays in direct contact with the surface of the disk as a song is being played. There is a perfect one-to-one correlation between the fluctuations of the analog signal and the vibrations picked up by the needle as it travels along an uninterrupted path. Analog recordings capture the entire sound wave, from beginning to end, as it propagates across time. Many people prefer analog recordings to digital recordings because they reproduce sound in a way that more closely resembles the way that people hear and process sound (see Figure 11.6).

Pulse-Code Modulation

In order for sound to be understood by a computer, it must be converted from its native analog format to a digital format that can be represented with discrete numerical values. *Pulse-code modulation* (PCM) is the most common method used for representing audio as a digital stream of binary data. British engineer Alec Reeves invented the technique in 1937 as a way of reducing noise during the transmission of speech over long-distance telephone lines. The PCM method relies on a technique called sampling to reduce a continuous signal into a sequence of discrete samples that can be defined mathematically. Each unit (or sample) represents a measurement of the sound wave's properties at a single moment in time (see Figure 11.7). Each measurement is recorded numerically as a binary string of 0s and 1s. The fidelity of a PCM audio stream is determined by two basic properties: the sampling rate, which indicates the number of samples that are recorded every second; and the bit depth, which refers to the number of bits used to encode the value of a given sample.

FIGURE 11.6
Audio recording technologies have changed often over the years. Physical media like vinyl records that you could hold and touch have been replaced with invisible data files that can be purchased online and downloaded to a portable MP3 player in a matter of seconds.

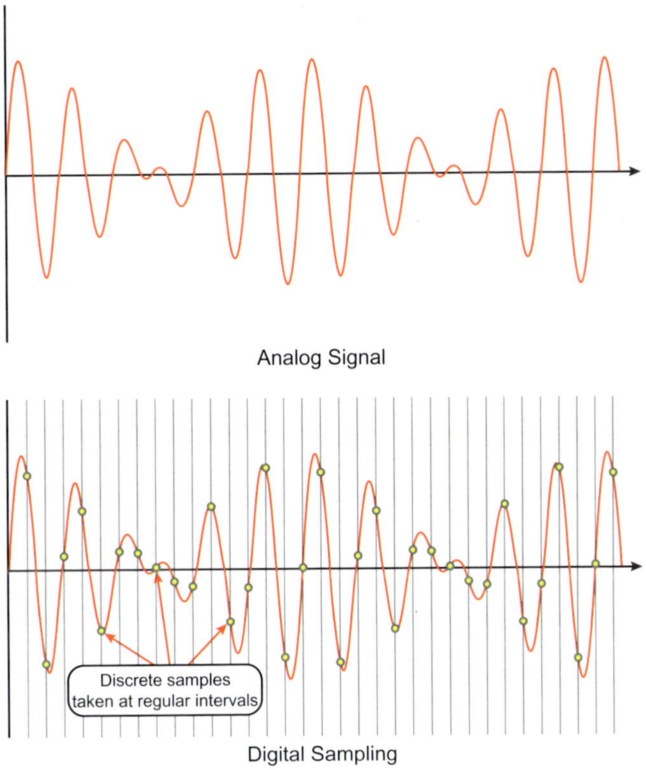

FIGURE 11.7
An analog audio signal is continuous without interruption (top). Sampling the analog signal at regular intervals is the first step in producing a digital recording (bottom).

Sampling Rate (or Sample Rate)

Audio sampling rates are designated in kilohertz (kHz) units. For example, a 48 kHz sampling rate indicates that the recording was sampled 48,000 times per second. While working for Bell Laboratories, engineer Henry Nyquist discovered that the sampling rate must be at least twice as large as the bandwidth (or frequency range) of the signal being recorded. Since human hearing has a frequency range of 20 Hz to 20 kHz, a minimum sampling rate of 40 kHz is required in order to effectively capture and encode all frequencies within this range. If the sampling rate is any lower, then frequency data (within the human hearing range) may be lost during the recording process.

Bit Depth

Whereas the sampling rate directly impacts the frequency response of a digital recording, *bit depth* affects its dynamic range and the amount of noise and distortion introduced during the recording process. Each audio sample is stored as a binary sequence of 0s and 1s. The bit depth setting determines how many 0s and 1s are used to represent the value of a waveform's *voltage signature* (or amplitude) at each sampling interval. The more bits you have to work with, the more descriptive the encoding can be to record subtle fluctuations in the waveform's amplitude. *Quantization* is a term that's often associated with bit depth, and is used to describe the mathematical process of assigning discrete numerical values to each voltage measurement.

An 8-bit binary sequence has 256 possibilities. A 16-bit sequence has 65,536 possibilities. And a 24-bit sequence can be arranged 16,777,216 different ways. The most common bit depth settings used in professional audio and video recording are 16-bit and 24-bit. While 24-bit recording is technically superior in terms of dynamic range, the higher bit depth also results in larger audio files. The additional data will demand higher performance from your computer system and editing software, potentially causing it to slow down if your system isn't powerful enough to handle 24-bit audio processing. While the difference between 24-bit

FLASHBACK

Industry Standards

Sony and Philips are familiar names in the consumer electronics industry. They joined forces to create the audio compact disc format in 1980. In doing so, they developed the infamous "red book" standard for the audio compact disc (CD), which specifies a bit depth of 16-bits and a sampling rate of 44.1 kHz. To this day, this is the industry standard used when distributing digitally recorded music to consumers. No matter what the bit rate and sampling rate are during production and editing, the final distribution file for your audio project should conform to 16-bit/44.1 kHz before being burned to a CD. In digital film and video production, a slightly higher sampling rate of 48 kHz was adopted as the industry standard. This rate conforms to the encoding standards set by Philips, Sony, Toshiba, and Time-Warner for the digital versatile disc (or DVD) recording platform in 1995. Because of this, camcorders are often programmed to encode the sound portion of a video recording at a sample rate of 48 kHz.

Since the introduction of HD television and Blu-Ray DVDs the concept of high-definition audio has grown more popular. The HD audio standard conforms to 24-bit/96 kHz encoding of the audio stream. While this standard is not yet universally supported, the added bandwidth is necessary for a number of advanced surround sound and multichannel applications. If your recording hardware supports 24-bit/96kHz encoding, then by all means choose this setting. Acquiring at the highest resolution possible is always a good idea. After your program is edited, you will have the option of exporting it as a standard definition product (16-bit/44.1 kHz).

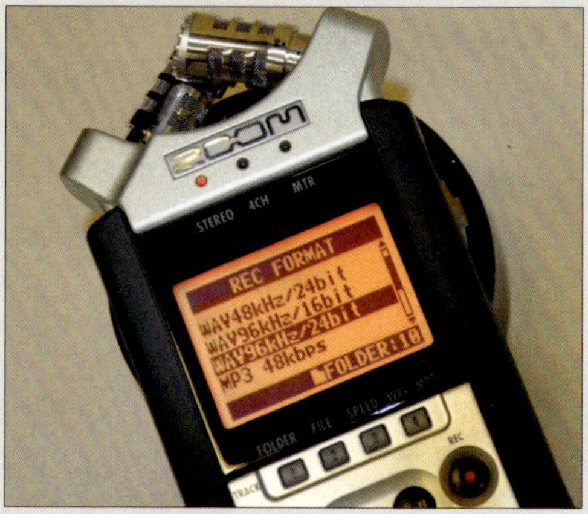

FIGURE 11.8
The recording format, sample rate, and bit depth settings are often located in the menu system of the recording device. Before you start recording, make sure that you review these settings. As a general rule, choose the highest quality setting that your device supports. You can always downsample to a lower resolution later in postproduction.

and 16-bit looks relatively small, at a sampling rate of 44,100 kHz, the amount of digital data stored every second becomes quite substantial. In a 16-bit/44.1 kHz recording, 700,600 bits of data are produced every second. In a 24-bit/96 kHz recording, the audio stream will contain more than 2.3 million bits per second. You may hear people refer to audio encoded at 24-bit/96 kHz or greater as *high-definition audio* because of its superior resolution.

CODECS AND CONTAINER FORMATS

This is a good time to make a distinction between two similar and often confusing terms: codec and container format. Pulse-Modulation is a *codec* (short for ***coder**-**decoder***), a computer program or algorithm designed for encoding and decoding audio and video into a raw digital *bitstream* (a sequence of data in binary form). Hundreds of codecs have been developed for digital video and audio applications over the years. Some audio codecs, such as AC3 and WMA, are proprietary and will only work with designated programs. Others, like PCM (Pulse-Code Modification), are open source, which means they are meant to work across all computer platforms and with most editing programs. Some codecs also perform *compression*—the process of reencoding data using fewer bits. A compression codec is designed to reduce the file size of a digital asset without adversely affecting its resolution. The popular MP3 audio format is a compression codec that's used to cut down the file size of a digital recording by a factor of 10:1, allowing you to fit thousands, rather than hundreds, of songs on your portable music player.

A *multimedia container* (or *wrapper*) format is a unique kind of file format used for bundling and storing the raw digital bitstreams that codecs encode. Container formats are widely used in multimedia production because of the necessity of keeping separate streams of related data together as they are processed and delivered to an end-user. For example, a digital stereo audio signal has two streams, one for the left channel and one for the right. Likewise, a 5.1 digital surround sound file has six streams. While the PCM codec can be used to create a stereo pair of encoded audio streams, a container format is required for keeping the streams together as a unit. A codec performs a single encoding/decoding function, while a container format can, and often does, support multiple codecs.

WAV and AIFF

The two most common container formats for digital audio are WAV and AIFF. The Waveform Audio File Format (WAV or WAVE) was developed jointly by Microsoft and IBM. The Audio Interchange File Format (AIFF) was codeveloped in large part by Apple. WAV and AIFF container formats are very similar. They both contain raw uncompressed PCM audio streams. When an audio file is converted from WAV to AIFF or vice versa, the underlying bitstreams are left mostly unchanged. Only the container file or wrapper is modified. You may have noticed that when you insert a professional audio CD into a Windows PC, the track icons for each song appear as WAV files. Take the same CD and insert it into a Mac and the tracks appear as AIFF files. While WAV and AIFF are rival container formats, they are

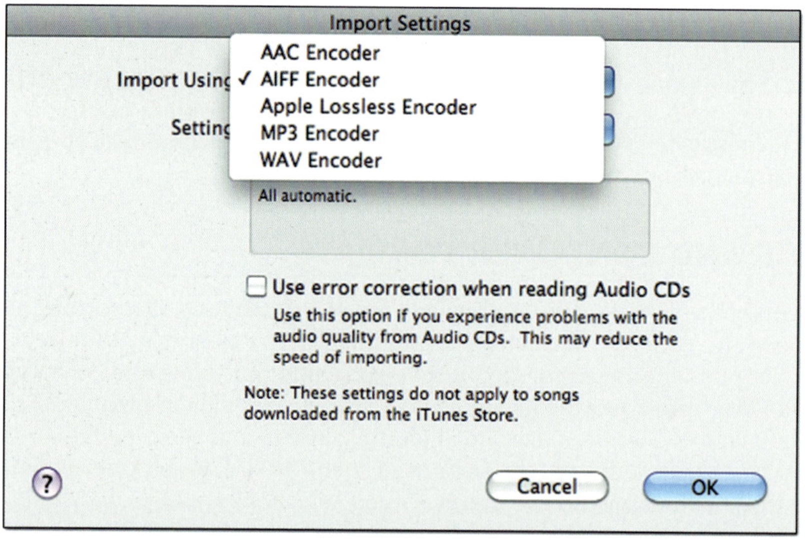

FIGURE 11.9
In Apple iTunes, users can convert audio sound files into any one of five formats: AAC, AIFF, Apple Lossless, MP3, and WAV.

largely interchangeable, and virtually all sound editing programs provide support for both of these uncompressed file formats (see Figure 11.9).

SOUND RECORDING

There are three main components to a sound recording system—a source, something or someone creating a sound; a microphone to convert physical sound waves into an analog signal transmitted via an electric current; and a recording device to store the sound imprint.

Microphones

A *microphone* is a recording instrument used to convert sound waves into an electrical equivalent that can be stored, transmitted, and played back through an audio sound system. Some microphones are designed specifically for use in a studio environment, while others are optimized for field use. Likewise, some microphones are better for voice work while others are designed primarily for instrument recording. While there's often more than one clear-cut choice, it's important to understand the fundamental differences in microphone design in order to choose the most appropriate tool for the job.

How Do Microphones Work?

While the digital revolution has radically transformed the design of nearly all of the production assets in the multimedia toolkit, professional microphones remain largely analog devices that have changed very little in design over the past 30 years. The microphone's job is to convert the acoustical waveform signature of the sound wave into an electrical voltage signal bearing the amplitude and frequency imprint of the recorded sound, a process called *transduction*. The signal coming out of a microphone is called an *analog signal*, because it is analogous to the variations in sound pressure and frequency present in the original

FIGURE 11.10
A boom arm and shockmount are used to support the microphone during this recording studio session. A pop filter is placed in front of the microphone to reduce plosives, vocal artifacts like those infamous "popping *P*s."

sound wave. And like the original sound wave, analog recordings provide a continuous and uninterrupted representation of the original sound.

Microphones are generally classified according to three main features or characteristics: (1) Transduction Method, (2) Polar Pattern, and (3) Form Factor.

Classifying Microphones by Transducer Type

Microphones use a *transducer* element to capture sounds. The transducer contains a moving diaphragm or ribbon that vibrates when exposed to a sound and encodes a sound wave's strength and frequency into electricity by modulating the current. The most common types of microphones, based on transduction methods, are dynamic microphones, moving-coil microphones, ribbon microphones, and condenser microphones.

DYNAMIC MICROPHONES

Dynamic microphones use acoustical energy and mechanical vibration as the means for producing the electromagnetic signal required for analog recording. Dynamic microphones do not require a power source. They are durable, relatively inexpensive, and moisture- and shock-resistant. Moving-coil and ribbon microphones are two of the most common types of dynamic microphones. Both rely on electromagnetic induction, which uses magnets to produce an electric current (see Figure 11.11-A).

MOVING-COIL MICROPHONES

In a *moving-coil microphone*, a diaphragm is attached to a coil (a metal core wrapped with copper wire) suspended in a magnetic field between the north and south poles of a fixed magnet. The diaphragm is a thin, circular membrane, typically made of paper, plastic, or metal. As the diaphragm vibrates, the coil oscillates in the magnetic field, producing a tiny current that's transmitted via copper wire to the microphone cable. The electromagnetic signal modulates in unison with the amplitude and frequency of the sound pressure wave, producing a copy of the original waveform.

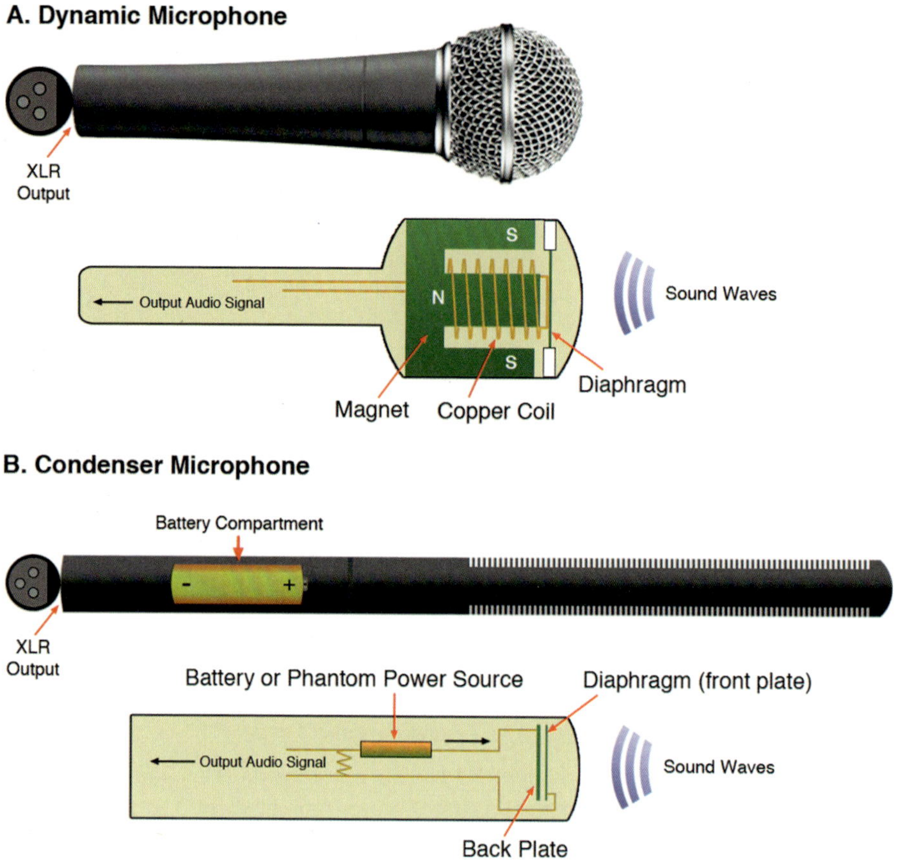

FIGURE 11.11
A) A dynamic microphone is less sensitive to sound because the transducer is self-powered by the sound of the subject's voice. B) A condenser microphone is more sensitive to sound because the transducer is powered by a battery or phantom power source.

RIBBON MICROPHONES

A *ribbon microphone* uses a thin metal ribbon of corrugated metal, usually aluminum, as the transduction element. The ribbon is suspended in a magnetic field between the opposite poles of a fixed magnet and generates an electromagnetic current when it pulsates in the magnetic field. Ribbon microphones are technically superior to moving-coil designs because they respond to sound bidirectionally, from both the front and the back of the element. While ribbon microphones are relatively expensive, broadcasting and recording professionals value them for their superior performance and natural sound reproduction. The metal elements in early ribbon microphones were quite delicate, and ribbon microphones had a reputation for being easy to damage. Newer ribbon microphones are more robust, though as with their predecessors, you need to be careful about picking up wind noise when using them outdoors (see Figure 11.12).

CONDENSER MICROPHONES

Condenser microphones use a capacitor to record variations in amplitude and frequency. The capacitor has two parts, the back plate (containing the electric charge) and the diaphragm. As the diaphragm vibrates, the distance between it and the

FIGURE 11.12
Vintage radio microphones like this one often have a ribbon transducer.

back plate changes, thus modulating the intensity of the voltage signal. Condenser microphones are much more sensitive to sound than dynamic microphones, and as a result can be positioned further from the source of the sound. Condenser microphones are separated into two groups based on diaphragm size. Large diaphragm condensers have a bigger form factor and are more often used in a studio recording environment, while small diaphragm condensers have a slender body profile and may be found in both field and studio environments (see Figure 11.11-B).

Condenser elements require an external power source to supply the electric charge to the back plate. For this reason, condensers are often equipped with an attached battery pack or built-in power module. A single AA battery is usually all that's required. As an alternative, condensers can receive phantom power directly from a connected mixer or recording device. Phantom power supplies a 48-volt (+48V) electric current to the capacitor through the attached microphone cable. Professional audio mixers and video cameras usually include this feature (see Figure 11.13).

Classifying Microphones by Polar Pattern

Microphones are also classified according to their *polar pattern* (or *pickup pattern*). Polar pattern refers to how well a microphone picks up sound within 360° of its central axis. Polar patterns are three-dimensional, so in effect, the sensitivity field includes the area above and below the microphone as well as to the right, left, front, and back. The narrower the pickup pattern is, the more directional the microphone will be, and the more effective it will be in sensing sounds along the central axis. In

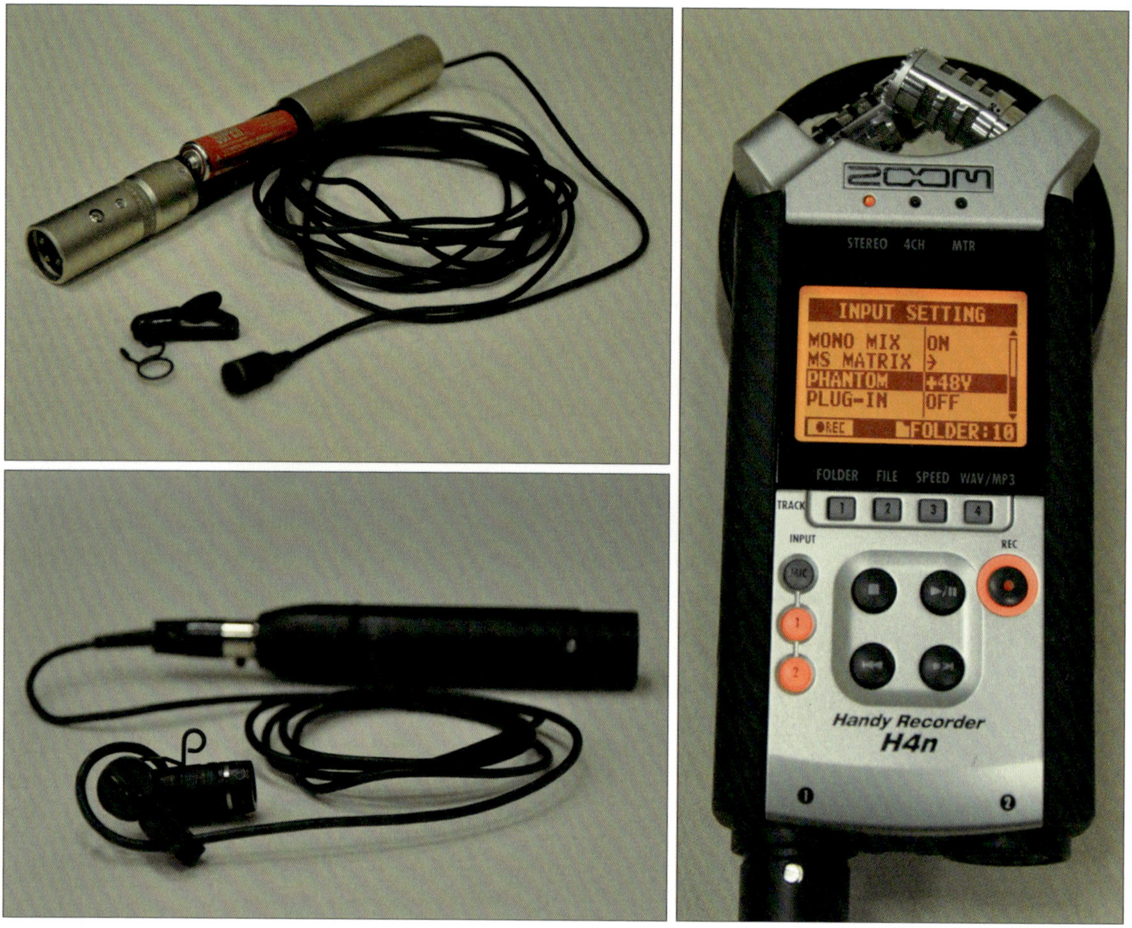

FIGURE 11.13
The two microphones on the left are condensers. However, the one pictured at the top can be powered with either a battery or phantom power. The microphone on the bottom does not have a battery compartment and must be powered by the camera or recorder it is connected to. Most professional recording equipment can provide phantom power, but it must be turned on to work. The phantom power switch may be located on the outside of the unit or, as shown on the right, within the menu system of the device.

short, the polar pattern of a microphone impacts how you use it and under which circumstances the microphone will function at its best (see Figure 11.14).

OMNIDIRECTIONAL

The pickup pattern of an *omnidirectional microphone* is a sphere around the microphone, though not an entirely perfect one. In theory, these microphones respond equally to sound in all directions. In practice, however, the microphone body, particularly on handheld microphones, can block or obscure the path of a sound wave. This can shield the microphone a bit from some frequencies. The smaller the microphone's body, the less of a problem this is. Because they pick up sound from all around, omnidirectional microphones are best used in situations where there is little to no ambient sound. You may also hear these microphones called *nondirectional*.

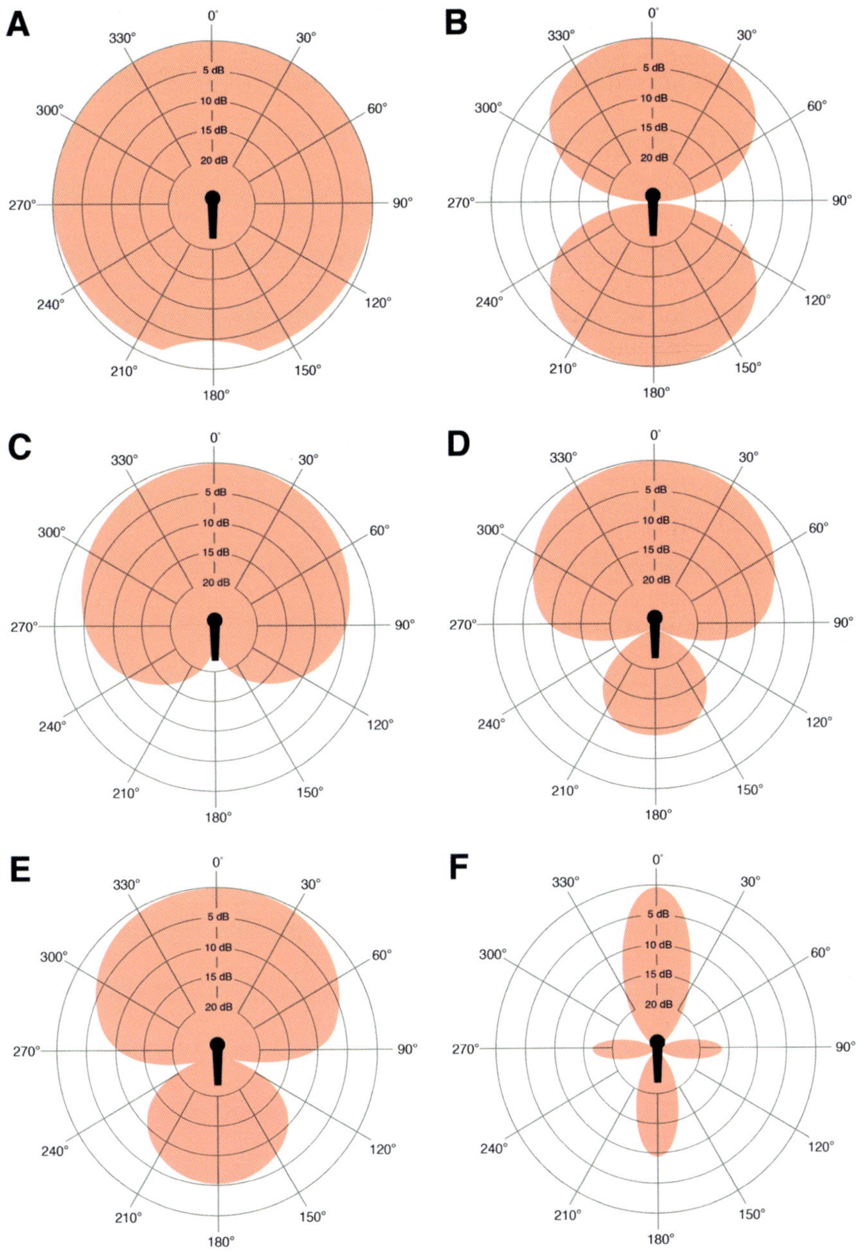

FIGURE 11.14
Six of the most common polar patters. (A) Omnidirectional. (B) Bidirectional. (C) Cardioid. (D) Supercardioid. (E) Hypercardioid. (F) Ultracardioid (or shotgun).

BIDIRECTIONAL

Bidirectional microphones pick up sound equally from the front and rear of the element. Most ribbon microphones are bidirectional. As a broadcast performance microphone, these are ideal for interviews where the host and guest are seated on opposite sides of a table or in situations where two people are required to share a single microphone.

CARDIOID (UNIDIRECTIONAL)

As the name implies, a *unidirectional microphone* picks up sound from only one direction. This makes it well suited for working in situations with lots of ambient (background) noise. There are a number of variants of this type of microphone. *Cardioid microphones* have a unidirectional polar pattern with a heart-like shape (hence their name). This pickup pattern favors sounds coming from the front and sides up to 130°. Cardioid microphones boast a relatively narrow pickup field and do a good job of rejecting ambient sound from the rear of the microphone. Cardioid microphones are ideal for recording single subjects and vocalists. Other members of the unidirectional family include *supercardioid*, *hypercardioid*, and *ultracardioid* (or *shotgun*) *microphones*. Each progression comes with a narrower pickup field and an expanded area of sound rejection from the rear of the microphone. The narrower the pickup pattern, the more proactive the operator needs to be in aiming the microphone directly at the sound source during recording.

Classifying Microphones by Form Factor

Microphones come in many different shapes and sizes, but in terms of practical application, there are four microphone styles that you will run into more than all the rest put together: handheld, lavalier, shotgun, and boundary microphones. If you are familiar with these, you will be ready to handle the vast majority of the recording challenges with ease and confidence.

HANDHELD MICROPHONES

Handheld microphones are designed for the talent or performer to hold during a recording session. Dynamic handheld microphones are ideal for rugged use and heavy handling, but they need to be held close to the mouth (3–6 inches) in order to generate enough sound pressure for a good recording (see Figure 11.15). The rugged construction of dynamic handheld microphones minimizes noise caused by sudden movement, rough handling, or when passing the microphone along from person to person. Reporters rely on this type of microphone most often when recording a standup interview or conducting field interviews. If you are interviewing someone using a directional handheld microphone, remember that you need to angle it toward the other person when he or she is talking.

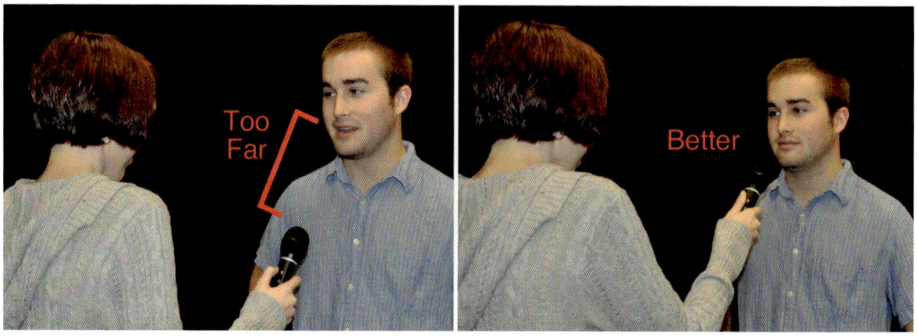

FIGURE 11.15
Reporters often use handheld microphones for conducting field interviews. Because handhelds are usually dynamic, they should be positioned a few inches in front of the subject's mouth.

Think about it as sharing an ice cream cone. If the other person is going to eat, you've got to put the cone in front of him or her.

Some handhelds are equipped with an electret condenser element. While this increases the microphone's sensitivity, it raises the risk of unwanted noise from outside forces. To reduce handling noise, condenser handheld microphones usually come with an internal shock mount. The shock mount suspends the element in mid-air with elastic bands, insulating it against sudden jarring movements (refer back to Figure 11.10).

Most handheld microphones are unidirectional. Handhelds work best when the microphone is positioned no further than 6 inches away from the mouth and slightly off-axis. Getting too close to the microphone grill (the shield) can produce annoying artifacts such as the infamous "popping *P*s" and other unpleasant plosives—the sound caused by releasing blocked air in speech, particularly from the pronunciation of the hard consonants *b, d, g, k, p,* and *t*. Remember, the microphone element is highly sensitive to sound pressure vibrations, and when a plosive ignites less than an inch away, vocal distortion and clipping is likely to occur. Using a windscreen or pop filter can help reduce or eliminate these types of negative consequences, but you still need to pay attention to your distance from the microphone (see Figure 11.16).

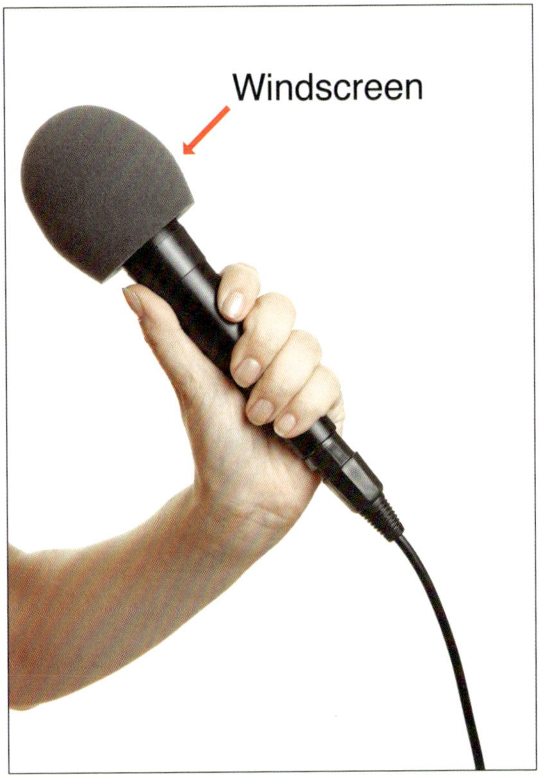

FIGURE 11.16
When using any microphone outdoors, it's a good idea to attach a windscreen.

FIGURE 11.17
A handheld microphone is supported by a microphone stand for hands-free use.

Up until now, we have assumed that a handheld microphone must be held at all times. While this is a common approach in field productions, concerts, and the like, handhelds can easily be attached to a floor stand, table-top stand, podium, or boom arm using a microphone clip, gooseneck, or other adapter (see Figure 11.17). Securing a handheld microphone to a stand or mount ensures hands-free operation and virtually eliminates the risk of handling noise, unless of course the stand topples over or the talent swats the microphone. It happens!

The downside to using stands, or handheld microphones at all, lies in the fact that most inexperienced users (nonprofessionals) vehemently shy away from close contact with a microphone. Most people feel nervous around microphones and assume they will work just fine if positioned 10 feet away from them. So if the keynote speaker for the annual fundraising banquet is an engineer, doctor, lawyer, or tax collector, you will need to remind him or her about the importance of moving in close to the microphone in order to obtain a usable recording. Even then, they may choose to ignore your instructions or simply forget them as the common fear of public speaking sets in. In either event, a better option awaits you in our discussion of the next form factor.

Tech Talk

The Proximity Effect The *proximity effect* is an acoustic phenomenon that boosts the bass frequencies of your voice as you move progressively closer to the microphone diaphragm. Next time you're in a recording studio, test this out by putting on a pair of headphones and listening to how your voice resonates more deeply as you narrow the gap between your mouth and the microphone. While the proximity effect is common with most unidirectional dynamic microphones, especially those with a single, large diaphragm, you'll particularly notice it with ribbon microphones, as both sides of the diaphragm are exposed to sound pressure. While you need to be close to a dynamic microphone when you use it, avoid leaning in too closely. When you are a quarter inch or closer to the microphone, it will lead to unnatural low-end distortion artifacts.

Whether the proximity effect is good or bad is simply a matter of taste and perspective. Radio disc jockeys, public-address announcers, and voice recording artists often get paid for having warm, larger-than-life voices. A professional can use the proximity effect to his or her advantage to enhance the overall warmth and presence of a performance or to increase the power and delivery of certain words and phrases. Over time, vocal artists develop an instinctive ability to control the proximity effect and to gauge when and how far to lean in on the microphone to mediate its intensity.

Too much bass, however, can muddy the audio. Over emphasized bass frequencies can cause the midrange and highs to be compressed, and the overall clarity and breadth of a vocal recording may suffer. Most professional microphones vulnerable to the proximity effect have a bass or low-frequency roll-off feature that gradually reduces the bass response as sound pressure increases. Mixers and recorders often include a similar control for attenuating (reducing) bass sounds or cancelling out excessive low-end frequencies. Because of the popularity of the bass roll-off feature with recording engineers, this feature is sometimes even included on microphones, resulting in little to no proximity effect distortion.

LAVALIERE MICROPHONES

Lavaliere microphones are designed specifically for speech and vocal acquisition. Also known as a *lapel* or *lav* microphone, this low-profile workhorse is designed with an electret condenser transducer element. Although they come in a variety of polar patterns, the most common ones have an omnidirectional, cardioid, or supercardioid element. Like all condensers, lavs require a battery pack or phantom power signal from the mixer or recording device.

Lavalier microphones have an extremely small form factor. Unlike handheld microphones, lavs are designed to be worn and are attached to the talent's clothing—often a tie, collar, or lapel—with the aid of a tiny metal clip. These microphones are too small to be handheld, as handling noise will produce unwanted artifacts during recording. Since they are physically attached to the talent, the distance from the microphone to the source is constant, removing an important variable from the recording process. Whether the subject is running, walking, sitting, or standing, the position of a lavalier microphone, relative to the source, will change very little. However, even when a lavaliere is properly attached, you have to be careful. The talent's physical actions (moving hands, feet, clothing, etc.) can cause unwanted noise if the microphone is suddenly bumped or jostled. Lavs are particularly popular with platform speakers who want the freedom to walk and talk at the same time without having to hold a microphone or stand behind a podium. They are also a good choice for recording interviews, especially when used indoors in a quiet setting (like a TV studio or office) and where the talent's physical movements won't interfere with a good recording.

Proper microphone placement is essential for maximizing performance and optimizing the rejection of unwanted ambient sound. Lavalier microphones should be attached 3–6 inches below the neckline. The microphone element should face upward towards the chin and be free of any obstructions from clothing and jewelry. Attaching a windscreen to the microphone capsule can help to alleviate wind or breathing noise. Lavs should be positioned so that the subject's voice projects directly over the top of the microphone. Most of the time, this means affixing it directly in the center of the upper body or chest. However, if the subject is turned off-axis to the camera, then the microphone should be positioned slightly to the left or right of center, so that it remains directly under the mouth or chin of the subject.

To maintain a professional appearance, lavalier microphones should be properly dressed. Dressing a microphone involves making it as attractive and obscure as possible (see Figure 11.18). At all costs, be sure to avoid the rookie mistake of allowing the microphone cable to dangle down the front of the subject's shirt or blouse. This is a telltale sign of an amateur production. With just a little bit of effort, and discretion, the microphone cable can be rerouted out of sight beneath clothing, or hidden behind a tie, lapel, jacket, or collar. Discretion is critical, because working with people in a professional production setting requires sensitivity to cultural norms and rules of etiquette. While you need to keep these issues in mind whenever you are working, you need to be particularly cognizant of these issues when working with people from other cultures or with different genders.

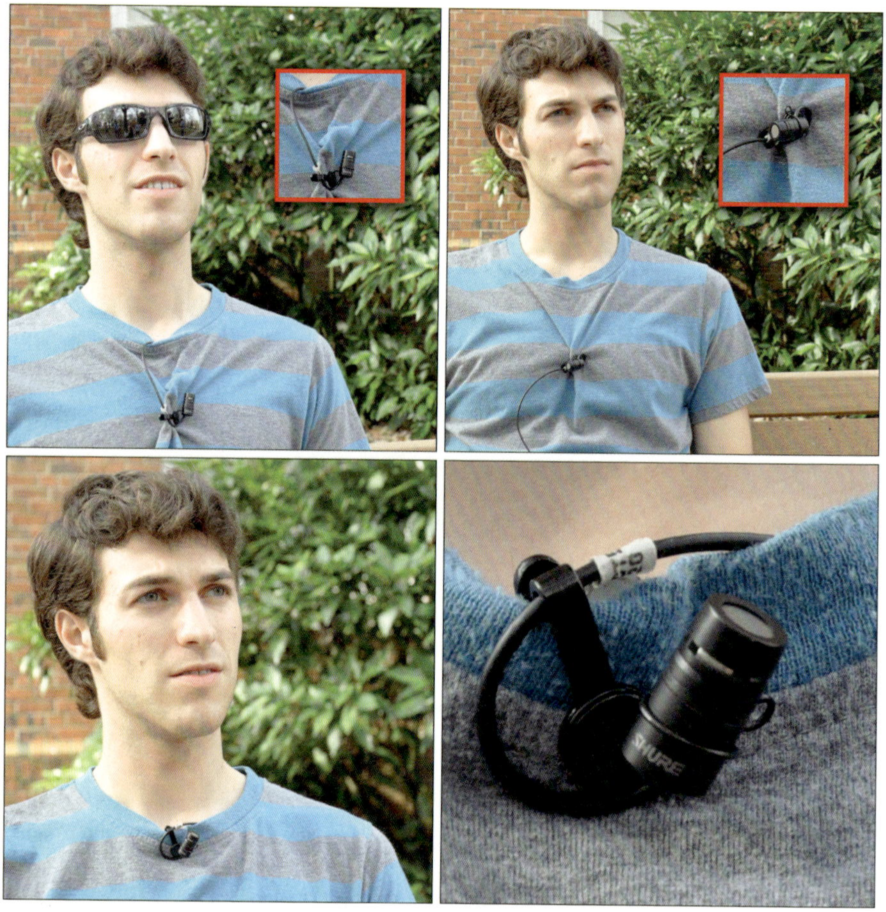

FIGURE 11.18
The lavalier is improperly attached and dressed in the top two photos. This is the mark of an amateur production. Taking the time to properly attach and dress a lavalier microphone, as in the bottom photos, improves the quality of the recording and the appearance of the subject during on-camera interviews.

In order to effectively hide the microphone cable, it may be necessary to conceal it under a shirt or blouse. Such a request needs to be made in a professional manner, with sensitivity to personal space and gender differences. Giving subjects clear instructions about microphone placement and offering them the option of moving to an off-set location (such as a dressing room or private area) is often appreciated. However, do not assume that the subject will know which way is up and which way is down. Do not expect them to understand the best technique for dressing the cable, or that they will have performed the task completely as instructed. In the end, this is your job, and before recording begins, you should make every effort to ensure that the microphone has been properly attached, positioned, and dressed. Leave nothing to chance.

SHOTGUN MICROPHONES

Shotgun microphones are among the most directional microphones. They feature a condenser element with an extremely narrow pickup pattern—in supercardioid, hypercardioid, and ultracardioid varieties. They are so named because of their long and slender form factor, which resembles the general shape of

FIGURE 11.19
A boom pole is used to position a shotgun microphone within a few feet of the subjects in this scene. The videographer works with the boom pole operator to ensure that the microphone does not dip down into the visible portion of the frame.

a shotgun barrel. Shotguns microphones are housed in a cylindrical capsule with a small diaphragm. While they are relatively expensive, film and video producers like these microphones because of their versatility and usefulness in complicated miking situations, particularly those in which more than one person in a scene is speaking. The main advantage of using this type of microphone is that it can remain hidden out-of-sight, beyond the camera's field of view. Some shotgun microphones (as well as other types of microphones) have interchangeable capsules that allow you to change the characteristics of the microphone on the fly.

Because of their narrow polar pattern, shotgun microphones need to be aimed in much the same way that a rifle has to be pointed towards its intended target. In a film-style recording setup, a shotgun is often mounted to a *boom* pole (or *fish pole*), a device that allows the audio operator to extend the microphone 6 to 12 feet into the scene where the subject or actors are located (see Figure 11.19). It can also be attached to a small *pistol grip* for handheld control, (see Figure 11.20) or mounted directly on top of a video camera. Using a boom pole or pistol grip, the audio operator is able to keep the axis of the barrel continually aimed at the subject as dialog moves from one person to another or as sound traverses along a linear path. The boom pole operator monitors the recording with headphones to assist with maintaining the "sweet spot" where the microphone is positioned at its optimal best. Remember to make sure the microphone stays out of the shot when you use a boom pole (see Figure 11.21).

Working alone, you may not have a second set of hands to operate a boom pole or pistol grip. In such cases, attaching it to the camera will allow for hands-free operation. While mounting a shotgun microphone directly to a camera is sometimes less than ideal, this technique can produce good results as long as the distance between the sound source and the camera remains fixed.

FIGURE 11.20
A pistol grip is used in lieu of a boom pole for acquiring the sound of footsteps on leaves. When using a shotgun microphone to acquire sound effects, the audio engineer usually wants to get the microphone as close to the source of the sound as possible.

FIGURE 11.21
Different techniques are used for positioning a microphone with a boom pole. Most often, the pole is held above the subjects or below them. Placing the microphone too close to the actors (bottom photo) may disrupt their concentration and potentially ruin a take.

Whether attached to a camera, boom pole, or handgrip, shotguns need to be secured in a sturdy shock mount in order to reduce the presence of mechanical noise transmission. Since they use a condenser element, shotguns require a power source, either phantom power or a battery—typically found in a compartment at the end of the microphone capsule. While broadcast and film producers have been using shotgun-style microphones for years, they are growing in popularity with corporate and prosumer productions. If you can only afford to have one microphone in your production arsenal, this is the one to choose.

BOUNDARY MICROPHONES

Boundary microphones, also known as *pressure zone microphones* (PZM), are condenser microphones intended to be placed on a flat surface, usually a table, ceiling, or wall. As you can see in the illustration, the microphone is mounted to a metal plate. The microphone points down at a metal baseplate and detects the sound pressure waves in between the microphone and the plate—the pressure zone (see Figure 11.22). This minimizes the effects of sound reflecting off other sources such as a wall by limiting the sound capture area. PZMs are usually used to record meetings and conferences and are good for recording multiple people at the same time. As you can see, they don't really look like what we typically think a microphone looks like. You can use this to your advantage—PZMs are less likely to make people nervous.

FIGURE 11.22
The Audio-Technica ES961 is a cardioid condenser boundary microphone designed for use on a flat surface such as a conference table or floor.
Source: audio-technica .com

Internal or External Microphones

The microphones we've talked about so far have been external microphones that you attach to a recording device, but many devices have built-in microphones, including laptop computers, cameras, cell phones, and voice recorders. In many cases, these are low-end condenser microphones. After all, if you are using a microphone for a phone call or video chat, it just needs to be good enough to be clearly understood. Even on many of the video cameras and audio recorders, built-in microphones are designed more for transmitting conversations, not recording them. There are, of course, exceptions. Be careful about relying on built-in microphones without carefully testing them before using them in production. That said, don't forget to test your external microphones as well. Just because a standalone microphone isn't built into a capture device doesn't automatically make it better. As the old adage goes, "you get what you pay for."

Regardless of the quality of a built-in microphone, however, it has some inherent limitations. One of the most important is that it *is* built-in. This means that in most cases the operator has little control over the location of the microphone, particularly with video cameras, and the closer the microphone is to the source, the better it will perform. Although professional external microphones are relatively more expensive, they are made with better transducers and components. There's simply no substitute for using a professional, high-quality, external

GREAT IDEAS
Why Should You Use an External Microphone?

Here are four reasons for using a professional-grade external microphone instead of one that is built into the recording device:

1. It gives you the ability to select the right type of microphone for the intended subject and recording application.
2. It gives you maximum control over microphone placement and distance to the subject, independent of where the sound or video recording device is located.
3. All things being equal, a professional external microphone will have better sound fidelity than the built-in microphone of a recording device.
4. It can help you avoid tape noise on tape-based equipment.

FIGURE 11.23
In the photo on the left, the producer uses the built-in microphone on his digital audio recorder. In the photo on the right, he uses the same recorder, but attaches an external handheld microphone. All things being equal, you will achieve better results using a professional external microphone to conduct interviews.

microphone. In fact, as a general rule in professional situations, you should avoid the temptation of ever using a built-in microphone to acquire primary audio content (actor dialogue, voiceovers, interviews, etc.) (see Figure 11.23).

Wireless Microphones

Although most of the time you are working with audio you'll be running a wire directly from the microphone to your recorder or mixer, you'll occasionally need to use a wireless microphone, particularly if you have talent who likes to walk around the room a lot. In some cases, you can plug your regular microphone into a wireless transmitter—essentially a tiny radio station that will send the audio to a radio receiver—which you'll plug into your mixer or recorder (see Figure 11.24). You may lose some of your frequency range when you switch to wireless. Like all battery-operated equipment, make sure you keep fresh batteries on hand for the transmitter and the receiver. If you use more than one wireless microphone at a time, you'll have to make sure they aren't using the same radio frequency. Just as two radio stations can't broadcast on 88.1 FM at the same time, you can't have two wireless microphones operating on the same radio frequency. The better the system, the more frequency options you'll have. Remember, you may not be the only one using a wireless microphone at some locations.

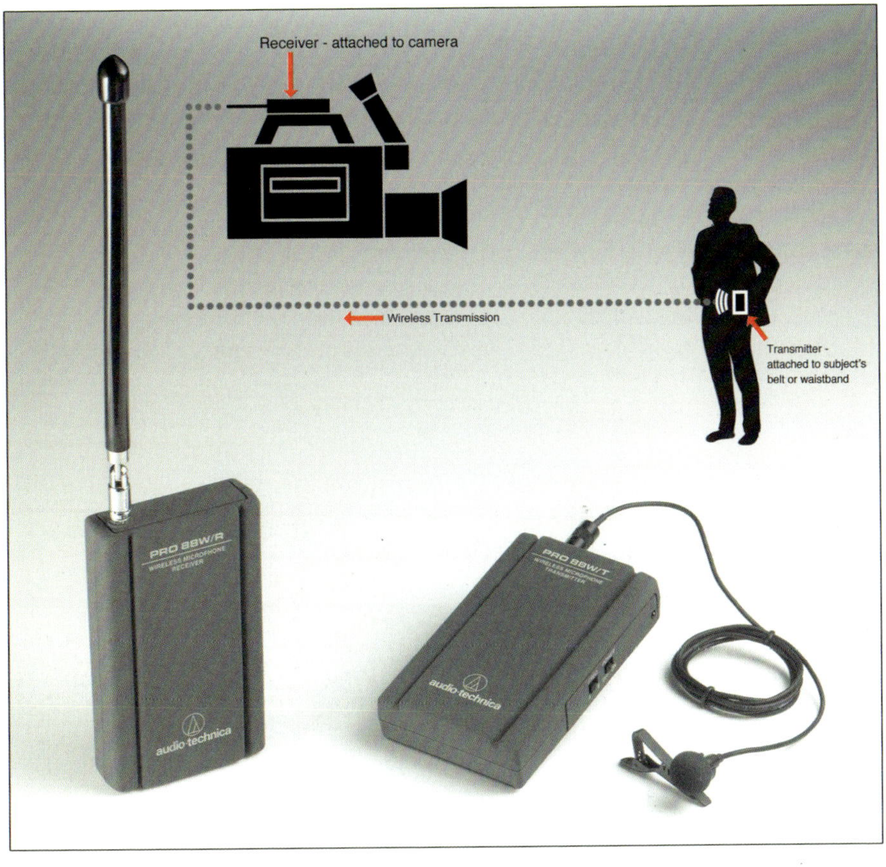

FIGURE 11.24
A wireless microphone like this one is designed for remote field production. The microphone and transmitter are attached to the subject. The receiver is attached to the camera.
Source: audio-technica .com

There are two basic transmitter types for professional equipment, UHV and VHF. Of the two options, UHF offers the most available frequencies. This may be helpful if you are using more than five wireless microphones at a time or are going to be in locations where others are using wireless microphones. On the other hand, UHF microphones are typically more expensive than VHF microphones. Be aware that some of the radio frequencies overlap with television station frequencies. Always test your equipment before you begin production. A third option for wireless is an *infrared transmitter*, which uses a beam of infrared light to send the signal. It's usually best to avoid infrared systems, as they require line-of-site transmission. If something gets between the transmitter and the receiver, it won't work, much like the remote control for your television. Infrared does have the advantage of being more secure—you can't pick it up from outside the room—and infrared transmitters don't typically interfere with each other.

Digital Microphones

One of the challenges with the move towards a digital workflow involves recording audio directly into the computer. While you can plug some microphones directly into a computer, a better solution is to use an A/D, an analog-to-digital converter, which translates the analog input into a digital format. These often rely on Firewire or USB connections. Using an A/D isolates the conversion process from the rest of the computer and lessons the chance of computer components such as the power supply introducing unwanted noise. Another option is to use a digital microphone—a microphone with the A/D built into it. These microphones are often called USB microphones because they typically connect to the computer via a USB connector (see Figure 11.25).

FIGURE 11.25
A student uses a USB microphone directly connected to the computer to record a voiceover.

AUDIO CONNECTORS

Microphones may be connected to audio recording devices by a variety of cables and connectors. Professional microphones use balanced connectors, while consumer devices use unbalanced connectors.

Balanced Audio Connectors

Professional microphones and audio devices are connected using balanced cables and connectors (see Figure 11.26). A *balanced microphone cable* has three wires encased in an outer rubber sheath. Audio signals flow in a loop, from the microphone to the recorder, and then back again. In a balanced system, a pair of twisted wires is used for conducting the signal path. The current travels down the positive wire in one direction and returns on the negative wire in the opposite direction. Since the impedance or resistance of the current is the same in both directions, this is called a *balanced line* or *circuit*. The third wire in a balanced cable is called the *shield* or *ground*. The ground wire is designed to "shield" the audio signal from electrical interference that can distort or weaken it in any way. The shield's job is to eliminate noise (buzzes, hums, hisses, etc.) by keeping interference from coming into contact with the audio signal. While using balanced wiring doesn't guarantee total noise rejection, it offers the best solution for protecting the integrity of the signal path. Balanced audio cables can be run for long distances with good results. This is particularly helpful in large rooms, fixed recording environments, or with live events and concerts,

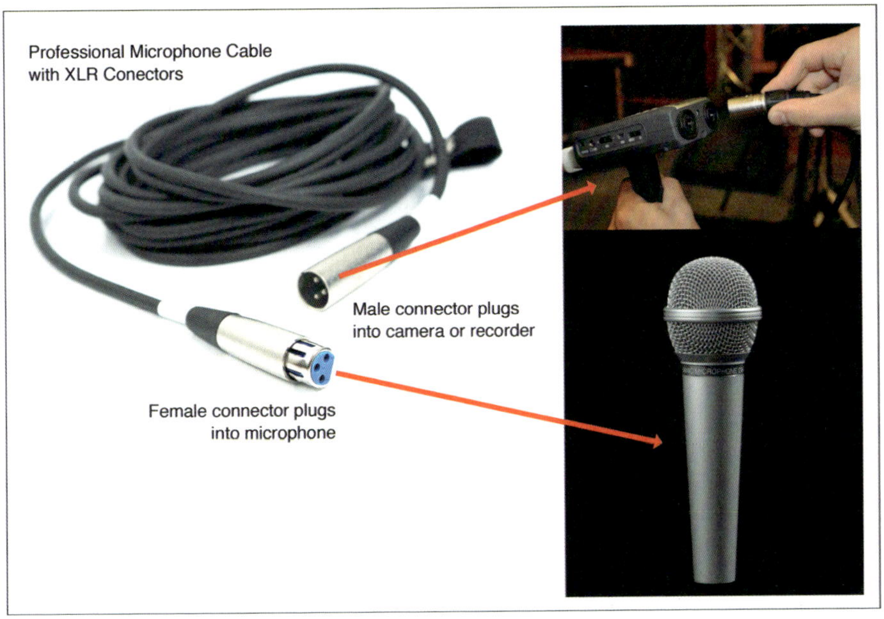

FIGURE 11.26 Professional microphones and recording systems have balanced XLR connectors.

where recording equipment is kept at some distance from the microphones and talent.

XLR CONNECTORS

Balanced microphone cables usually have XLR connectors on each end of the wire. The female XLR connector attaches directly to the end of the microphone or power adapter, while the 3-pin male connector plugs into the recorder or mixer. XLR connectors have a locking mechanism on the metal casing to keep it from coming loose during recording. To insert it, line up the pins and holes and push on the connector until you feel it snap in place. To disconnect it, press down on the safety lock while pulling back on the connector in a steady motion. Never pull directly on the cable wire when attempting to disconnect it. Doing so can weaken or sever the solder joint between the wire leads and the terminal posts, thus breaking the circuit and rendering the cable useless.

Unbalanced Audio Connectors

Most consumer microphones and electronic equipment use an unbalanced audio connector for patching analog sound sources. The male end of the connector is called the *plug* and the female end or receiving socket is referred to as the *jack*. An unbalanced cable uses two wires, a center conductor surrounded by a shield. The positive wire conducts the outbound signal flow, while the negative wire functions as both the return conduit and ground. Unbalanced cables are highly susceptible to interference when used across long distances. As a result, it's best to use them on patching runs of 20 feet or less.

TS AND TRS CONNECTORS

The ¼-inch phono plug has been around for over a century and uses a *tip and sleeve* (TS) design. This connector was originally made for the telephone industry for use by switchboard operators to patch telephone calls and is still used today for general purpose audio patching. The tip conducts the positive phase of the audio signal while the sleeve carries the negative phase and serves as the ground. An insulator ring separates the tip conductor from the sleeve. The stereo version of this connector uses a *tip, ring, and sleeve* (TRS) design. While a stereo signal requires a third wire, the circuit remains unbalanced. Stereo ¼-inch phone plugs are used for connecting headphones to the output jack of a portable listening device or sound system. TRS cables can also be used to carry a balanced mono audio signal.

As electronics have gotten smaller, TS and TRS connectors have evolved as well. In addition, to the traditional ¼-inch plug, both now come in an ⅛-inch (3.5mm) mini plug used on most MP3 players and computers, and a 2.5mm micro plug, which shows up on some mobile phones and other small devices. Adapters are available for converting any size of TS- or TRS-style connector to any other size (see Figure 11.27).

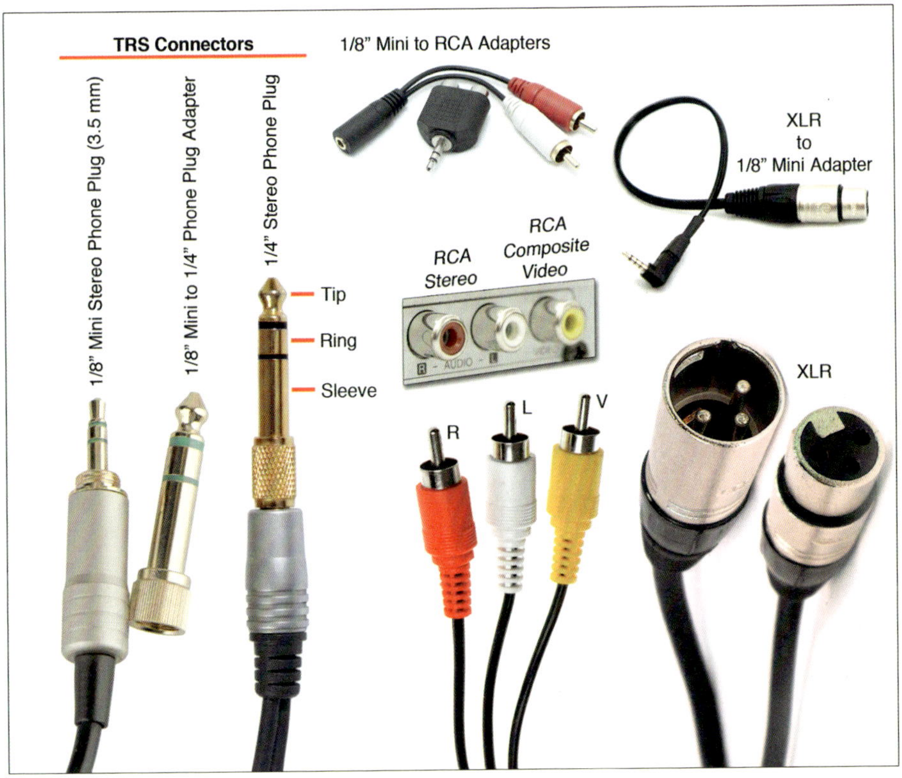

FIGURE 11.27
An assortment of connectors and adapters used often in audio production.

RCA CONNECTORS

In the early 1940s, the Radio Corporation of America designed the *RCA phono plug* for connecting phonographs (or record players) to amplifiers. Today, it is used for connecting both the audio and video signal paths of a diverse array of A/V devices, including television monitors, gaming consoles, projectors, and numerous other things. RCA plugs are often color-coded to match the receiving end of an RCA jack. Yellow designates the composite video channel, while red and white refer respectively to the right and left audio channels in a stereo system. You'll also find RCA plugs used for component video—a video format that uses a separate cable for the red, green, and blue signals.

ADAPTERS

While it's best to avoid using adapters, you'll sometimes need to use one for hooking up cables and devices with incompatible connectors, and it's a good idea to have some good quality adapters in your audio kit. One of the problems you may run into is the need to mix balanced and unbalanced audio gear. For example, the external microphone jack on a consumer camcorder (if it has one at all) is likely going to be a ⅛-inch mini plug. In order to use a professional microphone with a camera of this type, you'll need an XLR-to-mini plug adapter. Since the adapter is only traveling a short distance from the end of the microphone cable to the camera, you shouldn't have to worry too much about interference affecting the audio signal.

Still, adapters can complicate matters, as they introduce another potential failure point in the audio chain. If the adapter dies or comes undone, you'll lose your audio. To be safe, secure adapters with a small piece of gaffer tape to keep them from working lose during the recording. While gaffer tape looks similar to duct tape, don't confuse the two. Gaffer tape uses a different type of adhesive that doesn't leave a residue when you remove it. Mistake the two and you'll end up with messy gear. Make the mistake when taping cables down on a carpet and expect not to be invited back to the location.

Cable Management 101

While a microphone cable may seem like a rather inconsequential item, the role it plays in protecting the integrity of signal flow in the audio chain is critical to the success of a production. When properly cared for, cables will last longer, perform better, and be easier to handle and use. It pays to invest some time to learn the art and science of proper cable care and management. One of the best things I learned during my first internship as a young college student was how to wrap and store cables properly. The crusty broadcast engineer I was assigned to work with made no bones about how pitifully poor my cable-wrapping technique was. While I had to endure a bit of public humiliation and some colorful expletives along the way, I have always been grateful to him for taking the time to teach me the importance of cable etiquette, and even more importantly, for imparting to me a healthy sense of pride in regard to the proper use and care of equipment.

The most important lesson in cable management is learning how to properly wrap and secure a cable when you're finished using it. Scrunching it up into a chaotic heap simply will not do. The next person who uses it will not appreciate the time that he or she has to waste untangling the mess that you created. Instead, cables should be carefully wrapped in a uniform coil, 12 to 24 inches in diameter (depending on the length of the cable). For short cables less than 50 feet, each loop should be comprised of 30–36 inches of wire. For longer cable runs, the loops can be larger. The important thing is consistency. As you wrap a cable, each loop should be roughly the same length in order to preserve the circular shape of the coil when finished.

Proper wrapping keeps cables from twisting, kinking, creasing, or bending, which can cause permanent damage to the encased wires or weaken them over time. Cables retain a "memory" based on good or bad patterns of repeated winding. In the long run, it's easier to wrap a cable properly every time than it is to retrain a gnarled cable that has been poorly managed or abused. Once kinks and twists have been introduced into cable memory, they are difficult to undo.

Tech Talk

The Over-Under Wrap To prevent twists and kinks from developing, the method of *over-under wrapping* is used (see Figure 11.28). With this technique, each loop in the cable wrap is formed by twisting the wire in the opposite direction of the loop immediately before and after it. When the cable is unfurled, the alternating twists cancel each other out, allowing the cable to lie flat on the surface. Depending on whether you are right- or left-handed, the "over" loop runs in a clockwise or counterclockwise direction "over" the wire at the point where the loop began (Steps 1 and 2). The "under" loop runs the same way but is turned inward, causing it to twist in the opposite direction of the previous loop (Steps 3 and 4). In this pass, the cable is guided "under" the wire at the point where the loop began. This alternating pattern of over and under loops continues until the end of the cable is reached.

To complete the task, a cord or cable tie is used to secure the ends of the cable and keep the coil from coming undone. Once perfected, you will find that this technique can be used for all manner of video and audio cables. In fact, you may discover, as I have, that this method of coiling cables also works just as effectively on an extension cord or garden hose.

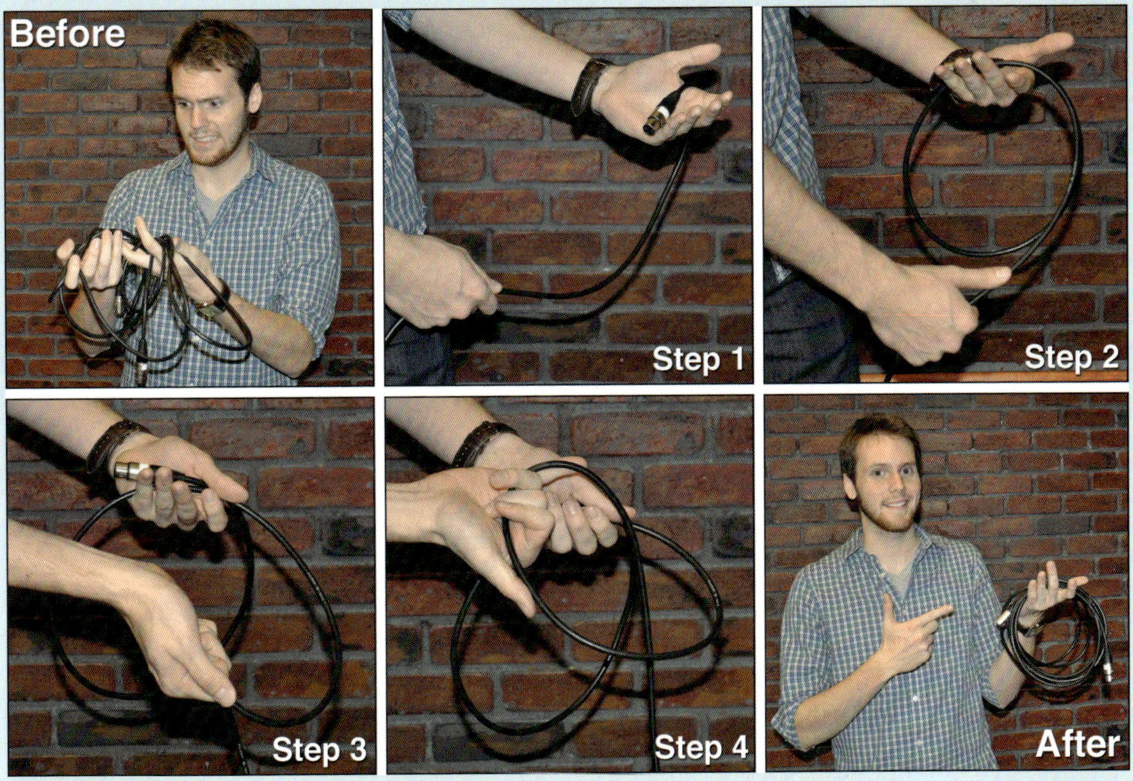

FIGURE 11.28
Nobody likes working with a tangled cable. Here, a student uses the over-under wrap to properly coil a microphone cable.

AUDIO MONITORING

One of the simplest recording scenarios is the one-person interview. All that's needed is a subject, a recording device (camcorder or audio recorder), a microphone, an XLR cable, and a set of headphones. The producer's goal is to acquire source material by interviewing the subject and recording his or her voice to disk. To achieve professional results, you need to monitor the audio signal as it is being recorded. Audio monitoring is a two-step process that includes (1) the objective act of measuring sound intensity and setting the record levels, and (2)the subjective act of listening to the audio signal as it is being recorded.

Audio Metering (Objective Monitoring)

The electrical signal produced by a microphone is very weak and must be amplified during the recording process. Audio mixing consoles and recording devices have a built-in microphone preamp for boosting the strength of the signal for audio processing. The *preamp setting* (or *record level*) is controlled with buttons or dials on the recording equipment (see Figure 11.29). In a stereo system, there are separate preamps and controls for the left and right channels. As the recording engineer or operator, it's your job to monitor the amount of amplification that's applied to the microphone signal. The levels you choose will depend on many variables, including the strength of the subject's voice, the type of microphone being used, the distance from the subject to the microphone, and the amount of background noise in the interview setting. For example, a soft-spoken person usually requires more amplification than a person with a naturally loud delivery. On professional systems, the preamp can be controlled automatically using *automatic gain control* (AGC), or manually using the *volume-unit* (VU) meter and record level controls. Given a choice, most professionals prefer the manual method.

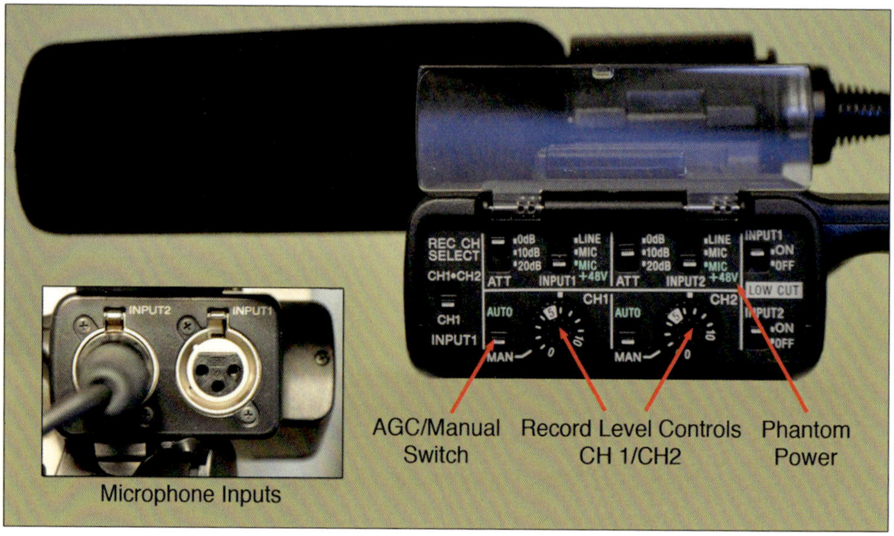

FIGURE 11.29
Like most professional camcorders, the Sony HXRNX70U comes with two XLR microphone inputs. An audio control panel provides user access to switches and dials for managing signal flow and setting record levels.

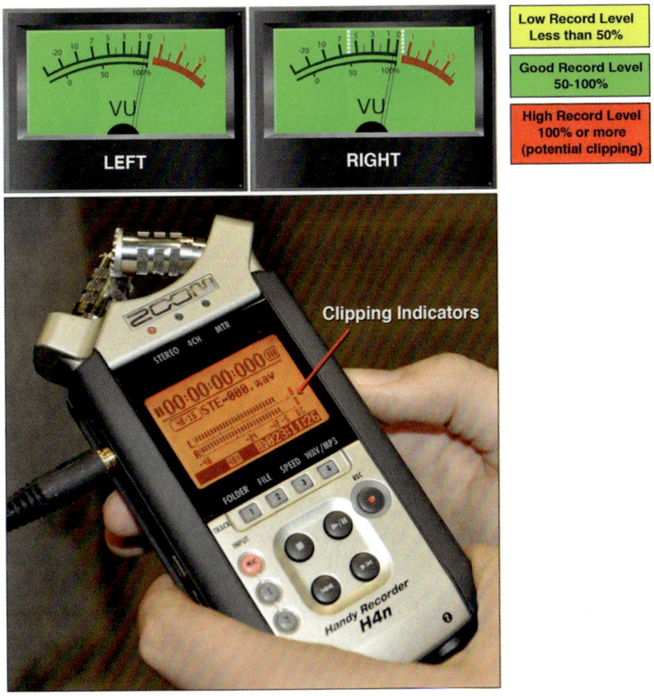

FIGURE 11.30
The analog VU meters shown on top have a range of –20 dB to +5 dB. The digital VU meter on the Zoom H4n audio recorder (bottom) has a wider range beginning at –48 dB and ending at 0 dB. Going past 0 dB doesn't mean clipping will occur, but it does mean you are getting precariously close to the distortion threshold. The Zoom recorder features a clipping indicator to the right of the scale. A red light turns on whenever clipping occurs.

A VU meter displays the strength of the microphone signal (in decibel units) after it has passed through the preamp (see Figure 11.30). An analog VU meter has a typical range of –20 dB to +3 dB. A bouncing needle indicates the loudness of the signal as it modulates throughout the full dynamic range of the recording (from the quietest moments to the loudest ones). Digital VU meters vary in style. Most of them have a wider range on the low end, starting at –48 or –36 dB. Instead of a needle, they often feature a row of colored LEDs.

On most VU meters, the region above 0 dB is color-coded red to indicate excessive amplification. If too much amplification is applied, waveform distortion can occur causing a phenomenon known as *clipping*. Clipping permanently corrupts the fidelity of the audio signal and cannot be repaired. On the opposite end of the scale, you need to also avoid setting the record level too low. A low audio signal will need to be boosted to acceptable levels in postproduction. Whenever you re-amplify a recorded audio signal, noise is introduced, and the quality of the original recording deteriorates. The lower your original record levels are, the more you will need to re-amplify them later, and the worse the results will be. Setting levels properly the first time is the key to getting professional results.

THE SOUND CHECK

Before starting the recording, conduct a *sound check* with your subject. Prompt them to speak in a normal tone of voice. Using the VU meter as a visual reference, adjust the record levels to the point where the loudest portions of their speech peak around 0 dB without going "into the red." After pressing record, continue monitoring the levels and adjusting them as necessary.

Listening (Subjective Monitoring)

A VU meter gives you a visual reference of what the electronic recording device is "hearing" and is an objective indicator of the recorded signal's intensity. The second step in audio monitoring involves the *art of listening* and is primarily concerned with the aesthetic properties of the recording. Monitoring a live recording with headphones allows you to hear the voice of your subject and any associated background sounds a split second after it has been recorded. The volume control is used to raise and lower your headphone levels and has no effect on the actual recording. Remember, just because the recording is loud to you in your headphones doesn't mean that the record levels are set properly. It might just be that the headphone volume is set to the maximum level, leading to a false impression. As a matter of practice, set your record levels first then adjust the volume of your headphones to the desired level.

HEADPHONES

You should invest in at least one set of good-quality headphones. Look for an over-the-ear rather than an earbud design. Professional video cameras and audio recorders will have headphone jacks that let you monitor your audio during the capture process—use headphones when you are working! Doing so will help you make sure nothing goes wrong with your audio. You can't rely on the VU meter alone to tell you that you are capturing good audio. It doesn't tell you that the audio is good or whether or not your microphone is working or picking up the main subject. You could just be picking up static or background noise. You might even be recording with the wrong microphone by mistake, for example, using an internal mic when you meant to be recording with an external mic. Try to keep the headphones on whenever you are capturing audio. Just because the audio sounded good when you started doesn't mean it will sound good all the way through. Batteries die, cables get unplugged, and microphones can slip. Oh, and cellphones can wreck havoc on your audio if you are not using RF-shielded microphones. You need to know if your audio has problems before you go back to the studio to edit.

Listen for potential audio problems—your headphones can help you here as well. Is your subject wearing metal bracelets that might clink together? What about background noise? Is the air conditioner making too much noise? What about that high-pitched electronic squeal from the video projector? Whenever possible, either eliminate the source of the unwanted sounds or find a better location. Whatever you do, don't just say "I'll fix it in editing." There's a good chance you won't be able to, at least not easily, particularly if the noise is in the same frequency range as your talent's voice. Watch for echoes in a room and pay attention to where you set up your equipment. Try to avoid recording in the middle of a large room with hard walls—instead move to the side of the room. Look for things that will absorb rather than reflect sound. Recording on a busy street? Your headphones will help you make sure you've placed your microphone in a position to minimize the traffic noise.

CHAPTER SUMMARY

All too often, newcomers to multimedia production don't pay enough attention to the quality of their audio work and it shows in the final product. To work in the industry, you need to understand the correct tool to use for a task. For audio, this means knowing which microphone to use when, and what the relative advantages are for each type. As an example, we've seen that a ribbon microphone is great for using as a tabletop microphone for conducting an interview in a studio. On the other hand, it is not a great microphone for conducting an interview outdoors, as it is very susceptible to wind noise. Make sure you know when to use a balanced cable and when you can get away with using an unbalanced cable—the short answer is, use balanced whenever possible, but by all means keep your unbalanced cable runs to around 20 feet or less. Use professional-grade equipment whenever possible—this doesn't mean the most expensive, just good quality—and avoid internal microphones when possible. Oh, and don't forget your headphones. They really are one of the most important tools you've got, not only when you are editing audio but when you are capturing it as well. Few things are worse in audio production than coming back from an assignment and realizing that the battery died in your microphone three minutes into the interview and, because you weren't wearing headphones, you didn't realize it.

CHAPTER 12

Sound and Video Recording

The current saturation of relatively inexpensive multimedia communication tools holds tremendous potential for destroying the monopoly of ideas we have lived with for so long.... A personal computer can be configured to act as a publishing house, a broadcast-quality TV studio, a professional recording studio, or the node in an international computer bulletin board system.

—Mark Dery, Author and Cultural Critic, (1993)

Key Terms

Advanced Video Coding (AVC)
Analog Tape
AVC-Intra
AVCHD
AVI
Betacam
Betamax
Blu-Ray
Camcorder
Codec
Color Sampling
Component Video
Composite Video
Container Format
Control Track
D1, D2, D3, D5, D5HD
Digital Betacam
Digital Tape
DNxHD
DV (Blue Book)
DVCAM
DVCPRO
DVD-Video
Generation Loss
GOP (I-, P-, and B-frames)
H.264
HD
HDCAM
HDV
Helical Scanning
Hi 8
Interframe Compression
Intermediate Format
Intraframe Compression
ISO/IEC

Chapter Highlights

This chapter examines:

- The history and evolution of videotape recording systems
- Formats used for recording audio and video to analog and digital tape
- Industry standards for the coded representation of audio and video on digital platforms
- Differences in formats created for consumer, prosumer, and professional use
- The transition from tape-based recording formats to file-based recording formats

MOTION PICTURE FILM RECORDING

Today, most television programs are shot, edited, and saved to tape (or disk) before being transmitted and delivered to a mass audience. However, in the early days of television broadcasting, programs were often produced and transmitted simultaneously. During a "live" production, the audience would see the on-screen performance as it was carried out in real-time, most likely in a remote television studio far away (see Figure 12.1). Recording technologies, like videotape, that have long been associated with television and video production were not invented until long after television was established as a viable commercial enterprise.

Prior to 1956, motion picture film was the only recording medium available for capturing and storing televised images. Using a device called a *kinescope*, a 16mm or 35mm motion picture camera was set up to record electronic images

Kinescope
M and MII
Magnetic Recording
MiniDV (DVC)
Motion Pictures
Experts Group
MP3
MPEG IMX
MPEG-1
MPEG-2
MPEG-4
Open Standard
P2/P2 HD
ProRes 4:2:2
Quadruplex Videotape
(QUAD)
QuickTime
Record Format
Spatial Redundancy
Telecine
Temporal Redundancy
Track Pitch
Transcoding
Transport Speed
Type-C Videotape
U-matic (¾ inch)
VHS/VHS-C
Videotape
VTR/VCR
XDCAM

FIGURE 12.1
The popular children's program *Howdy Doody* was telecast by NBC from 1947 to 1960. Prior to the invention of video recording, programs like this one were produced and transmitted "live" to the home television audience.

directly from the surface of a television monitor (see Figure 12.2). This pioneering method of video transcoding was used to generate a photographic archive of scanned television images in real-time. *Transcoding* is the process of converting media from one form, or format, into another. Thus, in the early days of broadcasting the only way to make a recording of a television signal was to transcode it from its native form, as a scanned projection on the surface of a cathode ray tube, to an optical reproduction of light on photographic film. While the filmed image represented aspects of the original form, transcoding resulted in the creation of something entirely different as well. For example, while a film could be shown to a local audience gathered in a theater using a mechanical

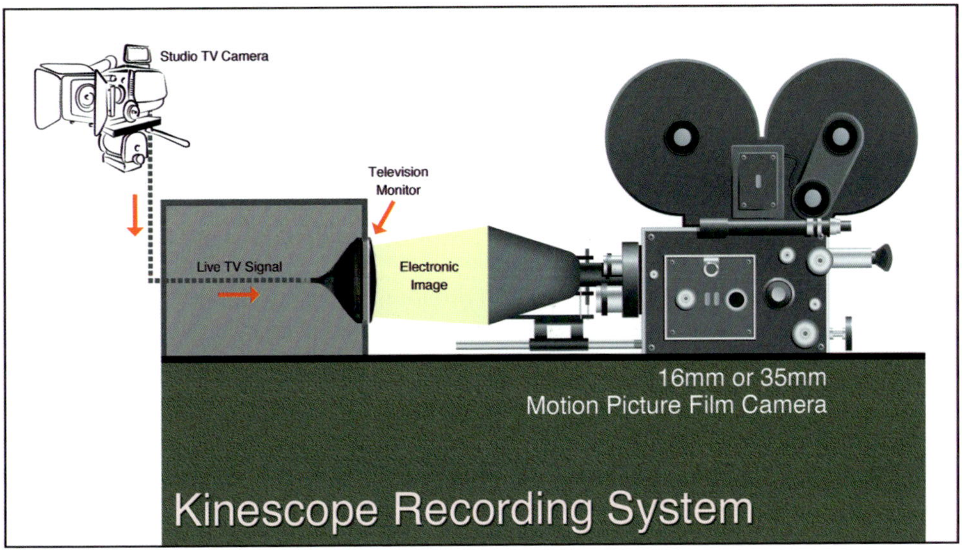

FIGURE 12.2
For many years, the kinescope was the only system available for recording a "live" television production.

projection system, it could not be transmitted electronically to a remote television audience. In order for a motion picture to be broadcast electronically, it had to undergo reverse transcoding, using a device called a *telecine*. As a companion to the kinescope, the telecine used a television camera to electronically capture and encode photographic frames of a film as they were projected. The telecine also gave broadcasters a tool for retransmitting film "live" over the air.

Transcoding is not without its problems. In the previous example, it doesn't take a great deal of imagination to realize that a 16mm reproduction of a scanned television image is going to look noticeably inferior to the quality of the original transmission in its native form. And in fact, this was often the case. With the kinescope, a mechanical shutter on the film camera was used to convert the native frame rate of U.S. television signals (30 fps) to the native frame rate of film (24 fps), resulting in the permanent loss of six frames of visual information every second. A slightly different version of the kinescope was used in England to accommodate the British television frame rate of 25 fps. While this early method of reproduction worked, the recorded copies were technically and visually inferior to the original.

Regardless of whether the transcoding methods are primitive, as in the early days of kinescopic reproductions, or sophisticated, as in the modern-day use of computer algorithms for manipulating streams of digital video content, the permanent loss of original image data and resolution are inevitable consequences of transcoding. Such observable losses in reproduction quality are referred to collectively as *transcoding artifacts*. While transcoding is a necessary task that's often associated with today's video production and postproduction workflows, one must always be mindful of the negative consequences that can occur whenever television signals or video files are converted from one format into another. Information is always lost during the process of transcoding.

MAGNETIC RECORDING

Ampex Corporation invented the world's first open-reel tape recorder in 1948. Dubbed the Model 200, it was used by the American Broadcasting Company (ABC) for the tape-delayed transmission of *The Bing Crosby Show*. The event went down in history as the first ever tape-delayed broadcast of a radio program in the United States. It took Ampex another eight years to release the first commercial videotape recorder, the VRX-1000 (or Mark IV), which they introduced at the National Association of Radio and Television Broadcaster's convention in Chicago in 1956.

With an audio recorder, the magnetic tape moves continuously across the path of stationary record and playback heads. Only the tape is in motion (see Figure 12.3). On a system like this, the audio signal is recorded longitudinally, across the length of a tape, as an uninterrupted stream of invisible data. Videotape recording is much more complex. Because of the large bandwidth requirements of television, video signals are written to tape using multiple record heads.

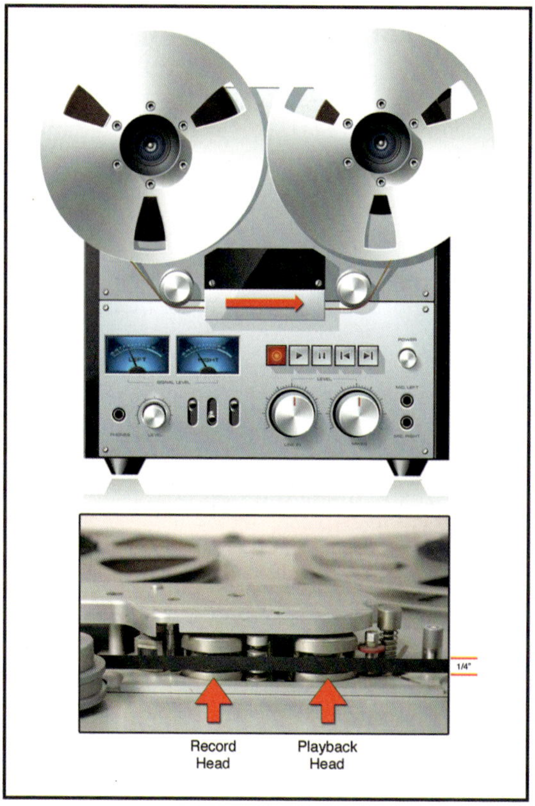

FIGURE 12.3
With an open-reel (or reel-to-reel) recorder, an analog audio signal is recorded to the surface of ¼-inch wide magnetic tape. The signal is captured on tape by the record head and played back a split second later by the playback head. During recording and playback, the tape is in constant motion. The heads, however, are stationary.

For example, the VRX-1000 was called a *quadruplex* (or *quad*) recorder because it used four record heads for writing data to a magnetic tape that was 2 inches wide. The record heads were mounted 90-degrees apart along the perimeter of a headwheel assembly that would spin at a high rate of speed as the tape (also moving) traversed in the opposite direction across its path. The invention of the videotape recorder was such an important breakthrough for the broadcasting industry that in 1957, the Academy of Television Arts and Sciences recognized Ampex Corporation with an Emmy award for its accomplishment.

GREAT IDEAS
Helical Scanning

With an audio tape recorder, the signal is recorded to tape as it travels past a stationary record head at a constant rate of speed. While this method worked well for low-bandwidth audio signals, it failed to meet the technical requirements of high-bandwidth video recording. In 1961, Ampex invented helical scanning, a technology that has been used in tape-based camcorders and VCRs ever since. *Helical scanning* records picture data diagonally across the width the tape, using a system of spinning record heads mounted on a slanted metal cylinder (see Figure 12.4). Helical scanning solved many problems for engineers who were seeking to design a reliable method of video recording. One problem it didn't fix was related to editing. Since audio tape is recorded longitudinally, it can be neatly edited by hand using a razor blade, splice block, and a piece of tape. In video recording, the audio and control tracks are longitudinal, but the video track is diagonal. Cutting the tape in half at any point in the recording will destroy

FIGURE 12.4
An inside view of a video cassette recorder (VCR) reveals the slanted headwheel assembly used in a helical scanning recording system.

(Continued)

a portion of several video frames. For this reason, unless you are performing a repair, and you know what you are doing, you should never attempt to edit videotape by hand.

Unlike motion picture film, the frame and track regions on a magnetic tape are invisible to the human eye. But just because you can't see them doesn't mean they don't exist (see Figure 12.5). For recording purposes, videotape is divided into four tracks. The *video track* is the widest region and is used to store the picture portion of a television program. Videotape also contains two audio tracks. The *audio tracks* can be used in tandem for recording a two-channel stereo signal or separately for recording two monaural feeds. For example, in a two-person interview, the microphone signal from Person A can be recorded to audio track one, while the signal from Person B is routed to audio track two.

The fourth region is designated as the *control track*. To understand the purpose of the control track, it is helpful to draw a comparison once again to motion picture film. Film contains two lines of sprocket holes lined up along each edge of the filmstrip. As a film is projected, moving gear like wheels engage the sprocket holes to advance one frame of film to the next. The sprocket holes keep the film aligned and moving at the appropriate speed. Like film, videotape is in constant motion during record and playback modes. As the video and audio signals are recorded to tape, an electronic synch pulse is written to the control track to mark the location of each video frame. NTSC video systems generate 30 frames (or still images) of picture information every second. The control track marks where these frames begin and end in order to ensure that the videotape plays correctly.

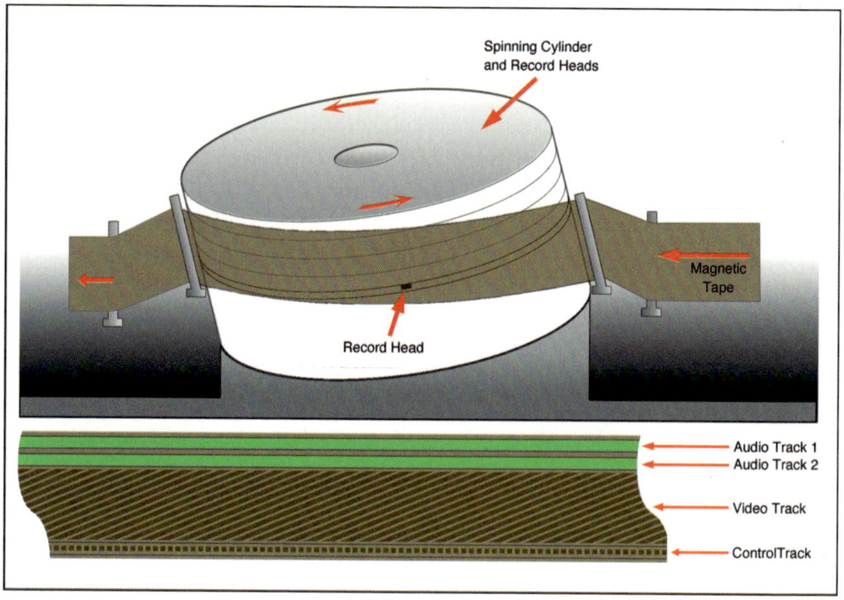

FIGURE 12.5
The surface area of a videotape is divided into linear regions called tracks. Most tape-based systems support two tracks for stereo audio, one track for video, and one track for synchronization or control data.

Tech Talk

Tape Recording Basics: Track Pitch and Speed In a tape-based recording system, *bandwidth* (the amount of recorded information that can be stored on tape) is primarily a function of two variables: track pitch and tape speed. Increasing either variable enables the production of a higher quality recording. *Tracks* are the linear regions of a tape used for recording different portions of an audio or video signal. *Track pitch* is the distance from the center of one record track to the center of the next. Tracks can be compared to the individual lanes of a highway. Increasing the number of lanes (or the width of the highway) automatically increases the amount of traffic that it can handle. For example, an eight-lane freeway can accommodate much more traffic than a two-lane country road, therefore it has greater bandwidth. *Speed*, the second variable, can be applied to this analogy as well. As traffic speed increases, more cars are able to travel along the same stretch of highway in the same amount of time.

In a two-track stereo system, ¼-inch reel-to-reel tape was the industry-standard recording format for many years. It was akin to a two-lane highway, where half of the tape was used for storing the left channel of a stereo signal while the other half recorded the right channel. For best quality, ¼-inch audiotape was designed to run at a maximum speed of 7.5 ips (inches per second). However, reel-to-reel recorders often came with multispeed transports. To conserve tape during longer recordings, an operator could run the unit at a slower speed. For studio sessions (also known as *multitrack recording*), where up to 24 tracks of stereo audio were needed, engineers developed a 2-inch audiotape format designed to run at a high speed of 30 ips.

The 2-inch quad format continued to evolve throughout the 1960s and 70s as features like color recording, helical scanning, and portability were incorporated into the design of newer, more advanced models. One of the biggest changes in open-reel designs occurred in 1976 when Ampex and Sony introduced the Type C videotape recorder (VTR). Type C VTRs used a narrower tape that was one-inch wide, cutting the physical size of the media and storage reels in half, while keeping the recording time the same (1 hour per reel). Sony also designed a portable model that was used for many years in remote field production. Type C VTRs included popular features such as stable freeze frames, variable playback speeds (slow-mo and fast motion effects), and advanced jog and shuttle control. The one-inch videotape format was the dominant recording medium for broadcast television for nearly two decades.

PROFESSIONAL VIDEOTAPE FORMATS

A brief review of the history of videotape formats is essential for understanding the relatively recent transition to tapeless recording. While most of these formats I'm about to discuss have reached their end-of-life (EOL), the previous decades of tape-based recording has produced a vast archive of content that was shot and edited using many different kinds of legacy camcorders and VTRs. Tape reels and cassettes continue to sit on shelves in closets, newsrooms, and film vaults around the world (see Figure 12.6). In your job as a multimedia producer, don't be surprised if one day you're handed a strange looking plastic cassette or metal reel containing video footage that a client wants to see restored or incorporated into a project. While tape may be dead as an acquisition format, videotape recordings will be with us for many years to come.

FIGURE 12.6
There have been numerous videocassette tape formats over the years. U-matic (top) seems large and bulky compared to newer digital tape formats like MiniDV (middle). As we've advanced into tapeless recording, the SD memory card is no doubt one of the smallest removable and reusable formats ever invented.

Two Japanese companies pioneered the development of nearly all of the professional cassette tape formats used in television production during the past 40 years. Sony and Panasonic have been fierce competitors in the tape-format wars, constantly trying to surpass the other in their quest to bring the next best product to market. While open-reel videotape formats were the bread and butter of broadcast studio operations for many years, the size and expense of these first-generation VTRs made them ill-suited for use in remote field production. After all, they were designed for indoor use and were best left in a studio facility where an engineer could keep close watch. For this reason, news organizations and documentarians relied on film-based recording formats well into the 1970s and beyond (see Figure 12.7). Unfortunately, film-based acquisition was expensive, time-consuming, and potentially disruptive to the natural flow of events. For example, press conferences and photo ops had to be scheduled early enough in the day to accommodate the needs of film crews. Before the age of microwave and satellite transmissions, news crews had to physically transport film of an event back to the station where it could be processed and edited in time for the early evening newscast. The phrase "film at eleven" served as a popular teaser for television audiences and meant that anything shot late in the day or early in the evening would not be aired until the last newscast of the day, which typically ran at 11:00 p.m.

Analog Tape Formats

Prior to 1986, when Sony released the first digital videotape format, all magnetic tape systems used analog methods of reproduction. The main disadvantage of analog tape formats was the problem of generational loss, which would occur whenever a program was copied from one tape to another. An analog copy was never as good as the original it was dubbed from. While in a first-generation dub (a copy of the original), the loss of quality was not too bad; signal degradation would get noticeably worse with each additional dub to the next generation. Thus, a fourth-generation dub (a copy of a copy of a copy), looked significantly worse than one that was reproduced directly from the original.

FIGURE 12.7
A producer conducts an interview as her camera operator records the subject. Prior to 1971, field recording like this was done entirely with film cameras. This meant a time-delay, because film had to be processed before it could be viewed, edited, and aired. Today, electronic images and sound can be shot, viewed, and transmitted instantaneously using either a tape-based or tapeless recording system like the one shown here.
Bruce C. Murray/Shutterstock.com

U-MATIC ¾-Inch

In 1971, the Japanese consortium of Sony, JVC, and Matsushita (Panasonic) led the way in pioneering a new era of electronic newsgathering (ENG) with their joint release of the U-matic videotape-recording format. U-matic, better known as ¾-inch because of its smaller tape width, offered field producers the first viable alternative to a film-based production workflow. The most appealing feature of the ¾-inch format was that the tape was enclosed in a portable plastic cassette. When inserted into a U-matic VCR (Video Cassette Recorder), the tape would be threaded automatically. The cassette housing provided protection for the tape and eliminated the process of threading by hand.

Compared to open-reel recording systems, ¾-inch decks were cheap and had a relatively small form factor. The portable version of the U-matic line was light enough to be carried by one person using a shoulder strap. By supporting the unit with the neck or shoulder, a tape operator could maintain convenient access to the controls while roaming freely during a mobile recording session. Before the invention of the camcorder, the video camera and recorder were two separate devices. A mobile production crew required at least two people—one person to

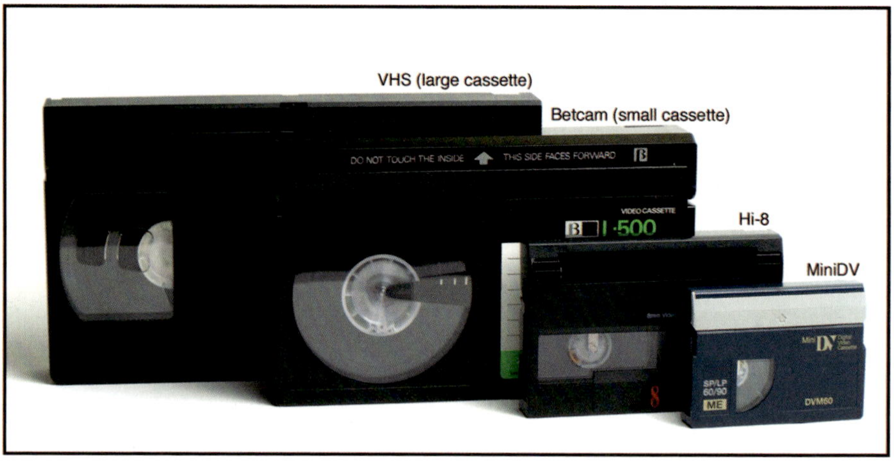

FIGURE 12.8
VHS, Betacam, and Hi-8 are analog tape formats. MiniDV is a digital tape format.

operate the camera and compose shots, and the other to monitor the video and audio signals during recording. The camera and VCR were tethered by a cable, which meant that the tape operator had to stay close to the shooter at all times. U-matic field recorders could be run on AC power or with a rechargeable Ni-Cad battery, further enhancing their usefulness in remote locations. The portable units used a small cassette with enough tape for 20 minutes of uninterrupted recording.

SONY BETACAM AND PANASONIC M

In 1982, Sony introduced Betacam, the first component video format designed specifically for professional use (see Tech Talk "Composite Versus Component Color Processing" on next page). In addition, Sony launched the first single-piece camera-recorder (or camcorder). The radically new design revolutionized field recording and meant that the physical cable connecting the videographer to the tape operator could be forever cut. This meant more freedom for the shooter and a reduction in the number of people required to physically operate the equipment. In response, Panasonic released the M format (or Recam). Both of these component formats used a new tape stock that was only ½-inch thick. Unfortunately for Panasonic, the M format never really took off.

U-MATIC SP

U-matic is regarded as one of the most successful and longest lasting video formats of all time. In 1986, Sony released U-matic SP (for Superior Performance), which used chrome tape and enhanced signal processing to produce a better picture. It remained, however, a composite videotape format.

BETACAM-SP AND MII

Also in 1986, Sony and Panasonic enhanced their professional line of recording formats with the release of Betacam SP and MII (pronounced *em two*). While MII

Tech Talk

Composite Versus Component Color Processing A color video signal has three primary components.

Brightness (or luminance). The first component is *brightness* and refers to the relative intensity or energy level of light in an RGB image. In the same way that a dimmer switch in your dining room can be used to vary the brightness of an overhead lamp, controls on a video camera or monitor can be used to adjust the brightness of a video image. Brightness can also be thought of as how much black or white is contained within the image.

Hue. The second component is *hue* and refers to the color tone of visible light as defined by its physical wavelength within the color spectrum. Adjusting the tint or hue control on a television monitor changes the color tone of the image on screen. Generic color values like red, blue, green, and orange are often used to describe the color tone or hue of an object.

Saturation. The third component is *saturation* and refers to the overall purity or intensity of a color. Modified values like navy blue, Carolina blue, royal blue, midnight blue, and true blue are used to differentiate between different shades of blue that can be achieved by varying the saturation level.

A composite video system combines the luminance values (brightness) and chrominance values (hue and saturation) into a single modulated signal. Once combined, it is difficult to adjust the value of one component without also affecting the value of the other two. Component video systems are typically much better (and more expensive) than composite systems because they keep the color signals separated throughout the recording process. As a composite video recording format, U-matic was unable to satisfy the needs of many high-end producers.

FIGURE 12.9
Like most professional nonlinear editing programs (NLEs), Avid Media Composer includes a color corrector interface for adjusting the color properties of a video clip. Color grading is the process of enhancing the color presentation of a film or video project during the final stages of the postproduction process.

fared better than its predecessor (the failed M format), Betacam SP became the dominant professional tape format throughout the 1990s.

Digital Tape Formats

The 1980s was a pivotal decade as the digital revolution forever changed the nature of broadcast technologies and production workflows. Digital recording held numerous advantages over traditional analog methods, but none perhaps was greater than the elimination of generational loss during editing or duplication. Digital recording reduced video and audio signals to discrete binary values that could be copied without error from one tape to the next. A data point was either a zero or a one, which meant that a copy of a copy of a copy would be virtually identical to the master recording every time.

D1 AND D2

In 1986, Sony and BTS collaborated in bringing the first digital tape format to market. Dubbed D1, the format provided a way for broadcasters to digitally write an uncompressed component NTSC video signal to tape. Unfortunately, D1 tape and the equipment required to use it was expensive and terribly inefficient in terms of managing bandwidth (1 MB of storage was required to write a single uncompressed frame of video). D1 had limited success, ultimately being adopted by only a relatively small number of high-end users who had deep pockets, and who were most interested in using it for motion graphics, compositing, and special effects. In 1988, Ampex and Sony released D2, the first digital tape format to be widely accepted by professional users. In their second attempt to design a cost-effective digital tape format, engineers succeeded by fixing the bandwidth issues that had plagued D1. They accomplished this by switching back to composite video sampling. D1 and D2 were cassette formats that used ¾-inch-wide tape.

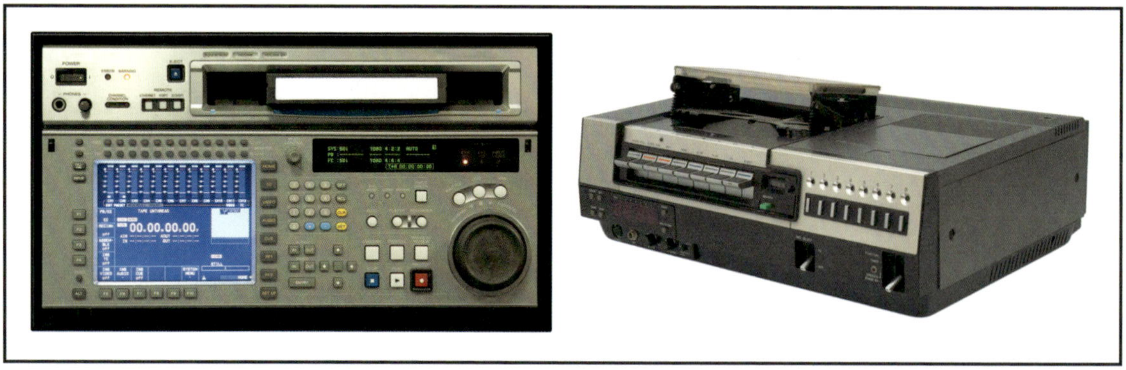

FIGURE 12.10
Tape formats are generally not interchangeable. For example, while the professional VTR on the left can record and play back HDCAM and Digital Betacam cassettes, it cannot be used to play a VHS tape. For that format, you will need a VHS unit like this vintage model pictured right.

PANASONIC D3

Panasonic released the D3 format in 1991. D3 decks were able to write uncompressed composite video onto a ½-inch wide tape, the narrowest yet for a professional digital format. Given its smaller form factor, Panasonic's D3 tape stock and recording equipment were considerably less expensive to buy and operate than D2. The ½-inch-tape width also meant smaller cassettes and longer record times.

SONY DIGITAL BETACAM, BETACAM SX, HDCAM

Sony took a giant leap forward in 1993 with its release of Digital Betacam (or Digibeta). Digibeta used a lossless 2:1 compression scheme to record component video to ½-inch tape. Whereas their first attempt to design a digital component recorder proved a dismal failure, Sony experienced great success with the release of Digital Betacam.

In 1996, Sony released Betacam SX, a cheaper version of Digital Betacam specifically designed for those working in electronic newsgathering (ENG). Some of the Betacam SX decks were even backward-compatible. This meant that the user could play back native digital SX tapes as well as older tapes recorded on legacy Betacam and Betacam SP equipment. This was an attractive feature for news organizations and others who had amassed a large library of legacy analog footage over the years.

FIGURE 12.11
Large-format camcorders have a larger form factor and are often easier to use for shoulder-mounted handheld camera work. Small-format cameras are less expensive, and until recent years have generally lacked the image quality and features that professionals need. However, the gap between high-end professional and low-end professional is shrinking as camcorder technology and recording formats continue to improve.

High-Definition Tape Formats

All of the legacy tape formats mentioned so far could record only in standard definition NTSC (720×486) or Pal (720×576). To address the needs of HD producers, Sony released HDCAM in 1997. As the name implies, HDCAM was marketed as a high-definition version of Digital Betacam, with the ability to record 1080i video at a native resolution of 1440×1080 (see Figure 12.12).

MPEG IMX

Marking a potential end to their long run of success in the professional videotape market, Sony released MPEG IMX in 2001. This advanced digital HD format is fully compatible with the DTV television standard. It is also provides full support for playing back all of the legacy Betacam formats (Betacam, Betacam SP, Digital Betacam, and Beta SX).

PANASONIC D5, D5HD

Panasonic released D5, a standard definition digital tape format, and D5HD, a high-definition companion product, in 1994. As an uncompressed component format, Panasonic D5 bore some similarity to Sony D1. However, in an effort to conserve bandwidth, D5HD video was compressed.

DV Formats

DVCPRO AND DVCAM

Sony and Panasonic developed competing professional variants of the DV format. Panasonic introduced DVCPRO in 1995. The format was marketed to low-end professional users (local ENG news crews, etc.) looking for an alternative to expensive digital formats like Digital Betacam. Panasonic achieved professional results with DVCPRO by switching to metal particle tape, widening the track pitch from 10 microns to 18, and increasing the speed of the tape transport by 80%. While the faster tape speed improved record quality, it cut record time on a mini-cassette from 60 minutes to 12. To compensate, Panasonic introduced a

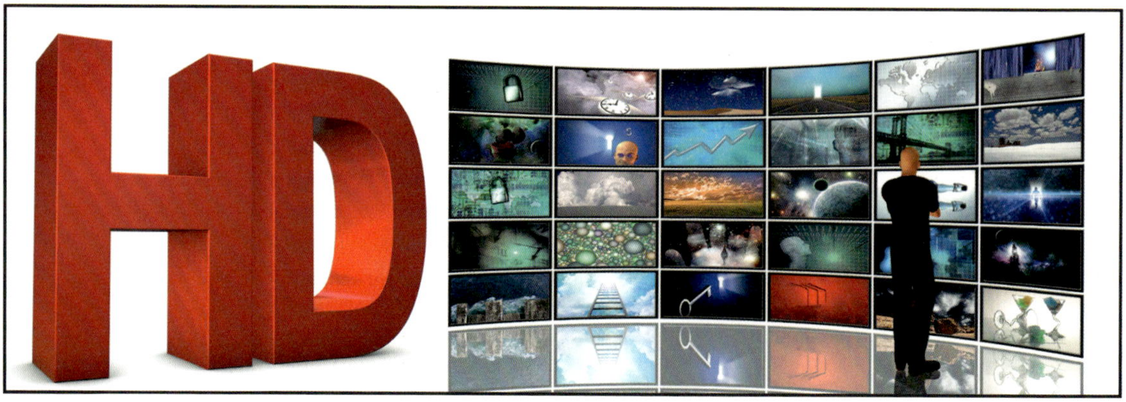

FIGURE 12.12 High-Definition signals require more bandwidth for recording. The old formats would once again be surpassed by new ones, with names such as HDCAM, DVCPRO HD, and HDV.

FLASHBACK

DV: The Blue Book Standard

In 1995, a large consortium of ten consumer electronics companies, including long-time rivals Panasonic (Matsushita) and Sony, released DV, an international set of standards for digitally compressing a component NTSC (720×486) or PAL (720×576) video signal to tape. DV (short for Digital Video), was more than just a tape format, it was a recipe book that manufactures could use for designing a variety of recording formats for different market segments. Known in engineering circles as *Blue Book* or IEC 61834, DV was quickly adopted by the consumer electronics industry and prosumer marketplace (see Figure 12.13).

DV uses *intraframe compression* to reduce spatial redundancy on a frame-by-frame basis. DV audio is recorded on one of two tracks as an uncompressed 16-bit Linear PCM stream with a sample rate of 48 kHz. The sample rate is slightly higher than the 44.1 kHz rate used in audio CDs. As a result, most NLEs have adopted 48 kHz as the native sample rate for the audio portion of a DV recording. When DV footage is ingested into a computer, it is saved either as raw data, or wrapped in a container format such as Audio Video Interleave (AVI), QuickTime (MOV), or Material eXchange Format (MFX). The NLE system determines which wrapper to use. For example, Final Cut Pro wraps DV in a QuickTime container, Apple's preferred video format; Avid Media Composer uses MXF.

While designed primarily for recording to digital tape, DV streams can also be written directly to optical disk, flash memory cards, and computer hard drives. It is a flexible hybrid format that helped to prepare the way for an industry transition from tape-based to file-based recording.

The Blue Book standard spawned a flurry of activity in both the consumer electronics and pro video markets as manufacturers sought to profit from the world's first digital tape standard with broad mass-market appeal.

FIGURE 12.13
The Canon XL-1 was a prosumer standard-definition camcorder made from 1997 to 2001. It used DV tape and was popular with corporate producers and independent filmmakers.

medium-size cassette format with a record time of 66 minutes. The larger cassette was designed for use with its professional line of DVCPRO camcorders. In 1997, Panasonic followed-up with DVCPRO50, a high-end professional format that doubled the bit rate and color sampling of recorded video.

Sony introduced DVCAM in 1997. In similar fashion, Sony achieved professional specs by widening the track pitch from 10 microns to 15 and increasing transport speed by 50%. Mini DVCAM cassettes have a record time of 41 minutes, while larger ones can run for three hours. Small format camcorders can only receive the mini cassette, but professional models can usually accommodate either size. DVCAM camcorders are fully backward compatible, allowing them to play back or record standard DV on a less expensive DVC cassette.

HDV

As the inevitable transition from SD to HD loomed on the horizon, a group of manufactures looked for a way to record high-definition television signals on standard DV tape. The answer came in 2003 when a consortium of four companies (Canon, JVC, Sharp, and Sony) announced the HDV standard. In order to record an HD signal within the same footprint as DV, engineers switched to an interframe compression scheme. They also decreased the resolution of the HD image to 1440×1080. Full HD has a native resolution of 1920×1080. HDV offered an affordable way for consumers, prosumers, and low-end professionals to work in HD without having to migrate to a full bandwidth HD workflow. And while HDV has been used, on occasion, in the production of professional broadcast programs, it is best to think of it as an advanced consumer or prosumer format. Most HDV devices are backward compatible, allowing users to record in standard DV as well.

DVCPRO HD

The final addition to the DV family of tape formats is DVCPRO HD, a low-compression format with features similar to Sony's HDCAM, such as 4:2:2 color sampling, a high bit rate, and intraframe compression. DVCPRO HD is used almost entirely by professionals.

TWO TYPES OF VIDEO COMPRESSION

The term *redundancy* refers to the amount of wasted space consumed by storage media to record picture information in a digital image. The goal of video compression is two-fold: (1) to reduce the file size of an image by eliminating or rewriting as much of the redundant information as possible; and (2) to retain the visible quality of an image. Redundancies can occur within the two-dimensional space of a single frame of video (as with a photograph), and also across time in a video sequence containing many frames.

Think for a moment about a five-second shot of a blue sky on a cloudless day. Thousands of blue pixels in an image like this would likely retain the same color value across the entire sequence of 150 frames. This phenomenon is called *temporal redundancy* and occurs whenever the value of a pixel remains unchanged from one frame to the next in a time-based sequence. And while the identical blue pixels in our video example extend forward over time, they also stretch outward within the space of each individual frame. This phenomenon is called *spatial redundancy* (see Figure 12.14).

The goal of video compression is to conserve bandwidth by eliminating spatial and/or temporal redundancies during the recording process (see Figures 12.15 and 12.16). Two methods of video compression are most commonly used today.

The first method is called *intraframe* (or *I-frame*) *compression*. This approach eliminates spatial redundancies "within" a video frame in much the same way that JPEG compression is used to reduce them in a digital photograph. I-frames are typically compressed at a ratio of 10:1. This means that a compressed I-frame consumes as little as 10% of the file space of a raw uncompressed frame. Since I-frames are fully defined by information from within the frame, they can be easily decoded and rendered onscreen during playback and editing. However, the overall amount of compression that's achieved with this approach is limited since temporal redundancies are not addressed.

The second and more common method is called *interframe compression*, a technique that exploits both spatial and temporal redundancies. Using the previous method of intraframe compression, all of the frames in a video stream are turned into I-frames. Each one is *intracoded* to eliminate spatial redundancy. Thus, compression is applied evenly to all of the frames within a video stream. With interframe compression, I-frames are created at fixed intervals (typically every 15 frames). An I-frame marks the beginning of a packaged sequence of adjacent frames called a GOP (Group of Pictures). The fully defined I-frame serves as a *keyframe* or reference for other frames in the group. Its job is to hold repeating color values in place that will not change across the sequence. Basically, it creates a digital marker on the frame that says "do not change the color of this pixel until you are told to do so."

HDV is a popular high-definition video format that uses an interframe compression algorithm called Long-GOP MPEG-2. With Long-GOP, each I-frame is followed by a sequence of 14 frames designated as either a *P-frame* or a *B-frame*. A *P-frame* is a predictive coded image that only stores data for pixels that are different from the preceding frame. For example, in a shot of a bird flying across a blue sky, only pixels related to the moving bird would be encoded to a P-frame. The unchanged background pixels simply carry forward from information stored in the previous frame. On average, a P-frame can be compressed twice as much as an I-frame. A B-frame is a bidirectional predictive coded image. It records changes from both the preceding frame and the one immediately following. On average, a B-frame can be compressed twice as much as a P-frame. With interframe encoding, all frames are not equally compressed. The more heavily compressed P-frames and B-frames require more processing power to encode and decode.

FIGURE 12.14
Spatial redundancy (top) is that which occurs within a single still image or video frame. *Temporal redundancy* (bottom) occurs over time across a sequence of motion picture frames. Video compression deals with both kinds of redundancy.

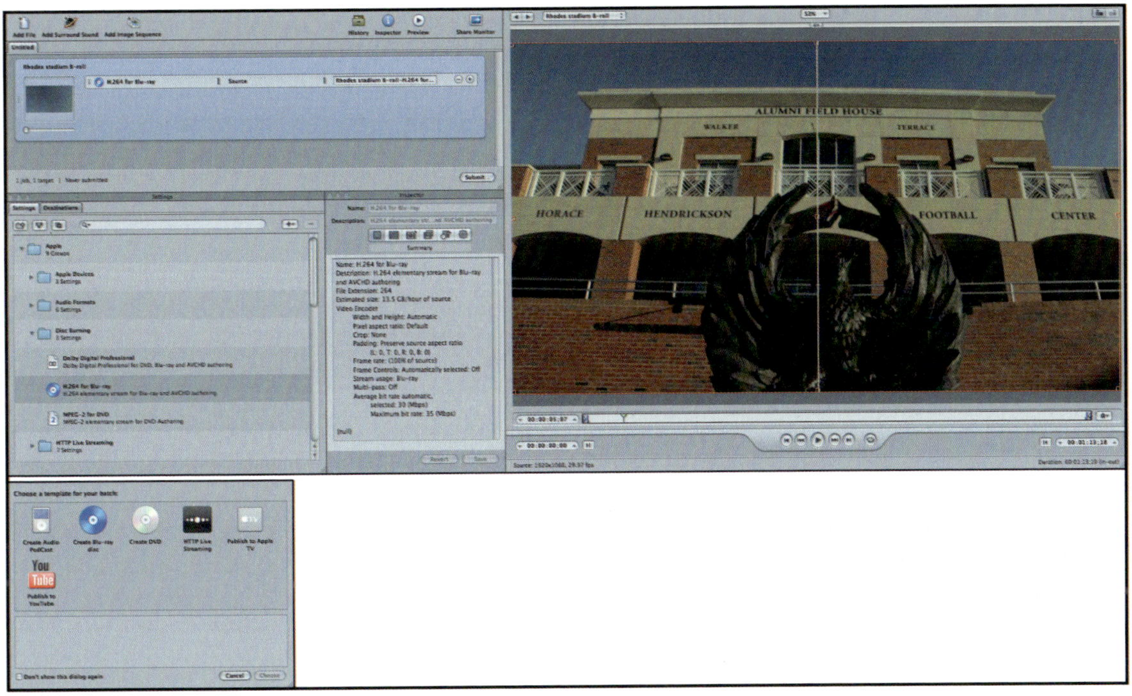

FIGURE 12.15
Apple Compressor 4 is a professional video compression and encoding tool. You can use this program or others like it to encode your video in any number of common distribution formats. For example, you may want to produce a DVD or Blue-Ray disc, upload the video online to YouTube or Vimeo, or save it to your iPad or Android tablet. Your video must be encoded in a format that is appropriate to each distribution channel you plan to use. For this reason, editors often find themselves creating multiple versions of a single project for different users.

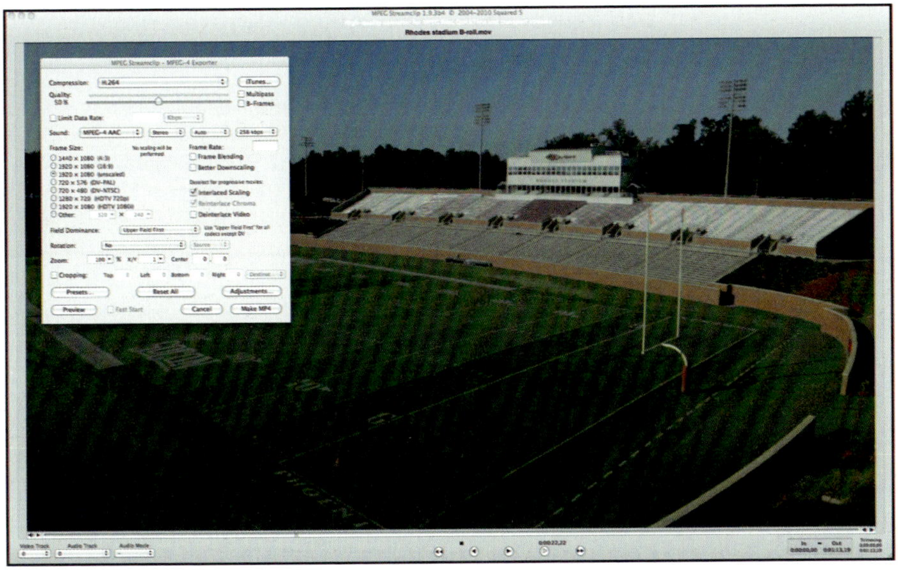

FIGURE 12.16
While Compressor 4 is a powerful encoder, it is a commercial product that will only run on a Mac. MPEG Streamclip (pictured here) is a free crossplatform video encoder. You can use it to convert digital video files to many of the common formats used today.

Depending on the power of the computer and the software being used, editing systems can experience difficulty when playing back interframe streams on the fly. Remember, only the I-frames are fully coded with all of the color information needed to render it on screen. In order to properly render P-frames and B-frames, the playback engine needs to access relevant picture data that's stored in other frames in the GOP sequence.

CONSUMER FORMATS

For the longest time, consumers had no ability to record television shows off the air in their homes. If you missed a show, the only option was to wait for the station to re-air it. A rerun might take several months or never happen at all. Likewise, if you missed the theatrical release for a motion picture film, chances were it would never be shown publically again. The likelihood of it appearing on television was just as remote. Home video recording formats would change this forever, giving consumers the ability to record a favorite program for viewing at a later time. This new consumer behavior would become known as *time-shifting*. The invention of the home VCR would also spawn the movie rental industry, giving Hollywood a profitable revenue source for the redistribution of motion picture films to audiences in the comfort of their own living rooms.

Betamax and VHS

The home video movement began with a battle of recording formats that pitted Sony against JVC. In 1975, Sony introduced Betamax, the first consumer-grade recording format. Within a year, JVC introduced a competing format called VHS

Tech Talk

Color Sampling The quality of a video format varies significantly by the amount of compression that's applied to separate components of a color video signal. As a rule, the human eye has a greater capacity for perceiving changes in luminance than it does in regard to color. Engineers exploit this phenomenon with a practice called *color sampling*, a technique that reduces bandwidth by applying more compression to the color channel of a video signal than it does to luminance. Known also as *chroma subsampling*, this technique uses strange looking ratios like 4:1:1 and 4:2:2 to convey a relative value for the amount of compression that's applied to each subchannel in a component video signal.

- **4:4:4** color space is fully uncompressed and is used in only a few high-end field cameras like RED, HDCAM SR, and network-level HD Studio cameras.
- **4:2:2** color space is much more common and is used in many professional formats including Beta SP (analog), Digital Betacam, Beta SX, IMX, DVCPRO 50, DVCPRO HD, HDCAM, and D-5 HD. As the name applies, it is also the basis of Apple's intermediate codec ProRes 4:2:2.
- **4:1:1** color space is used often in many consumer and prosumer formats including DV, DVCAM (NTSC), and DVCPRO 25.
- **4:2:0** color space is used for DV, DVCAM (PAL), MPEG-2, HDV, and XDCAM HD.

(Video Home System). For several years both formats competed side-by-side in a divided marketplace. Consumers were often confused. Video stores were required to stock two versions of a film. And film distributers had to deal with the hassle and expense of supporting two incompatible formats. Despite the fact that Betamax was first to market and that it produced a sharper picture, the marketplace eventually went with VHS. The decisive factor came down to record time. VHS offered two hours of record time in standard play (SP) mode. This was double what Betamax could deliver. In the end, VHS was a better fit for the movie industry. For twenty years, VHS reigned as the home recording format of choice throughout most of the world. VHS-C and Super VHS-C were compact versions of the larger cassette formats, designed for use in VHS camcorders.

MiniDV

DV was originally released to the public under the name of *DVC* (for Digital Video Cassette). DVC uses ¼-inch wide metal evaporated tape, which is capable of recording a high-quality video signal. The cassettes come in two sizes. The large cassette, designed primarily for desktop recorders, can hold three hours of recorded footage. The small cassette, called MiniDV, has a maximum record time of one hour and is intended primarily for use in consumer camcorders. However, because of its popularity as a flexible multiuser format, MiniDV tapes come in many different flavors ranging from consumer-grade to master-grade quality.

GREAT IDEAS

Optical Disc Formats

In 1995, Panasonic, Phillips, Sony, and Toshiba jointly released the DVD-Video standard. Identical in look to an audio compact disc, DVD was designed as a distribution format to replace Betamax and VHS (see Figure 12.17). DVD quickly became the new worldwide format for delivering standard-definition feature-length films to consumers.

The original DVD format uses a red laser beam to record and play back an MPEG-2 encoded video stream. The pitch of the record track is dependent on the wavelength of the laser beam and ultimately determines how much data can fit on a disc. Red light has a wavelength of 650 nanometers (nm), which by human standards seems small, but in physics is one of the largest wavelengths in the visible light spectrum. To put this in perspective, the average width of human hair is 100,000 nm. This is roughly 150 times wider than the record track of a red laser DVD, which has a capacity of 4.7 GB on a standard single-sided disc. While this is enough bandwidth for storing a standard-definition movie, it is far below the threshold for HD.

In order to increase the storage capacity of optical discs, engineers looked to the opposite end of the color spectrum. At 405 nm, blue light has a much smaller wavelength than red light, enabling a blue laser DVD recorder to write considerably more data in the same amount of space. In 2006, the Blu-Ray Disc Association

(Continued)

released the Blu-ray format, a high-density optical disc for distributing movies in HD. A Blu-ray disc is the same size as a standard DVD, but it can store more than five times as much data. A single-layer Blu-ray disc has a capacity of 25 GB, which is more than enough bandwidth to deliver a full-length high-definition motion picture. In addition, Blu-ray devices are fully backward compatible, which means they can play first-generation red laser DVDs and CDs.

FIGURE 12.17
DVD replaced VHS as the main distribution format for the motion picture industry. The market shifted again when consumers embraced Blu-ray and direct-to-home delivery of HD content via broadband cable and the Internet.

FILE-BASE RECORDING FORMATS

There is little room left in this chapter to cover all of the platforms, codecs, and recording formats associated with file-based recording (see Figure 12.18). So, for the sake of expediency, we'll look at just a few of the more ubiquitous formats that have made the greatest impact. In general there are two broad types of formats.

The first type is covered under the heading of open standards. An *open standard* is one that is publically released but that often stipulates specific conditions and applications for its use. Open standards are typically drafted and approved by a committee comprised of technical experts and stakeholders in the industry. These committees, or *working groups* as they're sometimes called, are usually tied to a nonprofit NGO (nongovernmental organization) whose mission is to help define international standards. When it comes to defining video and computer standards, two of the most well-known NGOs are the International Organization for Standardization (ISO) and the International Electrotechnical Commission (IEC).

Tech Talk

Container Formats With traditional tape-based recording methods, the videotape is divided into linear regions, called *tracks*, for separating the various components of a video signal (video, audio CH1, audio CH2, and control data). *Bandwidth* is controlled by the length of the tape, track pitch, and the transport speed of the VCR. File-based systems record video and audio signals as packaged streams of binary data on computer storage media. With this approach, bandwidth is defined largely by the circuitry of the recording device and the compression algorithms used to encode the various streams of digital information.

In tape-based recording, the tape itself serves as a container, keeping tracks together and in sync, as the tape moves from place to place. In file-based recording, a container (or wrapper) file serves the same function. A *container format* is a special kind of computer file designed to hold the contents of related media streams and data files in one place. Some container formats like WAV and AIF are designed specifically for wrapping audio streams, while other, more sophisticated ones like AVI and QuickTime are used to contain multiple video and audio streams. A video container file contains at least one video stream and two audio streams. However, additional streams are often generated to record things like *metadata* and *tags* (creation date, clip duration, exposure settings, GPS coordinates, etc.), subtitles, chapter markers, additional audio channels, and time-based synchronization data.

When a container format is created or updated, the owner of the format releases a white paper or specification sheet indicating which media formats and/or codecs are supported. For example, Apple QuickTime X supports the following video formats and more: H.264/MPEG-4 AVC, AVI, DV, and Sorenson Video. It also supports MP3, AAC, AIFF, and WAV for audio, and BMP, GIF, JPEG, PNG, and TIFF for graphics. As a result, the QuickTime media player will be able to decode and play back any media file recorded in one of these supported formats.

Physical tape formats are media-dependent, meaning that compatibility hinges on the hardware used to encode them. For example, a DV tape will only play back in a DV tape deck or camcorder. Try inserting it into a Betacam deck and you'll be out of luck. Not only will it not fit into the VTR, but DV and Betacam do not even speak the same language. Their system architectures are based on two incompatible codecs. Container formats are better than tape formats because they can be updated without having to reengineer the hardware used to play them back. As such, a file-based container format is said to be *media-independent*.

The second type of format you're likely to encounter is a proprietary standard that has been created by (a) a single manufacturer, or (b) a small group of companies who have formed a limited partnership for the purpose of jointly sponsoring and profiting from a new standard; or (c) a large consortium of manufactures with a shared stake in the deployment of a common format.

Open Standards for File-Base Recording

In 1988, the ISO/IEC established the Moving Picture Experts Group (MPEG) as a "working group" tasked with developing open standards for video and audio compression. While MPEG has published many compression standards for the recording and transmission of video, audio, and television signals over the years, we'll touch on only a few here.

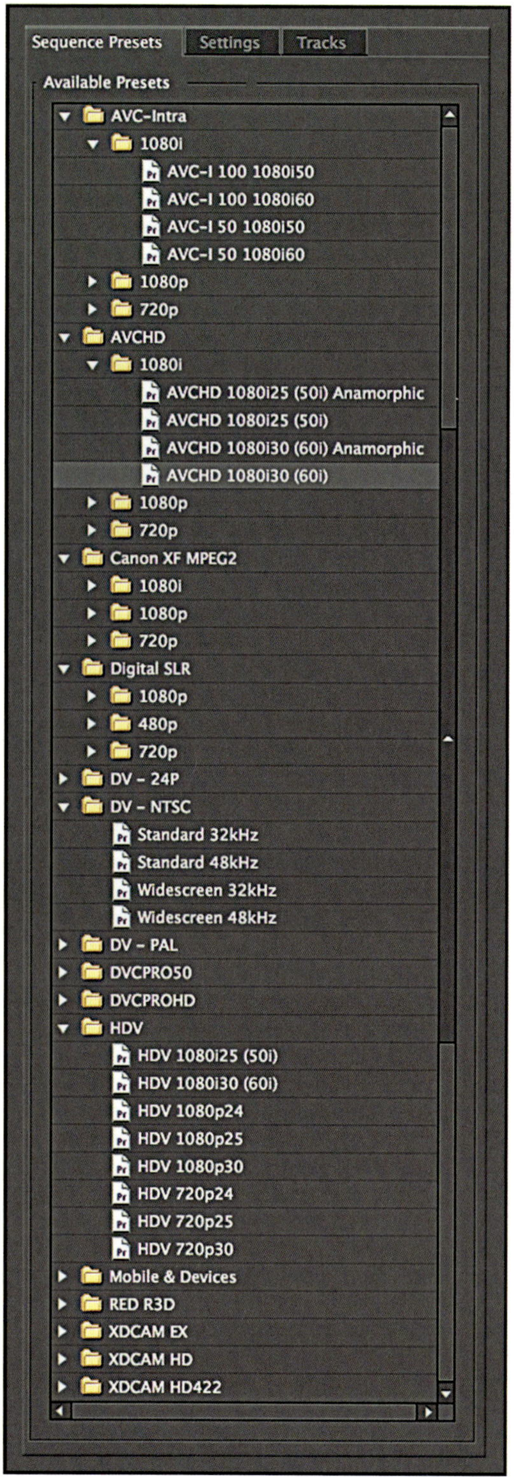

MP3

MPEG's first project was published in 1993 under the name of MPEG-1, which is most remembered for establishing the popular MP3 audio format. MP3 was the first digital codec designed for storing music on a portable audio player. MP3 offered users the ability to compress CD-quality audio (44.1 kHz) by a ratio of 10:1. In addition, MPEG-1 video was established, along with the first set of specifications for encoding SD video using intraframe or interframe encoding. Unfortunately, MPEG-1 video had a low bit rate of 1.5 Mbps, which was similar in quality to VHS.

MPEG-2

MPEG-2 was approved in 1993 as an advanced standard for encoding SD and HD video formats at a significantly higher bit rate. It would become the international standard for encoding SD video on a red laser DVD. Audio compression was enhanced as well. With MPEG-2, came Advanced Audio Coding (AAC), a format that extended the stereo capabilities in MPEG-1 to multichannel surround sound (Dolby Digital 5.1). In addition to its use as the encoding standard for DVD-Video, MPEG-2 has been incorporated into numerous other formats like HDV, XDCAM, consumer formats like MOD and TOD, and the terrestrial HDTV broadcasting standards ATSC and DVB. MPEG-2 is a fluid standard that has been amended several times since its initial public release.

MPEG-4 - ADVANCED VIDEO CODING (AVC)

The MPEG-4 initiative concerned itself primarily with developing a method for distributing full-bandwidth HD video to the home video consumer.

FIGURE 12.18
The sequence preset window in Adobe Premier CS 5.5 lists a slew of video formats supported by the NLE. While a list like this can be daunting at first to understand, most of the time you will find yourself working with a handful of trusted video formats and codecs. So don't worry, you don't need to know them all.

Tech Talk

Intermediate Formats As previously noted, a nonlinear editing system can experience problems when decoding interframe video formats like HDV and H.264 on the fly. Depending on the speed of your system and NLE software, it is possible to edit interframe streams natively. However, to reduce the likelihood of playback artifacts or rendering slowdowns, editors will often convert interframe video to an intermediate format prior to editing. For example, in legacy versions of Final Cut Pro (version 7 and earlier), HDV footage is automatically upconverted to ProRes 4:2:2 during the log and capture process. ProRes is Apple's intermediate codec for editing uncompressed full-width (1920×1080) HD video. It is comparable to DNxHD, the intermediate codec used in Avid Media Composer. Both of these intermediate codecs use intraframe compression, which is easier to decode, but which also produces a transcoded file that is considerably larger than the original source video. By upconverting to a higher quality uncompressed format, transcoding artifacts are kept to a minimum. Intermediate codecs are typically more robust in terms of rendering speed and color sampling methods.

The actual codec goes by many different names including AVC, H.264, MPEG-4, and H.264/MPEG-4. AVC is best known for being one of several native codecs supported by Blu-ray Disc. Both ATSC and DVB have approved AVC for use in terrestrial HDTV broadcasting. AVC is currently one of the most popular formats used for uploading video to online hosting sites like YouTube and Vimeo.

Proprietary Standards for File-Base Recording

Time will tell when the final gong will sound signaling the sale of the last tape-based camcorder on the planet. At the time of this writing, tape-based recording systems are still available for sale from professional distributers and big box consumer electronic stores. However, it is safe to say that the era of tape-based workflows is rapidly approaching EOL. You can now record hours of HD footage on a solid-state memory card that's not much bigger than the size of your thumbnail. Sony and Panasonic were instrumental in leading the professional marketplace to tapeless recording with their release of three solid-state, nonlinear, random access formats: SxS, Professional Disc, and P2.

PROFESSIONAL DISC AND SxS

Sony introduced XDCAM in 2003, a line of high-end cameras using Professional Disc, an optical recording medium like Blu-ray disc, capable of storing up to 50 GB of data. XDCAM supports recording in any of the following formats: DVCAM, MPEG IMX, and XDCAM HD. In 2007, Sandisk and Sony announced their joint release of the SxS (pronounced S-by-S) memory card specification. SxS is Sony's solid-state memory card format that bundles high-speed flash memory into a PCI Express (PCIe) case (see Figure 12.19).

FIGURE 12.19
In lieu of videotape, the Sony XDCAM EX series of professional camcorders records video to an SxS memory card.

P2

P2 is a solid-state memory card format introduced by Panasonic in 2004. These memory cards are capable of storing video streams in any of the following formats: DV, DVCPRO, DVCPRO25, DVCPRO50, DVCPRO-HD, or AVC-Intra. AVC-Intra is a master-quality recording format developed by Panasonic for its top-of-the line broadcast cameras. A P2 card contains multiple SD cards packaged together inside a large-format metal case known as a *PC* or *PCMCIA Card*.

PROPRIETARY CARD FORMATS

Professional Disc, SxS, and P2 are proprietary media formats designed for professionals and can only be used in a limited number of compatible cameras. Because of this, they are expensive. To their credit, however, these solutions are engineered to hold up well under the rigors of professional use, and as a result are physically more robust (see Figure 12.20).

AVCHD

One of the goals of the MPEG-4 initiative was to specify an open standard for recording HD video that would also be compatible with inexpensive flash memory card formats such as Secure Digital (SD and SDHC) and Compact Flash (CF).

FIGURE 12.20
Proprietary card formats like SxS and P2 are designed for professional users. These cards are significantly better than off-the-shelf SD memory cards, and as a result are more robust and reliable. Because of this, they are also more expensive, a fact that puts them out of reach for many low-budget producers.

This goal was realized in 2003 with the development of H.264/MPEG-4 AVC, a high-quality compression and recording standard that has become widely popular in recent years.

Three Reasons for the Rapid Rise of AVCHD

- Many professional editing programs provide support for a native AVCHD workflow throughout the entire postproduction process. Transcoding is kept to a minimum or eliminated altogether.
- Flash memory cards have increased in size and dropped in price (see Table 12.3).
- AVCHD is supported by a wide range of consumer electronic equipment, including Blu-ray players, gaming consoles, portable devices, and television systems.[1]

Tech Talk

Recording Variables in AVCHD

AVCHD Like many digital formats, AVCHD offers a broad set of parameters that can be individually controlled by the camera operator for defining how a video signal is encoded. These settings are often located in the menu system of the camera and may have different names and labels depending on the manufacturer. For example, a user may select any combination of the record options on the Sony-HXR-NX70U AVCHD camcorder listed in Table 12.1.

The image quality setting is very much like the JPEG compression setting on a digital still camera. Choosing the highest bit rate produces the best quality image with the least amount of compression. However, the higher setting also reduces the amount of recordable material that your SD card can hold (see Table 12.2).

(Continued)

[1]Sony Corporation. (2009). AVCHD Introduction Handbook (2nd Edition).

Table 12.1 Sony HXR-NX70U Record Options

Record Format	Image Quality (bitrate)	Resolution	Aspect Ratio	Frame Rate
High-Definition HD	FX – Highest (24 Mbps)	1920×1080	16:9	60i 60p 24p
	FH – High (17 Mbps)	1920×1080		
	HQ – Standard (9 Mbps)	1440×1080		
	LP – Long Time (5 Mbps)	1440×1080		
Standard Definition SD	HQ – Standard (9 Mbps)	720×480	16:9 4:3	60i

Table 12.2 A Comparison of Record Time (minutes), Record Format, and Memory Card Capacity for the Sony HXR-NX70U

	Memory Card Capacity		
HD Quality	8 GB	16 GB	32 GB
FX	40	80	170
FH	55	110	225
HQ	90	185	375
LP	145	295	590

The approximate recording time (in minutes) for each of the four quality settings on the Sony HXR-NX70U camcorder. Actual time depends on other variables such as frame rate and method of recording audio. (compressed or uncompressed)

Table 12.3 Secure Digital High Capacity (SDHC) Memory Cards Rated by Class

Class	Read Speed	Write Speed	Application
Class 2	16 Mbps	16 Mbps	Still Photography and SD video
Class 4	33 Mbps	32 Mbps	Full HD video recording
Class 6	48 Mbps	48 Mbps	Full HD video recording
Class 10	80 Mbps	80 Mbps	Full HD video recording

HD camcorders require the use of a class 4 card or higher. The higher the card's class, the more quickly data on the card can be transferred to a connected device such as a computer desktop or hard drive.

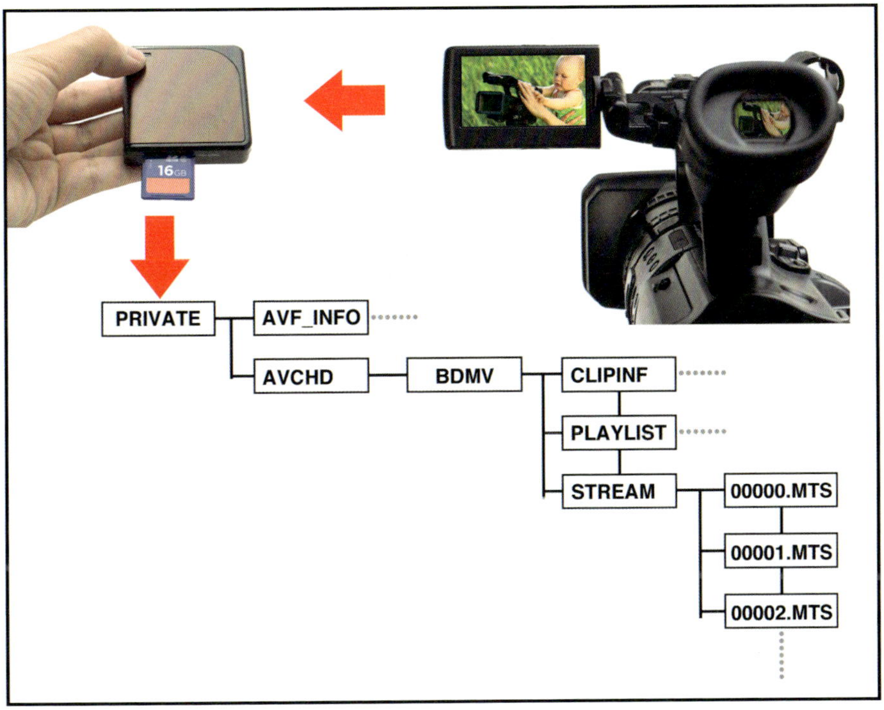

FIGURE 12.21 The AVCHD standard specifies this file directory structure for recording video and metadata to a solid-state memory card. It's important to keep this file structure intact. If any of the folder names is altered, your editing software may not be able to recognize the video files. With AVCHD, video files are saved to the STREAM folder in the .MTS format (MPEG Transport Stream).

In 2006, Sony and Panasonic jointly released a variation of the MPEG-4 standard called *AVCHD*. Originally designed for consumers, AVCHD is a proprietary format that has been incorporated into a new fleet of prosumer and professional camcorders. This format has grown quickly in popularity and has been licensed for use by other manufacturers, including Canon, JVC, and Hitachi. The AVCHD recording format is used in Sony's NXCAM line of cameras as well as Panasonic's AVCCAM series. A consumer-grade version of the standard, called AVCHD Lite, has a maximum resolution of 720p and is often used in digital still cameras for shooting HD video (see Figure 12.21).

CHAPTER SUMMARY

Video recording began in 1956. Since that time, a host of formats have come and gone as engineers and product developers have found newer and better ways of encoding video and audio signals. For many years, the recording device (the camera or VCR) was tied to a proprietary medium such as a magnetic tape reel or videotape cassette. A video recording could only be played back if you had the right hardware for viewing it.

The most significant development in recent years is the development of solid-state technologies that use file-based recording formats and codecs. Such formats have drastically driven down the cost of professional HD recording systems and media and are often more flexible and convenient to use. However, because they are more flexible, there is hardly ever just one way to record or transcode a video or audio signal. You can't just turn the camera on, press the record button, and expect the best results. You need to know a lot more information related to recording formats, codecs, container files, resolutions, frame rates, sampling rates, bitrates, etc. in order to make informed judgments about the best resolution and quality for a given job or assignment. The more you know now, the better positioned you will be when everything changes once again—and the next generation of recording technologies emerges.

CHAPTER 13

Time-Based Editing

As we get newer and better compression algorithms for video and still-frame images, we'll approach the next major leap in desktop computing: video on the desktop.

—John C. Dvorak, Technology Journalist and Radio Broadcaster, (1995)

Chapter Highlights

This chapter examines:

- The use of nonlinear editing (NLE) in video and audio production
- The visual interface components in an NLE workspace
- Strategies for project organization and asset management
- The relationship between project media files and clips in a nondestructive editing environment
- General concepts and principles related to the aesthetics of editing

Key Terms

Action Safe
Actuality
Alpha Channel
Audio Sweetening
Audio Track/Channel
B-Roll
Chroma Key
Clip
Codec
Color Correction
Compositing
Continuity Editing
Cut
Cutaway
Dissolve
Duration
Editing
Effect/Filter
Fade
Footage
Freeze Frame
Import/Export
In and Out Points
Insert
Jog and Shuttle
Jump Cut
Keying
Linear Editing
Lip Synching
Log and Capture
Marker
Mask
Matte
Mixing
Natural Sound
Nondestructive Editing
Nonlinear Editing (NLE)

NONLINEAR EDITING

Video editing is the art of arranging static and time-based media assets into a linear form of presentation for the purpose of telling a story or communicating a message. The goal of editing is usually to produce a thoughtful narrative with a clear beginning, middle, and end. Audio editing is similar but with a focus on sound-based media elements only. Many of the basic editing techniques used in video are applicable to audio, particularly if you are using professional audio editing software.

Motion picture editing began as a simple manual process. In the early days of film, an editor would review and edit footage using a hand-operated device (see Figure 13.1). Editing was performed by physically cutting film into sections, rearranging the pieces into a new linear order, then splicing them together again using clear tape or another type of adhesive—hence the term linear editing. This method was also used in audio tape editing. You'll find that many of the terms used in digital audio and video editing today have their origins from this era, particularly the use of terms such as the *razor blade tool* referring to the old cutting implements, and

Playhead
Render
Roll
Rough Cut
Scratch Disk
Scrubbing
Sequence
Shot
Slug
Sound Bite (SOT)
Sound Effects (SFX)
Split Edit
Talking Head
Timecode
Timeline
Title
Title Safe
Transition
Trimming
Video Track
Voiceover (VO)
VU Meter
Waveform

FIGURE 13.1
Motion picture editing used to be a physical act that required manually viewing, cutting, and splicing pieces of film together to make a movie. Today, film and video editing is done virtually using an NLE program. There's no more mess and no more film left behind on the cutting room floor.

the term *bins*, referring to the actual bins that film editors used to hold segments of film and audio tape.

While film editing began as a physical process, video editing started out as an electronic process. Unlike film, one cannot expose videotape to the light in an effort to view the semitranslucent frames of each still image. Video images are processed electronically, which means that viewing and editing has to be done using electromechanical players, recorders, and monitors. In the beginning, video editing was nothing more than systematic duplication. Material was copied section by section from a recorded tape in one VCR to a new tape in a second VCR, a process known as *tape-to-tape* or *machine-to-tape editing*. This technique was also used in audio production, though it was supplemented by multitrack recorders, which allowed multiple audio tracks to be recorded and edited on a single piece of audiotape.

Machine-to-machine editing worked pretty well for many years. The simplest machine-to-machine editing system involved five pieces of equipment: (1) a playback deck; (2) a playback monitor; (3) a record deck; (4) a record monitor; and (5) an edit controller. The edit controller was connected to both decks, allowing the editor to control them remotely. To perform an edit, the editor would begin by "electronically" marking the beginning and end of a selected shot on the source deck. This involved shuttling the deck (moving or *scrubbing* the tape backwards or forwards), pausing it at a specific spot on the tape, and pressing physical buttons to mark the respective IN and OUT points. The editor would perform the same procedure to set an IN point on the record deck. Pushing one last button allowed the editor to preview or perform the edit. During the pre-roll phase, both machines would back up 3–5 seconds ahead of the designated

IN points and then would roll (start to play) in unison. When the IN point was reached on the record VCR, recording would begin and continue until the OUT point triggered the end of the edit.

This type of machine-to-machine editing configuration was sometimes called a *cuts-only system*, because the only type of edit you could perform was a cut. If you wanted to create anything other than a straight cut transition, you had to use an *A/B Roll editing system*. The A/B Roll workstation had two source decks instead of one. The A-Deck was loaded with the primary footage (interviews, scripted dialog, etc.) while the B-Deck contained secondary support material (cover shots, establishing shots, cutaways, etc.) that would appear while the main person or character was talking on screen. This is where the familiar, yet sometimes confusing, term *B-Roll* comes from.

The computerization of media has made machine-to-machine editing a thing of the past. The edit controller is no longer a physical device sitting on a tabletop, but rather software powered by a computer. Welcome to the age of nonlinear editing (NLE), where programs such as Adobe Premiere, Avid Media Composer, and Apple Final Cut Pro, are used by professional editors to craft their stories. For consumers, the marketplace offers a number of simple-to-learn NLEs like Pinnacle Studio, Apple iMovie, and Windows MovieMaker. Professional NLE titles are designed for filmmakers and producers who want advanced tools and need to maximize their workflows. Audio editing software comes in a similar range, from consumer-level software such as GarageBand to professional-grade software such as Logic, Audition, or ProTools.

THE BUILDING BLOCKS OF AN EDITED SEQUENCE

Most professionally produced television shows or video programs contain basic components that when edited together, tell a story, communicate a message, or stimulate an emotion. Raw footage for a project is acquired during the production phase. The amount of raw footage you have depends on the type of project you are working on and your skill in keeping the number of "bad takes" to a minimum. For a one-hour documentary, you may have 10 hours of source material (interviews, B-Roll, etc.) to work with. We refer to this as a *ten-to-one* or *10:1 shooting ratio* because the amount of source footage is 10 times greater than the length of the finished product. For a 60-second news package, an editor will often have much less footage to work with. Although the shooting ratio might be the same at 10:1, the amount of material drops to just 10 minutes.

The media assets used to build an edited sequence fall into four categories: (1) scripted action and dialog; (2) unscripted action and dialog; (3) titles and graphics; and (4) music and sound effects.

Scripted Action and Dialog

Narrative films, television dramas, comedy shows, commercials, and educational and training programs are common genres that rely on prescripted action and dialog. During production, the actor, host, or talent will have to perform a

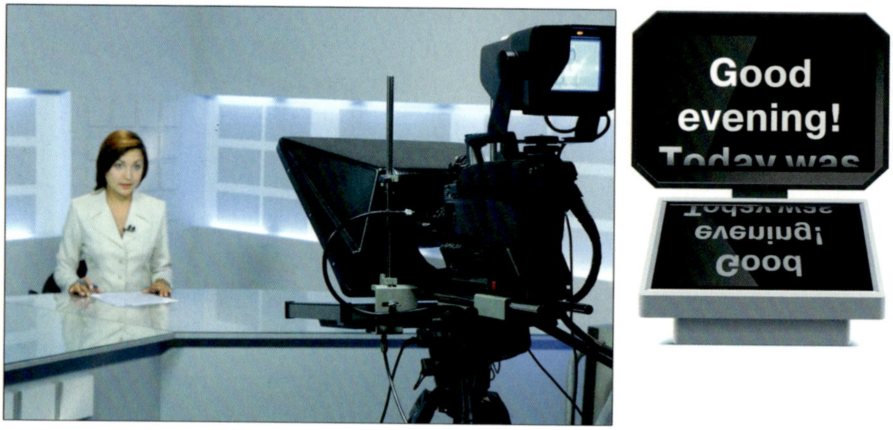

FIGURE 13.2
Television news anchors are able to maintain eye contact with the viewer by reading their scripts via a teleprompter mounted to the front of the camera.

scene *off-book*, or without the aid of a written prompt or script. This means that the talent will have to memorize lines and rehearse them prior to the actual recording. On-camera performances are rarely perfect, and directors often ask talent to make multiple attempts (*takes*) of a scene before he or she is satisfied with the performance.

In some situations, dialog may be performed with the aid of a teleprompter (see Figure 13.2). A *teleprompter* projects words onto the surface of a glass panel that's mounted in front of a television camera. The performer reads the text as it scrolls upwards and can still talk straight to the camera. Teleprompters are often used in studio productions (news, sports, talk programs, etc.), but can also be used in remote field production. While teleprompters can cut down on rehearsal time and speed production, their use doesn't guarantee perfect takes. Reading from a teleprompter is tricky. Some people are better at it than others.

Unscripted Action and Dialog

Nonfiction genres like journalism and documentary film rely heavily on unscripted dialogue and action. Footage is shot candidly using real-world subjects in a natural setting. The camera is there to capture a story, as communicated through the actions, behaviors, thoughts, ideas, feelings, and expressions of those involved. Content is acquired primarily through interviews, voiceovers, and B-Roll.

SOUND BITES

A *sound bite* is a short segment of a longer interview or speech that is inserted into a video program or news package. In television, a sound bite is denoted by the scriptwriting abbreviation SOT (pronounce as *S-O-T*) for *sound on tape*. In radio broadcasting, a short interview segment is called an actuality. Whereas interviews are shot or recorded during the production phase of a project, sound bites and actualities are "constructed" by editors during postproduction. A sound bite can be as short as a single word or several sentences long. The phrase *talking head* is used to describe an on-camera interview segment that goes on for too long, potentially causing the viewer or listener to lose interest and disengage from the message. The average length of a sound bite on network news programs is less than ten seconds. As a rule of thumb, sound bites should be kept to less than twenty seconds. Usually, the shorter, the better!

To avoid having a long sound bite of say thirty seconds, an editor can split (or cut) the sound bite into two shorter bites (roughly 15 seconds each). The editor can then insert natural sound, music, narration, reporter dialog, or another sound bite in between as a narrative bridge or cutaway. Using this technique, the content of the 30 second bite still gets communicated, but in a more dynamic fashion by intercutting it with other elements.

Sound bites from different people can be edited together in a sequence to form a continuous thought or interwoven narrative. The rapid intercutting of shorter sound bites in combination with other program elements is a great way to keep an audience engaged in the program. A skillful editor can even join noncontiguous sound bites in such a way as to make the person speaking sound as if they are saying something entirely different. In this regard, the editor is a potentially powerful gatekeeper and shaper of ideas, and as such, needs to follow the ethical standards and practices his or her profession and the organization they work for. Nowhere is this more important than in journalism, where reporters are expected to uphold the virtues of truth, fairness, and objectivity. An editor at Comedy Central may have more latitude and freedom in editing (under the cover of parody and satire) than a news editor working at CNN.

GREAT IDEAS
The Stand-Up

In television, a *reporter stand-up* or *on-camera host* segment can be used as an alternative to a voiceover or in combination with it. For example, a reporter may choose to use a stand-up at the beginning and end of a story and voiceovers throughout the rest of the package. The best stand-ups add meaningful visual value to the story by providing something other than a good look at the host. The stand-up can be used to demonstrate a key point or guide the viewer through a complex process, where video is not available or difficult to acquire.

FIGURE 13.3
A TV reporter prepares to deliver an on-camera stand-up.

VOICEOVER (VO)

The *voiceover* (or *VO*) is a narrative device used to describe an audio segment that's recorded off-camera without synchronized video. It is the sound of the hidden announcer, storyteller, reporter, narrator, or host, who guides the audience through the program—filling in details while adding color and continuity to the linear presentation of information. Voiceovers are often used in conjunction with sound bites to form longer strings of information. In news reporting, the *VO-SOT* (pronounced *VŌ-sät*) is a technique in which the television anchor reads a scripted story off-camera, while related images and sounds appear on screen. *VO-SOT-VO* describes a fundamental editing technique where voiceovers and sound bites alternate to form the basic narrative structure of a linear program.

B-ROLL

B-Roll is video source material that's used to fill holes in the timeline where synchronized video is not included, or as a source of supplemental footage to accompany a video sound bite. For example, when a voiceover is added to a sequence, B-Roll is used to supply the pictures. Likewise, in an interview segment, B-Roll can be used, in part or in whole, to replace the shot of the person speaking, effectively converting an SOT into a VO. B-Roll includes things like cut-ins and cutaways, which we will discuss later, and other footage that visually supports what is being said on screen. For example, as a reporter is speaking off-camera about a local bank robbery, the viewer sees a sequence of B-Roll shots depicting the scene of the crime. This could include material obtained from surveillance cameras along with other shots taken in the aftermath. There's a popular saying among editors that you can never get enough B-Roll. The more B-Roll an editor has to work with, the more options he or she will have for improving a story's pace and structure.

NATURAL SOUND

Natural sound (*nat sound*), or *ambience*, occurs in the background as a scene is being recorded. As humans, we are able to distinguish between foreground and background sounds. The sound of two voices, joined together in conversation, is registered as foreground sound. The sound of a car driving by is a background sound. When a camera operator records B-Roll, it is common practice to record audio that is simultaneously occurring in the background. You can use nat sound in both audio and video productions to help establish a sense of place.

TITLES

A *title* (or *super*) is a text-based graphic that is superimposed over video to identify visual content within the frame. One of the most common types of titles you see on nearly every television show is called a *lower third*—so named because of its usual placement near the bottom of the video frame. A lower third is used most often to identify the name and title of the person speaking on screen.

A title graphic is placed on screen through a process called *keying*. Keying replaces the background pixels in a title graphic (known as the *alpha channel*) with video from another source. This technique is similar to the superimposition of a weather map behind the weathercaster during the evening news. The

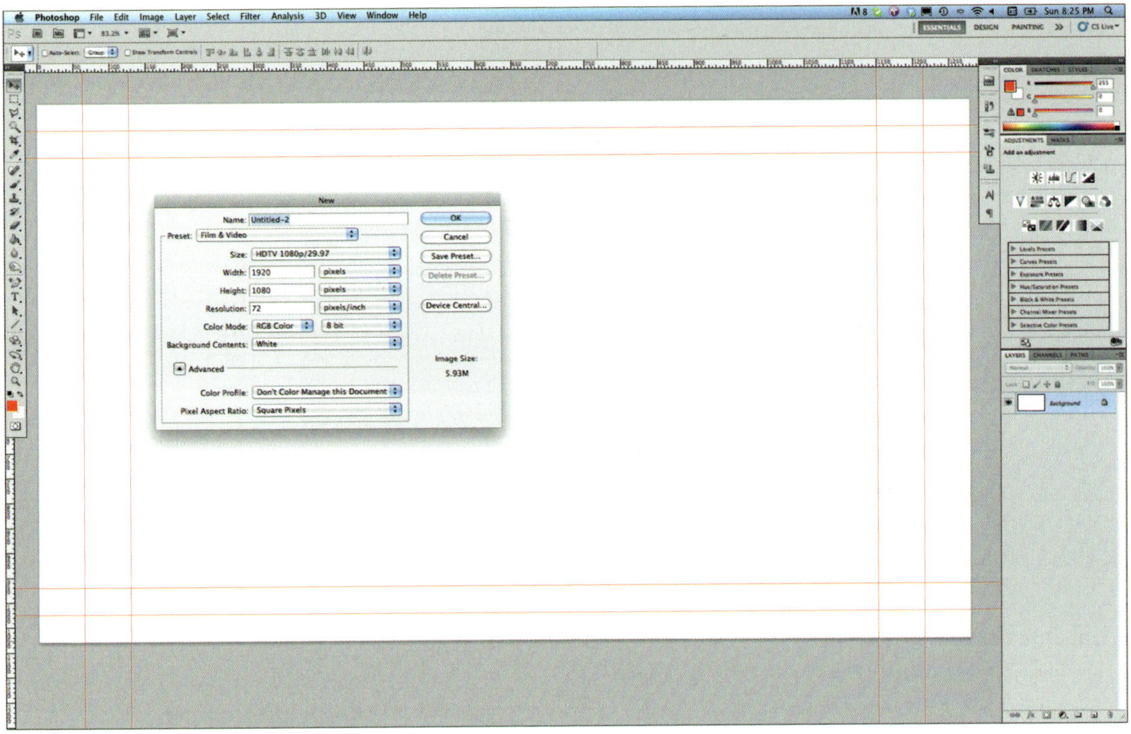

FIGURE 13.4
Adobe Photoshop includes several film and video presets. For example, if you need to create a full screen graphic for an HD television program, you can choose the one shown here. Film and video presets include visual guides for the action and titles safe areas.

weathercaster is actually standing in front of a green or blue wall. Using a technique called *chroma keying*, the colored wall is replaced with video of a weather graphic. For best results, the weathercaster cannot wear clothing with the same color as the wall. Can you imagine what that would look like? Like the green or blue wall in a TV studio, the alpha channel serves as a mask, allowing a title to be seamlessly merged with the video beneath it.

It's relatively easy to create simple titles in most NLEs. However, when you need a complex title, you may want to turn to a dedicated graphic design program such as Photoshop (see Figure 13.4). You can then use the NLE to import it into the project bin as a standalone media asset. NLEs can recognize most common graphic file formats including JPEG, GIF, TIFF, and PNG. In fact, most professional NLEs allow you to import Photoshop PSD files directly into the project bin and timeline. When an NLE opens a PSD file, it converts each layer to a corresponding video track, allowing the editor to have independent control of each layer element in the timeline.

Full-Screen Graphics

A *full-screen graphic* takes up the entire screen space and therefore does not have to be superimposed with another video source (see Figure 13.6). A matte (usually

FIGURE 13.5
A lower-third title graphic is superimposed over the video of a television reporter. This one was generated using a template in Apple Final Cut Pro X.

FIGURE 13.6
A full-screen graphic like this one fills the entire video frame.

a background image or color), still image, or freeze frame (a single frame from a video clip) can be used effectively as the background for a full-screen graphic in the timeline. Video tracks in the timeline function in much the same way that layers do in Photoshop. For example, you could place a solid color or gradient background on video track (V1), add text on V2, and place a still image on V3. Because each element in the composite is on a separate track, the editor retains independent control over the position and movement of each element.

GREAT IDEAS

Designing Graphics for Television

When designing television graphics, keep in mind that viewers may be watching the video on a low-resolution medium, or even in a small window on a computer monitor. Viewers have a short time frame in which to process information as it is flashes on the screen. Follow these tips when planning your graphics:

Avoid Clutter. Remember, less is more. Don't pack more information into the visual screen space than is absolutely necessary. Avoid long sentences and paragraphs. Instead, use short phrases and bullet points whenever possible.

Use Thick Sans-Serif Fonts. Select high-density fonts with a thick stroke. Scripts and other light stroke fonts don't translate well to video and lose much of their detail, making them hard to read and frustrating the viewer.

Use Large Font Sizes. Use font size to denote a visual hierarchy of information, but keep the sizes relatively large. It's better to use a readable font and break up information across several screens than to cram too much information into a single title screen or graphic.

Strive for Good Contrast. If the background is dark, the foreground text should be light. Separate the text from the background by using drop shadows, stroke, light, and texture. Text should pop off the surface of the background. Try using a high-contrast background matte behind text instead of superimposing the text directly over video and running the risk of making the text hard to read.

Use Video-Friendly Colors. White and yellow are popular colors for screen text because they are easy to read against a dark background. Black also works quite well when placed on white or a light-colored background.

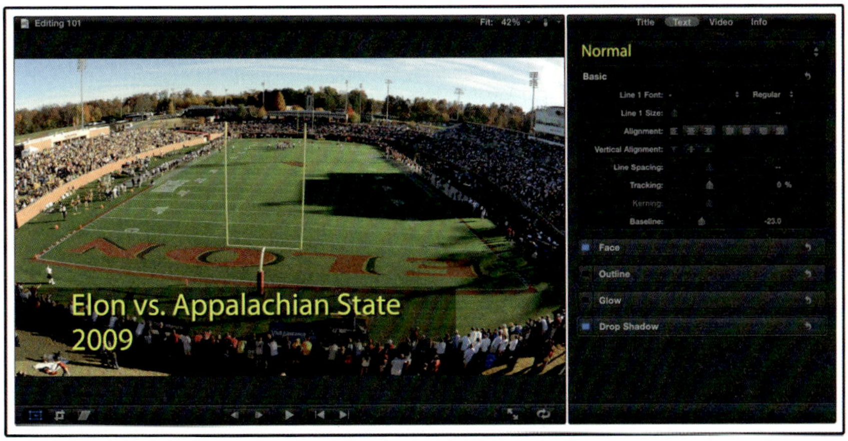

FIGURE 13.7
Your NLE software should include a character generator for composing on-screen titles like the one shown here in Apple Final Cut Pro X. This interface allows you to control the placement and appearance of the text within the frame.

(Continued)

Margins and White Space. Stay within the *title safe area* of the frame—the area where titles will display well—and don't forget to leave white space. Most NLEs will show you where the title safe area of the screen is. You'll also see marks for areas that are considered *action safe*, areas where it's safe to show action. The idea behind both of these terms is that older television sets didn't actually show the whole picture; a mask usually covered part of the picture tube. While newer flat panel displays don't have this problem, it's still a good idea to pay attention to these areas, particularly for titles, as they help give you some white space between your text and the edge of the screen.

Music and Sound Effects

Music and sound effects should be imported into the NLE project bin in an uncompressed file format such as WAV or AIFF. If you use a compressed format, particularly a lossy format such as MP3, you will be recompressing the audio when you export it at the end of the project and may accidently introduce unwanted artifacts into your audio. Pulse-Code Modulation (PCM) is the industry-standard codec used for encoding audio on a CD, DVD, or Blu-ray disc. The PCM standard stipulates a 44.1 kHz sampling rate and a 16-bit bitrate. WAV and AIFF audio files conform identically to the PCM standard. The only difference between the two is how a computer recognizes the file. On a Mac, a PCM audio asset is displayed using an AIFF container (or wrapper file), while on a PC, the same audio clip is displayed in a WAV wrapper (see Chapter 11 for more on PCM and container files).

Professionals usually avoid working with MP3 audio assets in video editing. MP3 is a consumer distribution format that is heavily compressed and technically inferior to WAV or AIFF.

CONTINUITY EDITING

The editing together of shots in sequence should be done in such a way that the linear presentation of visual and aural elements in a timeline is perceived as natural and coherent to the viewer. Bad edits can be disruptive to the narrative flow of a story, causing viewers to disconnect, get confused, lose their place, or stop watching altogether. There's a saying that "the best edits are the ones you never see." In other words, good edits are so seamless and logical, that the viewer doesn't even notice when they occur. And this is what editors often hope to achieve. *Continuity editing* is a term used to describe a wide range of practices and techniques that editors use to achieve smooth and natural transitions from shot to shot over time. When edits are performed well, the narrative continuity of the story is enhanced—leading to a more satisfying and enriching experience for the viewer (see Figure 13.8).

Cut-Ins

One of the techniques used in continuity editing is the cut-in. A *cut-in* directs the viewer's attention to a related object or alternative viewpoint within the current

FIGURE 13.8
The film *Chariots of Fire* won an Oscar for Best Picture in 1981. The movie included a one-minute scene, pictured here with still images, of two athletes competing in the Great Court Run. The runner's goal was to complete one lap around the main college square before 12 strikes of the courtyard clock (roughly 43 seconds). The edited scene was comprised of 30 shots from multiple camera angles. Through continuity editing, the director was able to portray the scene in real-time with continuous action, an amazing feat considering the scene was likely shot using only one camera. Notice how many cut-ins are interspersed with shots of the runners.

scene. For example, in a scene showing a woman getting onto an elevator, the sequence might begin with a wide shot of the elevator as the woman enters through the opening doors. She turns, glances down, and reaches out her hand; at which point we cut to a close-up shot of her finger pushing the button for the tenth floor. The cut-in of her finger may be framed from her point-of-view as if we are looking at it through her eyes, or through the eyes of someone standing nearby. A cut-in is often shot as a close-up that takes the viewer more deeply into the subject matter within a scene. Be careful when you are cutting your scene together. Avoid cutting between two shots that look almost the same—a *jump cut*. You'll see this error sometimes in the news, when the video editor is cutting down someone's speech. If you cut out a section of the speech and just splice the two pieces together, the speaker will appear to jump. This is one of the reasons cut-ins are so important—if you replace a small portion of the video on either side of the cut with video of the crowd (called a *cutaway*), you can get rid of the jump cut.

Tech Talk

Cutting-on-Action Cutting-on-action is a technique that editors often use to match continuous action in a scene as it unfolds across two sequential shots. In our previous example, the woman on the elevator performs a simple action by reaching out her hand to push a button on the control panel. Cutting-on-action means that the editor will cut from the wide-angle view to the close-up (or cut-in shot) while the hand is in motion. Typically, the best transition points occur at the apex of movement, when the action is most intense, and before the subject or object begins to decelerate or stop. The editor must ensure that the last frame of the action in the first shot matches the first frame of the continuing action in the second shot. For example, if the right hand is used to extend the finger in the first shot, the right hand should be shown completing the action in the second shot. If the actor uses a different hand in the second shot, then a continuity error will occur, drawing attention to the edit and disrupting the viewer's attention.

THE PROJECT FOLDER

In the process of shooting the footage for cut-ins and other camera changes, you will likely end up with a fair bit of material, and you need to learn how to effectively organize it. This means you need to understand how the NLE stores material. The project folder functions as a global container for all of the files associated with your project. It contains the project data file (also called the *EDL* or *edit decision list*) and subfolders for storing media content, such as video, music and sound effects, still images, titles, etc. In addition, NLE applications will often create nested subfolders for storing other data, including capture files, render files, and backup copies of the project file. As a general rule, each project you're working on should have its own designated project folder (see Figure 13.9).

Premiere and Final Cut Pro (prior to FCP X) use the term *scratch disk* as the name of the interface component for setting up the name and location of the project folder and subfolders. Hence, the phrase "setting your scratch disks" is synonymous with the process of linking to or creating the project folder at the beginning of an editing session. In Media Composer, the editor is prompted to use a "media creation settings" window to set up the name and location of the project folder. And not to leave audio editing out of the mix, Pro Tools refers to a work project as a "session" and requires the user to create a "session folder" at the beginning of each new project. Whatever the name or approach, be sure you understand how to set up the project management workflow for whatever NLE you are editing in. This step is critically important and will save you a great deal of time and frustration during the editing process if performed well. Consider using a secondary drive (i.e., not the one that your OS and NLE are located on) as your scratch disk. Using a dedicated scratch drive can help speed up rendering (more about that later), and using an external USB or Firewire drive may allow you to move your project between computers. Once you've created the project folder, be careful not to change its name or move it to a different location. This goes for all of the content within the project folder as well. Doing so could potentially confuse the NLE, causing it to lose track of important project files and assets.

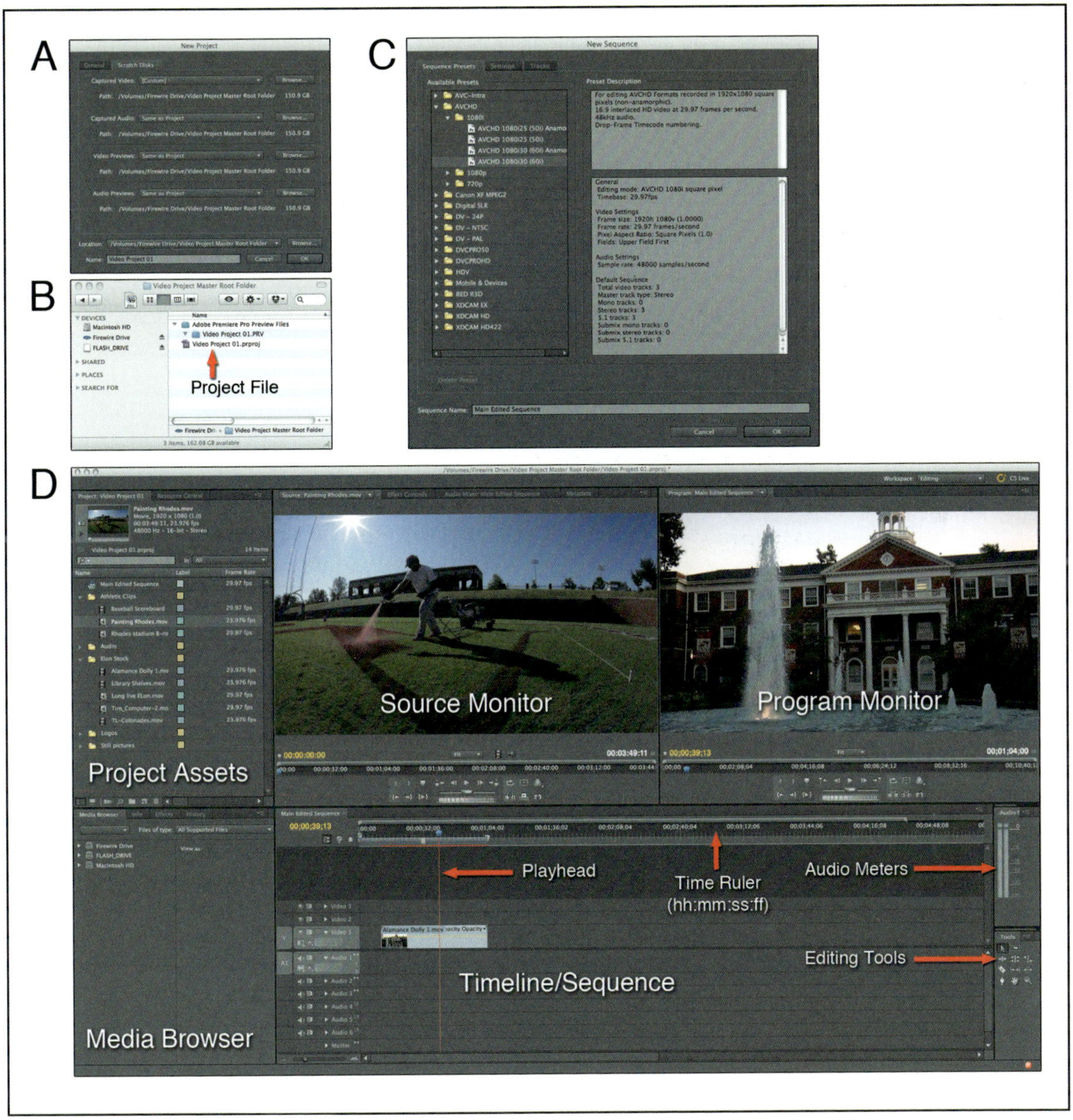

FIGURE 13.9

Starting a New Project in Adobe Premiere CS 5.5. (A) The editor is prompted to identify the scratch disk locations for the main project (captured video and audio, project file, etc.). All of the media assets and project files associated with a video project should be stored in a master project root folder. (B) Based on the information you provide in the scratch disk window, the NLE will create physical folders and files on your drive associated with the project. (C) The user is prompted to identify a video preset for the project sequence. Normally, you will choose a preset that conforms to the format you shot your footage in. Is your project shot in SD or HD? Which codec and record settings were used? (D) The program launches and editing can begin.

FIGURE 13.10
Apple did away with the concept of "scratch disks" with its release of Final Cut Pro X. By default, the program now stores media files in a master project folder called *Final Cut Events* and project files in a folder called *Final Cut Projects*. For each new video project, the user creates a new event folder where media (source footage) and other assets associated with the event will be stored. The project folder contains one or more sequences, the edited arrangement of media within the NLE timeline.

The Project File

The *project file* is a proprietary data file used for keeping track of every detail associated with an NLE project. Once an editing project is created, it can be revisited in later sessions by double-clicking on the project file icon. The project file can be thought of as a set of instructions for rendering media in the sequence timeline.

Media Files and Media Clips

Media files are the raw project assets that are created or acquired prior to the start of an editing session. These include the actual video and audio files captured from tape or through direct transfer from a video camera, memory card, or other digital source. Media files are typically the largest file assets associated with an editing project. For example, digital video (DV) requires 1GB of storage for every five minutes of recorded footage (or 250MB per minute). High-definition video files consume an even larger amount of digital real estate, which is why high-capacity hard drives are often used for storing the contents of video and audio projects.

When a media file is imported into an active NLE session, a clip is created and added to the media browser or project bin. A *clip* is a relatively small data file that "points" to a larger underlying media file on the hard drive. It functions as an alias or virtual representation of the real thing, and for this reason, it is sometimes called a *pointer file*. A clip can be placed in the timeline, trimmed, cut, and deleted without changing or destroying the actual media file it is linked with. The same clip can be added to a timeline sequence multiple times without adding to the physical size of the project file. Each instance of the clip is a stand-alone digital asset that keeps track of the pointer data for a particular event in the edited sequence. You can delete a media clip from the bin without deleting the media file. While deleting it makes the clip icon disappear from view in the project window or browser, the actual media file is safe and sound in its original

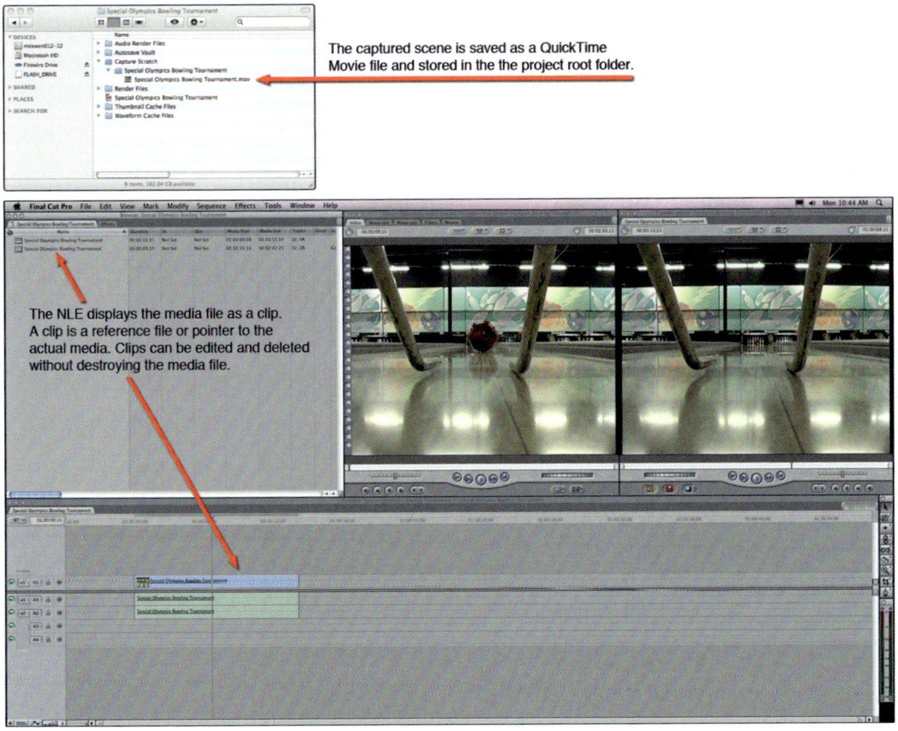

FIGURE 13.11
Nondestructive Editing. Clips can be copied, deleted, moved, cut, and edited numerous ways within the NLE without affecting the underlying media they refer to. If you delete a clip from the project window, simply import it again into the program.

location on the hard drive. A *media file* can be reconnected with a *media clip* at any time by re-importing it into the project.

CAPTURE FILES

Capture files are time-based media files that are created when footage is ingested into the computer through a connected camera or videotape recorder. The video and audio tracks recorded on tape exist as linear streams of digital information that are read and rendered in real-time as the tape is played back. Capturing involves converting these time-based streams (or video and audio tracks) into a digital file format that can be read and processed by the NLE program. Once captured, a media file can be easily moved and copied, allowing it to be used in other projects or saved in a digital archive for retrieval at a later time (see Figure 13.12).

Capturing-on-the-Fly

An NLE's capture interface provides the editor with numerous options for ingesting tape-recorded footage into the computer and saving it to the project folder.

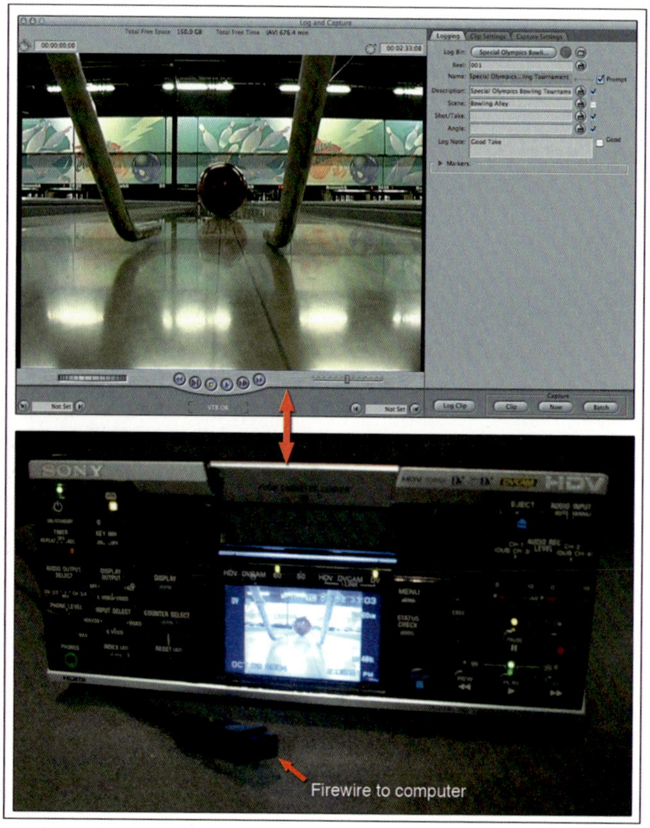

FIGURE 13.12
The Log and Capture interface in Final Cut Pro 7 allows users to ingest footage from tape via a camcorder or VTR connected by a Firewire cable. The virtual player controls in the software interface can be used to operate a connected device.

A virtual interface allows you to operate the playback and control functions of a connected camera or VCR. The simplest method is called *capturing on the fly*. With this process, the editor cues up the tape to the beginning, presses play, and begins capturing. Capturing will continue until the editor escapes from the procedure or the tape runs out of footage. The advantage of this method is that it's fast. A disadvantage is that it is fairly nonselective. The footage is captured in large chucks—bad takes and all—and the clips are rather long and unwieldy, which can slow down the editing process. For short projects with less than 30 minutes of footage, this method works well; but if you have lots of footage to ingest, you should consider the more advanced method of logging and batch capturing, which allows you to be more selective.

Logging and Batch Capturing

A simple scenario may help to illustrate the process of logging and batch capturing. An editor is handed a videotape recording with three scenes. Each scene was shot three times. The editor has been instructed to capture only the following shots: Scene 1, Take 3; Scene 2, Take 1; and Scene 3, Take 2. With capturing on the fly, the editor would have cued up the tape to the beginning and captured all nine takes as one continuous clip. In editing, the editor would then have to sort through all of the good and bad takes, slowing down the editing process and possibly wasting much of the time spent capturing the video.

With the *logging and batch capturing* method, the editor will preview the tape prior to capturing. He works his way through the footage one scene at a time, stopping at the beginning and end of each good take to set an IN and OUT point. In the logging fields, he can designate the tape or reel number, clip name, scene and take number, shot description, camera angle, and other notes or comments as desired. This information will be permanently attached as metadata to the captured media file. After viewing and logging the source footage, the editor will select the batch capture option. At this point, the NLE takes control of the VCR and begins to capture each of the scenes specified in the editor's logging notes. The bad scenes are skipped and the total capture time is cut down by roughly two-thirds. Instead of one long clip in the project bin, the editor sees three clips, properly named with logging notes attached. Batch capturing allows the editor to automate the capturing workflow, saving time and hard drive space, while creating valuable logging notes that will stay attached to the footage as long as it remains in its current digital form.

RENDER FILES

From time to time, the editing software creates new video files representing the placement of a transition, effect, filter, title, or multilayer composite. This process is called *rendering*. For example, when a one-second dissolve is attached to two adjacent clips in the timeline, a one-second video clip will need to be rendered showing the crossdissolve. A render file is a video clip created in the background by the NLE whenever part of the underlying media file needs to be copied, changed, or altered.

FLASH BACK

NLE Pioneers

Avid Technology is one of the oldest developers of nonlinear editing software. Its flagship program, Media Composer, was released in 1989 and continues to be one of the most recognized NLE applications used in the motion picture and television industries. Adobe's NLE solution is called Premier, which Adobe released in 1991. Adobe's chief competitor, Macromedia, was instrumental in developing a rival NLE called KeyGrip, a product designed to work natively with Apple QuickTime. KeyGrip was renamed Final Cut and eventually sold to Apple, who released it commercially as Final Cut Pro in 1999.

While there are many professional NLE solutions to choose from, Avid Media Composer, Adobe Premiere, and Apple Final Cut Pro have stood the test of time, and remain three of the most recognized names in nonlinear video editing.

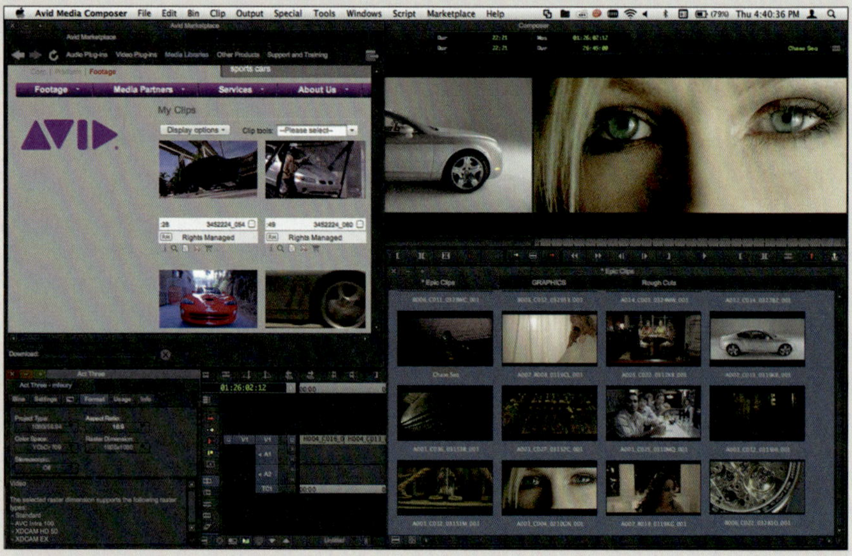

FIGURE 13.13
Avid Media Composer 6.

You can render clips as you go or wait until the end of a project to render everything at once. The more complex the effect or transition, the longer it will take for rendering to be performed. Depending on the speed of your computer, the NLE can often play back unrendered clips in real-time. However, the resolution may be low because the program has to process the transition or effect on the fly. It's a good idea to stop occasionally throughout a session to render all of the unrendered clips in the sequence.

COMPONENTS OF AN NLE INTERFACE

Project Window

The *project window*, as it's called in Media Composer, is the visual interface component of an NLE used for accessing media files located in the project folder. In Final Cut Pro, this window panel is called the *browser*. In Adobe Premiere, it's referred to as the *media browser*. When a media asset is imported into an NLE project, the clip icon—pointing to the media file—will appear in the browser. Deleting a clip icon from the project window will not remove the associated asset from the hard drive. This action merely severs the link that the NLE has established between the file and the clip alias. The project window serves as a media library, which an editor can use to quickly open clips for review, editing, or insertion into the timeline. It also allows an editor to organize clips into logical bins (or folders) that can be sorted, renamed, and viewed as a list or in thumbnail view.

The Timeline

Video and audio editing takes place in the *timeline*, a visual interface component that's divided into horizontal regions called *tracks*. When a video clip is added to the timeline, the video portion of the clip is placed on a *video track* while the audio portion is inserted directly below on an *audio track*. Audio tracks are normally grouped in linked stereo pairs. By default, the first track (or left channel) is sent to the left speaker and the second track (or right channel) is output to the right. For this reason, whenever a synchronized video clip (such as an SOT) is placed on the timeline, its content is usually spread across three adjacent tracks (one video track, and two audio tracks). If a single microphone was used in the recording, there will be only one channel of associated audio, and thus only one corresponding audio track. A mono track can be easily converted into a stereo pair within the NLE, sending it to both the left and right speakers.

When editing a synchronized video asset, you will normally want to apply the same action, simultaneously, to both the video and audio portion of a clip. For example, when a clip is split in two using the splice or razor blade tool, the edit will typically affect all three tracks at once. Likewise, when you reposition a video clip within the timeline, the linked video and audio segments will travel together in tandem, allowing them to remain *in sync*. Problems can occur when video and audio become unsynchronized. Even a slight shift of only a few frames can affect lip-synching in an SOT, causing the audience to squirm in discomfort.

Sometimes an editor will choose to unlink a clip in order to control the video and audio separately. For example, you may want to perform a *split edit*, by assigning different IN and OUT points to the video and audio clips. This technique is commonly used when editing sound bites. With a split edit, the audience might see a person talking for one to two seconds before they actually hear him. Another use of this technique would be to show B-Roll during the first five seconds of a sound bite before cutting to a synchronized headshot of the person speaking. Split edits are performed routinely and are extremely versatile and important in the aesthetics of editing. Just remember to relink the clips again when you're finished working on them to prevent accidentally unsynchronizing them later in the editing process.

In addition to synchronized clips, editors deal with a variety of standalone media assets. Digital images, for example, contain no corresponding audio. They are also static, meaning they have no duration (length), as compared to time-based media assets. Static clips like images, titles, backgrounds, and slugs (a solid black video frame) can be extended within the timeline to any length the editor desires. Audio assets, however, are always time-based, even if they contain no corresponding video clip information.

VIDEO COMPOSITING AND AUDIO MIXING

Compositing is the process of combining two or more video tracks together to form a new image or visual effect. Video tracks can be used as layers to segregate clips into different editable regions, thus allowing the editor to maintain individual control over each asset's appearance and placement in the timeline. In the timeline, content is rendered from the top down. For example, a clip placed on video track 2 (V2) will partially or completely obscure the view of content placed beneath it on video track 1 (V1). Let's look at a few examples.

Example 1: A Simple Two-Track Composite. The editor begins by placing an SOT on V1, the first video track in the timeline. Next, he inserts a lower third title graphic above the SOT on V2 (see Figure 13.14). The program monitor reveals a

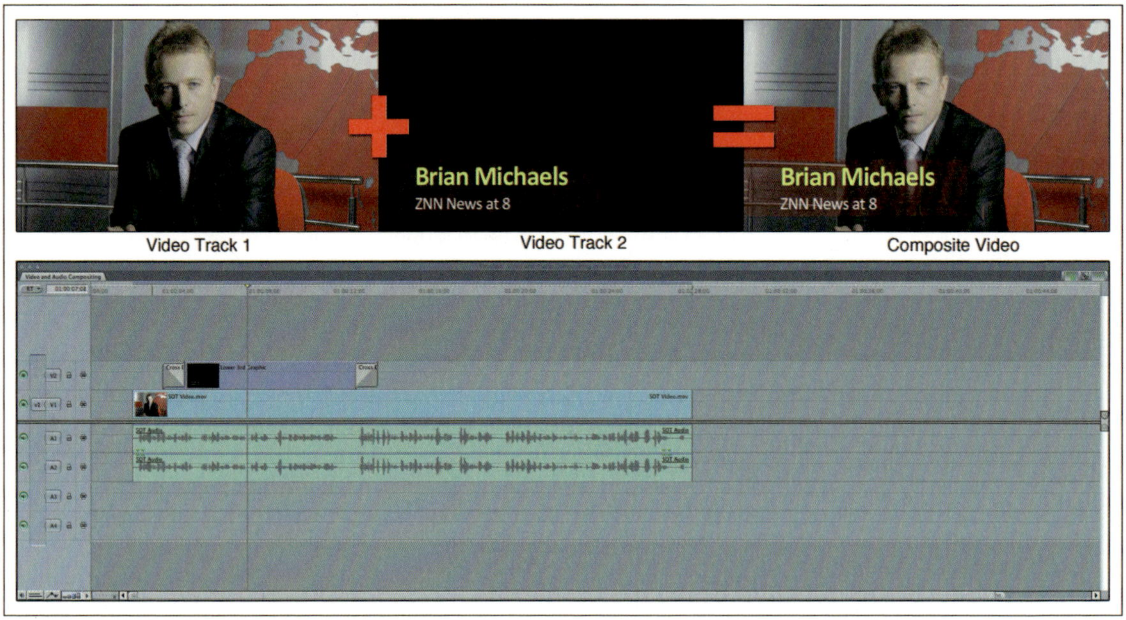

FIGURE 13.14
Example 1: Creating a two-track composite image in Apple Final Cut 7. An SOT and lower third title graphic are added to the editing timeline (bottom). After positioning the playhead over both clips in the timeline, we can look at the program monitor to see what the combined image will look like (top).

composite image, showing a superimposition of the title over the top of the person speaking. Because each component of the composite images resides on its own track, it can be edited independently without affecting other clips in the timeline.

Example 2: A Four-Track Composite. A color gradient background is positioned on V1. Next, an SOT is added to V2 (see Figure 13.15). The SOT image is scaled down to fit within the left side of the video frame, revealing the gradient background around it. A still graphic is added to V3 and positioned on the right side of the frame opposite the person speaking. Finally, a lower third is inserted on V4, showing the name and title of the person on screen. The composite image shows all four elements co-residing within the image. Incidentally, the four elements do not have to appear or disappear at the same points in the timeline. The editor can choose a different IN and OUT point for each object. The possibilities are endless.

Mixing is the audio version of compositing. With mixing, multiple audio clips can be combined in an unlimited number of ways to form a complex aural experience. For example, in a motion picture film, an action sequence often contains multiple

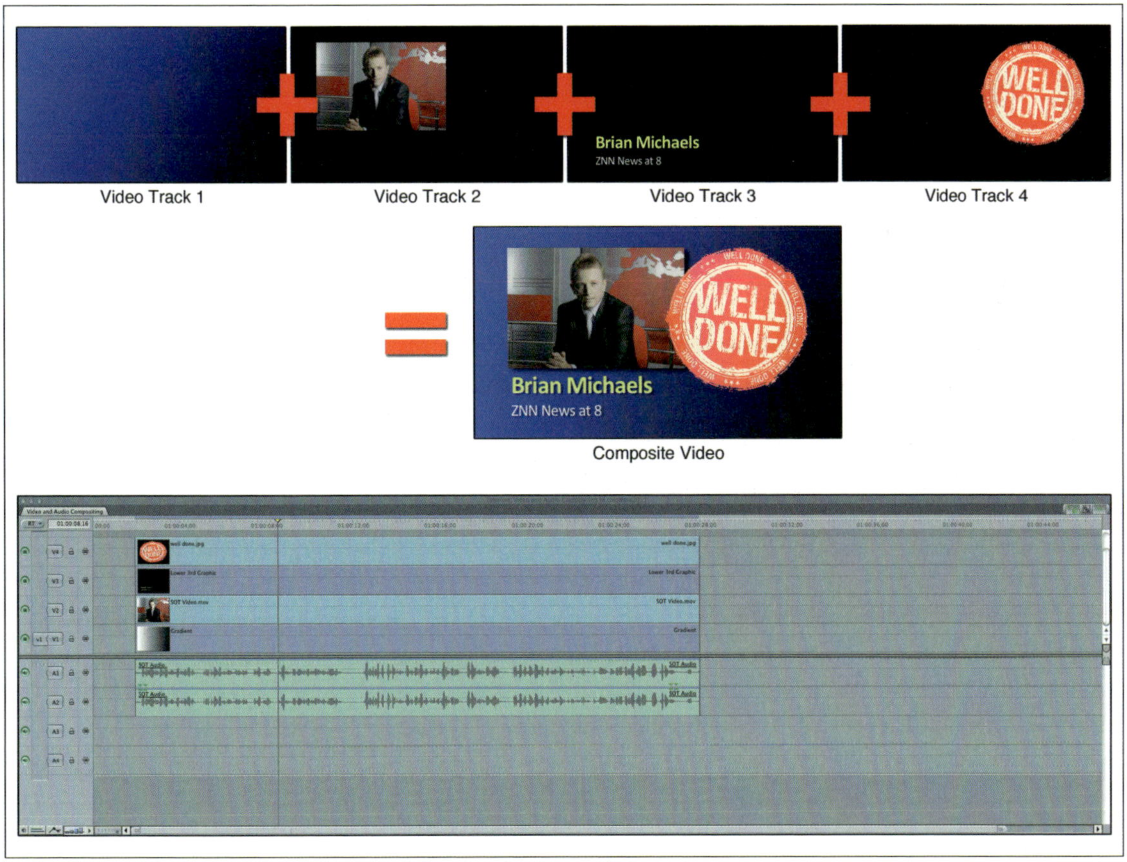

FIGURE 13.15
Example 2: Creating a four-track composite image in Apple Final Cut 7. This composite includes a background gradient, a foreground video frame, a lower third title graphic, and a foreground program graphic.

tracks of dialogue, background sounds, music, and sound effects (SFX). A sound editor is one of many people responsible for ensuring that the audio experience makes sense to the audience. Unfortunately, most of us don't have a sound editor standing by to perform the audio portion of video editing for us. We will need to do this ourselves. And it needs to be done well, lest the audience is overwhelmed by chaos and noise. Again, let's consider a common example.

Example 3: A Four-Track Stereo Mix. We begin a sequence by placing an SOT in the timeline. The audio portion of the SOT resides on A1 and A2 (see Figure 13.16). Music is then added to A3 and A4 and placed beneath the tracks of the person speaking. In this example, the primary, or foreground audio, is produced by the SOT. The editor wants this to stand out above the music and sets the channel volume (for A1/A2) to full. Music is a background element, and as such should not compete for the audience's attention. The editor adjusts the channel volume (for A3/A4) to a lower level appropriate for background music. As additional sources are added to the sequence, the editor will mix them accordingly, until he or she achieves the intended balance and effect that the program calls for.

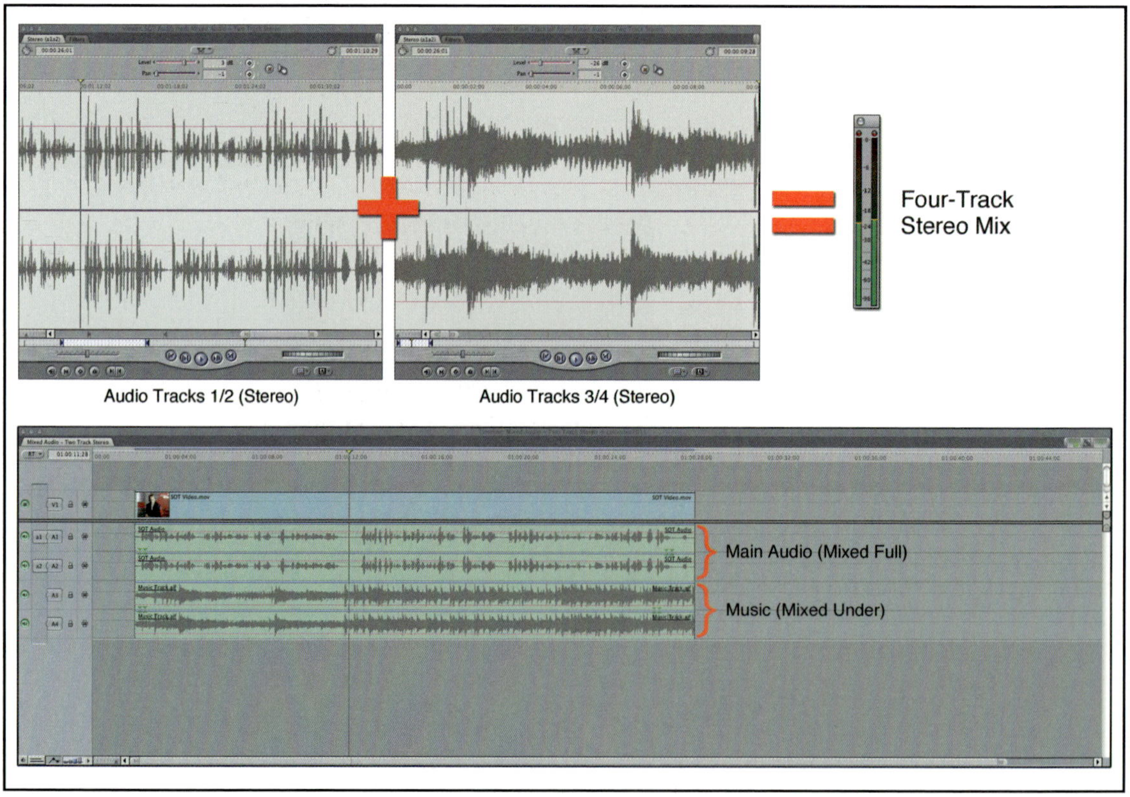

FIGURE 13.16
Example 3: Creating a four-track stereo mix in Apple Final Cut 7. Combining audio sources in editing is a common task. The editor needs to set the level of each stereo track pair independently to achieve an aesthetically pleasing mix. Since the SOT is the main element, tracks A1 and A2 are set to normal levels (full). The music tracks are set much lower to keep them from competing with the spoken word.

The Preview and Program Monitors

The NLE interface contains two virtual television monitors. The *preview monitor*, usually positioned to the left, is used for reviewing media assets imported into the project window and for trimming (shortening) and adjusting clips before adding them to the timeline. Double-clicking on a clip in either the project window or the timeline will open it in the preview monitor, where edits and changes can be performed. The *program monitor*, usually positioned to the right, is linked to the timeline. As you scan through the edited sequence in the timeline, the program monitor reveals what the audience will see and hear when viewing the program.

VIRTUAL MONITOR COMPONENTS

The preview and program monitor components contain a variety of controls for reviewing, trimming, and affecting the appearance of an open clip.

Transport Controls

The virtual *transport controls* act in much the same way as the buttons on a VCR or DVD player, allowing you to scan the contents of a time-based media clip. The editor has access to familiar functions like play, pause, stop, rewind, and fast-forward. The transport controls can be activated through keyboard input as well. Experienced editors prefer using keyboard shortcuts (see Table 13.1) because they're generally much quicker to execute than the virtual controls. *Shuttle* and *jog* are terms used to describe the speed at which you *scrub* (move) through a time-based clip. The jog control allows you to move through slowly, a few frames at a time, while the shuttle allows you to quickly scan through footage.

The Playhead

The *playhead* defines your position in a time-based clip. You can scrub slowly or rapidly through a clip by dragging the playhead horizontally in either direction. *Audio scrubbing* allows you to hear the audio portion of a clip as you move the playhead back and forth, and it's a useful technique for locating sound artifacts that you want to eliminate or isolate in editing. The preview monitor playhead allows you to scrub through the currently loaded clip. The program monitor playhead allows you to scrub through the entire length of the timeline. Because the program monitor is linked directly to the timeline, moving either playhead causes the other one to move in tandem.

Timecode Fields

Every frame of video is addressable via *timecode*. Whenever you mark an IN point or OUT point, the location is stored as a numerical series of eight digits denoting hours, minutes, seconds, and frames. A timecode display of 01:18:54:27 indicates a frame location of 1 hour, 18 minutes, 54 seconds, and 27 frames. This format is used to denote the duration of marked clips, transitions, and other program assets. For example, a one-second dissolve would appear as 00:00:01:00 in the duration field.

GREAT IDEAS

NLE Keyboard Shortcuts

Table 13.1 Keyboard Shortcuts Like the Ones Listed Here are Relatively Common in All NLE Programs and Help to Speed Up the Editing Workflow

Keyboard Shortcut	Action
Spacebar	Starts or stops the playhead while viewing (Play/Pause)
I Key	Marks the IN point
J Key	Plays backwards—pressing multiple times speeds up scrubbing
K Key	Stops playing
L Key	Plays forwards—pressing multiple times speeds up scrubbing
O Key	Marks the OUT point
Left/Right Arrow	Nudges the playhead one frame to the left or right

THE IMAGE FRAME

The largest area of the monitor control interface is reserved for the image or picture data. What you can do in this area is largely dependent on the features available in your NLE system. Typically, you will be able to transform the size and aspect ratio of the image through scaling, cropping, and wireframe controls. A *wireframe* acts like a bounding box that allows you to freely transform video within the frame, whether it's rotating the image, changing the playback speed, adding a visual affect or filter, or otherwise altering a clip's movement or appearance.

When an audio asset is loaded into preview, the visual interface is different. Instead of a video image you'll see an audio waveform. A *waveform* is a visual representation of the amplitude signature of the audio clip across time. The height of the waveform indicates the volume level. By looking at the waveform, you can often tell whether the audio was recorded at an appropriate level or not. Under-modulated audio (audio that is too soft) will have a short waveform pattern or perhaps none at all—simply a flat line. Over-modulated audio (audio that is too loud), which may be distorted, will have an intense waveform pattern that extends from the bottom of the track to the top (or from the "floor" to the "ceiling"). A waveform's repetitive fluctuations can provide the editor with a visual representation of timing and rhythm. In a musical asset, the waveform can reveal the beat structure and tempo of a selection, providing visual cues for determining transition points. In addition to having a waveform on the timeline, most audio and video editors will have a VU (volume units) meter that will let you monitor loudness while the audio is playing.

ADDING CLIPS TO THE TIMELINE

Editing a video program resembles the process of manufacturing a car. Before production of the car can begin on the assembly line, all of the individual parts that make up the car must be designed and assembled. A car is built from the ground up, beginning with the chassis and ending with the body panels, doors, windows, and trim. The chassis is the structural frame that everything else attaches to in some way or another. It must be assembled first. In a similar way, video editing moves forward in a linear fashion from beginning to middle to end. Because editing is also a nonlinear process, eventually you will be able to jump around your timeline—but first, you have to lay the foundation.

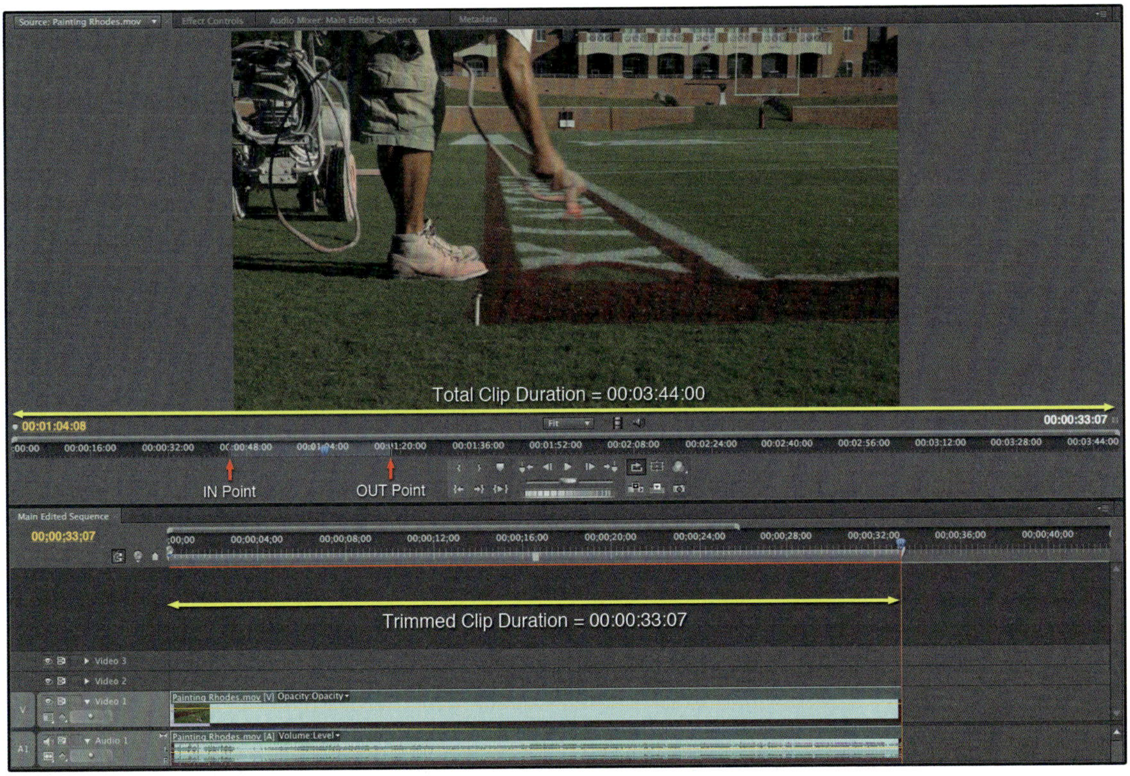

FIGURE 13.17
The source or preview monitor is used for screening and trimming clips before adding them to an edited sequence. The original clip shown here is 3:44, but the editor only wants to use a portion of it in the final edited sequence. He marks the portion of the clip he wants to use with an IN point and an OUT point. When the edit is performed, only the video and audio between these two points is added to the timeline.

In a video editing timeline, the audio portion of the narrative is the structural frame that everything else attaches to. It needs to be created first. Doing so allows you to edit video "in time" with the dialog, narration, music, and other audio elements in the sequence. The beat, tempo, and rhythm of the audio cues the editor to natural points in the timeline where transitions make the most sense. It is very difficult to edit video images without audio in the timeline. Once the audio portion of the narrative is established, editing the visuals becomes a snap.

A Simple Editing Scenario

Let's assume that the parts for our video (our media assets) have been created and imported into the project window and have been properly logged, labeled, and organized. Where do we go from here? While it's possible to start dragging clips willy-nilly directly from the project bin into the timeline, this is a bad habit and promotes an unproductive workflow. A better approach begins with first opening clips in the preview monitor, where they can be trimmed and marked, prior to being copied and placed in the timeline. Let's walk through the process of editing the following sequence: a voiceover, followed by a sound bite, followed by a second voiceover. To do this, we'll use three-point editing, a standard technique. (Note: You can view this editing example online at the Multimedia Foundations website.)

STEP 1: SET AN IN POINT AND OUT POINT IN THE PREVIEW MONITOR

I'll begin by opening the voiceover clip in the preview monitor. The clip is 3 minutes long and contains numerous voiceover segments along with several takes of each track (see Figure 3.18 top). Much of the material I'll never use.

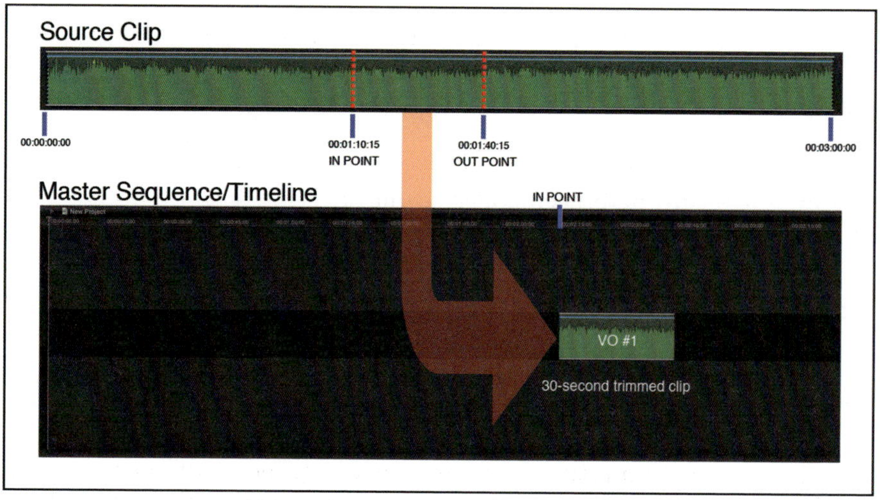

FIGURE 13.18
The three-point editing technique is used here to insert a 30-second portion of a 3-minute clip at a specific point in the timeline.

I scrub the playhead to the beginning of VO #1 (the best take) and mark an IN point by pressing the I key on my keyboard. Next, I move the playhead to the end of VO #1 and mark an OUT point by pressing the O key on my keyboard. The segment is now marked and ready to be placed in the timeline. The marked clip is 30 seconds long (00:00:30:00).

STEP 2: SET AN IN POINT IN THE TIMELINE

Next, I change the focus of the NLE to the timeline by clicking on it. Since this is my first edit, setting the IN point is relatively easy. I move the playhead forward one second into the timeline and mark an IN point by pressing the I key on my keyboard. Since the NLE knows the duration of my source clip **(00:00:30:00)**, there's no need to mark an OUT point in the timeline. It can figure this out on its own. Hence the term … three-point editing!

STEP 3: PERFORM THE EDIT

With three points marked, I'm ready to perform the edit. Doing so places a new version of the clip into the timeline at precisely the right spot (see Figure 13.18 bottom). This clip is shorter than the one in the preview monitor because it's been trimmed down to 30 seconds. The original 3-minute clip remains in the project bin and is still visible in the preview monitor. The clip in the timeline is an alias, with its own data file that can be changed without affecting the parent clip it was copied from. I can revise this clip by double-clicking on it to re-open it in the preview monitor. The preview monitor can only hold one clip at a time. As your project grows, and the number of clips and aliases increase, you will need to pay special attention to which version of the clip is loaded into the preview monitor. It's easy to get confused and make mistakes by inadvertently making changes to the wrong asset.

STEP 4: REPEAT STEPS 1–3 FOR SOT #2 AND VO #2

The next step in this example is to repeat steps 1–3 for the remaining clips in the sequence. In the timeline, the IN point for each subsequent edit will be the OUT point of the previous edit.

STEP 5: ADD B-ROLL OVER VO SEGMENTS

Once the three clips have been added to the sequence, I will need to return to the beginning of the timeline to insert B-Roll for each of my voiceover segments. The voiceover clips contain only audio, leaving the corresponding video track empty (or black). I'll use B-Roll to fill in the gaps. In addition, I want to include the natural sound that was recorded when the B-Roll was shot. To keep from replacing the voiceover clips on A1 and A2, the natural sound needs to be inserted on different tracks.

When editing B-Roll, I need to reverse my three-point editing technique. Since my goal now is to fill precise gaps in the edited sequence, I will mark both an IN point and an OUT point in the timeline. In the preview monitor, I will set only an IN point. When the edit is performed, B-Roll and natural sound will be inserted into the designated hole on tracks V1, A3, and A4 in the timeline.

STEP 6: ADD TITLES, TRANSITIONS, AND EFFECTS

Once the basic building blocks of the video and audio narrative have been established, I can begin the process of adding titles, transitions, effects, and other elements as required.

Transitions

A *transition* is an effect applied to the timeline at the beginning or end of a video or audio clip. Transitions are used to provide a sense of flow and rhythm to a project and to guide the viewer's senses through changes in the narrative structure of a story as it unfolds (see Figure 13.19).

CUT

The most common transition is called a *cut*. A cut is an instantaneous transition from the end of one shot to the beginning of another shot. Because of this, a cut has no duration per se. In fact, you can think of a cut as the invisible transition. Cuts are popular with editors because of their simplicity. When properly timed, the audience will hardly know that a cut occurred. Timing is critical, though.

FIGURE 13.19
(1) The first sequence (top) illustrates the visual effect of a 1-second dissolve transition at the midpoint between the end of one shot and the beginning of another. (2) The second sequence (middle) shows a timeline view of the attached dissolve. Transitions are usually attached to clips by dragging and dropping them into place on the timeline. (3) The third sequence (bottom) shows a few of the transitions available in Final Cut Pro X. While cuts and dissolves most often suffice, your NLE software will provide you with many basic transitions to choose from.

Cuts should be positioned at natural points in the narrative; for example, at the beginning or end of a sentence or concurrently with a sound effect or music cue. Cutting in the middle of a word or sentence, or on the wrong bar or beat in the underscore, can disrupt the continuity of a program and be self-defeating. Most often, the editor's goal is to make the presence of a cut invisible to the audience. Remember, the best edits are often the ones you don't notice. Incidentally, the first beat of a bar, called the downbeat, is the strongest point in a melody line and a great location for the placement of a cut or other transition.

FADE

The absence of picture data on a television screen is referred to as *black*. In television, the audience is cued to key program and scene changes by fading into or out of black, in much the same way that a lighting blackout is used during a theatrical production to signal the beginning or end of a scene or act. Programs usually begin with a fade-in from black and end with a fade-out to black. The *fade-in* is a gradual transition from black to a fully opaque television image, while a *fade-out* is a gradual transition in the opposite direction. Video and audio fades often occur simultaneously. For example, in an end-of-program fade-to-black, the video image should reach 100% black at precisely the same point in the timeline that the audio reaches 0 dB. In a case like this, it is standard practice to use the same duration time for both the video and audio fade.

DISSOLVE

A *dissolve* is a gradual transition from one shot to another that is created by overlapping the fade-out of one clip with a fade-in of the next clip in sequence. Dissolves are far less abrupt than cuts and are often used to signal a change in time, a change of location, or a change in tempo. Dissolves can be used to slow down the pace of a program when a gentler timing structure or rhythm is called for. However, short dissolves can be used in place of a cut to soften a transition without necessarily impacting an otherwise upbeat tempo.

WIPE

Most other transitions fall into the category of wipes or *3D effects*. A *wipe* uses a linear movement or sweeping pattern to replace the current image with a new one. For example a *vertical wipe* moves from the top of the frame down, or from the bottom of the frame up, as it replaces the current image with new pixels. A *horizontal wipe* does the same thing by sweeping left to right or right to left. A *circle wipe* moves in a radial direction from the center of the image outward and vice versa. Wipes come in a virtually unlimited assortment of shapes and patterns. There are *checkerboard* wipes, *clock* wipes, and *slide* wipes, which push the entire frame of video off-screen. A *spin* wipe is used to rotate the video frame as it moves out of view, while an *explosion* wipe shatters the picture into pieces before sending them off in every direction. If your selection of wipes is limited, chances are that a third-party software developer has produced wipes for your NLE that can be obtained for free or purchased and downloaded commercially.

Like wipes, *3D transitions* come in all shapes and sizes. Using powerful algorithms, video can be squished, stretched, warped, morphed, and distorted in any number of ways to achieve creative and unusual visual effects. *Page peel* transitions curl the edge of the video frame inward to simulate turning pages in a book. *Cube spin* transitions turn the video frame into a rotating object with multiple sides displaying different images or picture data. The list goes on and on.

Wipes and 3D transitions are visually very cool! They are fun to play with and can add legitimate value to a visual experience for the viewer. However, you must use them with caution. Anything you add into the video timeline should be motivated by the story and the impact you wish to make on the viewer. Simply throwing things into an edited sequence because you can, or because it looks cool, is not necessarily going to make it look any more professional. In fact, it's usually just the opposite. Until you gain experience, stick with cuts and dissolves for the most part. If you choose to use wipes, then be consistent. Do not use a pinwheel wipe in the first transition, a page peel in the second, and exploding video in the third. This sort of sporadic and random use of transitions will likely overwhelm the viewer's senses, potentially causing them to lose interest and disengage from the message.

TRANSITION PROPERTIES

Once a transition has been added to the timeline, it becomes a modular object with properties that can easily be changed. These values are saved in a data file that's stored in the render folder. While most transitions will play back in real-time, at some point before exporting your project, you will need to stop and fully render all of the transitions you've created. Once rendered, they will run more smoothly and appear sharper when playing through the video in real-time.

The most important property you will need to pay attention to is the transition duration. *Duration* is the amount of time that a transition takes to perform from beginning to end, as indicated in seconds and frames. The default transition in most programs is one second (or 30 frames). When adding a dissolve between two clips, I often use a 20-frame duration, which is roughly two-thirds of a second. This duration serves me well most of the time. For something heavily dramatic, I might use a longer increment of 1 to 3 seconds. Only rarely, will I use anything longer. You need to remember that transitions take time to execute and that this eats into your project's total runtime; robbing you of precious seconds and minutes, especially if the program is short. For example, if you produce a 60-second commercial with 10 default transitions (01:00 long), your program loses 1/6th of its content potential to transitions. The simple act of changing the default duration to 15 frames will save you 5 seconds of actual runtime. Five seconds in a 60-second spot is a lot of time.

In addition to the duration property, you can adjust a number of other variables. For example, you can change the direction of an edge wipe, causing it to start from the left, right, top, or bottom of the frame. The properties you have access to will depend on the transition you're working with. Each transition is unique, and therefore has different parameters and values that you can adjust or manipulate to change the way that it performs.

When applying a transition, make sure that the adjoining clips you're attaching it to touch. If there's a gap between the two clips that you can't see—because you're zoomed out too far, for example—then the transition may not attach properly. Zooming in to the timeline for a close-up view of the attachment point is really helpful. Once attached, transitions become visual objects you can modify. For example, you can change the duration of a transition by entering a new value in its properties window; or you can do it interactively in the timeline, by dragging the left or right edge of the transition in or out until the desired duration is obtained.

CHAPTER SUMMARY

Not surprisingly, you'll find that the interfaces for audio and video editing change between programs. What doesn't change, however, are good editing practices. For example, the need to use cutaways correctly and avoid unintentional jump cuts doesn't change when you switch from one NLE to another, nor does the need to carefully monitor your audio. In addition, you'll find that many of the core concepts are the same between NLEs. Most professional programs use a timeline for arranging clips linearly from beginning to end, allow you to organize your clips in bins, and mark in and out points in your video. The basic idea of a three-point edit is the same, regardless of your NLE. Keystrokes may even translate between NLEs, particularly the use of the space bar to start and stop the playhead. While you need to be able to use your NLE effectively, don't get too tied up in the software—if you don't understand basic editing concepts and theory, you won't be able to communicate effectively. Try to get experience on as many NLEs as possible, and avoid becoming too attached to a particular NLE. When you are looking for a job, you want to be as flexible as possible.

Index

Page numbers followed by *f* indicates a figure and *t* indicates a table.

A

B